S0-AHC-256

Social
Welfare:
Charity to Justice

This book is published in conjunction with
the Council on Social Work Education.

CONSULTING EDITOR: Martin Rein
Bryn Mawr College

RANDOM HOUSE New York

COUNCIL ON SOCIAL WORK EDUCATION, New York

SOCIAL WELFARE:

Charity to Justice

John M. Romanyshyn
University of Maine

with the assistance of
Annie L. Romanyshyn

Copyright © 1971 by Random House, Inc.
All rights reserved under International and Pan-American
Copyright Conventions. Published in the United States
by Random House, Inc., New York, and simultaneously
in Canada by Random House of Canada Limited, Toronto.

ISBN: 0–394–31026–8

Library of Congress Catalog Card Number: 73–141964

Manufactured in the United States of America by The
Kingsport Press, Inc., Kingsport, Tenn.

First Edition
9 8 7 6 5 4 3 2 1

ACKNOWLEDGMENTS

Extracts from Parts I and II of "Notes on a Post-Industrial Society," by Daniel Bell, from The *Public Interest,*
Vol. 6 (Winter 1967) and Vol. 7 (Spring 1967) were
reprinted by permission of the publishers. This material
appears in *A Great Society?,*
edited by Bertram M. Gross, published by Basic
Books, Inc., 1968.

Extract from *Man and Superman,* by Bernard Shaw,
reprinted by permission of The Society of Authors, on
behalf of the Bernard Shaw Estate.

Tables 20 and 21 are reprinted from "Legislative Analysis:
The Bill to Revamp the Welfare System" (Washington,
D.C.: American Enterprise Institute, 1970), by
permission of the American Enterprise Institute.

Comments of Dr. Frank Loewenberg are reprinted by his
permission.

Tables 4 and 5 are reprinted from the 1/16/69 and
2/3/70 issues of *The New York Times,* respectively.
Copyright 1969/1970 by The New York Times Company.
Reprinted by permission.

For
Vic, Mike, KK, and Cory

Foreword

Heine once wrote that "a book, like a child, needs time to be born. Books written quickly—within a few weeks—make me suspicious of the author." The present book need not be suspected by anyone for, unlike a child which takes only nine months from conception, the plans for this book were conceived almost a decade ago. The Council on Social Work Education (CSWE) was involved in various phases of development of this book. Shortly after its publication in 1962 of a *Guide* for undergraduate programs in social welfare, CSWE asked Professor Romanyshyn to provide a course outline for one of the curriculum areas suggested in the *Guide*. This course outline went through several drafts and incorporated many of the suggestions made by participants in CSWE-sponsored Faculty Institutes led by Professor Romanyshyn and members at the time of CSWE's Committee on Undergraduate Education and was one of the four syllabi published by CSWE under the title *Social Welfare as a Social Institution* CSWE, 1969. Social welfare as a social institution remains a key content area for the curriculum currently suggested by CSWE's revised *Undergraduate Programs in Social Welfare: A Guide to Objectives, Content, Field Experience and Organization* (1967).

After publication of that volume, Professor Romanyshyn was continuously urged by his colleagues to expand the syllabus into a textbook. The Council, without necessarily agreeing with every position taken by Professor Romanyshyn, encouraged him because it saw in his outline the potential for an outstanding contribution to the educational literature in social work. The final product now before us gives ample proof that the expectations of Professor Romanyshyn's colleagues have been justified. This volume provides a seminal reinterpretation of the nature and place of social welfare in American society. In the firm belief that there is no necessary conflict between the social sciences and social welfare, Professor Romanyshyn utilizes social science insights and findings to illuminate his study of social welfare as a social institution. While the issues in social welfare are constantly changing, Romanyshyn's basic approach will help students to raise the kind of questions and use the kind of analytical approaches that will always be needed and will be useful for many years to come.

The Council on Social Work Education is pleased and honored to publish this book by John Romanyshyn in conjunction with Random House.

Arnulf M. Pins
Executive Director
Council on Social Work Education

Preface

Upon completion of a book one wonders how he ever had the audacity to contemplate writing it. It is not quite the book I had started out to write, and portions of it I would wish to quarrel with now. I trust the reader will exercise this option. It is written for students who want to understand and critically examine social welfare issues and for the general reader seeking some perspective on questions of social policy. This is not a textbook in the usual sense of that term. On the other hand, I hope it will be more useful and more provocative than a lot of textbooks I've suffered through as both student and teacher. It is not a textbook because it offers a point of view, one to be challenged, criticized, and even condemned. It does not try to present the reader with a detailed overview of social welfare programs, although some of that may be found here. Social welfare is treated more as a moral ideal than as a collection of programs and services. I choose to see welfare primarily in terms of social issues rather than as professionally directed efforts to deal with social problems. It represents my conviction that this is the proper order of things. Programs and services change almost daily. For the most part the underlying issues remain.

Although social work as a profession and an occupation plays a central role in carrying out social welfare activities, relatively little is said in this book about methods and techniques of social work or other human service professions. That is the subject of another book—one I'd prefer to leave to someone else. Yet I hope social workers and social work students will find something of value in this book for them.

Social Welfare: Charity to Justice deals with issues that affect social work practice and the issues social workers accept the moral obligation to confront. In the final analysis these are public issues that require public resolution. Social work and other human service professions can make important contributions to the quest for the commonweal but they cannot totally embrace it.

How shall one thank all those who had some part in the making of a book such as this? I am first of all indebted to The Lois and Samuel J. Silberman Fund, Inc., for a generous grant and an equally generous amount of patience despite the long delay in completing this volume.   The Board of Directors and Grant Committee of the Fund must of course be relieved of any responsibility for its content.   At no time did the Fund seek to influence the direction of this work.   I thank them all, with special thanks to Mr. Samuel J. Silberman who will understand the meaning these few words are meant to convey.

The following will also understand my grateful acknowledgement; Katherine A. Kendall, Arnulf M. Pins, Frank M. Loewenberg, Donald Feldstein, Milton Chernin, and Betty Mandell.   Each made a special and important contribution.   It's impossible of course to discover, much less mention, all those to whom I am intellectually indebted.   The reader will recognize my dependence on a large group of writers.   I'm aware that Harold L. Wilensky and Charles N. Lebeaux introduced me to a new way of thinking about social welfare through their important volume, *Industrial Society and Social Welfare,* and that Ernest Becker through several of his incredibly scholarly and imaginative books deeply influenced my view of the science of man and its potential contribution to human welfare.   Richard M. Titmuss, Martin Rein, S. M. Miller, Erik Erikson, Abraham Maslow are among others of whose ideas I've borrowed freely.   Of course only the author can assume responsibility for his use or misuse of what they and others had to offer.

I'm especially grateful to Mrs. Jean Soule who typed most of the manuscript (sometimes under rather trying circumstances).   Others who should be mentioned include Phyllis McGrane, Cordelia Cox, Richard Steinman, Dennis Saleebey, and Edith Wilson.   To my children, Victor, Michael, Kathryn, and Coralie, I dedicate this volume with a poignant sense of what I spent in endless hours that properly belonged to them.   The last sentence is especially theirs— an expression of what I believe about man and what I hope they will realize in their own lives.   To my mother, Katherine Romanyshyn, the last word of thanks which really should have been the first.

Contents

Tables

ONE

Social Welfare
and Social Change

ONE

An Overview and a Point of View

This is a book about social welfare, analyzed in the context of our changing social system and evaluated in the light of our central concern with the development of human potential. Three questions are explored: (1) What is social welfare? (2) How has it developed and why? (3) What kind of social welfare philosophy and what programs do we require to contribute to a more democratic and more humane society? A brief overview of our tentative "answers" to these questions will provide the reader with an orientation to what is to follow.

The term *social welfare* expresses an ambiguous and changing concept. It has both a negative and a positive connotation. It may be narrowly defined to mean financial assistance and other services to the disadvantaged. It may, on the other hand, refer to collective responsibility to meet universal needs of the population. Elizabeth Wickenden, in 1965, defined social welfare as ". . . including those laws, programs, benefits, and services which assure or strengthen provisions for meeting social needs recognized as basic to the well-being of the population and the better functioning of the social order."[1] In this book we will use the broader definition of social welfare as including all those forms of social intervention that have a primary and direct concern with promoting both the well-being of the individual and of the society as a whole. Social welfare includes those provisions and processes directly concerned with the treatment and prevention of social problems, the development of human resources, and the improvement in the quality of life. It involves social services to individuals and families as well as efforts to strengthen or modify social institutions. Looking at it from a sociological point of view, social welfare functions to maintain the social system and to adapt it to changing social reality. From an ideological point of view, it is society's answer to that ancient and ever-recurring question, "Am I my brother's keeper?"

[1] Elizabeth Wickenden, *Social Welfare in a Changing World,* U.S. Department of Health, Education, and Welfare (Washington, D.C.: Government Printing Office, 1965), p. vii.

3

Historically our response to this question has embodied two antithetical concepts of community responsibility for the well-being of others. First, welfare may be seen as a *residual* function, that of policing deviants and dependents and/or alleviating their distress in some minimal way as an act of public or private charity. Traditionally this is the way we have tended to think of efforts to assist the "needy." Society intervenes through public or voluntary means to assure some a minimum level of personal well-being and social functioning. The poor, dependent children, the aged, and the handicapped have been some of the traditional recipients of welfare services. Charity, philanthropy, relief, and help to the disabled, deviant, and disadvantaged constitute part of our traditional welfare vocabulary—a vocabulary associated with the residual view that assumes that welfare programs exist to meet the emergency needs of individuals when they are incapable of providing for themselves through the normal institutions of the family and the market. In this view welfare ameliorates the problems of the "unfortunate classes" through middle- and upper-class benevolence. It tends to be a depreciatory term. Stigma is associated with client roles in those social agencies that provide services for "them" ("those poor devils"—or "the ne'er-do-wells"), not for "us" ("the self-reliant" and "normal" ones). Illustrations of such services are public assistance, foster care of children, corrections, and state mental hospitals.

The change in views is shown in a new vocabulary using such terms as *social planning, social utilities, community action.* These terms are associated with the *developmental* concept, which may be illustrated by social insurance and Medicare provisions under the Social Security Act and such supportive resources as day care and homemaker services. This is a positive concept that extends beyond services to the needy to the recognition that all citizens in an industrial society may require a variety of social services to develop their capacity to perform productive roles and to achieve and maintain a desirable standard of well-being. Since problems are rooted in the social structure as well as in individuals, emphasis is on planned social change, the provision of essential resources that support and enhance social functioning, as well as on such adjustment services as counseling and therapy. The antithetical nature of these two concepts is summarized in the statements:

> In current views of social welfare, two concepts predominate: the residual and the developmental. The first holds that social welfare activities should come into play only when the normal structures of society break down. This places social welfare activities in a residual role, ameliorating the breakdown and filling the gaps. The second, and far more promising view of social welfare defines welfare activities as a front line function of modern industrial society, in a positive, collaborative role with other major social institutions working toward a better society.[2]

Wilensky and Lebeaux use the terms residual and institutional:

> Two conceptions of social welfare seem to be dominant in the United States today: the residual and the institutional. The first holds that social

[2] *Social Development: Key to the Great Society,* U.S. Department of Health, Education, and Welfare (Washington, D.C.: Government Printing Office, 1966).

welfare institutions should come into play only when the normal structures of supply, the family and the market, break down. The second, in contrast, sees the welfare services as normal, "first line" functions of modern industrial society.[3]

Although the terms institutional and developmental are used interchangeably, the latter is a more dynamic concept, indicating a continuous process of social renewal.

Social welfare in the United States reflects both the residual and the developmental (or institutional) concepts. It is a system undergoing radical transformation in response to society's transition from scarcity to relative abundance and a revolution of rising expectations.

Social Welfare and Social Change

"The first century of the Machine Age is drawing to a close amid fear and trepidation. Its fabulous material success was due to the willing, indeed the enthusiastic, subordination of man to the needs of the machine. . . . Today we are faced with the vital task of restoring the fullness of life to the person, even though this may mean a technologically less efficient society."—Karl Polanyi [4]

Social welfare cannot be understood apart from society—its material, scientific, and human resources and its structure of values and power that allocates these among competing social ends. Economic growth and democratization of society have transformed our notions of welfare. In the transition from pre-industrial to nineteenth-century laissez-faire capitalism to our present post-industrial society, varying and often conflicting concepts of welfare have developed. Three general concepts—charity and corrections, welfare state, and welfare society—are briefly outlined below and will be expanded throughout the book.

Welfare as Charity and Corrections

Welfare as charity and corrections is essentially a pejorative concept. Its origin is in the Elizabethan Poor Law (1601) and in the nineteenth-century middle-class "benevolence" that was aimed at relieving destitution without reducing the incentive to work.[5] It continues in the present in such programs as public assistance and health services for the medically indigent. It involves measures influenced by the Protestant ethic and dictated by the imperatives of a market society to assist and control the poor within the dictum of "maximum work and minimum welfare." [6]

[3] Harold L. Wilensky and Charles N. Lebeaux, *Industrial Society and Social Welfare* (New York: Free Press, 1965), p. 138.

[4] Karl Polanyi, "Our Obsolete Market Mentality," *Commentary,* February, 1947, p. 109.

[5] Karl de Schweinitz, *England's Road to Social Security* (New York: A. S. Barnes & Co., 1961); and Samuel Mencher, *Poor Law to Poverty Program* (Pittsburgh: University of Pittsburgh Press, 1967).

[6] Charles Frankel, "The Transformation of Welfare," in John S. Morgan (ed.), *Welfare and Wisdom* (Toronto: University of Toronto Press, 1968), p. 176.

Based on an ideology of self-help and moral responsibility for failure it was geared to the central task of ". . . developing, controlling, motivating, and exploiting a labor force while necessary capital investment took place. . . ." [7] The ethic of minimum assistance to the needy was functional for disciplining the labor force to accept work they might otherwise reject as their only means of subsistence. It served also to reduce the burden of caring for others in a society of relative scarcity. Most important, it facilitated the transition from a feudal agrarian society characterized by enforced interdependence, ascribed status, and subsistence economy to an industrial society based on contract, a mobile supply of labor, and the promise—now fully realized in this society—of solving the problem of production. The Poor Law served both to defend the traditional obligations of status in the feudal society and to prepare for a market economy of free labor, free to face the hazards of insecurity as well as the hope of economic betterment.[8]

As Calvin Woodard has helped us to see, the philosophy of charity was adaptable for a society of scarcity bent on developing its powers of economic production. The central concepts of a laissez-faire industrial economy were (1) acceptance of the inevitability of poverty, a view realistic enough under the prevailing conditions, (2) belief that only through work could one aspire to improve his level of living, (3) insistence on moral responsibility for destitution, and (4) insistence on charity, especially its voluntary expression, as the right and proper way to ameliorate the conditions of the poor because it provided for discretion in the use of scarce resources to favor the "worthy poor"—those in need through "no fault of their own." [9] On the other hand the ideal of laissez faire did not mean the absence of government intervention but the use of government to create conditions for economic initiative and the development of the economy. Writing about the period between the American Revolution and the Civil War, Daniel Boorstin observes that there was little ". . . laissez-faire here. Private enterprise expected and obtained subsidies in capital or in kind from every unit of government, Federal, state, county, municipal. The history of canals, railroads, and banks bears obvious testimony to this." [10]

Welfare as charity, as fused in the nineteenth century with economic individualism and the gospel of wealth, was a curious mixture of benevolence and a defense of class inequality. The notion of the stewardship of wealth gave sanctity to large disparities in income, already justified on the basis of individual merit and moral responsibility for worldly success and failure. The act of giving to the needy was seen as a transfer of resources from those who produced the

---

[7] Alfred J. Kahn, "The Societal Context of Social Work Practice," *Social Work,* 10 (October 1965), 146. *See also* Roy Lubove, "Social Work and the Life of the Poor," *The Nation,* May 23, 1966, pp. 609–611.

[8] For a more scholarly presentation of this point *see* Karl Polanyi, *The Great Transformation* (Boston: Beacon Press, 1957) and Mencher, *op. cit.*

[9] Calvin Woodard, "Reality and Social Reform: The Transition from Laissez-Faire to the Welfare State," *Yale Law Journal,* 72 (December 1962), pp. 286–328.

[10] Daniel Boorstin, *The Americans: The National Experience* (New York: Random House, 1965). In short, public support of business and private philanthropy for the poor was perfectly consistent with the notion of laissez faire.

wealth to those who might deserve compassion but who were without rightful claim to the largess bestowed upon them.[11]   That charity clearly was a transaction between superiors and inferiors was evident in Josephine Shaw Lowell's comment that we could not be "charitable to our equals."[12]   Issues of justice related to the maldistribution of income, power, and privilege were concealed in the fiction that social well-being was best assured by the free operation of market forces that automatically transformed economic self-interest into the common good.   Since the individual was responsible for his own well-being, the community need concern itself only with those unable or presumably unwilling to provide for themselves.   Even the worthy poor—aged, widows, and children —tended to bear the stigma of failure because the primary breadwinners in their families, through work and thrift, should have provided for their needs. Though the ethic of self-reliance was a positive concept adaptive to scarcity and the imperatives of economic development, its companion, the ethic of charity for the "failures" of the system, became a depreciated concept that functioned to maintain an impoverished view of human relations and a conservative view of society.

Today welfare programs that continue to be organized around the residual philosophy of organized charity are regarded by some as those "despised services for the despised minority."[13]   The historic hatred of this concept of welfare by the poor is reflected in their rejection of the "bitter bread of charity."   It continues to be resented, as reflected in the contemporary criticism of "welfare colonialism," and is being vigorously challenged in relation to the human rights revolution and the further democratization of society.

Recent formation of welfare rights organizations and new concepts of welfare law seek to establish a citizen right to adequate assistance, protection against arbitrary exercise of authority, and full participation in American society.[14]

Welfare State

The concept of the welfare state has no clear meaning.   As Richard M. Titmuss observes, it is a term of abuse or an article of faith, depending on one's political beliefs.[15]   It can, however, be defined as ". . . government-protected minimum standards of income, nutrition, health, housing, and education for every citizen,

[11] Richard M. Titmuss, "The Role of Redistribution in Social Policy," *Social Security Bulletin,* 28 (June 1965), p. 14.

[12] Roy Lubove, *The Professional Altruist* (Cambridge, Mass.: Harvard University Press, 1965), p. 14.

[13] New York City Youth Board, *Proceedings of the Metropolitan New York Conference on Religion and Race,* 1964, p. 58.

[14] Charles E. Silberman, "The Revolt Against 'Welfare Colonialism,'" *Crisis in Black and White* (New York: Random House, 1964), pp. 308–348; Richard A. Cloward and Frances Fox Piven, "A Strategy to End Poverty," *The Nation,* May 2, 1966, pp. 510–517; Justine Wise Polier, "Problems Involving Family and Child," *Columbia Law Review,* 66 (February 1966), pp. 305–316; Charles A. Reich, "Individual Rights and Social Welfare: The Emerging Legal Issues," *Yale Law Journal,* 74 (June 1965), pp. 1245–1257.

[15] Richard M. Titmuss, "The Welfare State: Images and Realities," *Social Service Review,* 37 (March 1963), pp. 1–11.

assured to him as a political right, not as charity." [16]   It assumes a social rather than a moral explanation of difficulties in meeting needs, collective responsibility for shared problems, and a citizen's right to at least those minimum provisions essential for well-being and effective functioning in a society "where no one can be complete master of his own fate." [17]   The promotion of equality of opportunity has priority over protection of property rights as a basis for government intervention.   The best example of this concept is the social insurance and Medicare provisions of the Social Security Act, to which practically all Americans are entitled.

As nations achieve a relatively advanced technology, referred to by W. W. Rostow as a "stage of high mass consumption," [18] they may choose to devote an increasing share of resources to human and social development.   Some of this must go to the repair of human and social neglect created by a single-minded devotion to economic growth.   This shift from a regulatory to a developmental function of government is not only "humanitarian" but essential for economic and political stability.   Indeed, humanitarian motives may be minor or non-existent in the political decisions that lead to welfare legislation for such laws tend to arise ". . . from political necessity and not humanitarian predispositions. . . .   While love of fellowman may have been a motive for some individual reformers and welfare leaders . . . it was not the power that moved the men in power." [19]

The complexity of urban industrial societies and the need to maintain a high level of consumption for economic growth; the sense of relative deprivation that nourishes discontent, disorder, and the demand for political reform; and the need to invest in the development of those human capacities essential for maintaining an advanced technological system force the government into a direct concern with redistribution of income, creation of human services, and improvement in the physical and social environment.

The transfer of resources to human and social development does not occur automatically.   It results from political decisions that reflect values and the distribution of power.   Part of the pressure for welfare-state provisions comes from the increasing insistence that equality of citizenship be guaranteed by government.[20]   The welfare state is thus an affirmation of new citizenship status, even for that class once called pauper.   In turn it may represent a threat to the privacy and autonomy of individuals as government regulations may be concealed under the humanitarian rubric of "rehabilitation."   Further, the myth of the welfare state conceals the extent to which we have yet to assure minimum living standards or equal opportunity.

---

[16] Harold L. Wilensky, "The Problems and Prospects of the Welfare State," preface to the paperback edition, Wilensky and Lebeaux, op. cit., p. 9.

[17] Charles A. Reich, "The New Property," *Yale Law Journal,* 73 (April 1964), pp. 733–787.

[18] W. W. Rostow, *The Stages of Economic Growth* (Cambridge, England: Cambridge University Press, 1960).

[19] Martin Wolins, "The Societal Function of Social Welfare," *New Perspectives, The Berkeley Journal of Social Welfare,* (Spring 1967), pp. 1–18.

[20] T. H. Marshall, *Class, Citizenship, and Social Development* (Garden City, N.Y.: Anchor Books, 1965), especially "Citizenship and Social Class," Chap. 4, pp. 71–134.

Although the United States is the world's most affluent society, it has the most "reluctant welfare state" of any of the advanced industrial nations.[21] One out of every four children in the United States is growing up in a family living in poverty or just above the poverty line.[22] Nearly one-fourth of the wage and salary workers (16.3 million people) are not covered by unemployment insurance.[23] There is no public income protection against work injury for one out of five wage and salary workers.[24] Eight million social security beneficiaries live in poverty, even with their benefits.[25] Over 8 million poor people live in households in which the head of the family worked all year but did not earn enough to bring the family out of poverty.[26] The Select Senate Committee on Nutrition and Human Needs estimates that there are 10 million hungry Americans; yet in 1969 we spent eight times as much on subsidies to keep up farm prices as we did in helping the poor to receive adequate diets. One-third of our nation's population cannot afford adequate, nonsubsidized housing.[27] Almost all recipients of public assistance receive incomes below the poverty line as a result of public policy.

The rediscovery of poverty in the 1960s and the pressure of the civil rights movement are part of a changing political climate that appears to be moving us from the "social security" phase of the welfare state toward a "social planning" stage ". . . in which human preferences and values democratically determined, may guide allocation of consumption rights and other large areas of public policy." [28] In the light of more recent events this may be too optimistic since it appears that concern with "crime in the streets" and "law and order" may have replaced the "Great Society" and "War on Poverty" thrusts of the Johnson administration. Nonetheless the demand for full citizenship participation will be difficult to ignore. Measures of social reform may be delayed, but they cannot be long repressed without serious disruption of our democratic society.

Social Security Phase

The social security phase of the welfare state is best symbolized by the Social Security Act of 1935. It originated during the New Deal and was based on programs of social insurance more highly developed in Europe. Major goals are to protect individuals against the hazards of economic insecurity associated with old age, unemployment, disability, and loss of a breadwinner. However,

[21] Wilensky, in Wilensky and Lebeaux, *op. cit.* p. xvi.

[22] Mollie Orshansky, "The Shape of Poverty in 1966," *Social Security Bulletin,* 31 (March 1968), p. 6.

[23] *Manpower Report of the President,* U.S. Department of Labor (Washington, D.C.: Government Printing Office, 1968), p. 38.

[24] *Ibid.,* p. 42.

[25] Wilbur J. Cohen, "A Ten-Point Program to Abolish Poverty," *Social Security Bulletin,* 31 (December 1968), p. 3.

[26] *Ibid.,* p. 11.

[27] *Building the American City,* National Commission on Urban Problems, Ninety-first Congress, First sess., House Document 34 (Washington, D.C.: Government Printing Office, 1968), p. 9.

[28] Kahn, *op. cit.,* p. 148.

one-fourth of those 65 years of age or older live on incomes below the poverty line; we have yet to make adequate provisions even for those who, for the most part, cannot be expected to be self-supporting.[29]   Public assistance payments to families deprived of a breadwinner are considerably below the $3,335 minimum suggested for a nonfarm family of four.[30]   Facts such as these reveal the mythology of the welfare state.   At the same time, however, a new climate of acceptance of some form of guaranteed annual income that would place a floor below which no individual or family would fall seems to be developing.

From the Social Security Phase to the Social Planning Phase

The social planning phase would go beyond the assurance of a minimum income to a concern with raising the life chances of those who have been the casualties of the social system and would aim to create conditions that would nurture the development of all individuals.   This would require full employment and reallocation of resources to redress inequities in the distribution of income, housing, education, and medical and other essential human services.   The flood of social legislation in the mid-1960s in pursuit of the "Great Society" may be an indication of a trend in this direction.   In that period (1964–1966), Congress passed more basic legislation to combat poverty, raise the level of education, improve health, provide for the training of youth and the retraining of the unemployed, and develop new approaches to the myriad problems of living in a complex urban-technological society than at any other time in our history. Although hopeful, none of this yet denies that the welfare state is still more myth than reality.   We have yet to allocate resources sufficient for attaining the goal of equal opportunity or to accept the need for social planning and the establishment of priorities that might move us more rapidly in this direction.

Planning would raise the question of the goals toward which we direct our intelligence and resources.   This would lead us to consider going beyond the concept of the welfare state.   The promotion of equality of opportunity may help us establish a more just and more stable society, but it does not necessarily lead to a more human community.   Richard M. Titmuss has suggested that the basic ethic of the welfare state is equality of opportunity in education, access to medical care, and "equality of treatment in the natural and artificial adversities of life."   He adds that this is a past ethic, however unrealized: "The challenge of the second half of the twentieth century is to reinterpret the ethics of welfare in a more complex and wealthier society." [31]

Welfare Society

The concept of the welfare society stems from our aspiration to maximize the development of every individual.   Man is the central concern.   Human dignity and community, rather than property or equality of opportunity, are the central values.   Welfare in this sense is not a separate set of institutions, but the *goal* of society.   All institutions are evaluated in terms of their contribution toward

[29] Orshansky, *op. cit.,* p. 7.

[30] *Ibid.,* p. 4.

[31] Titmuss, "The Welfare State: Images and Realities," *op. cit.,* p. 11.

the development of the kind of human being we value and the social order we want. The term *welfare society* is borrowed from Harold L. Wilensky and Charles N. Lebeaux, who write:

> As the residual conception becomes weaker, as we believe it will, and the institutional conception increasingly dominant, it seems likely that distinctions between welfare and other types of social institutions will become more and more blurred. Under continuing industrialization all institutions will be oriented toward and evaluated in terms of social welfare aims. The "welfare state" will become the "welfare society" and both will be more reality than epithet.[32]

The issue of justice is conceived of in terms of optimum resources and experiences required for nurturing human potentialities. Such a principle is expressed in the purpose of the 1960 White House Conference on Children and Youth, which was ". . . to promote opportunities for children and youth, to realize their full potential for a creative life in freedom and dignity."[33] It is honored in the Judeo-Christian view of the dignity and worth of every human being and has roots in the earlier Greek notion of man as the measure of all things. A society that honors this principle accepts as its central task the adapting of life in an industrial civilization "to the requirements of human existence," thus ending the "subordination of man to the needs of the machine."[34] Such an aspiration must be the essential goal of social welfare however much its attainment remains in doubt. The imperatives of technology, the market society, and the warfare state all inhibit a closer approximation to such an ideal. New resources, new knowledge, and renewed awareness of human potentialities and human purposes beyond those functional for the production of goods may yet allow us to ". . . restore the habitability of the earth and cultivate the empty spaces in the human soul."[35] This would require a welfare ethic and a definition of charity and justice different from any we have so far been able to incorporate in our social life.

The nurture of life can only take place in a society that sees itself as a human community. This is not the kind of society in which we live, but perhaps it can become one. A human community honors charity and justice. Charity in this sense is the early notion of *caritas*. It signifies, as Charles Loch wrote, "good will toward members of the community."[36] It was an extension of sentiments of family members toward one another, developed in pre-Christian as well as in the Christian era. Only later was it to become synonymous with almsgiving and an attitude of *noblesse oblige*. *Caritas* as love, *philia* not *eros*, is to take delight in the existence of another human being and to wish to contribute to his fullest development. It requires what Lionel Trilling has called "the most

---

[32] Wilensky and Lebeaux, *op. cit.,* p. 147.

[33] "Theme of the Conference," *Children,* 7 (May–June 1960), p. 87.

[34] Polanyi, "Our Obsolete Market Mentality," *op. cit.*

[35] Lewis Mumford, *The City in History* (New York: Harcourt, Brace & World, 1961), p. 570.

[36] Charles Stuart Loch, "Charity," *The Encyclopedia Brittanica,* 11th ed. (Cambridge, England: University of Cambridge, 1910), Vol. V, pp. 860–891.

difficult thing in the world, making a willing suspension of disbelief in the self-hood of someone else." [37]   It is based on an ethic of sacrificial love, appropriate to "mothers, martyrs, and heroes," but not to the world of achievement and struggle for power.[38]   It is, however, the only appropriate human response to the needs of children.

Any decent society, much less a "great society," with resources sufficient for the task would meet the basic needs of all its children as a shared responsibility. But we permit over 12.5 million children to live in poverty; [39] develop a free school lunch program for low-income youngsters that fails to provide for two-thirds of all school-age children in poverty; [40] tolerate the scandalous treatment of children and youths in mental hospitals and correctional institutions; and ignore the invisible death of an untold number of children through social isolation and community neglect.

A human community does not require an impossible universal love, but it does require a decent measure of *caritas* that would not suffer the sight of needless deprivation in a society that congratulates itself on coming close to a trillion-dollar Gross National Product in the year 1970.   It also requires a decent measure of justice, the ". . . proper ordering of rights and obligations." [41]   The fundamental right is dignity.   One's obligation is to extend it to others, not only through personal behavior, but through the development of institutions that reflect a conviction that ". . . what men are entitled to by right is not the partial amelioration of their inequalities, but the full, equal realization of their capacities." [42]   Through creating such institutions, we all may become more fully human.

International Social Welfare

The concept of international social welfare is based on the transition from local to world society and the recognition that welfare problems at home cannot be solved in isolation from a concern with the entire family of man.

Until recently, welfare has been defined in national terms as the redress of inequities between the "haves" and the "have-nots" within a society.   Today the greatest challenge is international social welfare, the redress of inequities between the "have" and "have-not" nations.   Wide and growing disparities between the living standards of the rich and poor countries pose major threats to world security and crippling restrictions on world-wide human development. At the same time, though minimal in terms of needs, significant aid has been provided by the more affluent nations in support of a "Decade of Development"

---

[37] Lionel Trilling, *Freud and the Crisis of our Culture* (Boston: Beacon Press, 1955), p. 15.

[38] Reinhold Niebuhr, "Some Things I Have Learned," *Saturday Review*, November 6, 1965, p. 21.

[39] Orshansky, *op. cit.*, p. 16.

[40] Citizen's Board of Inquiry into Hunger and Malnutrition in the United States, *Hunger, U.S.A.* (Washington, D.C.:   New Community Press, 1968), p. 50.

[41] Richard Lichtman, *Toward Community* (Santa Barbara, Calif.:   Center for the Study of Democratic Institutions, 1966), p. 12.

[42] *Ibid.*, p. 45.

launched by the United Nations in 1960. In the past ten years some $60 billion was transferred from the rich to the poor nations. The results are invariably mixed, grounds for cautious optimism as well as deep concern for the future. As Sir Arthur Lewis has observed, underdeveloped countries have made miraculous progress in the light of expectations a decade ago. Yet, in the light of ". . . what is needed, and what has to be achieved, the underdeveloped countries are doing badly." [43]

The projected growth rate of 5 percent per annum in national income for the developing world has been attained by the end of the decade of the sixties. However, it has been undermined in varying degrees in some countries by excessive population growth. Still, the overall per capita growth rate is two and one-half, an impressive achievement since it exceeds the per capita rates of growth in the United States, England, and France. For some countries, like Pakistan, economic growth exceeds population growth. For others, like India, Egypt, and many Latin American countries, the reverse prevails. A recent report of the Agency for International Development on the Alliance for Progress (a program of economic development for Latin America supported by $9.2 billion in loans and grants from the United States from 1961 to 1969) concluded that economic progress is, in general, beyond reach until steps are taken to control population growth. [44] While the anticipated growth rate was more than attained, it was also more than absorbed in most countries by excessive population growth. The extent to which high birth rates may interfere with social development is revealed by the enrollment of school-age children in primary schools, which increased by about 50 percent between 1960 and 1967 in those countries participating in the alliance. Yet, because of high birth rates, there were in fact more children not enrolled in primary schools at the end of that period than at the beginning. In fact, throughout most of the underdeveloped world, population grows more rapidly than economic and social resources, leading to the prediction that despite "massive investments in education and jobs, the absolute number of illiterate and unemployed persons in the world is virtually certain to increase rather than diminish. [45]

The rate of population growth undermines the most heroic efforts at economic and social development. We were well into the nineteenth century (1830) before population attained the billion mark. In 1930 the second billion was added. In just 30 years (between 1930 and 1960) the population of the world increased by an additional billion. The fourth billion will be added by 1975 in the short span of only fifteen years. If current trends of high fertility and declining mortality continue, it will take only nine years to add the fifth billion, eight years for the sixth, and five years for the seventh. In that event, by the year 2000 the total human family will consist of around 7.5 billion individuals, about double the population in 1970. In the view of many, population growth combined with the technological assault on nature creates an ecolog-

[43] Sir Arthur Lewis, "Discussion" of "Priorities in an Affluent Society," *The Center Magazine,* 3 (January 1970), p. 78.

[44] *The New York Times,* March 16, 1969.

[45] *World Population: A Challenge to the United Nations and its System of Agencies,* A report of a National Policy Panel established by the United Nations Association of the United States of America, New York, New York, 1969, p. 23.

ical crisis. If we are to preserve the earth as a habitable planet and hold out some hope that man may yet live with dignity, world population control accompanied by technological restraint and massive aid in behalf of the poorer nations is essential. Throughout the world there is mounting concern over the population explosion, yet "not much more than a score of countries have population and family planning policies of any kind, only a handful of these have policies deliberately designed to have demographic impact, while the number with effective programs is even smaller." [46] Population control is not simply a matter of wide public acceptance and ready access to various means of contraception. Values and social structure influence rates of birth. Population growth is determined by the position of women in society and the range of careers open to them, as well as the degree of social acceptance of childless couples, small families and single status for adult men and women.

However effective population control may be, it cannot replace the need for a major redistribution of the world's resources. Some political conservatives, it is true, seek to avoid the issue of inequality on both the domestic and international scene, by focusing exclusive attention on overpopulation. The obligation of the wealthy nations to the underdeveloped world cannot be so easily denied. According to one observer this obligation to the family of man requires a fifteen-year tax equal to 20 percent on the national income of all developed nations.[47] This dramatizes the scope of the need for international aid but is probably unrealistic. The United Nations urges developed nations to contribute a modest 1 percent of their GNP to foreign aid, yet the current level of international assistance provided by the United States is equal to less than one-fourth of 1 percent. This is the lowest level during the post-World War II era. Indeed we seem to be retreating from the war on poverty both at home and abroad. Sentiments regarding foreign aid are complicated by the link between international warfare and welfare. Economic and military aid are sometimes difficult to separate. For example, in 1970 a $2.3 billion plan for military and economic aid was included in the defense appropriation bill.[48] Commitment to the preservation and expansion of American military power may motivate appropriations for foreign economic assistance rather than concerns for promoting international social welfare. In like manner, reactions against such motives may encourage some to oppose foreign aid, as in the case of Senator Mike Mansfield, the Senate Majority Leader, who is quoted as saying he "will vote against any foreign aid appropriations on the grounds that they lead only to foreign military involvements." [49] Ironically, without appropriate foreign aid aimed at economic and social development, world peace seems less assured.

With close to one-half the world's population suffering from hunger, crippling malnutrition, or both, world poverty is a life-and-death issue since ". . . the current international tensions generated by the have-nots of this world of expanding population could explode into the most dangerous forms of conflict,

[46] *Ibid.,* p. 16.

[47] Andrei D. Sakharov, *Progress, Co-existence and Intellectual Freedom* (New York: Norton, 1968), p. 47.

[48] *The New York Times,* July 2, 1970.

[49] *Ibid.*

including a nuclear war." [50]　The avoidance of such a holocaust may require a different war, one attacking world poverty.　In the words of Norton Long, "In the prosecution of this war, roles of dignity and meaning should be available to our whole society.　In a great and necessary task needing all our energies, The Great Society might come to be." [51]　Yet such an endeavor would have to be based on a conception of welfare that abjured any trace of international charity. At home and abroad we face a common issue, the right of citizens to an equitable share in the common wealth.

A Point of View

> Some confessions of a man seeking that golden mean between Pangloss and Don Quixote, where acceptance of reality is not acquiescence in the mutilation of mankind, the rationalization of self-interest, or the impoverishment of our ability to dream.　Some comments on the themes of inquiry, ambiguity, paradox, the tragic view of life and human potential.

Anyone who presumes to write about so controversial a field as social welfare ought to make explicit the ideological lens through which he sees or, perhaps, misperceives the world.　My approach is guided by the ethic of indignation and disciplined, I hope, by the principle of inquiry.　I mean the word "indignation" as Erik H. Erikson used it when he wrote:

> True *adaptation*, . . . is maintained with the help of loyal rebels who refuse to adjust to "conditions" and cultivate an indignation in the service of a to-be-restored wholeness without which psychosocial evolution and all of its institutions would be doomed. [52]

We need such rebels, loyal to the basic values of a free society, indignant over the extent to which our institutions violate our commitment to human dignity, and ready to pursue the ". . . vital task of restoring the fullness of life to the person . . ." [53]　Such was the mission of Jane Addams. [54]　She is the most noble and perhaps the most tragic figure in the history of social welfare; she symbolizes our highest aspirations and the dilemmas that confront a society ever hopeful about man, yet in many ways hostile to human values.　Our society

---

[50] Berton H. Kaplan, "Social Issues and Poverty Research: A Commentary," *Journal of Social Issues,* 21, (January 1965), p. 9.

[51] Norton Long, "Local and Private Initiative in the Great Society," in Bertram M. Gross (ed.), *The Great Society* (New York: Basic Books, 1966), p. 103.

[52] Erik H. Erikson, *Insight and Responsibility* (New York: Norton, 1964), p. 156.

[53] Polanyi, "Our Obsolete Market Mentality," *op. cit.,* p. 116.

[54] Jane Addams, *Twenty Years at Hull House* (New York: A Signet Classic, 1961).　For a sympathetic but critical analysis of her accomplishments, *see* Christopher Lasch, *The New Radicalism in America* (New York: Knopf, 1965), pp. 3–37. *See also* Robert M. Hutchins, "The Nurture of Human Life," *Bulletin* No. 10 (Santa Barbara, Calif.: Center for the Study of Democratic Institutions, March 1961), pp. 1–4; Henry Steele Commager, *The Search For a Usable Past* (New York: Knopf, 1967).

may be described as caught somewhere between "Cacotopia" and "Eutopia." [55] Cacotopia signifies the "bad place," the nightmare revealed in the literature of the absurd, as reflected in our expenditures to maintain the "warfare state" and the "culture of death," and implicit in Richard Hofstadter's description of our ". . . democracy in cupidity rather than a democracy of fraternity." [56] "Eutopia" is the "good place" (as distinct from "Utopia," which is "no place"). It is the reasonably decent society reflected in the real measures of social progress we have attained: relative political stability and freedom and economic security for the majority, facts of life that are rare in human history. Despite many imperfections, these do prevail in our society. This view of Eutopia is further reflected in our ideal values, perhaps progressively within our reach, as we learn to use our abundant intelligence and our economic resources for human purposes, purposes that can be attained only through a critical understanding and radical reform of our society. Historically, Americans have been resistant to the very idea of society. In the process we have created a culture hostile to the very idea of individuality. We misunderstand the relationship between self and society.[57] Our atomistic view of social relations, based on the myths of liberal capitalism, rests on an illusion that the celebration of the individual excludes an equal concern for creating the kind of society in which individual development can best take place. Thus we confuse individualism with individuality. Still driven by the imperatives of technology, the requirements of a market economy, and our Calvinistic ethos, we are less free than we think to develop our humanity. We find it difficult to perceive our social structures and the damage we do to one another, for we see through the narrow and distorted lens of an individualism bereft of an adequate sense of community. Individualism such as that seen by Alexis de Tocqueville, forces one ". . . back forever upon himself alone and threatens in the end to confine him entirely within the solitude of his own heart." [58]

We seem to be a culture that suffers from a tremendous discontent without an adequate language with which to register complaints or to imagine a better social order. Much of our protest is violent and psychosomatic. We have one of the world's highest rates of psychogenic deaths through murder, suicide, ulcers, high blood pressure, and cirrhosis of the liver.[59] Perhaps this is because we operate on a narrow and impoverished concept of human needs and social possibilities. It is difficult for us to see that we have a totalitarian technology in which man

---

[55] W. H. Ferry, Michael Harrington, and Frank L. Keegan, *Cacotopias and Utopias* (Santa Barbara, Calif.: Center for the Study of Democratic Institutions, 1965).

[56] Edward Albee, *The American Dream and Zoo Story* (New York: A Signet Book, 1959); Jules Henry, *Culture Against Man* (New York: Vintage Books, 1965); Richard Hofstadter, *The American Political Tradition* (New York: Vintage Books, 1948), p. viii.

[57] Paul E. Pfuetze, *Self, Society, Existence* (New York: Harper Torchbooks, 1961).

[58] Alexis de Tocqueville, *Democracy in America* (New York: Vintage Books, 1962), Vol. II, p. 106.

[59] Stanley A. Rudin, "The Personal Price of National Glory," *Trans-action*, 2 (September–October, 1965), pp. 4–9.

is subservient to the imperatives of an industrial economy that shapes our self-image; defines our needs; makes much of our education narrowly vocational, antidevelopmental, and antiintellectual; and determines the work we do and therefore the kind of human potentialities we can nurture.[60]   Much of our way of life, with important exceptions, becomes a celebration of mechanism over organism, of efficiency over creativity, of the instrumental over the expressive, and of the pragmatic over the pleasurable.   As a result, we may misdiagnose our problems and offer a narrow range of solutions.   We tend to ignore the insight of Jane Addams, who saw that much of what we call delinquency may be a normal, sad, or ugly expression of the natural human drive for pleasure, for enrichment of experience, for intensification of life, ". . . a protest against the dullness of life, to which we ourselves instinctively respond." [61]   She saw, as Christopher Lasch has written, ". . . that the outcry against juvenile delinquency . . . was more than anything else a profound indifference to youth and the resort to repression an index of cynical disregard for their welfare." [62] Perhaps this is less true today.   What remains true is our instrumental view, even of children.   Society, as Jane Addams thought, cares more for what young people may be able to produce ". . . than for their immemorial ability to reaffirm the charm of existence." [63]   We have an institutionalized incapacity to respond to such a poetic view of life, for our technologically induced categories of thought and central goals cannot quite accommodate such frills as the "charm of existence."   Robert Hutchins is surely right when he observes that ". . . the aims of the industrial society, no matter what methods are used to achieve them and no matter how far from or near to achievement they are, cannot now satisfy the aspirations of the human animal." [64]

Whatever man is, *homo sapiens, homo faber,* he is also *homo ludens,* man the playful animal.[65]   The challenge of life is to improve the quality of the games we play, make the rules more just and the stakes more worthy of human endeavor and dignity.   Reference to games should not be confused with mere child's play for, as Ernest Becker has so brilliantly demonstrated, man plays a "meaning game" through his participation in society, the norms and rules of which define the purpose of his life and provide either a narrow or rich source of possibilities for self-esteem and self-actualization.[66]

The combination of the Protestant ethic and the acquisitive market society has ceased to offer a definition of life's purpose that can provide a basis for in-

[60] Jacques Ellul, *The Technological Society* (New York: Knopf, 1965).   *Also:* Donald Michael, *The Next Generation* (New York: Vintage Books, 1965); Herbert Marcuse, *One Dimensional Man* (Boston: Beacon Press, 1964); Henry, *op cit.;* and Ernest Becker, *The Structure of Evil* (New York: George Braziller, 1968).

[61] Jane Addams, *The Spirit of Youth and the City Streets* (New York: Macmillan, 1909), p. 71.

[62] Lasch, *op. cit.,* p. 155.

[63] Addams, *The Spirit of Youth, op. cit.,* p. 305.

[64] Robert Hutchins, "Anatomy of the Post-Industrial Age," *The Center Magazine,* 2 (May 1969), p. 87.

[65] Johan Huizinga, *Homo Ludens* (Boston: Beacon Press, 1950).

[66] Ernest Becker, *The Revolution in Psychiatry* (New York: Free Press, 1964), p. 112.

dividual dignity or a viable community. Perhaps it never did. What it has accomplished in a magnificent way is the solution to the problem of economic scarcity. In the process it has created costs both human and social, which constitute much of the agenda of social welfare programs. This is hardly a novel observation. The "sickness of an acquisitive society" was noted by R. H. Tawney long ago.[67] The destructiveness of our image of man as "economic man," however functional for harnessing human energy for economic development, has been well described by a number of writers.[68]

Having solved the problem of production of goods we are in a position to devote our energies and wealth of resources to the development of man. Herein lies the basis for a more "eutopian" view of reality. We take seriously Jerome B. Wiesner's declaration:

> This is . . . one of the greatest, most exciting periods in man's history. We are the first generation with the resources to make almost any kind of world we want, including no world. Consequently the questions of what to make and what human values to honor are probably more important today than at any previous time in history.[69]

The major issue is what these values and goals are to be. The alternatives are not unlimited. Much of what we do seems to be functional for maintaining a technologically driven society. The goal of occupational achievement, compulsively affirmed, is functional for maintaining such a system. It may be gratifying for an intellectual elite and disastrous for those excluded by natural endowment, race and ethnic prejudice, class barriers, and lack of opportunity. As Donald G. McKinley puts it, our ". . . system of moral evaluation . . . produces the creative excellence and the brutal deviance . . ."[70]

If we organize society as a game called "occupational achievement," somebody has to be the "loser," at least relative to the position, power, and prestige attained by others. Welfare programs have functioned in part to keep the game going by maintaining the incentive to work, to cushion failure, and to control those who have tried to beat the system, withdraw from it, or seek revenge. Such programs have focused on defects to be corrected in individuals rather than on basic changes in the social system. This conservative orientation, however, is more of a political than a scientific problem. Richard Hofstadter has noted that modern industrial capitalism has been too successful to foster ideas hostile to its fundamental working arrangement: "Such ideas may appear, but they are closely and persistently insulated, as an oyster deposits nacre around an irritant." [71] All institutions, including education and welfare, tend to be in-

---

[67] R. H. Tawney, *The Acquisitive Society* (New York: Harcourt, Brace & Howe, 1920).

[68] Most notable are Tawney, *ibid.;* Polanyi, *The Great Transformation, op. cit.;* Becker, *The Structure of Evil, op. cit.,* especially pp. 238 ff. *Also,* poets from William Blake to Allen Ginsburg; novelists and playwrights, especially Kafka, Dostoevsky, Beckett, O'Neil, and scores of others. *See also* Archibald MacLeish, "The Revolt of the Diminished Man," *Saturday Review,* June 7, 1969, pp. 16–19 and 61.

[69] Jerome B. Wiesner, *Christian Science Monitor,* February 17, 1964.

[70] Donald G. McKinley, *Social Class and Family Life* (New York: Macmillan, 1964), p. 268.

[71] Hofstadter, *op. cit.,* pp. ix, xx.

herently conservative. They inhibit the development of a critical theory of society because their acceptability depends on their congruence with those norms around which we organize our social system.[72]

While this is a correct statement as far as it goes, it is too simple. Our basic values are conflicting and changing. Alfred North Whitehead wrote, "Mankind is now in one of its rare moods of shifting its outlook." [73] He added,

> It is the business of philosophers, students, and practical men to re-create and re-enact a vision of the world, conservative and radical, including those elements of reverence and order without which society lapses into riot; a vision penetrated through and through with unflinching rationality.[74]

In the ferment all around us; in the revolt of students, minorities, and the poor; in the anxious defense of fundamental values; and in the quest for new visions of social order, we see this shift in outlook of which Whitehead speaks. We are increasingly aware that our basic social institutions fail to realize our ideal values. Yet failure is relative. We perceive it in the light of altered conditions, new knowledges, and new aspirations. What may seem at least partially obsolete in terms of present realities may have served useful functions in the past. Those exhilarated by the perception of new social options are rarely kind to the Establishment. Still it is only the established order that makes a new one possible. To what extent we can experience this social revolution and direct its outcome with "unflinching rationality" remains in doubt.

Inquiry

Our quest is for understanding in a world characterized by ambiguity, para- dox, tragedy, and human potentials yet unrealized. The first step in any effort at inquiry into the nature of social institutions and the way they may be modi- fied is to recognize the difficulties we confront. There are serious limitations in our knowledge, dangers as well as promise in the application of science to the study and control of man and society. Deep anxieties underlie our resistance to giving up the illusions we all seem to need. We have no choice but act on the basis of the best knowledge available, to seek better understanding, and to constantly evaluate our efforts in terms of the end values we are pursuing. While we do have more knowledge than we are putting to use, we need a modest view of our intellectual grasp of the nature of man, society, and the processes of directed change.

Social and behavioral scientists are divided in their views of the world. There are more unsettled issues than agreed on theories, which makes for chal- lenging controversy for the scholar and difficult dilemmas for the man of action.[75] History continues to remind us that our hindsight is better than our

---

[72] *See* Robert L. Heilbroner, *The Limits of American Capitalism* (New York: Harper & Row, 1965).

[73] Quoted by Norman Cousins, "Editorial," *Saturday Review,* July 27, 1963, p. 16.

[74] *Ibid.*

[75] For one exploration of some issues in the psychologists' view of man, *see* Isidor Chein, "The Image of Man," *Journal of Social Issues,* 18 (October 1962), pp. 1–35.

foresight.   This is illustrated by the failure of most sociologists to predict the civil rights movement and the explosive demand of American Negroes for "freedom now."   Although it is possible and essential to apply reason and the scientific canons of observation and verification to the study of social phenomenon, there is disagreement about the extent to which the methods of the natural sciences are applicable to the social and behavioral sciences.[76]   It has been pointed out, for example, that natural science is the study of events that have causes whereas social science is concerned with understanding human behavior and experience that have meaning.

The scientist, more than the layman, must be expected to be disciplined in the encounter between reality and his image of what is or ought to be.   Yet we have the testimony of a major sociologist who insists that what the social scientist ". . . perceives to be the nature of that reality, is influenced by his own needs of which he may not be conscious and moreover he cannot help but change the reality just by his effort to define or redefine it." [77]   It appears that man is both a seeker of truth and a seeker of those illusions that will transform reality to fit his own needs and expectations.   Sigmund Freud helped us to understand how we defend ourselves from reality, and a review of what behavioral science tells us about man further comments on this point:

> For the truth is . . . that no matter how successful man becomes in dealing with his problems, he still finds it hard to live in the real world, undeluded: to see what one really is, to hear what others really think of one, to face the conflicts and threats really present, or, for that matter, the bare human feelings.[78]

Education ought to enable us to confront more of reality and to cope with it more successfully but, partly because of the kind of education most of us have experienced, we are not as open to new ideas as we like to think.   We are especially threatened by efforts to change assumptions on which we have so laboriously built our self-image and our view of the world.   A Zen story illustrates this point:

> Nan-in, a Japanese master during the Meiji era (1868–1912), received a university professor who came to inquire about Zen.   Nan-in served tea.

For an exploration of some issues in the sociologists' view of society, *see* Irving Louis Horowitz (ed.), *The New Sociology* (New York: Oxford University Press, 1964); Dennis H. Wrong, "The Failure of American Sociology," *Commentary*, November, 1959, pp. 375–380; Sidney M. Willhelm, "Elites, Scholars and Sociologists," *Catalyst*, No. 2 (Summer 1966), pp. 1–10; Irving Louis Horowitz, *Professing Sociology* (Chicago: Aldine Publishing Co., 1968).

[76] Bernard Berelson and Gary A. Steiner, *Human Behavior: An Inventory of Scientific Findings* (New York: Harcourt, Brace & World, 1964), p. 666.   *Also* John H. Madge, *The Tools of Social Science* (New York: Longmans, Green, & Co., 1953), chap. 1; and Arthur J. Vidich, Joseph Bensman, and Maurice R. Stein (eds.), *Reflections on Community Studies* (New York: Wiley, 1964).

[77] John R. Seeley, "Crestwood Heights: Intellectual and Libidinal Dimensions of Research," in Vidich, *et al., ibid.,* p. 163.

[78] Berelson and Steiner, *op. cit.,* p. 664.

He poured his visitor's cup full, and then kept on pouring. The professor watched the overflow until he no longer could restrain himself. "It is overfull. No more will go in!" "Like this cup," Nan-in said, "you are full of your own opinions and speculations. How can I show you Zen unless you first empty your cup?" [79]

Nothing so ambitious as Zen insight is promised through reading this book. The story simply reminds us that we are all so full of our own opinions and speculations that new insights, even if available and worth attention, are difficult to assimilate. We all need to develop the intellectual and emotional fortitude to examine critically our basic values. This is especially true in this era of rapid social change, for we tend to see the world in terms of concepts that are no longer appropriate to the new reality and we try to deal with new problems in terms of obsolete assumptions.

The quest for understanding assumes a capacity for tolerating the essential ambiguity of life and the uncertain nature of all social arrangements designed to ameliorate its hardships or enhance its quality. At every turn we are confronted with paradox, the ". . . inseparable mixture of good and evil, of true and false, of creative and destructive forces—both individual and social." [80] For example, the introduction of the wage economy produced freedom for the medieval serf and presented man with the problem of economic security. Industrialization and urbanization have helped to create our contemporary social problems, but are in turn the conditions for the development of the resources and knowledge that may allow us to deal with them more effectively. Alienation is a source of malaise and yet is a necessary condition of freedom from the restrictions of a traditional society. Division of labor and increasing specialization have made man more individual and more socially dependent. Richard M. Titmuss sees in the latter paradox the stimulus for much of the development of social welfare programs in the modern world.[81] Some of the new technology such as systems planning, cybernation, and social engineering provides tools for dealing with organized complexity, yet threatens to institutionalize a dehumanized image of man. The effort to promote social welfare must be based on the desire to increase the capacity of man to control the conditions of his life without making him a captive of social engineers, worshipping at the altar of efficiency.

To avoid a Pollyanna view of the world and a romantic optimism that can quickly turn into cynical despair, one must also face the tragic view of life. To confront the tragic is to recognize that fate is indifferent to the claim of any one individual to even a modest share of happiness, that men cannot live without doing injustice, and that frailty is the human condition in the face of an inexorable life cycle. Suffering and strife have always existed and must exist given the essential polarity of life, for we instinctively reject the Garden of Eden, even as we seek it. We must accept that there are limits within which

[79] Paul Reps, *Zen Flesh, Zen Bones: A Collection of Zen and Pre-Zen Writings* (New York: Anchor Books, 1961), p. 1.

[80] Paul Tillich, "The Ambiguity of Perfection," *Time*, May 17, 1963, p. 69.

[81] Richard M. Titmuss, *Essays on the "Welfare State"* (London: G. Allen, 1958), p. 41.

we may modify the human condition, however much these limits remain unknown.

Our inability to confront the tragic that we cannot change also means we frequently fail to face realistically that which is ugly and brutal but which might be modified if we were willing to bear the burden of change. We have an optimistic tradition that the "American Dream" will unfold painlessly to the advantage of all. This helps to account for our long neglect of the human cost of race discrimination and our unwillingness to accept the economic and social cost of changes that will redress this great wrong.[82] Whitney M. Young, Jr., describes his own involvement in this tendency to avoid seeing the negative:

> It has become necessary for me to face realistically the true state of America's development as it seeks to make operational and give honest meaning to its creed of equal opportunity and justice for all. Like most human beings and certainly most Americans, I seek the beautiful, the positive and the pleasant while avoiding that which is ugly, negative and sad.
>
> This is especially true when my own responsibility is clear, and when honest introspection arouses guilt. But there comes a time when the alternatives to facing ourselves frankly and seeing our roles clearly are so tragic, so dangerous, so foolish and so irresponsible, that even the most insensitive, the most blasé, or the most adept at rationalizing among us must stop and analyze both his attitudes and his actions or inactions.[83]

To accept the tragic is to accept man's fate. To learn to use knowledge in behalf of human welfare is to restrict the scope of fate in setting the limits within which we may design our lives. "The poor ye shall always have with ye," was a historical definition of man's fate. For Americans, this is now challenged by a new affluence in which poverty exists only so long as we tolerate it. To the extent that we cannot change the fate of man, the recognition of the tragic may allow us to become ". . . more humane and more realistic, more generous in our sympathies and more sober in our judgments."[84]

We need such counsel, for history has not acknowledged the wisdom of the eighteenth-century belief in progress and the perfectability of man. Neither has it destroyed, though it certainly has battered, the belief in fraternity and the possibility of establishing a human community. The writer assumes a compassionate view of man is to be preferred, though the cynic is not without his-

[82] My colleague, Dr. Frank Loewenberg, takes issue with this point of view. He writes, in a personal communication, "Racial discrimination was neglected for so long in America because (1) it was functional for many groups in American society, particularly industrial and agricultural employers, and (2) it fit the nonegalitarian culture which was the standard in many parts of the American society, the ideal egalitarian culture notwithstanding. Racial discrimination for many decades was not viewed as contrary to the American dream—neither by the discriminators nor by the discriminated. Hence, optimism is irrelevant in this discussion for all periods prior to World War I."

[83] Whitney M. Young, Jr., *To Be Equal* (New York: McGraw-Hill, 1964), p. 20.

[84] Herbert J. Muller, *The Uses of The Past* (New York: Oxford University Press, 1957), pp. 24–25. For a historian's view of the importance of the tragic view, *see* especially "The Method of Tragedy," pp. 21–26. For an alternate view, *see* Lionel Abel, "Is There A Tragic View of Life?," *Commentary,* December 1964, pp. 35–40.

torical support for a jaundiced assessment of man's best intentions. Compassion is not to be confused with sentimentality. "Sentiment," someone has said, "is jam on your bread, while sentimentality is jam all over your face." We discover our own humanity as we develop the capacity to identify with an ever larger group of our fellow-men, provided such identification allows for accepting in others the human foibles and frailties we dislike in ourselves. Expressions of humanitarianism are at times sentimental and tyrannical, seeking to purify humanity through moral reform, religious crusades, prohibitions against vice, wars of liberation, censorship, social uplift through social discipline, and other efforts to do good that may do great harm. Such efforts have led Sen. William Fulbright to protest that ". . . the world has endured about all it can of the crusades of high-minded men bent on the regeneration of the human race." [85]

The hostility toward do-gooders is not without foundation. It is partly a reaction against the repressive piety and the misguided idealism of those who would remake man without his consent and in an image he would not recognize, much less welcome. Sir Thomas More described this humanitarian fallacy when he wrote, "they not only invent ideal institutions for mankind, but invent an ideal mankind for their institutions." [86] Compassion, based on respect for the integrity of others, is a far different and urgently needed form of humanitarianism.

> If we are to avoid some of the distressing conditions in modern society, we must institutionalize and place in cultural pre-eminence, the compassionate concern for others. For aggression and rational exploitation beget regression and irrational assault. The slums do seek their revenge.[87]

How to do this in a mass society in which science, technology, and large-scale organization tend to support efficiency over humanitarianism as the dominant value orientation is not clear.

On the other hand, we need not depend on compassion alone to produce necessary social changes. Arthur M. Schlesinger, Jr., has observed that ". . . self-interest combined with humanitarian concern is the effective mixture for social reform." [88] Self-interest alone argues for more effective ways of dealing with our social problems whether we take a compassionate or a cynical view of man.[89]

[85] J. William Fulbright, "The Uses of Flexibility," *Saturday Review,* May 8, 1966, p. 19.

[86] Sir Thomas More, *Utopia* (New York: Everyman's Library, 1951), p. vii.

[87] McKinley, *op. cit.,* p. 269.

[88] Arthur M. Schlesinger, Jr., *The American as Reformer* (Cambridge, Mass.: Harvard University Press, 1950), p. 50.

[89] This dichotomy, of course, has the serious limitations of all efforts to make such simple divisions of mankind. Indeed, Alan W. Watts suggests that "gentle cynicism" characterizes the most cultured and the most humane who understand and accept that we are all rogues. ("The whole possibility of loving affection between human beings depends upon the recognition and acceptance of an element of irreducible rascality in oneself and others—though to parade it is just as much hypocrisy as the advertisement of one's virtues.") Alan W. Watts, *The Two Hands of God: The Myths of Polarity* (New York: George Braziller, 1963), p. 18. *See also* Thomas Mann, *Confessions of Felix Krull* (New York: Knopf, 1955).

Whatever our blend of cynicism and compassion, we all have a stake in the economic, social, and human cost of the failure to deal more effectively with poverty, unemployment, delinquency, crime, family breakdown, mental illness, and the host of troubles and issues included in what is called the urban crisis. Failure to operate the economy at full employment from 1953 to 1966 has meant a loss of $700 billion of total national production (GNP, measured in uniform 1965 dollars) and 35 million man-hours of unnecessary unemployment.[90] At the same time all levels of government thus lost over $200 billion in public revenues at existing tax rates. Without considering the suffering and social burden of illness and premature death, it is estimated that the economic cost of illness in 1963 was over $46 billion.[91] It takes over $3,000 a year to maintain a single delinquent child in an institution and estimates of the economic cost of delinquency and crime run into the billions.

In seventy-five disturbances in sixty-seven cities in the summer of 1967, there were eighty-three deaths and 1,897 injuries. Estimates of property damage were $40–50 million in Detroit and $10.2 million in Newark. These figures, according to the National Advisory Commission on Civil Disorders, should not obscure three important factors: (1) The dollar cost should be increased by the extraordinary administrative expenses of municipal, state, and federal governments. (2) Deaths and injuries are not the only measure of human costs—there were the costs of dislocation of people plus immeasurable costs of fear, distrust, and alienation. (3) Even low levels of violence may seriously disrupt a small community.[92] There is no way of calculating the total cost to society in wasted human resources and in the miserable quality of life characteristic of most of our cities.

But the issue is not primarily one of cost. Citing such figures as those above may not be particularly compelling. The burden of the waste and misery is not distributed equitably and may not be felt personally. In our increasingly interdependent and conflicted society—local, national, and international—the very condition of living at all requires that we learn to live together. This problem is both ethical and scientific: it is the problem of learning how to be effectively humane. This requires, writes Jerome Bruner, ". . . a working model of industrial society, of the limits and capabilities of science, of the constraints of history, of the possibilities of government." [93]

To be effectively humane requires some blending of compassion, self-interest, and competence. "In intensity of feeling," Charles Booth wrote in 1903, "and not in statistics, lies the power to move the world. But by statistics must this

[90] Leon H. Keyserling, "Employment and the 'New Economics,' " in Bertram M. Gross (ed.), *Social Intelligence for America's Future* (Boston: Allyn & Bacon, 1969), p. 339.

[91] U.S. Congress, *Economic Report of the President* together with *The Annual Report of the Council of Economic Advisers,* House Document No. 348, Eighty-ninth Congress, 2nd Session (Washington, D.C.: Government Printing Office, 1966), p. 103.

[92] *Report of The National Advisory Commission on Civil Disorders* (Washington, D.C.: Government Printing Office, 1968), p. 66.

[93] Jerome Bruner, "Character Education and Curriculum," in Jerome Bruner (ed.), *Learning About Learning,* Office of Education, U.S. Department of Health, Education, and Welfare (Washington, D.C.: Government Printing Office, 1966), p. 118.

power be guided if it would move the world aright." [94]   In like manner, Robert S. Morison observes that we must "develop the ability to feel statistics" [95] that is, to experience the full import of such statements as the following: Although the United States has one-sixth of the world's population we use up 50 percent of its irreplaceable natural resources to maintain our affluence.   Ninety-two percent of the children in a Head Start program were found to have vitamin A deficiencies on a level lower than that seen in children who were already blind because of the deficiency.[96]   "Mortality rates among nonwhite babies are 58 percent higher than among whites for those under 1 month old and are almost three times as high among those from 1 month to 1 year old." [97]   High crime rates in urban ghettos increase the probability of being a victim of a crime.   "For nonwhites, the probability of suffering from any index of crime except larceny is 78 percent higher than for whites.   The probability of being raped is 3.7 times higher among nonwhite women." [98]   In a 1967 sample survey of 3,000 women in forty-eight states who were receiving funds from Aid to Families with Dependent Children, nearly one-half said they would use an increase in payments to buy food; over one-third said they had postponed paying rent to buy food in the previous six months; almost one-half said there had been times during that period when they had no money to buy milk.   Seventeen percent reported some of their children had missed school in the previous six months because they lacked shoes or clothing; 30 percent did not have enough beds for every member of the family; 12 percent did not have enough sheets or blankets to have one for each bed; 25 percent did not have enough chairs to seat every member of their family at mealtime; 21 percent did not have enough tableware for their family; 13 percent had no inside running water; 14 percent had no flush toilet; 39 percent had not had needed dental care and 25 percent did not have eyeglasses because they could not afford the expense.[99]

Humanitarian concern, guided by scientific inquiry, represents our approach to the study of social welfare.   We hope, however, that we have warned the reader of some of the pitfalls in this seemingly noble statement of objectives.   One further difficulty remains to be more fully discussed—the relationship between inquiry and value judgments.

Inquiry and the Problem of Values

Concepts are tools that may enable us to find our way in an exceedingly complex reality.   They are essential because we can deal with reality only by simplifying it.   They are both useful and dangerous.   They sharpen our focus but

[94] Charles Booth, *Life and Labor of the People in London* (final volume): *Notes on Social Influences and Conclusion* (London: Macmillan, 1903), p. 178.   Quoted by Asa Briggs, "The Welfare State in Historical Perspective," in Mayer N. Zald (ed.), *Social Welfare Institutions* (New York: Wiley, 1965), 59*n*, p. 66.

[95] Robert S. Morison, "Where is Biology Taking Us?," *Science*, January 27, 1967, p. 433.

[96] *New York Times*, April 17, 1969, p. 37.

[97] *Report of the National Advisory Commission on Civil Disorders, op. cit.*, p. 136.

[98] *Ibid.*, p. 135.

[99] "AFDC" *Children*, 16 (May–June 1969), p. 122.

narrow our vision.   They are necessarily abstract, allowing us to relate seemingly dissimilar events, but by the same token, they obscure the rich detail and the actual complexity of human behavior.   They deal with classes of events and not the concrete individual.   As a result we often lose sight of the human being as we talk about social roles, social functioning, and social system—"ugly jargon," says Dennis H. Wrong, "that does not assure that we shall find the answers we are seeking." [100]   Such language is certainly not poetic.   Whether it does in fact provide some answers to the questions we ask in this book, we shall leave to the reader.   We think it does.   To see that welfare institutions function to maintain the social system gives us a perspective that is lost when we see it solely as a humanitarian enterprise.   On the other hand the individual's concrete experience with welfare programs and the *meaning* they have for him are of major importance and should not be lost.   In any event concepts are instruments that should be used only so long as they are useful.   The *kind* of concepts we use, however, invariably reflects our values.

Concepts are part of the cognitive map that allows us to order the world around us.   We have already noted that all of us tend to perceive reality in ways that meet our own needs and expectations.   For example, if one values the market allocation of jobs, he tends to "see" the unemployment of youths as a problem of *their* unemployability, *their* lack of appropriate education and job skills.   If he values the right of every individual to useful employment, he "sees" not only the need for education and training but the need for job creation that will utilize *existing* skills and aptitudes.   The major issue is the degree to which one searches for solutions to problems by dealing with the existing social system or by changing the social system to provide wider alternatives to individuals.   Values, as well as knowledge, will influence the kind of concepts or theories one will use in perceiving social problems and the avenues that are available for their alleviation.[101]   Our definition of the goals of welfare will invariably reflect both our knowledge and our values.

It is often thought that one must be value-free in order to attain an objective understanding of man and society.   Whether such ethical neutrality is possible or even desirable is doubtful.[102]   No one, of course, may intelligently argue for distorting facts to confirm dearly held prejudices.   That is not at issue.   What is at issue is the meaning of objectivity and the degree to which the student of society can or should be value-free.   The inability to maintain a separate subject-object relationship in studies of human behavior is clearly evident in the reports of research sociologists on their own efforts in this regard.[103]   However, the discovery of what is actually going on when people interact may well require an involvement of the researcher in a therapeutic or mutual-aid relation-

[100] Wrong, *op. cit.*, p. 376.

[101] Willhelm, *op. cit.*, pp. 5–6.

[102] Gunnar Myrdal, *Value in Social Theory*, Paul Streeten (ed.), (New York: Harper & Brothers, 1958).   *Also* Alvin W. Gouldner, "Anti-Minotaur: The Myth of a Value-Free Sociology," *The New Sociology*, *op. cit.*, pp. 196–217; Nevitt Sanford, "Social Science and Social Reform," *Journal of Social Issues*, 21 (April 1965), pp. 54–70; Horowitz, *Professing Sociology*, *op. cit.*

[103] Vidich, *et al.*, *op. cit.*

ship with those whom he would understand.[104] Such participation in the inner life of another is possible only when one feels free to reveal himself. It requires the "I-thou" rather than an instrumental relationship in which human beings are treated as objects.[105] It is at this point that the social scientist's concern for objective understanding meets the social worker's and therapist's concern with subjective involvement. But what about values?

Max Weber, perhaps the most influential spokesman in sociology for value neutrality, warns that ". . . whenever the man of science introduces his personal value judgment, a full understanding of the facts *ceases*." [106] This is a powerful statement from one of the world's great scholars and cannot be lightly dismissed. On the other hand the philosopher Morris R. Cohen saw the importance of clearly stated values for discovering the *significance* of social facts:

> We cannot disregard all questions of what is socially desirable without missing the significance of many social facts: for since the relation of means to ends is a special form of that between parts and wholes, the contemplation of social ends enables us to see the relations of whole groups of facts to each other and to the larger system of which they are parts.[107]

This is the position that we shall take. For example, the high concentration of Negroes as clients in public assistance programs, in institutions for dependent and delinquent children, in mental hospitals and in prisons, and in the ranks of the unemployed and underemployed are social facts that take on special significance with justice given as a goal. Briefly, the social system has functioned to recruit a disproportionate number of Negroes for some welfare programs, partly as a by-product of a division of labor that has met society's need for a supply of low-paid marginal workers. The system has exploited the Negro and concealed the inequities in distribution of opportunities and rewards through the fiction of individual responsibility for failure. This is fairly easy to demonstrate since the Negro has suffered from obvious forms of economic exploitation, segregation, and discrimination. A similar process of exclusion of those at the bottom of the class system may also help account for their high vulnerability to economic dependency, family breakdown, mental illness, and other problems in return for which they receive the dubious benefits of certain welfare services such as public assistance—benefits that may, in fact, further isolate them from society and further compound their difficulties. Justice requires acknowledgement of societal causes of such problems and collective responsibility for provisions sufficient in scope to redress inequities, develop capacities, and open new opportunities to participate in society. With this point of view, one focuses not on *problems* and how they may be alleviated or controlled, but on economic, social, and political *issues* and how they may be resolved in a manner consistent

[104] Seeley, in Vidich, *op. cit.*

[105] Martin Buber, "I and Thou," in Will Herberg (ed.), *The Writings of Martin Buber* (New York: Meridian Books, 1956), pp. 43–62.

[106] H. H. Gerth and C. Wright Mills (eds.), *From Max Weber: Essays in Sociology* (New York: Oxford University Press, 1946), p. 146.

[107] Morris R. Cohen, *Reason and Nature* (New York: Harcourt, Brace & Co., 1931), p. 343.

with our concept of justice.   Speaking about the American Negro, Dr. Kenneth Clark observes that in ". . . the transition period from injustice to justice, . . . we cannot pretend that there are no consequences of past injustices. We've got to face those consequences and do whatever is necessary to rectify them." [108]   One proposal was a "freedom budget" calling for an increased expenditure of $18.5 billion annually for ten years to assure a minimum adequate income to everyone, full employment, and health, housing, and educational opportunities for all.[109]   Although this was largely ignored by Congress, some such approach is necessary to meet the general problem of exclusion suffered by the rejects and the casualties of a system that has been "programed for their defeat."

A position of value neutrality tends to accept the definition of social problems as provided by society and leads to a search for solutions already existent within the system.   With a commitment to human values, we may translate problems into issues and perceive issues in terms of their human meaning, in this way discovering better ways of organizing our social life.[110]

Many of us have been taught an attitude of "cultural relativity," which suggests that such phrases as "better ways of organizing our social life" are suspect since they can only reflect individual preference and cultural conditioning.   In this view, all values are equally good, depending on one's culture.

It is true that awareness of the wide variation in possible forms of successful and relatively satisfying styles of life has, or should have, emancipated us from a narrow and crippling ethnocentrism.   This does not mean, however, that we are totally without basis for a critical analysis of values.   Cultural relativity, in rejecting ethnocentrism, is itself a value position.   It upholds respect for other cultures and is implicitly an affirmation of the essential unity of mankind. Only a naïve cultural relativity, however, would assume that man can adapt equally well to any society or that it makes little difference what style of life is available.   One may assert, as Nevitt Sanford does, that "If the purpose of culture is ". . . to make him [man] more human, then we may evaluate particular cultures in terms of how well they do what they are supposed to do." [111]   We focus on the culture of poverty without a sufficient awareness of the poverty of culture that deprives all of us of those meaningful symbols essential for the growth of personality and the enrichment of life.   When the historian Herbert J. Muller refers to America as having the "highest standard of low living in the world," [112] he echoes Emerson's judgment of our culture as a "life of toys and trinkets."   Human needs and the requirements of social life give rise to culture. Not all cultures, however, are equally expressive of man's unique capacity to meet his needs through the exercise of imagination and the creation of symbols

[108] Nat Hentoff, *The New Equality* (New York: Viking Press, 1964), p. 98.

[109] *A "Freedom Budget" for All Americans* (New York: A. Philip Randolph Institute, October, 1966).

[110] C. Wright Mills, "Troubles and Issues," in Paul E. Weinberger (ed.), *Perspectives on Social Welfare* (New York: Macmillan, 1969), pp. 46–47.

[111] Nevitt Sanford, *Self & Society* (New York: Atherton Press, 1966), p. 221. *See also* pp. xi and 220–224.

[112] Herbert J. Muller, *Freedom In The Modern World,* (New York: Harper & Row, 1966), p. 63.

that enrich life and endow his activities with meaning. When Erikson writes that for most of us the search for meaning is found in the ". . . subordination of ideology to technology" so that ". . . what works, on the grandest scale, is good," he helps us to see the extent to which the celebration of our technology leads to the impoverishment of our culture.[113] Social welfare must be part of an effort to create a social order more ". . . consistent with fundamental human needs for security, dignity and personal fulfillment." [114] This is the value position taken throughout this book. It should be emphasized, however, that a new form of ethnocentrism is not being proposed, nor is a blueprint for Utopia. There are probably a variety of ways to humanize our industrial society, many unknown and yet to be discovered in an ongoing experimental process of social innovation.

The reader is therefore forewarned. Though we shall try to be accurate in our facts and disciplined in presenting opposing points of view, no pretense of ethical neutrality is made. We are supported by Gunnar Myrdal, who writes:

> There is no way of studying social reality other than from the viewpoint of human ideals. A "disinterested social science" has never existed and, for logical reasons, cannot exist. The value connotations of our main concepts represents our interest in a matter, gives direction to our thoughts and significance to our inferences. It poses the questions without which there are no answers.[115]

In his monumental study, *An American Dilemma,* Myrdal takes the "American Creed" as his value premise, pointing out that since we cannot escape value judgments, we have an obligation to make them explicit. He writes: "There is no other device for excluding biases in social sciences than to face the valuations and to introduce them as explicitly stated, specific, and sufficiently concretized value premises." [116] Ideals of the essential dignity of the individual, of the fundamental equality of all men, and of certain inalienable rights to freedom, justice, and fair opportunity, are the principles that most Americans assume *ought* to prevail in society. They have roots in our Judaic-Christian heritage, the philosophy of the Enlightenment, and English law. They express aspirations of man both ancient and modern, in Eastern as well as Western civilizations. They are not American inventions, although perhaps America more than any other nation has made these a part of its national conscience. On the other hand there are deep ideological conflicts among those who adhere to the same abstract principles of democracy. Property rights and human

---

[113] Erik Erikson, "Youth: Fidelity and Diversity," in Erik Erikson (ed.), *Youth: Change and Challenge* (New York: Basic Books, 1963), p. 22.

[114] Herbert C. Kelman, "The Social Consequences of Social Research," *Journal of Social Issues,* 21 (July 1965), p. 21.

[115] Myrdal, in Streeten, *op. cit.,* p. 1. For a different point of view, *see* George A. Lundberg, *Can Science Save Us?* (New York: Longmans, Green & Co., 1947); and Glenn M. Vernon, *Human Interaction: An Introduction to Sociology* (New York: Ronald Press, 1965), pp. 23–25.

[116] Gunnar Myrdal, *An American Dilemma* (New York: Harper & Brothers, 1944), p. 1043. *See also* Appendix 2, pp. 1035–1065.

rights have not been given equal weight.   Although, for long periods in American history, property did tend to win in ". . . the ceaseless conflict between the man and the dollar, between democracy and property," [117] in the long run we have tended to favor a democratic over an economic individualism.   Though the conflict continues, it is Myrdal's conclusion that

> . . . taking the broad historical view, the American Creed has triumphed. It has given the main direction to change in this country.   America has had gifted conservative statesmen and national leaders and they have often determined the course of public affairs.   But with few exceptions, only the liberals have gone down in history as national heroes.[118]

The "triumph," it should be noted, is the direction of change, not any final attainment of the values of equality and dignity.   Indeed there are increasing numbers of those who declare the failure of the "American Dream," pointing to the apparently unbridgeable gap between the official rhetoric and the structured inequalities, the destructive function of a harmonizing ideology that conceals socially tolerated injustices, and the narrow vision of human possibilities contained in the traditional definitions of freedom and equality.[119]

Each generation has the responsibility to redefine the meaning to be given to equality and freedom in the light of new resources, new knowledge, and higher aspirations for the development of human potential.   The ethic, we may discover, that urges us toward a critical view of our social institutions lies not only in democratic values, but in the very nature of the human organism and the possibility of ". . . an optimum relation of inborn potentialities and the structure of the environment." [120]

We may discover that the humanistic values of the American Creed correspond to the basic needs of individuals everywhere.   In any event they provide the value base for our study of social welfare.   The values of equality, freedom, and dignity are radical in their import, although this society has tended to apply them conservatively.

To understand and to humanize our society, we need a more radical expression of these values.   Radical in the sense in which we mean it has no reference to political dogma.   It refers to a set of attitudes nurtured by science

[117] Vernon L. Parrington, *Main Currents in American Thought,* Vol. 3, *The Beginnings of Critical Realism in America, pp. 1860–1920* (New York: Harcourt, Brace, 1939), p. 410, as quoted in Myrdal, *ibid.,* Vol. I, p. 7.

[118] Myrdal, *ibid.*

[119] Marvin E. Gettleman and David Mermelstein (eds.), *The Great Society Reader: The Failure of American Liberalism* (New York: Random House, 1967).   *See* especially Tom Hayden, "Welfare Liberalism and Social Change," pp. 476–501.

[120] Erikson, *Insight and Responsibility, op. cit.,* p. 2.   *See also* Sanford, *Self and Society, op. cit.;* Laura Thompson, *Toward a Science of Mankind* (New York: McGraw-Hill, 1961); Abraham H. Maslow, *Motivation and Personality* (New York: Harper & Brothers, 1954); Gardner Murphy, "Human Potentialities," *Journal of Social Issues,* Supplement Series No. 7, 1953, and *Human Potentialities* (New York: Basic Books, 1958); Hadley Cantril, "The Individual's Demand on Society," in Seymour M. Farber and Roger H. L. Wilson (eds.), *Conflict and Creativity,* (New York: McGraw-Hill, 1963).

and ethics that prefers the exercise of intelligence to the "conventional wisdom"; that accepts an experimental attitude toward society; that regards intellect and social institutions as the servant of the human being; that honors the pursuit of a community of men, not the control of man over man.   It rejects a sentimental view of human beings or any notion of automatic progress, yet believes in the indestructible spirit of man.

TWO

Changing Concepts of Social Welfare

Summarizing Chapter 1, we have seen that there is no agreed-upon definition of social welfare. The range of needs, the methods, and the degree of adequacy with which they are met, as well as the definition of who are the proper recipients of communal concern and the designation of those charged with the responsibility of performing welfare functions, varies with societies and changes over time. Programs designed to carry out welfare purposes have developed as a result of many piecemeal reforms during different historical periods that have been influenced by varying concepts of communal and political responsibility.

Social welfare in the United States has fallen in a large measure within the residual concept, with its patchwork system of programs based on the assumption that social obligation extends only to meeting the emergency needs of that portion of the population that is regarded as incapable of meeting its own needs through the traditional means of the market and the family. The residual view accepts the poor as incompetent second-class members of society for whom second-class services may be provided.

Increasingly, however, we are moving toward an *institutional* (or developmental) concept, by which social welfare performs the normal and necessary first-line functions of a modern industrial society in order to assure economic and political stability, provide its citizens with essential supportive resources, equalize opportunities, and redress class-related inequities in the distribution of income and power. The newer view is part of the quest for equality and accords to all a citizen's right to an equitable share in the benefits and obligations of his society. The conflict between inequalities of class and the equalities of citizenship is a major factor, accounting for the democratization of charity and leading to the more positive views of welfare that are now evolving.

The Evolving Role of Social Welfare

As we have moved from the preindustrial society characterized by economic scarcity toward a complex interdependent postindustrial society of high mass consumption and a revolution of rising expectations, the awareness of needs

33

requiring social intervention has broadened.   The terms charity, corrections, welfare state, and welfare society symbolize the changing and conflicting approaches to and concepts of social welfare.   The transition of welfare in its charity role to the broader contemporary and more positive view may be seen on a continuum as a gradual movement from a residual to an institutional concept, evolving from the notion of gratuity to that of citizen right, from special programs for the poor to a concern with the universal needs of the population, from minimum to optimum provisions and services, from individual to social reform, from voluntary to public auspices, and from welfare for the poor to the concept of a welfare society.

From the Residual to the Institutional Concept

The residual view, as we saw in the first chapter, places welfare outside the "normal" institutions of society.   Welfare is seen as a last resort for those presumably incapable of meeting their needs through the normal structures of the market and the family.   The residual welfare services tend to be characterized by colonial attitudes toward the poor, crisis intervention, and a "character defect" view of the needy.   William Blake provided a poet's definition of residual welfare services when he wrote:

> For this is being a friend just in the nick,
> Not when he is well but waiting till he is sick.
> He calls you to his help, Be you not moved
> Until by being sick His wants are proved.[1]

The institutional view of welfare, on the other hand, is predicated on the assumption that a modern industrial society requires a variety of services as first-line supports to enable individuals to cope successfully with a changing economic and social environment and to assure the stability and development of social institutions.

Charity to Citizen Right

Whereas welfare as charity is in the tradition of nineteenth-century middle-class benevolence, a gratuity provided to the worthy or unworthy poor, the notion of a citizenship right to welfare benefits can be seen as part of a long historic process of transforming an ever larger group of people from subjects to citizens.   In the view of T. H. Marshall, citizenship consists of three sets of rights and duties—civil, political, and social.[2]   The rise of the middle-class in the eighteenth century saw the establishment of civil rights: liberty, freedom of speech, equality before the law, and the right to own property.   Political rights in the form of universal manhood suffrage developed primarily in the nineteenth century, partly in response to the demands of the newly organized working class.   Social rights make up the dominant theme of the latter part of this century.   The question involves citizen rights to economic security, education,

[1] *William Cowper, Esquire,* stanza 1.

[2] T. H. Marshall, *Class, Citizenship, and Social Development* (Garden City, N.Y.: Anchor Books, 1965), pp. 78–91.

and access to the benefits and obligations that accompany full participation in society. The notion of such rights is implicit in the concept of the welfare state, an idea that many people find morally repugnant precisely because of its moral originality.[3] The notion that people should have the right to what they need violates the moral sensibility of those who uncritically accept the Protestant ethic. Nonetheless such rights have been affirmed by a number of national commissions, such as the National Advisory Commission on Civil Disorders, the President's National Advisory Commission on Rural Poverty, the National Commission on Community Health Services, the National Commission on Technology, Automation and Economic Progress, the President's Commission on Law Enforcement and Administration of Justice, and the President's Commission on Income Maintenance. They have also been affirmed by prominent leaders in all walks of life and constitute the major agenda of the organization of welfare recipients themselves.

Special to Universal

We tend to think of social welfare as consisting of special services for the poor. Increasingly, however, social welfare programs are developed to meet universal needs of the population. Such universal programs tend to focus on certain common social contingencies that are consequences of living in an industrial society, with such related risks as unemployment, old age, disability, loss of the breadwinner, the high cost of medical care, and so forth. The Social Security Act of 1935 symbolized the first national venture in the direction of universal social welfare programs. It is important to observe that, in declaring the Social Security Act constitutional, the U.S. Supreme Court in May of 1937 defended the act on the grounds of the "general welfare" provision of the Constitution, pointing out that "needs that were narrow or parochial a century ago may be interwoven in our day with the well-being of the nation." [4] Whether social welfare programs should be special or universal remains an issue. Special services tend to isolate the poor from society and to be inferior in quality. Universal social welfare programs are free of stigma and integrate the poor into society. Currently at issue is whether the income needs of the poor shall continue to be met through special programs aimed at the poor, however modified in form, or through such universal instruments as social insurance. The idea of a negative income tax and the Nixon administration's version of it—the Family Assistance Plan—are examples of the former. The idea of a children's allowance illustrates the latter. This issue is examined in Chapter Six.

Minimum to Optimum

In the new view of social welfare, we move away from the restricted notion that only minimum resources are to be made available to individuals and we

---

[3] *See* Charles Frankel, "The Welfare State: Postscript and Prelude," *The Democratic Prospect* (New York: Harper & Row, 1962), pp. 125–144.

[4] "Helvering et al. v. Davis: Opinion of Benjamin N. Cardoza for the Supreme Court, 1937," reprinted in Stuart Gerry Brown (ed.), *We Hold These Truths*, 2nd ed. (New York: Harper & Brothers, 1948), p. 354.

concentrate on examining the degree to which optimum social environments and resources can be created to nurture and develop human potentialities and to achieve some desirable level of well-being for all. Given the increased knowledge of the relationship of relatively rich and relatively deprived social environments to an individual's development, attention is focused on early infancy and childhood in order to make available to all children those optimum conditions that may make it possible for them to develop to the fullest their capacities.

Individual to Social Reform

The older view of social welfare operates on the assumption that problems are created by individuals with moral defects who require social uplift. Character defect was the diagnosis of the nineteenth century, and psychological defect was the diagnosis of the mental health movement of the twentieth century. Today we tend to see that social problems are structural, that is, they result from defects in institutional arrangements. Consequently reform of the society rather than reform of the individual tends to be emphasized as social science theory replaces the moral assumptions of the past.

Voluntary to Public

Although public responsibility for welfare dates back to the sixteenth- and seventeenth-century English Poor Law, during most of the nineteenth and early twentieth centuries, America tended to rely more heavily on voluntary social welfare efforts. This was consistent with the laissez-faire emphasis and the influence of Social Darwinism, which insisted on minimum government and minimum government intervention in behalf of the victims of the "free play" of market forces. No such fear prevented the powerful from using government in behalf of their interests, whether this was in the form of tariff protection, enforcement of zoning regulations, or government subsidies to promote business expansion. The belief in laissez faire, as both Asa Briggs and Calvin Woodard observe, did not mean the absence of government but the use of government to create the conditions for economic initiative and the development of the economy.[5] The social costs of industrialization, the democratization of society that accompanied economic development, and the inability of voluntary middle-class benevolence to provide in spirit or in quantity the kind of resources that would satisfy the needs stimulated by rising expectations in the context of more abundant possibilities have created political pressures to expand the welfare functions of government. With the trend toward a national society, the federal government rather than state and local governments becomes the major dispenser of welfare provisions and services, posing dilemmas in the uses of national power to promote equality without limiting freedom.

[5] Calvin Woodard, "Reality and Social Reform: The Transition from Laissez-Faire to the Welfare State," *Yale Law Journal,* 72 (December 1962), pp. 286–328; Asa Briggs, "The Welfare State in Historical Perspective," in Mayer N. Zald (ed.), *Social Welfare Institutions* (New York: Wiley, 1965), p. 53.

From Welfare for the Poor to a Welfare Society

In the concept of the welfare society all social institutions are critically evaluated in terms of their contributions to maximizing development of all individuals. We are certainly far from achieving this kind of perspective in our current social welfare philosophy and programs. Nonetheless the trend in this direction in thought if not in action is unmistakable. For example, writing on the transformation of the concept of philanthropy, Aileen D. Ross observes that

> The basic problem of philanthropy has changed from that of caring for the physical needs of a relatively few destitute people living in simple society to attempting to meet the physical, social, and psychological needs of total populations living in highly complex society. The emphasis is now being placed on securing a better, happier, or healthier, world for all: and the focus has shifted from the relief of immediate wants to long term planning that will prevent future wants.[6]

Stages in the Evolution of Social Welfare

In moving toward the idea of social welfare as social development, it appears that the United States is following certain common stages in the evolution of welfare that seem to characterize, with wide variations, all advanced industrial societies. Alva Myrdal describes this evolution in the following way:

> [Social reform policies may be conceived as passing through three stages: A paternalistic conservative era, when curing the worst ills was enough; a liberal era, when safeguarding against inequalities through pooling the risks is enough; and a social democratic era, when preventing the ills is attempted.] The first was the period of curative social policy through private charity and public poor relief; the second was the period of social insurance, broad in scope but yet merely symptomatic; and the third may be called a period of protective and cooperative social policy. Some phases of all these types may be found incidentally during each of the different epics. This schematization is true only on broad lines.[7]

Such stages are suggestive only. They are overlapping and nothing like a law of social development is being proposed. Nonetheless, with such cautions in mind, it is helpful to identify such stages in the development of our concept of social welfare in order to be aware of residues of the past and possibilities for the future. The charity stage has been primarily concerned with the alleviation of economic destitution. The welfare state attempts to assure some minimum level of economic security for all as a citizen right. Planned social development recognizes the essential interdependence of people in a complex urban-industrial society and the need for intelligent intervention to create a social order more consistent with basic human needs and new aspirations for higher

[6] Aileen D. Ross, "Philanthropy," *International Encyclopedia of Social Sciences* (New York: Macmillan and Free Press, 1968), Vol. XII, p. 80.

[7] Alva Myrdal, *Nation and Family* (New York: Harper & Bros., 1941), p. 152.

levels of living for all. It is not suggested that this development may go only in one direction. There are reactions to the welfare state, reflected in efforts to place greater reliance on individual choice, self-help, and free play of the market. Federal responsibility may be increasingly shared with local communities through new forms of so-called creative federalism. The continuum is highly general and the outlook for the future is always in doubt. Nonetheless certain major changes in our concepts of social welfare may be clarified by reference to the above stages.

Such changes in the concepts of social welfare have been accompanied by more drastic changes in the very nature of society itself. It is evident that the ideology of residual social welfare has hardly kept pace with the basic shift from a rural agrarian society to an increasingly complex industrial one. In a relatively simple rural frontier society it was necessary and possible to be self-reliant. No individual, however, is ever totally independent. Patterns of informal mutual aid through the extended family, church, and community provided a supportive network of primary group ties as well as emergency assistance in periods of stress. In complex, urban, industrial wage economies the individual loses control over the material conditions of his survival and is uprooted from traditional ties of kinship and community. Problems of economic insecurity, deprivation, and breakdown of social control accompany the industrialization and urbanization of society. Loss of income through unemployment, illness, disability, and old age became shared risks for which social welfare provisions through social insurance and public assistance have been made. These are in a sense functional equivalents of earlier patterns of mutual aid and are social adaptations to the requirements of living in an industrial society. They substitute for income normally derived through work. Even when work is available, however, it does not necessarily provide the resources essential for maintaining and developing self and family. Access to such essential resources (material resources in terms of food, shelter, medical care, etc., as well as symbolic goods in the form of status, self-esteem, and power) are dependent on the breadwinner's position in the occupational structure and on his capacities to compete for occupational achievement. Opportunities for upward mobility and the capacities to exploit such opportunities are influenced, however, not only by native endowment; they are also influenced by factors over which the individual has little or no control, such as accidents of birth related to complications of pregnancy associated with poverty and lack of adequate prenatal care. In addition, the family into which the child is born and the capacities of the parents to play their parental roles are related to the social-class position of the family and its access to resources of income, housing, medical care, and education. Racial and ethnic membership and community attitudes toward minorities are additional factors influencing the individual's life chances. Most important perhaps is the opportunity structure itself, that is, the roles available to individuals and the societal supports and resources to enable the individual to participate in society. For example, even in time of relatively full employment, work is not available to 3–4 percent of the labor force or to about 8 percent of the Negro labor force. Opportunities for stable marital roles are limited for lower-class women if lower-class males are denied access to a living wage and to the education and training necessary to acquire the skills for occupational achievement. All this means that the fate of the individual is intimately tied to the structure of his society, its available roles, its social provisions for developing and sustaining capacities for role performance—such provisions as education, medical care, income maintenance, housing, day care, homemaker services, and so forth. The eighteenth- and nineteenth-century versions of self-reliance are no longer relevant for conditions that prevail in an urban, bureaucratized, technological, highly interdependent society. Community responsibility is necessary to develop individual capacities and to provide opportunities for their fullest expression. Social welfare may be seen as the exercise of such responsibility. We need, therefore, a twentieth-century concept of self-reliance based on knowledge of what human beings require to develop their capacity for self-actualization. The continued adherence to an ideology of individual self-help, despite the increasing interdependence of an industrial society, often obscures the extent of our needs for social intervention and for new forms of mutual aid.

A clear example of the extent to which the fate of individuals is intimately tied up with the structure of society is revealed by a report of the President's National Advisory Commission on Rural Poverty. The plain and poignant fact is that most people in rural areas are trapped, victims of technological advance over which they have had little or no control. In short, as the commission notes, some 14 million rural Americans, who make up half our population living in poverty, are ". . . outside our market economy. So far as they are concerned, the dramatic economic growth of the United States might as well have never have happened. It has brought them few rewards. They are on the outside looking in, and they need help." [8] Social legislation that has helped large-scale farmers, industrial workers, and vast segments of the middle class has discriminated against the rural poor, who have been ". . . denied unemployment insurance, the right of collective bargaining, . . . and the protection of workman's compensation laws." Millions of rural residents, the commission points out, are simply denied the opportunity to earn a living. Not only does society have the responsibility to assure them greater access to employment opportunities but, as the commission goes on to state, ". . . the United States has the resources and the technical means to assure every person in the United States adequate food, shelter, clothing, medical care, and education, and, accordingly, recommends action toward this end." [9]

Social Welfare and Value Conflicts

Welfare had its origin in efforts to deal with poverty and the problems related to it. *This is still the priority concern,* although our aspirations ought to extend beyond that.

In this country the provisions we have made for dealing with poverty and economic insecurity reflect our historic conflict between a self-reliance philosophy and community responsibility for promoting human well-being. Welfare programs developed as a series of compromises between the conflicting values

[8] *The People Left Behind,* President's National Advisory Commission on Rural Poverty (Washington, D.C.: Government Printing Office, 1967), p. x.

[9] *Ibid.,* p. xi.

inherent in democratic capitalism: ". . . economic individualism and free enterprise on the one hand, and security, equality and humanitarianism on the other." [10]   Welfare may be seen as an "aim-inhibited" enterprise, caught between the organizational and humanitarian mores.[11] [We have sought to alleviate poverty without reducing the incentive to work; to socialize the poor into a work culture in a society that has never guaranteed full employment; to strengthen family life without providing parents with essential supporting resources; to assure the "rights of childhood" without disturbing the market allocation of income, housing, and medical care; to reduce social conflict without upsetting the class distribution of opportunities and privileges; to redress inequities without confronting the issue of justice.]

Emphasis on economic individualism has been a positive force in our society, permitting us to mobilize human energy and intelligence toward the maximum production of goods.   In Karl Polanyi's judgment, it was part of a market ethos that enriched society at the ". . . price of impoverishing the individual." [12]   It was adapted to a society of scarcity, but not to one of affluence.   Our approach to meeting the basic needs of human beings is no longer tolerable in a society that professes to value the dignity and worth of every individual.   It is no longer viable in a society that faces the crisis and the challenge of revolutionary change, both technological and social.   We must redress inequities not only because the "slums do seek their revenge" [13] but because we are all involved in a social system that does violence to our sense of dignity.   It implicates us in the denial of life to some and in the failure to nurture the fullest development of all.

Today we have the resources to abolish poverty in this country.   Paradoxically, the technology that offers this opportunity also moves us toward a credential society in which the acquisition of formal symbols of educational attainment provides the tickets of admission to status and rewards.   This may mean increasing affluence and advantages for those who will be in a position to participate in the "educated society."   It can mean more barriers and relative deprivation for the excluded minority poor, a disproportionate number of whom are Negro.   Forces beyond individual control determine life opportunities.   This presents us with the issue of social justice.   Rising expectations and a human rights revolution provide us with the challenge and the urgent need to examine how we organize our social life and allocate resources and opportunities.   We are in the midst of a great transformation of society, which creates new human problems and new potentials for improving the quality of life.   Having solved the problem of production we face the problem of distribution and, beyond that, the greater need to turn our attention to the development of human potential.   What would this mean for our concept of social welfare?

[10] Harold L. Wilensky and Charles N. Lebeaux, *Industrial Society and Social Welfare* (New York: Free Press, 1965), pp. 138–139.

[11] Willard Waller, "Social Problems and the Mores," *American Sociological Review,* 1 (December 1936), pp. 922–933.

[12] Polanyi, "Our Obsolete Market Mentality," *Commentary,* February, 1947, p. 116.

[13] Donald Gilbert McKinley, *Social Class and Family Life* (New York: The Macmillan Co., 1964), p. 269.

Social Welfare As Moral Concept

In a sense social welfare is an empty concept. We define it according to our moral ideals.[14] To be concerned with welfare is invariably to be involved in ". . . large judgements about the proper ends of life." [15] From this point of view it is possible to understand how we may have both negative and positive concepts of welfare. In the light of the importance given to the ethic of work and self-reliance, welfare is perceived as immoral. To be defined as a welfare recipient is to be relegated to the pale of society. "The stigma which clung to poor relief expressed the deep feeling of a people who understood that those who accepted relief must cross the road that separated the community of citizens from the outcast company of the destitute." [16] The nineteenth-century notion of charity, as we saw, was expressive of this moral view, one that accepted work as an end in life and especially the obligation of the poor to accept whatever work was available. It was part of a larger moral ideal, that of a liberal economic society organized around maximizing economic development through the free play of market forces, with a view of human needs and motivation that ascribed to man a consuming appetite for material goods but a natural reluctance to engage in hard work to attain them. Thus the presumed inherent laziness of man, especially of the poor, militated against a too-generous welfare provision. Welfare has continued to be restricted by the ill-founded assumptions of the Poor Law dilemma, defined by Frederick H. Wines in 1872 as the ". . . great problem of all charity, public or private, . . . how to diminish suffering without increasing by the very act, the number of paupers, how to grant aid, in case of need, without obliterating the principle of self-reliance and self-help." [17]

The dilemma reveals a humanitarian concern inhibited by the greater priority given to the values of work and self-reliance around which the market industrial society was organized. The Puritan ethic probably played an important role in creating the morality attached to labor.[18] However, all industrial societies, as Wilensky notes, tend to develop an ideology favorable to work.[19]

The collapse of the market economy in the Great Depression of the 1930s modified, through bitter experience, the intensity with which Americans ad-

---

[14] Eugen Pusic, "The Political Community and the Future of Welfare," in John S. Morgan (ed.), *Welfare and Wisdom* (Toronto: University of Toronto Press, 1968), p. 82.

[15] Charles Frankel, "The Moral Framework of Welfare" in Morgan, *ibid.,* p. 164.

[16] Marshall, *op. cit.,* p. 88.

[17] Quoted in Robert H. Bremner, *From The Depths: The Discovery of Poverty in the United States* (New York: New York University Press, 1964), p. 46.

[18] For a discussion of Puritan sources of American values *see* Richard H. Tawney, "Economic Virtues and Prescriptions for Poverty," in Herman D. Stein and Richard A. Cloward (eds.), *Social Perspectives on Behavior* (New York: Free Press, 1958), pp. 266–87. This is an abridged portion of R. H. Tawney, *Religion and the Rise of Capitalism* (New York: Harcourt, Brace & World, 1926).

[19] Harold L. Wilensky, "Work as a Social Problem," in Howard S. Becker (ed.), *Social Problems: A Modern Approach* (New York: Wiley, 1966).

hered to self-reliance.   During that period the economy denied employment
to one-fourth of the labor force.   The Social Security Act of 1935 produced a
modest welfare state that gave some recognition to the need for social provisions against common risks to loss of income.   Government has expanded its
welfare functions and we are in some measure a "social service state," yet the
ideology of self-help and economic individualism remains a potent force in
American life.   L. K. Frank has observed that we are in the curious position
of having accepted government responsibility for promoting human welfare
without having developed a new political theory that would rationalize and
justify these as proper ends of organized political society.   Thus each new
public welfare program is perceived as an illicit encroachment on our traditional definition of the proper, limited obligations of government.[20]

In any event our moral values conflict, which helps to explain the confusion
around the concept of welfare.   As Wilensky and Lebeaux have observed:

> Contemporary definitions of welfare are fuzzy because cultural values re-
> garding the social responsibility of government, business, and the individual
> are now in flux.   The older doctrines of individualism, private property
> and free market, and of minimum government provided a clear-cut defi-
> nition of welfare as "charity for unfortunates."   The newer values of social
> democracy—security, equality, humanitarianism—undermine the notion
> of "unfortunate classes" in society.   All people are regarded as having
> "needs" which ipso facto become a legitimate claim on the whole society.
> Business and government as channels to supply these needs have vastly
> broadened their responsibilities.   Both the older and newer doctrines co-
> exist today, creating conflicts and ambiguities in values which are reflected
> in loose definitions of social welfare.[21]

The "newer values of social democracy" make up the more positive moral
ideals contained in concepts of welfare embodied in notions of the welfare
state and that of the welfare society.   Such ideals from the humanistic tradition are part of the American Creed, as we noted in Chapter One.   One must,
however, avoid a simplistic notion of ideals.   They are invariably conflicting
and contradictory.   Each value we uphold may have antitheses that we also
support.   Our commitment to equality is matched by our preference for a
system that supports inequality.   We are confronted not only with a gap
between our ideals and reality but our attachment to opposing ideals.   Yet
such opposition may provide a source of tension and a dynamic force for
change, preventing the rigidity and tyranny that may accompany consensus on
a single value system.   Given plural and contrasting ideals, all values cannot
be simultaneously maximized, which forces us to constantly make moral
choices.   Key social welfare issues invariably involve questions of moral
priorities.   We proclaim a long-range, ethical priority to the dignity of the
individual.

> The paramount goal of the United States was set long ago.   It is to guard
> the rights of the individual, to ensure his development, and to enlarge his

[20] Lawrence K. Frank, "The Need for a New Political Theory," *Daedalus*, 96 (Summer 1967), pp. 809–816.

[21] Wilensky and Lebeaux, *op. cit.*, p. 139, *n* 1.

opportunity. . . . All our institutions—political, social, and economic—must further enhance the dignity of the citizen, promote the maximum development of his capabilities, stimulate their responsible exercise, and widen the range and effectiveness of opportunities for individual choice.[22]

If all our institutions were in fact adapted to the above goals we would achieve the welfare society. It is simple enough to point to enormous gaps between such expressions of ideals and social reality. It would be a mistake, however, to dismiss such statements as mere rhetoric or to ignore changes that have taken place, at least in part, through the action of humanitarians and social reformers who represented the conscience of society. One needs to be reminded that there had to be campaigns against the exploitation of child labor, insistence on compulsory school laws, a fight for maximum hours and minimum wage laws. Jane Addams described the conditions of her time as ". . . the stupid atrocities of contemporary life, its arid waste, its meaningless labor, its needless suffering, and its political corruption." [23] If such conditions seem to be with us still, they are of a somewhat different order from the social evils she and others fought against.

Some child labor continues, as evidenced by a report of the U.S. Department of Labor, which revealed that 5,500 children under sixteen years of age were working in agriculture during school hours, 18 percent of whom were nine or younger. In 1965–66, 18,500 children were employed in violation of the child labor provisions of the Fair Labor Standard Act.[24] Unnecessary poverty, ill health, inadequate housing, and even hunger and malnutrition are still with us in an otherwise affluent society. Although only a minority in the United States can be said to be truly poor, the total number is large (over 22 million) and, for the individuals concerned, their condition is all the more depressing given the obvious power of this nation to meet their economic needs.[25] That some children continue to go hungry is attested to by Dr. Raymond M. Wheeler, who, reporting on a visit with a team of doctors to investigate the claim that Negro children in Mississippi were malnourished, declared, "We do not want to quibble over words, but 'malnutrition' is not quite what we found; the boys and girls we saw were hungry-weak, in pain, sick. . . . They are suffering from hunger and disease and, directly or indirectly, they are dying from them—which is exactly what 'starvation' means. . . ." [26]

Both old and new social evils are now part of the urgent social welfare

[22] President's Commission on National Goals, *Goals for Americans* (New York: Prentice-Hall, 1960), pp. 1–3.

[23] Jane Addams, *The Second Twenty Years at Hull House* (New York: Macmillan, 1930), p. 12.

[24] *Children,* 14 (March–April, 1967), p. 83.

[25] If the increase in real income for the nonpoor is lowered from 3% to 2½% annually (or ½ of 1%) and that differential effectively transferred to the poor, the poverty gap could be eliminated in four–eight years. *Economic Report of the President* together with *The Annual Report of the Council of Economic Advisors* 91st Congress, 1st Sess. House Document No. 28 (Washington, D.C.: Government Printing Office, 1969), p. 160.

[26] *The New York Times,* July 16, 1967.

agenda and require a new commitment of economic resources and political power to the quest for equality, dignity, and social justice. Such aspirations are world-wide in scope and are not confined to the United States.[27] This is revealed by the following portion of the United Nations Declaration of Human Rights:

> Everyone has the right to a standard of living adequate for the health and well-being of himself and of his family, including food, clothing, housing and medical care and necessary social services, and the right to security in the event of unemployment, sickness, disability, widowhood, old age or other lack of livelihood in circumstances beyond his control.[28]

It is also of interest to observe that the United States had to defend, before U.N. delegates, its support of the Declaration of Human Rights. In reply to a Tanzanian charge that the United States ignored economic and social rights, Morris Abram told the Commission on Human Rights that Americans had broken away from the unrealistic doctrine of laissez faire that, he said, originally denied government a role in promoting a people's welfare. Mr. Abram conceded that when the Universal Declaration was adopted by the General Assembly in 1948, many Americans had misgiving over provisions stating that everyone had the right to work, rest, and leisure, to an adequate standard of living, to social services, to education, to participation in cultural life, and to enjoyment of the arts. Mr. Abram insisted, however, that the United States was now living up to the declaration "very well indeed." [29]

For much of the world's population the Universal Declaration of Human Rights may seem a utopian ideal, but it can serve to remind us of our obligation to international social welfare and to the entire family of man. The immediate concern, in the words of Lord William Beveridge, architect of the post-World War II British welfare state, is with abolishing the "five giants oppressing mankind: disease, ignorance, squalor, idleness, and want." [30] Beyond that there is the claim of each individual to equal opportunity to develop his potential to the fullest. The goal must be ". . . to make persons out of nonpersons . . . to validate them as full participating members of the social order, with all the rights, privileges, benefits, and obligations that accompany full citizenship. Anything short of that goal must be regarded as a failure." [31] A revolution of rising expectations and the refusal of the poor and minority groups to be satisfied with less than full participation in society gives a new urgency to the struggle for social justice.

[27] Pope Paul VI, "On the Development of Peoples," Encyclical Letter, *Populorum Progressio* (Boston: St. Paul Editions, 1967).

[28] United Nations, *The Universal Declaration of Human Rights: A Standard of Achievement*, Special Fifteenth Anniversary Edition (New York: United Nations, 1955), Article 25, p. 37.

[29] *New York Times*, February 23, 1967.

[30] Walter A. Friedlander, *Introduction to Social Welfare* (Englewood Cliffs, N.J.: Prentice-Hall, 1968) 3rd ed., p. 46.

[31] Bernard L. Diamond, "The Children of Leviathan: Psychoanalytic Speculations Concerning Welfare Law and Punitive Sanctions," *California Law Review*, 54 (May 1966), pp. 368–369.

Social justice, while subject to various interpretations, includes at the minimum the elimination of the arbitrary exercise of power, principles that assure equity in the distribution of the benefits and obligations of society, and compensation for losses and injuries for which one cannot be held personally responsible.[32] Its essence is equality. This is not to be confused with identical treatment that fails to take into account relevant differences such as individual needs and capacities. Justice requires that differential treatment be justified on the basis of such considerations. Thus children, the aged, and the disabled have rights to income and other necessities without the obligation of work that is expected of others—rights not yet fully honored in this society. Social justice is a test of a democratic society, for equality is at the core of both.

The challenge before us is to see whether we can go beyond ideological pronouncements to a critical assessment of our social institutions. What action might we take to translate ideals into social reality? What kinds of action are politically feasible? What are the implications for social policy? This issue is forcefully brought to our attention by a report of another national commission.

> The list of public needs which have not been adequately met is a long one. While the lists of different persons might vary somewhat, there is a general consensus on a number of "human and community needs." Most of them are related to the growing problems of urbanization: education, health, crime, low-income housing, air and water pollution, mass transportation, and waste disposal—problems arising out of the fact that a preponderant part of our population now lives in cities, and that many cities have been unable to expand the range of necessary services to meet the needs of the new members. Why have not these needs been met? Our conviction, growing out of the spectacular achievements in military technology and our success in the conquest of space, is that the obstacles are not primarily technological. . . . Just as the concentration of research efforts produced such radically new innovations as intercontinental ballistic missiles and Polaris submarines, concentrations of similar scale on more difficult economic and social problems could contribute to meeting our human and community needs *if the political consensus could be implemented.*[33] [Emphasis added.]

Ideals are useful in establishing directions for social reform. At some point they must be incorporated into the way we organize our social life. As of the present the older values of a business civilization continue to make up a large portion of our "organization mores," the values that are the very substance of daily existence, around which the essential activity of society is transacted, rewards and punishments meted out, life chances determined.[34] Given the limits imposed by our continuing reliance on the ethics of a market society, the outlook, thinks Robert Heilbroner, ". . . is still for a society of narrow am-

---

[32] Morris Ginsberg, *On Justice in Society* (Ithaca, N.Y.: Cornell University Press, 1965), p. 10.

[33] *Technology and the American Economy,* National Commission on Technology, Automation, and Economic Progress (Washington, D.C.: Government Printing Office, 1966), Vol. I.

[34] Waller, *op. cit.*

bitions and small achievements, a society in which we belatedly repair old social ills and ungenerously attend to new ones." [35]

To a large degree the positive ideals of welfare remain aspirations, though they are increasingly becoming part of a new human rights revolution that seeks basic changes in the structure of opportunity and the distribution of societal rewards. It is even possible that what we are experiencing is a cultural revolution, a reordering of fundamental values, a redefinition of the "proper ends of life." Or there may be, in response to the unsettling turmoil, an iron determination to repress discontent and minimize the need for basic changes. The very stability of our society, however, would seem to require that a larger measure of social justice be implemented in social policy.

Social Welfare As Social Policy

Social welfare as social policy refers to collective decisions that have a direct concern with promoting the well-being of all or part of the population. Thus the decision to expand the federal highway system or to conserve natural resources, however much they indirectly affect the well-being of individuals, are not part of social welfare policy, though admittedly the line is indeed thin. Decisions to increase social insurance benefits, to provide rent supplements, to expand maternal and child health services, and to subsidize a school lunch program, all "meet direct consumption needs" of individuals and in this sense are more clearly social welfare policy.[36] With the recognition of the interrelatedness of all of social life, it is increasingly difficult to maintain the distinction between welfare and other forms of social policy. The failure to provide adequate rapid mass transportation deprives the poor of access to employment while business and industry move to the suburbs. The priority given to highways is a subsidy to the auto industry, maintains our auto-based culture, adds to air pollution, helps to maintain the slaughter on the highways (55,000 deaths in 1968 and 4.4 million injured),[37] and—by building expressways on land of least value—destroys low-rent property, which further adds to the congestion and misery of the urban ghetto. All decisions to allocate resources will affect social welfare. Thus those who would advance social welfare policy are in competition with the claims of national defense, space exploration, and other concerns of society.

Values and power affect the allocation of resources among competing social needs. Federal expenditures for national defense in 1969 were at $81.2 billion, while $1.96 billion was spent for community development and housing, $6.82 billion for education and manpower, $11.69 billion for health, and $37.86 billion for income security—a total of $57.86 billion. An additional $7.6 billion was spent for veterans' benefits and services.[38] Decisions to escalate

[35] Robert L. Heilbroner, *The Limits of Capitalism* (New York: Harper & Row, 1965), p. 60.

[36] Wilensky and Lebeaux, *op. cit.*, p. 145.

[37] *Statistical Abstract of the United States, 1969*, U.S. Bureau of the Census (Washington, D.C.: Government Printing Office, 1968), Table 834, p. 567.

[38] *New York Times*, February 3, 1970, photographic text of President Nixon's Budget Message.

the war in Vietnam had a notable impact in resources available for the War on Poverty and the urban crisis.   The ideology of individualism has limited the amount of resources devoted to social welfare and has influenced the nature of the programs that have attempted to meet social needs.   Social welfare programs almost invariably have been conceived of in terms of meeting needs of individuals rather than family units.   Even a program like Aid to Families with Dependent Children, clearly a family-focused program, continues to ignore the needs of the entire family since about half the states do not provide assistance when an unemployed father is in the home.   As part of the Social Security Act of 1935, grants were initially authorized for each dependent child, with no consideration given to the needs of the mother.   It was not until 1950 that this was corrected.   Unemployment compensation benefits, as another case in point, are usually paid in relation to the individual worker's wages, not the number of dependent family members.   Wages of course are distributed on the basis of the work people do, not their family needs; but the United States alone, among advanced industrial nations, has so far failed to develop a family allowance system that would supplement wages in relation to total family needs.   Here, too, attention has increasingly been given to this problem, and it is possible that some such family policy will develop.   Unlike European nations the United States has no family policy in the sense of a politically conscious effort to consider the welfare of families and to allocate resources accordingly. For example, in Norway,

> . . . most branches of public policy are today influenced by social welfare measures, and especially by the opinions and evaluations connected with family policy.   This influence can be traced in the policies governing economics, taxes, prices, wages, employment, schools and housing.   In all these fields the authorities keep their eye on how the family's interests can best be served.   Just as society has accepted its duties toward the rising generation, so has it recognized the family as the social corner-stone.[39]

While we take it for granted that the power of government ought to be used in the protection and support of the economy through deliberate social policy, from tariffs to subsidies, to favorable government regulations and the application of the science of economics through such means as the Council of Economic Advisors, socially conscious efforts to protect and strengthen families or to promote general social development are only beginning to be part of the "American Way."   Concern may shift from exclusive preoccupation with social policy related to expansion of the Gross National Product and the needs of the private sector of the economy to social needs and the requirements of the public sector.   This is an issue that is central to social welfare and one that John Kenneth Galbraith has analyzed so well.[40]   It is clear that a critical question in social welfare has to do with the ordering of national priorities and

[39] Magne Langholm, *Family and Child Welfare in Norway* (Oslo: Norwegian Joint Committee on International Social Policy, 1963), p. 17.

[40] John Kenneth Galbraith, *The Affluent Society* (Boston: Houghton Mifflin, 1958).   *See* especially Chap. 19, "The Theory of Social Balance," pp. 251–269.

the resources to be devoted to social needs. Howard J. Samuels, former Under Secretary of Commerce and a businessman, recognized the problem when he suggested that if we were serious about dealing with the urban crisis we would take half the annual increase in resources that go into private consumption and devote them to the public sector in expenditures for such things as schools, housing, day care centers, and health programs. The annual output of goods and services in 1968, he said, would increase at about $35 billion, of which $20 billion would be spent for personal consumption. Half that amount could be devoted to vital needs in the public sector. Such a distribution by 1972, with continued growth in the economy, would yield $50 billion a year for investments in public needs and human resources. "The question is," he said, "are we going to spend that money on even more elaborate plastic packaging and on things like color television or on better schools and housing and other social needs?" [41]

Social policies that would overcome "the private gorge and the public famine" are at the heart of social welfare concerns, indicating the extent to which social welfare is a study in political economy. To define welfare as humanitarianism is to ask how we may help individuals in need. To think of it as a study in political economy is to ask how we may influence political decisions to reallocate resources consistent with the developmental needs of children, the requirements of stable family life, and the goals of a humane and democratic society. Attention, then, is directed at both values and power and the process of resolving conflicts over definitions of the proper ends of social life.

It is largely power that determines national priorities. The distribution and uses of power, however, have not until recently been a chief concern of students of social welfare or practitioners of the human service professions. If anything, ideologies of welfare have tended to conceal questions of power. The perception of welfare as an activity directed at helping people with problems almost invariably has focused attention on individuals and their defects, on therapy and rehabilitation, rather than on social structure and institutionalized power and privilege that allocates advantages and disadvantages. It is true that the history of social welfare and social work demonstrates a dual concern with individual change and social reform. The question of power, though never entirely neglected, now comes increasingly to the front as a central issue; conflict is now more visible and the power of privileged groups to resist demands for a new set of national priorities is more manifest.

Issues of social welfare no longer can be seen simply as a conflict over individual versus collective responsibility. We live in a society of rugged collectivism, of organized groups that compete for advantage and are able to use political power to influence social policy in ways that favor their interests. A new function of a democratic welfare state is to redress imbalances in the distribution of power. A corresponding concern of voluntary groups is to see to it that the state itself does not wield excessive power. The guarantee of the right of collective bargaining provided the labor movement with legitimate power to enable workers to bargain on a more equal plane with management. What the functional equivalent is for those poor who are essentially outside the labor force is, as we shall see later, a troubling issue. In any event the

[41] *The New York Times*, April 11, 1968.

more equal distribution of power to influence questions of social policy in a society in which government makes the major welfare decisions is of primary importance. Questions of equitable distribution of power in all areas of life touch on social welfare concerns. To Charles Frankel the business of liberalism has always been

> . . . to correct imbalances of power, and to organize social institutions in such a way that no one has too much power. For the major source of social injustice is the monopoly of power by any group, political, economic, or ecclesiastical; and the only way to prevent social injustice is to counter power with power. Only by diffusing power in the community does one expand the area in which men act by free choice and not by coercion.[42]

Coercion is often invisible however, concealed especially by the ideologies of a free market and a free political system. Robert H. Bremner gave recognition to the first portion of this statement when he wrote of the positive function of the welfare state in protecting individuals from the arbitrary though hidden power of the market. "Men," he said, "can be victimized as much by the law of supply and demand as by the arbitrary whim of a despot." [43] Social welfare legislation has to some degree protected individuals from such coercion through protection of collective bargaining, social insurance, minimum wage laws, pure food and drug regulations, and so forth. Much concealed coercion remains because economic decisions determine capital investments, plant relocation, rates of unemployment, and pollution of the environment and have other consequences that exert influences on individuals beyond their control.

The power of government may also, in concealed ways, contribute to human ill-fare rather than welfare. Social policy provides for guaranteed poverty since grants for those dependent on public assistance are legislated levels of subsistence below the poverty line. More important because less visible is the extent to which social policy creates inequalities and forces individuals and families into conditions defined as "social problems." Billions of dollars spent in agricultural support programs have had the effect of displacing southern white and black farm laborers, forcing them to search for employment in the cities, where considerably less has been spent in their behalf through welfare services. To a considerable degree rates of unemployment today are managed or manageable by the federal government through fiscal and monetary controls. The hardships imposed on the unemployed and subemployed are consequences of commission or omission in social policy. Individual responsibility for failure to work is difficult to sustain when the government could provide for full employment but fails to or when, through deliberate efforts to curtail inflation, it imposes higher rates of unemployment on those least able to protect themselves. The notion of social compensations for socially imposed hardship might replace the pejorative concept of welfare for the failures of society. Social policy has produced approximately 700,000 public housing units since

[42] Frankel, *op. cit.*, p. 30.

[43] Bremner, *op. cit.*, p. 267.

this program began in 1937.   In addition the Federal Housing Authority has helped another 235,000 families in both low-income and middle-income projects.   Whereas less than one million low-income families have benefited from housing policy, the FHA, since 1935, has helped some 9 million, chiefly suburban, families to purchase homes and has permitted an additional 28 million to secure low-cost loans for home improvements.[44]   We shall return to this issue later when we ask, Who are the welfare recipients?

It is important to emphasize that much of our way of life today and some of its ills are a consequence of social policy decisions that allocate advantages and disadvantages, determine life opportunities, and influence the quality of life.   To the extent that social conditions are subject to deliberate social policy, we cannot escape the moral responsibility to assess the consequences of our acts.   We often expect this of individuals when they lack resources and opportunities to act otherwise.   Can we avoid social responsibility for social acts, particularly when resources and opportunities are available for alternative choices, or at least for compensating benefits?

Social welfare, then, focuses attention on issues of social policy, the values that define them, and the distribution of power that determines how they will be resolved.   ·

But knowledge, as well as values and power, influences social policy.   We have moved from a moral to a secular scientific approach to social problems in the degree to which social science concepts influence our perception of problems and the proper avenues for their treatment or prevention.   Ultimately social policy decisions are made through the political process.   In the view of some, however, social science knowledge may increasingly play an influential role as we develop a form of "social intelligence" to guide social policy, just as economic intelligence through the Council of Economic Advisors now guides national economic policy.   Proposals for a "social report" equivalent to the Economic Report of the President have been incorporated in legislation and in a number of scholarly efforts.[45]   Political decisions that take into account the findings of social science, it is hoped, will facilitate an emerging politics of relevance based on well-ordered information and careful analysis, and will permit an open and experimental approach to achieve social goals.   Emphasis will be on incremental improvements through continuous efforts to modify attempts at social reform based on knowledge of positive and negative outcomes. Since the consequences of action cannot be fully anticipated, a premium is placed on continuous and rapid feedback of information in order to correct for the inevitable errors that will occur.   Thus some gap between intentions and outcomes is recognized as inevitable, and a method is developed to permit a continuous approximation toward some desired state.   This places failure in

[44] Martin Nolan, "A Belated Effort to Save Our Cities," *The Reporter,* December 28, 1967.

[45] U.S. Congress "Full Opportunity and Social Accounting Act," S843, introduced February 1967 by Senator Walter F. Mondale of Minnesota; Walter F. Mondale, "Reporting on the Social State of the Union," *Trans-action,* 5 (June 1968), pp. 34–38; Bertram M. Gross (ed.), *Social Intelligence for America's Future* (Boston: Allyn & Bacon, 1969); *Toward A Social Report,* U.S. Department of Health, Education, and Welfare (Washington, D.C.:   Government Printing Office, 1969).

an entirely different perspective, with the possibility of freeing program developers from the paralyzing fear of not succeeding and from the defensiveness and concealment of damaging information that so often accompanies this state of mind. The appeal of this approach will be "cerebral rather than visceral." Its weakness is its lack of passion, which moves men to ". . . accomplish that which reason suggests is impossible." Its strength lies in the lack of "passion that allows men to commit monstrous crimes in the name of just causes." [46] This is an essential part of the view of social welfare as social development, to which we shall return when we ask whether a passion for human freedom may not properly direct social intelligence.

Knowledge, values, and power influence social policy. Social policy issues involve questions of strategies and programs. How much of our effort should involve expansion of the economy and job creation, redistribution of income and other services, enhancement of social competence and social resources for more effective participation in society, reform of institutions to alter the status, power and opportunity of individuals? We look now at various social welfare programs and strategies—social provisions, social services, and social action.

Social Welfare as Programs and Services

Social welfare may refer to those socially sponsored programs and activities that reflect social policy decisions. They are forms of intervention through public or voluntary means that meet socially recognized needs not provided for through the free market or the family system. Social welfare programs may be understood in terms of the social functions they perform and may be evaluated in terms of the ideal values we are trying to realize. Three interrelated and overlapping functional areas that make up the social welfare system may be identified: (1) social provisions, (2) social services, and (3) social action.

Social Provisions

Social provisions substitute for, supplement, or replace the market allocation of income, medical care, housing, and other resources. Illustrations are public assistance, social insurance, public housing, and public provision of medical care. Such programs may be residual (public assistance) or institutional (social insurance). They may be directed at problems of destitution, poverty, insecurity, or inequality. A variety of means may be used to promote economic well-being, which may include fiscal and occupational welfare programs. The ideal goals of social provisions are social security and social justice. They are not necessarily concerned with changing people, improving their character, or making them into more competent citizens. They may simply be intended to assure all individuals, as a citizen right, equitable access to those provisions essential for some defined level of well-being. On the other hand, as we shall see, adequate social provisions is a basic underpinning for more effective social functioning and is thus interrelated with other concerns of social welfare.

[46] This view of social intelligence is based on Bertram M. Gross (ed.), *Social Intelligence for America's Future* (Boston: Allyn & Bacon, 1969).

Social provisions direct our attention to the economic function of social welfare and to the relationship between social policy and the operation of the market economy. This theme is explored in Chapter Five.

Social Services

Social services support, supplement, or substitute for the family and our educational institution and are part of socialization and social control mechanisms. They are essentially "people-changing" institutions designed to equip individuals with the competence and resources essential for effective social participation or to control those whose participation is defined as a threat to society. A residual definition of social services focuses on control, whereas a developmental view emphasizes assuring societal resources and life experiences that enhance social functioning. By social functioning we mean role performance. Through social roles society distributes those functions (e.g., work and parental care of children) that must be performed if it is to maintain itself and realize values embodied in its institutions. The family, school, and social services are part of the socialization structure designed to provide personal and social resources essential for effective performance of social roles.

This structure may be seen as (1) developmental, (2) remedial, (3) supportive, or (4) substitutive. Education is usually considered as belonging to the first category because it seeks to facilitate the normal growth process and to equip individuals with those skills and attitudes essential for successful adaptation to role requirements. Family counseling agencies and child guidance clinics are remedial services aimed at "compensatory socialization." Day care and homemaker services are supportive resources supplementing the family and facilitating its functioning. A foster home substitutes for the family. These services are overlapping, of course. A day care center may enable a mother to enter the labor force and it may provide both educational and remedial services for a child and his parents. Schools, especially in the inner city, are increasingly being pressured to take on expanded social service functions that will help deprived children and their families overcome both educational and social handicaps.[47] A social service that was once defined as remedial may take on a developmental concern, focusing attention not so much on defects to be corrected but on strengths and potentialities to be developed. A case in point might be some of the new efforts at creating child and family development centers in which parents and children are involved together, not as clients to be treated but as learners to be exposed to new opportunities in order to develop new skills and competencies.[48] Parents may also be helped to focus on deficits in community resources in employment opportunities, schools, and medical care that prevent them from achieving goals for themselves and their children. In this event attention may be given to parental involvement in social action in efforts to alter institutional arrangements or to develop new institutions to meet needs.

[47] Peter Schrag, *Voices in the Classroom* (Boston: Beacon Press, 1965), pp. 59, 93, 96, and 282.

[48] *See* articles in *Children,* 16 (March–April 1969); *also* Charles V. Hamilton, "Race and Education: A Search for Legitimacy," *Harvard Educational Review,* 38 (Fall 1968), especially pp. 681–684.

Social Action

Although an absolute distinction is not possible between service and action, the former may be said to be primarily concerned with changing people, while the latter directs attention at system change. One seeks to develop capacities and to provide enabling resources for better functioning within the system; the other seeks to alter the structure of roles and the distribution of power, prevent problems, expand opportunity, and enhance the quality of life. The two are often interrelated. Targets of change may be formal organizations (e.g., schools and social agencies) and larger social systems such as communities and even the society itself.

The connection between service and action may be illustrated by the following: Helping to organize low-income parents to form an action group directed at improving the quality of education for their children is a social service to that group and leads to social action aimed at producing institutional change. In the process parents may acquire a new self-image and enhanced social skills with opportunities to play new social roles if they achieve, for example, the right to participate in formulating school policy. The school system, in turn, may change its approach to both children and parents, thus facilitating their social participation.

Efforts at system change may be through citizen participation in organized efforts using both the normal political process and varying degrees of norm-violating action, from civil disobedience to violent revolution. While the attainment of social welfare goals might require radical alterations in the social structure, particularly in the distribution of income and power, the use of violence or revolutionary tactics are not ordinarily considered part of social welfare methods. Society rarely sponsors a revolution against itself. The action of militant blacks or students, however much they may be related to the goals of social justice, are not usually regarded as part of the social welfare process. Through the Community Action Program portion of the Economic Opportunity Act of 1964, however, some attempt was made under social auspices to organize the poor for political action. The effort which has had mixed results and uncertain outcome, will be considered more fully in Chapter Eight.

Efforts at social reform may be through planned social change that relies on expert knowledge and skills and the coordinated effort of professionals and citizens. An example is the Model Cities effort under the Demonstration Cities and Metropolitan Development Act of 1966, which provided for

> . . . comprehensive city demonstration programs containing new and imaginative proposals to rebuild or revitalize large slum and blighted areas; to expand housing, job, and income opportunities; to reduce dependence on welfare payments, to improve educational facilities and programs; to combat disease and ill health; to reduce the incidence of crime and delinquency; to enhance recreational and cultural opportunities; to establish better access between homes and jobs; and generally to improve living conditions." [49]

[49] Demonstration Cities and Metropolitan Development Act of 1966. Public Law 89–754. Title 1, Sec. 101.

Social reform is the order of the day, an urgent necessity, yet difficult to realize and problematic at best, whether attempted through political action or professional planning or both.

Social provisions, social services, and social action may be seen as different though interrelated social welfare strategies. They also identify some of the chief issues. The relative emphasis to be given to redistribution of income and other resources, to social services or basic alterations in social structure, are among the critical social welfare questions.

Organization of Social Welfare Programs

There are a number of social welfare systems whose functions are interrelated, overlapping, and poorly coordinated. These are (1) public welfare, involving programs of financial aid and other services to the destitute, (2) social insurance, providing a variety of work-related benefits, (3) employment and manpower development programs, (4) housing and urban renewal, (5) health and medical care, (6) mental health, including state mental hospitals and newer forms of community mental health programs, (7) vocational rehabilitation, (8) delinquency and corrections, (9) recreation and leisure-time activities, (10) family and child welfare services, and (11) community organization and planning.

These and other such programs may be under public or voluntary auspices or both. They may be organized around a social problem (e.g., poverty) or focused on a target population (e.g., children or the aged). They may be restricted to the poor or may be designed to meet universal needs. They may be essentially remedial, seeking to restore individuals to normal functioning, or developmental, providing resources to enhance the capacity of citizens to participate in society. They may offer social provisions or social services or may seek to stimulate social action and planned social change.

We are moving toward a recognition that the essential purpose of social welfare must be human development, just as our past history has been a successful effort at economic and technological development. To implement such a goal requires attention to issues concerning adequacy and equity in social provisions, comprehensive high-quality social services provided as a citizen right, critical evaluation, and radical alteration of social institutions to maximize self-actualization. All require greater concern with social planning, clarification of value choices, confrontation with the issue of power, and resistance to change. All contain dilemmas that are not easily resolved.

Social Welfare and Social Work

Social work refers to an occupation and a profession concerned with improving social relationships. It thus has a social service and a social action focus. The field of social welfare may be thought of as encompassing the functions of the various human service professions and occupations: teaching, medicine, psychiatry, clinical psychology, rehabilitation, counseling, and so forth. Social work is one of several professions operating within the social welfare network of programs and activities.

Social work, however, does have some unique features that may distinguish it from other service professions. It has an integrative function and a clearly articulated moral ideal in which man is the center of concern, however much the practice of social work may have failed to live up to its value aspirations.[50] Of all the human service professions it also has the longest historic association with social welfare concerns, so that not too long ago the terms social welfare and social work were used synonymously.

Social work may be said to stand at the interface between the individual and social institutions. Ideally, social work knowledge, skills, and values are used to help individuals adapt to social institutions; in turn, social work seeks to modify social institutions to meet human needs.

The activities of social workers are oriented toward almost every major social institution. That is, public assistance is oriented toward the economic functioning of individuals; family and child services are, of course, concerned with the family; probation, parole, and correctional social work is directed at the relationship between the individual and the law; school social work is concerned with the relationship between the educational institution and the individual; medical social work is oriented toward the relationship between the individual and health institutions. Even the army has its social workers to help soldiers adapt to the role requirements of military life.

Social workers are also found in a variety of agencies concerned with character development, recreation, and leisure-time activities (e.g., neighborhood and settlement houses) and in social agencies providing community-planning services. The need for a profession with an integrated view was noted by Dr. Richard Cabot, when he wrote that social work ". . . takes no special point of view; it takes the total human point of view." [51] He thought that social work must contribute a holistic approach, precisely because doctors and other professionals take so specialized a view. While social workers as individuals inevitably must perform specialized functions (e.g., in the placement of children in foster care, marital counseling, group work, probation, community action, etc.), they do so, ideally, with a concern for the individual's total needs. Moreover, the profession seeks to maintain an integrated view of the individual in society, directing its attention to improving services to individuals and families and to broad issues of social policy and social action.[52]

Social welfare and social work are historically related and are sometimes still used synonymously. Today we distinguish social welfare institutions from the profession and occupation of social work. This is, however, a distinction of recent origin that accompanied the general professionalization of social work

[50] For a discussion of some distinctions between the values of educators and those of social workers, for example, *see* David Street, "Educators and Social Workers: Sibling Rivalry in the Inner City," *Social Service Review,* 41 (June 1969), pp. 152–165.

[51] Quoted in Mary E. Richmond, *Social Diagnosis* (New York: Russell Sage Foundation, 1917), pp. 35–36.

[52] *Social Action Guide* (New York: National Association of Social Workers, 1965); *also Goals of Public Social Policy* (New York: National Association of Social Workers, revised 1966). The 1969 Delegate Assembly of the National Association of Social Workers (April 20–24, 1969, Atlantic City) adopted social action as the association's top priority.

and the rise of experts in an increasingly complex, bureaucratized, and scientifically oriented society. When Edward T. Devine wrote his definition of social work in 1922, he did *not* make this distinction.

> Social work . . . is the sum of all the efforts made by society to "take up its own slack," to provide for individuals when its established institutions fail them, to supplement those established institutions and to modify them at those points at which they have proved to be badly adapted to social needs. It may have for its object, the relief of individuals or the improvement of conditions. It may be carried on by the government or by an incorporated society or by an informal group or by an individual, or it may be a temporary excrescence on some older institution which exists primarily for some other function. It may be well done or badly . . . It may be inspired by sympathy or expediency or fear of revolution or even of evolutionary change, or by a sense of justice and decency. It includes everything which is done by society for the benefit of those who are not in a position to compete on fair terms with their fellows, from whatever motive it may be done, by whatever agency or whatever means, and with whatever result.[53]

This comprehensive and realistic definition could easily apply to social welfare today. Social work, however, must have a more restricted definition as a major profession providing knowledge, skills, and leadership in the broad social welfare field.

The intimate association of social work with social welfare is illustrated by their common stages of development, as noted by a United Nations survey of training for social work, which makes the following observations regarding the development of the functions of social work:

> . . . the stages through which social work has passed in many of the countries in which it is today most fully developed, may be broken down into three major categories: (a) social work as individual charity; (b) social work as organized activity, under governmental and non-governmental auspices, directed towards the solution of problems associated with economic dependency; and (c) social work as professional service, under governmental and non-governmental auspices, potentially available to every member of the community, irresponsive of his means, to assist him in achieving his full potentialities for productive and satisfying living.[54]

Today, however, social work must ally itself with a variety of other professions and scientific disciplines. It may be said that social work stands in relation to social welfare as the medical profession stands in relation to the field of health. The interrelationship of social problems and the requirements of achieving a more comprehensive, effective, and positive effort to promote welfare require collaboration with related human service professions and a better link between science and practice.

[53] Edward T. Devine, *Social Work* (New York: Macmillan, 1922), pp. 21–22.

[54] United Nations Department of Social Affairs, *Training for Social Work: An International Survey* (New York: United Nations, 1950).

Ideally, social work is committed to the ethical use of knowledge for problem-solving and the enrichment of life.   It has a historic identification with social reform, yet it often has been constrained to be more conservative than innovative.   Society endows social work with the mandate to maintain social stability and to meet human needs—functions that often conflict.   Social work and other service professions often fail because society does not wish to pay the price for solving its social problems.   On the other hand, we cannot ignore the problems.   Consequently something has to be done, partly to alleviate misery, partly to meet threats to the social order, and partly to assure ourselves that we are humanitarian after all.   Now social work, as well as other human service professions, faces a crisis.   The accumulation of human neglect and the aspirations for redressing old grievances and expanding our commitment to equality challenge social work to alter its own practice.   Both within the profession and without, there are critics who see social work as excessively preoccupied with its own professional advancement, fixated on individual casework and therapy to the neglect of social reform, and resistant to basic modification in its own modes of operation.   Ferment characterizes the field as it seeks to meet the new challenge being voiced by the once dispossessed client, now speaking with the voice of the consumer, and by members within the profession who are asking for ways to fulfill their social action commitments.[55] Important changes have been taking place in social work education and practice over the past several years, with increasing emphasis on developing skills and modes of practice for system change as well as for more effective delivery of social services.[56]   There is a new concern with the development of knowledge and skill for changing institutions.   Recognizing that social problems result from system defects as well as individual maladjustments, greater attention is being given in professional schools to preparing people who can be agents of social change.   This may mean helping to organize people for involvement in solving their own problems, from staging a rent strike to developing new community resources.   Among the new settings for field experiences are comprehensive community mental health centers, antipoverty programs, offices of local or state government officials, community action settings, and civil rights movements.   In the words of one student, the "new definition of social work is the nitty-gritty approach."   A new approach also means the ability to analyze a community and its needs and to contribute to

[55] Increasingly, clients are disagreeing freely with professionals.   For example, in a letter to the editor commenting on an earlier article describing the attempts of the Philadelphia Chapter of NASW to support her organization, the chairman of the Philadelphia Welfare Rights Organization, Mrs. Roxanne Jones, said, "What disturbs me are the many sentences like 'The aim was for NASW to help the two organizations (WRO and the Union) see their mutual interests in a welfare system that meets clients' needs and respects the rights of workers.' I want to say from the ghetto that we at Philadelphia WRO are dedicated to destroying the welfare system that has oppressed the poor and continues to destroy poor families in Philadelphia every day." *NASW News,* 14 (May 1969), p. 23.

[56] As an indicator of this change *see* recent issues of the *Journal of Education for Social Work,* 5 (Spring 1969), and *Social Work* 14 (April 1969), which contain articles with titles such as "Societal Crisis—Strategies for Social Work Education" and "Social Work's New Role in the Welfare Class Revolution."

planning and action that take into account the human dimension. The emphasis of the Demonstration Cities legislation on *social* as well as physical planning is an indication of the need for this kind of competence.[57]

New models of agency service based on a more sophisticated understanding of the relationship between social disability and the opportunity structure have been established and in some measure evaluated.[58] Even with the passage of time we may not produce the data essential for thorough evaluation, partly because of inherent difficulties in such efforts and partly because we are not always eager to find out how well we are doing. Moreover programs aimed at producing basic changes in social institutions quickly lose the support of dominant groups in the community. If social reform proceeds too well, threatening to upset the existing distribution of power and privilege, there are likely to be efforts to curtail social workers and others who are too militant in their advocacy of social change. How to mobilize sufficient power for social reform without at the same time invoking the superior power of backlash from those who are in basic control of social institutions is a persistent dilemma. At the same time society's commitment to equality of opportunity, the social and political unrest created by exclusion, and the mounting problems of an urban society offer possibilities for directed social change. Social workers with skill in social system intervention as well as those equipped for direct service to individuals, families, and groups are increasingly in demand. Both functions require more sophisticated understanding of the value and limitations of social science knowledge than ever before. New recruits to the field must have the imagination, competence and courage to develop and apply new methods and to participate in more effective collaboration with professional, nonprofessional, and politically active groups. Social work's traditional regard for both the individual and society, as well as its roots in both science and values, could make it a strategic profession in a period that seeks to adapt social institutions to human needs. How successfully it can carry this responsibility is a major question.

Social Welfare Expenditures

The nature of social welfare and its place in American society may be clarified by a brief look at the expenditures made for programs that carry this label. Welfare expenditures express the value we place on human beings. The kind

[57] Demonstration Cities and Metropolitan Development Act of 1966, Public Law 89–754. Title I, Sec. 103, states that programs must be of sufficient magnitude to make an impact on physical and social problems; ". . . to contribute to the sound development of the entire city; to make marked progress in reducing social and educational disadvantages, ill health, underemployment, and enforced idleness; and to provide educational, health, and social services necessary to serve the poor and disadvantaged in the area; widespread citizen participation in the program, maximum opportunities for employing residents of the area in all phases of the program, and enlarged opportunities for work and training." It must be noted that these objectives are not necessarily realized in current programs, but they do recognize the need for competence in social planning.

[58] Harold H. Weissman (ed.), *The New Social Work* (New York: Associated Press, 1969), 4 vols.

and amount of such expenditures reflect the extent to which human values are honored in our society. Controversy over social welfare expenditures forces us from time to time to determine to what ends we wish to devote our resources and, in the process, to choose those values we wish to be reflected in our own lives.

To ask how much we spend on social welfare, however, is to bring us back to the problem of definition. Data on social welfare expenditures are provided annually in the *Social Security Bulletin*. In this very useful series of reports, social welfare is defined as follows:

> Social welfare, as defined for this series, is limited to those activities that directly concern the economic and social well-being of individuals and families. Not included in this concept are programs aimed at the general welfare of the population and only indirectly affecting the welfare of the individuals, such as enforcement of law and order, promotion of economic growth and price stability, and provision for national security.[59]

Thus the definition is intended to include expenditures for all public and nongovernmental programs that have a direct concern with the "economic and social well-being of individuals and families." [60] Education, however, is included, as explained by the following statement:

> Education is included in this series, in part to make the data comparable with social welfare data used in other countries and in the United Nations. In discussions of the share of national income a country is or should be using for social welfare purposes—compared with economic development or military expenditures, for example—the term social welfare usually includes not only public welfare and social security, as defined in the United States, but also health and education. In many countries widespread public education is a much more recent development than it is in the United States. Here its social welfare aspects, which had been recognized in the early debates about public schools, are now largely taken for granted. Increasing concern with school dropouts, the quality of education in slum areas, and the interrelationship of social and eco-

[59] Ida C. Merriam, "Social Welfare Expenditures, 1964–65," *Social Security Bulletin,* 28 (October 1965).

[60] However, some things are excluded that do have a direct concern with economic and social well-being, such as certain manpower and development programs under the auspices of the U.S. Department of Labor that are conducted outside educational institutions. Understandably not included, since they are related to a different set of purposes, are education, medical care, and other services provided by the military; they do, however, make a major impact on many lives. Paradoxically, the military is from one point of view one of the largest and possibly the most successful social service agency in the country. According to research reports, the military's efforts in training men who received low scores on classification tests (and were formerly rejected) have been uniformly successful. Just as many become useful servicemen as the average, normal members of groups with which they have been regularly compared.

Ivar Berg, "Rich Man's Qualifications for Poor Man's Jobs," *Trans-action,* 6 (March 1969), p. 49

nomic circumstances with educational aspirations and achievements, however, again point up the relevance of education to social welfare.[61]

How much do we spend on social welfare as defined in these annual reports? It may surprise some to note that total public expenditures in 1968–1969 were expected to exceed $126 billion (Table 1). This represented 14 percent of our total Gross National Product for that year and an increase of $38.9 billion over expenditures for 1965. With adjustments for population growth and price changes, total expenditures in 1969 were 41 percent above those for 1965. The increase from 1968 to 1969 alone was $14.8 billion, the bulk of this was due to expansion of social insurance and state and local increases in expenditures for education.

Expenditures for health, education, income maintenance, and other services related to the well-being of individuals and families are both public and private. In 1969 this amounted to $181.6 billion or 20 percent of our Gross National Product. This amount includes employee benefit plans (or the occupational welfare state, which we will discuss later), private expenditures for health and education; and the cost of voluntary social welfare programs and philanthropy. Voluntary contributions that largely support a variety of social services and some cash payments amounted to $1.9 billion in 1969. The largest share of all expenditures comes from federal, state, and local governments (Table 2). Public expenditures account for 83.3 percent of the cost of education and 85 percent of organized income maintenance and other welfare programs. Private expenditures continue to account for the largest share of the total spent for health, with government paying 37.5 percent.

Concern about the increasing public cost of social welfare must be seen in relation to the Gross National Product and to total government expenses (Table 3). As already noted public expenditures in 1969 accounted for 14 percent of GNP, a significant increase over the past several decades. In relation to government expenditures for all purposes, social welfare in 1969 accounted for almost 45 percent, compared to 36 percent in 1929. In 1969 social welfare expenditures accounted for 38 precent of the total federal budget. However, in the 1930s, the era of economic collapse, it amounted to almost half.[62]

Most revealing is the proportion of the total federal budget directly devoted to the welfare of individuals. Budgets are instruments for setting national priorities. They deal, as James Reston has observed, "not only with the economics, but with the philosophy, psychology and character of the nation." [63] In this regard a look at the federal budgets for fiscal 1970 and 1971 may be instructive, provided we can make a distinction between the apparent and the real. In presenting the 1971 budget, President Richard M. Nixon declared that it marked a beginning in "the necessary process of reordering our national priorities." The federal government, he contended, will "for the first time in two full decades . . . spend more money on human resource programs than

[61] Merriam, *op. cit.,* p. 3.

[62] Ida C. Merriam, Alfred M. Skolnik, and Sophie R. Dales, "Social Welfare Expenditures 1967–68," *Social Security Bulletin,* 31 (December 1968).

[63] James Reston, "Washington: Another Case for Raising Taxes," *The New York Times,* December 11, 1966.

Table 1. Social Welfare Expenditures Under Public Programs, Selected Fiscal Years, 1928–1969.

PROGRAM	TOTAL EXPENDITURES (IN MILLIONS)				
	1928–29	1949–50	1965–66	1967–68	1968–69*
Total	$3,921.2	$23,508.4	$87,948.7	$112,044.5	$126,801.7
Social insurance	342.4	4,946.6	31,878.6	42,692.9	48,720.0
Public aid	60.0	2,496.2	7,301.1	11,091.7	13,442.9
Health & medical programs	351.1	2,063.5	6,938.0	8,271.3	8,817.5
Veterans programs	657.9	6,865.7	6,360.4	7,361.6	8,036.5
Education	2,433.7	6,674.1	32,820.7	38,756.6	43,033.0
Housing	0	14.6	334.8	427.9	555.8
Other social welfare	76.2	447.7	2,315.0	3,442.5	4,196.1
Vocational rehabilitation	1.6	30.0	298.7	469.6	557.7
Institutional care	74.7	145.5	736.7	1,038.2	1,521.4
School meals	0	160.2	537.4	705.9	795.4
Child welfare	0	104.9	400.6	503.0	550.4
Special OEO programs	0	0	287.3	608.1	647.5
Social welfare not classified elsewhere	0	7.1	54.2	117.5	123.6

* Preliminary estimates.

SOURCE: Alfred M. Skolnik and Sophie R. Dales, "Social Welfare Expenditures, 1968–69," *Social Security Bulletin,* Vol. 32 (December 1969), p. 5. Table 1 is adapted from a much more comprehensive table in the *Social Security Bulletin*'s annual article on social welfare expenditures. Many subheadings as well as footnotes are omitted. It should be noted that this table includes all public federal, state, and local expenditures. Major items included under social insurance and their estimated amounts for 1968–1969 are old age, survivors, disability, and health insurance—$33.4 billion, including health insurance for the aged—$6.6 billion; railroad retirement—$1.5 billion; public employee retirement—$7.5 billion; unemployment insurance—$2.9 billion; workman's compensation—$2.6 billion. Public aid includes public assistance—$12 billion including vendor medical payments of $4.4 billion, and other (Job Corps, Neighborhood Youth Corps, work-experience programs under OEO, surplus food for the needy, food stamps, repatriate and refugee assistance)—$1.5 billion. Over thirty-four billion dollars of the education total is spent for elementary and secondary education.

Table 2. Total Expenditures for Health, Education, and Welfare, 1968–1969, and Percentage of Public and Private Funds

TYPE OF EXPENDITURE	TOTAL EXPENDITURE (BILLIONS)	% PUBLIC	% PRIVATE
Total	$181.6	69.0	31.0
Health	60.3	37.5	62.5
Education	52.4	83.3	16.7
Income—maintenance and welfare	71.1	85.0	15.0

SOURCE: Alfred M. Skolnik and Sophie R. Dales, "Social Welfare Expenditures, 1968–1969," *Social Security Bulletin,* Vol. 32 (December 1969), Table 10, p. 17.

Table 3. Social Welfare Expenditures Under Public Programs as Percent of Gross National Product, Selected Fiscal Years, 1939–1940 through 1968–1969.

	1939–40	1949–50	1959–60	1966–67	1967–68	1968–69 [a]
Gross national product (billions)	$95.1	$263.4	$495.6	$771.1	$827.6	$900.6
Social welfare expenditures as % of GNP						
Total [b]	9.2	8.9	10.6	12.9	13.5	14.1
Social insurance	1.3	1.9	3.9	4.8	5.2	5.4
Public aid	3.8	.9	.8	1.1	1.3	1.5
Health and medical programs	.6	.8	.9	1.0	1.0	1.0
Education	2.7	2.5	3.6	4.6	4.7	4.8
Other social welfare	.1	.2	.2	.4	.4	.5

[a] Preliminary estimates.
[b] Includes housing and veterans programs.
SOURCE: Alfred M. Skolnik and Sophie R. Dales, "Social Welfare Expenditures, 1968–1969," *Social Security Bulletin*, Vol. 32 (December 1969), Table 3, p. 9.

on national defense." Indeed as a comparison of Tables 4 and 5 reveals, a new item, human resources, was introduced in the 1971 budget, and it appears that it does replace national defense as the leading contender for the federal budget dollar. In fact expenditures for defense have been reduced from a 1969 actual outlay of $81.2 billion to estimated expenditures in 1970 and 1971 of $79.4 and $73.5 billion. At the same time, the prominence given to human resources in the 1971 allocation of the budget dollar does not quite reflect the apparent major reordering of priorities in the direction of welfare

Table 4. The Budget Dollar, Fiscal Year 1970 Estimate

WHERE IT COMES FROM	
Individual income taxes	46¢
Social insurance taxes and contributions	23
Corporate income taxes	19
Excise taxes	8
Other	4

WHERE IT GOES	
National defense	41¢
(Vietnam)	(13)
Social insurance trust funds	22
Education and other major social programs	12
Other	11
Interest	6
Veterans	4
International	2
Debt Reduction	2

SOURCE: *The New York Times*, January 16, 1969.

Table 5. The Budget Dollar, Fiscal Year 1971
Estimate

WHERE IT COMES FROM	
Individual income taxes	45¢
Social insurance taxes and contributions	24
Corporate income taxes	17
Excise taxes	9
Other	5
WHERE IT GOES	
Human resources	
(education, manpower, health)	41¢
National defense	36
Physical resources	
(rural development, natural resources)	10
Interest	7
Other	5
Debt reduction	1

SOURCE: *The New York Times,* February 3, 1970.

rather than warfare. As Carl T. Rowan has noted, the item for human resources includes approximately $50.4 billion for income security, a large
portion of which is social insurance trust funds provided almost entirely from
payroll taxes and employee contributions. While these are properly regarded
as investment in human resources, they are essentially funds committed by law
for this purpose, "and no President is entitled to take credit for it as evidence
of his changing priorities." [64] He further observes that out of a total $200.8
billion 1971 fiscal budget, some $78 billion represent "relatively controllable
outlays," funds that an administration can reallocate to new purposes. "Of
this 'controllable' money, $46.7 billion will go for national defense and only
$21.8 billion for civilian programs. That is a more accurate reflection of where
our national priorities now stand than the misleading pie showing national
defense taking a back seat to human resources." [65] This is not to say that a
small beginning had not been made in the reordering of priorities, for, along
with cuts in national defense, civilian programs were increased by $200 million
in fiscal 1971. Yet this is not quite the basic redirection in resource allocation
required for meeting human needs in this era. It seems reasonably clear that
these cannot be met without continued reductions in the cost of military expenditures. In 1969, for the first time, Congress began to raise critical
questions about the size of the military budget, its relative efficiency in meeting
legitimate needs of national defense, and the degree to which it supports the
narrow interests of the military-industrial complex. Outcomes of the conflict
regarding the proportion of the national income to be devoted to defense over
domestic concerns will continue to influence the adequacy with which social
needs can be met. In the meantime, with an expanding economy, government
involvement in social welfare has continued to grow.

[64] Carl T. Rowan, "Nixon Budget Is Misleading," *Portland Press Herald,* February
7, 1970.

[65] *Ibid.*

Some measure of the growth of government involvement in social welfare is revealed by noting that in 1928–1929 government at all levels expended in constant 1967–1968 prices, a per capita amount of $69.58, while in 1968–1969 the figure is $616.01, more than an eight-fold increase.[66]   It is important to observe, however, that $445 of that amount goes for education and social insurance—both universal programs.   This sizable increase in public expenditures for social welfare might seem sufficient to convince anyone that we are indeed a welfare state.   Although it is impossible to deny the significant expansion of government involvement in the broad field of social welfare, a look at the items for which funds are expended and the level at which various social needs are met is important before any judgment can be made about the degree of public commitment to welfare.   The broad definition used to determine social welfare expenditures, in the series prepared by the Social Security Administration, has the merit of focusing attention on the related programs directly concerned with economic and social well-being.   As a rule, the public tends to restrict the label of welfare to financial aid and other services to the needy.   The great bulk of social welfare expenditures in 1968–1969 were in support of education ($43.0 billion) and social insurance programs ($48.7 billion).   Both education and social insurance also account for a major portion of recent increases in the total cost of social welfare.   In the popular lexicon, neither of these are ordinarily considered to be welfare programs, although in this book they are so defined.   Social insurance payments are usually thought of as work-related benefits, as in the case of unemployment compensation, and contributory, as in the case of OASDHI.   Education tends to be thought of as separate from welfare.   Since the public becomes concerned about how much we are spending on welfare, meaning expenditures in behalf of the poor, it is important to extract from total social welfare expenditures those in support of programs oriented primarily toward the low-income population.   These are the programs listed under Public Aid and most of those included under Other Social Welfare.   (Table 1).   The bulk of the expenditures for Public Aid are in support of public assistance including vendor medical payments.   In addition, some OEO programs (e.g. Job Corps, Neighborhood Youth Corps) and others such as surplus food, food stamps, refugee assistance are also included.

Though the largest share of these expenditures goes for programs directed at various groups of the poor, not all listed under other social welfare are restricted to those who meet some test of need.   School meals are subsidized in behalf of children other than the poor.   The Vocational Rehabilitation Act Amendments of 1965, which authorized new and expanded vocational rehabilitation programs for the physically or mentally disabled, eliminated the federal requirement that financial need be determined before certain services are provided.[67]   Nonetheless most of these programs (public aid and other social welfare) are those the public tends to regard as welfare.

The label, welfare, is especially applied to public assistance involving financial

[66] Skolnik and Dales, *op. cit.,* p. 9.

[67] *Vocational Rehabilitation of the Disabled: The Public Program,* Reprint, *Health, Education, and Welfare Indicators* (Washington, D.C.: Government Printing Office, December 1965, and April 1966), p. 2.   The goal is to make services available to all handicapped people who want and need them by July 1975.

aid, medical care, and other services to the aged, blind, disabled, and needy families. In 1968–1969, expenditures for public assistance were $13.4 billion, or about 1.5 percent of GNP. (Tables 1 and 3). When the public refers to welfare recipients, it has in mind programs that represent less than 10 percent of our total social welfare expenditures as defined by the Social Security Administration.

Only those receiving public assistance are identified as welfare recipients by the general public. These are the people on welfare. As of January 1970, there were 10 million welfare clients in the four federal-state-local public assistance programs: (1) Old Age Assistance, (2) Aid to Families with Dependent Children, (3) Aid to the Permanently and Totally Disabled, and (4) Aid to the Blind (Table 6). An additional 912,000 were recipients of financial aid under

Table 6.   Public Assistance Recipients and Average Money Payment, January 1970

PROGRAM	NUMBER OF RECIPIENTS	U.S. AVERAGE MONEY PAYMENT (PER RECIPIENT)	HIGH	LOW
Old Age Assistance (OAA)	2,064,000	$ 74.95	$155.50 (N.H.)	$46.30 (Miss.)
Aid to the Permanently and Totally Disabled (APTD)	811,000	91.40	135.15 (Iowa)	51.00 (Ala.)
Aid to the Blind (AB)	80,400	100.15	159.75 (Calif.)	54.80 (Miss.)
Aid to Families with Dependent Children (AFDC)	7,479,000	45.80	70.90 (Mass.)	12.00 (Miss.)
Total	5,530,000			
Families	1,919,000			
General assistance	912,000	50.95	120.70 (N.J.)	3.70 (Ark.)
Total	11,346,400			

SOURCE: *Social Security Bulletin,* Vol. 33 (June 1970), Table M-26, 43.

the state and local general assistance programs, sometimes known as local relief or poor relief. Table 6 reveals the number of individuals involved in each public assistance program and the average monthly payment for which they earn their welfare status.[68]

To be a recipient of welfare, in this restricted sense, means a special identity, special treatment, and a special kind of exclusion. It is not likely, however, that most recipients feel very special. Those on welfare are among the poorest of the poor and are maintained in poverty through deliberate social policy. As noted

[68] The number of public assistance recipients in any given month is lower than the total number who receive aid at any time during the year. Thus for 1968, total recipients of the categorical programs and general assistance came to over 12 million. The President's Commission on Income Maintenance Programs, *Poverty Amid Plenty, The American Paradox* (Washington, D.C.: Government Printing Office, 1969), p. 115.

in Table 6, average payments to the aged are $74.95; to the blind, $100.15; to the disabled, $91.40. Families with dependent children get considerably less, with an average monthly payment of about $1.50 a day per recipient. Public assistance programs not only keep people poor, they may perpetuate dependency, deprive clients of hope, destroy self-respect, invade privacy, violate constitutional rights, contribute to family breakdown, encourage physical and mental illness, and cripple children through public indifference and neglect. They conceal social injustice by defining dependency as a personal problem.[69] For example, how do we account for the fact that over 40 percent of all public assistance recipients are Negro and that the risk of a Negro child becoming a recipient of public assistance is at least six times that of a white child? Is it lack of self-reliance that accounts for the fact that almost two-thirds of the increases of Aid to Families with Dependent Children between 1948 and 1961 were nonwhite families?[70] To believe this is to discount all the known economic and social barriers that prevent the Negro from participation in society; it is to ignore the fact that 63 percent of nonwhite children under 18, compared to 21 percent of white children, were living in poverty or near poverty in 1966.[71] It is also to ignore the fact that ". . . the Negro frequently faces unemployment rates which if faced by all workers would be considered a national scandal." [72] Thus, to condemn people as welfare recipients is to deflect attention from basic economic and social reforms essential for equalizing opportunity.

It should be made clear that in varying degrees public assistance programs may try to provide useful services to the poor and that the complex problems associated with poverty and societal neglect of that "other nation" are beyond

[69] Sherman Barr, "Budgeting and the Poor," *Public Welfare*, 23 (October 1965), pp. 246–250, 293–294; Winifred Bell, *Aid to Dependent Children* (New York: Columbia University Press, 1965); Walter C. Bentrup, "What's Wrong With the Means Test?," *Public Welfare*, 23 (October 1965), pp. 235–242; Gil Bonen and Philip Reno, "By Bread Alone, and Little Bread: Life on AFDC," *Social Work*, 15 (October 1968), pp. 5–11; M. Elaine Burgess, "Poverty and Dependency: Some Selected Characteristics," *Journal of Social Issues*, 21 (January 1965), pp. 79–97; Arthur Greenleigh, "Does the ADC Program Strengthen or Weaken Family Life?," *Casework Papers, 1961* (New York: Family Service Association of America, 1961), pp. 9–16; Robert D. Hess, "Educability and Rehabilitation: The Future of the Welfare Class," *Journal of Marriage and the Family*, 26 (November 1964), pp. 424–434; Gerald Kahn and Ellen J. Perkins, "Families Receiving AFDC: What Do They Have to Live On?" Reprint from *Welfare in Review*, 1 (October 1963); Daniel P. Moynihan, "The Crisis in Welfare," *The Public Interest*, No. 10 (Winter 1968), pp. 3–29; National Institute of Mental Health, *Mental Health in Appalachia*, (Washington, D.C.: Government Printing Office, 1965); Justine Wise Polier, "Problems Involving Family and Child," *Columbia Law Review* 66 (February 1966), pp. 305–316; Charles A. Reich, "Midnight Welfare Searches and the Social Security Act," *Yale Law Journal*, 72 (June 1963), p. 1347; *Report,* National Advisory Commission on Civil Disorders (Washington, D.C.: Government Printing Office, 1968).

[70] Daniel Patrick Moynihan, "Employment, Income, and the Ordeal of the Negro Family," *Daedalus* 94 (Fall 1965), p. 766.

[71] Mollie Orshansky, "The Shape of Poverty in 1966," *Social Security Bulletin* 31 (March 1968), p. 5.

[72] Mollie Orshansky, "More About the Poor in 1964," *Social Security Bulletin*, 29 (May 1966), p. 4.

the scope of existing public welfare programs. At the same time there are increasing doubts whether public assistance in its present form is a viable instrument of social policy, those doubts being expressed by social workers, political and civic leaders, and by welfare clients themselves. A new welfare rights movement is pressing for major reforms in the system, more adequate aid, and an end to the humiliating status historically associated with welfare in the United States. This crisis in welfare will be explored in later chapters. What is significant here is the recognition that out of the wide range of programs that may be broadly defined as social welfare, a special category of services associated with an indigent status and second-class citizenship exists. These are the public welfare services, consisting of financial assistance and other forms of aid to the needy. This is the traditional use of the term welfare, with its historical roots in the English Poor Law and the long-standing hostility and distrust of those defined as paupers. It was perpetuated in the 1965 Amendments to the Social Security Act, which provided a dual program of medical care, one available as a citizen right to all persons 65 years old and over, and a special program for the medically indigent.[73] The first is conceived as a social insurance program, financed as part of the social security system through a special payroll tax paid by the employers, employees, and the self-employed. The basic hospital insurance plan applies to all the elderly, aged 65 and over, who are eligible for monthly social security or railroad retirement benefits. An additional 2 million elderly who attained age 65 prior to 1968 but who are not covered by railroad retirement or the social security system are included in the same protection, with the cost to be paid from general funds from the treasury.

In addition, ". . . the 1965 Amendments to the Social Security Act contain important *welfare provisions* which authorize increased Federal aid for medical care and other programs benefiting persons with low incomes in all age groups." [74] The distinction between Medicare under the OASDHI program and medical care provided under the residual welfare label is made clear by the remark of President Lyndon B. Johnson regarding provision of Medicare, which, he noted, means that ". . . every senior citizen will be able to receive hospital care—not as a ward of the state, not as a charity patient, but as an insured patient." [75] The special and restricted use of the word "welfare," with its invidious connotations of help for the failures of society, may eventually disappear from our vocabulary, as suggested by Wilbur J. Cohen, former Secretary of the U.S. Department of Health, Education, and Welfare. He writes:

> We can—and I believe eventually we will—eliminate the terms "welfare," "relief," and "categories" from our governmental programs. The State *public welfare agencies* will become *Departments of Social Services* or Departments of Individual and Family Services. They will include homemaker services, foster homes and day care for children, and family home

[73] Melvin A. Glasser, "Extension of Public Welfare Medical Care: Issues of Social Policy," *Social Work,* 10 (October 1965), pp. 3–9.

[74] *1965 Social Security Amendments, Welfare Provisions,* U.S. Department of Health, Education, and Welfare, (Washington, D.C.: Government Printing Office, 1965).

[75] *New York Times,* June 16, 1966.

care for adults among a wide and varied range of social services, which will be *available to every person* in the community who chooses to use them.[76]

This is not to suggest that some of the new programs to aid the poor are without value. On the contrary they do extend the range of services available, as in the case of medical assistance under Title XIX of the Social Security Act. However, the provision of welfare is predicated on the notion of second-class citizenship; it is hurtful to pride, destructive of self-respect, and further alienates the poor from society. To restrict the term welfare to services for the poor is to exaggerate their dependency, conceal its societal roots, ignore the degree to which the poor may be deprived of access to the preferred public benefits and social services, and mask the extent to which all of us are recipients of social welfare programs broadly defined. Farm workers, for example, are still not protected by unemployment insurance, were not protected by minimum wage legislation until 1966, and still do not have the same protection afforded other workers under the minimum wage law.

Deprived of economic security by virtue of their work and lacking social protection afforded others, farm workers may be especially vulnerable to the need for public assistance, as noted by a study of that program in the state of Washington.[77] The study points out that only a small percentage of public assistance recipients are in the labor force. Those who are have only marginal employment, yet their work is essential to the economy of the state. Since social insurance benefits are related to level of earnings, those with the poorest wages and most unstable employment are invariably least protected by our basic social legislation. Thus the welfare state tends to benefit the stable working class and the middle class rather than the poor. Martin Rein describes this as the "iron law of welfare"—those most in need get the least.[78]

In any event social welfare benefits and services are not restricted to the poor, and the better services may go to the advantaged rather than the disadvantaged. In fact it is charged that the best family counseling and community mental health services staffed with the most highly trained professionals are most likely to serve the middle class.[79] This seems to be true, despite the fact that the poor are viewed as society's social problem group, having the highest rates of mental illness, delinquency, and family breakdown. Some of the recent federal legislation, such as the Economic Opportunity Act and the City Demon-

[76] Wilber J. Cohen, "Social Policy for the Nineteen Seventies," *Health, Education, and Welfare Indicators,* May 1966, (reprint ed., Washington, D.C.: Government Printing Office, 1966), p. 5.

[77] Greenleigh Associates, Inc., *Public Welfare: Poverty-Prevention or Perpetuation* (New York: Greenleigh Associates, Inc., December 1964).

[78] Martin Rein, "The Strange Case of Public Dependency," *Trans-action,* 2 (March–April, 1965), pp. 16–23. The point may be debated. Some light on this issue is provided by Robert J. Lampman, "How much Does the American System of Transfers Benefit the Poor?," Leonard H. Goodman (ed.), in *Economic Progress and Social Welfare* (New York: Columbia University Press, 1966), pp. 125–157.

[79] Richard A. Cloward, "Social Class and Private Social Agencies," *Education for Social Work, 1963* (New York: Council on Social Work Education, 1963), pp. 123–137.

strations Act, are in part efforts to bring the social services to those who need them most. It is claimed that one such measure, the Community Mental Health Centers Act, may in fact develop in a way that will ". . . restrict services to a favored few in the community." [80] The American Psychological Association, in expressing this concern, offers the following assessment of services for the mentally ill:

> The more advanced mental health services have tended to be a middle-class luxury; chronic mental hospital custody, a lower-class horror. The relationship between the mental health helper and the helped has been governed by an affinity of the clean for the clean, the educated for the educated, the affluent for the affluent. Most of our therapeutic talent, often trained at public expense, has been invested not in solving our hard-core mental health problem—the psychotic of marginal competence and social status—but in treating the relatively well-to-do educated neurotic, usually in an urban center.[81]

The need for service, of course, is not restricted to any social class and all are entitled to appropriate community resources. There are questions of priority needs that we must postpone until later. At this point our concern is with questioning the popular tendency to define social welfare as services for the poor. We have in fact a dual welfare system, one provided as a citizen right, the other institutionalizing a special stigmatized status for the poor. Many of the poor are badly served by existing programs or not served at all. Some community services presumably aiding the poor are in fact oriented toward the more advantaged members of society. The economic benefits of the welfare state provided through various social insurance provisions are designed for those with access to stable and preferred employment. The assumption that only the poor benefit from social welfare is a neat device for maintaining the questionable distinction between the dependent and the independent. We may indeed ask, Who are the welfare recipients?

Who Are the Welfare Recipients?

Are college students welfare recipients when they receive financial aid or when they participate in subsidized work-study programs? Since 1958 more than 1.4 million students who needed financial assistance to meet college expenses have been aided under the provisions of the National Defense Education Act—395,000 in 1967.[82] The Higher Education Act of 1965 provided funds to ex-

[80] Public Law 88–164, Public Law, 89–291.

[81] M. Brewster Smith and Nicholas Hobbs, *The Community and the Community Mental Health Center* (Washington, D.C.: American Psychological Association, 1966), p. 14.

[82] *Health, Education, and Welfare Trends,* 1966–1967 ed., Part I, National Trends, U.S. Department of Health, Education, and Welfare (Washington, D.C.: Government Printing Office, 1968), p. 11.

Unfortunately it now appears that "money for needy students will be tighter than ever" since funding for loans has been cut back for 1969–1970 and because of the quiet elimination in 1968 of most of the interest subsidy. This means students will be

pand the work-study program originally initiated under the Economic Opportunity Act, as well as a subsidized low-interest insured loan program.   In 1967, 300,000 students participated in the college work-study program.   It is estimated that 500,000 students received benefits of the loan programs in 1968.[83] This program is not solely for students who come from poor homes.   Those from families with adjusted incomes of less than $15,000 may receive loans with all interest paid by the federal government prior to the repayment period.   Are the various forms of financial assistance to college students essentially different from expenditures for the education and training of low-income youths through programs such as the Job Corps or the Neighborhood Youth Corps?

Are farmers welfare recipients when they receive several billion dollars a year in income support payments?   The total cost of federal subsidies for agriculture was over $4.2 billion in 1967.[84]   Direct cash farm subsidies in 1966–1967 included five payments of over $1 million, eleven payments of between $500,000 and $1 million, and 258 payments of between $100,000 and $500,000.[85]   Such payments have been described as a "vast system of outdoor relief." [86]   The nation spends about eight times as much propping up farm prices (through subsidies) as it does helping the poor receive adequate diets (surplus commodities and food stamps).   The cost of farm subsidies was 86 percent of the total money payment for public assistance and was about twice the amount received by child and adult recipients through the Aid to Families with Dependent Children program in 1967.   Public assistance payments, excluding vendor medical payments, were $4,931,404,000, while payments in the AFDC program in that year were about $2.25 billion.[87]   It is ironic that, in some instances, payments to farmers to reduce their production of crops create unemployment for farm workers, forcing some families to become welfare recipients.   This is the case for southern cotton farmers and farm workers.   For example:

> The Mississippi State Employment Security Commission says that by Spring the number of tractors and farm mechanic jobs in 18 Delta counties will have declined by 25 percent to 19,500 and the "hired work force" of cotton choppers by about 50 percent to a total of 7,000.   Such reductions appear inevitable, according to the Commission's labor analyst, because of continuing farm mechanization and *a new federal subsidy program* [emphasis added] that is attacking cotton surpluses by offering

charged the full 7% interest rather than the 3% previously charged.   *New York Times,* June 8, 1969.

[83] HEW *Trends, op. cit.*

[84] *Statistical Abstract of the United States: 1968,* U.S. Bureau of Census (Washington, D.C.: Government Printing Office, 1968), Table 547, p. 385.

[85] *Congressional Record,* 90th Congress, 1st sess., Vol. 113, No. 108 (July 13, 1967), S 9619.
There is now increasing concern about these payments, and attempts are being made in Congress to place a ceiling on them; however, such payments have been made for over three decades.

[86] S. M. Miller and Martin Rein, "Change, Ferment, and Ideology in the Social Services," *Education for Social Work* (New York: Council on Social Work Education, 1964), p. 9.

[87] *Social Security Bulletin,* 32 (April 1969), p. 63.

farmers $1.05 a pound on average cotton yield for production cut-backs of up to one-third. . . . "We can't buy no nothing!" said 51 year old Sam Watts, speaking for the 16 Negroes who were huddled around the coal-burning stove in the dim cafe. "There ain't one of us that's hit a lick of work since before January. The white man got all the jobs." [88]

He might have added that the white man got the best public *subsidies* as well. It is curious that we have found a means to meet the need of those whose problem is surplus crops but not the need of those whose problem is surplus labor. From 1940 to 1967 nearly 20 million people migrated from rural to urban areas, most of them as a result of the technological revolution in agriculture. One of the major migration routes has been from the southeastern states to northeastern cities, accounting for some of the sharp increase in welfare rolls in urban centers. Of central importance is the failure to provide adequate public subsidies to ease the forced relocation of millions of such migrants.

Subsidies are traditional in American society for those who have sufficient political power to gain favorable government intervention. The great American continental railway was built with the aid of enormous land grants. Subsidies, both direct and indirect, continue to benefit business and industry today. Direct subsidies to business for 1969 are estimated to have been over $1.5 billion.[89] These and other subsidies to the nonpoor may be justified. James Reston, however, has questioned "the fat cat subsidies" that are continued at a time when mounting costs of the war in Vietnam require cuts in programs to aid the poor. Such subsidies include federal support amounting to about $5,000 per plane per year for private and business aircraft (total cost $160 million a year), $79 million a year for a special milk program for schoolchildren of middle-class families, and subsidies for irrigation water amounting to as much as $100,000 a year for some of the large factory farms. "It is," he writes, "the old story: the vested interests of the farmers, the merchant marines, the impacted school districts, and big business help put together large enough voting combinations in Congress to carry on expensive programs that may have been sensible at one time but need to be revised if not eliminated." [90]

The farm workers wonder who really receives the welfare benefits and question programs that provide huge new irrigation systems at taxpayers' expense, government subsidies (handouts) for cotton growers, and the use of tax money to develop machines that increase growers' profits and force workers to go on welfare.[91] In 1967 the J. G. Boswell Company in King's County, California, received $4 million in diversion payments, and Rancho San Antonio in Fresno County received $3 million.[92] The average monthly money payment per recipient in the Aid to Families with Dependent Children program in California was $48.40 in December 1968.[93]

[88] *The New York Times*, February 7, 1966.

[89] *Statistical Abstract, op. cit.*

[90] *New York Times*, December 7, 1966.

[91] *El Malcriado* (The Voice of the Farm Worker, Delano, Calif.), March 15, 1967, pp. 6–7, 18.

[92] *New York Times*, February 24, 1969.

[93] *Social Security Bulletin*, 32 (April 1969), p. 64.

A great many Americans benefit from government subsidies that do not carry a welfare label. For example, little recognized is the fact that federal subsidies through FHA have made possible the ". . . low-density middle-income living in suburbs, and have thereby financed the flight of white population from the city." [94] Nor is the extent to which such subsidies helped to build the urban ghettos by discriminating against low-income families, especially the Negro poor, generally recognized.[95]

One may even ask who gets the dollars that are clearly regarded as welfare expenditures. In 1960 the average rent for whites in Cook County, Illinois, was $65 per month. Negro families receiving public assistance were paying $83 per month for poorer housing. It is estimated that such higher rents increased public assistance costs by $3.4 million per year, a form of welfare payment to slum landlords.[96] Before a Senate subcommittee, Robert C. Weaver, former Secretary of the Department of Housing and Urban Development, was asked whether government welfare checks are helping to subsidize the slums. He replied, "I think that they probably are to some degree." [97] Evidence from New York City indicates the extent to which this may be so. According to Mitchell Ginsberg, formerly Commissioner of the Human Resources Administration, the city *subsidizes* the landlord by paying $150–$180 a month for housing worth about one-fourth of this.[98]

The attention given to dependence on public assistance programs cannot be seen in perspective without consideration of the enormous growth of similar forms of dependence on the largess of government. According to Charles A. Reich, an increasing number of Americans in business, industry, and the professions, in the labor market and out, depend on ". . . valuables dispensed by the government." This "new property"—government-provided income, benefits, jobs, licenses, franchises, contracts, subsidies, use of public resources, and so forth—is "steadily taking the place of traditional forms of wealth." [99] Included are subsidies to business, agriculture, the shipping industry, local airlines, and housing, which are "analagous to welfare payments for individuals who cannot manage independently in the economy." [100]

Those who benefit from one form of subsidy may be ardently critical of those who benefit from another. This is especially true if subsidies appear to be unrelated to current or potential contribution to the Gross National Product. Subsidies that seem to have the character of investment in future productivity are more likely to be sanctioned. It is interesting to note, for example, that Congress appropriated for fiscal 1965 a little over $29 million to support NDEA

[94] Bernard Weissbourd, *Segregation, Subsidies, and Megalopolis* (Santa Barbara, Calif.: Center for the Study of Democratic Institutions, 1964), p. 7.

[95] Scott Greer, *Urban Renewal and American Cities* (Indianapolis: Bobbs-Merrill, 1965), pp. 135, 144.

[96] Alvin Schorr, *Slums and Social Insecurity* (Washington, D.C.: Government Printing Office, 1963), p. 84.

[97] *The New York Times,* August 17, 1966.

[98] *The New York Times,* July 30, 1967.

[99] Charles A. Reich, "The New Property," *Yale Law Journal* 73 (April 1964), p. 733.

[100] *Ibid,* p. 735.

(National Defense Education Act) Language Institutes and $15 million for project grants for health care to low-income expectant mothers.

Participants in the Language Institutes receive $75 per week plus $15 for each dependent, while the maximum weekly subsidy for MDTA (Manpower Development and Training Act) trainees is on the average about $50 a week plus $5 per dependent. Grants under the AFDC public assistance program average nationally about $10.50 a week per recipient.

Subsidies to mothers with dependent children have little public blessing at the present time. If a mother becomes a domestic and cares for someone else's child, she is productive according to the norms of a market society. If, with the assistance of public aid, she remains at home to care for her own, she is dependent. The value of publicly provided day care services for children of working mothers is reflected in an increase in the Gross National Product. Private child care provided by mothers has no monetary value that can be recorded in our system of economic accounts. However, the merits of day care or of working mothers is not at issue here. The need for adequate day care services can easily be documented. One-third of the women with children are in the labor force. Others would enter if jobs and suitable care for their children were available. But the notion that a mother is productive only when in the labor force, and that subsidies ought to be attached only to efforts related to economic activity, is a curious distortion of values.

The norms of a market society that link income to work define the productive and the nonproductive, the self-reliant and the dependent. They constitute the criteria that tends, in the popular view, to distinguish the welfare recipient from the remainder of society. Society is seen as divided between those who earn their own way and those who do not. How to integrate those outside the labor market so that they are respectable and self-respecting members of society is a major social welfare problem. The negative connotation attached to welfare makes it difficult to provide both subsidy and self-respect for those who are unable to obtain adequate income through work. Before we examine this problem more carefully, it may help to see some other forms of social welfare that exist in society. The distinction between the dependent and independent may seem less clear-cut.

Social Division of Welfare [101]

Some attention must be paid to the various institutional means used to directly promote the economic and social well-being of all or part of the population. Richard M. Titmuss has suggested that these may be divided into three major categories—fiscal, occupational, and social. In his view, what is to be identified as social welfare ought to be determined by the goals and not by the ". . . administrative methods and institutional devices employed to achieve them." [102] For example, tax allowances for dependents, union-negotiated retirement benefits, and public assistance payments share the common goal of promoting eco-

[101] This section draws heavily on an essay by Richard M. Titmuss: "The Social Division of Welfare: Some Reflections on the Search for Equity," *Essays on the Welfare State"* (London: G. Allen, 1958), pp. 34–59.

[102] *Ibid.,* p. 42.

nomic security. To be sure, they may serve other purposes as well and are not equally valued. The first is provided as a citizen right without stigma; the second may be defined as deferred wages to which the worker is entitled; and the third is more likely to be seen as relief for those incapable of providing for themselves. The differences in the institutional means are important. At this point we focus on some of the similarities that tend to be ignored.

Fiscal Welfare: Tax System as a Welfare Instrument

It is not usual for Americans to think of tax deductions or exemptions as welfare benefits. However, tax savings that accrue to an individual through such allowances are in effect an indirect subsidy similar to cash payments that might be made directly. Tax deductions and public assistance payments for dependent children are both collective provisions that may express a common social purpose—the wish to redistribute the economic burden of child rearing. Income tax laws may promote a variety of social purposes. Eveline M. Burns observes that there has been ". . . a growing tendency to use the tax system as a welfare instrument" through special deductions for dependents, exemptions for persons aged sixty-five and over, allowances for medical expenses, and complete relief from tax liability for social insurance and other types of socially provided income.[103] Thus the federal income tax is a welfare instrument, conferring benefits on children, the aged, the blind, homeowners, and those with major medical expenses. Benefits are not only provided in behalf of the nonpoor, but the wealthiest of taxpayers tend to receive the greatest benefits. This is substantiated by a study of the tax system made by Joseph A. Pechman, Director of Economic Studies for the Brookings Institution. He reports that tax provisions to help the aged actually help well-to-do older persons considerably more than they help those in modest circumstances. The double exemption for the aged, the nontaxable status of social security payments, and the special tax credit for other retirement income benefit those with high incomes more than those with low incomes.[104] Tax subsidies for major medical expenses also tend to favor the upper-income groups.[105] Additional inequities are related to the fact that low-income families cannot take full advantage of exemptions and deductions available to higher-income groups.[106] For example, the $600 federal income tax exemption permitted for each dependent child, an indirect form of a children's allowance, provides higher net allowances for families in higher-income groups. Families without income receive no benefits. For families in the 14 percent tax bracket, the cash value of this exemption is $84 per year, or $7 per month per child. For those in the 20 percent tax bracket it rises to $120 per year, or $10

---

[103] Eveline M. Burns, "Social Security in Evolution: Toward What?," *Social Service Review,* 39 (June 1965), pp. 135–136.

[104] *The New York Times,* September 12, 1966.

[105] Eveline M. Burns, "The Role of Government in Health Services," *Bulletin of the New York Academy of Medicine,* 41 (July 1965), p. 17.

[106] Burns, "Social Security in Evolution, *op. cit.,* p. 136. *See also* Alvin Schorr, "Alternatives in Income Maintenance," *Social Work,* 11 (July 1966), 27, and Alvin Schorr, *Poor Kids* (New York: Basic Books, 1966), p. 131.

per month per child. Those in the 50 percent bracket reap a benefit of $240 per year, or $20 per month per child.[107]

Inequities in subsidies for housing are revealed in data supplied by Alvin Schorr, who calculates that in 1962 the federal government spent an estimated $820 million to subsidize housing for poor people (this includes public housing, housing costs of public assistance, and savings by income tax deductions) and an estimated $2.9 billion (savings from income tax deductions only) to subsidize housing for those with middle incomes or more. This is about three and one-half times as much for those who were not poor as for those who were. "That is very nearly the relative proportion of the poor and nonpoor in the population, so one might say that the federal government spends equally per capita for the rich and the poor." [108]

While the tax system adds to the welfare of the well-to-do, it forces some into poverty. Estimates are that the combination of social security and income taxes drives 600,000 families into poverty.[109] Proposals for some form of negative income tax, to be discussed later, would equalize the tax system as a welfare instrument. Basic inequities in our tax structure are beyond the scope of this book. The relevance of tax policy for economic welfare, however, needs to be emphasized. Certain myths associated with the notion of the poor as tax-eaters supported by taxpayers are challenged by studies that reveal the poor may pay more taxes than commonly assumed.

> The tax system by itself redistributes income away from the poor. As a share of income, higher taxes are paid by households in the lower income classes than by those with incomes between $6,000 and $15,000. This reflects the heavy tax burden of low income families from State and local taxes—primarily sales, excise and property taxes. Federal taxes also contribute to this burden through the social security payroll tax.[110]

For example, one study of the real property tax discovered that the impact of that tax falls most heavily on the poor. The property tax, according to the study ". . . is the equivalent to an excise tax of nearly 24 percent on rental housing," falling especially hard on low-income renters. In this research report, prepared for the National Commission on Urban Problems, Professor Dick Netzer of New York University indicates that the heavily regressive nature of the property tax absorbs a "much higher fraction of the incomes of the poor than of the rich." For all renters in the United States, property taxes in 1959–1960 accounted for 8.5 percent of the income of those with less than $2,000 per year and 1.4 percent of the income of those with incomes over $15,000.[111] Un-

[107] I am indebted for this information to Dr. David Gil, who made this available in a special report to the Model Cities staff of Portland, Maine, in 1969.

[108] Alvin Schorr, *Explorations in Social Policy* (New York: Basic Books, 1968), p. 274.

[109] Christopher Green, *Negative Taxes and the Poverty Problem* (Washington, D.C.: Brookings Institution, 1967), pp. 26, 33.

[110] *Annual Report of the Council of Economic Advisors,* 1969, *op. cit.,* p. 160.

[111] Dick Netzer, *Impact of the Property Tax,* prepared for the National Commission on Urban Problems, 90th Congress, 2nd sess. (Washington, D.C.: Government Printing Office, 1968), pp. 18–19.

recognized is the degree to which industry receives indirect subsidies through the social costs of private enterprise, environmental pollution, unemployment, and so forth.   The inequities in the tax structure and in loopholes in tax laws are beyond the scope of this discussion but are worthy of note.   Inequities also exist in the access to fringe benefits, the private welfare state available to selected groups in the labor force.

Occupational Welfare: The Private Welfare State

One of the interesting incongruities of the social scene in America today is the business community's decrying the welfare state that it fears is being imposed by government.   The truth is that industry itself has entered the welfare areas with a vengeance.   If welfarism is supposed to destroy the individual's responsibility to provide himself and his family with security and the appurtenances of a good life, then surely industry is much more the culprit than the government.[112]

There are a variety of fringe benefits that make up the private welfare state. They accompany occupational status and reflect not only the value society attaches to work, but also the power of groups differently located in the economic system to command ever-increasing shares of the valuables of society in a manner that may or may not be related to actual productivity.   One report suggests that employee fringe benefits ". . . are paid out on a basis other than current productivity and are financed largely out of factor income (employer and employee contributions) but with a public (tax subsidy) contribution." [113] It is common to define such work-related provisions as deferred wages or substitutes for money payments to which individuals are entitled as a result of their occupational effort.   It is also possible to see them as functional equivalents of socially provided welfare measures designed to promote income security and other benefits on the basis of one's citizenship status, that is, one's membership in a collectivity.   The desire to promote income security may be institutionalized in a variety of ways, including seniority provisions in collective bargaining agreements, which are ". . . almost universally regarded by employees as a valuable property right." [114]   It should be noted in passing that monopolistic practices and other measures employed by the business community represent other forms of assuring income security, the shibboleths of competition and free enterprise notwithstanding.   More closely related to social welfare are such benefits as private pension plans, which now cover approximately 25 million workers.   An illustration of what it might mean to get a union-negotiated benefit as a right, rather than be dependent on public charity, is revealed by the following letter from a retired West Virginia miner.

I am glad after spending 47 years in the coal mines that I can walk with my head straight up and feel a little sunshine in my heart, instead of

---

[112] Frederick Herzberg, *Work and the Nature of Man* (Cleveland: World Publishing, 1966), p. 8.

[113] Lampman, *op. cit.,* p. 127.

[114] National Commission on Technology, Automation, and Economic Progress, *op. cit.,* p. 63.

seeing a hopeless road before me which leads only to the poorhouse or the bread line. The pension I get from the welfare fund makes all the difference in the world.[115]

Not all former coal miners are so fortunate. Harry M. Caudill has documented the plight of unemployed coal miners who, denied the right to work, are forced to accept demeaning public welfare as their only hope.[116]

Occupational welfare may also include life insurance; various degrees of comprehensive medical care; accident, sickness, and maternity benefits; supplemental unemployment insurance; subsidies for housing, travel, entertainment, recreation, meals, holidays, sabbaticals, education, and training. For example, in addition to prenatal and postnatal care and convalescent and nursing home care, the United Auto Workers negotiated the first national program of inpatient and out-of-hospital mental health benefits.[117] Recently the Chicago Joint Board of the Amalgamated Clothing Workers of America announced a college scholarship plan providing $600 a year for one hundred students whose parents belonged to the union for at least thirteen years. Provided without consideration of high school grades, the intent is clearly to equalize opportunities for working-class youths. According to one union member, "We'd like to see union members' children have the same educational opportunities as children of the employers." [118]

Fringe benefits also include a variety of social services designed to enable the upwardly mobile to adapt to new social environments. In addition to paying for moving expenses, major universities, government bureaucracies, and corporations assist new employees and their families in a variety of ways to locate housing, schools, and other community resources. Efforts may be made to acquaint the employee and his family with the community and to generally facilitate their social integration. If problems in adaptation develop ". . . an effort will be made to help without requiring the executive to become a client who must prove that he cannot help himself. Service is given as a matter of right, not as a favor." [119] Provided in cash, in kind, or in services, these occupational benefits add to economic security, health, and the amenities of life for those in a position to take advantage of them. What other consequences they may have are not clear. Frederick Herzberg points to the fact that, while the social security system does not limit the worker's freedom to change his employment, ". . . company pension plans tend to have the vicious consequence of embedding the employee in a company in which he is no longer able to maximize his potentiality." He asks, "Which is more restrictive of individual freedom?" [120]

[115] *New York Times,* August 12, 1966.

[116] Harry M. Caudill, "The Rise of the Welfare State," chap. 18 *Night Comes to the Cumberlands* (Boston: Little, Brown, 1962), pp. 273–301.

[117] Melvin A. Glasser, "Problems and Prospects for Mental Health Coverage Through Collective Bargaining Agreements," *American Journal of Orthopsychiatry,* 36 (January 1966).

[118] *New York Times,* September 5, 1967.

[119] Joseph W. Eaton, "The Immobile Poor" in Thomas D. Sherrard (ed.), *Social Welfare and Urban Problems* (New York: Columbia University Press, 1968), p. 77.

[120] Herzberg, *op. cit.,* p. viii.

An increasing proportion of the dollar paid to employees in recent years has gone into welfare contributions and benefits.[121]   Gross amounts of employee fringe benefits are variously estimated at between $8 and $11 billion.[122]   A measure of the increasing importance of this private welfare state is the data that indicates that "expansion of cash benefits under private employee benefit plans, and especially under private pension plans has more than matched percentagewise the growth of social insurance benefits" (Table 7).[123]

Table 7. Expenditures from Public and Private Funds for Cash Transfer Payments (Excluding Administration) for Selected Fiscal Years, 1949–1968 (in billions)

SOURCE OF FUNDS	1949–50	1959–60	1966–67	1967–68 *
Total cash transfer payments	$10.1	$28.7	$48.7	$53.8
Public funds	9.1	25.2	41.5	45.6
Social insurance	4.4	18.2	31.9	35.3
Veterans programs	2.4	3.8	4.98	5.0
Public assistance	2.2	3.2	4.6	5.3
Private employee benefits	.97	3.55	7.2	8.2
Percent of total				
Public funds	90.5	87.7	85.2	84.8
Private funds	9.5	12.3	14.8	15.2

* Preliminary estimates.

SOURCE: Ida C. Merriam, Alfred M. Skolnik, and Sophie R. Dales, "Social Welfare Expenditures, 1967–1968," *Social Security Bulletin,* Vol. 31 (December 1968), Table 7, p. 26.

It is interesting to note the democratization of industrial "welfare work." [124] The term welfare, used in that context, referred to the voluntary efforts of employers to improve the living and working conditions of their employees. Such efforts were often regarded with suspicion as a form of paternalism and as an attempt to avoid wage increases or prevent labor organization. With the rise of labor unions, workers preferred to bargain for fringe benefits as a right rather than to receive them as an act of employer charity.[125]

In general labor unions have also preferred to pursue economic security and improvement in life conditions through collective bargaining rather than through publicly supported services. In most European countries, on the other hand, especially in Britain and in Scandinavia, the working class has pressured for the development and expansion of the welfare state.[126]

[121] Harry L. Lurie (ed.), *Encyclopedia of Social Work* (New York: National Association of Social Workers, 1965), Vol. XV, p. 740.

[122] Lampman, *op. cit.,* p. 128, and Merriam, *et al., op. cit.,* p. 26.

[123] Merriam, *et al., op. cit.,* p. 26.

[124] *Encyclopedia of the Social Sciences* (New York: Macmillan, 1931), Vol. XV, pp. 395–399.

[125] *Ibid.,* p. 396.

[126] Briggs, in Zald, *op. cit.,* p. 69.

Since labor unions in the United States have worked primarily to help "their own," this has limited their political significance and retarded the development of comprehensive social services. In the opinion of Richard Titmuss, the development of the private welfare state conflicts with the ". . . aims and unity of social policy; tends to divide loyalties and nourish privilege, and to narrow the social conscience as they have already done in the United States, in France and in Western Germany." [127]   At the same time the political power of the labor unions has been used in some degree to promote various forms of government-sponsored measures of social security, adding benefits of the welfare state to occupational welfare programs. The poor, without access to favored employment, enjoy the benefits of neither.

Occupational welfare, of course, is not restricted to the fringe benefits negotiated by labor unions. It includes similar benefits available to business executives as well. The line between occupational welfare and the opportunity exercised by some corporation executives to award themselves unusually high salaries, extra compensation, and generous savings and retirement plans may be a thin one indeed.[128]

Critics of government provisions for security and the amenities of life ought not ignore some similarities between the private and the public welfare state. The tendency to focus on the tax burden of public programs conceals the problem of equity in access to the variety of institutionalized means for achieving economic security and a desirable level of well-being.

The Significance of Our Welfare Vocabulary

The way welfare is defined has political consequences. Our welfare vocabulary influences our attitudes toward recipients and helps to determine both the goals and the allocation of resources for program development. Welfare may be seen as emergency assistance to the poor and the handicapped or as essential services from which we may all benefit, directly or indirectly. It may be thought of as a tax burden or as an investment in human beings, as benevolence or as a citizen right. The political significance of our welfare vocabulary has been pointed out by Martin Rein. He writes:

> Labels are matters of political decisions—is public assistance a form of public subsidy for an economic system that cannot provide jobs, or adequate wages for all—or is it politically wiser to refer to it as a form of welfare for those without capacity to compete effectively thus shifting the onus of responsibility on the poor themselves.[129]

The residual vocabulary of welfare focuses attention on problems rather than political issues, on poverty instead of inequality, on helping rather than social reform, on changing individuals instead of changing systems. This vocabulary

---

[127] Titmuss, *op. cit.,* p. 52. Note the increasing share of private expenditures for cash transfer payments (Table 7) from 9.5 percent of the total in 1949–1950 to 15.2 percent in 1967–1968.

[128] Heilbroner, *op. cit.,* p. 37.

[129] Martin Rein, "The Social Service Crisis," *Trans-action,* 1 (May 1964), pp. 3–4.

reflects the moral ideals of a previous era. It maintains a distorted view of human possibilities and a conservative view of society. If welfare recipients are seen as "tax-eaters" living off handouts, economic dependency is seen as an individual problem and a personal fault. Programs of amelioration or rehabilitation organized around this conception substitute for basic social reforms that would redress inequities, assure economic security, and provide opportunities for the fuller realization of human capacities. Preoccupation with dependency as a form of pathology conceals the degree to which it is a normal by-product of an industrial society requiring new institutionalized means for the satisfaction of basic needs. To take this view is to adopt a new moral ideal regarding the proper relationship between the individual and society. Welfare conceptions invariably reflect the kind of human being we value and the social order we want. This chapter has demonstrated that the distinction between the dependent and the independent is far from crystal clear, that we all benefit from a variety of social welfare programs, and that we have a dual system of welfare. Social welfare, then, is a system for the unequal distribution of advantages and disadvantages. It helps to perpetuate the very inequalities now under attack as we live through the crisis and challenge of this era.

THREE

Change, Crisis, and Challenge in Contemporary Society

Introduction

Our current social welfare programs were developed to deal with economic insecurity, the breakdown of socialization and social control, and the decline of community that accompanied the industrialization and urbanization of society. To cope with economic and social dislocations created by the Industrial Revolution we built a patchwork welfare state, partly out of regard for democratic and humanitarian mores and partly to stabilize and maintain our capitalistic market system. Though not without their value, our social welfare measures have never been adequate to meet the requirements of a complex society or of a humane polity. They are even less adapted now to new imperatives of social order and our higher aspirations for human fulfillment. They must be improved in the light of better understanding of the shape of our society, the social and human cost of change, the new possibilities open to us for humanizing our urban-technological system, and the consequences of decisions we make or fail to make.

We live in an era of upheaval, of enormous problems and great promise. We are challenged to respond to a series of related urban, racial, moral, and political crises, with realistic recognition of their dangers and with creative regard for the opportunities they present. In part, this means giving up ideas suitable to the past but unrelated to the present. For example, we cling to the notion of rugged individualism, and confuse it with individuality, while we should cope with the interdependence thrust upon us by our intricately specialized division of labor; promote identity and autonomy in an increasingly organized and depersonalized society; and develop individuals having the creative capacity to master a complex and changing environment.

How revolutionary this era will be is unpredictable, for at best we "see through a glass darkly." We know that institutions will resist change, which will assure some necessary stability but will also prevent essential adaptations to new conditions. We are also reminded to avoid the mystique of change, for, as

Charles Malik has written, though we fancy that everything changes, perhaps change only touches the surface of our lives ". . . never the essence, never the grounds of sorrow and joy, of ecstasy and fulfillment." [1]

Nonetheless we do live in a new era. What is new is a revolution in our aspirations for extending the full benefits of society to all. One may see this as a new phase in the long historic quest for equality. What is also certainly new is the enormous increase in our scientific knowledge and in our material resources, which could contribute to the extension of equality and to the greater freedom to redesign our social order so that man would be the true center of concern. Also new is the relationship between science and morality. Daniel Bell suggests that perhaps the ". . . most important social change of our time is the emergence of a process of direct and deliberate contrivance of change itself." [2]

As we become more scientifically conscious of the probable consequences of alternative courses of action, we must accept the moral responsibility for the decisions we make or fail to make. For example, we have increasing knowledge of the probable relationship between nutrition and the development of intelligence; between prenatal care and birth anomalies; between work, income, and family stability; between unemployment and economic dependency; between relative deprivation and violence; and between the structure of opportunity and individual life chances. To the degree that we can alter the social environment, we cannot plead that the invisible hand and individual will are the arbiters of human fate.

There are, of course, limits to the degree to which man may intelligently shape his society that are inherent in inadequate knowledge, uncertain outcomes of directed change, and conflicts over the kind of social order best suited to a pluralistic and democratic polity. There are also critical questions regarding who will be in a position to make crucial decisions, to exercise power and leadership, to determine the shape of the future society. How much democratic participation is possible and desirable in the advanced industrial society? A brief summary of the characteristics of such a society, based on the writings of Donald Michael, Daniel Bell, and others, follows.

It is in the context of a postindustrial society that we will shape our social welfare programs.[3] It seems clear that we shall be an increasingly urbanized and rationalized society following patterns that, in varying degrees, seem to operate in all highly complex technological systems. A scientific revolution may make it possible to plan, coordinate, and control the social environment. Rapid change, population mobility and density, the increasingly complex, unstable,

---

[1] Charles Malik, "Reflections on the Great Society," *Saturday Review,* August 6, 1966, p. 12.

[2] Daniel Bell, "Notes on the Post-Industrial Society (I)," *The Public Interest,* No. 6 (Winter 1967), p. 25.

[3] *Ibid.;* Daniel Bell, "Notes on the Post-Industrial Society (II)," *The Public Interest,* No. 7 (Spring 1967), pp. 102–118; Donald N. Michael, "Urban Policy in the Rationalized Society," *Journal of the American Institute of Planners,* 31 (November 1965), pp. 283–288; Harvey Wheeler, *The Rise and Fall of Liberal Democracy* (Santa Barbara, Calif.: Center for the Study of Democratic Institutions, 1966).

and interrelated urban-technological society, and the urgency of meeting priority social needs makes such planning likely.

Government, as the major agency capable of exercising control of the social environment, will have vastly increased power to be used for good or ill. The basis for such control will be theoretical knowledge, which means that scientists and professionals may be part of a new elite; that the university may become the central social institution (as the church was in the feudal society and the corporation in industrial capitalism); that scientific knowledge, not capital, will be the scarce resource; and that control over the production and utilization of scientific knowledge may determine the future shape of society. The power to make major decisions will increasingly rest with scientists, professionals, and politicians, although considerable power will probably continue to reside in the hands of giant corporations. How much citizen participation will be feasible and in what form and how much access to knowledge and power will be shared in order to democratize decision-making will be major questions. Knowledge generated by social scientists, on the basis of which policy decisions may increasingly be made, is not readily available to any citizen. Access to such knowledge requires not only improved education but new structures for democratizing the distribution of this new kind of capital. It seems clear that better understanding of the distribution of knowledge and the power to make decisions as well as the decision-making process itself, are keys to understanding both the shape of society and the avenue for its reconstruction.

Our expanding Gross National Product (estimated to be about 977 billion dollars in the year 1970) will provide resources that could be allocated to rebuilding and beautifying cities, developing human resources, and increasing the amenities of life. In 1968 the GNP rose by almost $34 billion (in 1958 prices). Resources, however, are never unlimited, despite the relative affluence of American society. For example, a 1960 commission established by President Dwight D. Eisenhower to report on desirable "goals for Americans" selected fifteen areas in which goals might be established for assessing improvements in the quality of American life.[4] In a study of the economic cost of achieving such goals, it was estimated that over a trillion dollars would be required by 1975, or approximately $150 billion more than the anticipated Gross National Product for that year. We suffer, said the director of that study, from a myth of "economic omnipotence." The reality is that priorities must be established and "their choice is a matter of public debate." [5]

Efforts at planning will sharpen the issues of priority needs both within our society and in terms of international commitments, which will intensify the conflict of values and of group interests. Efforts to conceal such conflicts may militate against confronting issues of priorities. Avoided or resolved, such conflicts will provide a major dynamic of change, peaceful or violent, for in the new era of rising expectations conflicts are stimulated and not easily repressed.

Higher material standards of living (barring a catastrophic war) seem assured

[4] President's Commission on National Goals, *Goals for Americans* (New York: Prentice-Hall, 1960).

[5] "The Myth of Economic Omnipotence," *The Public Interest*, No. 1 (Fall 1965), p. 135.

to those who will qualify for work that may be increasingly specialized; such work will demand ever higher educational credentials as well as the personal attributes needed for adapting to complex formal organizations. Such organizations (bureaucracies) are now and will increasingly be the instrument through which major social functions, including welfare, are performed. Adapting them to meet individual and social needs poses serious problems, but there are indications that, as we move from a society of "earning a living" to one characterized by "learning a living," new structures for organizing the complex division of labor will be developed. These structures will be less hierarchical, providing for greater equality among co-workers and increased autonomy for the individual.[6] Those most proficient in skills required for work in a scientific and educated society and with the best opportunities to acquire them will reap the largest share of rewards, which will increase the gap that already separates the affluent from the excluded poor. The uneducated, relatively unskilled, deprived and discriminated against will continue to share, as they do now, some measure of increased prosperity, but unless greater efforts are made to redress economic, political, and social inequities and to create new forms of work, they will continue to face insulting barriers to more full and just participation in society.

In like manner, the disparity between the rich and poor nations is almost sure to increase in accord with the principle that "he who hath shall receive."   John W. Dyckman has described the process that accounts for the increasing gap between the haves and the have-nots or, better still, the haves and the have-more.

> . . . the more effectively the economy is organized and rationalized, the more disadvantaged are the weaker competitors, whether they are firms, regions of a federal system, or nations in a world economy.[7]

As he notes, without ". . . an explicit equalization mechanism, based on other than efficiency," it is almost impossible for deprived individuals, groups, regions, or nations to catch up.[8] This draws attention to the redistributive function of welfare to promote social justice and maintain domestic and world stability.

Domestic and world instability is the consequence of such relative deprivation. The demand for equality at home is likely to be pressed more forcefully and more violently. We probably will continue to take social measures to promote equality of opportunity and to further democratize society. Whether such measures will be sufficient in scope is the burning question. Resistance to paying the cost of equalizing opportuinties through redistribution of income, power, and privilege and the subordination of social needs to priorities given to maintaining and expanding our position as a world power may continue to severely restrict efforts to cope with inequality. Equality of opportunity, how-

---

[6] Eugen Pusic, "The Political Community and the Future of Welfare," in John S. Morgan (ed.), *Welfare and Wisdom* (Toronto: University of Toronto Press, 1968), pp. 80–81; Warren Bennis, "Beyond Bureaucracy," *Trans-action,* 2 (July–August 1965), pp. 31–35; Warren Bennis, "Post-Bureaucratic Leadership," *Trans-action,* Vol. 6 (July–August 1969), pp. 44–51.

[7] John W. Dyckman, "Some Conditions of Civic Order in an Urbanized World," *Daedalus,* 95 (Summer 1966), p. 806.

[8] *Ibid.*

ever, may prove to be an inadequate goal for the future, for it is the quality of life that may be the center of concern of an increasing number of people. Industrial society continues to honor man as producer and consumer and to neglect his needs for ever richer symbolic gratification. The restricted opportunities for realizing man as *homo poeta* is noted by Ernest Becker when he declares that Western culture

> . . . has historically been diminishing the reservoir of meaning upon which the individual can draw. While we thought that the increasing individualism should make personal life richer and more meaningful, it has actually done the opposite. Both in range of objects and in richness of shared performance, modern man has been increasingly narrowed down.[9]

It is possible to see the crisis and challenge of our times as, in part, an effort to subordinate technology to the requirements of human existence, to honor man over machine, and to devote attention to the quality of life through a quest for new and richer definitions of its meaning. The quest for meaning may intensify value conflicts, putting to a severe test our capacity to tolerate and nurture a variety of styles of life. Major conflicts may arise between the rationalizers concerned with an efficient, productive, and orderly society and the various existentialists who give priority to experience and meaning. Fullness of opportunity, rather than equal opportunity to pursue the single goal of occupational and material success, would be a value worth considering.[10] It is possible, as Dennis Wrong suggests, to conceive of a society in which upward mobility may be optional rather than socially compelled, provided the general standards of living are high, a reasonable floor on income is assured, and inequalities are reduced to some acceptable limit. In such a case, a "diversified value system which recognizes and honors human qualities other than functional intelligence and single-minded ambition will be more likely to flourish." [11]

Some of these trends are reasonably certain (e.g., urbanization, progress of science, increasing demand for education, expanded power of government); others are more doubtful. Within certain limits set by the structure of society, there is an unknown area of freedom of choice, of exercise of individual and collective will. The future is not predetermined. Decisions we make or fail to make will influence the course of events. Only from the vantage point of some future historian will those decisions now open to us seem to have been inevitably determined by social and other impersonal forces.

Social change produces the problems with which we are concerned since institutions relatively adapted to a past era no longer function to meet the requirements of living in the present. As a result, as John Kenneth Galbraith has said, ". . . we do many things that are unnecessary, some that are unwise and a few that are insane." While residual welfare programs deal largely with the

[9] Ernest Becker, *The Structure of Evil* (New York: George Braziller, 1968), p. 230.

[10] Dorothy Lee, *Freedom and Culture* (Englewood Cliffs, N.J.: Prentice-Hall, 1959), pp. 39–52.

[11] Dennis H. Wrong, "The Functional Theory of Stratification," *American Sociological Review,* 24 (December 1959), p. 781.

consequences of change and the symptoms of institutional defects, social welfare as social development is an effort to direct change itself and to alter institutions or to develop new ones that are more consistent with social needs and human values as they may be currently defined. Understanding some of the dynamics of change (and resistance to change) may enable us to recognize some limits and possibilities of social reconstruction.

Some Ideas About Social Change

While there are no adequate theories of social change, there are some useful ideas that may illuminate changes that have taken place and factors that may influence future directions of society. Wilbert E. Moore provides a framework for the consideration of social change.[12] In his view, with the exception of cataclysmic changes caused by natural disaster or enemy attack, the major sources of change are to be found in the social system.

The term *social system* implies organized or patterned behavior. It directs our attention to the fact that individuals are embedded in social relationships, that their behavior is to a considerable degree influenced by their position (status) in an organized system of relationships and by the accompanying role requirements (norms) that function to direct activity toward certain socially valued ends. This structure of roles has its own dynamics, somewhat independent of though interrelated with individual personality factors. Thus a feudal social structure (rural, manorial, aristocratic, traditionally oriented with extended family system and little mobility) will produce behavior different from that which one would expect to find in a democratic, capitalistic, urban, industrialized, secular society with high mobility and a nuclear family system. Such structures will produce their unique social problems and characteristic ways of dealing with them. The system changes as it adapts to its own internal conflicts and to innovations in its environment. We shall return to this seminal social system concept later.

It is well to remind ourselves, however, that human beings may be regarded as the ultimate source of change. One may easily fall into the trap of regarding man only as social product, conditioned by society and reacting to change, rather than seeing man as creating social order, responding to it, disrupting it, and inventing modes of relationship to it in order to enact a new vision of human possibilities. Karl Marx recognized that men make their own history, limited by circumstances "directly found, given and transmitted from the past." As Emerson put it, "men are free to collaborate with necessity." The requirements of social order are part of such "necessity." After given societal arrangements have been established, their maintenance will impose limits on human behavior as well as provide opportunities for the satisfaction of needs. As institutions are altered a new, possibly better, balance between freedom and con-

---

[12] The basic framework for the consideration of social change is based on Wilbert E. Moore, "A Reconsideration of Theories of Social Change," *American Sociological Review,* 25 (December 1960), pp. 810–818.

We have liberally modified and supplemented his presentation with apologies to Dr. Moore and with full personal acceptance of responsibility for the use, or misuse, of his very helpful article. We have also drawn on other writers, as noted.

straints may be created—better at least for some if not all members of society. As Leonard Duhl states, man is shaped by his environment; he in turn makes his own environment and is further influenced by his own creation.[13] Man creates symbols that pattern behavior, providing order and meaning. He creates institutions for the gratification of both biological and cultural needs. Once we see that man creates his own symbolic world to make action possible and to give meaning to his life, we see the paradox inherent in man-made culture. On the one hand, the structure he invents frees him to act. On the other hand, man becomes the prisoner of his own definitions of reality, which prevent him from seeing alternative courses of action for the greater gratification of his needs. In any event men are embedded in social systems through which they strive to meet needs and attain ideal values. While human striving may be said to be the ultimate source of change, its nature and direction, though dimly understood, are influenced by the structure of society. Drawing loosely on Wilbert E. Moore, we may explore the dynamics of change with reference to the following set of ideas: (1) efforts to resolve persistent problems in the human condition, (2) flexibilities in the system, and (3) social system strains.[14]

Efforts to Resolve Persistent Problems in the Human Condition

Everywhere man seems to strive for the satisfaction of at least two essential needs: (1) his material need to assure survival and to achieve some culturally defined level of economic well-being and (2) the symbolic need for order and meaning. Though both are present and interrelated, different cultures may emphasize one or the other. In the view of Ernest Becker, the basic human striving is the quest for meaning and for a positive definition of self. He sees alienation, which evolved as industrial man's self-concept became narrowly identified with production and consumption, as the root of social ills. From this perspective one may see the frequently criticized materialism of the Western world as an economic and a sociopsychological phenomenon. The apparently endless and compulsive quest for higher standards of living is not simply the pursuit of consumption needs, it may also be the more basic quest for identity and self-esteem on whatever terms society may provide. Thus the profit motive is as much a psychological motive as an economic one: Economic success is the symbol by which individuals know how well they are doing and, at the same time, it is a major medium by which our society distributes dignity, a sense of self-respect, and a direction for human activity.

This is hardly a fair summary of a brilliant analysis of the human malaise. The reader is again referred to Becker's *The Structure of Evil*. Frederick Herzberg has somewhat the same view. The basic needs of the human are (1) material, which stem from his animal disposition to avoid loss of life, hunger, pain, and sexual deprivation, and (2) symbolic, which express higher needs for self-actualization and enrichment of life. The first, he identifies as the Adam view of man. The latter, as the Abraham view. In his opinion, the industrial-

---

[13] Leonard Duhl (ed.), *The Urban Condition* (New York: Basic Books, 1963), p. 62.

[14] Moore, *op. cit.*

commercial society, in celebrating the Adam image of man, destroys man's potentialities for continuous psychological growth.[15]

While industrial man seems preoccupied with economic development, the aspiration to improve the material conditions of life is common if not universal. Not everywhere, of course, has man accorded equal value to such a goal. In some places it has been minimized because of different philosophies of life and the beliefs, real or otherwise, that scarcity and hardship are part of man's unalterable fate. Interestingly enough, however, a cross-cultural study of human aspirations reveals that people in a variety of societies seem to want essentially the same things: better health, a longer life, improved material conditions, and better opportunities for their children.[16] Throughout the world a revolution of rising expectations is advancing faster than the technological capacity to fulfill them.

The happy peasant satisfied with poverty is largely a myth. A poet of ancient Greece may have been giving expression to a personal feeling when he wrote, "Better to hurl oneself into the abysmal sea or over a blunt cliff, than be a victim of poverty." If peasants were poets they might agree; in any case it is unlikely they would sing of the wonders of being poor.[17] It is rather likely that they might ask, along with Ntoni in Giovanni Verga's *The House by the Medlar Tree,* why it is some are "born lucky and . . . able to enjoy themselves while others were born penniless and had to spend their lives pulling wagons with their teeth." [18] Today almost every society throughout the world is committed to material progress through development and application of science and technology. In turn, science and technology may dehumanize life if allowed to become ends rather than means to human fulfillment. Industrialization thus has its social consequences, its gains and costs.

Industrialization and Changing Social Structure

The capacity of a society to fulfill human aspirations for higher levels of material well-being depends on its stage of industrial development. W. W. Rostow has identified three stages: (1) takeoff, (2) maturity, and (3) high level of mass consumption.[19] The first stage is characterized by the rise of investment rate exceeding population growth; development of fundamental and applied science; existence of entrepreneurs ready to apply inventions to productivity; a people prepared to risk investments; and a disciplined labor force motivated to accept specialized narrow and recurrent tasks.[20] Welfare as charity, geared to

[15] Frederick Herzberg, *Work and the Nature of Man* (Cleveland: World Publishing, 1966).

[16] Hadley Cantril and Lloyd A. Free, "Hopes and Fears for Self and Country," Supplement to the *American Behavioral Scientist,* 6 (October 1962).

[17] See Carolina Maria de Jesus, *Child of the Dark* (New York: Dutton, 1962) for a view of poverty from a remarkable woman who lived in the *barrio* of Brazil.

[18] Giovanni Verga, *The House by the Medlar Tree,* (1881; reprint ed., New York: Grove Press, 1953), p. 184.

[19] W. W. Rostow, *The Stages of Economic Growth* (Cambridge, England: Cambridge University Press, 1960).

[20] *Ibid.,* p. 20.

the primary task of maintaining the motivation to labor at work not freely chosen, has its roots in this stage of industrialization. The second stage, economic maturity, is attained when a society has developed a basic capital goods industry with the ". . . technological and entrepreneurial skills to produce . . . anything that it chooses to produce." [21] The third stage, high-level mass consumption, is signified by a shift toward durable goods and services; surplus income for large numbers of people, which permits consumption beyond essential food, shelter, and clothing; increasing urbanization; and a change in the structure of the work force toward skilled factory and white-collar jobs. At this point further development of technology need not be of primary concern. A nation, however, may move toward a new takeoff stage of technological development. This may be true of the United States to the degree that automation and cybernation became the new modes of production.

It was probably Henry Ford's assembly line that symbolized the attainment in the United States of an economy of high-level mass consumption (1913–1914). In the 1950s we became identified as the "affluent society." The median income of the population was over $5,000 per year, and we achieved the first "service economy," in which more than half the labor force was not directly involved in manufacturing.[22] An economy, having attained high-level mass consumption, need no longer give priority to the development of technology, but may allocate increasing resources to consumption, including provisions for meeting social needs. In such a context Western societies, for example, have chosen to develop social welfare measures through the political process, for the ". . . emergence of the welfare state is one manifestation of a society's moving beyond technical maturity." [23]

Societies do not necessarily go through such a specific sequence of stages, nor are social welfare programs developed solely in response to stages of economic development, since unique political and cultural factors in each society influence such provisions. Some of the emerging underdeveloped nations, just embarking on industrialization, are welfare states in their aspirations and, to a degree, in the way they allocate resources. The economic, scientific, and human resource capacities of a society will determine the degree to which welfare objectives can be materialized. Furthermore, there is a reciprocal relationship between economic development and the investments in health, education, and other social welfare resources. Improvements in human resources may lead to increased economic productivity, providing even more resources that could be invested in meeting social needs. Newly developing nations may have an opportunity to exploit this reciprocity, one largely ignored in our own industrial development and only now being given some attention.

Economic development is accomplished by a related process of modernization of society, which produces basic alterations in the social structure. Traditional institutions no longer meet needs, and norms governing behavior break down, creating dislocations: e.g., insecurity and unemployment, as work-for-wages replaces dependence on the land, and deviant youths, as traditional family and

[21] *Ibid.*

[22] *Ibid.*, p. 11; and Victor R. Fuchs, "The First Service Economy," *The Public Interest,* No. 2 (Winter 1966), pp. 7–17.

[23] Rostow, *op. cit.,* p. 11.

extended kinship control are attenuated in response to conditions of urban-industrial living. These and similar conditions may come to be defined as social problems requiring amelioration or prevention.

Seymour Martin Lipset describes the concept of modernization in the following way; he emphasizes that he means this as an "ideal type" statement and that variations in both developed and underdeveloped societies should not be overlooked.

> The very concept of modernization refers to the social conditions characteristic of an urbanized, economically advanced society, in which there has been a great deal of social differentiation, division of labor, and social change, in contrast to the institutions of a traditionalist rural or preindustrial society, with its relative lack of differentiation and its emphasis on social stability.[24]

Such modernization fundamentally alters the modes of social relationships, involving costs and gains—inequitably distributed—that attend the development of an urban-industrial society. Drawing freely on Lipset and Hauser,[25] the following trends may be identified.

INSTRUMENTAL RATHER THAN PERSONAL RELATIONSHIPS. As secondary groups take precedence over primary group affiliation, people tend to relate to one another primarily in terms of the functions they perform. As Emile Durkheim put it, "The division of labor does not present individuals to one another, but social functions." [26] Relationships tend to be instrumental rather than personal, while rights and obligations tend to be limited rather than diffuse. Even the modern nuclear family may take on some secondary features; for example, the husband's job may be seen as more important to the wife than the kind of man she married.[27] A major study reveals the need for instrumental relations.

> As our data . . . suggests, what a modern society needs for successful development is flexibility in a man's role relationships. His entire network of relations to others should not be traditionally determined by his caste or even by his occupational status. Instead he enters into relationships for particular reasons which should provide for greater efficiency in working out the network of relationships among people. To use the unpleasant language of Marxism, interpersonal relationships are reduced to a "cash basis"; they have a particular reason for being, so that in a sense they seem calculated rather than warm and diffuse. . . .[28]

[24] Seymour Martin Lipset, "Introduction," in T. H. Marshall, *Class, Citizenship, and Social Development* (Garden City, N.Y.: Anchor Books, 1965), p. viii.

[25] Lipset, *ibid.,* and Philip M. Hauser, "Social Problems of Urban Development," speech given at National Conference on Social Welfare, Chicago, Illinois, May 29, 1966.

[26] George Simpson, *Emile Durkheim on the Division of Labor in Society* (New York: Macmillan, 1933), p. 407.

[27] Helena Znaniecki Lopata, "The Secondary Features of a Primary Relationship," *Human Organization,* 24 (Summer 1965), pp. 116–121.

[28] David McClelland, *The Achieving Society* (Princeton, N.J.: Van Nostrand, 1961), p. 194.

What is functional for economic development may not be functional for human development, particularly when the imperatives of economic growth may not need the same order of priority once attached to them. Having solved the problem of production, our own society may focus on the nature of the social bond and seek ways to reestablish a sense of community characterized by a greater regard for persons as ends rather than as means. If man becomes human only through transactions with others, then the quality of these social relationships is crucial. What we perceive to be social problems or private troubles may in a more critical perspective turn out to be, as Ernest Becker suggests, issues regarding the kind of social bond or social structure that facilitates or impedes personal growth and human freedom.[29] We may discover that problems in human relations, around which we have developed many social service programs and the practice of social work and other human relations professions, are symptoms with deeper systemic roots than these strategies can touch.

RATIONAL RATHER THAN TRADITIONAL NORMS. In preindustrial societies, decisions are predetermined and roles are part of the "cake of custom." In developed societies individuals have the freedom and the burden of numerous decisions in regard to the kind and extent of education to undertake, vocations to pursue, marital partner to select, and life goals to pursue. These are to be rationally calculated rather than traditionally determined. Helping professions develop to provide expert information, guidance, counseling, and therapy around such complex and problematic decisions. At the same time, this freedom may be more apparent than real to the degree that it is limited by the lack of capacity and resources with which to make decisions and by the lack of socially structured alternative opportunities to exercise choice. For example, the poor may be said to be that group in society with the least freedom in the choice in jobs, education, housing, and life opportunities. The ideal goals of social welfare ought to be directed at maximizing their freedom of choice as well as that of others whose freedom may be more restricted than generally recognized. Residual welfare programs, however, tend to police the poor into conforming to norms established by the middle class. The middle class, in turn, may be prisoners of their own value system. Socialization and education may function to distort and limit the perception of life's possibilities, and roles available for even the relatively advantaged may not be consonant with their own preferred life styles or with the full range of human needs one may wish to satisfy. A technological society ". . . committed to the quest for continually improved means to carelessly examined ends," as Jacques Ellul puts it, moves in the direction of the increasing rationalization of life, with economic efficiency as the ultimate value.[30] Yet this very rationalization, based on the application of the most efficient means for the attainment of specified ends, enables us to achieve a variety of social purposes otherwise beyond our reach. Formal organizations are such instruments for rationalizing social life.

CREATED RATHER THAN CRESCIVE INSTITUTIONS: TREND TOWARD AN ORGANIZATIONAL SOCIETY. In traditional societies institutions are a product of col-

[29] Becker, *op. cit.,* p. 315.

[30] Jacques Ellul, *The Technological Society* (New York: Knopf, 1965), p. vii.

lective experience over generations. They are "crescive rather than created" that is, products of history and tradition rather than rational calculation.[31]   A central characteristic of modern societies is the high moral value given to "rationality, effectiveness, and efficiency," and the application of organizational techniques to the planning, coordination, and control of human activity that makes possible a highly specialized and interdependent division of labor for the pursuit of social goals.[32]   Thus we may speak of a trend toward an organizational society as major social roles are performed within such formal organizations, as major social transactions occur not between individuals but between organizations, and as major decisions involving the allocation of resources and opportunities become dependent on the power of various organizations to compete for advantage and political influence.   In this sense, as we have noted, rugged collectivism replaces rugged individualism as one's fate is linked to one or more bureaucracies, primarily by way of one's occupational status. Formal organizations have their own imperatives that may complement or conflict with the needs and value aspirations of individuals, thus posing some of the major dilemmas of modern society.

Daniel Katz and Robert L. Kahn have identified four such dilemmas: (1) the maximization dynamic that leads to the increasing size of organizations, richer material life, and the threat of organizational totality foreshadowed in Orwell's *1984*; (2) the use of role systems as rational devices for handling all problems, which produces greater efficiency but may lead to loss of self-identity and to impersonal relations; (3) complexity and specialization of large-scale organizations, restricting policy decision to an elite with access to knowledge and competence for decision-making, limiting grass roots participation at a time when there are increased aspirations for a more full participation as a symbol of one's first-class citizen status; and (4) the need for pragmatic conformity to a variety of bureaucratic roles with an emphasis on compromise and practicality rather than on idealized moral standards, which may undermine the moral integration of society.[33]

Each dilemma poses a problem, each may contain gains as well as costs; adaptations to such strains are available if society is willing to make necessary changes.   We've already noted that formal organizations may be humanized as new kinds of work engender more flexible structures characterized by greater equality, autonomy, and participation in decision-making.[34]

SECONDARY RATHER THAN PRIMARY GROUP SOCIALIZATION.   The family becomes less well-equipped to prepare children for social roles demanded by an industrial society.   In an advanced scientifically oriented society, serious questions are even raised about the possible necessity of an almost complete shift of the socialization function to schools and other formal organizations.   Thus, some of the social problems with which we deal are a result of a failure to develop a

---

[31] Hauser, *op. cit.*

[32] Amitai Etzioni, *Modern Organizations* (Englewood Cliffs, N.J.: Prentice-Hall, 1964), pp. 31–34.

[33] Daniel Katz and Robert L. Kahn, *The Social Psychology of Organizations* (New York: Wiley, 1966), pp. 459–472.

[34] Bennis, *op. cit.;* "Beyond Bureaucracy" Pusic, *op. cit.*

socialization structure that functioned as well as the family in preindustrial society. In the words of Philip A. Hauser, educators, social workers, and others are ". . . fumbling to discover alternative mechanisms as effective" as the family had previously been in traditional societies.[35] The bulk of social services have developed in response to the impact of industrialization on family life. As long as society holds the family primarily responsible for child rearing and other functions, services tend to be residual in nature, provided only at the point of crisis and breakdown. As recognition is given to the inextricable connection between family functioning and social structure and to the fact that families can be held responsible for performance only of those functions that capacities and resources permit, greater attention may be given to social provisions and social services as essential social utilities that enhance the capacity of parents to carry out their responsibilities.[36]

There is always the danger, however, of a romantic view of the traditional family and of primary group societies. Some of the dynamics of change surely come from youths eager to escape from family and community once the opportunity presents itself. It has never been easy to keep them down on the farm once other alternatives become available. While mechanisms of socialization and social control are more effective in reducing deviant behavior in traditional societies, such societies are also characterized by little individuality or freedom of choice.

FORMAL RATHER THAN INFORMAL SOCIAL CONTROL. Advanced societies have to rely to an increasing degree on such formal instruments as law, police, courts, social workers, and other professional agents to control deviant behavior as the traditional forms of control exercised through kinship ties, church, and community become less effective. Residual social services have developed partly in response to the need for new forms of social control. Ideally, we may see the social services as representing a quest for a more adequate socialization structure that will enable individuals to develop those inner controls compatible with the degree of order essential for a free society, yet sufficiently flexible to promote that measure of individual autonomy that, in David Reisman's terms, allows one the "capacity to conform and the freedom to choose." In this event the function of social services shifts from a primary concern with social control to an increasing concern with social competence, a point to be elaborated later.

ACHIEVEMENT RATHER THAN ASCRIPTION. In preindustrial societies, the division of labor is determined by tradition, and roles are assigned by age, sex, class, or caste. Individual merit tends to be the actual or proclaimed criterion for occupational assignment in modern societies. Since society cannot know in advance who will be most qualified, all may be encouraged to compete for position, creating opportunities for upward mobility as well as status discontent, risk of failure, and associated problems. Advanced societies, of course, vary in degree of openness and occupational mobility. Especially when associated with

[35] Hauser, *op. cit.*

[36] Alfred J. Kahn, "New Policies and Service Models: The Next Phase," *American Journal of Orthopsychiatry*, 35 (July 1965), pp. 652–662.

political democracy, a pressure for equality of opportunity develops. Some of our social welfare measures are a response to such a demand, while the crisis in welfare, at the same time, indicates the degree of our failure. As the post-industrial society moves toward a "meritocracy" of talent, distributing coveted rewards to those most highly endowed and best educated for the performance of valued functions, the quest for equality of opportunity not only becomes more urgent but it also raises difficult issues and dilemmas. Some of these have to do with a body of knowledge that suggests a link between early sociali-zation and educability, with implications for intervention in infancy and early childhood.[37] Others have to do with the problem of transforming schools so they can assure equality of results rather than merely equal opportunity, a challenge that focuses attention on the tension between meeting the needs of the middle class and of a managerial society as opposed to the special needs of the poor.[38]

Perhaps of key importance is the issue of the credential society, one that dis-tributes occupational status on the basis of educational credentials—diplomas and degrees—rather than actual capacity to perform specific job requirements. There is evidence that the common assumption that jobs increasingly require more highly educated personnel is something of a myth. Some complex jobs can be done with relatively little formal education, many people are over-educated for the tasks they perform, and employers tend to raise educational qualifications not so much in response to the demands of the job but to chang-ing educational qualifications of the labor supply.[39] The issue is not the value of education, but the value of educational credentials as a measure of job per-formance. There is evidence that many employers have unrealistic educational qualifications that arbitrarily restrict admission to entry positions and that equalizing job opportunities might be more effectively promoted, not by at-tempting to change individuals, but by focusing on system change through efforts to expand job opportunities and to alter ". . . employers' policies and practices that block organizational mobility and seal off entry jobs." [40] How-ever, so long as educational credentials are taken seriously as a screening device for access to coveted social roles, schools are the gatekeepers into the oppor-tunity structure. We may thus value education for the wrong reasons and create a "tyranny of schooling," as Lewis Dexter has suggested, characterized by a constant exposure to tests and fear of failure, and most of all to a paralyz-ing dread of being regarded as stupid. This may account for a good deal of ". . . inferiority complexes, self-contempt, self-depreciation, and despair" with

[37] James Coleman, "Toward Open Schools," *The Public Interest,* No. 9 (Fall 1967), pp. 20–27; Hess, Robert D., "Educability and Rehabilitation: The Future of the Welfare Class," *Journal of Marriage and the Family,* 26, (November 1964), pp. 422–429; Morison, *op. cit.;* J. McVicker Hunt, "Black Genes—White Environment," *Trans-action,* 6 (June 1969), pp. 12–22.

[38] Thomas F. Green, "Schools and Communities: A Look Forward," *Harvard Educational Review,* 39 (Spring 1969), pp. 221–252.

[39] S. M. Miller, "The Credential Society," *Trans-action,* 5 (December 1967), 2; Ivar Berg, "Rich Man's Qualifications for Poor Man's Jobs," *Trans-action,* Vol. 6 (March 1969), pp. 49–51.

[40] Berg, *ibid.,* p. 50.

an unknown, but probably significant, impact on the mental health of the nation.[41] In an achievement-oriented society in which people are processed and screened for occupational status, one's sense of self-esteem is always in jeopardy. Probably a fair amount of the demand for casework, counseling, and therapy from the human service professions is the result. As Richard Titmuss has observed, ". . . perhaps one of the oustanding social characteristics of the twentieth century, . . . [is] the fact that more and more people consciously experience at one or more stages in their lives the process of selection and rejection." [42]   Through this screening process, with its built-in class bias, the failures and rejects of society are shifted to the residual welfare programs.

Further issues have to do with the limits of our knowledge about appropriate and politically feasible measures for promoting equality. The value of equal opportunity itself may be questioned, as we have already suggested. In the meantime the pressure for equality continues and extends to the notion of citizenship rights to social benefits—a concept that has major implications for social welfare.

EQUALITY RATHER THAN TRADITIONAL ELITISM: CITIZENSHIP FOR ALL.   According to Seymour Martin Lipset, all modern political systems are constrained to promote equality of opportunity or at least to claim this as a basic tenet.[43] A commitment to economic growth and to science and technology as the means to attain it inevitably leads to the destruction of structures that support traditional elites and to the establishment of a status system rooted in competition for occupational attainment.   Although questions may be raised about the assumption of any inevitable trend toward equality inherent in industrialization, the experience of Western democracies does seem to be characterized by a progressive evolution of the idea of common citizenship.[44]

In preindustrial societies, citizenship status tends to be restricted to a hereditary elite, which tends to monopolize various rights, powers, and privileges. Modernization tends to encourage the admission to citizenship of additional strata of industrial society, so that one may see a long historic process of transformation of people from subjects to citizens.

We have already introduced Marshall's notion of citizenship, but it might be well to briefly review it here. Citizenship, in his view, consists of three sets of rights and duties—civil, political, and social. The rise of the middle class in the eighteenth century saw the establishment of *civil rights*—liberty, freedom of speech, equality before the law, and the right to own property. *Political rights* in the form of universal manhood suffrage developed in the nineteenth century, partly in response to the demands of the newly organized working class. *Social rights* (social justice) has been the dominant theme of the latter part of this century. It involves a citizen right to economic security, education, and the benefits and obligations that accompany full participation in society.

[41] Lewis Anthony Dexter, *The Tyranny of Schooling* (New York: Basic Books, 1964).

[42] Richard M. Titmuss, *Essays on the "Welfare State"* (London: G. Allen, 1958), p. 43.

[43] Lipset, *op. cit.*, p. xiii.

[44] Marshall, *op. cit.*

All hereditary privileges come under attack with the advance of the equalitarian ideal. Only merit is accepted as a legitimate basis for superior rewards, but here too the democratic ideal tends to set limits on the degree of differential prestige, material benefits, and the power that may accompany occupational status. A basic dynamic for further equalization of the opportunities to participate in the benefits of social membership and a major dynamic of change is the conflict between the inequalities inherent in social class and the ideal of citizenship, a point we shall discuss later. This tension between the culturally defined ideal and social reality may be particularly applicable to the United States for, in the words of Gunnar Myrdal,

> . . . America, relative to all the other branches of Western civilization, is moralistic and "moral-conscious." The ordinary American is the opposite of a cynic. He is on the average more of a believer and a defender of the faith in humanity than the rest of the Occidentals. It is a relatively important matter to him to be true to his own ideals and to carry them out in actual life.[45]

At the present time it is the gap between our belief in equality of opportunity and the institutionalized inequalities in jobs, income, education, medical care, housing, and other benefits and privileges of membership in society that creates a major dynamic for social change.

The excluded seek full citizenship, demanding that the belief in equality, which de Tocqueville saw as central to American life, be more fully implemented. Daniel Bell has written that "One of the reasons why the predictions of Tocqueville, made more than 130 years ago, are still so cogent, is that he had hit upon the great 'master key' to American society—the desire for equality." [46] This democratic stress on equality conflicts with the inequalities inherent in the operation of social class systems. It is a major factor in reducing class privileges in all modern industrial societies in which, increasingly, the notion of civil, political, and social rights for all citizens takes precedence over the rewards and privileges associated with social class.[47]

The gap between our ideals of equal opportunity and structured inequality is not the only source of tension and efforts toward change. Equally important perhaps are the protests, not of the excluded, but of the alienated youths—those who have access to the opportunity structure but reject what they see as the gross material values of society, its hypocritical denial of dignity and humanity, its vulgarization of the ideal of progress, its celebration of military power and technology, and its restrictions on open, honest, and genuine relationships. Some are activists seeking change, others withdraw from any commitment to society, but many respond not simply to the gap between the promise and the reality of equality but also to what they see as the need for a new moral order, however difficult it may be for them to articulate this. Their protest is not simply economic, social, or political. It may be aesthetic. What they may be

[45] Gunnar Myrdal, *An American Dilemma,* 2 vols. (New York: Harper & Brothers, 1944), p. xiii.

[46] Bell, "Notes on the Post-Industrial Society (II)," *op. cit.,* p. 111.

[47] Marshall, *op. cit.*

saying is that the entire human drama built on the dream of material progress has lost its moral power and is no longer convincing. To the extent that this is a shared feeling, we may be in for a cultural revolution of unpredictable proportion and uncertain outcome. At a minimum, there will be increasing conflict between those who wish to preserve their perception of the existing moral order and the dissidents who wish to radically alter it.

In any event students seem to constitute the major voice for the liberal conscience of our society. This is demonstrated in a report to President Nixon on campus violence by twenty-two young Republican congressmen of varying political and social ideologies, ranging from moderate to ultraconservative. They said that students complained that "The university, like society in general, failed to practice what it preached." The "neglect of human problems and a preoccupation with material wealth" was the largest single factor behind student unrest. The congressmen added that students question unchallenged defense expenditures while cuts are made in domestic and educational programs. Questions were raised everywhere regarding society's hypocrisy toward the disadvantaged, minority groups, and developing nations. The report said that the great majority of students were "decent and intelligent young people who believed that injustices could yet be put to right." [48]

We have reviewed thus far some of the social consequences that accompany industrialization—an effort, largely successful in this society, to overcome the historic problem of scarcity. So long as there is ". . . a strong commitment to the value of economic progress, and to the belief that the adoption of technological change is the best way to get it," technological change may be regarded as the "basic cause of change." [49]

Flexibilities in the System

Moore identifies other problems in the human condition that he sees as a source of social change. These are the inconsistencies that invariably exist between ideal values and patterned social behavior.[50] Human beings require some kind of moral order, and no society is possible without some consensus on values and goals. While cultures are more or less integrated, they are rarely completely so. All cultures have some discontinuity between their moral ideals and social reality, which is itself a source of change as efforts are made to alter social reality to conform more closely to ideal images.

The remarkable quality of this society, however, is the degree to which the system itself is flexible, allowing for a wide range of tolerable behavior. We institutionalize roles that permit and encourage dissent (e.g., conscientious objector, organizer of the poor in a community action program) as well as those deliberately designed to produce change (scientist, city planner, social planner). In no society are individuals all socialized in the same mold. Socialization in a pluralistic and dynamic society such as ours, with its high valuation on the uniqueness of the individual, its belief in individual freedom, and its conflicts

[48] *New York Times,* June 19, 1966.

[49] Harold L. Wilensky and Charles N. Lebeaux, *Industrial Society and Social Welfare* (New York: Free Press, 1965), p. 344.

[50] Moore, *op. cit.*

over philosophies of parenthood and pedagogy, is even less likely to produce uniformities in individuals, concern over the conforming American notwithstanding.   Urbanization undermines social control, and our cultural pluralism prevents any uniform value system.   A society that encourages and facilitates individual expression can expect greater social change, creativity, deviation, and instability.   A social system like that of the Hutterians, with roles more carefully detailed and enforced by group pressure and with change deliberately guarded against, will be characterized by greater social stability and individual security, limiting the degree of individual freedom and social change that is possible.[51]

It is difficult for Americans to accept the degree to which various deviations are a natural consequence of the very freedom and individuality we value.   It is possible that some of our social problems might be more humanely and efficiently handled, not through repression or rehabilitation, but simply through greater tolerance of different life styles and modes of individual expression.   It is difficult to know, however, at what point a system ceases to be flexible and becomes characterized by anomie, a state of normlessness, where essential socialization and social control functions are not performed in even a minimally adequate way.

Harvey Wheeler, for example, sees the collapse of the family as a socializing force when he writes that the "American family has become an agency for the decivilization of children, rather than their civilization." [52]   Wheeler, Urie Bronfenbrenner, and others believe that we must now plan for the socialization of children.[53]   In such a view the target of change is not simply the poor and disadvantaged families, whose socialization patterns are presumably dysfunctional, but the average American families, whose child-rearing practices may be unsuited to developing the kind of human being who can creatively participate in our changing social reality.   Little is known about this, and thus far direct efforts to change families are not impressive.

At the same time individualism that is self-centered and oblivious to social consequences disrupts the fabric of society.   The need to cope with the complexities of an increasingly interdependent society leads to new forms of social control to restrict the flexibility of the system and to guide change in some desired fashion, raising difficult questions around the never-ending issue of the relationship between individual freedom and social order.

Social System Strains

Other sources of change may be found in social system strains.   Moore identifies three: (1) demographic imbalances, (2) universal scarcities that create

[51] John W. Bennett, "Communal Brethren of the Great Plains," *Trans-action,* 4 (December 1966), pp. 42–47.

[52] Wheeler, *op. cit.,* p. 19.

[53] *Ibid.,* p. 22; Harry C. Bredemeier, "Proposal for an Adequate Socialization Structure," *Urban America and Planning of Mental Health Services* (New York: Group for the Advancement of Psychiatry, November 1964), Symposium, Vol. V, No. 10, pp. 447–469; Urie Bronfenbrenner, "The Split-Level American Family," *Saturday Review,* October 7, 1967, pp. 60–66; Morison, *op. cit.*

the struggle for order and equity, and (3) conflicting principles of social organization.

DEMOGRAPHIC IMBALANCES. Population growth, mobility, and density are likely to be sources of stress and consequent change. In the past fifty years the population in the United States has doubled, and there have been great regional shifts from rural to urban, South to North, as we moved from a nation of farms to an industrial urban society.

In 1865 only about one-fourth of the population was urban. In 1969 it was estimated that only about 5 percent of the total population lived on farms. By the year 2000, 60 percent of the population of some 311 million may live in three gigantic urban regions on 7.2 percent of the land in the United States. More immediate is the possibility that each of the country's ten metropolitan areas may soon have "from 30 to 50 million people compacted into them. Traditional interventionist devices simply cannot cope with demographic disequilibrium on such a scale." [54]

Philip A. Hauser has called this population mobility and increasing density a social morphological revolution, accounting in part for the changes in social structure that we reviewed earlier. Such population shifts alter social structures, help create social problems, and require some form of intervention for dealing with their consequences. Intelligent and planned intervention could reduce the unnecessary human cost and the social dislocations that follow population changes. This is illustrated by the rational and comprehensive way the federal government undertook to facilitate the assimilation of Cuban refugees.

By mid-1966 more than 200,000 Cubans had been resettled in over 2,000 United States communities under the Cuban Refugee Program administered by the Welfare Administration of the U.S. Department of Health, Education, and Welfare. Once resettled, less than 5 percent required any further public assistance. A variety of services given the refugees had cost a total of over $177 million by the end of 1965. "Had they merely been given refuge and a bare subsistence income, $40 a month, without the resettlement, vocational, education, health and other services included in the program, the cost would have been more than double—$400 million." [55]

No equivalent program has ever been designed to assist Puerto Rican, Negro, or other migrants who are in special need of facilitating resources to enable them to adapt to the requirements of urban life. An increasing proportion of those in the inner city are Negro migrants from the South; they are handicapped by the personal and social disabilities that accompany racial discrimination, exploitation, and the denial of opportunities to acquire the skills to adapt to a competitive urban technological society. In 1910 Negroes were 73 percent a rural population; in 1960 they were 73 percent urban. They were driven from rural areas by an agricultural revolution that destroyed their livelihood without compensating benefits and were pulled to the urban centers by the hope for jobs and education for their children, often without the resources and op-

[54] Harvey Wheeler, *The Restoration of Politics* (Santa Barbara, Calif.: Center for the Study of Democratic Institutions, 1965), p. 20.

[55] *Programs and Services,* U.S. Department of Health, Education, and Welfare (Washington, D.C.: Government Printing Office, September 1966), p. 351.

portunities to realize their dreams.   They are concentrated in the urban ghettos, are increasingly hopeless about gaining admission to a society in which the basic credentials are a white skin and ever-higher educational qualifications, and resent the inadequate attention to their plight on the part of privileged whites.   One response has been the violent riots that have taken a heavy toll in lives and property damage.   Harlem in 1964, Cleveland in 1965, Watts in 1966, Newark and Detroit in 1967 are only some of the most dramatic instances of the breakdown of order following shattered hopes and unfulfilled promises. In recent years it appears that violent discontent may be taking the form of guerrilla warfare directed primarily at the police, who are regarded by the more militant blacks as symbols of a repressive society.   The very stability of society is threatened by the failure to respond compassionately and sensibly to the needs of human beings who made the great migration and who had every right to expect that they would be treated as citizens.

If the problem of the urban ghetto can be seen partly in the light of a demographic disequilibrium, it is not only the Negro who is involved.   It is estimated, for example, that each month enough people move into Los Angeles to make up a sizable town.   The services they require in housing, health, education, sanitation, and so on are not brought with them.   This nation is not adequately prepared to plan ahead to provide essential resources, to restrict migration to ease pressure on limited community facilities, or to establish priorities to distribute more equitably the scarce manpower and other community resources required to accommodate to the population pressures that are due to growth and migration.

The rate of population growth has been declining (4.3 million births in 1957, 3.6 million in 1966), but we still add each year a total equal to the population of Chicago.   An increasing proportion of our population is aged (almost 10 percent) and children under 18 (over 35 percent).[56]   The needs of the aged cannot be provided solely through the operation of the market.   Societal provisions for employment, income, medical care, housing, recreation, and most important of all, some opportunity for continuing participation in society are required.   We have only begun to respond to these needs through such means as Medicare legislation and a modest commitment of resources to the noble objectives embodied in the Older Americans Act of 1965.[57]

[56] Derived from U.S. Bureau of Census, *Population Estimates,* Series P–25, No. 359, February 20, 1967, p. 14.

[57] This act (P.L. 89–73) establishes for the first time an Administration on Aging in the Department of Health, Education, and Welfare and provides for a commissioner appointed by the President. Grants to states were authorized for community planning, services, and training, and grants to public and private nonprofit agencies were authorized for research and development projects and for training personnel.

The purpose of the act, as stated in Title I, is the following:

The Congress hereby finds and declares that, in keeping with the traditional American concept of the inherent dignity of the individual in our democratic society, the older people of our nation are entitled to and it is the joint and several duty and responsibility of the governments of the United States and the several states and their political subdivisions to assist our older people to secure equal opportunity to full and free enjoyment of the following objectives:

The increase in the birthrate following World War II has had continuing re-percussions as school enrollments have outpaced educational resources and as the number of entrants into the labor force has exceeded employment op-portunities. An increase in the rate of juvenile delinquency has reflected both the population increase and the inability of society to meet the needs of youth. Between 1950 and 1960 the young labor force (16–21) increased by about half a million. More than that number are expected to enter the labor force each year in the decade from 1960 to 1970. In the early 1960s youth being out of school and out of work was a problem of crisis proportions; for ghetto youth the problem remained especially severe throughout the mid- and late 1960s. By 1967 economic growth, an accelerated draft, and a variety of antipoverty programs, including the Job Corps and the Neighborhood Youth Corps, had absorbed hundreds of thousands, yet over one in eight white youths and almost one in three Negro youths were still unemployed.[58] An unknown number found jobs only in the slum rackets. Malcolm X, in his autobiography, speaks of the hustlers in Harlem, the pimps, thieves, racketeers: "All of us—who might have probed space, or cured cancer, or built in-dustries—were, instead, black victims of the white man's American social system." [59] For the near future the continuing trend of out-of-school, out-of-work, out-of-hope young people poses an issue for which this society has yet to devise an appropriate solution.[60] The cynicism and despair of one such out-cast from society, a 21-year-old unemployed Negro, is reflected in the follow-ing comment: "If they give a colored boy a job, it's going to be the kind of

1. An adequate income in retirement in accordance with the American standard of living.
2. The best possible physical and mental health which science can make avail-able without regard to economic status.
3. Suitable housing, independently selected, designed and located with reference to special needs and available at costs which older citizens can afford.
4. Full restorative services for those who require institutional care.
5. Opportunity for employment with no discriminatory personnel practices because of age.
6. Retirement in health, honor, dignity after years of contribution to the economy.
7. Pursuit of meaningful activity within the widest range of civic, cultural, and recreational opportunities.
8. Efficient community services which provides social assistance in a co-ordinated manner, and which are readily available when needed.
9. Immediate benefit from proven research knowledge which can sustain and improve health and happiness.
10. Freedom, independence, and the free exercise of individual initiative in planning and managing their own lives.

Total authorization for fiscal year 1967—$11 million.

[58] *Manpower Report of the President,* U.S. Department of Labor (Washington, D.C.: Government Printing Office, 1968), p. 237.

[59] Malcolm Little, *The Autobiography of Malcolm X* (New York: Grove Press, 1965), p. 91.

[60] Eli E. Cohen and Louise Kapp (eds.), *Manpower Policies for Youth* (New York: Columbia University Press, 1966), pp. xiii–xiv.

work a white boy doesn't want to do. They say we're supposed to go to Vietnam and fight for our country. Hell, this ain't our country." [61]

About half of our population is under twenty-five years of age. Our increasingly youthful population raises a special problem in the light of our expanding knowledge of the central importance of early nurturance, socialization, and education. More and more we shall face the issue of the extent of collective responsibility we must take to assure all children equal access to all the basic resources and life experiences that are crucial for human development. There will be major questions about the societal roles of youth, the ability of society to enlist their loyalty by offering worthy goals, and our degree of tolerance for a variety of life styles.

Major social changes are not likely to be produced by the middle aged and the established. Although they are more apt to be the accompaniments of youth, the sense in which this is so is open to dispute. F. Musgrove, in *Youth and The Social Order,* quotes Karl Mannheim only to disagree with him.[62] Mannheim assumed that static societies in which the rate of change is relatively slow rely mainly on the experience of the old; if progress and change are to be achieved, youths must be accorded high status. Musgrove argues that youth are sources of change, not when they are included in society, but when they are excluded. He states that when the status of youths is low and "their seniors can effectively block their access to adult statuses and impede their assumption of adult roles, then there is likely to be a predisposition to change, to social innovation and experimentation. . . ." Musgrove seems to demonstrate the relatively simple principle that groups tend to accept and preserve the social order when they have a vital stake in its reward system. The irony, as he notes, is that a society that provides rewarding opportunities for upward mobility to its youth and others tends to be conservative. Oppression and exclusion tend to create pressure for change.

The principle has implications for the alienated youth in the ghetto who are denied admission to society and those from the suburbs who reject the kind of adult roles available to them. What the increasing proportion of youth in our society portends for the future is a matter of conjecture, but it seems clear that how we approach the question of acculturation and integration of youth in society will influence the kind of changes that will take place and the degree to which these will be regarded as creative or problematic.

UNIVERSAL SCARCITIES: STRUGGLE FOR ORDER AND EQUITY. Universal scarcities and the struggle to allocate them within some system of order and equity is a further source of change. Even in a relatively affluent and democratic society all wants, material and other, cannot be fully satisfied. Norms must govern the distribution of relatively scarce economic goods, power, prestige, and other valuables either through the market, via work and property, or through the political process and government social welfare intervention based on concepts of social needs and citizen rights. In a period of scarcity it is possible to promote someone's welfare only at the expense of someone else. However, a

[61] *San Francisco Chronicle,* April 1, 1966.

[62] F. Musgrove, *Youth and the Social Order* (Bloomington: Indiana University Press, 1964), pp. 125–127, 143, and 149.

society of relative affluence, such as ours, can afford to allocate an increasing proportion of its expanding Gross National Product toward equalizing income and other resources.

In an advanced industrial society there may be a greater complementarity between economic and social development, as Myrdal suggested when he wrote ". . . at this juncture of history there is a striking convergence between the American ideals of liberty and equality of opportunity on the one hand, and of economic progress on the other. Indeed the chief policy means of spurring economic progress will have to be huge reforms that are in the interest of social justice." [63] Values associated with a past era of scarcity, however, may continue to govern allocation of resources in a way that intensifies conflicts generated by a new awareness that neither poverty nor inequality is inevitable.

In a period of rising expectations a share of the benefits of society, once accepted as more or less legitimate or beyond effective protest, may become a center of overt conflict. Demands may be made for guaranteed wages, guaranteed incomes, more equitable distribution of quality education, medical care, job opportunities, housing, and so on. Such a condition, now dramatically evident in the United States, is seen in developing nations as well. As changed circumstances stimulate ". . . new horizons and hopes among the members of less privileged groups and their sense of being frustrated by the established organizations . . . increases, social conflict inevitably arises." [64] Thus economic growth brings with it special problems in maintaining order, a condition noted by Durkheim when he warned against the "perils of prosperity." If there are no normative limits on human aspirations, the discontent generated by unattainable goals may lead to anomie:

> Because prosperity has increased, desires are inflamed. The richer prize offered to them stimulates them, makes them more exacting, more impatient of every rule, just at the time when the traditional rules have lost their authority. The state of rulelessness . . . or *anomie* is further heightened by the fact that human desires are least disciplined at the very moment when they would need a stronger discipline. [65]

The situation may be aggravated by both real and imagined injustices; by knowledge that deprivation once accepted fatalistically could be remedied; by socially fostered discontent endemic in a consumer-oriented, profit-driven economy that endlessly stimulates material desires and imputes inferiority to those who cannot display the material symbols of belonging; and by bold political rhetoric of a War on Poverty and, at the same time, timid allocation of resources.

The sense of inequity may sharpen at the very moment when the groups most

[63] Gunnar Myrdal, *Challenge to Affluence* (New York: Pantheon Books, 1964), pp. 10–11.

[64] Ward Hunt Goodenough, *Cooperation in Change* (New York: Russell Sage Foundation, 1963), p. 103.

[65] Emile Durkheim, "On Anomie," in C. Wright Mills (ed.), *Images of Man* (New York: George Braziller, 1960), p. 456.

afflicted are experiencing a general economic and social advance. It is the sense of *relative deprivation,* not the absolute progress made over the past, that may be most acutely felt. This may be stimulated not only by new aspirations but by an improvement in self-image that unleashes previously repressed resentments. The docile slave, serf, resident of the ghetto, welfare recipient may have accepted with resignation a humiliating inferior status, feeling not only powerless to change it, but unworthy of anything better. However, a new awareness of citizenship status and consumer right has contributed to the powerful feeling of relative deprivation that energizes not only the Negro revolution but a general awakening of the poor.

The relationship between the distribution of rewards and the morale of group members was studied by Samuel Stouffer in *The American Soldier,* from which we now derive the scientific data on the significance of relative deprivation for social structure. The key idea is expectations. In the Military Police, for example, promotions were slow and piecemeal, while in the Air Corps they were rapid and widespread. Which service had the highest troop morale? One might have assumed it would be the Air Corps. On the contrary, it was the Military Police. Because expectations were lower there were fewer sources of discontent. Higher expectations in the Air Corps, due to more frequent and rapid promotions, left the men relatively dissatisfied.[66]

The notion of relative deprivation is not new. Invidious comparisons of the deprived to the rich and the powerful are ancient. Tocqueville wrote the following observation of sentiments that are perhaps felt even more keenly and acted upon more vigorously today:

> The sight of their own hard lot and their weakness, which is daily contrasted with the happiness and power of some of their fellow creatures, excites in their hearts at the same time the sentiments of anger and of fear: the consciousness of their inferiority and their dependence irritates while it humiliates. . . .[67]

What is critical is that aspirations may rise more rapidly than the access to means essential for their fulfillment. This is especially true for the American Negro. While gains in income, employment, education, and health have been substantial when measured against past conditions, today some Negroes are ". . . relatively more deprived than they were before the last twenty-five years of racial progress."[68]   A few statistics may illustrate this point: For example, the median family income of nonwhites increased from $1,614 in 1947 to $5,177 in 1967, but that of whites increased from $3,157 to $8,318. The median family income of nonwhites was 51 percent of that of whites in 1947, and by 1967 it was 62 percent; yet the difference in income was $1,543 in 1947 and $3,141 in 1967 (Table 8). Furthermore, according to the President's

[66] This summary of the Stouffer study is taken from the account in Thomas F. Pettigrew, *A Profile of the Negro American* (Princeton, N.J.: Van Nostrand, 1964), p. 178.

[67] Alexis de Tocqueville, *Democracy in America,* 2 vols. (New York: Vintage Books, 1962), Vol. I, p. 24.

[68] Pettigrew, *op. cit.,* p. 179.

Committee on Urban Housing, nonwhite families must earn about one-third more than whites in order to be assured of standard housing (Table 9). This

Table 8.　Median Family Income by Color of Family Head, 1947 and 1967

YEAR	MEDIAN INCOME		NONWHITE as % OF WHITE	ACTUAL MONEY DIFFERENCE
	White	Nonwhite		
1947	$3,157	$1,614	51	$1,543
1967	8,318	5,177	62	3,141

SOURCE: *The Negroes in the United States,* U.S. Department of Labor, Bureau of Labor Statistics, Bulletin 1511 (Washington, D.C.: Government Printing Office, June 1966), p. 138; *Current Population Reports,* U.S. Bureau of the Census, Series P-60, No. 55, "Family Income Advances, Poverty Reduced in 1967" (Washington, D.C.: Government Printing Office, 1968), p. 5.

Table 9.　Minimum Annual Incomes Required to Assure Standard Housing for White and Nonwhite Households by Household Size, 1960 (Based on Expenditure of 20% of Income for Housing)

RESIDENCE AND RACE	MINIMUM INCOME NEEDED BY HOUSEHOLD SIZE (1960 DOLLARS)				% OF HOUSEHOLDS BELOW MINIMUM INCOMES UNABLE TO FIND STANDARD HOUSING
	1–2	3–4	5	6+	
Inside SMSA					
White	$2700	$3400	$4100	$4600	55.8
Nonwhite	3800	4700	5500	6200	43.8
Outside SMSA					
White	$3900	$4800	$5600	$5900	26.0
Nonwhite	5300	5800	6300	6500	74.5

SOURCE: GE Tempo, "United States Housing Needs 1968–1978," from the President's Committee on Urban Housing, *A Decent Home* (Washington, D.C.: Government Printing Office, 1969), Table 1–6, p. 43.

is the economic penalty the nonwhite family must pay for racial discrimination.

Another dramatic illustration is the maternal death rate. Although it has decreased greatly for all women in the past quarter century, in 1940 the rate was more than twice as high for nonwhite women than for white; by 1966 it was more than three times higher.[69]

Another illustration of relative deprivation is the fact that in 1966, 50.4 percent of the nonwhite children under 18 were poor, compared with 12.3 percent of the white children. It should be borne in mind, however, that the

[69] *Statistical Abstract of the United States, 1968,* U.S. Bureau of the Census (Washington, D.C.: Government Printing Office, 1968), p. 55.

number of poor white children (7.3 million) is still greater than the number of poor nonwhite children (5.2 million).[70]

The most dramatic indication of the gap between Negro aspirations and access to opportunities is their educational and occupational advance relative to whites. It is estimated that they lag about fifty years behind and that existing discrepancies are ". . . so great that the prospects of substantial equality during the present century are not particularly promising." [71]

Practically all of the net growth in nonfarm employment during the 1950s among white men occurred at the skilled level or above, while among Negro men only two-fifths of equivalent growth occurred in the skilled or white-collar occupations.[72] The 1967 studies by the Equal Employment Opportunity Commission reveal still more recently a bleak picture of Negro employment in nine major metropolitan areas. Negroes occupied 2.1 percent of the white-collar jobs in Kansas City and 8.4 percent of such jobs in Washington. In Cleveland, where blacks make up 13 percent of the population of the metropolitan area, they hold 3.2 percent of the white-collar jobs. In Los Angeles, Negroes make up 7.6 percent of the population but hold 2.8 percent of the white-collar jobs.[73] Such discrepancies in occupational advantage, which reflect differences in education, job skills, and opportunities, are likely to continue for the next half century. That is a long time for those whose quest is "freedom now." Since work is the major avenue for participation in society, relative deprivation in access to those jobs that provide security, achievement, and self-respect is likely to be a continuing source of tension and conflict. Nevertheless significant gains have been made by Negroes. From 1961–1968 total Negro employment increased about 20 percent; white employment rose 15 percent. In 1967, for the first time, substantially more than half of all nonwhite workers were employed in white-collar, craftsman, and semiskilled occupations.[74]

Social order in democratic, advanced industrial systems is dependent on (1) cooperative interdependence, (2) democratic ethic, and (3) the existence of nation-states prepared to adjudicate conflict and equalize opportunities.[75] Cooperative effort is provided through the division of labor with its functional interdependence, thus pointing up the central importance of adequate employment opportunities. Carried beyond a certain point, of course, such efforts may produce a reaction from those threatened by loss of valued advantages. However, nation-states that adjudicate conflict and equalize benefits and opportunities through fiscal and social welfare measures serve to relieve the pressures that underlie the feelings of relative deprivation.

[70] *Ibid.*, p. 329.

[71] Dale I. Hiestand, *Economic Growth and Employment Opportunities for Minorities* (New York: Columbia University Press, 1964), p. 57.

[72] Hiestand, *op. cit.*

[73] *New York Times,* August 7, 1967.

[74] *Manpower Report of the President,* U.S. Department of Labor (Washington, D.C.: Government Printing Office, 1969), pp. 39, 193.

[75] Katz and Kahn, *op. cit.,* p. 467. A serious omission here is the role of power. See Ralf Dahrendorf, *Class and Class Conflict in Industrial Society* (Stanford, Calif.: Stanford University Press, 1959).

These components of social order replace the collective sentiments that provided the moral integration of preindustrial societies, as Durkheim informed us. More than anything, as he wrote, order must be attained through social justice:

> What we must do to relieve this anomy is to discover the means for making the organs which are still wasting themselves in discordant movements harmoniously concur by introducing into their relations more justice by more and more extenuating the external inequalities which are the source of the evil.[76]

In the United States we tend to define problems of social order as individual deviations requiring repression or rehabilitation. Thus we resort to a mixture of police power and residual social services, seeking to control or "cool out" discontent. Issues of social justice are concealed through an ideology of individual success and failure. Such issues are increasingly being violently placed on the public agenda and must be dealt with through methods of social reform that get at underlying grievances. The quest for social justice, however, is a continuing one, providing a constant dynamic for social change as conflicts are generated around new definitions of an equitable and legitimate distribution of universal scarcities.

The conflict of contending interest groups may be a major dynamic of change, one largely ignored in the American perspective that places so much emphasis on democratic consensus, individualism, and the myth of the melting pot. A consensus view of society deflects attention from the reality of the continuing conflict of interests. The ideology of individualism conceals the degree to which position, privilege, and power are distributed on the basis of one's group membership, while the melting pot assumption hides the extent to which we continue to be a plural society of racial and ethnic groups with strong identifications and loyalties:

> Given America's unprecedented ethnic pluralism, simply being born American conferred no automatic and equal citizenship in the eyes of the larger society. In the face of such reservations, ethnic minorities had constantly to affirm their Americanism through a kind of patriotic ritual which intensified the ethnic competition for status. . . . America's tightened consensus on what properly constituted "Americanism" prompted status rivalries among the ethnic minorities which, when combined with economic rivalries, invited severe and abiding conflict.[77]

These subgroup identifications and loyalties stimulate intergroup conflict and consequent changes as some accommodation is made to such contending forces. Conflict seems to be inherent in the human condition and in the nature of social systems. It may be dealt with creatively or otherwise, but it cannot be

[76] Simpson, *op. cit.*, p. 409.

[77] Hugh Davis Graham and Ted Robert Gurr, *Violence in America.* A Report to the National Commission on the Causes and Prevention of Violence (Washington, D.C.: Government Printing Office, 1969), Vol. II, p. 625.

eliminated. In Freud's view, "Human relations are seen in terms of clashing intentions, which society at best can regulate but can never suppress." [78]

Conflict may exist between individuals, between an individual and society, between groups within a system, and, as any news headline will testify, between nations. The more open a society, the greater the opportunities for overt conflict, but also the more likelihood that this may lead to further integration and adaptive change. The more democratic a society, the more tolerant it is of social conflict and the more prepared it is to institutionalize mechanisms for its expression and adjudication. Ralf Dahrendorf has suggested, in fact, that the essential difference between free and totalitarian systems is the difference in attitude toward social conflict, a difference that may characterize not only nations but also institutions within a society.[79] Though our society is ridden with conflict, most Americans are ill-prepared to understand and accept it or to cope with it in ways that maximize the values of a free and pluralistic society. Herbert J. Gans makes this clear in his study of a largely middle-class suburb. He writes:

> Like the rest of the country, Levittown is beset with conflict: class conflict between the lower-middle class groups and the smaller working and upper-middle class groups; generational conflict between adults, children, adolescents, and the elderly.[80]

It is not the existence of conflict that poses a problem but the inability of Levittowners to accept it as inevitable and to deal creatively with it. Gans writes, "Insisting that a consensus is possible, they only exacerbate the conflict, for each group demands that the other conform to its values and accept its priorities." In part, conflict is mishandled because people continue to perceive a greater scarcity of resources than is actually the case: "Since resources are not so scarce, however, the classes and age groups could resolve their conflicts more constructively than they do, giving each group at least some of what it wants." Unfortunately so long as ". . . people think that resources are scarce, they act as if they are scarce, and will not pay an extra $20 a year in taxes to implement minority demands." In addition, Gans documents the inability of Levittowners to recognize or accept the pluralism of American society, and consequently they cannot cope with conflict. Instead, when conflict occurs, each group struggles to impose its values in the "ultimate consensus."

It is important to understand what is at stake here for it will help us to see the sense in which people strive to achieve and maintain their definition of moral order and the degree to which their quest for identity and purpose in life underlies the dynamics of change and resistance to it. It is doubtful that major change can occur in society unless people are provided with a new

[78] Sigmund Freud, *The Mind of the Moralist* (New York: Viking Press, 1959), p. 33.

[79] Ralf Dahrendorf, "In Praise of Thrasymachus," The Henry Failing Distinguished Lecture, delivered April 25, 1966, mimeographed (Eugene, Ore.: University Press, 1966).

[80] Herbert Gans, *The Levittowners* (New York: Pantheon Books, 1967), pp. 413–415.

cultural image around which they may fashion a new identity and thus re-direct their energies toward its maintenance and enhancement. This seems supported by the study by Herbert J. Gans.[81]   Gans observes that, when conflict occurs, each group struggles to assure that community institutions reflect its conception of moral order.

> Each group wants to put its cultural stamp on the organizations and institutions that are the community, for otherwise the family and its culture are not safe. In a society in which extended families are unimportant and the nuclear family cannot provide the full panoply of personnel and activities to hold children in the family culture, parents must use community institutions for this purpose, and every portion of the community therefore becomes a battleground for the defense of familial values.[82]

Thus it is common in the United States to think of conflict as inherently destructive while consensus may be regarded as the hallmark of the good society.   A more complex and realistic view suggests that the kind of harmony ". . . best suited to a democratic society . . . comes from many-sided inner tensions, strains, conflicts, and disagreements." [83]   A *cooperative* society and a *consensus* society are not synonymous.   As Irving Louis Horowitz points out, cooperation allows for pluralism because it legitimizes differences, whereas consensus insists on "the principle of unity and unilateral victory."   Further, as he notes, consensus may be the "idealization of coercion," concealing societal repression of vital differences.[84]   According to Lewis Coser, conflict may in fact serve to integrate society, provided that contending parties share the most fundamental values that give legitimacy to the system and provided that the system itself is flexible enough to tolerate conflict and develop ways of adjudicating it so that changes in norms and new accommodations in the balance of power may occur.[85]   Students of social welfare and others interested in social reform are increasingly recognizing the societal functions of conflict. Most important is the notion that conflict may help to structure the large social environment by facilitating social participation.   Organized conflict, as illustrated by the civil rights movement, the black protest, and the action for welfare rights, may reduce social isolation by channeling discontent through associations and coalitions and thus unite diverse groups to press for needed changes.   Negative consequences may also follow if strategy is poorly conceived and if conflict provokes a serious backlash from those threatened by the demand for change.   Needless to say, gains and costs of conflict, as in most things, are not easily determined or equally distributed.

---

[81] For a somewhat similar view *see* Goodenough, *op. cit.,* especially Chap. 9, "Identity Change," pp. 215–251.

[82] Gans, *op. cit.,* p. 414.

[83] Frank Tannenbaum, quoted in Clyde Kluckhohm, *Mirror for Man* (New York: Whittlesey House, 1949), p. 241.

[84] Horowitz, *Professing Sociology, op. cit.,* pp. 6, 16.

[85] Lewis A. Coser, "The Functions of Social Conflict," in Lewis A. Coser and Bernard Rosenberg (eds.), *Sociological Theory: A Book of Readings* (New York: Macmillan, 1957), pp. 199–203.

Conflict and Resolution

Conflict, within certain limits, is vital to a democratic society because it enables people to clarify issues and to support proposals for change. Without conflict, disadvantaged groups are powerless to produce change. One may think of the emancipation of women, not yet fully achieved, as one of the great conflicts that have had radical impact on social structure. It may be that further development of the egalitarian ethic, including equality in personality development, sexual expression, career choice, and freedom from drudgery, will have even further major impact for society. The long and often violent struggle between labor and management produced major accommodations in the allocation of income and power and new mechanisms for the arbitration of conflict, such as the National Labor Relations Board. It might be added that increasing prosperity has accompanied the rise of the labor movement.

In recent years there has been a new effort to organize the poor for various self-help efforts and to produce changes in the structure of public assistance, education, courts, public housing, police, and other community resources. Such efforts recognize the function of conflict, the importance of organizing to effect change, and the value of participation on the part of the poor in efforts to overcome their powerlessness. Results are invariably mixed, having both positive and negative consequences, and little evidence exists for the adequate appraisal of such efforts. Since power accompanies function and since many of the poor are without vital functions in society, it is difficult to effectively organize those who play no important role in the occupational structure. On the other hand some of the poor who have been organized around vital issues regarding quality education, housing, urban renewal, and consumer rights have been able to effect some changes, such as some community control of schools, changes in welfare regulations, and alterations in urban renewal practices. Political organization in a society in which political decisions are increasingly decisive in the distribution of opportunities, is, of course, of central importance.

Social order, then, is dynamic, derived not only from consensus around basic values, but from a continuing accommodation among conflicting interest groups. Hans L. Zetterberg defines the vested-interest group and its import for social change in the following way:

> Persons sharing a common style of life centered on their particular reward pattern form a "vested interest.". . . Their concern with the elaboration and protection of their reward patterns generates much of the dynamics in a society.[86]

Interest groups, however, are not solely concerned with preserving or enhancing their material rewards, prestige, or influence. They may also strive to promote values that they identify with the common good. Some of the motivation for the establishment of middle-class-dominated voluntary social services, however much it may have been in part protective of the interests and values of a particular class, was also in pursuit of some disinterested vision of community well-being. In a democratic plural society, no one group has the right to

---

[86] Hans L. Zetterberg, *Social Theory and Social Practice* (New York: Bedminster Press, 1962), p. 119.

define the common good or to determine what methods shall be used to achieve it. In the social welfare field, the conflict between middle-class control of social agencies and the rising demand on the part of the poor for a consumer control over services is a major dynamic of change.

Conflict reflects differential power to maintain or advance group interests and values. Democratic societies are characterized by a considerable dispersion of power. Yet power tends to be inequitably distributed and to be a continuous source of friction. The redistribution of power is a major goal of social reform movements. While classical liberalism was directed at the abuse of political power, contemporary liberalism is concerned with inequities in economic and social power. The distribution and exercise of power is central to understanding any social system. Changes in the social system occur as a new distribution of power and authority develops out of an accommodation between those who wield the power and those who are subjected to it, those who challenge and resist, for the ". . . dialectics of power and resistance determine the rate and direction of change." [87]

Resistance to social change reflects differences in the power of groups variously located in the social structure to adhere to their preferred social patterns, privileges, and values. Societies may conceal the existence of power and privilege through the use of various myths that give legitimacy to the reward system and justify decisions as being in the public interest. Social welfare philosophy and programs, for example, have developed in disregard of the relationship between economic power and the problems and needs of client groups. Thus to conceive of public assistance as a form of charity for the incompetent and disabled is to conceal inequities in the distribution of income and life chances. Proposals for generous and dignified assistance may be degraded as handouts, while decisions to punish the poor by withholding resources from them are rationalized as measures to promote self-reliance and work incentive.

While conflict among vested-interest groups is part of social reality, so is cooperation among diverse groups for the promotion of the commonweal. Some concept of the common interest must transcend parochial interests if society is to be more than the war of each against all. The determination of what is public interest and what is special advantage requires that differential power be recognized and that institutions be designed to control it ". . . rather than to camouflage it with a harmonizing ideology." [88] On the other hand, perhaps there are limits to which any society can face all the issues that divide it, so that some use of fictions that conceal conflicts and inequities is probably an inevitable device for assuring stability. A democratic and increasingly educated society, however, will find it difficult to be taken in by the platitudes that are meant to pour oil on troubled waters. As knowledge is disseminated and inequities are revealed, conflict is more likely to become overt and pressure for change is more likely to increase. To some degree then, change is the outcome of conflict, while justice never finally attained is ". . . the permanently changing outcome of the dialectics of power and resistance." [89] Efforts to plan

---

[87] Dahrendorf, *In Praise of Thrasymachus, op. cit.*, p. 14.

[88] *Ibid.*, p. 29.

[89] *Ibid.*, p. 31.

social change and to promote social reform invariably must deal with the issue of power in society.

An important source of conflict that leads to change can be found in competing principles of social organization.

COMPETING PRINCIPLES OF SOCIAL ORGANIZATION.   Society may be organized around competing principles.   One principle tends to be dominant while the other, posing a constant challenge, stimulates effort at change.   Of special importance for students of social welfare is Willard Waller's formulation of this idea.   He suggested that attempts to solve social problems were handicapped by a conflict between the organizational and the humanitarian mores. The organizational mores (private property, free market, individualism, limited government, monogamy, Christianity, nationalism) create social problems. This is to say that social problems result from the way we organize our basic social institutions.   Humanitarian ethics require that we take some action to alter the problems that are created by social arrangements.   However, Waller wrote, since humanitarians neither question nor are prepared to alter the basic mores giving rise to problems, their efforts at best are palliative.[90]

Social reform movements have been stimulated by ideals embodied in the culture but have been in conflict with existing social, economic, and political realities.   Whether the changes they have produced have been as limited as Waller suggests may be open to question.   Perhaps the function of the social reformer, as Calvin Woodard has suggested, is not so much to produce change but to enable society to recognize the existence of a new social reality that permits it to aspire to change conditions once accepted as unalterable.[91]   Certainly this is true of poverty in the midst of affluence.   It is true that proposals for reform are more likely to be accepted if they do not threaten the basic mores around which the society is organized or the privileges of those with power to resist, unless accompanied by sufficient power to overcome resistance. Thus compromises tend to be made between self-reliance, for example, and collective responsibility, property and equality, competition, and security.   Such compromises, however, may produce fundamental reforms within the limits set by the social system, as Arthur Schlesinger observed by his comment that social welfare developed out of a largely successful effort to make the "capitalistic system more humane and more democratic."   How humane or democratic such reforms have been must be reassessed in the light of new awareness of poverty and inequality and a new definition of our social obligations that casts a more critical light on the accomplishments of social welfare.   For the most part social welfare has been conservative in an effort to redress the worst abuses of a laissez faire society while seeking to avoid the presumed dangers of socialism.[92]

The dominant mores of the society in the nineteenth century and into a good part of the twentieth have been those of a business civilization.

---

[90] Willard Waller, "Social Problems and the Mores," *American Sociological Review,* 2 (December 1936), p. 226.

[91] Calvin Woodard, "Reality and Social Reform: The Transition from Laissez-Faire to the Welfare State," *Yale Law Journal,* 72 (December 1962), p. 287.

[92] Sidney Fine, *Laissez-Faire and the General-Welfare State* (Ann Arbor, Mich.: University Press, 1964), p. 376.

Such a statement conceals, of course, the complex shifting and conflicting value system that has tended to characterize American society. The observation by President Coolidge that "the business of America is business, but the chief ideal of the American people is idealism" suggests something of the contradictions often noted in American life. Nonetheless, society has been largely organized around economic activity. Rewards have been tied to functions in the market system and power has been concentrated in the corporate elite, though it has been increasingly shared with others and regulated by government. Perhaps most important is the fact that

> . . . the major decisions affecting the day-to-day life of the citizen—the kinds of work available, the location of plants, investment decisions on new products, the distribution of tax burdens, occupational mobility— have been made by business, and latterly by government, which gives major priority to the welfare of business.[93]

It is the opinion of Robert Heilbroner that, despite important changes that have occurred through the increased power of labor and government, social welfare measures, and the rise of a scientific and professional elite, this is still a business civilization. Without serious intellectual opposition to business power and privilege, and without serious alternatives to business ideology, future social policy, he thinks, will be restricted by the more liberal yet still basically conservative business establishment philosophy that tends to set the limits of public debate.[94]

He notes, however, that there is an inherent conflict between the principles that underlie our modified market system and the new social functions that must be performed if we are to meet the priority needs of this society. Such new priorities are in the realm of scientific exploration, national power, planned economic growth and stability, conservation and development of physical and human resources, urban redesign, extension of equality and dignity to minority groups and the poor, and a basic improvement in our cultural life.

Social systems change as their basic functions change. A market system effectively solved the problem of production. New functions are linked to the primacy increasingly given to science, technology, education, and planned social development. New social priorities cannot be met through the market mechanism as we have traditionally understood it. While the market will continue in modified form, it may become increasingly subordinated to the needs of a scientifically oriented and educated society. The kinds of decisions made and the principles governing such decisions help determine the character of a society. Decisions oriented toward the maintenance and enhancement of a free market system are in some measure opposed to those that must be made to develop an educated, scientifically based, and socially planned society. Daniel Bell puts it in the following way:

> To say that the major institutions of the new society will be intellectual is to say that production and business decisions will be subordinated to, or

---

[93] Bell, (I), *op. cit.*, p. 30.

[94] Robert L. Heilbroner, *The Limits of American Capitalism* (New York: Harper & Row, 1965), pp. 55, 58–59.

will derive from, other forces in society; that the crucial decisions regarding the growth of the economy and its balance will come from governments, but that they will be based on the government's sponsorship of research and development, of cost-effectiveness and cost-benefit analysis; that the making of decisions, because of the intricately linked nature of their consequences, will have an increasingly technical character.   The husbanding of talent and the spread of educational and intellectual institutions will become a prime concern for the society; not only the best talents, but eventually the entire complex of social prestige and social status, will be rooted in the intellectual and scientific communities.[95]

Thus the principles that underlie a business society and the imperatives of the new social system that seems to be developing are to some degree in conflict.   Society's commitment to technological development and to the democratic ethic conflicts with its remaining adherence to laissez faire and free enterprise.   Technology is disruptive.   The social and human costs of the change it creates require social intervention.   It can be anticipated that the competing principles that allocate resources on the basis of the market and those oriented toward social needs in a scientific, technologically driven, educated, and increasingly welfare-oriented society will provide the dynamic for some of the major changes that are likely to occur.   As Daniel Bell observes, we may move increasingly toward a communal society in which social rights determine the allocation of rewards as disadvantaged groups acquire political power to protect themselves from the hazards and inequities of the market, much as farmers and organized labor were able to use the political process in their behalf.[96]   Thus the principle of common citizenship and social rights is an increasingly powerful force in American society, but it conflicts with the more powerful principle of class inequality rooted in the business civilization.

T. H. Marshall has observed that, in the twentieth century, citizenship and the capitalist class system have been at war.[97]   The opposing principles of class inequality and equality of citizenship are conflicting, and yet in some measure they are complementary.   These competing principles account for change and stability since they permit compromises consistent with an ideal of social justice and yet make possible legitimate differentiation of rewards functional for maintaining incentive and for distributing power.   Citizenship is the status of full membership in society, with entitlements to all rights and duties of membership, to equality of opportunity that challenges all hereditary privileges, and to an equitable share in the social heritage.   Inequalities can be tolerated in an egalitarian society provided they are regarded as legitimate and are not sources of intense dissatisfaction.[98]

At this juncture in our history, however, we seem to be caught in a particularly intense conflict between these opposing principles, for existing inequalities are increasingly defined as illegitimate by those relatively outside the system of rewards.   Their demand for fuller membership in society is resisted

[95] Bell, (I), *op. cit.*, p. 30.

[96] Bell, (I) *op. cit.*, p. 34.

[97] Marshall, *op. cit.*, p. 93.

[98] *Ibid.*, pp. 94, 127.

by various groups who seek to protect whatever security and advantages class inequalities provide. The clash between the claims of equality of citizenship justified on the basis of a democratic ethic conflicts with the strongly felt claims of inequality justified on the ethic of individual effort and achievement. The outcome of this tension will help determine the shape of this society and the possibilities of social reform. The preservation of social-class values and the self-image organized around such values accounts for much of the resistance to proposed reforms. This can be, in one way, illustrated by reactions to a proposal to place low-cost homes in the "good" neighborhoods of Stamford, Connecticut, which produced some of the following reactions.[99]

> The city's trying to take away the things the good working people have fought a lifetime to achieve. . . . May God now assist us in our struggle.
>
> I used to live in that central city neighborhood that these people are coming from . . . I didn't like it, but I was poor. So I worked, I worked hard, and I pulled myself out of it. Now I haven't got much, but I'm O.K. and so the Mayor wants to take away what I've given my life's work to.
>
> They'll put the low-class unemployed, those noisy welfare cases in my back yard, but you don't see them up north (i.e. north of the Merritt Parkway—the elegant portion of Stamford)—and you know why? Because that's where the powerful people live. And they don't want it.

Most threatened are upper-working-class and lower-middle-class whites, whose antagonism toward the poor is intimately associated with questions of social status and prized self-image. Adam Walinsky has suggested, as long as identity is so intimately related to one's social class position there are absolute limits to overcoming poverty and redressing inequities.[100] Self-enhancement, he suggests, requires that visible distinctions be retained, for ". . . the middle-class is defined largely by the fact that the poor exist." Minor improvements in the opportunity structure are supported because they ". . . reaffirm the existence of the depressed who need help and serve as further 'proof' that their inferior position is the result of inherent inferiority." [101] Here we have a contemporary version of William Blake's reminder that

> Pity would be no more
> If we did not make somebody Poor;
> And Mercy no more could be
> If all were happy as we.

Adam Walinsky suggests that the middle class will not support any major effort to raise the status of the poor until such time as they no longer need to cling to their social position as the major claim to self-worth. Only a new life

[99] *New York Times*, September 15, 1966.

[100] Adam Walinsky, "Keeping the Poor in Their Place: Notes on the Importance of Being One-Up," in Arthur B. Shostak and William Gomberg (eds.), *New Perspectives on Poverty* (Englewood Cliffs, N.J.: Prentice-Hall, 1965), pp. 159–168.

[101] *Ibid.*, pp. 160–161.

style capable of offering the middle class other criteria for self-esteem will overcome the resistance to reducing the distinction between those who have made it and those who have failed.   Thus, in keeping with our earlier point, it is dignity, self-respect, and a sense of personal significance that people are striving for, on whatever terms society makes them available, which may well account for change and resistance to change.   Resistance by the more affluent to giving up advantages and the challenge by the underclass to such inequality stem from the common wish to preserve or enhance identity, however narrowly it may be defined.   We agree with Walinsky when he writes that any serious program

> . . . must offer the middle class a new life style in return for the raise in status it would give the poor; it must deal not only (or even primarily) with pockets of economic poverty, but with the poverty of satisfaction, purpose, and dignity that afflicts us all.[102]

This is not to say that relative deprivation cannot be mitigated or that more equal opportunity for occupational mobility is not possible.   Planned economic growth that expands the annual increment in the GNP allows for reducing inequities without depriving anyone of current levels of living.   Improved education, elimination of artificial credentials, expansion of higher-quality on-the-job training programs, and creation of new forms of work are all possible and can make some significant impact on structured inequality.   None of these can touch the ultimately more significant problems of life goals and life styles that are the crucial ingredients in any definition of well-being.   No program, of course, can accomplish this.   No social planner should determine for others what their life styles ought to be.   As we attempt to direct social change toward some defined goal, however, it is well to be aware of some possible limitations in goals we may take for granted and ask instead how we can maximize freedom of choice to select satisfying life styles consistent with some essential degree of social order.   How much tolerance for varying life styles is possible in the existing structure is open to question.   The changes taking place, however, may offer opportunities for a wider acceptance of cultural pluralism, for the fullness of opportunity we have referred to, and for the development of life goals more consistent with an individual's potentials and perceptions of life's possibilities.   We shall return to this question.

We may sum up our discussion of change by noting that the basic sources of change are to be found in human aspirations as they are culturally defined as men strive to attain some ideal version of life goals to meet their own needs for self-enhancement and symbolic meaning; these ideals invariably conflict, requiring some accommodation, usually determined by the relative power of competing groups to uphold their moral view of the world and maintain any advantages that may accrue from that view.   In this sense man is the source of change, but the social system in which he is embedded influences the direction of his aspirations.   Most of all the system provides the ". . . conceptual model which the members of that social order are continually trying to attain in living, are always revising and improving, testing its adequacy by its failure to

---

[102] *Ibid.,* p. 168.

exhibit the desired qualities." [103] Thus our individual lives and the operation of social systems are goal directed, but the quality of life is determined by the quality of our goals and the relative freedom with which we may choose them. It is possible that it is the quality of the goals of this society that is at the root of many of our difficulties and the lack of freedom in the choice of those goals we might prefer if real alternatives were available. It is possible that ". . . advances in a social order . . . occur when the members of that group accept a new or different model which they attempt to realize in daily living. . . ." [104]

[103] Lawrence K. Frank, "Research For What?," *Journal of Social Issues,* Supplement Series No. 10, 1957, Kurt Lewin Memorial Award Issue, p. 20.

[104] *Ibid.*

FOUR

Social Change, Social Costs, and Issues of Freedom and Justice

In the previous chapter we reviewed some ideas about social change and their implications for social welfare. In this chapter we shall examine the link between the social costs of change and the issue of social justice. We explore the urban crisis and define it, in part, as a failure to deal adequately with the human costs of our changing urban-technological system. Attention then is given to the crisis in social welfare, the failure of traditional methods of social intervention, which leads to a consideration of new forms of social welfare more relevant for the era in which we live.

Any society that values freedom and equality must look at the costs of social change, the distribution of these costs, and the consequences that flow from the failure of existing institutions to adapt to meet the needs of the population, in particular those who have the least protection against shifts in technology and altered patterns of community life. There is concealed coercion and concealed inequality in the impact of social change on groups, and varying resources and power to cope with social dislocation. Some groups are offered new opportunities, others are forced into poverty and unemployment; some gain advantages, others bear a disproportionate share of the cost. There would be little point in noting such consequences if they were beyond the control of man. Such consequences, however, result in large measure from the way society is structured, and many of them are subject to social policy. It is common to refer to social problems as the price we pay for social change, but the key issues are who pays the price, whether such costs are necessary, and the extent to which social compensations may more nearly equalize the costs and gains of change.

The observation by Richard Titmuss that the poor bear "part of the social

119

costs of other people's progress,"[1] raises the issue of social justice. Earlier we defined social justice to include the concept of compensation for losses and injuries for which one cannot be held personally responsible. In significant ways this society has acted on this concept: first in compensating for damage to property rights; later and less adequately, for injuries to human beings. Property is protected, for example, in procedures established to compensate owners when the state exercises the right of eminent domain. Tariff barriers have traditionally protected industries from foreign competition. Individuals are compensated for losses through such measures as workman's compensation legislation, unemployment insurance, and veteran's pensions and benefits. Of special importance is the GI Bill, which helped to promote the upward mobility of returning servicemen following World War II. This vast investment in human resources deserves some special mention. It may be seen as a means of social compensation and as a universal social welfare measure designed to provide supportive resources for a major role transition. It has significance in the light of its great success and our relative failure to design equivalent programs to avoid social dislocations that accompany similar social upheavals such as the rural-urban migration.

The Serviceman's Readjustment Act, or G.I. Bill, was intended to ease the transition from military to civilian life in three major ways: (1) provide financial support for education, (2) ease the purchase of homes, and (3) provide support for those who could not get jobs immediately. More than 11 million veterans have received some form of training under the GI Bill: 4.8 million in below-college schooling, 1.6 million in on-the-job training, 785 thousand in farm training, and over 5.1 million in college. This is almost half of all male college students over the years. The government has spent over $20 billion in direct benefits for education under the provisions of the GI Bill. Over the twenty-five-year period since enactment of the law more than 7.3 million home loans totaling more than $73.6 billion have been guaranteed. About $3.2 billion was collected by servicemen in unemployment allowances. Although this was the subject of much criticism of the kind usually directed at welfare programs, only 10 percent exhausted their full benefits and the amount spent was equal to about one-third of their full entitlement. This provision was dropped in the later bill covering veterans of Korea and Vietnam.

The Veteran's Administration estimates that the taxes on the higher earnings of the college-educated GIs will more than repay the federal investment in their education. General Omar Bradley said, on the quarter-century anniversary of the bill,

> They [veterans] took heart in the knowledge that the nation stood ready to back their civilian chances in making good. . . . [GI Bill] was an investment in human beings. It has paid unparalleled dividends. . . .[2]

Not all social costs that people bear are necessary. Some could be avoided by preventive action, which almost invariably stirs up controversies related to

[1] Richard M. Titmuss, "Social Policy and Economic Progress," *The Social Welfare Forum,* 1966 (New York: Columbia University Press, 1966), p. 33.

[2] (Portland) *Maine Sunday Telegram,* June 22, 1969.

economic cost and the uses of political power.   An illustration of this is the discovery that some 70,000 coal miners in this country are suffering from miners' pneumoconiosis, or black lung disease, a disabling and frequently fatal condition that is not reversible in advanced stages.[3]   The disease results from coal dust that could in large measure be controlled, but at a considerable cost to mine operators.   Death due to mine accidents, many of them preventable, has also been a cost borne by coal miners.   Over 100,000 miners have died as a result of injuries suffered in coal mines from 1897 to 1956.[4]   Although the number of men employed has declined drastically since 1940, there were 543 fatal injuries in coal mines in 1966.[5]   Harry M. Caudill has documented, in *Night Comes to the Cumberlands,* the social and human costs created by the coal industry, which irresponsibly exploited a region and failed to bear a fair share of fiscal responsibility for its own ravages or for the support of essential community resources.[6]   This illustrates the concept of diseconomies, that is, the economic and other costs created by private industry but borne by the public or some portion of it.   Environmental pollution, unemployment, and technological displacement are some others.   Needless to say these are costs that accompany gains on which the society in general places value, but the issue here is the equitable distribution of such costs and gains.

As we have noted, social devices may compensate for at least part of the costs of changing technology and of the operation of the industrial system through such measures as workman's compensation and unemployment compensation.   About one-fifth of the wage and salary workers, however, are without protection from industrial accidents and health hazards, and only thirty-two states cover all occupational diseases.   Only two states, Alabama and Pennsylvania, provided workmen's compensation for black lung disease in 1967.   Average benefits in unemployment insurance pay less than half the wage lost; farm labor is not protected, and much of the burden of technological change that adds up to economic gain for the majority has been borne by the poor and minority groups.   This is dramatically and poignantly illustrated by the plight of technologically displaced agricultural workers, a disproportionate number of whom are Negro, crowded into the ghettos of the inner cities of the North and West.

The migration from farm to metropolis, and the resulting pile-up of problems, failed to register on our social consciousness until it reached crisis proportions. A dramatic aspect of the larger agricultural revolution is the fact that the index of farm output per man hour increased from 36 in 1940 to 167 in 1967.   A

---

[3] *New York Times,* March 6, 1966; June 17, 1967; May 17, 1968.

[4] *Historical Statistics of the United States, Colonial Times to 1957,* U.S. Bureau of the Census (Washington, D.C.: Government Printing Office, 1960), p. 372.

[5] *Statistical Abstract of the United States: 1968,* U.S. Bureau of the Census (Washington, D.C.: Government Printing Office, 1968), p. 673.

[6] It might be noted that there have been recent efforts on the part of some coal-mine operators to lobby for stringent safety regulations, illustrating a point we made earlier about the relationship between self-interest and humanitarian reform.   It appears that an effort to rationalize mine operations and to avoid the inefficiency resulting from wildcat strikes in protest against mine conditions are the forces behind this political move on the part of major oil concerns, who now control a significant portion of the mining industry. (*The New York Times,* June 22, 1969.)

half century ago, about one-fourth of the labor force was employed in agriculture. In 1968 this was true of less than 5 percent. Only about 5 percent of the population still reside on farms. Since 1950 there has been a decline of over 4 million jobs in farm employment. This agricultural revolution has in particular affected the southern Negro, pushed off the land and pulled to the urban North and West by the promise of economic opportunity. In 1910 four out of five Negroes lived in rural areas of the South. By 1960 almost three out of four were living in cities.[7] Two-thirds of adult Negroes living in northern cities in that year were born in the South. During the early 1960s alone, there was an estimated annual net migration of 816,000 people from the Mississippi Delta and other areas. Many of these were Negro farm families.[8] Nowhere were appropriate measures designed to facilitate this social transition.

One should not assume that Negroes were necessarily better off before changing technology forced them off the land. Herman P. Miller observes that

> So long as Negroes lived in rural southern hamlets it did not seem to matter how their lives were wasted. Even the statisticians in the Census Bureau did not count them as unemployed since they were ostensibly farming.[9]

Many were attracted to the cities by jobs created during World War II. In the late 1950s and early 1960s technological change destroyed some jobs of the semiskilled. Lagging economic growth and the passive policy of the Eisenhower administration, plus the growth of the labor force, produced average rates of unemployment of over 5 percent and at least twice that for Negroes. The human cost of high unemployment in the decade 1954–1964 is yet to be determined, but one can be reasonably sure of two things; it was considerable, and it was largely avoidable because government policy could have prevented a rise in unemployment by monetary and fiscal policy, as the 1964 tax cut by the Kennedy administration clearly revealed.[10] The urban migration continued in the 1960s. In this decade alone, an estimated million farmers will have moved to the cities—a majority, whether white or black, without the education, skills, and other resources with which to adapt to an entirely new environment. Nowhere do communities adequately share the cost of this great transition, and hardly anywhere is there sufficient awareness of the importance of investing ample resources in the new arrival to enable him and his family to gain a firm foothold in the urban society.

[7] Figures from *Statistical Abstract,* 1968, *op. cit.*

[8] Earl E. Huyck, "White-Non-white Differentials: Overview and Implications," *Demography,* 3 (1966), p. 551.

[9] Herman P. Miller, *Rich Man, Poor Man* (New York: Signet Books, 1965), pp. 211–212.

[10] *Technology and the American Economy,* National Commission on Technology, Automation, and Economic Progress (Washington, D.C.: Government Printing Office, 1966), p. 15. Leon Keyserling points out that this was not the most equitable or the most economically efficient way to stimulate economic growth; nevertheless it demonstrated the government's ability to exercise some control over the economy. *See* Keyserling in Bertram M. Gross (ed.), *Social Intelligence for America's Future* (Boston: Allyn & Bacon, 1969), p. 342.

This demographic disequilibrium and this failure in social consciousness account for a good portion of the current urban crisis.

Although various manpower programs of the Labor Department and special programs of the Office of Economic Opportunity and the Department of Health, Education, and Welfare were aimed at ghetto youths and the hard-core unemployed in the 1960s, none of these met the mounting crisis in the ghettos.[11] This was partly so because an undue share of the cost of the agricultural revolution was left to fall on former farm workers and their families. While they live with the costs of technological displacement from rural areas and the consequences of social and technological barriers to employment in the cities, other Americans enjoy the benefits of economic progress. The *Report of the National Commission on Technology, Automation, and Economic Progress* takes note of this:

> Because society gains from the flexibility and responsiveness which are the sources of displacement, it is society's responsibility to see that alternative opportunities are available and that blameless individuals do not bear excessive costs.[12]

The report of another commission reminded the nation of "the people left behind" in rural poverty. These are victims of change who are effectively barred from gaining from the expanding industrial economy.[13] Freedom of choice can mean little to people who find themselves living in a world that provides no place for them or resources with which they can adapt to changed circumstances. When resources are provided through such demeaning residual welfare programs as public assistance, they may serve to increase a sense of powerlessness.

One of the costs of change is dependence on welfare. Technological displacement, the increasing rationalization of the economy, and the movement of business and industry to the suburbs are some factors that force people to become welfare recipients. We have already commented on the tendency to ignore society's responsibility in this regard by an insistence on individual responsibility for failure. We shall return to the relationship between dependency and social structure. Here the central point is the need for a continuing assessment of the consequences of social change and the development of social policies to avoid unnecessary hardships and to more nearly equalize gains and costs.[14]

As we noted in Chapter Two, social policy may itself create change and be

[11] Job Corps, Neighborhood Youth Corps, Concentrated Employment Program, Job Opportunities in the Business Sector, Cooperative Area Manpower Planning System, Work Incentive Program, Special Impact Program, Concerted Services Program, Human Resources Development Program, Operation Mainstream, New Careers, Manpower Development and Training, Testing, Information, Discussion and Evaluating Program, Opportunity Line, Opportunities Industrialization Centers, etc.
See Manpower Report of the President, 1968, *op. cit.,* pp. 193–212.

[12] *Technology and the American Economy, op. cit.,* p. 48.

[13] *The People Left Behind,* President's National Advisory Commission on Rural Poverty (Washington, D.C.: Government Printing Office, 1967), pp. ix–xiii, 11–14.

[14] Titmuss, *op. cit.*

responsible for the costs incurred.   This is a consequence of our increasingly managed economy and directed society and introduces the paradox that efforts to solve problems may create other problems.   Costs and gains of urban renewal, for example, are far from being distributed equitably, as noted in that oft quoted phrase "urban renewal becomes Negro removal." [15]   This is documented by the fact that, of the total number of families displaced by urban renewal in the fifteen years ending in 1963, two-thirds of those for whom color was reported were nonwhite.   In fact, urban renewal programs have succeeded in destroying more low-income dwellings than they have managed to create, increasing the difficulty of attaining the goal of a "decent home and suitable environment for every American family."   As of June 30, 1967, approximately 400,000 dwelling units had been demolished in urban renewal areas; the majority of the units were low- or moderate-income housing.   Of the 195,999 dwelling units planned for these same sites, 18,766 (less than 10 percent) will be public housing, and only 10,760 of these public housing units were in existence in June, 1967.   Of the total units planned 62.3 percent will be for middle- and upper-income residents.[16]

The unequally distributed benefits and social costs of the FHA program have already been noted.   Management of the economy to maintain certain given rates of unemployment in efforts to control inflation or to maintain farm prices produced inequities, also noted in Chapter Two.   A society mobilized for the warfare state with major allocations in both economic and human resources directs the lives and fortunes of individuals in ways that reflect the distribution of power in society.   The war in Vietnam has meant a sizable increase in corporate profits after taxes ($38.7 billion in 1964 to $48.3 billion in 1966) and a restriction on resources available for the War on Poverty.   The Vietnam War has meant a greater risk of death on the battlefield for low-income youth.   For Negro youths, the risk of death in Vietnam has been higher than for white servicemen.   While the army in Southeast Asia was 10 percent Negro as of March 31, 1968, the Negro death rate there was 14 percent through April 1968.[17]   There is tragic irony in this distribution of advantages and sacrifices, especially in the remark of a Pentagon official, who, in commenting on the higher death rates of Negro soldiers, stressed that the statistical count was not a reflection of discrimination in battle assignments but ". . . perhaps a measure of Negro valor in combat." [18]

Social change, planned and unplanned, produces accumulated costs, which if unattended may reach crisis proportions.

[15] Harold Wilensky points out that while urban renewal means "Negro removal" it does increase the tax base of cities.   Harold Wilensky and Charles N. Lebeaux, *Industrial Society and Social Welfare* (New York: Free Press, 1965), p. xxiii *n*.

[16] *Building the American City,* National Commission on Urban Problems, 91st Congress, 1st sess., House Document 34 (Washington, D.C.: Government Printing Office, 1968), p. 163.

[17] "Recent Trends in Social and Economic Conditions of Negroes in the United States," *Current Population Reports,* Series P–23, No. 26, U.S. Bureau of the Census, and Bureau of Labor Statistics Report No. 347 (Washington, D.C.: Government Printing Office, 1968), p. 28.

[18] *The New York Times,* March 10, 1968.

Urban Crisis

The urban crisis is a challenge to the social system, a test of its capacity to hear, understand, and respond to danger signals. It may be seen, in part, as a result of past failures to deal with the accumulated human costs of industrialization and urbanization and to recognize and deal adequately with the unequal distribution of advantages and disadvantages associated with technological change. It results from our single-minded devotion to the goals of economic growth and national power, with too little critical scrutiny of such goals and too little attention to the processes by which a society must maintain the motivation and commitment of its citizens to a democratic social order. It reflects a possible breakdown of the social order itself in its apparent incapacity to effectively deal with the problems it has identified in many voluminous reports of scholars and presidential commissions.[19] This crisis casts a critical light on traditional modes of social intervention, creates a corresponding crisis in the field of social welfare, and prompts professionals, politicians, and consumers of services to challenge existing structures and to seek new ways to meet human needs. Such efforts invariably reflect conflicting ideologies, so that the urban crisis puts to test the moral ideals of this nation.

One may view the urban crisis as a state of mind as well as a set of interrelated social problems and political issues that are dramatically enacted in the cities but that are of national and even international scope and significance. As a state of mind, it reflects the perception of many students and critics that our cities are in serious trouble. As Charles Abrams put it in a review of four books on American cities, one is left ". . . with the sad feeling that the richest nation now has the poorest cities—poor in aspect, poor in prospect, and poor in purse."[20] To members of the Urban Coalition, who include large-city mayors and leaders in business, labor, religion, education, and civil rights, our "sick" cities require massive federal aid and a reordering of national priorities to make possible action commensurate with the urgent problems.[21] The majority of Americans, however, whose lives may seem more comfortable and promising than ever, may feel no great sense of urgency about saving the cities; this is especially so since an increasing number have fled to the suburbs. In 1968 only about one-fourth of the white population lived in the central cities, compared to 55 percent of the Negroes. If the majority of Americans sense any crisis at all, they tend to perceive it primarily as a breakdown of law and order.[22] Their political preferences for dealing with the urban unrest do not necessarily agree with the prescriptions of professionals and others who tend to see a need to deal with fundamental grievances in a way that may require some basic alterations in economic, social, and political institutions. Needless to say professionals disagree on the nature and cure of urban ills. In the final analysis the problems of the cities turn out to be national problems, inseparable from the total fabric of society. Political decisions will determine the action we take, and this will

---

[19] *See* Chapter Two, p. 35.

[20] Charles Abrams, *The New York Times Book Review,* July 16, 1967, p. 21.

[21] *The New York Times,* August 2, 1967.

[22] James Q. Wilson, "The Urban Unease: Community vs. City," *The Public Interest,* No. 12 (Summer 1968), pp. 25–26.

depend primarily on how Congress perceives the urban crisis and the sense of urgency it feels.[23] Prescriptions for the urban unrest seem increasingly and all too simple to polarize between proponents of law and order versus supporters of basic reforms, with serious consequences for the entire body politic.

It is evident that cities have serious problems. When the President's National Commission on Urban Problems reports that ". . . after our inspections, hearings and research studies, we found conditions much worse, more widespread and more explosive than any of us had thought" they confirm signals, violent and otherwise, that communicate the same urgent message.[24] The heightening crisis may be said to consist of a number of interrelated problems. Cities are in a financial crisis; they are without adequate structures for carrying out the functions of governing and managing the increasingly large, complex, and interdependent urban environment; they face the explosiveness of poverty and racism in a period of a human rights revolution; and they cannot deal adequately with problems of order, crime, riots, and student unrest. Perhaps one should add that the most serious problem of all may involve a spiritual crisis, "a sense of boredom and thinness of self," the protest against the rationalization of life and the lack of community.[25]

Cities are without sufficient resources to provide adequate education, medical care, welfare, and police protection or to carry out other expanding functions of local government. The flight of the middle class to the suburbs deprives the central cities of essential tax resources to meet the needs and rising demands of the remaining population, an increasing proportion of whom are black. There are some indications that, prior to 1960, the major motivation for movement to the suburbs was the attraction of better housing, space, and freedom from congestion. By 1966 the primary motives may have been fear of racial integration, race and class conflict, the wish to escape civil disorder, crime, conflict over community control of schools, and the increasing cost of welfare and other municipal expenditures. In the years 1960–1968, the number of whites in central cities declined from 47.5 million to 46.1 million, while nonwhites increased in number from 10.3 to 13.5 million.[26] The 1970 statistics will provide a more accurate picture of these trends, but predictions are that central cities will increasingly be black, surrounded by a noose of white suburbs. This ignores the

[23] Martin Nolan observed that "If Congress really believed there is an urban crisis, it would have responded as it did in the last national "crisis," the uproar following Sputnik in 1957. Congress established the National Aeronautics and Space Administration and created House and Senate committees to deal with it. NASA's budget rose to $5 billion and spawned a major aerospace market. HUD's budget is considerably smaller and problems of housing and urban affairs are still concealed within subcommittees to committees on Banking and Currency. Thus Congress tends to treat housing and urban affairs as an appendage to economics." Martin Nolan, "A Belated Effort to Save Our Cities," *The Reporter,* December 28, 1967.

[24] *Building the American City, op. cit.,* p. 30.

[25] Donald Michael, *The Next Generation* (New York: Vintage Books, 1965), p. 41; John Dyckman, "Some Conditions of Civic Order in an Urbanized World," *Daedalus,* 95 (Summer 1966).

[26] *A Decent Home,* President's Committee on Urban Housing (Washington, D.C.: Government Printing Office, 1969), p. 40.

fact that much of the flight is class related rather than purely racial, since indications are that some middle-class Negroes may share the same desires and the same reasons to move to the suburbs. The flight to the suburbs not only deprives central cities of desperately needed financial resources, but the wish to escape the critical problems of the cities depletes the moral and political commitment to essential action. John W. Gardner, former Chairman of the Urban Coalition speaks of the "irresponsibility of the middle class":

> Here is a class that has been done pretty well by in economic terms. But typically they are not doing much to make this a thriving society. They get out to the suburbs and they don't give a damn what happens. They're not citizens anymore in a Periclean sense. They're not responsible members of a city in a civic sense. They conceive of the city's problems as something you can run away from. But there just isn't a far enough place to run.[27]

Mr. Gardner would probably be the first to admit he is not speaking of the entire middle class and that the wish to escape the problems of the city represents something more than simple irresponsibility. It may reflect a positive quest, however narrowly conceived, to maintain or achieve some stability and order and to find those conditions that allow for the pursuit of life goals. As one middle-class resident put it, "I want to live a decent life, send my kids to a decent school and give them a chance to grow up to become decent adults." The irony is that these are the similar goals of the deprived and disadvantaged, whose militant demands for equal life opportunities are in part responsible for the flight to the suburbs. A society that has traditionally conceived of individual pursuit of life goals, without equal emphasis on preservation and enhancement of a sense of community, is ill prepared to recognize or accept the degree to which the law of reciprocity governs the probability that anyone can achieve his ends without regard for his fellow-man. In this sense we have never had the Periclean ideal of civic responsibility.

Part of the urban crisis stems from the inability of local governments to deal with metropolitan and regional problems. We are becoming increasingly megalopolized. Three-fourths of our population by 1980 will be living within metropolitan areas, the boundaries of which in no way conform to traditional political units. We deal with critical ecological and social problems that are ". . . incapable of adequate solution within the constraints of arbitrary political boundaries of city and state."[28] The New York metropolitan region, for example, includes 6,900 square miles, 22 counties in the states of New York, New Jersey, and Connecticut, and over 16 million people, with employment opportunities concentrated in jobs affected by national markets.[29] The proper management of cities in order to control traffic and environmental pollution and to humanize

[27] *New York Times,* June 7, 1969.

[28] Michael, *op. cit.,* p. 47.

[29] Benjamin Chinitz, "New York: A Metropolitan Region," *Scientific American,* 213 (September 1965), pp. 134–148. Robert M. MacIver observes that this is the key international problem. National political boundaries in no way accord with social and economic interdependence, as each country becomes more bound up with the welfare of each. *Politics and Society* (New York: Atherton Press, 1969).

the urban environment involves complex questions of appropriate political structures, zoning, code enforcement, taxation and financing, and planned land use.
A central issue has to do with the possibilities of social planning in the interest
of redirecting cities toward their historic function ". . . as centers of community, civility, and culture." [30]   But this conflicts with our present concept of the
city as an arena for private real-estate speculation and as the medium for promoting values associated with the self-regulating market.

When President Johnson declared that the ". . . city is not an assembly of
shops and buildings. . . . It is a community for the enrichment of the life of
man," and adds, ". . . Our task is to put the highest concerns for our people at
the center of urban growth and activity," he expresses a noble aspiration. [31]
What he is not free to point out is the extent to which the concept of the city as
an economic efficiency system that has successfully organized economic activity,
despite all the social and human costs, conflicts with the notion of the city beau-
tiful, dedicated to ends other than the market place. [32]   Here the humanistic concept of the city conflicts with the organizational mores of private profit and technological efficiency.   Nor is he free to outline the vested interests that would
have to be overcome in order to alter the basic function of the city as we conceive of it.   This may be illustrated by the different experience in Stockholm,
Sweden, where a city planning office has existed since 1640.   The ability to plan
in Stockholm is attributed to one all-important factor—public ownership of
land. [33]   Finally, there is no evidence that most Americans really wish to fundamentally alter cities even if this could be accomplished without excessive costs.
In fact:

> . . . there is a great deal of evidence to indicate that most of the models
> of improvement proposed for the American city are nothing more than
> projections of the desires of certain articulate minorities. . . .   Traffic
> jams and urban sprawl are not high on the agenda of complaints of
> American people—because those are not great problems to most of the
> people who are defined as "urban dwellers" in the United States today. [34]

It is possible that the pressure of accumulated social and human costs, particularly those related to poverty and race, may force at least some redirection
of priorities and values.   The problems of poverty and race are at the heart of
the urban crisis.   While the majority of the poor are white, almost all major
social problems today have racial overtones, partly because Negroes and other

[30] Herbert J. Muller, *Freedom in the Modern World* (New York: Harper & Row,
1966), p. 66.

[31] "Problems and Future of the Central City and its Suburbs," Message from the
President of the United States to the House of Representatives, 89th Congress,
March 2, 1965; House Document No. 99.

[32] Dyckman, *op. cit.*

[33] Goran Sidenbladh, "Stockholm: A Planned City," *Scientific American,* Vol.
213 (September 1965), p. 107.

[34] Daniel J. Elazar, "Are We a Nation of Cities?," *The Public Interest,* No. 4
(Summer 1966), p. 46.

minorities bear a disproportionate share of the conditions we define as social problems, partly because whites tend to perceive problems in terms of race when in fact they are economic, social, and political.

Part of the heavy financial burden on cities is the rising cost of welfare. Although they remain at about 12 percent of the total costs, local (excluding state) expenditures for public assistance increased from $451 million in 1960 [35] to $1.4 billion in 1968.[36] The burden of the increases fall principally on our central cities. This increasingly becomes a political and racial issue because of the resentment over higher taxes and because people prefer to believe that the characteristics assigned to minority groups account for the problem.

The number of blacks who are forced to depend on welfare is symptomatic of and interrelated with the fact that Negroes bear an inequitable share of those conditions defined as social problems: unemployment and subemployment, marginal incomes, family disorganization, inadequate housing, education, and other public services, and most of all systematic exclusion from opportunities for self-respect through positively acknowledged and rewarded social participation. As a consequence they figure not only high on the caseloads of public assistance agencies but also represent a disproportionate number of clients of a vast array of residual welfare and correctional programs.

Negro children, as compared with white children, have at least six times the risk of being dependent on public assistance. They are also more likely to be in foster homes and institutions. Although in 1960 nonwhite children under age twenty made up about 13 percent of the child population, they constituted one-fifth of the children in institutional care. Their rates of institutionalization were 6.3 per 1,000 children, compared to 4 per 1,000 for white children—a rate 58 percent higher for nonwhites. In the decade 1950–1960 the white child population increased by 31 percent, and their number in institutions increased by 9 percent. For nonwhite children the corresponding figures were 43 and 69 percent. In correctional institutions, nonwhite children in 1960 accounted for almost one-third of the inmate population, an increase from 1950 of 76 percent compared to a corresponding increase for white children of 11 percent.[37]

Negro rates of first admission to psychiatric hospitalization are ". . . consistently and overwhelmingly higher than white rates for both sexes and for virtually every age group." [38] Although these figures seem to reflect the fact that Negroes suffer the most extreme forms of deprivations and threats, current data indicate that the majority of Americans prefer to believe that Negroes have fairly equal opportunity. For example, according to a recent study 56 percent of the whites interviewed in fifteen major cities felt that the fact that Negroes have worse jobs, education, and housing than whites was mainly due to

[35] *Statistical Abstract, 1968, op. cit.,* p. 298.

[36] U.S. Bureau of the Census, *Statistical Abstract of the United States: 1969* (Washington, D.C.: Government Printing Office, 1969), p. 299.

[37] Seth Low, *America's Children and Youth In Institutions,* U.S. Children's Bureau, Publication 435 (Washington, D.C.: Government Printing Office, 1965), pp. 8–9.

[38] Marc Fried, "Social Problems and Psychopathology," *Urban America and the Planning of Mental Health Services,* Vol. IV, Symposium No. 10 (New York: Group for the Advancement of Psychiatry, November, 1964), pp. 403–446.

Negroes themselves; another 19 percent felt it was due to a mixture of discrimination and to Negroes themselves.[39]

Intense feelings of prejudice become mixed with intense resentment over the cost of welfare payments for Negro families. In a city like New York, where a high proportion of people on welfare are black and Puerto Rican, this is a moral affront to the stable working and middle classes, who ascribe their own preferred status to hard work and self-reliance. Negroes and others reject the stigma of welfare and insist on welfare rights, which increases their visibility and inflames deeply embedded prejudices. Hostility and conflict are thus further aroused. The concept of black power and the struggle for control of major social institutions, like schools, further identifies urban problems with the issue of race.

Whitney Young suggests that the "Negro in America . . . has become the barometer that will predict whether this nation can guarantee the democratic heritage and the good life for the masses of its citizens." He makes the point even more forcibly when he states:

> The most crucial social problem facing the nation today is the problem of the Negro in America. And this does not mean "the Negro problem" per se . . . The problems of crime and delinquency, poverty, dependency, the deterioration of the inner city, the broken family, and unmarried mothers—all of these and others are faced by whites and Negroes alike. But the Negro is in the more exposed position and suffers disproportionately because, in addition to his deprivation, he encounters racial discrimination . . . the degree to which this dilemma is resolved for the Negro will point the way toward resolving it for all citizens.[40]

The tragic irony is that all of this is well known, and yet such knowledge by itself does not necessarily move men to act with greater justice. Facts alone are not persuasive in a society that jealously guards inequality as much as it aspires to equality. In such a society, to mistreat Negroes is acceptable to many, especially since social responsibility is so readily converted into individual moral fault. Delinquency, crime, family breakdown, economic dependency, and riots may be seen by some as justification for further exclusion or repression.

Riots are symptomatic of a general discontent of lower-class Negroes, only a few of whom actively have participated in violence and many of whom have in fact been the direct victims of such disasters. Moreover, in the 1967 Detroit uprising, the violence was not simply racial (if indeed it was anywhere). Some reports were that whites also participated in the sniping, looting, and burning. As one observer put it, "It's really the have-nots of American society saying, 'We're going to have a piece of the American affluence, and if it means rioting, then we'll riot.' "[41] What distinguished the violence of the late 1960s from the

[39] *Supplemental Studies,* National Advisory Commission on Civil Disorders (Washington, D.C.: Government Printing Office, 1968), p. 30.

[40] Whitney M. Young, Jr., "Racial Discrimination," in Nathan E. Cohen (ed.), *Social Work and Social Problems* (New York: National Association of Social Workers, 1964), p. 340.

[41] "The Talk of the Town, Notes and Comments," *The New Yorker,* August 5, 1967, p. 21.

racial conflict that occurred in Detroit in 1943 when Negroes and whites fought each other, as Bayard Rustin observed, is that the attacks in 1967 were on symbols of white power and privilege, namely, police and property.[42] Morris Janowitz views earlier race riots as communal clashes between blacks and whites and describes the 1964–1967 riots as commodity riots because of the widespread looting. He sees, in 1968, the development of a new form—a more selective terroristic use of force by small organized groups of blacks.[43]

It would be a mistake to concentrate on riots as the center of the urban crisis. They represent, to be sure, a danger signal that points to serious imbalances in society that affect not only Negroes but all of us.

The central problem, as the Report of The National Advisory Commission on Civil Disorders tried to make dramatically clear, is that ". . . Our Nation is moving toward two societies, one black, one white—separate and unequal." [44] Most Americans found it difficult to accept the charge that white racism is essentially responsible for the explosive mixture that has accumulated in our cities since the end of World War II.[45] The President of the United States, who had commissioned the report, chose for the most part to ignore its anaylsis of the complex of factors associated with racial discrimination and exclusion and the series of recommendations made to assure ". . . the realization of common opportunities for all within a single society." [46] A one-year follow-up study of the nation's response to the report noted that some important action had taken place, including open-housing legislation and some programs to hire the hardcore unemployed. On the whole however, it found that the nation had ". . . not yet made available to the cities or the blacks themselves the resources to improve the neighborhoods enough to make a significant change in the residents' lives. Nor has it offered those who might want it the alternative of escape." Observing that most of the recommendations of the commission— from reform of the welfare system to assuring employment for everyone who wished it—had yet to be implemented, the study saw a nation closer to the prediction of "two societies." [47] The fact is that two societies have existed for a long time. Racial violence, commission reports, and relative inaction are not new. Dr. Kenneth B. Clark made this clear when he appeared before a recent commission and commented:

> I read that report . . . of the 1919 riot in Chicago and it is as if I were reading the report of the investigating committee on the Harlem riot of '35, the report of the investigating committee on the Harlem riot of '43, the report of the McCone Commission on the Watts riot [1965]. I must

[42] Bayard Rustin, "A Way Out of the Exploding Ghetto," *The New York Times Magazine,* August 11, 1967.

[43] Morris Janowitz, "Patterns of Collective Violence," in Hugh Davis and Ted Robert Gurr (eds.), *Violence in America,* 2 vols., a report to the National Commission on the Causes and Prevention of Violence (Washington, D.C.: Government Printing Office, 1969), Vol. II, pp. 317–340.

[44] *Report,* National Advisory Commission on Civil Disorders Report, *op. cit.,* p. 1.

[45] *Ibid.*

[46] *Ibid.*

[47] *The New York Times,* February 23, 1969.

. . . in candor say to you members of this Commission—it is a kind of Alice in Wonderland—with the same moving picture reshown over and over again, the same analysis, the same recommendations, and the same inaction.[48]

Yet not all things are the same. The Negro is no longer invisible; improvements have occurred, and it is clear that his status will be at the center of efforts at social reform in a way that was never before true. Indeed, according to C. Van Woodward, no reform movement until the 1960s paid serious attention to the Negro. The Progressive Movement of the late nineteenth century either ignored him or contributed to his exploitation, so in that period of liberal and idealistic reform ". . . the Negro's status deteriorated steadily. With Progressive connivance, or permission, or encouragement, Jim Crowism made its most rapid gains. . . ." The record of the New Deal is not impressive, although ". . . some of its reformers made the Negro a special object of concern in welfare programs." Still, ". . . the fundamental approach of the New Deal toward the Negro was paternalistic rather than equalitarian and it easily accommodated itself to white supremacy." [49]

There have been improvements, though far from adequate. In one survey two out of every three Negroes reported that things had improved for them since 1963, especially in schooling, jobs, voting registration, and public accommodations; but housing, especially in northern big-city ghettos, continued to be a sore point.[50] What has also changed is the new self-image of blacks. "A new mood has sprung up among Negroes, particularly among the young, in which self-esteem and enhanced racial pride are replacing apathy and submission to 'the system.' " [51] This may be illustrated by the remark of Mrs. Lela May Brooks of Sunflower, Mississippi, who refused to accept the comment of Senator James Eastland that Negroes were satisfied in his state. "We're not. No sir. No more working $3 day, sun to sun, going home to roaches and rats. They put their tractors in better houses than we live in. Sorry! No! We've been assassinated all along." [52] The new self-image as citizen is increasingly the mood of other minorities and of the poor in general. It can lead to increased frustration and possible violence as long as equal opportunity seems to lag behind aspirations.

The majority—mostly white, comparatively affluent, equipped with education and the social position to command increasing rewards and to seize new opportunities—have a strong stake in the society. The minority poor—two-thirds of

[48] *Report,* National Advisory Commission on Civil Disorders, *op. cit.,* p. 13.

[49] C. Vann Woodward, "Flight from History," in David Boroff (ed.), *The State of the Nation* (Englewood Cliffs, N.J.: Prentice-Hall, 1965), pp. 179–180. It might also be noted what little attention has been paid to questions of race in social welfare literature until relatively recently. For example, in the most scholarly work produced on the history of social welfare [Samuel Mencher, *Poor Law to Poverty Program* (Pittsburgh: University of Pittsburgh Press, 1967], neither the words "Negro" or "race" appear in the index.

[50] *The New York Times,* August 16, 1966, Report of a Louis Harris survey conducted for *Newsweek.*

[51] *Report,* National Advisory Commission on Civil Disorders, *op. cit.,* p. 5.

[52] *Portland* (Maine) *Press Herald,* May 22, 1968.

them white, with a disproportionate number black, Puerto Rican, Indian, and Mexican—are excluded by prejudice, poor education, inadequate job skills, and most of all by the class distribution of power that maintains existing inequities. They confront barriers to participation in the reward system precisely at the moment when they have been led to hope for a more equitable share in the "American Dream." Mass media invite the poor into a society of consumer abundance. The rhetoric of a War on Poverty proclaims an end to deprivation and second-class citizenship. Despite some gains, those at the very bottom of society have experienced little significant improvement in their lot.

Three major social trends contribute to the explosiveness of the deprived inner city in the midst of an affluent metropolitan area: the human rights revolution, the changing character of work and opportunity for work, and the development of a credential society. The human rights revolution demands citizenship status of equal participation in the benefits and obligations of society. It is being most forcefully advanced by blacks and increasingly by Puerto Ricans, Chicanos (Mexican Americans), American Indians, and other ethnic and racial groups. Combined with a revolution of rising expectations and deep resentments about current relative deprivations as well as past injuries, insults, and humiliations, it presents both an unprecedented threat and challenge to American society. Only major and far-reaching efforts to assure full participation in society can hope to deal creatively with this new force in American life.

Changing technology and educational credentials impose barriers to rewarding employment, which is the major means of participating in this society and of achieving the style of consumer living to which an increasing number of Americans aspire.

Technology is altering the character of work although work itself, at least for the foreseeable future, is far from obsolete as some prophets of the automation revolution have predicted. Nor can we anticipate the disappearance of unskilled jobs. Estimates are that between 1964 and 1975 ". . . the overall demand for less-skilled workers will not decrease . . . although it will decline somewhat as a percentage of the total." [53] Over the past fifty years the proportion of factory employment has remained remarkably stable, about a third of the labor force. What is significant is that such jobs have not increased at a rate fast enough to absorb increases in the labor force, particularly in areas with surplus labor. What is more significant is that white-collar jobs are growing at about twice the rate of manufacturing jobs. In 1967 the major employment gains were made by the best-trained and best-paid white-collar workers and skilled craftsmen. Unskilled and semiskilled workers found practically no additional opportunities.[54] As migrants from the rural areas moved into the urban ghettos they found little demand for their labor. While the remainder of the nation enjoyed relatively full employment, the inner city has been characterized by high rates of unemployment and subemployment.

A new statistical measure, the subemployment index, was introduced in

[53] *America's Industrial and Occupational Manpower Requirements 1964–75*, U.S. Department of Labor, Bureau of Labor Statistics (Washington, D.C., Government Printing Office, 1966), p. 3.

[54] *Manpower Report of the President*, U.S. Department of Labor (Washington, D.C.: Government Printing Office, 1968), p. 184.

1967.[55]   It was redefined in 1968 to include only those workers who were unemployed 15 weeks or more during the year and those who earned less than $3,000 for year-round full-time work.[56]   According to this conservative measure, the subemployment rate fell from 17 percent in 1961 to 10 percent in 1967, when it included over 6.8 million low-earners and 2.3 million long-term unemployed.   In 1967 the male subemployment rate for white men was 8 percent, while nonwhite men had a rate of 19 percent, nearly two and a half times as high.[57]   The National Advisory Commission on Civil Disorders calculated the actual number of subemployed nonwhites in disadvantaged areas of all central cities in 1967 to be over one million persons.[58]   Relatively full and economically rewarding employment for the majority obscures the severe problems of unemployment for the poor, particularly the Negro lower class.   In 1967

Table 10.   Unemployment Rates by Sex,
Color, Age, 1957 and 1967

	NONWHITE	WHITE
Males 20 years and over		
1957	7.5	3.2
1967	4.3	2.1
Females 20 years and over		
1957	6.3	3.8
1967	7.1	3.8
Both sexes 16–19 years		
1957	19.1	10.6
1967	26.5	11.0

SOURCE: *Manpower Report of the President,* U.S. Department of Labor (Washington, D.C.: Government Printing Office, 1968), p. 226.

nonwhite workers made up 11 percent of the civilian labor force and represented 21 percent of the unemployed and 23 percent of the long-term unemployed.[59]

There has been little change in these figures since 1957.   Table 10 shows the ratio of nonwhite to white unemployment, indicating that Negroes tend to have twice the unemployment rate of whites, and that, for women, especially for youths of both sexes between 16 and 19, there has been a widening gap in rates of unemployment.   These are, of course, official rates of unemployment and do

[55] The components of the first subemployment index were unemployment, part-time work, subminimum earnings (on a weekly basis), nonparticipation in the labor force (able-bodied adult men only), and undercount of adult men.   In a survey of ten slum areas in 1966, the average rate of subemployment was 34 percent.   *See Manpower Report of the President,* U.S. Department of Labor (Washington, D.C.: Government Printing Office, 1967), pp. 74–76.

[56] *Manpower Report,* 1968, *op. cit.,* pp. 34–36.

[57] *Manpower Report of the President,* U.S. Department of Labor (Washington, D.C.: Government Printing Office, 1969), p. 171.

[58] *Report,* National Advisory Commission on Civil Disorders, *op. cit.,* pp. 126–127.

[59] *Current Population Reports,* Series P–23, No. 24, U.S. Bureau of the Census, and Bureau of Labor Statistics Report No. 332 (Washington, D.C.: Government Printing Office, 1967), p. 37.

not reflect the more severe problems that are revealed in the subemployment index. Until recently we have consistently underestimated the problem of unemployment and subemployment in the poverty areas, rural and urban; we have preferred to focus on overall national rates that reflect general levels of economic well-being while concealing the desperate problems of those excluded from work. For example, nonwhite workers are twice as likely as white workers to be not only unemployed but also to be among the long-term unemployed.[60] The difficulty has been not so much a lack of jobs in the nation as a whole, but a lack of appropriate employment opportunities for ghetto residents, who are often separated from jobs by lack of transportation, racial discrimination, and unavailable credentials. The problem has been particularly severe for Negro teen-agers. From 1960 to 1968 their numbers (in the age group sixteen–nineteen) increased in the inner cities by over 60 percent.[61] Nationally, a fourth of the Negro youths are unemployed, with higher rates of unemployment and subemployment existing in the urban slums. Thus a complex mix of factors—discrimination in employment and housing, poor education and job skills, arbitrary credentials, migration of industry to the suburbs, inadequate mass transportation, failure to develop comprehensive manpower training and placement programs or to create new jobs, plus the rejection by Negroes of menial work that carries the stigma of inferiority—helped to maintain high rates of unemployment and subemployment and to feed ghetto discontent.

Those with qualifications for white-collar jobs have the best opportunities for work that produces income to support the affluent style of life and to assure self-respect and decent status. For blacks the problem is complicated by discrimination. Even when educational credentials are acquired they do not assure equal opportunity. The common assumption that education is the answer to Negro unemployment and subemployment is belied by the following fact: Although at each educational level nonwhite men have less income than white men, the disparity is greatest at the college level (Table 11). The nonwhite male who has attended college earns less than the white who did not complete high school. In central cities between 1959 and 1967 there was no significant narrowing of the income gap between white and Negro men at any level of educational attainment.[62] Upward mobility is further blocked for both the black and white underclass by arbitrary educational credentials that unnecessarily restrict entry into the opportunity system. At the same time, the most rapidly expanding opportunity sector and the most lucrative in terms of lifetime rewards is the area of white-collar employment. Daniel Bell has noted the status upheaval that has occurred as an increasing proportion of the male labor force have become professional, technical, and managerial white-collar workers: from 15 percent in 1900, to 25 percent in 1940, and an estimated 40 percent in 1970.[63] We are moving from a society in which one earns a living to an edu-

[60] *Ibid.*

[61] "Trends in Social and Economic Conditions in Metropolitan Areas," *Current Population Reports,* Series P–23, Special Studies No. 27, U.S. Bureau of the Census (Washington, D.C.: Government Printing Office, 1969), p. 9.

[62] *Current Population Reports,* Series P–23, No. 27, *op. cit.,* p. 26.

[63] Daniel Bell, "Notes on the Post-Industrial Society (1)," *The Public Interest,* No. 6 (Winter 1967), p. 28.

Table 11.   Median Income of Men 25 Years Old and Over,
by Educational Attainment, 1966

	Median Income, 1966		Nonwhite Income as a Percent of White
	NONWHITE	WHITE	
Elementary school—			
Total	$2,632	$3,731	71
Less than 8 years	2,376	2,945	81
8 years	3,681	4,611	80
High school—			
Total	$4,725	$6,736	70
1 to 3 years	4,278	6,189	69
4 years	5,188	7,068	73
College—			
Total	$5,928	$9,023	66

SOURCE: *Current Population Reports*, Series P–23, No. 24, U.S. Bureau of the Census and Bureau of Labor Statistics, Bureau of Labor Statistics Report No. 332, "Social and Economic Conditions of Negroes in the United States" (Washington, D.C.: Government Printing Office, 1967), p. 21.

cated society in which "learning a living" is the mode which involves a capacity to handle and exchange information. Enormous changes will take place in the structure of society with likely positive outcomes for those with essential qualifications and, at best, uncertain outcomes for others. Some of the credentials are arbitrary and unrelated to actual performance requirements. To some degree educational qualifications are an artificial, not an inherent, barrier to useful employment. Efforts to alter such obstacles are already part of a strategy to include the poor in the opportunity structure.[64] Such efforts have as yet had only limited success. Unrealistic credentials are not easily eliminated. In any event opportunity for useful and satisfying work is likely to be a critical, though by no means the only, strategy for enabling the excluded to get into the society. It will involve the creation of new forms of employment and possibly even some basic redefinitions of the meaning of work in an advanced industrial society.

Modern societies maintain integration largely through functional interdependence and through a system of rewards and sanctions that accompany occupational status. Values, such as the democratic ethic, are also an important source of social cohesion. Where traditional moral codes are attenuated, the discipline of work and its accompanying rewards are major sources of integration. To be effective, work must be available, and the rewards and sanctions that accompany occupational roles must be accepted as legitimate. The more secular, rationalized, and materialistic the society becomes the more central are issues of equity, or social justice, for the maintenance of social stability. Since rewards are in-

[64] *Putting The Hard-Core Unemployed Into Jobs*, Part 1, National Citizens' Committee for Community Relations and the Community Relations Service of the U.S. Department of Justice (Washington, D.C.: Government Printing Office, 1967).

variably differential, there must be justification for unequal allocations of income and other rewards, such as prestige, power, and autonomy, that accompany occupational stratification. Who gets what and why become major concerns in maintenance of the system itself. The egalitarian ethic not only supports a more equitable distribution of rewards, but it limits the capacity to use authority or repressive sanctions as a means of enforcing conformity, as police have discovered in their efforts to control the Negro ghetto. Coercive power may be an effective force temporarily, but to win the loyalty and support of populations excluded from what they would define as a fair share of the benefits of society, a more equitable distribution of these benefits is essential. Those excluded from satisfying work and from an equitable share of rewards attached to the occupational structure can be expected to be alienated from society. All developing societies find they can maintain stability only with an increasingly equitable allocation of resources, for with economic growth ". . . disturbing tensions in society . . . can be resolved only if the increased output is used to secure more equitable distribution. . . . Those who have accepted the advice of impatient economists have found themselves with riots on their hands." [65] Work provides a sense of social participation and self-respect in a society in which one's position in the division of labor is the major determinant of socioeconomic resources available for personal development and family stability. Those rebelling against exclusion from rewarding work and/or an equitable portion of other benefits that accompany full social participation now challenge the society to deliver on its promise of equality.

The nature of the challenge and the response to it draws our attention to the fact that we are dealing not so much with social problems as with political issues. When one focuses attention on problems there is a tendency to separate them from the functioning of the entire system and to assume these can be solved without basic alterations in ourselves and in our way of life. A problem is something someone else has, and often the problem condition becomes translated to mean "problem people"—the poor, the blacks, the dissident minorities, the welfare recipients—all of whom need to change in order to fit into the society. But part of the existence of the urban crisis stems from the fact that the excluded are no longer defining themselves as problems to be treated by social agencies or controlled by the police. Many see themselves as victims of class distribution of status and power.

The issues involve class conflict over the distribution of status and power, of access to education, work, income, and the amenities of life. It is likely that the basic conflict has to do with the class distribution of opportunities to acquire and enhance one's sense of self-respect. S. M. Miller and his colleagues recognize this when they write, "The differential distribution of positive feelings about one's self is perhaps the essence of inequality." [66] So long as identity is so intimately tied to status there will be pressures to escape stigma associated with inferior class position and at the same time resistance to giving up this differential distribution of self-respect. Since government is increasingly regarded as an

[65] W. A. Lewis, quoted in Paul Fisher, "Social Security and Development Planning: Some Issues," *Social Security Bulletin,* 30 (June 1967), p. 18.

[66] S. M. Miller, Martin Rein, and Pamela Roby, "Poverty, Inequality and Conflict," in Gross, *op. cit.,* p. 326.

instrument for equalizing advantages, class conflict is politicalized.   In New York City and elsewhere the backlash of working-class and middle-class protest against mayors who seem too identified with the poor has occurred.   To blacks in the ghetto, the whites have all the advantages.   To a white storekeeper, the "blacks are trying to get everything for themselves."   As attempts are made to equalize opportunities for the poor and the Negroes, ". . . the middle class has felt cheated and threatened.   And when attention has been turned to the middle class, the blacks and the poor felt abandoned, helpless and hostile." [67]   Perhaps the conflict is most intense at the interface between ". . . those who stand just above and those just below the line dividing power from impotence," for, as Ralf Dahrendorf suggests, no boundary is more cruelly felt than this one.[68]   It is difficult to know how this problem can be met, if at all, without changing the values that define one's sense of self.   To meet the problem of the flight of the middle class to the suburbs, a proposal by the City Planning Commission in New York City would create a new middle class by expenditures of $1.9 billion a year for direct payments to the poor, development of public service jobs, subsidies to expand jobs in private industry, and stipends to the poor to facilitate advanced training.[69]   This has intriguing possibilities, but so long as there is a sizable group with political power who feel any threat from such a move, it is doubtful that it could succeed even if resources could be found to finance such a bold effort.

The dimensions of the urban crisis may go deeper than we have thus far suggested, and it is possible that it involves social trends beyond the power of government or any community group to control.   Problems of the urban environment and of inequalities suffered by the minority poor do not necessarily constitute a crisis so far as many are concerned.   What does trouble a great many, possibly the majority, if James Q. Wilson is correct, is the breakdown of social order, the decline of appropriate standards of behavior, of common notions of decency and decorum.   When asked what was the biggest problem facing the city, in a poll of over a thousand homeowners in Boston, the ". . . issue which concerned more respondents than any other was variously stated—crime, violence, rebellious youth, racial tension, public immorality, delinquency.   However stated, the common theme seemed to be a concern for improper behavior in public places." [70]   Though some of this was disguised anti-Negro feeling on the part of whites, Negro respondents tended to share the same concerns.   It is difficult to know what this means or how widely prevalent this is.   To James Q. Wilson this indicates that, to the majority of people, the urban crisis involved a failure of community, that is, a decline in common standards of behavior. Cities, of course, have always been perceived as centers of evil and this may mean no more than that.   On the other hand, whatever their source, crime, delinquency, riots, and student unrest may signal to many a basic disruption of their moral universe.   Since people act on their perception of problems and issues rather than on any professional analysis, and since politicians are natu-

[67] *The New York Times,* January 7, 1969.

[68] Ralf Dahrendorf, "Recent Changes in the Class Structure of European Societies," *Daedalus,* 93 (Winter 1966), pp. 225–270.

[69] *The New York Times,* June 7, 1969.

[70] Wilson, *op. cit.,* p. 39.

rally sensitive to the mood of the voters, the political climate does not suggest that it will be easy to win public support for the massive reordering of priorities needed to deal with the urban crisis. Indeed it will be easier to focus public attention on crime in the streets and on issues of law and order than to deal with fundamental grievances. An illustration of the tendency to focus on violence in order to avoid examining the social roots of disorder may be seen in a decision of the Senate Permanent Investigations Subcommittee. Chosen to conduct the chief congressional inquiry into the cause and cure of urban rioting, the committee rejected by a vote of 6 to 2 a resolution proposed by John Sherman Cooper, Republican from Kentucky, to search specifically for economic and social factors. Some of the committee members urged that to stress social factors would amount to "condoning lawlessness." [71] Civil rights, racial integration, and the pursuit of the Great Society were the domestic issues of the early 1960s. By 1968 these had been replaced by crime in the streets and law and order, themes that are not likely to focus public attention on the need for basic social reforms.

A commission appointed by the President to study violence in America produced an assessment of the American people that does not sit well with our prized self-image. The National Advisory Commission on Civil Disorders bluntly told us we were a racist society, which accounted for the violence in the ghetto. The National Commission on the Causes and Prevention of Violence informs us that we "have never been a very law-abiding nation and illegal violence has sometimes been abundantly rewarded." Violence is part of the American heritage, a common means used by all groups to promote their own ends, although rarely has violence been successful. Americans like most nations, say the authors of the study, suffer from an "historical amnesia," screening our violent past in order to maintain the historic vision of ourselves "as a latter day Chosen People sent . . . to create a new Jerusalem." [72] The conclusion of this staff report suggests two general ways of responding to outbreaks of violence by political leaders: forceful social control or efforts to alleviate the conditions leading to the violence. While popularly supported public force may contain specific outbreaks, it is unlikely to prevent violence.

> At worst, public force will so alienate a people that terrorist and revolutionary movements will arise to challenge and ultimately overthrow the regime. . . . The effort to eliminate the conditions that lead to collective violence may tax the resources of a society, but it poses less serious problems than increased resort to force.[73]

If our past response to similar studies is any indicator, we are likely to ignore the report. We shall do so, however, at our own peril. The crisis we face is one of social integration, not in the narrow sense of racial integration, however important that objective may continue to be, but in the sense of creating a social structure ". . . in which every individual will feel valued and none will feel

[71] *The New York Times,* August 2, 1967.

[72] Graham and Gurr, *op. cit.*

[73] *Ibid.,* p. 639.

rejected." [74]   We face the Hobbesian problem of order, for we approximate the war of each against all, and it is difficult to believe that any response to this crisis that ignores the claims of social justice can maintain a free society.

Crisis in Social Welfare

The urban crisis may be seen as an indication of social breakdown, a reflection of the relative inability of this society to deal effectively with the problems it has identified. Rapid and unsettling change produced by expanding technology and urbanization, plus new claims for human rights, require new modes of intervention to deal with complex and interrelated environmental, economic, and social problems. Social intervention directly concerned with meeting human needs is our special concern, yet this is inseparable from other efforts to alter the environment or regulate the economy. Physical planning, illustrated by urban renewal, has consequences for human beings who are dislocated and for the poor in general, whose supply of low-income housing is affected. Economic policy influencing rates of economic growth and levels of employment may have greater significance for the disadvantaged than certain specific social welfare measures. In this latter illustration we see that if our focus is on goals such as equalizing opportunity, preventing deprivation, and promoting full participation in society, institutionalized means other than those specifically identified as social welfare may be the most direct way to attain our ends. The disadvantages and deprivations that make up the human side of the urban crisis are a consequence of deficits in all our institutions, including those directly concerned with meeting social needs. Social welfare measures, developed to a considerable extent as part of the New Deal response to the crisis of the 1930s, cannot deal now with the radically new forces generated by technological and democratic revolutions. Although issues related to the excluded minority poor are critical, the problem of humanizing the urban environment extends beyond specific concerns with poverty and inequality. There are indications that some aspects of the urban environment itself, at least as it has been created under the twin imperatives of technology and the market, are hostile to health and well-being. Environmental pollution with its hazards to health, excessive population density with its threats to privacy and mental health, social instability and impersonality that undermine identity, and the increasing complexity and organizational authority that create feelings of powerlessness are possible risks to all individuals. [75] Without question, one's position in the social structure determines the degree to which one can cushion whatever strain is related to living in an urban setting. An occasional trip to Bermuda fortifies one for coping with the hardships of city life. So does a sympathetic psychiatrist at $30 an hour.

In a period in which we must give increasing attention to meeting human needs and to democratizing access to resources and the amenities of life, those

[74] The Ad Hoc Committee on the Triple Revolution, *The Triple Revolution,* Santa Barbara, California: 1964.

[75] Leonard S. Cottrell, Jr., "Social Planning, The Competent Community, and Mental Health," in *Urban America and the Planning of Mental Health Services, op. cit.,* pp. 399–400.

organizations ostensibly designed for these purposes come under critical scrutiny and attack. This is especially so as recipients of service acquire a new image as citizen-consumers having the right to pass judgment on the quality of service being rendered. In this light all the human services are found seriously wanting. Yet inadequacies must be understood in the context of a radically altered social reality in which programs are being asked to meet needs beyond those for which they were established.[76] The relative inability of social welfare programs to effectively respond to critical social problems and to meet needs and aspirations stems from a series of interrelated gaps between reality and some attainable ideal.[77] These are gaps in (1) strategy, (2) structure, (3) ideology and power, and (4) knowledge and manpower.

Strategy Gap

The strategy gap refers to the failure to develop policies and programs that deal with the real problems and issues. This can be illustrated by an inappropriate reliance on social services as a substitute for economic policy and programs that would assure adequate employment and provide decent incomes. Social services are those helping or enabling efforts and resources directed at changing individuals and increasing their social competence. They are useful and necessary. However, when employment is not available and income is too meager to sustain life or hope, narrowly conceived social services may be a *dis*service if they direct our attention away from issues of economic policy and decent social provisions. This can be illustrated by the 1962 Public Assistance Amendments. In the words of President John F. Kennedy, as he signed the new law in July 1962, "This measure embodies a new approach—stressing services in addition to support, rehabilitation instead of relief, and training for useful work instead of prolonged dependency." What the 1962 amendments did not and could not provide were decent jobs and decent incomes, critical unmet needs both then and now. The limited training they did authorize could not create employment opportunities. No significant attention was paid to the depressed levels of assistance grants. In a period of relatively high unemployment, the emphasis given to a social service strategy could only intensify deprivation and contribute to the crisis we now confront.[78] In 1962 the unemployment rate was 5.5 percent of the labor force, 4.9 for whites and a critical 10.9 for nonwhites. There was a sharp increase in unemployment from 1957 to 1958 (from 4.3 to 6.8, and

[76] It should be made clear that the evaluation of programs in no way is intended as criticism directed at individuals, nor does it deny useful accomplishments. Society pretty much has the kind of programs it is willing to pay for and individual practitioners, whether in social work, education, or the field of health sometimes perform remarkable services in the face of limited resources. It should be added that, in the field of social welfare, social workers have been aware of severe deficiencies in many programs and have been extremely self-critical as professionals.

[77] It is not assumed that it is possible or even desirable to create a "perfect" social system, free of strain, "problems," or "deviations." Such a system would be static and totalitarian, free of creativity as well as nonconformity.

[78] It is not being suggested that adequate social services were provided or that they were not needed.

rates continued at 5.5 or above through the early 1960s). Subemployment figures are not available for those years, but relatively high subemployment rates in the ghettos during later, more prosperous, years indicate that inadequate employment as well as unemployment have been chronic problems for the lower class in general and the black poor in particular. However valuable the 1962 amendments may have been on other grounds, they avoided the central problems of work and income. In that year and continuing into the present, grants in public assistance were well below the poverty line and large groups of the poor were not eligible for financial aid. The amendments did nothing to raise grants, and other income programs were not improved. For example, as late as 1968, unemployment insurance did not cover one-fourth of the wage and salaried workers. National average weekly benefits in that year represented 36 percent of the average weekly wage in covered employment. Because Negroes have a greater risk of being confined to jobs not covered by unemployment insurance, they are also least protected by even this inadequate social measure. Alvin Schorr has pointed out that the nation has continued to rely on a social service strategy rather than on appropriate economic policy directed at expanding employment and income. This is so because it is cheaper and because it permits us to deal with the dilemma of full employment versus inflation by forcing the poor to accept increased unemployment in order to protect the nation from rising prices.[79]

Social work and the mental health professions in general have contributed to an excessive reliance on case services because all professions tend to perceive and to promote solutions to problems in terms of their particular expertise. For the most part such expertise has relied excessively on a medical model of treatment of individuals, who are diagnosed as suffering from some form of pathology; the degree to which behavior defined as sick may be a normal adaptation to social system strains has been largely ignored.[80] Increasing attention in social work and among community-oriented mental health practitioners is being given to the social in social problems. We return to these issues later. Here it is important to recognize that part of our current crisis is due to our unwillingness to pay the cost of dealing appropriately with our problems.

To some degree the social services are blamed for failures, when in fact they are being misused for economic, political, and professional reasons. It is not simple to determine what our real problems are or which strategies would be the most effective. In general we have tended to deal with symptoms rather than causes, with individual rather than institutional defects. We have focused on meeting the social system's need for stability rather than adapting the system to meet human needs. It is possible that the best hope of dealing effectively with social problems will lie in efforts at redesigning social institutions to give primacy to the human being and his needs. Strategies that begin with this concept may look quite different from the ones now employed.

[79] Alvin Schorr, "Social Services Are No Substitute for Economic Policies," *Social Work*, 14 (April 1969), pp. 2, 128.

[80] For an excellent discussion of the value and limitations of the medical model see Nevitt Sanford, Chap. 19, "Social Action to Promote Individual Development," *Self and Society* (New York: Atherton Press, 1966), pp. 313–336.

Structural Gap

The organization of social welfare programs makes them relatively incapable of meeting the needs of those whom they serve or of reaching large groups of people whose needs go totally unmet through any social intervention. Residual welfare programs in particular suffer from the too mean—too little—too late syndrome, contributing perhaps as much to ill-being as to well-being. Such programs may be criticized on the grounds that they are often insulting, inadequate, and irrelevant.

Perhaps it is the stigma associated with residual welfare programs that is the chief issue. This is seen in the bitter charges of welfare colonialism, directed especially at public assistance programs, on the part of newly organized client groups who insist in the status of citizen and consumer.[81] The insult to self-respect institutionalized in residual welfare programs may be seen as part of society's stigmatize-rejection mechanism in the service of maintaining invidious class distinctions and a labor force confined to menial work. Separate services for the poor invariably turn out to be poor services. Incorporating a social paternalism that reflects the definition of the poor as weak and unworthy and offering a treatment service based on a diagnosis of individual defect, such programs distribute stigma along with service. It seems clear that we have reached a point in our economic development at which punitive welfare is no longer necessary; we have reached a point in our democratic aspirations at which pejorative welfare will come increasingly under attack.

The relative inadequacy of social welfare programs may be seen in their inability to meet desirable standards of benefits or service for those they reach, in the large numbers of persons who are not reached at all, and in the tendency to be so organized that at times the needs of agencies have priority over the needs of the target population. Social provision of income, medical care, and housing fails to attain acceptable standards for those who are served. In public assistance, grants vary from levels of destitution to standards approximating the poverty line. Nowhere do they allow for a reasonably decent minimum level of living. In addition large groups of the poor are not reached by these programs at all. In 1967 at least two-thirds of those whom we call poor or near-poor received no public assistance, and it is estimated that at least one-half of those who were eligible did not receive any assistance. The conditions under which assistance is granted to those eligible are frequently restrictive and repressive, leading the National Advisory Commission on Civil Disorders to conclude that ". . . our present system of public assistance contributes materially to the tensions and social disorganization that have led to civil disorders."[82] Other social provisions such as housing and medical care are also inadequate. In the past twenty years we have succeeded in building only about two-thirds of the public housing units originally authorized for the six year period, 1949–55.[83] Often only a demeaning quality of life is made possible by such housing

---

[81] Charles Silberman, *Crisis in Black and White* (New York: Random House, 1964), pp. 304–358.

[82] Report of the National Advisory Commission on Civil Disorders, *op. cit.*, p. 252.

[83] *Building the American City*, National Commission on Urban Problems, *op. cit.*, p. 14.

because of paternalistic and restrictive public housing administration and because such dwellings become stigmatized as homes for the poor.[84]

Inadequacies cited in this section are generalizations that are not uniformly true, so a note of caution is required. For example, although many of the poor dislike public housing, some studies indicate that a significant proportion of residents value what they have.[85] It must be emphasized that public housing has provided some low-cost dwellings not otherwise available. Indeed, a recent report suggests that we shall have to continue to rely on public housing as the only way to meet the need for low-cost dwellings.[86] Medicaid legislation under Title XIX of the Social Security Act has extended health services to the poor, but it has also perpetuated and expanded a dual system of medical care, one for citizens and one for the indigent. It has been criticized by Dr. John H. Knowles as having perpetuated "welfare medicine for the poor" and as having failed ". . . to provide a standard of quality in health care," which could lead to a ". . . frozen destructive confrontation between the needy and the medical establishment as the poor perceive that they are not getting what they deserve." [87]

Social welfare programs may be so organized as to be relatively inaccessible to those who wish to use them and unresponsive to the needs that clients may bring. The poor often have least access to quality professional counseling and therapy. Treatment services, when they are rendered, seem to have little significant impact, as measured by the admittedly limited evaluative research so far available.[88] Such facilitating resources as day care and homemaker services are in short supply. The care of children who cannot or should not remain with their own parents is an especially critical problem. Evidence of community neglect of the young is formidable.[89] Information about services may not be widely distributed, and clients without cars may have difficulty getting to agencies not located in their neighborhoods. When people do find their way to agencies, services may be fragmented or irrelevant to their real needs. At times the needs of the agency supersede those of the client. Agencies need to maintain the support of those in the community who control vital resources that determine the survival of the program. The needs of the supporting public, however, may conflict with the needs of the public to be served. Saving tax dollars frequently has priority over the needs of recipients.

[84] "Pruit-Igoe: Survival in a Concrete Ghetto," *Social Work,* 12 (October 1967), pp. 3–13.

[85] Daniel Thurz, *Where Are They Now?,* (Washington, D.C.: Health and Welfare Council of the National Capital Area, 1966), pp. 77–92.

[86] *A Decent Home,* President's Committee on Urban Housing, *op. cit.*

[87] *Portland* (Maine) *Press Herald,* June 23, 1969.

[88] Gordon E. Brown (ed.), *The Multi-Problem Dilemma* (Metuchen, N.J.: Scarecrow Press, 1968); Henry J. Meyer, Edgar F. Borgotta, and Wyatt C. Jones, *Girls At Vocational High* (New York: Russell Sage Foundation, 1965).

[89] Henry S. Maas and Richard E. Engler, Jr., *Children in Need of Parents* (New York: Columbia University Press, 1959); Harold Lewis, "Parental and Community Neglect," *Children,* 16 (May–June 1969), pp. 114–118; Alfred J. Kahn, "The Social Scene and the Planning of Services for Children," *Social Work,* 7 (July 1962), pp. 3–14.

The education of low-income children, and of the black poor in particular, has been described by Dr. Harold Taylor as "a national scandal," and, he added, "the evidence of years of neglect is now exploding into public consciousness." [90] To a considerable degree failures in our educational system account for those human beings who are labeled failures and relegated to our residual welfare programs. But the failure of public education is not restricted to the poor. A study sponsored by the Carnegie Corporation concluded that America's schools and colleges ". . . destroy spontaneity and joy and fail to educate." The author of the study, Charles E. Silberman, declares that the ". . . public schools are quite literally destructive of human beings . . . they are the most grim, joyless places on the face of the earth." [91] While failures of the educational system particularly with regard to low-income youths can be documented, explanations for why these failures occur and how they can be remedied are not so readily available. [92] It is easier, of course, to point to failures in all of the human service programs than to offer realistic solutions, and in a period of crisis it is failure that is highlighted, not success. With regard to education, it seems clear that schools function reasonably well to prepare most middle-class youths for participation in society. The values and goals of society itself may need to change significantly before education can alter its primary function of processing young people to fit into the social system. [93]

Human services other than education also reflect the total organization of society, whose failures in some measure are linked to the more or less successful operation of other institutions we value and wish to preserve. For example, the successful operation of the American economic system requires a certain measure of unemployment and subemployment, forcing some families to rely on public assistance, which is charged with their rehabilitation—an almost impossible task without changes in basic economic policy. Such changes are resisted. In turn, however, resistance to necessary changes are found in social welfare organizations as well.

Like all formal organizations, social agencies are relatively resistant to change. Though there is much rhetoric about the need for innovation in services to people and some solid accomplishments, functionalism, professionalism, and standpatism are common pathologies that afflict human service organizations. Agencies find it difficult to relate to needs outside their defined functions. Spe-

---

[90] *The Washington Post,* September 15, 1963.

[91] Charles E. Silberman, *Crisis in the Classroom* (New York: Random House, 1970).

[92] James S. Coleman, *et al. Equality of Educational Opportunity* (Washington, D.C.: Government Printing Office, 1966); Patricia Cayo Sexton, *Education and Income* (New York: Viking Press, 1961); Jonathan Kozol, *Death At An Early Age* (Boston: Houghton-Mifflin, 1967); Robert Rosenthal and Lenore F. Jacobson, "Teacher Expectations for the Disadvantaged," *Scientific American,* Vol. 218 (April 1968), pp. 19–23; Harvard Educational Review, 31, (Winter 1968); *Racial Isolation in the Public Schools,* U.S. Commission on Civil Rights (Washington, D.C.: Government Printing Office, 1967), Vol. I; Estelle Fuchs, "How Teachers Learn to Help Children Fail," *Trans-action,* 5 (September 1968), pp. 45–49.

[93] Thomas F. Green, "Schools and Communities: A Look Forward," *Harvard Educational Review,* 39 (Spring 1969), pp. 221–252.

cialization, though necessary, complicates the problem of coordination and the need for some comprehensive approach to people and their needs. Professionalism develops useful loyalties to one's occupation but serves the negative purpose of limiting the ability of people from related human service professions to cooperate. Standpatism refers to a natural conservative tendency in all organizations to seek stability and to preserve those structures that have been developed and have proven more or less useful in the past. When change is required that poses a threat to such structures and to whatever vested interests have developed around them, there is inevitable resistance.

In a sense we have a highly irrational social welfare system. This is partly because it has developed historically on an ad hoc basis as various powerful groups in the community perceived problems and organized solutions on the basis of their values and assumptions; partly because it is highly specialized, fragmented, and overlapping, with no mechanism to provide for overall co-ordination or for adaptation to change; and partly because it is more responsive to the politics of problem-solving than to the logic of problem-solving, more sensitive to the ideology of the groups in power than to human values. It has served in some measure to relieve distress and to provide a variety of useful supports. Efforts to make social welfare programs more responsive to human needs confront an ideological and power gap.

Ideological and Power Gap

It is common to observe that we have the resources to solve our problems but lack the will to do so. This is a half-truth, or perhaps only a third of the truth. All the resources—material, human, and scientific—are not quite there to solve all our problems. Yet they are there in sufficient quantity to solve at least the problems related to poverty and inequality. Here the issue is one of national priorities, of commitment of resources to human beings and their needs. The problem is both moral and political. Where there is the will there is not the power; where there is the power there is frequently not the will.[94] Those in control of our institutional life—economic, political, or social—including our human service agencies, seek to maintain or enhance their control. Threats to such control and to the privileges that accompany power are resisted, which poses a basic dilemma in social reform. To insist on the necessary radical reforms may destroy support for those modest reforms that may be possible. In many human endeavors—in the conduct of war, in space exploration, in the

[94] The American commitment to equal opportunity frequently flounders on the lack of power to accomplish stated goals. For example, although the Equal Employment Opportunity Commission has been described as a "poor, enfeebled thing," "very new, very weak and very small," (Richard P. Nathan, *Jobs and Civil Rights,* prepared for U.S. Commission on Civil Rights by the Brookings Institution, Clearinghouse Publication No. 16 (Washington, D.C.: Government Printing Office, 1969); Senator Everett Dirksen (Ill.), on March 27, 1969, accused the chairman, Clifford L. Alexander, of "punitive harassment" to bring businessmen into compliance with antibias provisions of the Civil Rights Act of 1964. Senator Dirksen went on to say, "I'm going to the highest authority in this government and get somebody fired." *The next day* the White House announced Mr. Alexander would be replaced as chairman. *Christian Science Monitor,* April 29, 1969.

promotion of economic growth, in scientific research—it is axiomatic that strategies must be consistent with the requirements of successful problem-solving. In the approach to social problems we are faced with the need to do what is politically feasible. This may have little relationship to what is required. For example, the major strategy in the War on Poverty, developed through passage of the Economic Opportunity Act of 1964, paradoxically provided very little economic opportunity. The priority needs for jobs and income were sacrificed for the politically more acceptable emphasis on education and rehabilitation of the poor. Included was an ill-defined community action component, portions of which unexpectedly turned out to be politically not so feasible.[95] What is politically feasible in the short run may turn out to be socially and politically disastrous in the long run. Unattended human costs accumulate, and resentments are compounded by awareness of the gap between what society can do and what it has the political will to accomplish to the point where the very structure of society is threatened. Political feasibility involves questions of values and power and draws our attention to the moral ends we seek and the power available to various groups in society to have their needs effectively represented in choices that are made. To understand the politics of problem-solving is to see that our failures are not simply due to lack of knowledge. The popular bromide of education and the scientist's insistence on additional research may conceal the degree to which power, not stupidity, lies at the root of our difficulty.[96]

Knowledge and Manpower Gap

Yet the degree of our social stupidity is something to behold and should not be slighted. "The real enemy of the human spirit is man's own stupidity in regard to his social arrangements."[97] It is stupid to adhere to social institutions that were developed in the past and do not function to meet the needs and aspirations generated in the present. It is equally senseless to deny the utility of any social arrangement simply because it has become part of the Establishment. Directed change is needed, but since outcomes are always uncertain we require some means for assuring as best we can that efforts at social reform are guided by "social intelligence."[98] At this point such expertise is crude at best. Our socially useful knowledge is limited, since knowledge of how social systems work does not necessarily tell us how they may be changed. Efforts to solve social problems may have unanticipated side effects, both positive and negative. Thus the argument for additional knowledge is self-evident. What is not self-evident is the kind of knowledge required or how it may be distributed to assure democratic participation in decision-making. Social work and other human service professions of necessity rely increasingly on the social and behavioral sciences. The notion that these sciences as they are now organized will invariably lead to socially useful knowledge may be questioned. Our fragmented,

---

[95] Peter Marris and Martin Rein, *Dilemmas of Social Reform* (New York: Atherton Press, 1967).

[96] S. M. Miller, "Stupidity and Power," *Trans-action,* 1 (May 1964).

[97] Ernest Becker, *Structure of Evil,* (New York: George Braziller, 1968), p. 248.

[98] Gross, *op. cit.*

discipline-based, "value-free" social science is not likely to add up to the kind of social wisdom we need. Years ago Robert S. Lynd asked, "knowledge for what?" Ernest Becker's persuasive answer is that

> . . . the science of man in society must be a superordinate value science; one which has opted for human progress, and which has a clear and comprehensive, compelling idea of what constitutes such progress. The task of such a science would be the incessant implementation of human well-being.[99]

While such a bold assertion should arouse skepticism, one may agree with Archibald MacLeish that all science must be subordinated to some conception of human purpose.[100]   In any event, it is clear that increasing power shall be granted the social and behavioral scientist, for we shall soon face truly critical problems ". . . and only the behavioral sciences . . . will have the expertise to deal with them." [101]   How to enable the nonexpert to have access to knowledge that will permit him to make an informed judgment about issues that vitally affect his life raises complex questions about the democratization of power that accompanies knowledge in the postindustrial society.[102]

The social welfare crisis may also be seen as a manpower crisis, a shortage in the number and quality of people required to provide the wide range of human services necessary in a society that aspires to pay increasing attention to the needs of people.   Indeed, one of the many ways we may characterize our age is to see it in terms of a developing human service society.   An increasing proportion of the labor force is involved in education, health-related activities, recreation, and a variety of social services designed to enhance human competence and contribute to the amenities of life.   Both our changing technology and egalitarian aspirations may move us in this direction.   In a postindustrial society in which routine and repetitive tasks can be automated and human labor power is diminished in importance, the conservation and development of human resources is given greater priority.[103]   A rapidly changing, increasingly interdependent society may have to place a premium on developing people with a high degree of interpersonal competence capable of knowledgeable and flexible adaptations to change.   New forms of *transactional* work involving the use and exchange of knowledge require individuals with high capacity to carry on learning tasks and to relate to others in productive ways. The concept of transactional work comes from Jean Gottman, who defines it as

[99] Robert S. Lynd, *Knowledge for What?*, (Princeton, N.J.: Princeton University Press, 1939); Becker, *op. cit.*, p. xiii.

[100] Archibald MacLeish, "The Great American Frustration," *Saturday Review*, July 13, 1968.

[101] Michael, *op. cit.*, p. 166.

[102] Donald N. Michael, "On Coping With Complexity: Planning and Politics," *Daedalus*, 97 (Fall 1968), pp. 1179–1193.

[103] This can be seen in the increasing attention being paid to the notion of investment in human resources and to specific programs designed to overcome disabilities and to expand capacities. *See*, for example, Burton A. Weisbrod, "Investing In Human Capital," *Journal of Human Resources*, 1 (Summer 1966), pp. 5–21; and *Manpower Report of the President*, 1968, *op. cit.*, p. 199.

involving "competent understanding and correct exchange" of information.[104] The term also implies transacting with others, a relationship of reciprocity in which one can accomplish his work well only by obtaining needed information from another. Thus competence in human relations as well as in some area of expertise is implied. The degree to which an advanced society will make possible such new careers for the vast segment of its population and the extent to which only an elite will have opportunity for useful work of this kind are unclear. Critical problems of work and leisure may need to be resolved.

In any event an egalitarian society will be faced with pressures to find a place for all of its members through creation of new forms of work or other legitimate pursuits. It will certainly have to pay increasing attention to assuring that all individuals have access to education and other developmental experiences that equalize their opportunities to participate in society. The demand for equality extends to the full range of education, health, and social services that are ever more important for one's life chances and for a sense of well-being. Manpower to provide quality human services will require increasing attention.

We already face serious shortages in the number of teachers, physicians, dentists, nurses, paramedical personnel, social workers, and related human service practitioners.[105] In addition there are critical problems of reeducating existing human service manpower and educating those who enter the human service field to be responsive to rapidly changing practice dictated by new knowledge and a new social reality that radically alters the traditional relationship between the professional and the consumer of services. The power and authority of all professions are being challenged by citizen-consumers.

A variety of proposals have developed to meet the manpower gap, including the promising if highly problematic plan for massive creation of "new career" opportunities for the poor in the human services. It is hoped that the development of new career ladders in education, health, law enforcement, recreation, social work, and so forth, with planned provision of continuing education and training to promote upward mobility, will both meet the need for decent career opportunities for the poor and help expand the supply of human service practitioners.[106] There are a number of unsettled questions, including issues of financing, of differentiating among tasks appropriate for the various levels of education and training, and of restructuring human service agencies to promote a new deployment of staff. We turn to these later. Let us note here, though, that as a result of the Economic Opportunity Act, Elementary and Secondary Education Act, and legislation related to Medicare, there were by 1968 over

[104] Jean Gottman, "The Corrupt and Creative City," *Center Diary: 14* (Center for the Study of Democratic Institutions, September–October 1966), p. 35.

[105] *Closing the Gap in Social Work Manpower*, U.S. Department of Health, Education, and Welfare (Washington, D.C.: Government Printing Office, 1965); National Commission for Social Work Careers, *Manpower: A Community Responsibility*, 1968 Annual Review (New York: National Commission for Social Work Careers, 1968); National Commission on Community Health Services, *Health is a Community Affair* (Cambridge, Mass.: Harvard University Press, 1966), pp. 77–100.

[106] Arthur Pearl and Frank Riessman, *New Careers for the Poor* (New York: Free Press, 1965); *also* Frank Riessman, *Strategies Against Poverty* (New York: Random House, 1969).

50,000 new nonprofessionals recruited from the poor; they were working as community aides, teacher aides, home health aides, and so on.

Credibility Gap

Perhaps it is the credibility gap that is the most critical. This is the gap between the rhetoric of a War on Poverty and the continuing unnecessary deprivations, between the ideology of equality and the experience of inequality for so many. The mid-1960s were characterized by an unusual flurry of new social welfare programs launched in pursuit of the Great Society. The momentum was soon lost, overtaken by the claims of the war in Vietnam, the arms race, and civic disorder. Attention to racial violence, student unrest, and crime in the streets tended to emphasize disturbances that required repressive control, not the degree to which these were symptomatic of grievances that required remedy. Expectations have been aroused by a national policy that declared an end to poverty and frustrated by strategy and resources that touched only a portion of the problem. Aaron Wildavsky has stated it well:

> A recipe for violence: Promise a lot, deliver a little. Lead people to believe they will be much better off, but let there be no dramatic improvement. Try a variety of small programs, each interesting but marginal in impact and severely underfinanced. Avoid any attempted solution remotely comparable in size to the dimensions of the problem you are trying to solve.[107]

This tension between rhetoric and reality will continue to provide a dynamic that will force new accommodations to demands that we live up to the declared values of the society. If they do not come soon enough we may lose confidence in the ability of this society to deal with its problems at all. In some measure that has happened. A small but unknown number of militant critics have given up on the American Dream. For some blacks, our social institutions are not inadequate but irrelevant. Revolution, not reform, seems the only answer to some dissident students, black power advocates, and others in the New Left. There has been a loss of confidence on the part of liberals and conservatives in the capacity of the programs we have mounted to deal at all adequately with the problems at hand. There is disenchantment with the capacity of government itself to deal with urban and human problems, and there are severe doubts whether the welfare state, however much its protections and services may be valued, can do much about producing basic changes that might improve the quality of life. Our challenge is to assure economic security plus a greater measure of social justice for those excluded from the system and to expand opportunities for self-actualization for all. Government can provide the means for the former. The latter goal is more elusive and focuses our attention on the functioning of all our social institutions. Social provisions, social services, and social action are social welfare strategies related to these goals. In Part II we examine these interrelated and overlapping approaches to meeting social needs.

---

[107] Aaron Wildavsky, "The Empty-head Blues: Black Rebellion and White Reaction," *The Public Interest,* No. 11 (Spring 1968), p. 3.

TWO

Social Welfare Needs, Programs, Policy Issues

Social welfare programs may be understood in terms of the social functions they perform and may be evaluated in the light of ideal values we are trying to achieve. As shown in figure, three interrelated and overlapping functional areas may be identified: (1) Social provisions substitute for or supplement and replace market allocation of goods and services. Ideally these represent a quest for social security and social justice. (2) Social services support, supplement, or replace the family. They are part of society's means for socialization and social control and represent people-changing institutions. They may be seen as a quest for an adequate socialization structure to equip people with the personal competence and societal resources needed for effective functioning in a period of rapid change. (3) Social action represents those efforts at system intervention designed to prevent problems, expand opportunities, and enhance the quality of life. They may be seen as a quest for community and a better polity. All these approaches, however, are caught between social welfare's conservative function of helping to maintain the social system and its innovative function of helping to adapt social institutions to new conditions and higher aspirations for the self-fulfillment of all.

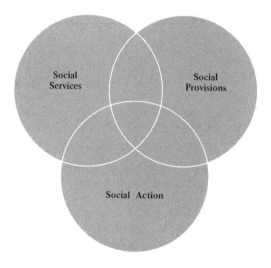

Social Provisions—Quest for social security and social justice.
Social Services—Quest for an adequate socialization structure.
Social Action—Quest for community.

153

Our first concern is with the relationship between social welfare and the market economy, in particular with efforts to deal with the poverty and inequality that are in large measure rooted in the operation of our economic system. Social welfare may be seen as an effort to regulate the market system to meet the need of democratic capitalism for a stable and expanding economy and the need for a greater social balance between the private and public sector. The relationship between poverty and our political economy is explored in the next chapter. In Chapter Six we examine the various social provisions that supplement and substitute for the market allocation of resources and raise some issues about their adequacy in the light of the claims of social justice. In Chapters Seven and Eight we turn our attention to social services and the quest for an adequate socialization structure. The concern is with human development, a goal that is inseparable from social development and the quest for community, which is the focus of Chapter Nine.

FIVE

Social Welfare and Political Economy

Industrialization

An industrial society requires a wage economy, with its risk of income insecurity; a mobile labor force, which creates problems in adaptation to new social environments; nuclear families, with the risk of social isolation in times of stress; and achievement orientation, with success for some and failure for others; instrumental relationships and large-scale organization that increase the likelihood of depersonalization; and an urban environment that adds to anonymity and breakdown of social control. Industrial society uproots people, destroys traditional institutions, promotes individual freedom while creating new forms of dependencies, and requires for its own survival a variety of social provisions and services that carry functions previously performed by the family and by patterns of mutual aid in agricultural economies. Industrialization has also produced an economic revolution by raising general levels of living and a social revolution by stimulating rising expectations. It may conceivably be the catalyst for a cultural revolution as we discover that the Protestant ethic and associated values adaptive to the problem of scarcity are not suited to the requirements for coping with social realities and the political and moral aspirations of this era.

It is industrialization within a market economy that has created our particular problems and influenced the character of our social welfare measures. We have increasingly moved from a laissez-faire toward a politically managed market economy, a form of welfare capitalism. The social dislocations attendant upon advancing technology require new instruments for the planning and direction of society, which raises serious questions about the ability of the market decision mechanism to function in socially useful ways. The aspiration to humanize our social order requires a new image of man and of social possibilities that transcends both the market mentality and our current methods of social intervention.

155

Social Welfare and the Market Economy

The quest for social security and social justice is a response to the economic insecurity and inequities characteristic of industrial capitalism. The ethos of such a system gives priority to economic individualism, property, and profit. It promotes an ideology extolling the virtues of the free market, however much the economic system may, in fact, have departed from the classical model of free enterprise. One measure of our mixed economy is the degree to which opportunities for employment are increasingly less dependent on the private sector. Between 1950 and 1960 one out of every ten new jobs was created in the private sector; the public and private nonprofit sectors accounted for the remainder. By 1965 a third of the labor force, compared to 15 percent in 1929, worked for employers outside the private profit sector of the economy.[1] The rates of economic growth, the stability of the economy, and the extent of full employment are highly dependent on the government's fiscal and monetary policy. Modifications in the operation of the "self-regulating" market have occurred in part through social welfare provisions that make available goods and services on principles other than those that characterize the private sector of the economy. In this respect, social welfare functions in relation to the market system, providing supports toward its more effective operation and supplementing or replacing the market allocation of goods and services to assure some measure of security or equity in economic distribution. The structure of a market society, its business ideology, and its distribution of power and privilege set certain limits within which social reform is possible. At the same time, social needs created by two major dynamic forces—a technological and a human rights revolution—will force increasing modifications of the market mechanism, expanding political control over the creation and distribution of goods and services. Since societies without market economies pose quite different welfare problems, some understanding of the nature and significance of the market society is essential. Relatively little attention has been paid to this central institution in most studies of social welfare.[2]

Karl Polanyi has depicted the social and human significance of the great transformation of man and society that accompanied the development of industrial capitalism and the creation of a market mentality.[3] Little appreciated is the extent to which the image of man and society was fundamentally altered, the degree to which the economic was severed from the social to become, for the first time in human history, so powerful and directing a force that one might speak not simply of an economy, but of an economic society. The "laws" of the self-regulating market system were founded on acquisitive self-interest, individual competition, and a profit-oriented price system that allocated commodities of land, labor, and capital so as to produce the goods society presumably wanted at a price it was willing to pay. Enormously successful in

[1] Robert L. Heilbroner, *The Limits of American Capitalism* (New York: Harper & Row, 1965), p. 52.

[2] For an exception *see* T. H. Marshall, *Class, Citizenship, and Social Development* (Garden City, N.Y.: Anchor Books, 1965), especially pp. 303–323.

[3] Karl Polanyi, *The Great Transformation* (Boston: Beacon Press, 1957; Polanyi, "Our Obsolete Market Mentality," *Commentary*, February, 1947, pp. 109–117.

promoting economic development, it was disastrous in its severing of social bonds and in converting social into economic relations. This transition from status to contract, however much it destroyed the cohesion of society, did free men from the bondage of feudal obligations and traditions, thus allowing new liberties at the cost of economic insecurity for the laboring classes. Although the self-regulating market is in some measure a social fiction, having been modified by monopolistic practices and government regulation, the essential economic structure of society and the values associated with the market image of man continue in the persisting game of self-aggrandizement. The rules of the game have been considerably altered by the growth of large and powerful corporate structures and by the intervention of a regulatory welfare state.[4] The ideology associated with the rise of the market society may continue long after economic activity ceases to be governed solely by principles of free enterprise. The market produces not only goods and services but values. It helps to structure not only buying and selling, but our image of man and society and our vision of alternate possibilities. We are still in the grips of a legacy of a market mentality that imposed a fundamental heresy, however utilitarian.[5] The image of man as essentially economic man, driven by motives of hunger or gain, obscures the degree to which man and his motives are essentially social and inhibits our capacity to imagine alternate ways of structuring society. To the degree that this image of economic man is still functional for maintaining and expanding our vast industrial enterprise, it is difficult to create new concepts that might allow for the development of other than material motives and pursuits.[6] Moreover, the assault on self-esteem continues to the degree that the economic structure treats man as a commodity whose welfare can be determined by the price his labor can bring in the market. Here, as we shall see, lies much of the discontent of the underclass and possibly of others as well.

The market image of society, based as it was on an atomistic view of individuals freely engaging in pursuit of self-interest that was automatically transformed into the well-being of all, created a grand illusion about the very nature of social order. Society became, as Polanyi has said, "invisible."[7] All behavior, it seemed, could be explained by acts of individual initiative, while order was assured through the operation of the self-regulating market. Yet this essentially utopian view of social reality could not be sustained very long. Men were forced to protect themselves from economic insecurity and the social dislocations of an uncontrolled market system.

> Capitalism, do not forget, is the only society in human history in which neither tradition nor conscious direction supervises the total effort of the community; it is the only society in which the future, the needs for

---

[4] John Kenneth Galbraith goes so far as to suggest that the market is dead as an instrument for regulating economic activity. Instead he asserts that it is technology that determines the nature of economic society, ". . . so that in all modern states the economy is planned and managed in much the same way." John K. Galbraith, *The New Industrial State* (New York: Houghton Mifflin, 1967).

[5] Polanyi, "Our Obsolete Market Mentality," *op. cit.,* p. 110.

[6] Heilbroner, *op. cit.,* pp. 95 and 125.

[7] Polanyi, "Our Obsolete Market Mentality," *op. cit.,* p. 116.

tomorrow, are entirely left to an automatic system. Scant wonder then that no sooner had the boat been set adrift than the passengers began to worry. A ship without a captain might work very well—at least so the designers promised—but suppose it did not? Suppose, for example, that its social results were not so pleasing as its economic ones—or suppose the economic ones were not so pleasing to some as to others? Then what?[8]

In a sense we were forced to rediscover society. Various forms of social intervention, including those we identify as social welfare, were part of this new awareness of the reality of society. Man meets his needs, not through individual initiative, but through social institutions. When these cease to function in some adequate way, regulatory and protective measures are essential. The commercial industrial revolution disrupted the traditional patterns of mutual obligation. Distrust of government notwithstanding, political control over the hazards created by a laissez-faire economy became necessary. Government intervention took many forms, such as factory legislation, industrial accident insurance, protective tariffs, protection of women and children in industry, minimum-wage laws, zoning and building codes, and regulations regarding pure foods and drugs.

Social dislocations and economic insecurity required protective and stabilizing measures, through such forms as tariff protection or social legislation. A regulatory welfare state gradually emerged aimed at social control of economic activity and its disruptive consequences. Polanyi saw it as reincorporating ". . . economy in society by controling markets, assuring a minimum level of income to all as a matter of political right, and enlarging the redistributive sphere of the economy by allocating medical and some other social services on non-market criteria." [9] Needless to say the timing, nature, and degree of such social control and the political motives for state intervention varied with societies.

It is not suggested that the operation of industrial capitalism alone accounts for the various forms of social intervention. Religious and other cultural factors in varying industrial societies influenced social policy and welfare measures. In Catholic France, relief of the poor did not bear the stigma associated with welfare because it was viewed as assistance to neighbors and parishioners.[10] The British Poor Law and its American version, both strongly influenced by Protestantism, had its origins in preindustrial economies; yet in each country assistance to the poor became influenced by the need of a market society for a disciplined labor force. Help was rendered outside the market system and in a way that would not interfere with its normal operation. In the United States more than in any other industrial nation social policy has been influenced by the ethos of capitalism and the commercial ideal of the Protestant ethic.[11] In the

[8] Robert L. Heilbroner, *The Worldly Philosophers,* rev. ed. (New York: Simon and Schuster, 1961), p. 281.

[9] George Dalton (ed.), *Primitive, Archaic and Modern Economies: Essays of Karl Polanyi* (New York: Anchor Books, 1968), p. xxvi.

[10] Marshall, *op. cit.,* p. 315.

[11] Samuel Mencher, *Poor Law to Poverty Program* (Pittsburgh: University of Pittsburgh Press, 1967), p. 132.

absence of other traditional institutions and lacking a feudal past, with its acceptance of status privileges and obligations, capitalism became "the principal dynamic force in American society." [12]   Economic individualism, distrust of government, free enterprise in business, and voluntarism in social welfare delayed public responsibility for control of the economy and for minimum provisions of economic security.   Yet, here too, the outlines of the welfare state took shape in the 1930s by the passage of the Social Security Act and other New Deal measures designed to preserve the capitalistic system from total collapse.   Establishing measures of income security, social legislation in this period also served to bolster a badly shaken economy and to preserve rather than dismantle the market system.   One may indeed say that social welfare is, in part, the answer of liberal capitalism to the challenge of socialism.   It helps to account for the "failure of the Marxist prediction that capitalism would destroy itself." [13]   In fact, democratic capitalism has shown itself increasingly capable of assimilating socialist ideas without radically altering its own structure. [14]   In a sense social welfare measures, along with other forms of social intervention designed to stabilize and regulate the market economy, are the product of the "golden mean of social reform," an effort to ". . . steer a middle course between the known evils of laissez-faire and the anticipated evils of socialism." [15]   Some major business leaders have come to accept this. Thomas J. Watson of IBM has put it this way:

> Much as we may dislike it, I think we've got to realize that in our kind of society there are times when government has to step in and help people with some of their more difficult problems.   Programs which assist Americans by reducing the hazards of a free market system without damaging the system itself are necessary, I believe to its survival. . . .[16]

What these remarks do not point out is the degree to which government intervention sustains and promotes the market economy by maintaining high rates of employment, stimulating economic growth, subsidizing various economic activities, and providing guaranteed markets for certain products, particularly those of agriculture and the defense industry.   Those measures defined as social welfare, ostensibly aimed at promoting individual well-being, may also function to stabilize the economy or act as a stimulus for economic expansion.   Margaret S. Gordon notes this in the following way:

[12] Stanley M. Elkins, *Slavery* (New York: Grosset & Dunlap, 1963), p. 43.   For another viewpoint *see* Henry Steele Commager (ed.), *Lester Ward and the Welfare State* (Indianapolis: Bobbs-Merrill, 1967).

[13] Richard M. Titmuss, "The Welfare State: Images and Realities," *Social Service Review,* 37 (March 1963), p. 2.

[14] Norman Thomas, once the grand old man of the American Socialist Party and perennial candidate for the office of the President, was fond of pointing out that when Franklin Delano Roosevelt took office the first thing he did was to help enact some of the major planks of the Socialist Party.

[15] Sidney Fine, *Laissez-faire and the General-Welfare State* (Ann Arbor, Mich.: University Press, 1964), p. 376.

[16] Quoted in Heilbroner, *The Limits of American Capitalism, op. cit.,* p. 34.

Although older humanitarian and social considerations continued to play a role, public welfare programs have come to be regarded as part of a battery of instruments available to the modern state in its efforts to maintain economic stability. This attitude has clearly played a significant role in connection with the marked expansion and liberalization of social security programs which has characterized the period since World War II.[17]

In the present era investments in human resources and other forms of social welfare may be seen as economic multipliers that contribute to economic growth. They tend to be identified as social welfare measures to the degree that they directly serve the individual by promoting economic security and by equalizing opportunities. The hazards of the free market and the demand for equality are twin forces that have moved government to substitute social policy for the "invisible hand," leading increasingly to a social market economy in which political allocation of resources may be made on the basis of democratic values, social needs, and sensitivity to the distribution of power. Social provisions of income, medical care, and housing represent efforts of government to alter the operation of the market in behalf of disadvantaged groups or to assure some minimum level of economic well-being for all citizens. Provisions in the United States tend to be largely residual emergency substitute measures that meet needs normally provided for through the operation of the market and family system. Social insurance is regarded as an "institutional" provision available without stigma. But here too, one's function in the market influences the availability and adequacy of these measures. Perhaps the British National Health Service is the true "symbol of the welfare state" because it is a universal service, that is, it is equally available to all regardless of income.[18] It ignores class and replaces the calculus of the economic market with "a calculus of needs."[19] To what extent universal social provisions may continue to replace the market is uncertain. In Britain for example, there is some swing away from the principle of universality in favor of services restricted to the most needy.[20] In the United States, social provisions have been especially restricted by the continuing influence of market values on social policy.

Political decisions are not responsive to any single ideology or center of power in society; yet despite the increasing social consciousness of the business community, its relatively conservative values have tended to set the limit of our social vision. This may be seen in the timid way we implemented the Employment Act of 1946 and in the fact that, upon assuming the office of President, after having campaigned for a bold attack on social problems, John F. Kennedy

[17] Margaret S. Gordon, *The Economics of Welfare Policies* (New York: Columbia University Press, 1963), p. 2.

[18] Yet services available to all may not be used by all; as Titmuss notes, "middle income groups make more and better use of all services . . ." in all countries. Richard M. Titmuss, *Commitment to Welfare* (New York: Pantheon Books, 1968), Chap. 5, pp. 59–71.

[19] Marshall, *op. cit.*, p. 320.

[20] Timothy Raison, "The British Debate the Welfare State," *The Public Interest,* No. 1 (Fall 1965), pp. 110–118, and "British White Paper on Social Security Reform," *Social Security Bulletin,* 32 (May 1969), pp. 3–15.

felt constrained to assure the business community that he was not hostile to free enterprise. The mores of the market society continue to have priority over the values of social democracy. Nowhere is this more clearly seen than in our efforts to deal with poverty. To a considerable degree the problem of poverty is created by our economic system, while the values of the market and its companion—the Protestant ethic—continue to inhibit development of appropriate social measures for its alleviation and prevention. It is an open question whether we can effectively deal with poverty and related problems within the present structure of welfare capitalism. Incremental changes are possible but may not produce the required degree of social justice. Radical changes in the direction of social democracy may be required but may not be politically feasible. Beyond the issue of poverty and inequality are the gnawing problems of lack of community and noble purpose, neither of which are susceptible to solution within the restricted world view of a commercial industrial society.

The Anatomy of Poverty

Social Welfare and the Discovery of Poverty

Social welfare has its origin in concern with poverty and in measures for the relief of the poor. Yet throughout the early history of this society it was not poverty so much as pauperism, not economic need so much as dependency that occupied the attention of humanitarians and reformers. In Great Britain too, especially with the rise of industrial capitalism and the development of a laboring class tied to a wage system, economic dependency became a moral issue, a threat to the integrity of a market system in which income through employment, however insecure, became the normal means of survival. Until the latter part of the nineteenth century, in both England and the United States, there was less concern with mass poverty than alarm over pauperism. In this country attention shifted to poverty and insecurity in the post-Civil War period. The condition of the poor became defined as a social rather than a moral problem. The discovery of poverty as a social problem was made possible by industrialization and new levels of economic prosperity that nourished the belief that poverty might be abolished. At the same time, attention was drawn to the gap between existing deprivation and new definitions of feasible social policy.[21] However, throughout most of the nineteenth century the philosophy of Social Darwinism with its belief in the natural law of competition, survival of the fittest and automatic evolutionary progress, tended to prevail. In this view, society mirrored nature. Evolutionary progress could be assured only if social competition were unfettered to permit the elimination of the unfit. Consequently humanitarian inclinations had to be held in check to avoid interfering with nature's grand design for ultimate human well-being. Measures that might go beyond restrictive public and private charity were viewed with suspicion, particularly if aimed at relieving the economic insecurity of able-bodied workers.

By the early twentieth century, however, some attention was given to various

---

[21] Robert H. Bremner, *From the Depths—The Discovery of Poverty in the United States* (New York: University Press, 1964).

ways of dealing with the economic insecurity that accompanied the boom and bust propensity of the market economy. Public works, social insurance, and proposals for minimum-wage legislation were given serious consideration.[22] For the most part it was not until the rediscovery of poverty in the 1930s that many of the proposals for promoting economic security and more equal opportunity were realized in social legislation. In the context of calamitous unemployment and general economic collapse, many of the social reforms first promoted by the late nineteenth- and early twentieth-century Progressive Movement now seemed more acceptable. It is difficult to realize, in this era of Keynesian economics and managed economy, that unemployment in March of 1933 was variously estimated to include from 13.5 to 16 million workers. White-collar workers sold apples and shined shoes. The unemployed and homeless welcomed arrest, ready to exchange liberty for assured survival. Over 100,000 workers applied for jobs in the Soviet Union. The problem then was not mass poverty in the midst of plenty but threats of mass starvation in the midst of plenty. Emergency soup kitchens and lines of people waiting to be fed were a common sight in many communities. There were organized hunger riots and open talk of revolution.[23] Yet it was probably economic mobilization for World War II rather than any specific New Deal measure that did the most to restore full employment and extend the fruits of economic progress to the poor and disadvantaged. Poverty as a social problem was not on the public agenda again until the 1960s. It was affluence, not deprivation, that was a popular theme for the public, politicians, and professional social scientists during the 1950s. Few books on social problems written by sociologists in that period paid any serious attention to poverty. A best seller written by an outstanding economist brilliantly portrayed the new affluence that had converted poverty from a problem for the majority to an affliction for a minority. Published in 1958, *The Affluent Society,* though clearly sympathetic to the lot of the existing poor, noted that poverty in its modern form was no longer a massive problem but rather ". . . more nearly an afterthought." [24] Only a few years later (1962) Michael Harrington aroused the American conscience by making the poor once again visible through his book *The Other America.*[25] For Harrington the problem of poverty was a massive one because it affected a sizable minority in a society that could afford to spend the considerable resources it would take to abolish intolerable deprivation in the midst of plenty. Shortly after the book was published a combination of factors, especially an increasingly militant Negro movement for political, economic, and social rights, transformed poverty from an afterthought into an explosive social issue involving not only controversies surrounding appropriate strategies but the very definition of the problem itself.

[22] Mencher, *op. cit.,* p. 279.

[23] David A. Shannon, *The Great Depression* (Englewood Cliffs, N.J.: Spectrum Books, 1960).

[24] John Kenneth Galbraith, *The Affluent Society* (Boston: Houghton Mifflin, 1958), p. 323.

[25] Michael Harrington, *The Other America* (New York: Macmillan, 1962).

What is Poverty?

Poverty has no single meaning. Deficits in income, social competence, political power, or opportunity for full participation as a self-respecting member of society may be stressed. More specifically poverty may be seen as material deprivation, as inequality, or as a style of life (the culture of poverty). Whatever poverty may be, the starting point for discussion in a money society is inadequate income. The issue hinges around the meaning to be assigned to "inadequate." Two approaches may be taken. One assumes some poverty line or income level that separates the poor from the nonpoor. The other concerns itself with inequality, that is, with the relative share of income and other valuables available to those at the bottom, usually the lowest fifth of income receivers.[26] While most of public discussion rests on some assumed poverty line, the critical issue now seems to be inequality, not only in income but in access to resources and opportunities that determine life chances. But the traditional social welfare vocabulary of poverty is preferred to the politically disturbing language of inequality.[27] Our vocabulary reflects our values and values are central in formulating our concept of poverty.

With expanding economic resources, the standard defining the poverty line increases. Only two centuries ago poverty meant not having enough to eat, a subsistence level below 3,000 calories a day for a workingman. Poverty is therefore relative to resources and aspirations. This is small comfort, however, to those with the least in material goods or decent life prospects. Beyond the minimum requirements for survival, our needs are socially determined and it is in the context of a given society, with its standards for acceptable functioning, that the poor must measure their own well-being. When Charles Booth made his famous survey of the poor in London in the late nineteenth century, he used a standard of poverty that was approximately five times higher than the standard of living prevailing for the average person in Calcutta today.[28] Values define what we take to be some desirable level of living below which no one should be permitted to fall or they suggest some equitable distribution of the good things of life. Invariably standards conflict so that politics determine the concept of poverty that guides public policy. The poverty line in the United States today exceeds by a considerable degree the standard prevailing in London almost a century ago or in India today, which documents the fact that there are no fixed criteria for poverty; but it is not likely to ease the sense of deprivation the American poor experience. Poverty is the gap between our needs and our resources, but needs are experienced relative to prevailing standards.

In a sense the relativity of poverty means that it can never be abolished. Joseph S. Berliner has suggested that a cultural definition might draw the pov-

[26] S. M. Miller, Martin Rein, and Pamela Roby, "Poverty, Equality, and Conflict," in Bertram M. Gross (ed.), *Social Intelligence for America's Future* (Boston: Allyn & Bacon, 1969).

[27] *Ibid.,* p. 284.

[28] Peter Townsend, "The Scale and Meaning of Poverty in Contemporary Western Society," *Dependency and Poverty,* Colloquia 1963–1964, The Florence Heller Graduate School for Advanced Studies in Social Welfare (Waltham, Mass.: Brandeis University, 1965), p. 14.

erty line at that point at which people no longer define themselves as poor no matter what the gap is between what they and others may have.[29]   The challenge for each generation is to redefine its concept of social justice and to critically evaluate the needs it seeks to satisfy.   The value assumption we take in this book would argue that our commercial, consumption-oriented society does stimulate pseudo-needs that do not lead to an enrichment of experience. Any assumption about needs is, after all, based on some notion of life's purpose. While ethical ideals conflict, a democratic society must maximize freedom of choice.   The poor, then, may be seen as that group having the least freedom of choice to determine those needs they wish satisfied or to define and pursue their life goals.

While definitions of poverty invariably conflict, most would admit that hunger and malnutrition are indications of severe deprivation.[30]   It has been common in recent years, when speaking of the problem of hunger, to confine discussions to underdeveloped nations.   Studies, however, indicate a surprising amount of malnutrition and even hunger in the United States.   An extensive survey produced the following conclusions:

> Nonetheless, it is possible to assert, with a high degree of probability that we face a problem which, conservatively estimated, affects 10 million Americans, and in all likelihood, a substantially higher number.
>   Magnitude: available evidence indicates that the percentage of poor affected by hunger and malnutrition range between one-third and one-half of the poor.
>   Where income is low, where postneonatal mortality rates are high, and where participation in welfare and food programs is low or non-existent, it seems safe to suggest that hunger and malnutrition are prevalent.   On this basis we have identified hunger counties (256) requiring immediate and emergency attention.[31]

While hunger clearly marks a level of abject poverty, the common standard for counting the number of poor in the United States is the poverty line established by the Social Security Administration.   This poverty threshold for a nonfarm family of four was an annual income of $3,130 in 1964.   Revised to take price increases into account, the poverty line had risen to more than $3700 in 1969.   The basis for this poverty index is an Agriculture Department economy food plan that allows for $.75 a day per person (in an average four-person nonfarm family) for total food expenditures.[32]   Twice that amount is

[29] Joseph S. Berliner, "Some Aspects of Poverty in the United States," in *Dependency and Poverty, op. cit.,* p. 21.

[30] We may learn that many of us are more deprived than we think.   Senator George S. McGovern (S. Dak.) called for an inquiry into the nutritional quality of the food available in U.S. supermarkets, stating that "the dietary status of the nation as a whole appears to have deteriorated."   He expressed concern regarding food additives and the inability of the consumer to determine the nutrient value of purchases.   *Portland* (Maine) *Press Herald,* July 14, 1969.

[31] Citizen's Board of Inquiry into Hunger and Malnutrition in the United States, *Hunger, U.S.A.* (Washington, D.C.: New Community Press, 1968), pp. 32, 37–38.

[32] Mollie Orshansky, "The Shape of Poverty in 1966," *Social Security Bulletin,* 31 (March 1968), pp. 3–31.

budgeted for all other expenditures. To measure the adequacy of this standard, the reader may wish to assess how much he spends on food in an average day. Using this index, it is estimated that almost 30 million individuals were poor in 1966. In addition some 15 million were counted as near-poor.[33] While the poverty level is set at $65 a week for a nonfarm family of four, a similar family with less than $85 a week is regarded as near-poor.

There are conservative and liberal critics of this and other commonly accepted standards. For example, on the basis of a "nutritive adequacy definition of poverty," Rose D. Friedman estimates that in 1962 only 10 percent of families in the United States were poor. Her conservative criteria of poverty are intended as a criticism of the President's Council of Economic Advisers for their $3000 poverty line which produced an estimate that in 1964 20 percent of Americans were poor.[34] Any definition of poverty, however, must reflect some definition of social goals. Subsistence, no matter how defined, is no longer an adequate criterion for this society. Alan Haber has analyzed the Social Security Administration's poverty line and has declared it defective as an instrument for measuring poverty and as a guide to social policy.[35] He points out that the index is based on an unrealistic economy food plan, with a one-to-two ratio of food to total expenditures, thus allowing a total of $1.50 per day per person for all expenditures other than food (for the four-person nonfarm family). The poverty line based on the economy food plan has further deficiencies since it unrealistically assumes "skillful nonwaste food preparation," superior consumer skills, as well as time and resources with which to shop for the best buys.[36] It fails to recognize the dependence of the poor on neighborhood grocers, where prices are often higher and where dependence on credit restricts freedom to shop for bargains. It ignores the fact that the poor pay more and are exploited by some merchants.[37] The economy plan provides for no meals away from home, and it unrealistically assumes that the amount remaining after food expenditures meets minimum needs. The poor often can afford only relatively cheap durable goods, which require more frequent repair and replacement. Not only do the poor have limited resources to meet the normal emergencies that cut into any family's budget, but their hazardous existence compounds emergencies and intensifies the problem of meeting contingencies. Moreover they do not benefit from the occupational welfare system and thus lack the security and protection of fringe benefits that accompany more stable work patterns. To take a day off to go to a clinic, to visit the school, to attend court, to attend to an illness in the family is more costly for the poor than for others.

The present poverty line reflects a social goal far too limited to meet explosive demands and rising aspirations. A definition of poverty must give

---

[33] *Ibid.*

[34] Rose D. Friedman, *Poverty: Definition and Perspective* (Washington, D.C.: American Enterprise Institute for Public Policy Research, 1965), p. 34.

[35] Alan Haber, "Poverty Budgets: How Much is Enough?," *Poverty and Human Resources Abstracts,* 1 (May–June 1966), pp. 5–22.

[36] *Ibid.,* p. 6.

[37] David Caplovitz, *The Poor Pay More* (New York: Free Press, 1963).

realistic consideration to the resources required for effective functioning in our contemporary social environment.   Such a definition would consider social goals beyond biological maintenance and would include ". . . individual fulfillment and satisfying involvement in the larger society." [38]   While no adequate measure of the resources required for the attainment of this goal is available, some indication of the gap between the poverty line and what might be required may be derived from a comparison of the standard of living available to the poor compared with a family living on a moderate-income budget in 1967. The poverty budget in that year was $3,410.   In the same year a moderate family budget according to the Bureau of Labor Statistics required an annual income of $7,836 for an urban family of four.   In neither budget are allowances made for costs related to employment or for taxes paid.   In the following table (Table 12) the amount of money available for each major consumption item is shown for both the poverty and the moderate-income budgets.

Table 12.   Monthly Budgets, Poor and Moderate-Income
Urban Families of Four, 1967

CONSUMPTION ITEM	POOR [a]	MODERATE [b]
Total	$284	$653
Food	122	175
Housing	91 [c]	199 [d]
Transportation	6	77 [e]
Clothing and personal care	57	82
Medical care	0	40
Gifts and contributions	0	21
Life insurance	0	13
Other consumption (recreation, education, tobacco, etc.)	9	46

[a] Based on budgeted need for an AFDC family of four in Los Angeles, California.
[b] Moderate living standard defined by the Bureau of Labor Statistics for a family of four.
[c] Renter.
[d] Homeowner.
[e] Automobile owner.
SOURCE: President's Commission on Income Maintenance Programs, *Poverty Amid Plenty: The American Paradox,* (Washington, D.C. Government Printing Office, 1969), TABLE 1–3, p. 14

While the moderate-income budget may define what Americans take to be the amount of money necessary for an average way of life, one cannot imagine public acceptance of a poverty line that would approach that standard of living. A useful suggestion has been advanced by Victor Fuchs, who proposes that the poverty line be set at one-half the median family income.[39]   In 1968 median family income was $8,937.   While admitting that this is as arbitrary as any

[38] Haber, *op. cit.,* p. 8.

[39] Victor Fuchs, "Redefining Poverty and Redistributing Income," *The Public Interest,* No. 8 (Summer 1967), pp. 88–95.

standard, it has the merit of focusing attention on the distribution of income and it makes explicit a concern with assuring those at the bottom an equitable share in the expanding economy.[40] For example, the average income of four-person families increased by 37 percent between 1959 and 1966. In the same period, the poverty line was upwardly adjusted by only 9 percent; it took into account the changes in cost of living but not the relative increases of income going to the nonpoor.[41] An issue of social justice is raised by the recognition that a significant portion of the population has either marginal or no attachment to the labor force and therefore does not benefit from economic growth. Do they not have a citizen right to share in the common wealth of the nation? A significant portion are aged and others, female heads of households with dependent children. In addition a large segment of the poor are living in households having a breadwinner employed year round yet receiving wages that maintain the family in poverty. What right should they have to supplemental income?

If the concern is with inequality rather than with raising the income of the poor to some fixed level, then the comparative measure suggested by Fuchs would provide an index of our progress in this direction. Although, in 1947, 30 percent of all families had incomes under $3,000 compared to 12.3 percent in 1967, the percent of families with incomes below one-half the median has remained approximately the same (about 20 percent). Yet for most Americans inequality in income distribution is not a major issue. We prefer to believe that general economic progress will benefit all. "Alas, if that progress should come to the poor at the same pace as during 1946–65! Then it would be well along in the 21st century before the average income of the poorest fifth of American families reached $80 a week." [42]

Inequality of income and inequality in other life opportunities are issues we prefer to avoid because they focus attention on socially structured advantages and disadvantages, on the institution of power and privilege, and on the painful question of income redistribution and social reform. We fix our attention on the expanding economy or on programs of education and rehabilitation that may correct disabling characteristics of the poor to enable them to enter the system without altering its fundamental structure. There is some basis for this. The number of the poor, as measured by the poverty-line yardstick, is declining; there were 18 million fewer poor in 1969 than in 1960.[43] Real income has increased for all groups in society; special programs do aid some individuals to acquire skills that lift them out of poverty. In addition, improvement in social security measures could remove an increasing number of the aged from levels of poverty as now defined. In the meantime relative deprivation, not poverty in any absolute sense, has become the central political issue to an increasing number of those who view the world from the lower depths. Whether articulated or not, the hurt and humiliation of galling

---

[40] *Ibid.*

[41] Orshansky, *op. cit.,* p. 6.

[42] Oscar Gass, "The Political Economy of the Great Society" *Commentary,* (October 1965), p. 36.

[43] Wilbur J. Cohen, "A Ten-Point Program to Abolish Poverty," *Social Security Bulletin,* 31 (December 1968), p. 13.

disparities in life styles and life prospects nourish the alienation of the poor and the seeds of revolt.   It is doubtful that we can deal with this without policies and programs aimed directly at reducing inequalities.   Although it is possible to raise the income of the poor to some poverty line, to alleviate inequality and restore the poor to their membership in society is far more difficult.   Although scholarly attention is being focused on this more and more, our social welfare measures are geared for dealing with the consequences of poverty and inequality, not for redressing inequities.

Inequality has come to be broadly defined, in this era of the human rights revolution, to include unacceptable disparities in such things as income, decent employment, quality education and social services, participation in decision-making, and opportunities for self-esteem.   Measures of inequality are only now being developed that include not only income, but the quality of community services available, as well as real opportunities for upward social mobility and for rewarding participation in society.[44]   Income, however, remains an important indicator; but it is not a totally adequate measure.   It excludes certain less visible forms of wealth that function as multipliers of advantage.   These include such items as capital appreciation, perhaps ". . . the major source of the wealth of the rich in the 1950s and 60s; fringe benefits available through the occupational welfare state, expense accounts, stock options, tax exemptions that favor the wealthy; spread of income into retirement; conversion of income into lower-taxed capital and capital gains." [45]   Rather than focus solely on annual income, Richard Titmuss has suggested a need to consider resources available to individuals and families over time.[46]   Such resources would include not only money income and various forms of personal property but also access to quality community resources and services.   One's real income is money income plus available community resources.   The level of living is increasingly determined by the quality of life made possible through the social provision of education, medical care, police protection, parks, recreation facilities, and clean water and air.   Unlike the Scandinavian countries, with their provision of quality public services as a means of assuring some minimum level of well-being for all, to have relatively low incomes in the United States is also to be exposed to inferior and even damaging social provisions of education, medical care, police protection, and the like.[47]   We shall suggest later that, if we wish to look at poverty from the perspective of a concern for human development, the definition of deficits would need to consider command over strategic resources at the time most critically needed: adequate nutrition and medical care in the first trimester of pregnancy; critical inputs of nutrition, affection, and sensory stimulation for the infant; education that promotes cognitive development and creative social adaptation among the young; supplemental income, adequate retraining, and other supportive resources to ease

[44] S. M. Miller, *et al,* in Gross, *op. cit.*

[45] Townsend, in *Dependency and Poverty, op. cit.,* p. 3.

[46] S. M. Miller, *et al.,* in Gross, *op. cit.,* p. 286.

[47] Carl G. Uhr, *Sweden's Social Security System,* Social Security Administration Research Report No. 14 (Washington, D.C.: Government Printing Office, 1966); George R. Nelson (ed.), *Freedom and Welfare* (The Ministries of Social Affairs of Denmark, Finland, Iceland, Norway, Sweden, 1953).

the transition for a breadwinner and his family from one job to another, and so forth.

Attention to income requires some consideration not only of its adequacy, but of its stability and source.[48] Income received from a stigmatized public assistance program, even if adequate in amount, will add to material well-being but may destroy self-respect. There is some evidence, for example, that more generous public assistance grants tend to lower the school dropout rate for whites but increase it for Negroes. Black youths, it is suggested in *Big City Dropouts,* tend to perceive public assistance as a mark of their bondage to the white man.[49]

To define poverty in terms of income equality is to draw attention to the share of income received by the lowest one-fifth of income receivers. While invariably there must be some group at the bottom so long as income is distributed on the basis of some assumed differential contribution to society, critical questions are Who is at the bottom? How do they happen to be there? What share do they receive? Contrary to the common assumption of an increasing equalization of income in the United States, there has been no significant change in income distribution for almost twenty years.[50] As indicated in Table 13, the share of income received by the lowest fifth of families

Table 13. Percent of Aggregate Income Received by Each Fifth and Top 5 Percent of Families and Unrelated Individuals: Selected Years, 1947–1966

ITEM AND INCOME RANK	1947	1950	1960	1963	1966
	%	%	%	%	%
Families	100	100	100	100	100
Lowest fifth	5.0	4.5	4.9	5.1	5.4
Second fifth	11.8	12.0	12.0	12.0	12.4
Middle fifth	17.0	17.4	17.6	17.6	17.7
Fourth fifth	23.1	23.5	23.6	23.9	23.8
Highest fifth	43.0	42.6	42.0	41.4	40.7
Top 5%	17.2	17.0	16.8	16.0	14.8
Unrelated individuals	100	100	100	100	100
Lowest fifth	1.9	2.3	2.6	2.4	2.9
Second fifth	5.8	7.0	7.1	7.3	7.6
Middle fifth	11.9	13.8	13.6	12.7	13.3
Fourth fifth	21.4	26.5	25.7	24.6	24.2
Highest fifth	59.1	50.4	50.9	53.0	52.0
Top 5%	33.3	19.3	20.0	21.2	21.8

SOURCE: *Statistical Abstract of the United States,* 1968.   U.S. Bureau of the Census, (GPO), 1968 Table No. 471, p. 324.

[48] S. M. Miller, *et al.,* in Gross, *op. cit.,* pp. 292–295, 322–327.

[49] Robert A. Dentler and Mary Ellen Warshauer, *Big City Dropouts and Illiterates* (New York: Center for Urban Education, 1965), pp. 31–35.

[50] Herman P. Miller, *Income Distribution in the United States,* a 1960 Census Monograph (Washington D.C.: Government Printing Office, 1966), p. 2.

has remained near 5 percent since 1947. The highest fifth of families receive over 40 percent of the income; the share of the bottom fifth is eight times lower. The gap is even wider with unrelated individuals; the lowest fifth receive only 2.9% of the income, over seventeen times less than the highest fifth's share of 52%. One observer writes:

> As a citizen I judge this American income distribution—one of the foundation stones of our society—to be against good conscience. But I participate in it . . . so far as my eyes can reach, no politically significant group of Americans, young or old, finds this income pattern—not as a statistic, but as experienced in the day's encounters—in conflict with its operating conceptions of a democratic society.[51]

Income did become more evenly distributed in the period 1929–1941, during which time the major redistribution involved families in the top and middle brackets. The share received by the lowest income group increased somewhat during World War II, but no significant change has occurred in the past quarter of a century.[52] It is important to note that the increase in two-earner families accounts for some of the rise in family income. This is especially true for Negro families. In 1967 the median income of Negro two-earner families residing in central cities was $7,225, roughly equal to that of white central-city families having one earner ($7,285).[53]

This does not mean, of course, that there has been no economic progress. Real incomes have increased significantly for all groups in society. In contrast 1967 dollars, the median total money income of families increased from $6,210 in 1959 to $8,017 in 1967.[54] Nevertheless neither our social welfare measures nor our tax structure seems to have any significant impact on the distribution of income to the poor. On the other hand the degree of income inequality should not be exaggerated. According to H. P. Miller there is no evidence that incomes are more widely distributed in any country than they are in the United States.[55]

Since one can enjoy an average way of life only with income that makes this possible, the gap betwen the incomes of those at the bottom and those above them is more critical than the absolute amount available to the poor. Relative deprivation is an especially critical problem for nonwhites. While the ratio of nonwhite to white family income has risen in recent years from 54 in 1959 to

[51] Oscar Gass, "The Political Economy of the Great Society," *Commentary,* October 1965, p. 25.

[52] *Income Distribution, op. cit.,* p. 2.

[53] "Trends in Social and Economic Conditions in Metropolitan Areas," *Current Population Reports,* Series P–23, Special Studies No. 27, U.S. Bureau of the Census (Washington, D.C.: Government Printing Office, 1969).

[54] "Family Income Advances, Poverty Reduced in 1967," *Current Population Reports,* Series P–60, No. 55, U.S. Bureau of the Census (Washington, D.C.: Government Printing Office, 1968), p. 4.

[55] Herman P. Miller, *Rich Man, Poor Man* (New York: Signet Books, 1965), p. 53.

62 in 1967, the gap is still considerable.[56] The difference between white and nonwhite median income (in 1965 dollars) was $2,174 in 1947 and $3,036 in 1966.[57] Poor Negroes in central cities are relatively worse off than poor whites. In central cities the average poor Negro family had an income $1,100 below the poverty line. The comparable figure for whites was $700.[58] An important factor, previously referred to in Table 9, that vitiates use of any overall poverty line and increases the inequality of income distribution is that

> according to the 1960 census statistics, nonwhites—regardless of income —must earn *one-third* [emphasis mine] more than whites in order to afford standard housing (based on allocation of 20% of earnings for mortgage payments or rent).[59]

This represents one quantifiable price of discrimination, paid in cash by the victims of race prejudice.

Life opportunities as measured by a variety of indices consistently show serious relative gaps despite significant improvements over the past. While income inequality is an important indicator of social inequality, it is the life style and life circumstances created by this inequality that merit attention. The market does not simply distribute income, it allocates life and death, health and disability, opportunity for self-fulfillment and self-destruction. Opportunities for upward mobility are severely restricted for children in families at the bottom of the occupational hierarchy. The chance of getting a white-collar job for the son of a white manual worker is a little better than half that of a son born to a white family supported by a white-collar job. The equivalent chance of a black boy born to a man with a manual job is less than a fourth. Even more distressing is the fact that ". . . among Negro sons of white-collar fathers, 72.4 percent went into manual occupations, as compared with 23.4 percent of non-Negro sons, indicating an unusual rate of downward mobility." [60]

On the other hand significant gains have been made. There has been a marked and continuing drop in the number of families living at subsistence levels. In 1929 at the peak of prosperous 1920s some 31 percent of the families and individuals had incomes under $2,000. By 1961 this had dropped to 12 percent, a figure based on adjustments made for changes in cost of living.[61]

---

[56] "Recent Trends in Social and Economic Conditions of Negroes in the United States," *Current Population Reports,* Series P–23, No. 26, U.S. Bureau of the Census, and Bureau of Labor Statistics Report No. 347 (Washington, D.C.: Government Printing Office, 1968), p. 6.

[57] "Social and Economic Conditions of Negroes in the United States," *Current Population Reports,* Series P–23, No. 24, U.S. Bureau of the Census, and Bureau of Labor Statistics Report No. 332 (Washington, D.C.: Government Printing Office, 1967), p. 18.

[58] *Current Population Reports,* P–23, No. 27, *op. cit.*

[59] *A Decent Home,* President's Committee on Urban Housing (Washington, D.C.: Government Printing Office, 1969), p. 8.

[60] S. M. Miller, *et al,* in Gross, *op. cit.,* p. 315.

[61] *Income Distribution, op. cit.,* p. 12.

Income under $1,600 defined the poorest 20 percent of all families in 1947. The cut-off point for the bottom fifth in 1960 was $2,800. Thus, increases in real income have been widely distributed and even the poor today may enjoy certain amenities of life either unavailable a few decades ago or confined solely to the wealthy.[62] Yet the problems we have to deal with are those felt deprivations that are experienced by the poor, who live with ugliness, dreariness, and humiliation. To refer to improvement over time seems insulting to those who continue to live without bare necessities and the pain of social exclusion.

> You ask me what is poverty? Listen to me. Here I am, I am dirty, smelly and with no "proper" underwear on and with the stench of my rotting teeth near you. I will tell you. Listen to me. Listen without pity. I cannot use your pity. Listen with understanding. Put yourself in my dirty, worn out, ill fitting shoes, and hear me. Poverty is getting up every morning from a dirty and illness stained mattress. . . . Poverty is being tired. They told me at the hospital when the last baby came, that I had chronic anemia caused from poor diet, a bad case of worms, and that I needed a corrective operation. I listened politely—the poor are always polite. . . . Poverty is dirt. You say in your clean clothes coming from your clean house, "anybody can be clean." Let me explain about housekeeping with no money. . . . Poverty is asking for help. Have you ever had to ask for help, knowing your children will suffer unless you get it? . . . Poverty is remembering. It is remembering quitting school in junior high because "nice" children had been so cruel about my clothes and my smell. . . . Poverty is looking into a black future. . . . Poverty is an acid that drips on pride until all pride is worn away. . . .[63]

It is poignantly clear from the above quotation that the experience of poverty is not solely one of material deprivation but of an assault on self-respect. The new poverty with which we deal is not a question of material deprivation, though this remains important, but of status deprivation. Economic and social inequalities create a socially excluded and stigmatized underclass. The claims of common citizenship now challenge class inequality. The imperatives of self-esteem now energize the social revolution that abhors the residual welfare measures designed by one class on behalf of its inferiors, no matter how adequate we may seek to make such programs. The issue now is one of two nations. To see proverty in terms of some fixed income line is to ignore Disraeli's advice that ". . . the condition of classes must be judged by the age, and by their relation with each other." [64] Lee Rainwater recognizes this when he writes:

> What has become clear in the past decade is that the relative deprivation of the underclass goes to the heart of their marginality and alienation.

[62] Herman P. Miller, *op. cit.,* pp. 73–74.

[63] Jo Goodwin Parker, "What Is Poverty?," U.S. Congress, House, *Congressional Record,* Vol. 112, (September 14, 1965), pp. 21617–21618.

[64] Benjamin Disraeli, *Sybil or the Two Nations* printed as Vol. IX of the Bradenham Edition (London: Peter Davies, 1927), p. 200, originally published by Mayday, 1845.

No matter how much the incomes of the underclass rise, as long as there exists in the society groups of people whose level of living is far below the going average, we will continue to have the misery and the problems of an underclass.[65]

Who Are the Poor?

The poor are not all alike although they do have one thing in common—too little money. Not all those considered poor today will be poor tomorrow. Some are young heads of households who are temporarily in poverty. Not all those considered poor today were poor throughout their lives. A number are aged with smaller incomes because of retirement. Too little is known about those individuals and families who move in and out of poverty. We do know that the poor vary enormously and that certain groups are characterized by a relatively high risk of being poor. Identification of such groups aids in recognizing that different strategies are required for different groups. Groups with a high risk of poverty are women and children, nonwhites, aged and disabled, families living in rural areas, particularly in the South, those with more than four children, female-based households, those with least education, and the unemployed and underemployed.

Special attention should be paid to the high risk of poverty for women and children. It is not commonly recognized that poor women outnumber men by 8 to 5.[66] This raises questions about the extent to which women have been truly emancipated. With increasing knowledge about the critical importance of early childhood, the fact that in 1966 one-fourth of all children under 18 were living in poverty or near-poverty is startling.[67] Two out of three female-headed households with children under six are poor.[68] For nonwhite children the risk of poverty is roughly four times that for white children (Table 14). Over 60% of all nonwhite children in 1966 were poor or near-poor (Table 15). Children in families headed by a woman have a particularly high risk of poverty and of remaining in poverty. While poverty has declined for families headed by a male, those headed by a female have increased as a proportion of all families in poverty. From 1959 to 1966 there was a drop of 2.4 million families headed by a male counted as poor. In that same period the number of poor families headed by a woman remained unchanged (about 1.5 million) and the number of poor in female-headed families increased by one-tenth.[69]

The aged continue to face serious problems of inadequate income, with one-third of those 65 and over counted as poor. Nearly 30 percent of the 25.9 million persons counted as poor in 1967 lived in households with an aged or disabled head. Most of these could be removed from poverty through expanded social insurance and other financial assistance programs.[70]

[65] Lee Rainwater, "Looking Back and Looking Up," *Trans-action,* 6 (February 1969), p. 9.

[66] Orshansky, *op. cit.,* p. 16.

[67] *Ibid.,* p. 6.

[68] *Ibid,* p. 16.

[69] *Ibid.,* pp. 8–9.

[70] Cohen, *op. cit.*

Table 14.   Who Are the Poor?   1967 (in thousands)

	TOTAL		WHITE		NONWHITE	
	Number	%	Number	%	Number	%
Total poor persons	25,929	13.3	17,584	10.2	8,344	35.3
Poor children	10,666	15.1	6,184	10.3	4,482	42.9
Unrelated individuals 65 and over						
Male	553	42.4	450	40.2	103	56.0
Female	2,149	57.1	1,941	55.7	208	75.4
Families						
Total	5,266	10.6	3,730	8.3	1,536	30.6
Male head	3,544	8.0	2,724	6.7	820	22.2
Female head	1,723	32.3	1,007	25.1	716	54.1
6 children or more	438	35.0	213	24.9	225	56.5

SOURCE: *Current Population Reports,* Series P–60, No. 55, U.S. Bureau of the Census, "Family Income Advances, Poverty Reduced in 1967" (Washington, D.C.: Government Printing Office, 1968), pp. 4, 7.

Table 15.   Poor and Near-Poor Children by Race and Family Head, 1966 *

	(NUMBERS IN THOUSANDS)					
	TOTAL		WHITE		NONWHITE	
	Number	%	Number	%	Number	%
Children under 18	69,771		59,578		10,193	
Poor	12,539	18.0	7,526	12.6	5,014	49.2
Near poor	6,637	9.5	5,222	8.8	1,413	13.9
With male head	62,521		55,103		7,419	
Poor	8,117	13.0	5,280	9.6	2,837	38.2
Near poor	5,932	9.5	4,732	8.6	1,201	16.2
With female head	7,251		4,475		2,776	
Poor	4,423	61.0	2,246	50.2	2,177	78.4
Near poor	705	9.7	492	11.0	213	7.7
Children under 6	23,550					
Poor	4,386	18.6	2,564		1,823	
Near poor	2,300	10.0	—		—	
Male head	21,534					
Poor	2,964	13.8	1,893		1,071	
Near poor	2,196	10.2	—		—	
Female head	2,018					
Poor	1,423	70.5	671		752	
Near poor	164	8.1	—		—	

* Poor, as defined by the Social Security Administration, means an income of $3,335 for a nonfarm family of four.   Near-poor is about $20 per month higher for the same-size family.

SOURCE: Mollie Orshansky, "The Shape of Poverty in 1966," *Social Security Bulletin,* Vol. 31 (March 1968), pp. 5, 6, 17.

Those with the highest risk of poverty have been called the "immobile poor"; they suffer from the most severe socially imposed handicaps to participation in an expanding economy. These are nonwhites, aged and disabled, families headed by a woman, and the underemployed and the unemployed.[71]

Perhaps the best way of classifying the poor is in terms of their relationship to the labor force, since work is the major means by which income, self-esteem, and the opportunity to fully participate in the life of this society is acquired. The adult poor may be divided into two groups: those with an attachment to the labor force and those temporarily or permanently outside the labor force because of age, disability, or the need to care for dependent children. Where work is not possible at wages above the poverty line, the only way to immediately relieve poverty is to provide generous transfers of income supplemented possibly by social provisions of housing, medical care, and so on. For those in the labor force the only hope is improved employment opportunities or supplementation of marginal wages.

In the American mythology the poor consist primarily of those too lazy to work, which ignores the fact that the majority of the poor (57 percent) live in families with an adult in the labor force. About a third were living in families in which the head worked year-round in 1967. A fourth of those called poor were in families in which the head worked part of the year.[72]

In 1967, almost a third of the poor were in families with an aged or disabled head—individuals unable to participate in the economy, not subject to society's expectations about work, yet denied access to decent levels of income. An additional 14 percent of the poor were in families in which the head of the household was not employed. Most of these (3.1 million out of a total of 3.7 million individuals) were in families with a woman at the head. The remainder (600,000) were living in families with a male head, most of whom were not employed because of illness.[73] Try as one might, it's simply impossible to come up with facts to support the persistent myth about the "sturdy male beggar," too lazy to work, as the prime cause of poverty. The facts are that 80 percent of the working-age men who are poor have jobs and 75 percent are in full-time employment.[74] The remainder are for the most part, ill, disabled, or seeking employment.

Why Are People Poor?

Historically, and all too simply, there have been two approaches to explaining poverty: one focusing attention on the moral, psychological, or cultural character of the poor; the other focusing attention on the structure of society itself, its level of economic development, and its system of values. Clearly the explanation one chooses depends on the kind of poverty under discussion and one's moral perspective. Poverty in this society is not the problem of scarcity

[71] Joseph W. Eaton, "The Immobile Poor," in Thomas D. Sherrard (ed.), *Social Welfare and Urban Problems* (New York: Columbia University Press, 1968), pp. 64–65.

[72] Cohen, *op. cit.*

[73] *Ibid.*

[74] *Ibid.*, p. 1.

that characterizes a primitive society, an agricultural economy, or a nation just beginning its capital accumulation. It is not mass poverty awaiting economic development.[75] The poverty we confront cannot be understood except in the context of our rapidly changing society. We are dealing with a new problem by relying on outmoded categories of thought. The new problem involves a minority rather than majority poor, consisting primarily of those excluded from participation in a relatively affluent, postindustrial society of high mass consumption and rising expectations. Critical issues are the manner in which people may be compensated for the unemployment and subemployment forced upon them, the extent to which dignified work as a career may be offered to those now confined to dead-end jobs, and the degree to which income may be redistributed to whose who cannot be expected to participate in the labor force.[76] We must now deal with inequality in access to decent work, income, education, and other valuable goods and services; unequal power to influence decisions; and most of all inequality in opportunity to develop self-respect and one's maximum capacities as a person. We are now on a collision course between rising aspirations and resistance to essential social reforms. Great barriers to social progress are the values and attitudes of yesterday. Though poverty is a structural problem we persist in viewing it through the Puritan lens of moral defect.

The Moral View of Poverty

The new problem we are trying to deal with tends to be viewed in old categories of thought more appropriate to the eighteenth and early nineteenth centuries. The older view saw poverty in moral terms through the lens of the Puritan ethic that focused on defects in the individual character of the poor.

In a world of scarce goods that required the labor of all it made sense to insist that he who did not work would not eat. To work became a moral obligation, to fail to work became a sin. In a land of apparent unlimited opportunity, a self-reliant individual could not help, it was thought, to provide adequately for himself and for his dependents. Although some recognized that economic and social conditions, inadequate wages, unequal distribution of property, chronic and cyclical unemployment were linked to poverty, the general belief was that work was available to all who wanted it. Yet from the late eighteenth through the early twentieth centuries, economic insecurity due to periodic depressions was the common lot of the working class. In the depression of 1807–1809 it was estimated that some 500,000 were unemployed. Two decades later another economic decline forced many workers to apply for assistance. As *The New York Times* recorded it:

> Thousands of industrious mechanics who never before solicited alms, were brought to the humiliating condition of applying for assistance, and with tears on their manly cheeks, confessed their inability to provide food or clothing for their families.[77]

[75] Pierre L. Van Den Berghe, "Poverty as Underdevelopment," *Trans-action*, 6 (July–August 1969), pp. 3–4 and 62.

[76] Marc A. Fried, "Is Work a Career?," *Trans-action*, 3 (September–October, 1966), pp. 42–47.

[77] Quoted in Mencher, *op. cit.*, p. 137.

Despite periodic lack of employment the able-bodied man was held responsible for the support of his family. Self-reliance in the face of economic adversity became the hallmark of character. Even to demand the right to work was viewed with suspicion and alarm. In 1873 a spokesman for the New York Association for Improving the Conditions of the Poor referred to unemployed workers who demanded jobs through public employment as a "vast hydra-headed class ready to strike at property and all we value most." [78] The misery of the poor, it seemed, could be easily explained by their defect of character. Most studies of the causes of poverty in the early nineteenth century emphasized the idleness, intemperance, and improvidence of the poor. In 1853 in Newburyport, Massachusetts, 10 percent of the population received public aid. Wages were so low that women and children had to work; 20 percent of the expenditures of laboring families were financed by the labor of children under fifteen. Yet the general view of poverty, as expressed in a newspaper in 1856, was that it was "not a want of means but a want of will—of real manliness and self-control." [79] Some early nineteenth-century studies in England emphasized social rather than moral considerations. A study by Mathew Martin of mendicity from 1800 to 1803, which was based on interviews with 2,000 beggars, concluded that mendicity was ". . . more misfortune than choice or roguery." [80] On the other hand a study in London in 1833 could not discover a single case that could not be explained by improvidence of some kind, "the great improvidence being marriage." [81] Important scholars and writers contributed to this moral view of poverty. Malthus believed the lower class was "ruled by passion and sinful desire." [82] Ricardo insisted that the poor needed to be consistently reminded ". . . that the most effective remedy for the inadequacy of their wages is in their hands." [83] The volume *Self-Help* by Samuel Smiles, published in 1860, sold 300,000 copies and conveyed the popular message

> . . . that there is no power of law that can make the idle man industrious, the thriftless provident, or the drunken sober; though every individual can be each and all of these if he will, by the exercise of his own free power of action and self-denial.[84]

William Graham Sumner contributed the authority of the sociology of his day to the philosophy of Social Darwinism. In the *Forgotten Man* and other essays, he celebrated the ideology of self-reliance and contributed to an at-

[78] Herbert G. Gutman, "The Failure of the Movement by the Unemployed for Public Works in 1873," *Political Science Quarterly,* 80 (June 1965), p. 254.

[79] Stephen Thernstrom, *Poverty and Progress* (Cambridge, Mass.: Harvard University Press, 1964), pp. 20 and 73.

[80] David Owen, *English Philanthropy, 1660–1960* (Cambridge, Mass.: Belknap Press, 1964), pp. 109–110.

[81] *Ibid,* p. 138.

[82] Mencher, *op. cit.,* p. 170.

[83] Calvin Woodard, "Reality and Social Reform: The Transition from Laissez-Faire to the Welfare State," *Yale Law Journal,* 72 (December 1962), p. 317.

[84] Quoted in Crane Brinton, *Ideas and Men* (New York: Prentice-Hall, 1950), p. 433.

titude of contempt for those who fell by the wayside.[85]   Granting that paupers and the physically incapacitated are an "inevitable charge on society," he warned against excessive sympathy or generosity for the ". . . weak . . . the shiftless, the imprudent, the negligent, the impractical, . . . the inefficient. . . the intemperate, the extravagant and the vicious . . . a drunkard in the gutter is just where he ought to be."   Any capital diverted to the support of the "shiftless and good-for-nothing" is diverted from some other useful employment.[86]   Such ideas fell on fertile ground, prepared since the eighteenth and nineteenth centuries not only to view the poor with suspicion and contempt but to regard the able-bodied poor as petty criminals and to define destitution as a crime.   The law incorporated this view in such decisions as *City of New York v. Miln* (1837), which granted the State of New York the right to regulate the entry of those regarded as potential paupers on the grounds that it was entitled to protect itself from their "moral pestilence."   It was not until a hundred years later, in *Edwards v. California* (1941), that the power of the state to restrict entry of indigents was declared unconstitutional.[87]   The view of poverty as a crime has persisted to the present day.[88]   Law and public opinion, however, are increasingly recognizing the poor as persons and citizens.[89]   Contempt for the poor may be seen to this day, as in the remark allegedly made by the head of a large citrus farm operation: "Migrants are the scum of the earth.   Anything they get over forty cents an hour is gravy." [90]

To many of the nineteenth-century humanitarians who sought to aid the poor, ". . . poverty was but the material result of their sinful self-indulgent lives." [91]   From their observations of the poor, one might easily conclude ". . . that if the poor did not drink so much, would use the savings banks, and would wash more frequently, social distress would at least be markedly alleviated." [92]   To the founders of the late ninetenth-century Charity Organization Society, it was the "sheer incapacity" of the lower class "which makes and

[85] For an earlier but in many ways a more contemporary view *see* Ralph Waldo Emerson, "Self Reliance," in Brooks Atkinson (ed.), *The Selected Writings of Ralph Waldo Emerson* (New York: Modern Library, 1950), pp. 145–169.

[86] William Graham Sumner, *The Forgotten Man* (1919; reprint ed., New Haven, Conn.: Yale University Press), pp. 11, 16.

[87] City of New York v. Miln, 36 U.S. (11 Pet.) 102, 142 (1837); Edwards v. California, 314 U.S. 160 (1941).

[88] Betty Mandell, "The Crime of Poverty," *Social Work,* 7 (January 1962), 3–11; Jacobus tenBroeck and Floyd W. Matson, "The Disabled and the Law of Welfare," *California Law Review,* 54, (May 1966), pp. 832–833.

[89] Bernard L. Diamond, "The Children of Leviathan: Psychoanalytic Speculations Concerning Welfare Law and Punitive Sanctions," *California Law Review,* Vol. 54 (May 1966), pp. 368–369; Charles A. Reich, "Individual Rights and Social Welfare: The Emerging Legal Issues," *Yale Law Journal,* Vol. 74, No. 1 (June 1965), pp. 1245–1257; A. Delafield Smith, *The Right to Life* (Chapel Hill, N.C.: University of North Carolina Press, 1955).

[90] Steve Allen, *The Ground Is Our Table* (New York: Doubleday, 1966), p. 131.

[91] Mencher, *op. cit.,* p. 197.

[92] Owen, *op. cit.,* p. 462.

keeps them poor." [93]   To meet their material needs was only to risk increasing their dependency. The task instead was the development of sobriety and industry. It is possible to suggest, as Woodard does, that moral improvement in the middle and late eighteenth century was a critical factor in the production of wealth. Such character traits as frugality, diligence, temperance, and sexual restraint were "affected with a public interest," insofar as they were attributes that accompanied the discipline of work.[94]

While the legitimate needs of the "worthy poor" might be a proper obligation of philanthropy, one must be ever alert against material assistance that might undermine the individual initiative regarded as so essential to an individualistic and competitive society. Some doubt was even cast on the prudence of relieving the economic distress of widows, for if ". . . the head of the family makes no provision in case of his death, part of the responsibility falls on his wife and it is doubtful whether the widow ought to be relieved of the consequences by charitable aid." [95]   Similarly, a spokesman for the Chicago Relief and Aid Society declared in 1873, in the midst of serious unemployment, that "if the manifest destiny of a man is the poor house we must let him go there. To aid some men will do them no good." [96]   The notion of the poor as the degraded and dangerous classes and the cult of self-help and rugged individualism had its forceful opponents in the late nineteenth-century founders of social settlements; in the proponents of the Social Gospel, who attacked the social Darwinism of Sumner and Spencer; in such social reformers as Jane Addams, Henry George, Edward Bellamy; and in the sociology of Albion Small, Edward A. Ross, and Lester Ward. It was the latter part of the nineteenth century that gave us the "most audacious belief of the age," the belief in the possibility of abolishing poverty. The initial attack in the battle against poverty, says Robert H. Bremner, "came from the new profession of social work.[97]   By the last decade of the nineteenth century the swing was away from a moral to a scientific view of poverty, from laissez faire to a positive conception of the function of government to contribute to the well-being of its citizens. In the words of Francis G. Peabody, at the dawn of the twentieth century, never before had so many people been stirred by the "recognition of inequality in social opportunity, by the call to social service, by dreams of a better social world." [98]   A new view of poverty, combined with a more optimistic view of human nature and the possibilities of government, was aided by the economic growth that seemed to promise the end of the ancient curse. Society was no longer seen as the automatic product of an invisible hand. Declaring the death of laissez faire, Albion Small asserted that popular judgment was "intoxicated

[93] Mencher, *op. cit.,* p. 202.

[94] Woodard, *op. cit.,* pp. 299–300.

[95] From the manual of the London Charity Organization Society, quoted in Philip Klein, "Social Work," *Encyclopedia of the Social Sciences* (New York: Macmillan, 1937), Vol. XIV, p. 166.

[96] Gutman, *op. cit.,* p. 256.

[97] Bremner, *op. cit.,* p. 201.

[98] Quoted in Fine, *op. cit.,* p. 378.

with the splendid half truth that society is what men choose to make it." [99]

Although social reform has been the emphasis in approaches to poverty and related problems in the first two decades of the twentieth century, during the crisis of the Great Depression of the 1930s, and again in some measure during the early phase of the War on Poverty in the 1960s, the moral view of the poor has never been obliterated. Recent studies indicate that a significant proportion of Americans continue to perceive the problems of the poor and particularly the Negro poor in terms of individual moral responsibility. As noted in Chapter Four, a majority of whites interviewed in fifteen major American cities felt that Negroes themselves were responsible for their low-status jobs, poor education, and housing.[100]

The myths of the nineteenth century, useful in some respects in their day, now continue like the dead hand of the past to prevent us from seeing the actual conditions of the poor and blind us to a perception of the societal factors that account for unnecessary deprivations. At the same time, such ideologies tend to be protective devices designed to avoid confrontation of facts that threaten self-interest. Therefore they are not easily changed. So long as we continue to blame the poor for their plight or see poverty as an individual problem we shall not see that we are dealing with a new problem calling for new kinds of action.

This brings us to the anatomy of poverty, an anatomy that focuses attention not on the character of the poor but on the character of society. We can see, if we want to, that poverty is a social problem. This is not to suggest that all the evidence is in on the causes of poverty or that social scientists agree on causal theories. Students of poverty tend to be divided between those who focus on structural causes and those who, while not necessarily denying the validity of the former, tend to emphasize the importance of the culture of poverty, the values and life styles of the poor that they see as central in perpetuating the cycle of poverty.[101] We are partial, for reasons we shall outline, to a structural analysis, although in a later chapter we shall pay some attention to the concept of the culture of poverty and its implications.

The Social View of Poverty

> The problem of poverty . . . is not a problem of individual character and its waywardness, but a problem of economic and industrial organization. It has to be studied first at its sources, and only secondly in its manifestations.[102]

[99] *Ibid.,* p. 377.

[100] *Supplemental Studies,* National Advisory Commission on Civil Disorders (Washington, D.C.: Government Printing Office, 1968), p. 30.

[101] Oscar Lewis, "The Culture of Poverty," *Scientific American,* 215 (October 1966), 19–25; Elizabeth Herzog, "Some Assumptions About the Poor," *Social Service Review,* 37 (December 1963), pp. 389–402; and Charles A. Valentine, *Culture and Poverty* (Chicago: University of Chicago Press, 1968).

[102] R. H. Tawney, quoted in Richard M. Titmuss, *Essays on the "Welfare State"* (London: G. Allen, 1958), p. 18.

Poverty is linked to social institutions that determine the allocation of personal and social resources required for living in an industrial economy and for competing for position and power.[103] An ecological approach enables us to see that the lower class is an integral part of the functioning of the total society. The disorganization we attribute to the poor is a direct consequence of the organization the rest of us participate in and take for granted. Personal resources, biological competence, intelligence, health, motivation, and social and occupational skills are as much socially allocated (within limits set by genetic potential) as are community resources and opportunities, education, employment, medical care, income, and paths to social mobility. For example, Dr. George James estimates that poverty is the third leading cause of death in American cities. An infant born of poor parents has twice the risk of dying before reaching his first birthday than does the child of more well-to-do parents. Furthermore, although 5 percent of all the children born in the United States are mentally retarded, by the age of thirteen 9 percent will be retarded. "We produce as much retardation as is born and 75 percent of mental retardation among children comes from areas of poverty." [104]

The reciprocal nature of personal and social resources and their availability on the basis of one's group membership and location in the social structure require emphasis. Children born to low-income mothers deprived of adequate nutrition and decent prenatal care have a high risk of birth anomalies, including mental retardation, cerebral palsy, epilepsy, behavioral disorders, and reading disability.[105] To be born into a minority group denied access to adequate education is to suffer restrictions on the development of personal resources, with consequent limitations in the competition for rewarding employment and the influence that flows from membership in functionally significant occupational groups. To be poor is to belong to powerless groups with little command over social resources that can effect a change in life conditions, with consequent restrictions on capacity and opportunity for upward mobility.

---

[103] Acknowledgment is made of the generous use of central concepts provided by Jack Meltzer and Joyce Whitley, "Social and Physical Planning for the Urban Slum," in Sherrard, *op. cit.,* pp. 161–185. This article has helped enormously to clarify the author's long effort to understand the process that created the lower class and to see the reciprocal relationship between the personal and the social in the so-called culture of poverty. It has also helped to support the conviction that radical alteration in allocation of resources is central if human development is to be a goal of this society. In this light, social welfare is concerned with the optimum possible relation between human needs and the institutional flow of supportive and nurturing resources, a point to be expanded on later.

[104] Joseph T. English, M.D., "Health Among the Poor: The Challenge to U.S. Medicine," *Poverty and Health* (New York: National Tuberculosis and Respiratory Disease Association, 1969), pp. 3–5.

[105] Benjamin Pasamanick and Hilda Knoblock, "Epidemiological Studies on the Complications of Pregnancy and the Birth Process," *Prevention of Mental Disorders in Children* (New York: Basic Books, 1961), p. 74; *National Action to Control Mental Retardation,* President's Panel on Mental Retardation (Washington, D.C.: Government Printing Office, 1962), pp. 47–72; Florence Haselkorn (ed.), *Mothers-At-Risk* (New York: Adelphi University School of Social Work, 1966).

Motivation for achievement, so often identified as a central problem in the "failure" of the poor, is itself a function of structured opportunities that are perceived as realistically available. When real opportunities *are* made available the problem often has been, not lack of motivation, but insufficient opportunities for those who respond. Soon after it was set up in late 1964 the Job Corps received 280,000 cards from youths indicating their interest. By January 1966 only 17,500 had been permitted to enroll.[106] Thus the problems confronting the poor are not so much individual defects as defects in institutional arrangements that control the flow of supportive, nurturing, and enabling resources. To focus on defects in the poor compounds the problem by further undermining self-respect. To approach people in terms of their weakness only further alienates them from those who would seek to help. Efforts to reverse the so-called culture of poverty and to alter attitudes of apathy and hopelessness without changing the social situation in which the poor find themselves is to ignore the possibility that the behavior and attitudes of the poor may be a realistic adaptation to their life circumstances, their way of coping with a poverty of satisfactions and the prospect of a bleak future. Efforts to change the poor without changing the resources and opportunities at their command seem futile. Social scientists and the rest of us have

> . . . failed to recognize that one of the crucial problems for understanding modern industrial society is to know what resources are necessary for a person before he can behave in ways that will allow him to become a full member of that society.[107]

The goal of change, given this view, must be to redirect the institutional flow of resources in order to develop capacities, expand opportunities, and maximize freedom of choice. To the extent that it is a valid analysis, the problem of poverty turns out to be an economic and political issue; economic because the market mechanism allocates income, employment opportunities and other resources in a manner that creates and maintains the underclass; political because, although we have the power to alter such allocations, we do not do so to a degree sufficient to make a significant difference in the life prospects of the poor. In fact all social institutions are implicated in the social arrangements that function to produce the underclass. Families adapt to damaged work roles in ways that may limit the child's capacity for upward mobility.[108] Race and ethnic discrimination restricts access to avenues that promote rewarding social participation. Public schools contribute to educational failure at the same time society establishes the cult of academic credentials. Poverty is maintained by public policy that restricts public assistance grants and creates a residual welfare system that may compound rather than relieve problems associated with economic dependency. Our system of justice is weighted against the poor. All institutions reflect our values, which give greater priority to considerations other than those related to human needs. Once again we meet the conflict between our organizational and our humanitarian mores.

---

[106] *Manpower Report of the President,* U.S. Department of Labor (Washington, D.C.: Government Printing Office, 1966), pp. 104–105.

[107] Rainwater, *op. cit.,* p. 9.

[108] Rodman, *op. cit.*

The organizational values of our political economy direct employment opportunities, income, and other resources in ways that maintain severe deprivation and class inequalities. The basic cause of poverty lies in our political economy, which directs resources away from those with the greatest needs to those with the greatest power. The pressure for reform meets the structure of profit and privilege and its organized resistance to change. Even though we have acted on our humanitarian ethic in significant ways, the structure of our political economy is such that it inhibits the decisions that would abolish material want and eliminate a special class of "superfluous" people. Nowhere is this more evident than in our inability to feed the hungry, provide full employment, or to allocate sufficient funds to those for whom work is a nonexistent or inadequate source of income.

Poverty and Political Economy

It is possible that within a short while we shall find ways to eliminate hunger in the United States. Our difficulty, in the face of resources more than sufficient to accomplish the task, is the resistance with which the structure of our political economy deals with compelling issues of basic human needs. A profit-oriented market system has been enormously successful, with the aid of stabilizing and supportive government intervention, in creating the affluent society. The same market system, by allocating goods and services on the basis of effective demand, that is, the ability to pay, produces the inequities that create poverty and deprivation. Political decisions may alter the flow of resources and income, as has been done through economic and tax policy and a variety of social welfare measures. However, as late as 1969, though hunger had become a political issue, the power to distribute sufficient food to those who needed it most could not be marshaled. Hunger, as John A. Hamilton observed, ". . . must be seen as consequences of a political and economic system that spends billions to remove food from the market to limit production, to retire land from production, to guarantee and sustain profits for the producer." [109] The issue goes beyond the anomaly of hunger and malnutrition in a country where, for most people, the problem is too many rather than too few calories. It goes to the heart of the issue of social justice. Does an individual have the right to a superfluous gratification of needs before a fellow citizen has satisfied even his most basic ones.[110] It seems clear that further political modifications of the market system are needed to deal with poverty and inequality. Expansion of the public sector to assure adequate employment, income, and a variety of essential services is needed to create the social balance that will produce community resources the market does not provide and assure a greater allocation of resources to meet the needs of those to whom the market mechanism is indifferent.[111] How radical these changes may need to be is unclear. Dilemmas cannot be avoided. These may be seen in the efforts to make

[109] John A. Hamilton, "The Politics of Hunger," *Saturday Review,* June 21, 1969, p. 21.

[110] Richard Lichtman, *Toward Community* (Santa Barbara, Calif.: Center for the Study of Democratic Institutions, 1966), p. 16.

[111] Galbraith, *The Affluent Society, op. cit.,* Chap. 18.

available two basic resources that underlie the central problems of the poor—decent employment and decent income. Writing of the very poor, Lee Rainwater observes that ". . . Social scientists have been very slow to provide detailed knowledge on what has become apparent as the central fact about the American underclass—that it is created by and its existence is maintained by, the operation of what is in other ways the most successful economic system known to man." [112]

In every industrial society access to basic resources for most citizens is determined by one's occupational role and the income received from work. Yet no advanced industrial society permits the essentials of life to be distributed solely on the basis of income. The heart of social welfare programs is the social provision of income, housing, medical care, and other social services that supplement or substitute for resources earned through work. Of all the Western nations only the United States continues to rely so heavily on the ethic of work for determining one's share of the nation's wealth. As Nathan Glazer observes, basic resources in this country, housing and medical care for example, ". . . are to a much larger degree allocated by the free market." In England and other countries in northwestern Europe a much greater reliance is placed on providing a standard floor of services—family allowances, pensions, subsidized housing, unemployment insurance, nationalized health services—below which, in theory at least, no one may fall.[113] The life of the lower class, like the life of other classes in society, is linked to the larger system primarily through employment. How a man earns his living will influence family structure, child rearing, the place of the family in the community, and the life prospects of his children. The difference between the stable working class and the unstable poor is in large measure a reflection of different work patterns that produce regular income and a measure of economic security rare among the very poor.[114] It is important to note that there is no such thing as a clearly defined lower class of homogenous individuals. We use this as a shorthand term for those at the very bottom of society, but they vary enormously. While noting the relationship between employment patterns and the life of the very poor, S. M. Miller prefers to distinguish the lower class by an income criterion rather than an occupational one.[115] Where the concept of a basic floor is accepted, continuing poverty is blamed on inadequate social provisions rather than on the personal attributes of the poor.

We live in a social system in which work is the major norm defining the individual's rightful access to income and other resources essential for life, personality development, family stability, and social participation. It would be difficult to exaggerate the importance of work in American society. Indeed, Harold Wilensky suggests that "the shape of American society can be understood through understanding work" and, he adds, "every other social problem

---

[112] Rainwater, *op. cit.*, p. 9.

[113] Nathan Glazer, "Paradoxes of American Poverty," *Public Interest,* No. 1, (Fall 1965), pp. 71–81.

[114] Herbert Gans, "A Survey of Working- and Lower-Class Studies," and S. M. Miller, "The American Lower Classes: A Typological Approach," in Riessman, Cohen, and Pearl, *op. cit.,* pp. 119–127 and 139–154.

[115] *Ibid.,* pp. 141, 147.

may have some connection to work and its discontents." [116]   Studies indicate the relationship between unemployment and alienation.   Chronic unemployment in a society that values work disrupts the normal ties to community institutions.[117]   Marginal occupational status may be an even more serious problem, tied as it is to society's "stigmatize-rejection mechanism" and the damaged self-esteem that accompanies the damaged work role.[118]   Although it is often assumed that inferior people do inferior work, it may be that the occupational role itself creates the very inferiority it ascribes to the occupant. Narrow and debased demands of a job have their own self-fulfilling prophesy. An efficiency expert describing the kind of person suited for handling pig iron declared he should ". . . be so stupid and so phlegmatic that he more nearly resembles an ox than any other type." [119]   Lower-class life is an adaptation to occupational failure and to one's sense of personal failure.   The relatively high incidence of social pathology often noted in urban ghettos is, in some measure, a reflection of the alienation produced by the disesteem with which society regards those assigned to marginal employment.   A study of the New York City Harlem ghetto observes that ". . . if all the residents of Central Harlem were employed at their present level, it would not materially alter the pathology of the community." [120]   Central issues are thus status and social participation, not simply material poverty.   Work in this society is the avenue to both.   Unemployment and subemployment seem to be related to such social problems as delinquency, illegitimacy, mental illness, and breakdown in family life.[121]   The most damaging consequence of unstable and menial work may be the harm suffered by the family, although evidence is inconclusive.   In his study, *Social Class and Family Life,* Donald McKinley develops the theory that differences ". . . in rewards received by the father in his occupation feed back into and influence family life." [122]   Such rewards are not only material but include self-esteem, prestige, status, power, and autonomy.   These may be seen as inputs available for investment in parental roles.   A poorly paid and low status laborer cannot derive from his job critical resources that society fails to invest in his work or make available in other ways.   We are becoming more and more

[116] Harold A. Wilensky, "Work as a Social Problem" in Howard S. Becker (ed.) *Social Problems: A Modern Approach* (New York: Wiley, 1966) p. 118.

[117] Philip Selznick, "Institutional Vulnerability in Mass Society," in Philip Olson (ed.), *America as Mass Society* (New York: Free Press, 1963), pp. 13–29.

[118] Leo Srole, Thomas Langner, Stanley T. Michael, Marvin K. Opler, and Thomas A. C. Rennie, *Mental Health in the Metropolis: The Midtown Manhattan Study* (New York: McGraw-Hill, 1962), Vol. I, p. 360; and Rodman, *op. cit.*

[119] Quoted in Lichtman, *op. cit.*, p. 7.

[120] Harlem Youth Opportunities Unlimited, Inc., *Youth in the Ghetto* (New York: Haryou, 1964) p. 159.

[121] Rodman, *op. cit.;* Belton M. Fleisher, *The Economics of Delinquency* (Chicago: Quadrangle Books, 1966), p. 43; Marc Fried, "Social Problems and Psychopathology," *Urban America and the Planning of Mental Health Services,* Vol. 5, Symposium No. 10 (New York: Group for the Advancement of Psychiatry, November 1964), p. 417.

[122] Donald G. McKinley, *Social Class and Family Life* (New York: Macmillan, 1964), p. 3.

aware of the relationship between work and well-being, a key dimension of which is the nature of job authority and the opportunity for the exercise of some autonomy.[123]   Erik Erikson notes, for example, that the ". . . kind and degree of a sense of autonomy which parents are able to grant their small children depends on the dignity ánd sense of personal independence which they derive from their own lives." [124]   In the Child Rearing Study of Low Income Families in the District of Columbia, researchers

> . . . found that few low income Negro men received significant satisfaction from their work, that their jobs offered not only small pay, but little, if any, dignity or status.   Thus the cement finisher, after overhearing a conversation between two CRS workers about criminal law, said that he "didn't even know what (the workers) were talking about."   When one of the workers told him that a lawyer or doctor would not know anything about pouring a sidewalk, the cement finisher replied: "Maybe so, but when was the last time you saw anybody standing around talking about concrete?" [125]

Material, social, and psychic deprivations related to inferior occupational status limit the competence and confidence with which parents may play their essential roles.   Any number of studies have noted that to deprive a breadwinner of his capacity to support his family is to destroy his manhood and undermine his status in the family.[126]   The transition from "machismo" to "matriarchy," sometimes within a very short period, has been observed among Puerto Rican families who migrate to the United States when the male breadwinner is unable to perform his traditional economic function.

Since roles are reciprocal, the capacity and manner in which women play their roles are in turn dependent on the adequacy with which their men can perform.[127]   Children in turn tend to admire and emulate parents who are powerful providers of material and psychosocial satisfactions.   The relative powerlessness of lower-class fathers to meet the basic needs of their children means a greater reliance on physical punishment to maintain control.   Donald McKinley sees little hope of enabling lower-class families to change child-rearing practices without some fundamental alterations in the material, psychic, and social resources available to parents.[128]   Nor is it likely that the relatively high incidence of female-based households among the poor can change without enabling low-income males to acquire stable and satisfying employment.   Society tends to focus on the broken family as representing a form of pathology,

[123] Wilensky in Becker, *op. cit.;* S. M. Miller, *et al.,* in Gross, *op. cit.,* p. 322.

[124] Erik Hamburger Erikson, "Growth and Crises of the 'Healthy Personality,' " in Clyde Kluckhohn and Henry A. Murray (eds.), *Personality in Nature, Society and Culture,* 2nd ed. (New York: Knopf, 1954), p. 203.

[125] Luther P. Jackson, *Poverty's Children* (Washington, D.C.: Cross-tell, 1966), p. 37.

[126] Rodman, *op. cit.;* Liebow, *op. cit.;* Helen Icken Safa, *Profiles In Poverty: An Analysis of Social Mobility in Low-Income Families* (Syracuse, N.Y.: Syracuse University Youth Development Center, 1966); McKinley, *op. cit.*

[127] Liebow, *op. cit.,* p. 133.

[128] McKinley, *op. cit.*

ignoring the fact that it is functional—perhaps not so much a problem to the poor as a solution to a problem, a means of adapting to ". . . basic occupation-earner problems inherent in the damaged work role of the lower class male." [129] As Hyman Rodman puts it:

> Alternative marital and quasi-marital relationships develop . . . because these . . . make it easier for men and women to enter and leave a relationship in accordance with the changing occupational-earner circumstances of the man or woman or both.[130]

Economic insecurity is a major factor in the marital instability among the poor. When a husband becomes, in the eyes of his wife, a "no-good man" by virtue of his inability to support, there are natural incentives to desert. The ranking order of attributes that identify a "no-good man," according to the Child Rearing Study, are inadequate work or wages, mismanagement of money, problem drinking, and contacts with other women.[131] To be a poor provider and remain with one's family is to face daily the evidence of one's failure to be a man, a husband, and a father. One mother of six children, chiding her husband for not showing enough initiative to get a second job to add to the family's income, observed that his pay stub looked ". . . more like a receipt for a woman's paycheck instead of a man's." [132] A husband's wish to escape from his home may be fostered by the knowledge that a public assistance program, however inadequate, may be a more reliable provider. As one public assistance worker in Washington, D.C., where no assistance is provided an unemployed father, put it: "If your husband were not with you, we would help you." On the other hand, low-income couples do not break up for the sole purpose of obtaining financial assistance. Long periods of financial difficulty are likely to precede the break. The inability of the family to receive income so long as the father is in the home only adds stress to an already intolerable situation.

Since the economy does not assure adequate opportunities for work for lower-class males, the opportunities for stable marriages for lower-class women are limited, which increases the risk of illegitimacy and female-based households. Consequently such families have a high risk of needing public assistance. In turn, such assistance has been provided in a manner consistent with the self-reliance ethic of our market society that has assumed that minimum and humiliating aid is essential to deter pauperism and to maintain the incentive to work, even if employment is not available. Though claiming to strengthen family life, public assistance has often had the opposite effect; in most states grants have been so low as to fail to meet basic needs of dependent children, thus contributing to the deprivation and social isolation of the poor.

Children growing up in welfare and other lower-class homes may be deprived of the kinds of socialization experience essential for occupational and family roles in society. Although the structure of lower-class families is

---

[129] Rodman, *op. cit.*

[130] *Ibid.,* p. 5.

[131] Jackson, *op. cit.,* p. 31.

[132] *Ibid.,* p. 30.

adaptive to the struggle for economic survival, it may be less adaptive for socializing children for upward mobility. Although too little is yet known about child-rearing practices among the poor or about consequences for their life chances, there is increasing evidence of the critical importance of the early years for all children and some indication that a significant portion of the poor inadvertently socialize their children in ways that help to compound their failure in life. Child-rearing practices that may be more or less adaptive for survival in poverty are less likely to be functional for participating in an achievement-oriented society, should such opportunities for achievement be genuinely available. Robert Coles sympathetically portrays the anguish of a Negro mother speculating on the future of her son:

> I think Peter could go and do better for himself later on, when he gets older, except for the fact that he just doesn't believe. He don't believe what they say, the teacher, or the man who says it's getting better for us . . . I guess it's my fault, I never taught my children, any of them, to believe that kind of thing; because I never thought we'd ever have it any different, not in this life.[133]

On the other hand, as his mother tried to get Peter to believe in the possibility of opportunity, she sought the aid of a neighbor who supported the skepticism of her son by noting that ". . . all you have to do is look around at our block and you'd see all the young men, and they just haven't got a thing to do. Nothing!"[134]

Patterns of child rearing reflect the occupational status of the major family breadwinner and expectations about the child's future. In turn early socialization helps to determine the future occupational status of the child. Emphasis on achievement motivation may not characterize lower-class child-rearing patterns partly because occupational roles that seem available hardly require it and partly because parents may not have acquired the skills for supporting and guiding the ambitions of their children. The parent's own job is not likely to be an inspiring model. For most, their only experience is ". . . the dull, repetitious work of the porter, domestic, laborer, construction worker, or dishwasher."[135]

Most parents may aspire, at best, for a secure job for their child and, if goals are more ambitious, there is the desperate humiliation of not being able to offer concrete help in guiding the acquisition of appropriate skills. Low-income parents are not unaware of the importance of education but they are keenly aware of their own educational inadequacy and their impotence in the face of requests for assistance from their children: "It hurts me when they bring a hard question and I cannot help them. I don't want them to know that I can't help them."[136]

It appears that children may be socialized in ways that tend to perpetuate a lower-class style of life. Crucial variables seem to be not only economic and

---

[133] Robert Coles, "Like It Is in the Alley," *Daedalus,* Vol. 97 (Fall 1968), p. 1324.

[134] *Ibid,* p. 1325.

[135] Jackson, *op. cit.,* p. 24.

[136] *Ibid,* p. 25.

social deprivation but a style of verbal communication that affects cognitive development, restricts educability, and sets in process a series of failures in school and at work, which ultimately leads to a high vulnerability to public assistance.[137] According to Robert D. Hess, the teaching styles of lower-class mothers seem to develop a ". . . passive attitude toward learning on the part of the child in which his own imagination, curiosity, and assertiveness are discouraged, and he is taught to assume the stance of waiting to be told, to receive and to be acted upon." [138]

Language structures what and how a child will learn, setting limits within which future learning may take place; the kind of communication pattern to which many lower-class children are exposed may limit their success in school and therefore in later life. On the other hand there is some evidence that lower-class children may be deprived of formal language patterns used in middle-class schools but that this is no necessary indication of inability to learn. There may be instead a rich capacity to use language patterns that do not fit the middle-class ideal.

Sheer deprivation, the stress of unrelieved poverty, may account for much of the difficulty in child rearing.

> The inadequate incomes, crowded homes, lack of consistent familial ties, the mother's depression and helplessness in her own situation, were as important as her child-rearing practices in influencing the child's development and preparing him for an adult role. It was for us a sobering experience to watch a large group of newborn infants, plastic human beings of unknown potential, and observe over a five year period their *social preparation to enter the class of the least-skilled, least-educated, and most-rejected in our society*.[139] [Emphasis mine.]

This social recruitment for the underclass is reinforced by the public school system, which functions to compound rather than reverse the educational failure that may have begun in the family. On the basis of his research, James S. Coleman concludes that

> (1) minority children have a serious educational deficiency at the start of school, which is obviously not a result of school; and (2) they have an even more serious deficiency at the end of school, which is obviously in part a result of school.[140]

The sad part of such social preparation, in addition to its heavy human cost, is that to some extent it has been functional for maintaining the occupational system. This will continue to be true so long as society requires that someone

[137] Robert D. Hess, "Educability and Rehabilitation: The Future of the Welfare Class," *Journal of Marriage and the Family,* Vol. 26 (November 1964), p. 422.

[138] *Ibid.,* p. 429.

[139] H. Wortis *et al.* quoted by Bettye M. Caldwell, "The Effects of Infant Care," Martin L. Hoffman and Lois Wladis Hoffman (eds.), *Review of Child Development Research* (New York: Russell Sage Foundation, 1964), Vol. I, p. 71.

[140] James S. Coleman, "Equal Schools or Equal Students?," *The Public Interest,* No. 4 (Summer 1966), pp. 72–73.

do the dirty work and so long as we insist on assigning that work on the basis of race and class. The class system functions to protect white middle-class children from downward mobility and to restrict upward mobility on the part of the poor, especially the nonwhite poor.

The emphasis on occupational achievement conceals the extent to which some are not expected to achieve. Public schools may function to discourage aspirations for upward mobility on the part of lower-class children, reinforcing a pattern possibly already established in the family. Much of the work that needed to be done in the past (and to a lesser degree in the present) required a relatively docile labor force, with a set of attitudes and a self-image that would accept conditions of marginal employment, low pay, little status, and not much hope. Negroes were especially exploited in this way. Today many reject low-paid, unskilled work because they know they ". . . would have been equipped for something better if (they) . . . had a fair chance earlier, and because their work is itself a symbol of previous economic bondage." [141]   The National Advisory Commission on Civil Disorders has noted that ". . . the concentration of male Negro employment at the lowest end of the occupational scale is . . . the single most important source of poverty among Negroes." [142]

Broken families function to produce the kind of people society requires for such menial work. Both male and female products of these families perform the demeaning duties assigned to them:

> On a rough and conservative estimate, our present economy requires some 10 million people to fill job slots at the lowest skill levels (125,000 kitchen workers; 200,000 gardeners and groundkeepers; 350,000 parking attendants and auto service workers; 240,000 guards, watchmen and doorkeepers; etc.). The mothers . . . bring into the world, care for, and provide the early training of the men and women who do this work. This is the job they do for society, and, with some exceptions, they do it well. They have, in general, made an effective adaptation to the difficult task of rearing children in a low-occupational-skill, low-income milieu. [143]

The controversial and much-abused program of Aid to Families with Dependent Children is itself, according to Sydney E. Bernard, a system that functions ". . . as an adaptation to the requirements of a certain set of occupational roles—the unskilled, the unstable, and the poorly paid." [144]   Contrary to common assumptions, many mothers on public assistance are in the labor force, coping with marginal and insecure work, using public assistance as part of their pattern of economic survival. [145]

[141] Former Secretary of Labor Willard Wirtz, *The New York Times,* February 9, 1966.

[142] National Advisory Commission on Civil Disorders, *op. cit.,* p. 125.

[143] Walter Miller, Foreword to "Fatherless Families: Their Economic and Social Adjustment," by Sydney E. Bernard, *Papers in Social Welfare,* No. 7, The Florence Heller Graduate School for Advanced Studies in Social Welfare, Brandeis University, 1964.

[144] Bernard, *op. cit.,* p. 10.

[145] *Ibid.;* and *Manpower Report of the President,* U.S. Department of Labor (Washington, D.C.: Government Printing Office, 1968), pp. 97–98.

Thus the much deplored life style of the poor has its social uses. In view of the evidence accumulated by Walter B. Miller and others, the broken family seems ". . . functionally related to demands of the lower-class occupational system and thus appears highly resistant to change."[146] It is fascinating to realize that in 1786 Joseph Townsend made a similar observation. In that instance, however, it was in a candid defense of keeping the poor in their place. In "A Dissertation on the Poor Laws By a Well-Wisher to Mankind," which was to exert major influence on attitudes toward the poor and on measures for relief of poverty, he wrote:

> It seems to be a law of nature, that the poor should be to a certain degree improvident, that there may always be some to fulfill the most servile, the most sordid, and the most ignoble offices in the community. The stock of human happiness is thereby much increased, whilst the more delicate are not only relieved from drudgery, and freed from those occasional employments which would make them miserable, but are left at liberty, without interruption, to pursue those callings which are suited to their various dispositions, and most useful to the state.[147]

He argues against any adequate and secure provision of assistance that would undermine the distress and poverty that reconcile the poorest to the meanest occupations because

> . . . a fixed, a certain, and a constant provision for the poor weakens this spring; it increases their improvidence, but does not promote their cheerful compliance with those demands, which the community is obliged to make on the most indigent of its members.[148]

Not without compassion (he argued against the use of the roman P in scarlet cloth upon the shoulders of the poor to discourage their use of poor relief), he nonetheless offered a comforting rationale for the preservation of inequality:

> If a new and equal division of property were made in England, we cannot doubt that the same inequality which we now observe would soon take place again: the improvident, the lazy, and the vicious, would dissipate their substance; the prudent, the active, and the virtuous, would again increase their wealth.[149]

The division of labor and its concomitant differential rewards generates inequality in any industrial society. At issue is the degree of justice inherent in the process by which individuals are allocated to occupational roles and the extent of inequality in the distribution of rewards that accompany work.

Here we are confronted with something of a dilemma. The process of social

---

[146] Walter B. Miller, "Implications of Urban Lower-Class Culture for Social Work," *Social Service Review*, 33 (September 1959), p. 226.

[147] Joseph Townsend, "A Dissertation on the Poor Laws," in J. R. McCulloch (ed.), *A Select Collection of Scarce and Valuable Economic Tracts* (London, 1859), p. 416.

[148] *Ibid.*

[149] *Ibid.*, p. 420.

competition that underlies our division of labor and distribution of rewards has positive consequences for most but negative consequences for others. It is functional for maintaining our achievement-oriented society and dysfunctional for the casualties of the system. An achievement-oriented society inevitably rewards some and rejects others. For most people this society seems to work tolerably well. We are not eager to upset the social structure for the benefit of those who suffer most from its defects. This social system has enabled an ever-increasing number of people to achieve an adequate standard of living and a preferred status relative to a diminishing number of those at the very bottom of society. How to provide social roles for the excluded, roles that will offer access to material and symbolic rewards, is a critical question especially when there is a declining need for unskilled labor.

Through social roles society distributes those functions that must be performed if the social system is to work at all effectively. How does a society determine its division of labor? Allocation of tasks in preindustrial societies is relatively simple; it is based on birth, age, sex, and traditional norms that ascribe roles for various members. An industrial society depends to some degree on role ascription since women, for example, are still expected to perform the traditional roles of child rearing and other domestic tasks. For the assignment of occupational roles an industrial society must emphasize occupational achievement. It must also "make a virtue of discontent," according to Richard A. Cloward and Lloyd Ohlin. To understand "why this is so is an important key to understanding both normal and deviant behavior." [150] Since there is no way of knowing in advance who is best suited for various tasks, industrial societies seek to motivate all individuals to strive for common success goals. Competition for occupational success functions to select candidates for work roles, in this way assuring at least some rough "correlation between talent and occupational position." [151] Increasingly the competition takes place by means of educational attainment and the acquisition of academic credentials (Table 16). Such competition is of course far from perfect, which lends support to the need for programs that will compensate for past inequities and assure more nearly equal opportunity in the present. This poses grave difficulties and dilemmas. For example, to the degree that a child's early experience in his family is a limiting factor on the development of social competence, the way to assure equality of opportunity without invading family rights and responsibilities is a major dilemma.

Although the injustices in the distribution of opportunities and rewards are real enough, what people may sense most poignantly is not the inadequacies of society but their own relative impotence. This is even true when the objective reality clearly indicates that equal opportunities are not available. Studies of long-term unemployed men deprived of work because of the inability of society to assure the right to employment have found that the men tend to blame themselves for their failure as breadwinners.[152] Status anxiety and status discontent

[150] Richard A. Cloward and Lloyd E. Ohlin, *Delinquency and Opportunity* (Glencoe, Ill.: Free Press, 1960), pp. 80–82.

[151] *Ibid.*, p. 81.

[152] Richard C. Wilcock and Walter H. Franke, *Unwanted Workers* (Glencoe, Ill.: Free Press, 1963).

Table 16. Education and Poverty—Median Money Income of Families by Color of Head and Years of School Completed, 1966

	WHITE		NONWHITE	
	Median Income	% Below $3,000	Median Income	% Below $3,000
Elementary school				
less than 8 years	$ 4,477	33.1	$3,349	45.2
8 years	6,103	19.9	4,399	31.9
High school				
1 to 3 years	$ 7,267	11.9	$4,418	29.8
4 years	8,217	7.2	5,886	18.1
College				
1 to 3 years	$ 9,252	6.1	$7,043	11.0
4 years or more	11,697	4.3	9,510	7.6

SOURCE: *Statistical Abstract of the United States, 1968,* U.S. Bureau of the Census (Washington, D.C.: Government Printing Office, 1968), p. 327.

may well make up the most critical deprivation suffered by the poor. Commenting on his own sense of failure one of the "street-corner" men describes his envy of a man with "position":

> It's not the money. It's position. I guess. He's got position. . . . People respect him. . . . Thinking about people with position and education gives me a feeling right here (pressing his fingers into the pit of his stomach).[153]

The "rage of the disesteemed" may well account for much of the "deviant" behavior observed among the deprived.[154] With the new consciousness of social injustice, the rage now turns against society itself, either in the form of violent uprising or in the form of militant demands for basic reforms. A sense of both personal impotence and rage at exclusion from society is illustrated in the remarks of a Negro following the violent uprising in the Watts area of Los Angeles in 1965.

> "I'm 38 and I'm dead," says the man in the neat white shirt with the frayed tab collar. "But my kids ain't. They ain't going to have to take the——— I took. You work and it's $60 bucks a week. 'Honey,' the wife says, 'buy us a new car.' You can't. But if she goes on welfare, they give her $300 a month. Who needs you? She knows it, you know it, the kids know it." He pauses and suddenly starts talking about the riots. "You should've seen them flames, a mile high! I guess we showed we was men." [155]

The agony of the American Negro, according to some, is not simply his struggle for equality. For the majority of the unskilled, it is a struggle to

[153] Liebow, *op. cit.,* p. 61.

[154] Harlem Youth Opportunities Unlimited, *op. cit.,* p. 387.

[155] *San Francisco Chronicle,* January 18, 1966.

avoid becoming superfluous.   The problem is severe economic dislocation, ". . . change from an economics of exploitation to an economics of uselessness." [156]   In the past unskilled work was for many an avenue into the society. Today a dead-end job may mean just that.   For Negroes the chance of achieving occupational equality with whites in this century, at the current rate of progress, is far from promising.   According to Dale L. Hiestand, Negroes lag about fifty years behind whites in occupational positions; they tend to acquire jobs whites leave behind as they move into preferred positions, and the leftover jobs Negroes get tend to be those most vulnerable to technological displacement.[157]

While the public is conscious of the relatively high rates of illegitimacy, female-based households, and dependence on public assistance among lower-class Negroes, it is not conscious of the degree to which these reflect the class position that follows the organized process of recruitment for and exclusion from the world of work.   The myth of moral irresponsibility conceals the tragic irony that the greater one's commitment to the ideal of an adequate bread-winner, the greater one's sense of failure and defeat when one has at best "a piece of a job" that leaves one feeling like less than a person.[158]   The recruits for occupational roles at the very bottom of society have suffered a double insult.   The system has restricted their potential as human beings.   In turn they have had to bear the personal shame and the social scorn of failure.   Their marginal work has kept them from acquiring self-respect, the social competence required for improving their condition, and the material and psychic resources essential for contributing to the well-being of their families.

The family, as Donald Gilbert McKinley documents, is to a considerable degree dependent on its position in the occupational reward structure in a society concerned primarily with achievement.   Though failure may be cushioned through a variety of supportive and ameliorative efforts, to the extent that we support an achieving ideology we ". . . participate in the resentful deprivation of the disesteemed and murderous elements of a society." [159]   The prospects for altering the emphasis we give to achievement is not promising.   Nor is it clear we would want to even if we could.   It might be possible to alter the content of achievement from a narrow concern with material success to broad support and rewards for the widest development of human potentials and talents. In this case, new definitions of work and occupational success and broadened opportunities for entry into new careers may be a strategic way to meet the problem of poverty.[160]   The creation of new work roles, upgrading of existing work, abolition of artificial racial and credential barriers to employment, and expanded opportunities for vital education for young and old hold some hope that the stigmatized underclass may be reduced in size if not eliminated.

Yet employment alone is not the answer.   A significant portion of the poor

[156] Sidney M. Willhelm and Edwin H. Powell, "Who Needs the Negro?," *Transaction,* 1 (September–October, 1964), pp. 3–6.

[157] Dale I. Hiestand, *Economic Growth and Employment Opportunities for Minorities* (New York: Columbia University Press, 1964), p. 114.

[158] Elliot Liebow, "Fathers Without Children," *The Public Interest,* No. 5 (Fall 1966), p. 19.

[159] McKinley, *op. cit.,* p. 268.

[160] Riessman, *Strategies Against Poverty, op. cit.,* Chap. 3, pp. 21–42.

are not and cannot be in the labor force. Social provisions that assure to all a level of living not too far below that enjoyed by the average citizen are essential if we are to confront the issue of inequality. Massive investments in people, particularly those who have borne the heavy cost of serving society at the very bottom of the occupational system, are essential.

Special attention must also be given to minority groups. Racism has been so interwoven with our system of labor force recruitment and utilization that it is an integral part of the organized process that leaves minority groups exposed to the greatest risk of occupational failure and exclusion. Such groups have borne the heaviest share of the cost of wage exploitation, economic insecurity, unemployment, and subemployment that a market industrial economy imposes on the least protected. For this reason Gunnar Myrdal relates the problem of the underclass to the issue of social justice. Our affluence, he reminds us, is "heavily mortgaged." This society ". . . carries a tremendous burden of debt to its poor people. Not paying the debt implies risks for the social order and for democracy as we have known it." [161] Those now left behind, with only a marginal attachment to the labor force or excluded entirely, cannot benefit from continuing economic progress since they have no way of acquiring the occupational positions that command the disproportionate share of rewards. Depressed economic conditions, social exclusion, and the assault on self-respect that is generated by an ideology of self-reliance and self-blame create a ". . . vicious circle tending to create . . . an underprivileged class of unemployed, unemployables and underemployed who are more and more hopelessly set apart from the nation." [162] Largely regarded as expendable by the system, they nonetheless represent a terrible waste of human lives, of potential unrealized. Investments in their development are in the interest of social justice and in the interest of furthering the social development of this nation.[163]

In some respects the underclass poses the problem found in underdeveloped nations; it requires sufficient capital investment to "leapfrog into the modern world." [164] To achieve this degree of commitment of resources to people requires a critical examination of our values and priorities, especially those that are dictated by the operation of our market system. Poverty is an economic problem to the degree that it is a consequence of market allocation of employment and critical resources away from the poor. The answers are, however, social and political. Eli Ginzberg puts it in the following way:

> . . . It is unlikely in the second half of the twentieth century that the answers to complex economic problems can be found completely within the traditional confines of economics. With the possibility of a war of unbelievable destruction never more than a few minutes away, with human injustice at home and abroad crying for remedy, with the affluence of the few uneasily counterpoised by the want and misery of the many, with technology at once a promise and a threat, our nation cannot permit its

[161] *New York Times,* October 4, 1967.

[162] Gunnar Myrdal, *Challenge to Affluence* (New York: Pantheon Books, 1964), p. 10.

[163] *Ibid.,* pp. 10–11.

[164] Hiestand, *op. cit.,* p. 119.

economy to operate under its own momentum, solely responsive to the maximization of profit. For better or worse, economics must once more embrace political economy and even moral philosophy.[165]

Yet to some degree we have a political economy. It is the moral philosophy guiding it that is subject to question. This may be seen in the 1964 tax cut, a political regulation of the economy that acted on the moral assumption that the best way to aid the poor was by favoring the rich. The option was to reduce unemployment by expanding the demand for consumers goods or to give priority to the public need for vital services, education, medical care, housing, the rebuilding of cities, and so forth. The choice was, as John Kenneth Galbraith put it, to pay attention to those whose income ". . . makes them more sensitive to taxes paid than to public services foregone." [166] The result was to increase the gap between "private well-being and public squalor" and to further deprive the poor of access to quality public services upon which they depend the most.[167] In the view of at least some economists, the public spending route would have perhaps been slower but both economically and ethically preferable. The moral principle that underlies the 1964 tax cut is the "trickle down" theory, which acts on the assumption that the best way to feed the sparrows is to gorge the horses.[168] More recent political efforts to control inflation continue to take for granted that the poor should bear the cost in increased unemployment without sufficient regard for the need to compensate them for this politically imposed patriotism.[169]

The key problem is "the great refusal," as John Dewey put it, to critically examine the moral foundations of our economic order in search of ways to remake the profit system into one that would not only serve the needs of consumption, however important that is, but also the need for ". . . positive and enduring opportunity for productive and creative activity and all that signifies for the development of the potentialities of human nature." [170] The continuing adherence we give to the values of a market society deflect attention from critical inquiry into the relationship between the operation of the economy and our inability to solve pressing human problems. Furthermore, it constricts our moral vision. John Maynard Keynes saw the eventual need for a basic change in our socioeconomic system that would enable us to ". . . rid ourselves of many of the pseudomoral principles which have hagridden us for two hundred

---

[165] Eli Ginzberg, Introduction to Hiestand, *op. cit.,* p. xv.

[166] *The New York Times,* May 14, 1969; *see also* Leon H. Keyserling, "Employment Goals and the 'New Economics,' " in Bertram M. Gross (ed.), *Social Intelligence for America's Future* (Boston: Allyn & Bacon, 1969), pp. 330–351.

[167] Galbraith, *The New York Times,* May 14, 1969.

[168] For a defense of an improved trickle-down theory *see* Alan Altshuler, "The Potential of Trickle Down," *The Public Interest,* No. 15 (Spring 1969), pp. 46–56.

[169] Gertrude S. Goldberg with Carol Lopate, "Strategies for Closing the Poverty Gap," *IRCD Bulletin,* 5 (March 1969), p. 7.

[170] John Dewey in Joseph Ratner (ed.), *Intelligence in the Modern World: John Dewey's Philosophy* (New York: Modern Library, 1939), p. 428.

years, by which we have exalted some of the most distasteful of human qualities into the position of the highest virtues." [171]

It is not that we do not sense the moral crisis. It is all around us. One has only to read the many scholarly commission reports on the various social crises to recognize the anguish reflected in such statements as "Putting our nation back on the right track will not be easy. The difficulties are great. It is a struggle for the soul of America." [172]

What is difficult to confront is the degree to which the market creates and sustains inequality not only in access to resources but in the very possibility of developing one's full humanity. The relatively higher incidence of disease, disability, mental illness, delinquency, and crime that accompanies the social class distribution of life chances exposes the very principle of the market to moral judgment. Most of our social welfare measures are essentially reactive, seeking to deal with the symptoms of social inequality, but are unable to touch the structural sources of maldistribution of life opportunities. Welfare capitalism is designed to sustain not replace the market mechanism. The issue is not the total rejection of the market mechanism but its subordination to moral principles that transcend the market, that is, to social values that reflect a vision of love and justice and the community of men.[173]

Social values embodied in our welfare measures are subordinated to the demands of the market system, seeking to ameliorate injustice without raising the issue of justice. So long as we define welfare in terms of forms of assistance to inadequate individuals, the injustices in the system of distributing resources and opportunities remain protected.

Beyond the issue of economic justice lies the more complex question of the quality of life available to all of us. The market harnessed to awesome technology can add to our material comforts and at the same time compound the social and human costs that accompany uncontrolled economic expansion. The market uncontrolled by some moral ideal that transcends sheer expansion of the GNP can only vulgarize the ideal of human progress. It continues to foster the narrow values of economic man and economic society and to conceal the basic moral problem. The moral problem before us is the problem of socal order. Society is nothing but moral relations among men, consisting of ethical rules that guide interaction and define human purpose. The market society supplants social order by economic order, and our political economy, geared to sustaining and expanding the market, can offer no effective alternative. Missing is the guiding social vision, the ethical ideals that would harness economy and technology to some noble end and enable all of us to transcend narrow self-interest.

Somehow man must be again at the center. The moral allegiance we give to our common humanity and to its fullest expression must be incorporated in the economic and political structure of society. Harvey Wheeler helps us to see

[171] Quoted in Robert Theobold (ed.), *The Guaranteed Income* (Garden City, N.Y.: Doubleday, 1966), p. 86.

[172] *Building the American City*, National Commission on Urban Problems, 91st Congress, 1st sess., House Document 34 (Washington, D.C.: Government Printing Office, 1968), p. 163.

[173] Lichtman, *op. cit.*, p. 12.

that our concern for the kind of human being we develop is the measure of a decent society. He writes:

> The Athenians were fond of saying of themselves that although other states might know how to make better products, only Athens knew how to make human beings. All any social system really makes, well or ill, is human beings. This is the product on which it must stand or fall, the one that demands and deserves its largest capital investment and its most sedulous attention.[174]

All men must be part of a society that recognizes that institutions exist to serve human needs and that no man may be treated as superfluous. A better balance must be established between allocation of resources on the basis of achievement and on the basis of one's right to life. Required is a new welfare ethic committed to human development that would direct our attention to resources and life opportunities essential for assuring self-actualization to all. From this perspective social welfare is concerned with the optimum possible relationship between human needs and the individual's command over resources at critical stages of his development. For example, Gerald Caplan has written that in order to promote mental health a person needs continual supplies (resources) commensurate with his stage of growth and development. These may be specified as physical, psychosocial, and sociocultural.[175] Social problems may be seen as a result of defects in structures for the delivery of vital resources. Social systems may be critically analyzed in terms of the way they distribute life opportunities. Structures functional for maintaining a market society, with its built-in multipliers of advantage, may not be functional for human development. For example, the imperatives of child development ought to determine the structure for meeting basic needs of children as nearly as possible. In system terms one may speak of the appropriate inputs of resources for children at different stages of development. We may then critically examine the extent to which we nurture or damage a child's capacity to grow. At a minimum this calls for a generous meeting of the basic needs of children as a shared responsibility, the "almost unanimous agreement that the prior satisfaction of the so-called basic needs is necessary before human beings can become concerned with and perform higher level functions" has led to recommendations for assuring to all children proper food, clothing, medical care and other essentials prerequisite to learning.[176] To accomplish this we cannot rely as heavily as we have on the market mechanism or on a residual welfare system that at best provides for only minimum alleviation of the maldistribution of resources. Abraham Maslow and others offer us a concept of human needs that might guide social policy.[177]

[174] Harvey Wheeler, *The Restoration of Politics* (Santa Barbara, Calif.: Center for the Study of Democratic Institutions, 1965), p. 21.

[175] Gerald Caplan, *Principles of Preventive Psychiatry* (New York: Basic Books, 1964), p. 31.

[176] Benjamin S. Bloom, Allison Davis, and Robert Hess, *Compensatory Education for Cultural Deprivation* (New York: Holt, Rinehart & Winston, 1965), p. 8.

[177] Abraham H. Maslow, *Motivation and Personality* (New York: Harper & Bros., 1954); Nathan E. Cohen, "A Social Work Approach," in Nathan E. Cohen (ed.),

We return to this theme later. We recognize that there are dilemmas and conflicts that cannot be fully resolved. The tension between the inequality of class and the equality of citizenship, between the market principle of profit and the social welfare principle of human needs, between what is politically feasible and morally desirable, are dynamic tensions that are essential for promoting new accommodations between reality and the ideal. We do not pretend to any final solutions to these dilemmas for there probably are none. What is sadly missing is public debate that gets to the core of the moral assumptions that underlie our system—a system that produces so much and allocates so badly, that creates products we could do without at the cost of opportunities foregone for improving the quality of our lives.

Social Work and Social Problems (New York: National Association of Social Workers, 1964), p. 384.

SIX

Economic Needs and Social Provisions: The Quest for Social Security and Social Justice

"The age of the industrial revolution is drawing to a close; that of the scientific revolution is crashing in on us. Holding fast to our makeshift welfare state, like a man attempting to go over Niagara Falls in water wings, we are trying to face the scientific revolution with the primitive tools left over from the Great Depression." [1]

The Quest for Social Security and Social Justice

A major function of social welfare programs in all industrial countries is to protect individuals and families from such contingencies as unemployment, illness, death of a breadwinner, and other hazards that interfere with the flow of income derived from work. When wages from work are not adequate to meet socially defined needs, legislation providing for minimum wages or wage supplementation may be part of a gamut of provisions designed to assure some level of economic well-being. A wide variety of other social provisions, including medical care, housing, meals, subsidized vacations, and special tax deductions may contribute to the economic welfare of some or all of the population. The extent and adequacy of social provisions reflect the stage of economic development and the ideology of the nation. Where values support the idea of collective provisions to assure a floor beneath which no citizen may fall, continuing poverty is seen as a failure of social policy to adequately redistribute essential goods and services. In the United States, with its persistent ideology of self-

[1] Harvey Wheeler, *The Restoration of Politics* (Santa Barbara, Calif.: Center for the Study of Democratic Institutions, 1965), p. 19.

help and moral responsibility for poverty, the tendency is to pay less attention to defects in social provisions and to give intense devotion to presumed defects in individuals.

The dominant ideology in American society, however complex, conflicted, and incapable of being captured in a single phrase, continues to give priority to the individualism associated with the Protestant ethic and the ideals of a commercial society. Inherently conservative, it functions to maintain the present socio-economic order and the pattern of power and privilege embedded within it. Yet our egalitarian ethic provides a constant challenge to this conservative ideology. Inequality of class and equality of citizenship provide the major tensions that underlie the quest for social security and social justice. Although our dominant beliefs tend to place the welfare state in some disrepute, on an operational level Americans do accept the idea that government has responsibility for meeting a variety of social needs. According to a study conducted by Lloyd A. Free and Hadley Cantril, we are a paradoxical mixture of "operational liberals and ideological conservatives," favoring some programs of social reform yet believing that the basic American institutions require little change.[2] Following is a brief summary of the findings of Free and Cantril.[3] Specific government programs to meet social needs tend to be favored, especially if they are perceived as furthering one's own purposes. The majority of Americans are in favor of maintaining or increasing the present level of support for the antipoverty programs. They favor expanded federal aid to education, compulsory medical insurance, low-rent public housing, and urban renewal. Yet at an ideological level, Americans remain profoundly conservative. Only about 16 percent are classified as ideological liberals. There is relatively little popular support for comprehensive social measures that would eliminate poverty or promote social justice. Despite approval of some specific programs, the world view of the average American, his conceptual understanding of the operation of the economic and political system, tends to be rooted in the mythology of free enterprise and individual initiative. In a period when 5 percent of the labor force was unemployed and when Negroes were facing a critical unemployment rate of 15 percent, three-fourths of the population maintained that ". . . any able-bodied person who really wants to work in this country can find a job and earn a living." The same myth was held by 70 percent of the people in relatively low-income groups (with family incomes of less than $5,000 a year) and by 60 percent of all Negroes.

This fact is testimony to the highly effective miseducation of the American people by our schools and mass media concerning the realities of economic and social life. Education, which is often appealed to as the solution to our social problems, has in fact prepared Americans to see the economic and political world through the myopic lens of an economic individualism that protectively conceals a hierarchical social order and a maldistribution of economic and political power.[4] Most of our public schools do not equip citizens with the

[2] Lloyd A. Free and Hadley Cantril, *The Political Beliefs of Americans* (New Brunswick, N.J.: Rutgers University Press, 1967), p. 22.

[3] *Ibid.*, pp. 11–15, 22, 26, 36, and 40.

[4] Rush Welter, *Popular Education and Democratic Thought in America* (New York: Columbia University Press, 1962), p. 335.

capacity for critical social inquiry.   Since man is social man, with his very nature dependent on the kind of society in which he lives, his very freedom to actualize himself requires a critical awareness of his social environment, its constraints and opportunities for action.   American education has fostered the mythology of individualism out of its timid compliance with the need of society to restrict social awareness for its own protection.   The fear of "un-American" ideas and the uncritical celebration of the American Dream has substituted ideology for inquiry in most of our public schools.   The myth of individualism conceals the structure of opportunity, power, and privilege that functions to allocate social resources and social rewards.   It serves to dampen social discontent through the paralyzing inhibition of self-blame.   We now confront questions of social justice that cannot be appropriately understood or responded to with an ideology that deals with social issues by converting them into individual moral problems.   We are at a point in our history at which ". . . our economic progress needs to be shared with low-income groups," as Walter W. Heller, former Chairman of the Council of Economic Advisors, recognized.[5]   Beyond that there are critical questions of the goals of the society, the quality of life we can offer our citizens, and the ideals we can hold out to our young.

Issues of social justice arise as the existence of relative abundance conflicts with the degree of asceticism demanded of the poor.   When Emerson wrote of the "lame pauper haunted by overseers from town to town," he lived in a society whose Gross National Product was about $6 billion.   Today our GNP expands each year by five times that amount.   Yet, despite the fact that our social welfare expenditures have increased considerably, they do not approximate the share of national income other nations devote to social welfare. (Table 17).   It is estimated that, at the ". . . present rate of retarded social progress in the United States, it will be 1984 before we reach welfare state minima comparable to those now provided in most Western European countries." [6]

Individualism combined with a historic distrust of government has limited the social uses of political power for the promotion of freedom and equality. Social security, essential for freedom of action, is a functional equivalent of property rights.   Liberty is protected since social provisions available as a citizen right assure that one individual is not dependent for survival on the whim or coercion of another.   Yet in the context of an ideology of individual free enterprise, public provision of economic security may be seen as a threat rather than a friend of liberty, especially when equality of opportunity is regarded as an American accomplishment rather than a goal yet to be fully attained.   In this view an individual has only to take advantage of the opportunity all around him. In this way he may measure his self-worth against the possibilities open to him. Although the shibboleths of free enterprise and individual initiative were battered by the hard realities of economic insecurity and inequality, they have remained remarkably persistent as part of the American world view.   Despite increasing acceptance of specific government social welfare measures, in partic-

[5] *Twentieth Anniversary of the Employment Act of 1946*, U.S. Congress, Joint Economic Committee, 89th Congress, 2nd sess. (Washington, D.C.: Government Printing Office, 1966), p. 67.

[6] Bertram M. Gross (ed.), *A Great Society?* (New York: Basic Books, 1966), p. 331.

Table 17.   Social Security Expenditures of Common Market Countries, Sweden, the United Kingdom, and the United States as a Percent of National Income by Major Types of Coverage, 1962

COUNTRY	TOTAL	OASDI	SICKNESS AND MATERNITY INSURANCE *	UNEMPLOYMENT INSURANCE	WORK ACCIDENT INSURANCE	FAMILY ALLOWANCE
Belgium	13.4	4.7	3.6	1.1	1.0	3.0
France	13.4	3.9	4.1	—	1.1	4.3
Germany (West)	14.4	8.1	4.5	.4	.8	.6
Italy	12.0	4.7	2.9	.6	.6	2.9
Luxembourg	13.7	6.3	3.1	—	1.8	2.5
Netherlands	12.0	5.7	3.6	.6	.4	1.7
Sweden	9.2	5.1	2.2	.2	.2	1.6
United Kingdom	10.6	4.2	5.1	.3	.3	.6
United States	4.8	3.6	.1	.7	.3	—

* U.S. figure on sickness and maternity insurance, i.e., temporary disability, for four states and for railroad workers.

SOURCE: *European Social Security Systems,* U.S. Congress Joint Economic Committee, Economic Policies and Practices, Paper No. 7, (Washington, D.C.: Government Printing Office, 1965), p. 11.

ular our social security programs, we have yet to develop a positive philosophy of government that would sanction the uses of political power for the development of social democracy. Despite the expansion of the welfare state it remains in disrepute, its legitimacy challenged by the ideology of individualism. A narrow and distorted definition of self-reliance, no longer functional in an interdependent urban technological environment, prevents us from exploring ways we can create social environments that will support and nurture the self-reliance that develops from compassionate attention to meeting basic human needs and developing human capacities. For this kind of regard for all human beings we need to restore a sense of community, without which neither security nor justice can be assured. It is perhaps our lack of a sense of community more than anything else that makes us so morally oblivious to the human cost of our continuing economic insecurity and injustice. Our cultural pluralism is a divisive rather than a uniting force for, in truth, we honor not the diversity of our backgrounds but the myth of the melting pot. In reality this has come to mean the chauvinism of white Anglo-Saxon Protestants and the social denigration of other ethnic groups, which have had to struggle to enter the society and proclaim their citizenship. The struggle for status, although a positive and dynamic force in economic development, disrupts the social fabric, the ties that bind men to one another. It may be that our need for achievement and for affiliation are forever in conflict, calling always for efforts to attain some balance.

Out of the recurring tension between the values of capitalism and those of social democracy we have developed social provisions that contribute to economic well-being and some that may have, at best, mixed results. Our basic programs increasingly come under critical scrutiny. Major reforms are being demanded and receive support from a fairly wide spectrum of political opinion, however much such proponents may still be in the minority. Our social provisions have developed in a manner consistent with our market-oriented, work-dominated, individual-centered culture. Income maintenance programs for the most part have been designed to reward the most economically productive and to relegate those with marginal attachment to work or those essentially outside the occupational structure to residual and demeaning programs. Yet this understates the degree to which recipients of our residual welfare programs are work related, as we shall see. In any event, like all industrial nations, we have had to come to some terms with the basic problem of economic insecurity characteristic of such economies. In the process we have created the American version of those social provisions that are used by all Western countries to deal with the twin problems of poverty and economic insecurity.

Public Assistance and Social Insurance

Public assistance and social insurance are the twin programs we use to respond to poverty and income insecurity. They are related, but public assistance is clearly the poor relative; it is relegated to the back room of the welfare state and only grudgingly acknowledged as a member of the family of measures used by society to meet its needs. Yet it is the forerunner of all our social welfare programs. The characteristics that are said to distinguish social insurance from public assistance have been summarized in the following way: [7] (1) Social insurance is *work related*. Past employment determines a worker's entitlement to benefits, and the amount he and his family may receive are related to earnings in covered employment. Thus the underlying rationale is that the worker assures security for himself and his family through his own work. (2) There is *no means test*. Benefits are defined as an earned right, paid regardless of income from sources other than employment, such as savings, investments, pensions, home ownership, and insurance. One does not have to prove that he is needy or undergo any investigation of resources. (3) It is *contributory*. The apparent contributory nature of OASDHI is a major social fiction that accounts for its general public acceptance. It reinforces the notion of earned right and maintains the respectable aura of insurance, thus avoiding the stigma of public welfare. (4) It is *compulsory*. For the most part coverage is a requirement justified on the grounds that such a provision assures financial soundness of the program because it forces both the good and the bad "risks" to be included. A further argument is that this requirement prevents dependency by compelling a breadwinner to save a portion of his income to cover future contingencies. (5) *Rights are clearly defined by law*. One of the most notable distinctions between public assistance and social insurance is the relative absence of administrative discretion in the determination of eligibility or benefits. The law clearly defines conditions of eligibility and amount of benefits.

The Mythology of Social Insurance

The general acceptance of social insurance rests on certain useful social fictions consistent with the American ethos of work and self-reliance. It is the

[7] *Social Security Programs in the United States,* U.S. Department of Health, Education, and Welfare (Washington, D.C.: Government Printing Office, 1966), pp. 21–22.

analogy with private insurance rather than with public assistance that gives to the OASDHI program its stamp of respectability. The analogy, never entirely accurate, has become less so, yet the mythology persists to protect the program from the stigma of welfare. Professor Eveline Burns distinguishes three stages in the evolution of social insurance.[8] In the first stage the analogy to private insurance has some distinct relevance since benefits are closely geared to contributions; equity is emphasized over adequacy; coverage is restricted to those whose substantial employment record indicates good risk; and potential beneficiaries and their employers bear the total cost. In the second stage principles and policies governing eligibility, benefits, and methods of financing that maintain the analogy with private insurance are modified to meet the pressure to extend coverage. The relationship between benefits and earnings becomes more tenuous as the low and marginal wage earner is brought into the system and efforts are made to assure him some acceptable level of benefits. The question of contributions from general revenues may become a political issue in the latter part of stage two. The third stage ushers in the doctrine of an assured minimum income for all as a result of universal acceptance of a social provision without a means test.

Thus social insurance may pave the way for a universal system of guaranteed income as a citizen right, although no claim is made that these are invariably evolutionary stages. The American provision of OASDHI rests somewhere in the second stage. Public expression is increasingly being given to the notion of some form of guaranteed income. Once regarded as a clearly un-American idea, the serious consideration being given to new forms of income maintenance by prominent politicians and business and civic leaders suggests that the third stage is not entirely a utopian ideal.

In the meantime the social security program continues to be defined in terms of insurance rather than public assurance of income. It is generally recognized that, unlike the basic principle of equity that governs private insurance, social insurance schemes are concerned with the social adequacy of benefits in order to assure all a certain standard of living irrespective of contributions. The tendency is to move away from equity toward social adequacy. Yet social insurance may be said to qualify as a form of "insurance" if it is seen as a broad mechanism for pooling collective resources to protect against common contingencies. Unlike private insurance there is no binding contract. There is no constitutional protection of insurance rights. In *Flemming v. Nestor* the U.S. Supreme Court declared that OASDHI benefits could be withheld on the grounds of subversive activities because the social security system was ". . . enacted pursuant to Congress' power to spend money in aid of the general welfare."[9] According to the Court, covered employees have a noncontractual interest that ". . . cannot be soundly analogized to that of the holder of an annuity, whose rights to benefits are bottomed on his contractual premium payments." The analogy to private insurance may still be maintained to some degree on the basis of the following similarities: (1) widespread pooling of common risks, (2) specific and detailed descriptions of all conditions regarding coverage, benefits, and fi-

[8] Eveline M. Burns, "Social Security in Evolution: Toward What?," *Social Security Review*, 39 (June 1965), pp. 129–140.

[9] Flemming v. Nestor, 363 U.S. 603, 1960.

nancing, (3) mathematical calculations of benefit eligibility and accounts, and (4) specific contributions that are calculated to meet projected costs of the system.[10]

The amount beneficiaries pay into the system may be defined as contributions that resemble premium payments or they may be seen simply as forms of taxation, not essentially different from other tax revenues that go to the support of public programs. Charles Schottland defends the contributory idea on the grounds that it is an important psychological principle that accounts for widespread support of the social security system. Moreover, in his view, it helps to maintain a responsible and disciplined attitude on the part of voters, who refrain from insisting on enlargement of benefits since they clearly recognize their share in paying the cost. Nations that earlier had rejected the principle of contribution in favor of support through general taxation are to some degree viewing it with increasing favor.[11] The British are now considering major changes in their social security system that would relate contributions and benefits to earnings, partly because support from general taxation has not been as great as originally envisaged. To be gradually achieved over a period of twenty years, the new plan, based on pay-as-you-go financing, has as its goal benefits adequate enough to eliminate supplementation for those who have no other means of support.[12]

On the other hand, it can also be argued that, although social insurance has an appealing image, its analogy to private insurance is distorted and misleading and impedes ". . . intelligent consideration of alternative means of shaping the course of the program." [13] In the view of Joseph A. Pechman and his colleagues, social security is

> . . . a mechanism for transferring financial resources from the working generation to those who cannot work because of age, disability or dependency status. This is a point that has been emphasized by many economists and is no longer in serious dispute.[14]

The key issues, they insist, concern criteria for deciding the size of the transfer and for financing and allocating benefits. Despite the positive value of the insurance analogy in securing widespread public support for social security, the image ". . . is strained and, in the end, seriously misleading."

Though the fiction continues to be maintained that each individual pays for his own benefits, which he receives as an earned right rather than as public charity, our social security program in fact, ". . . is not an insurance system, but a transfer payment system that distributes to the aged a share of the gains

---

[10] Robert J. Myers, *Social Insurance and Allied Government Programs* (Homewood, Ill.: Irwin, 1965), p. 9.

[11] Charles I. Schottland, *The Social Security Program in the United States* (New York: Appleton-Century-Croft, 1963), p. 58.

[12] "British White Paper on Social Security Reform," *Social Security Bulletin,* 32 (May 1969), pp. 3–15.

[13] Joseph A. Pechman, Henry J. Aaron, and Michael Taussig, "The Objectives of Social Security," *Old Age Income Assurance,* U.S. Congress Joint Economic Committee, 90th Congress, 1st sess., Part III: Public Programs (Washington, D.C.: Government Printing Office, 1967), p. 5.

[14] *Ibid.*

from the growth in the overall productivity of the economy." [15]   Beneficiaries under our present OASDHI program receive benefits in excess of the taxes they paid, or that were paid in their behalf.   Congress is likely to continue to raise benefit levels to correspond to higher wage levels so as to distribute more equitably some of the increased common wealth of society.

The extent to which there is an appropriate analogy between private insurance and social security hinges on whether individuals now in the labor force and paying taxes into the social security trust fund are storing up reserves for their future and that of their families or simply paying for current benefits distributed to others through the program.   The facts are that, for sound fiscal reasons, the social security program is financed on an almost complete pay-as-you-go basis, which means simply that current participants in the labor force pay for the benefits that go to those presently eligible.   They in turn will receive transfers of income from those employed in the future at rates that will reflect economic growth.[16]   The currently employed will simply be taxed at a rate sufficient to allow political judgments about the degree of social adequacy to be provided under the social security system.   The recognition of this fact means that benefits going to the current recipients ". . . need not, and should not, depend on their past taxes; they should be based on an explicit decision reached by democratic political processes as to how much of the Nation's total income should be allocated . . ." [17] for the social purposes intended by the legislation.   The tax ought to be considered not as an insurance premium but as one method of financing to be evaluated along with other devices for the support of essential social provisions.   Given this perspective the distinction between social insurance and public assistance turns out to be largely a social fiction, useful in some respects, harmful in others.   To the degree that it maintains the invidious and largely fallacious distinction between earned right and charity and continues to sort out the worthy and the unworthy, it disrupts rather than binds the community of men.   As one examines the structured inequalities that assign some to dependency on the residual and demeaning public assistance programs, the stigmatizing distinction between social insurance and public assistance is even less supportable.   The trouble with the mythology of social insurance is not that it is a form of social fiction, since all of social life rests on some binding myth, but that in the new era in which we live it may be an obsolete and harmful myth.   The value of a citizen right to life is that it may provide a social ideal that will release human energies for the pursuit of goals beyond those now included in our narrow definition of work and establish a basis for the fullest social participation of all.   The distinction between the worthy and the unworthy, the taxpayers and tax-eaters, will be seen for what they are—social definitions ill suited to a society that aspires to honor the dignity of man and his fullest development.   But this may be too radical a myth even for our revolutionary era, which continues to rest on the fiction that each man produces his own wealth and is entitled to what he receives—no more, no less, except as charitable impulse may alleviate the self-imposed suffering of the weak and the indolent.   Of course this overstates the case.   Recognition of

[15] *Ibid.*

[16] *Ibid.*, p. 19.

[17] *Ibid.*, p. 20.

socially created hardships and risks over which one has no control has inspired a variety of social provisions for meeting economic needs. First we will look at the various programs of social insurance directed primarily at those who are defined as productive members of the labor force, and then we will examine the residual programs of public assistance that are directed at those defined as the failures and rejects of society. This is not to suggest that the programs are completely distinct. In many ways they overlap, as illustrated for example, by the fact that approximately one million OASDHI beneficiaries are also recipients of public assistance through Old Age Assistance grants. Moreover there is a trend toward endowing public assistance with some of the characteristics of social insurance through measures that assure entitlement. Further as we shall see, social insurance and public assistance are both income transfer programs serving a social purpose.

Social Insurance Programs

OASDHI. A third of a century ago the idea of social security seemed, to some, subversive of the traditional American emphasis on individual initiative. Today the Old Age, Survivors, Disability, and Health Insurance Program, the major expression of this idea, has become an accepted institution, a universal and popular social welfare measure. Its acceptability reflects the degree to which the program evolved in a manner that seemed consistent with conventional values and concepts: "self-help, mutual aid, insurance, incentives to work and save." [18] Part myth, part reality, the belief that people earned what they receive has given legitimacy to a program that has been extended to cover almost all Americans.

The program has three related but distinct objectives: (1) It assures some minimum income support for those eligible to receive benefits—the aged, disabled, and dependent survivors. (2) It moderates the decline in living standards when income is interrupted because of retirement, disability, or death of a breadwinner. (3) More recently it has taken on the objective of protecting the aged from the high cost of medical care. With increasing national concern about poverty, greater attention is being given to the first goal. The success of the program is in part measured by its ability to lift beneficiaries above the poverty line. In the view of Robert M. Ball, this social security system has been ". . . our most effective weapon in the war on poverty to date." [19] It is estimated that social security benefits lift some 10 million Americans above the poverty line. About 6.5 million remain in poverty despite their social security benefits. Of all beneficiaries, only about a fourth have incomes that would enable them to live above the poverty line without social security payments.[20]

OASDHI is the basic national social insurance program. Financed through a tax on employers, employees, and the self-employed, it provides monthly cash benefits when earnings are interrupted by retirement, disability, or death. In 1965 health insurance for those sixty-five and over was added. The program

[18] Robert M. Ball, "Social Security Perspectives," *Social Security Bulletin,* 31 (August 1968), p. 3.

[19] *Ibid,* p. 3.

[20] *Ibid.*

evolved in various stages, as Dr. Burns has suggested. In its origin in 1935 it covered only retired workers. Four years later it became a family program with benefits provided for a worker's dependents and his survivors; today it represents part of our patchwork family policy, a point to which we will return later. During the 1950s and 1960s coverage was extended so that now about 90 percent of those in paid employment or self-employment are covered. In 1967 about 87 million workers paid social security taxes. In that year all but 5 percent of young children and their mothers were eligible for monthly benefits in the event of the death of the family head. All but 8 percent of those who reached sixty-five in the same year were eligible for retirement benefits.[21] Basic retirement benefits are paid to eligible workers sixty-five years and over and to their dependents. Reduced benefits are available to those who retire at age sixty-two, a fact of some concern since now more than half of all those who retire do so before the age of sixty-five and consequently receive reduced benefits. Indications are that early retirement is forced by ill health or inability to secure employment.[22] Widows are eligible for benefits at age sixty or at any age so long as they have children under age eighteen or twenty-two who are attending school.

Benefits reflect the distinct goals of social security. On the one hand they reflect past average monthly earnings and thus serve to relate retirement income to the level of income during the working years. On the other hand they are weighted in favor of low-wage earners in order to assure some minimum level of retirement income. Table 18 shows the number of beneficiaries and the amounts of payments under OASDHI in 1969–1970.

The addition of health insurance for the aged in 1965 brought to a climax a long battle against such a provision by the American Medical Association.[23] Proposals for national health insurance had been made during the deliberation of the original Social Security Act, more than three decades before a partial plan was realized. The 1965 Amendments to the Social Security Act set up a basic hospital insurance program financed through a separate tax on earnings. Provisions were also made for funds from general revenue for those sixty-five and over who were not eligible for social security payments. A program of voluntary supplemental medical insurance was also introduced. Financed through small monthly premiums and federal contributions, it covers part of the cost of services from a physician as well as other related medical and health services.

A number of issues are inherent in the OASDHI program, particularly as we search for better mechanisms to deal with questions of social security and social justice. Although social security benefits have been raised, almost 8 million OASDHI beneficiaries are poor. Retired couples face a rising gap between their benefits and modern standards of living. In 1950 the average monthly social security benefit of $75 allowed a retired couple one-half the cost of a moderate living standard as determined by the Bureau of Labor Statistics. In 1968 the ratio was about a third. In that year the average benefit was about

[21] *Health, Education, and Welfare Trends,* 1966–1967 ed., Part I, National Trends, U.S. Department of Health, Education, and Welfare (Washington, D.C.: Government Printing Office, 1968), p. 21.

[22] Ball, *op. cit.,* p. 5.

[23] Richard Harris, *Sacred Trust* (New York: New American Library, 1966).

Table 18. OASDHI—Beneficiaries and Payments

	MARCH 1970	MARCH 1969
Total beneficiaries (monthly)	25.7 million	24.7 million
Age 65 and over (total)	17.2	16.7
Retired workers	11.8	11.3
Survivors and dependents	4.8	4.6
Persons with special age—72 benefits	.6	.7
Under 65 (total)	8.5	8.1
Retired workers	1.2	1.1
Disabled workers	1.4	1.3
Survivors and dependents	5.9	6.6
Total monthly benefits (billions)	2.6	2.1
Average benefits in current payment status		
Retired workers	$116.93	$ 99.36
Disabled workers	130.21	111.98
Aged widows and widowers	100.96	86.63
Children of deceased workers	81.86	70.80
Average Benefit awarded		
Retired workers	$106.11	$105.20
Disabled workers	120.89	116.87
Aged widows and widowers	92.74	90.65
Children of deceased workers	72.55	68.50

SOURCE: *Social Security Bulletin,* Vol. 33 (July 1970) p. 1.

$120, while the cost of a moderate living standard was $365.[24] Most retired or disabled couples with two children and totally dependent on OASDHI are poor. Although widows with dependent children are economically better off than other fatherless families, their level of living remains considerably below that of the average American family.[25] Over one million persons receive public assistance because their social security grants do not meet minimum state or local welfare standards. A special problem confronts the low-wage earner now retired or about to retire. He faces minimum benefits because of low earning patterns and because his employment became covered under the program relatively late.

An issue, then, is the degree of compromise to be established between conceiving of this social security program as a wage-related contributory system designed to maintain some relationship of retirement income to past earnings and conceiving of it as an antipoverty mechanism. If it is to assure a more adequate income to beneficiaries, general revenue funds will be required at some point; this would further undermine the conception of the program as a contributory insurance mechanism. How important is it to maintain the analogy to insurance? As increasing attention is given to social adequacy over

[24] *Aging,* No. 175 (May 1969), p. 6.

[25] Erdman Palmore, Gertrude L. Stanley, and Robert H. Cormier, *Widows with Children under Social Security,* Social Security Administration, Research Report No. 16 (Washington, D.C.: Government Printing Office, 1966), pp. 63–64.

equity will it be possible to maintain the fiction of insurance? What should be the relationship between OASDHI to public assistance? How will it relate to other programs being proposed to assure all Americans a decent income and the right to life?

UNEMPLOYMENT INSURANCE. The Social Security Act also established a federal-state system of unemployment insurance financed through a tax on employers and federal grants to the states to cover costs of administration. Nothing like a uniform system has developed because states determine coverage, eligibility requirements, and duration and amount of benefits. Three-fourths of all jobs in wage and salary employment are covered. Excluded are employees in state and local government, domestic service, farming and processing of agricultural products, those in very small firms, and those in nonprofit organizations. Unprotected too are the self-employed, young workers unsuccessfully seeking their first job, reentrants into the labor force, and unpaid farm workers. In 1967, 40 percent of the unemployed were in these groups.[26] In that year over 16 million workers had no protection under this program. Although the modest aim has been to cover one-half the gross weekly wage lost due to unemployment, the national average weekly benefit in 1967 was $41.25, or a little over a third of the average weekly wage in covered employment. Little security here. Most states provide a maximum coverage of twenty-six weeks in any one-year period—a provision tied, however, to length of previous employment. In 1966 over half of all claimants who exhausted their benefits had received unemployment compensation for less than 26 weeks. Only eleven states, in 1965, augmented the weekly benefit by including an amount for dependents. Such augmented maximum weekly benefits ranged from $43 in Indiana to $75 in Connecticut and to as much as 100 percent of the claimant's average weekly wage in Massachusetts.[27] The moral is clear: choose your state carefully if you are going to be unemployed.

Relatively few basic changes have been made in the program over the years, despite its inadequacy as a social provision. It is estimated that no more than one-fifth of all wage loss due to unemployment is recovered through this program. As the 1968 *Manpower Report* observes, a significant number of workers, unemployed through no fault of their own, may find themselves ". . . sooner or later thrown on . . . (their) . . . own resources." The Report goes further to declare:

> For millions of workers . . . the U. I. system does not meet its original objectives. It often fails to restore even as much as one-half the weekly earnings to those who lose their jobs, and even that inadequate payment often stops before the workers are again earning wages.[28]

[26] *Manpower Report of the President,* U.S. Department of Labor (Washington, D.C.: Government Printing Office, 1968), p. 38.

[27] *Summary Tables for Evaluation of Coverage and Benefit Provisions of State Unemployment Insurance Laws as of December 31, 1965,* U.S. Department of Labor, Manpower Administration, Bureau of Labor Statistics, U-256 (July 1966), p. 6.

[28] *Manpower Report of the President,* 1968, *op. cit.,* pp. 40, 42.

Such statements are important recognition of the failure of this society to acknowledge fully the ordeal of unemployment and to provide adequately for this contingency. Statistical data support the conclusion. Yet it is difficult to translate the problem in human terms, to reflect the meaning of unemployment to a breadwinner and his family, to convey the stress of loss of wages, the lowered standard of living, the failure to provide for those who depend on you. One study of unemployed men who had to resort to public assistance because they were ineligible for or had exhausted their unemployment insurance benefits offers the following remarks:

> I clear out of the house before the kids go to school. I know they haven't got the right clothes to wear. Their clothes are more like rags than anything else.

> When the kids ask me for something extra, I get mad. It isn't their fault, is it? Getting mad doesn't help. It makes me feel worse.

> When you don't have the money you buy stuff that sticks to the ribs.

> I'm afraid I'll go buggy not doing anything all day. You sit around thinking and worrying. It's enough to make a guy go nuts.[29]

In this study most of the respondents preferred work to more adequate social provision. Yet, for some, even when work is available it does not produce wages sufficient for meeting basic needs. Minimum wage legislation is an effort to meet this problem.

MINIMUM WAGE LEGISLATION. This form of social legislation is not a method of social insurance as that term is ordinarily understood, but it is part of the battery of instruments used to secure some minimum level of living. Such legislation is directed at protecting those in the labor force whose work produces substandard wages because of economic exploitation or, as is more common in this era, because they are employed in marginal sectors of the economy that may not be able to pay a living wage. Lack of strong labor unions among low-wage earners is also a factor. In 1968 as many as 10 million workers, about two-thirds of whom were in full-time employment, were earning less than $1.60 an hour. Of the over 2 million people engaged in domestic service, 92 percent received less than the minimum wage of $1.60 per hour and over 1.9 million of them received less than $1 an hour.[30]

In 1966, for the first time, the federal minimum-wage legislation was extended to cover a portion of farm labor—some 390,000 workers out of an estimated 1.5 million. Those covered included only workers on large farms and big migratory labor crews. In all, this legislation extended coverage to 8 million workers to bring the total covered to some 30 million. Newly covered farm and nonfarm workers under this law are to attain $1.60 an hour by 1971. For

---

[29] Harry A. Wasserman, "Social-economic Effects of Unemployment" (Dissertation submitted in partial satisfaction of requirements for DSW degree, University of California, Berkeley, 1965).

[30] *Manpower Report of the President,* 1968, *op. cit.,* p. 27.

others, already covered under the law, the minimum wage was raised in steps until the level of $1.60 an hour was attained in 1968.

There is disagreement about the merit of minimum-wage legislation. In the view of some, it is not a very effective way to assure a reasonably decent level of living for a worker and his family. It may have the effect of increasing the risk of unemployment for some workers having the least education and skills. Where labor productivity does not warrant increased wages, the net effect may be to force marginal workers out of employment as their jobs become mechanized or as their industries contract. It has been argued that the political energy ". . . that has spent itself in successive increases in the minimum wage would probably have done more for the poor had it been used to build some kind of explicit floor under incomes." [31] Although he accepts the notion of a floor under incomes, Leon H. Keyserling, former Chairman of the Council of Economic Advisers, argues for expanded minimum-wage legislation as one among several ways of assuring that those at the bottom of the occupational ladder share more equitably in the economic growth of the nation.[32] Tax concessions to marginal enterprises unable to bear the added cost of higher wages would, in his judgment, be a desirable form of public subsidy. Whatever the form, it is clear that some social provision must be made for those in the labor force whose work fails to provide a decent level of living and an equitable share in the expanding economy. Minimum wages cannot meet the needs of large families, which indicates the need for additional provisions.

WORKMEN'S COMPENSATION. It is estimated that out of one hundred young people who enter the labor force at age twenty only one-fourth will complete their working lives without disability or injury: one will die, six will suffer permanent impairment, and sixty-eight will experience one or more disabling injuries.[33] At the turn of the century, before any social provision had been made to protect workers against industrial illness and accidents, the risk was even greater.

Although we include workmen's compensation last among the list of social insurance programs, it was the first to be developed. It originated in Europe a third of a century before this country undertook similar protection of workers. A law established in 1908 provided workmen's compensation for federal employees. Three years later several states enacted similar legislation. In 1948 Mississippi was the last to step in line. The principle underlying the program is that occupational injury is a cost that must be borne by industry regardless of the cause. Earlier common law had placed primary responsibility on the worker, whose only recourse was to involve himself in an expensive and lengthy suit to recover damages; he could successfully accomplish this only if he could prove that he was not negligent when the accident occurred. All states have workmen's compensation laws today, but each is different in the extent of its coverage and range of benefits. No state covers all jobs and only thirty-two cover all occupational diseases. One out of five workers in the

---

[31] "The Minimum Wage," *The Public Interest,* No. 5 (Fall 1966), p. 121.

[32] Leon H. Keyserling, *The Role of Wages in a Great Society* (Washington, D.C.: Conference on Economic Progress, 1966), pp. 17–19.

[33] *Manpower Report of the President,* 1968, *op. cit.,* p. 42.

nation, 12 million in all, plus all self-employed workers have no such protection. Excluded are domestic employees, agricultural workers, those in small firms and in nonprofit enterprises. In 1966 the national maximum weekly benefit averaged 48 percent of the average weekly wage. In fifteen states, maximum benefits, measured in constant 1965–1966 dollars, were actually lower in 1966 than in 1940—an example of the retrogressive welfare state. In thirty-five states a worker with a family of four who becomes injured at work will be well below the poverty line if he has to depend on the maximum weekly benefit derived from workmen's compensation.[34] Benefits are generally inadequate, for ". . . the evidence today is that the average worker is still meeting out of his own resources the larger share of the cost of work injuries." [35]

For some there is no compensation at all. Once again we meet the special plight of the farm laborer who, after a lifetime of toil in the fields, reaps a harvest of bitter hardship. Ironically, among the hungry in America are those whose labor feeds the nation. The use of pesticides in the fields is a hazard to those who pick the crops, a risk unprotected by workmen's compensation. Thus the poverty of low wages may be aggravated by the unprotected risk of disability. A woman who was briefly in the nation's spotlight when the Senate Committee on Nutrition and Human needs studied the problem of hunger described the situation of her husband, who suffered blindness in one eye and damaged vision in the other as a result of working in a field freshly sprayed with pesticides:

> "He don't get much work anymore. . . . He don't see too good. Picking tomatoes, they say he misses too many of the pinks. . . . He knowed it had been sprayed but he was hot and sweaty on the bus riding back from the field and he forgot hisself. He took out a handkerchief and wiped it over his face. That's when he said it happened. He said a skim come over his eye." [36]

GAPS IN SOCIAL INSURANCE. Our social insurance programs make a significant contribution to economic security. Life would be a good deal meaner without them. Yet none of them are fully adequate, and some social insurance programs common in other nations are absent in the United States. Levels of benefits are too low; there are excessive and inequitable variations among states; and without automatic cost of living adjustments benefits tend to lag significantly behind the rising cost of living. Significant portions of the labor force remain unprotected by such programs as unemployment insurance (onefourth) and workmen's compensation (one-fifth). In several instances programs that protect workers do not include benefits for dependents, reflecting our tendency to orient our social provisions toward individuals rather than family units. About one-third of the states provide supplemental benefits to workmen's compensation for dependents, and about one-fifth of the states

[34] *Ibid.,* p. 44.

[35] Alfred M. Skolnik, "Twenty-Five Years of Workmen's Compensation Statistics," *Social Security Bulletin,* 29 (October 1966), p. 26.

[36] John A. Hamilton, "The Politics of Hunger," *Saturday Review,* June 21, 1969, p. 19.

provide family supplements to unemployment insurance. There are no social provisions covering the entire population to protect those with inadequate incomes against the increasing costs of medical care and child rearing. Other countries recognize some degree of shared responsibility for both of these ". . . common but unpredictable or irregularly occurring costs." [37] We have no national comprehensive health insurance and no national provision to cover loss of wages due to temporary disability or illness. When a group of social workers meeting in 1915 asked "What next in reform?" the unanimous reply was health insurance. They soon discovered they had seriously underestimated the strength of the opposition, which included employers' and taxpayers' associations, organized labor (until the 1930s), insurance firms, Christian Scientists, producers and dispensers of drugs and patent medicines, and the medical and dental professions.[38]

It was fifty years before the 1965 Amendments to the Social Security Act established Medicare, a program of health insurance for the aged, and Medicaid, medical assistance for the poor and near poor. Most Americans remain unprotected from the high cost of medical care by any national insurance provision, and the risk of the loss of wages due to illness and disability is for the most part uncovered by any social provision. Only four states (California, Rhode Island, New Jersey, and New York) provide temporary disability insurance covering most wage and salary workers in private industry. About three-fifths of wage and salary workers in private industry have some extremely limited protection against short-term nonoccupational disability.[39] Unlike most European and many African countries we have no national recognition of the need for social provisions for maternity leaves and benefits. About sixty-five countries have some type of sickness and maternity benefit program. Some kind of maternity benefit only is available in an additional twenty countries, including fourteen African countries.[40]

Except for tax deductions for dependent children, there is no national program of family allowances, nor any "fatherless insurance" that protects all children against the risk of being without a male breadwinner in the family. Children whose fathers die are economically better off than those who lose their fathers through family disruption. In either case, children without a father tend to be economically worse off than those in families headed by a male. Nonwhite children suffer the greatest risk of being without a father and thus are without adequate social protection against a socially structured handicap.

New kinds of risks previously given little attention are those associated with automobile accidents and crime. Some states do require drivers to carry auto insurance, but there is no comprehensive national public protection against the risk of injury or death in automobile accidents. (In 1968, 4.4 million persons were injured and 55,000 died in car accidents.) There have been a few state

[37] Burns, *op. cit.,* p. 135.

[38] Robert H. Bremner, *From the Depths—The Discovery of Poverty in the United States* (New York: New York University Press, 1964), p. 259.

[39] *Manpower Report,* 1968, *op. cit.,* p. 44.

[40] *Social Security Programs Throughout the World, 1967,* U.S. Department of Health, Education, and Welfare, Social Security Administration (Washington, D.C.: Government Printing Office, 1967), p. xviii.

laws passed to compensate victims of crimes.[41] Such laws would be of special benefit to the poor, who are more likely to be victims of crimes and the least likely to carry private theft or sickness and hospital insurance.

Public Assistance

"Welfare is where you go when you are going nowhere"
Paul Good [42]

If our social insurance programs are inadequate, our public assistance programs are a disaster. We write about them at a time when, for different reasons, almost everyone acknowledges that these programs are in a state of crisis. The Report of the National Advisory Commission on Civil Disorders declared that our public assistance measures have aggravated the tensions and social dislocations that underlie civil disorders. "The failures of the system," the commission wrote, "alienate the taxpayers who support it, the social workers who administer it and the poor who depend on it." [43]

This welfare crisis may lead to major modifications in the public assistance programs or to the establishment of some new form of income maintenance that may reduce, but will not in all likelihood abolish, this residual social provision.

Facts and Fiction About Welfare

We are a nation of contradictions. We declare a war on poverty, yet we deliberately maintain our welfare poor at a level below the poverty line. We believe in family life, but design our basic family support program—Aid to Families with Dependent Children—in ways that seem to contribute to the disruption of family life. We believe in the ethic of work, yet do not guarantee the right to work. We are a child-centered culture and are endlessly sentimental about children, but it does not strike us as unconscionable that children should live in destitution or that they should suffer punishment for the presumed sins of their parents. We are a rich and powerful nation, at times generous and humanitarian, yet we cannot mobilize ourselves and our resources to treat the poor decently and with dignity. The contradictions of our society are mirrored in our approach to the welfare poor, our superfluous people, the failures and rejects of our social system. They are both a source of embarrassment and a necessary source of reassurance that self-reliance has made the rest of us what we are. Consequently we do not like to know what their lives are like, how badly we treat them, and how much like the rest of us they really are. Instead

[41] The first such state law was passed in California (effective January 1, 1966), to compensate persons with dependent children. A New York City law (December 1965) set no limit on compensation. Laws were being considered in New York, New Jersey, California, Rhode Island, and Michigan. *The New York Times,* January 2, 1966.

[42] Paul Good, *Cycle to Nowhere,* U.S. Commission on Civil Rights, Clearinghouse Publication No. 14 (Washington, D.C.: Government Printing Office, 1968).

[43] *Report,* National Advisory Commission on Civil Disorders (Washington, D.C.: Government Printing Office, 1968), p. 252.

we prefer to believe in a series of myths. These ease our conscience, justify the punishment and humiliation accorded the welfare poor, and rationalize their exclusion from participation in the social game that we uncritically accept as the only one worth playing.

Who Are the "Welfare Poor?"

They are recipients of five public assistance programs: Old Age Assistance (OAA), Aid to the Permanently and Totally Disabled (APTD), Aid to the Blind (AB), Aid to Families with Dependent Children (AFDC), and General Assistance (GA). The first four are federal-state programs, with some local participation. The last one is primarily administered and financed locally; it is the most residual of residual programs, with a close affinity to the punitive and restrictive Elizabethan Poor Law. As Table 6 reveals, over 11 million individuals, as of January, 1970, received some form of public assistance.[44] If one accepts the Social Security Administration poverty line, this amounts to a little under half of all the poor in the United States, which means that a considerable number of people in need receive no financial assistance.

To be eligible for the federal-state categorical programs one must meet the test of need, variously defined by the states. One must also meet other eligibility requirements that are established for each program: age sixty-five or over in Old Age Assistance; medically certified blindness or disability in the case of AB and APTD; and a variety of conditions that govern receipt of AFDC, especially those surrounding the absence or unemployment of a male breadwinner. A dependent child, according to the Social Security Act, is "a needy child who has been deprived of parental support or care by reason of the death, continued absence from the home, or physical or mental incapacity of a parent;" who is living with any of fifteen specified relatives; who is under age eighteen, or twenty-one if in school; and (as of 1961 and optional for the states) is deprived of parental support because of unemployment of a parent (changed to father in 1967).[45] In short, it is not possible to get welfare simply because one is in need. Even those who are technically eligible for help under the categorical programs may not receive financial assistance. They may be uninformed of its availability, may shy away from the stigma associated with welfare, or may be arbitrarily denied assistance by a discretionary interpretation of rules designed to keep the cost as low as possible. Although the federal government establishes broad guidelines and provides about 55 percent of the total cost of the categorical programs, the states administer them with a considerable degree of freedom and with wide variation in conditions of eligibility and amounts of grants. For example, an estimated 8.5 million individuals would qualify for assistance under the federal guidelines but are denied assistance because they do not meet the more restrictive requirements established

---

[44] Of greater importance than these figures, which quickly become obsolete, is recognition of the precipitous and apparently continuing rise in public assistance largely attributable to increases in the AFDC program. By June 1970 there were 12.2 million public assistance recipients. Of these, 8.3 million were AFDC recipients, an increase of more than one-fourth over June 1969.

[45] Social Security Act, Title IV, Sections 406, 407.

by the states. In order to assure receipt of federal funds, a state must meet certain requirements: (1) It must ascertain that persons receiving assistance are in need (the definition of need is left to each state). (2) It must consider all of a person's income and resources (certain small amounts may be exempted at the discretion of the state, and the first $85 of monthly earnings of the blind must be exempt). (3) It must submit a state plan for administering the program. (4) It must operate its program on a statewide basis. (5) The state must participate financially. (6) Administration must be by a single state agency. (7) Opportunities must be provided for fair hearings for persons whose applications are denied.[46] Federal grants to the states vary and are based on type of program (with greater benefits for the elderly) and state's per capita income. As a result of this the percentage of assistance payments from federal funds in 1968 varied from 39.1 percent in New Jersey to 82 percent in Mississippi.

The welfare poor share the conditions that confront all the poor in society, yet in some respects they represent a distinct group by virtue of their association with the welfare system. Of primary importance is their depreciated social role as welfare recipients. Despite the expansion of the welfare state that provides a variety of services and benefits for all Americans, those receiving public assistance are the only members of society defined as welfare recipients, a label deliberately intended to convey the fact that they are not quite full members of society. Their welfare benefits are not regarded as legitimate rewards accorded to those who are defined as normal participants in society. The pejorative role of a welfare client sustains the fictional separation of the self-reliant from the dependent. A variety of myths, highly resistant to fact, has historically been associated with residual welfare. In this way we help maintain the morality play organized around the theme of the Protestant ethic and the struggle for status.

Seven interrelated myths may be identified. These are the myths of (1) the sturdy beggar, (2) runaway fathers, (3) promiscuous mothers, (4) the gravy train, (5) the chiseler and free-loader, (6) chronic dependency, and (7) rehabilitation as the answer to the problem of dependency.

THE STURDY BEGGAR. The notion that most welfare recipients are able-bodied workers living off the sweat of honest, hard-working taxpayers has been alive for over three hundred years and probably has a good future. About a third of public assistance recipients are aged, blind, and/or disabled. One-half are dependent children. The remainder are mothers caring for these children. A small number, less than one percent of all recipients, are unemployed fathers; they are eligible under a special category (AFDC-UP) that permits families with unemployed fathers to receive assistance. About half the states have adopted this provision. In short, there are relatively few able-bodied males receiving assistance.[47] Most of them would work if adequate jobs and suitable

---

[46] *Social Security Programs in the United States, op. cit.,* p. 87.

[47] These figures do not include those receiving General Assistance (about 800,000) because it is impossible to know how many are women, children, aged, disabled, recipients of one fuel or food order, etc.

education and training were available.   Yet the public persists in its notion that "The relief rolls are loaded with chiselers and people who don't want to work." [48]   An opinion poll testing the acceptance of this statement found that two-thirds of those interviewed agreed with it.[49]   This is a deeply felt prejudice, as revealed by such statements as the following:

> Now people won't work for fear of losing government handouts.

> We need to do something about this welfare business.   If people don't want to work, they shouldn't be fed.

> Establish CCC camps again.   And, instead of these people standing around drawing relief, make them work for it.   There's plenty of jobs for them that need doing.   Let's quit handing everything out on a platter.[50]

Periodically there are local quests for sturdy male beggars, based on the assumption that relief rolls could be materially reduced if they could be rooted out and put to work.   One such effort in Newburg, New York, received considerable national notoriety.   Its proclaimed intention was that of getting ". . . a large and lazy labor force back to work."   It succeeded in locating one employable male, who was put to work for the city.[51]

What about mothers on AFDC?   Can't they work?   As increasing numbers of women join the labor force, there is less tolerance for a publicly supported program that enables mothers to remain at home with their children in the absence of a male breadwinner.   Once upheld as a measure to preserve the home life of worthy widows and their children, the Aid to Dependent Children program (changed to Aid to Families with Dependent Children in 1962) became increasingly under attack as it developed into a social provision for broken families, an expanding portion of which have been black.   Mothers receiving welfare are now also defined as sturdy beggars.   Their dependency is viewed as deviant, and measures of social control have been devised to encourage or force them to work.   This is seen in the 1967 Amendments to the Social Security Act and in the proposed Family Assistance Plan, which we shall discuss later.   Public anxiety about the failure of AFDC mothers to work ignores the degree to which they are in fact in the labor force, occupying marginal and insecure jobs, and using public assistance as one of their sources of survival.   The U.S. Department of Labor, in its *Manpower Report,* makes the following observation:

> Employment and welfare are systems which mesh in complex ways.   Welfare is a form of social provision when income is absent, interrupted or inadequate, not simply a cash transfer system operating outside the world of work.[52]

[48] Free and Cantril, *op. cit.,* p. 27.

[49] *Ibid.*

[50] *Ibid.,* p. 27.

[51] Meg Greenfield, "The 'Welfare Chiselers' of Newburg, New York," *The Reporter,* August 17, 1961.

[52] *Manpower Report of the President,* 1968, *op. cit.,* p. 99.

Current data on the extent and kind of labor force participation on the part of AFDC mothers is not readily available. The most thorough study of characteristics of dependent families, done in 1961, reported that 20 percent of white and 40 percent of Negro AFDC mothers were employed.[53]

The concern with the sturdy beggar ignores the deeper problem of adequate employment opportunities and sufficient community resources to make freedom of choice a reality for AFDC mothers. Studies indicate that many such mothers would prefer to work. One study in Cook County, Illinois, reports that "most of the ADC recipients strongly desire personal and economic independence." Almost half of the families had potentialities for full or partial self-support if vocational training (needed by two-fifths of them) could be arranged, if medical and dental problems could be overcome, and if adequate day care (required by 90 percent of these families) could be provided.[54] Public insistence that AFDC mothers work may be an insistence that they continue to perform the menial work that has been the traditional lot of lower-class women. While work as a career has been associated with the emancipation of middle-class women, for lower-class women, as Gisela Konopka observes, work has been traditionally associated with drudgery and exploitation.[55]

Among persons who worked full time in 1965, 29 percent of the women and 11 percent of the men had incomes under $3,000 per year, while 2 percent of the women and 17 percent of the men earned over $10,000. Although the employment of women in professional and technical occupations more than doubled between 1950 and 1966, the women's share of the jobs fell from 45 percent to 37 percent of the total. At the same time the portion of women in low-paying service jobs outside the home rose from 40 to 55 percent.[56] Dignity that accompanies freedom of choice and opportunities for decent work at adequate wages is the central issue. Facing the investments it would take to create the day care facilities, the education and training programs, and the career-oriented employment opportunities, is avoided by focusing on the presumed indolence of the indigent poor. Conservative critics have exaggerated the idleness of AFDC mothers; liberal supporters have underestimated the importance of work. Both need a different perspective and all need to recognize that the special handicaps facing any working mother are intensified for the low-income fatherless family.

The hostility toward the sturdy beggar is largely aimed at the "invisible males," the fathers of dependent children absent from the home mostly because of some form of family disruption: divorce, separation, desertion, or because they are not married to the mothers. As Table 19 reveals, almost three-fourths of all children receiving AFDC are living in families with an absent father. In

[53] M. Elaine Burgess and Daniel O. Price, *An American Dependency Challenge* (Chicago: American Public Welfare Association, 1963), p. 30.

[54] Greenleigh Associates, Inc., *Facts, Fallacies and Future* (New York: Greenleigh Associates, 1960), pp. 3, 23.

[55] Gisela Konopka, *The Adolescent Girl in Conflict* (Englewood Cliffs, N.J.: Prentice-Hall, 1966), pp. 70–74.

[56] *Manpower Report of the President*, U.S. Department of Labor (Washington, D.C.: Government Printing Office, 1969), p. 198.

1940, death of the father accounted for the largest share of families dependent on ADC; By 1968, primarily because of the expansion of OASDHI, this had declined to a relatively minor factor. In 1968 almost 3 million children were beneficiaries of OASDHI. From 1940 to 1968 their number per thousand of population had increased from one to forty-one.

RUNAWAY FATHERS. Most of the AFDC families are eligible for assistance because of an absent father. He is no myth. The runaway father, however, is a myth to the degree that this concept is based on the assumption that lower-class males exercise freedom of choice between supporting their families or abandoning their breadwinning responsibility. To be sure, the absent father is a mote in the eye of the taxpayer. In the previous chapter, however, we traced at some length the relationship between employment opportunities and one's capacity to perform the obligations of husband and father. Elliott Liebow has documented in a persuasive way the degree to which denial of access to decent work has deprived the lower-class male of the resources with which he might carry out his traditional obligations.[57] He has also demonstrated that most of the lower-class males aspire to being adequate breadwinners, husbands, and fathers, for this is the definition of masculinity in this society. We shall need much more than a call to moral rearmament among the poor to re-establish the male as a decent provider and head of his family. The occupational structure and the educational system that feeds into it deprive the lower-class male of opportunities to perform as an adequate breadwinner. The welfare system, by denying financial assistance to an unemployed father, as is done in about twenty-two states, contributes to the stress that may lead to marital separation.[58]

At a hearing conducted by the U.S. Civil Rights Commission, a mother on welfare was asked if the program encouraged fathers to leave the home. She replied:

> Sure, because a man doesn't want to feel that he is going to take bread out of his child's mouth if he is really a man. This means that he leaves. If he is not able to support his family adequately, he usually leaves.

Another mother testified as follows:

> This is how me and my husband got separated when he got out of his job and he went to relief to get help and they refused to help . . . this is one reason we separated and divorced. He couldn't afford four, so he just left.

There is no research that adequately substantiates the relationship between public assistance and family disruption, and we have already cautioned against the assumption that men abandon their families solely to enable them to get welfare. On the other hand, a program that penalizes a family by refusing

---

[57] Elliott Liebow, *Tally's Corner* (Boston: Little, Brown, 1966).

[58] *A time to listen . . . a time to act,* U.S. Commission on Civil Rights, (Washington, D.C.: Government Printing Office, 1967), p. 33.

Table 19. Population Under Age 18 and Number Receiving AFDC Money Payments by Status of Father, June of Selected Years, 1940 through 1968

	TOTAL CHILDREN RECEIVING AFDC				NUMBER OF CHILDREN RECEIVING AFDC BY STATUS OF FATHER				
	Population Under Age 18	Number	Number Per 1,000 Population Under 18		Dead	Absent from Home	Incapacitated	Unemployed	Other
1940	41,409,000	835,000	20		347,000	253,000	227,000	—	8,000
				%	42	30	27		1
1950	48,225,000	1,660,000	34		350,000	818,000	455,000	—	37,000
				%	21	48	29	(1961)	2
1960	65,697,000	2,322,000	35		202,000	1,493,000	569,000	89,000	58,000
				%	9	64	21	4	2
1968	72,125,000	4,207,000	58		195,000	3,051,000	556,000	234,000	171,000
				%	5	73	13	6	3

SOURCE: *Trend Report, 1968*, Social and Rehabilitation Service, National Center for Social Statistics Report A-4, (Washington, D.C.: Government Printing Office, 1968) p. 47.

assistance so long as a father is in the home can hardly be said to encourage family stability.

A small proportion of absent fathers contribute to the financial support of their families. Some maintain contact with the family and continue to play some parental role, but little is known about this. One of the few studies on support from absent fathers reveals that the men most likely to contribute to their families are those who are divorced or separated rather than those who have deserted, who are living in the same county as the family, and are subject to a court order or agreement to support. Support is also more likely if the agreement is voluntary.[59] The noncontributing father is described as follows:

> The typical non-contributing father is likely to be a man who left his family without entering into any agreement to support them. He has been gone a fairly long time. If his whereabouts is known, he is probably unable to provide support because of illness, unemployment, or low income. If his whereabouts is unknown, which is more often the case, he may never be located despite intensive efforts. If he is located, he will probably be brought before a court and ordered to support his family. He may comply with the order for a while but the burden of compliance becomes irksome and before long he leaves the jurisdiction of the court for parts unknown.[60]

Concern regarding the runaway father has led to increased reliance on detection and control. For example, the 1967 Amendments to the Social Security Act now make Social Security Administration files available to courts in nonsupport hearings. Such studies as we have indicate that the absent father is without much in the way of resources and that law enforcement, however vigorous, cannot create income. As Winifred Bell observes, unemployment and underemployment remain the pressing problems.[61]

PROMISCUOUS MOTHERS. Most AFDC children are not illegitimate, and most illegitimate children do not receive AFDC. In 1961 less than one-fourth of all child recipients were illegitimate, and only one-fifth of all illegitimate children in the nation received assistance.[62] The myth of the promiscuous mother exaggerates the degree of illegitimacy characteristic of AFDC families, ignores the socioeconomic basis for the higher incidence of unmarried mothers among the poor, and obscures the degree to which the sexual deviancy of the middle class is more easily concealed.[63] Wherever economic opportunities are insecure, consensual marriages are more common and illegitimacy more fre-

[59] Saul Kaplan, *Support from Absent Fathers of Children Receiving ADC,* Public Assistance Report, No. 41 (Washington, D.C.: Government Printing Office, 1960), p. 5.

[60] *Ibid,* p. 8.

[61] Winifred Bell, *Aid to Dependent Children* (New York: Columbia University Press, 1965), p. 214.

[62] Helen E. Martz, "Illegitimacy and Dependency," Reprint *Health, Education and Welfare Indicators* (September 1963), p. xxiv.

[63] Clark Vincent, *Unmarried Mothers* (New York: Free Press of Glencoe, 1961).

quent.[64] While this alone does not account for the problem of illegitimacy, it helps to account for the relatively higher rate of illegitimacy among the poor and their consequent vulnerability to public assistance. Lower-class women, particularly those receiving public assistance, function as a scapegoat for a society conflicted about its own sexual mores.

The public image of the promiscuous AFDC mother is based also on the existence of the "boyfriend," a not uncommon though little studied feature of lower-class life. The boyfriend as male boarder or regular visitor may help pay the rent, provide some extras in the way of small luxuries, and in some instances may play the role of father substitute. He may marry the mother and assume full responsibility for the family. Marriage is often out of reach for the AFDC mother, however, and this poses a problem that has helped to cast a shadow of suspicion on the AFDC program. Most of the AFDC mothers must adapt to the fact that they do not have a husband upon whom they can depend for support, companionship, love, or sexual gratification. The AFDC mother may devote herself to her children and to getting whatever satisfactions she can from contacts with family, friends, or participation in community activities. Many women are socially isolated, however, and their inadequate assistance grants do not encourage community participation. On the other hand she may seek a man who can assume some responsibility for her and her children, either through marriage or through a consensual union. In some instances she is not free to remarry; or she may wish a husband but fear a repetition of desertion. She may find a boyfriend but not one able or willing to assume financial responsibility for a family. Until recently, the policy in most states that terminates assistance for children living with a stepfather has acted as a deterrent to marriage. Thus, the boyfriend is part of the way of life for some among the poor when males cannot be relied upon to be steady providers or stable marital partners.

THE "GRAVY TRAIN." The most ironic myth of all is the myth of the "gravy train," the belief that welfare recipients are living on easy street. This assumption may well reflect the repressed discontent with work and the pain of unwelcome discipline it exacts for many. It certainly reflects resentment at bearing the cost of welfare expenditures, especially since such expenditures are easily the most vulnerable target because they allocate resources to the least powerful segment of the community. The facts about the amount of money available to the welfare poor are clear. They are among the poorest of the poor, although the degree of their poverty varies enormously depending on the region in which they live. Their poverty is easily explained. It results from the political decisions their fellow citizens make that allow too little money for decent social provision. All states establish their own standards to define the minimum income essential for maintaining a level of health and decency. Yet in a number of states welfare payments fail to meet the state's own standards because of inadequate legislative appropriations. For example, in 1966 the Department of Public Welfare in Ohio considered $224 a month an amount

---

[64] Helen Icken Safa, *Profiles in Poverty,* An Analysis of Social Mobility in Low-Income Families (Syracuse, N.Y.: Syracuse University Youth Development Center, 1966), pp. 94–105.

necessary to provide a mother and three children with a minimum standard of health and decency based on 1959 prices. The maximum payment that could be made to a family of four, however, was only $170. In Indiana $237 a month was considered the minimum essential for a mother and three children. The maximum payment to such a family in that state was $126. One AFDC mother, commenting on the statement that "ADC mothers have it pretty easy," had this to say:

> I have heard people say it lots of times. They think we have it so easy. I would like to see anyone, anyone, to step forward, to change his good job for my position, his nice home, you know, just his nice position. In other words, if he wants my place, let him take it for a couple of months. Just a couple of months that's all. Let them come forward, smell the garbage in the summertime, fight the rats, freeze in the winter time . . . let him take it, let him try to feed five children from 17 to 5 on $167.00 a month.[65]

In 1965 the Council of Economic Advisers noted that the average annual total income of an aged public assistance recipient was $970 a person; for a blind recipient it was $1,110; for a disabled recipient, $910; and for a four-person family receiving AFDC, $1,680. This meant that a mother and three children had available $1.15 a day, for each member of the family, to cover the costs of food, shelter, clothing, and all other essentials.[66] In recent years this has improved somewhat, but not uniformly, and not by much. Average monthly payments in the nation in January, 1970 for public assistance recipients in the adult categories ranged from about $2.50 a day in Old Age Assistance, to roughly $3.35 a day per recipient in Aid to the Blind. In AFDC, average monthly payments per recipient were about $1.50 a day. As Table VI indicates it made a good deal of difference whether a child lived in Mississippi. where he received $12.00 a month, or in Massachusetts, where he received $70.90 a month. It makes a difference, too, whether one is a child deprived of a father due to death covered by social insurance or a child with an absent father covered by public assistance. In January, 1970 the average OASDI monthly benefit for a child of a deceased worker was $71.16. In the same period the average money payment per recipient of AFDC was $45.80. Although public assistance grants have been raised over the years, they do not adequately reflect the increasing cost of living and expansion of the economy. In fact, the standard of living of an AFDC family has declined one-third relative to the rest of the population since 1938. It has been estimated that the average monthly payment for an AFDC family of $163 in March 1968 should have been $250 if it were to reflect the AFDC standard prevailing in 1938, considering 1968 prices, family income, and growth in the GNP.[67]

Although the 1967 amendments to the Social Security Act required the states to raise their standards for determining need in accordance with costs

---

[65] *A time to listen, op. cit.,* p. 30.

[66] *Economic Report of the President* together with the *Annual Report of the Council of Economic Advisers,* House Document No. 348, 89th Congress, 2nd sess. (Washington, D.C.: Government Printing Office, 1966), p. 115.

[67] Jean Rubin, "Prospects for Children," Editor's Page, *Child Welfare,* 42 (December 1968), p. 568.

of living the amendments do not require implementation nor prevent subsequent reduction of actual grants.[68]

Once again the issue of social justice: Do people have a citizen right to share in the expanding economy? Do children have such rights if their parents are so located in the economic structure as to be deprived of opportunities to participate in economic growth?

While public assistance grants prevent absolute destitution they do not enable most recipients to escape poverty. In some low-income states the level of living provided for a public assistance family is less than a fourth of the official poverty line. After a study of the AFDC program in Cuyahoga County, Ohio, where the average grant for a family of four attains 71 percent of the federal poverty level, the United States Commission on Civil Rights declared that cash payments under the program were ". . . grossly inadequate to provide support and care requisite for health and decency." The commission concluded that this inadequacy resulted in ". . . families being reduced to deficient diets, insufficient clothing, and substandard housing accommodations." [69] During this investigation mothers testified about their difficulties in making ends meet, which at times meant resorting to ". . . old basic of potatoes or . . . biscuits and grits and staples like that. . . ." In order to secure adequate clothing for her children one mother said:

> Mostly I go around asking people if they know anybody who has clothes to fit my child. This is how I get clothes for my children.

Asked whether she had enough money to pay school expenses one mother replied:

> No, I don't because my boy don't have no gym clothes to go to school to play gym.
>
> What does your son do if he doesn't have gym clothes?
>
> He stands on the sidelines.
>
> The school doesn't provide him with the gym clothes?
>
> No, It doesn't.

The commission also heard testimony on poor housing conditions.

> Would you tell the commissioners why you keep trying to find a better apartment?
>
> I don't see any sense in paying $80 to $90 a month for four to five rooms and they are in such condition where you have to have a lamp in every room. Every time I got ready to wash my face in the face bowl, we have to plunge it down. The commode was overflowing all the time and so was the tub.

[68] *See* Rosado V. Wyman, 38 U.S.L.W. 4266 (U.S. April 1, 1970).

[69] *Children In Need,* Urban Studies: Cleveland, U.S. Commission on Civil Rights (Washington, D.C.: Government Printing Office, 1966), p. 25.

One mother summed it up as well as anyone might:

> We are not even accepted as human beings. . . . We should be accepted as other human beings and because a child is poor doesn't mean that he doesn't get hungry.   Because a child is poor doesn't mean that he doesn't need shoes.   Because a child is poor why should he get an F in Gym because he doesn't have tennis shoes and suit and things, and we don't think it is fair for our children to have to suffer these things.[70]

When interviewed, AFDC mothers make it clear that their main problem is money. As one woman put it:

> The main problem is money. . . . That is our main problem, money. . . . But even with my working, the money I get from work and the money I get on AFDC, it is still not sufficient to live decently.[71]

In the southern states, the situation is even more serious. As a special report of the Southern Regional Council notes, the rules of public assistance in the poorest section of the United States have one obvious purpose: "to keep as many people as possible from getting help." [72]   In Alabama, for example, a mother and six children are expected to exist on $54 a month. One such woman used $22 of this amount to buy food stamps worth $72, in this way supplementing the meager grant. With the remaining $32 a month she was expected to meet all other needs. Commenting on the "state of welfare" in Alabama, a report for the U.S. Commission on Civil Rights had this to say:

> Welfare in Alabama is where you go when you are going nowhere. It is what you are when you are nobody. It is the logical extension of the poverty cycle from black men denied a living on farms and in factories to their black women and children consigned to a limbo of hungry days endlessly reiterated where need always exceeds have and hope never catches up with is.[73]

In a review of the relationship between community resources and mental health, the human significance of inadequate public assistance grants is further pointed up:

> Among the resources crucial in maintaining mental health are those providing financial assistance to persons in need. The benefits and grants under these public welfare programs are frequently too small to supply the minimum necessities of life. In our view, the strains placed on individuals and families by these below-subsistence grants are inimical to the maintenance of the mental health of adults and to the social and emotional development of the children involved.[74]

[70] *Ibid.,* p. 22.

[71] *Ibid.,* p. 27.

[72] "Charity Doesn't Begin at Home" *Trans-action,* 6 (November 1968), 7.

[73] Good, *op. cit.,* p. 39.

[74] Reginald Robinson, *Community Resources in Mental Health* (New York: Basic Books, 1960), p. 2.

"CHISELERS AND FREE-LOADERS." Despite the low level of public assistance payments, the myth that welfare recipients are chiselers and free-loaders is also common. In fact, so deep is the mistrust of the poor that until recently applicants for welfare in San Diego, California, were interviewed first by the district attorney's office.[75]

Although there are cases of fraud, as one might expect to find in any program involving money, there is no evidence that the amount of chiseling can equal the degree of income tax violation and evasion or the amount of white-collar crimes committed by the more powerful and more affluent members of society, which involve such things as illegal stock manipulation, fraud in government contracts, and price-gouging by some corporations. Studies of established fraud cases in Califorina resulting in convictions by district attorneys amount to less than one-thirtieth of 1 percent of the total Aid to Families with Dependent Children caseload in the state.[76] A national review of AFDC eligibility in 1963 revealed that, nationwide, 5.4 percent of families receiving aid were not technically eligible for assistance. It should be noted that people may be seriously in need yet not eligible for public assistance. The amount of actual fraud is not known though it is undoubtedly minimal. Some of it may well be a strategy for survival and a strategy for manipulating a system one defines as unjust. In any repressive system those who are its intended victims find ways to outsmart, outwit, and outmanipulate the oppressors. Some of this may well characterize behavior identified as chiseling, although little is really known about this. At the same time, we have only recently begun to make clear the degree to which the welfare system itself may be accused of its own kind of chiseling and law violation. For example, in defiance of federal guidelines a number of states have ". . . succeeded one time after another in outwitting the federal government in devising policies that fell most heavily on Negro and illegitimate children." [77] Arbitrary and illegal denial of rights to assistance and violation of constitutional rights of welfare recipients have characterized the administration of some public welfare programs.[78] Only recently have we begun to establish administrative procedures and legal support for the notion that welfare recipients have certain citizen rights as defined in various state laws as well as in the constitution. The violation of such rights constitutes an institutionalized form of crimes against the poor, which should be considered together with the allegations that the poor are chiseling and free-loading on welfare.

CHRONIC DEPENDENCY. The notion that public welfare recipients are chronically dependent, or products of a generational dependency cycle is another myth. Like many myths, there may be some truth to this notion, one that is little

[75] *Communities in Action,* 5 (April 1969), p. 9.

[76] California State Department of Social Welfare, News Release, December 10, 1965.

[77] Bell, *op. cit.,* p. 189.

[78] *See* Charles A. Reich, "Midnight Welfare Searches and the Social Security Act," *Yale Law Journal,* 72 (June 1963), p. 1347; and "Individual Rights and Social Welfare: The Emerging Legal Issues," *Yale Law Journal,* 74, (June 1965), pp. 1245–1257.

researched and little understood. Such data as we have undermines the generalization that welfare is a permanent life style for most recipients.[79]   The more common pattern for AFDC recipients is to use public assistance until other sources of income become available through employment, marriage, return of an absent husband, and so forth, and in many instances to resort to welfare again when another crisis occurs. Data from the 1961 Burgess and Price study showed that the median length of time families remained on AFDC was under two years: fifteen months for white and twenty-two months for Negro recipients.[80]   A 1967 survey revealed that most AFDC families had remained on assistance for less than three years, with 45 percent remaining for a longer duration. The same survey revealed the on again, off again pattern, almost 40 percent of the families had received assistance at least two different times.[81]   Thus for most recipients AFDC is not a way of life but an emergency source of income. The "high users" of AFDC, the women most likely to resort frequently to this resource for economic survival, according to Sydney E. Bernard, are those at the very bottom of the occupational system: "Public assistance serves these families as a buttress and provides necessary supplementary income to those who supply the economy with casual labor."[82]   Public assistance does become a reliable form of income security for some—usually those living under the most severe conditions of economic insecurity and with the least access to family and other forms of support in times of stress.[83]   A number of recipients have grown up in families in which public assistance performed this function. The picture of "generational dependency" is derived from this group, but here too, the data are not very clear. The facts we have do not support the notion of a high proportion of generational chronic dependency with families subsisting solely on welfare, but they do reveal a significant number of recipients whose families had at some time resorted to public assistance. Patterns of generational assistance were found for more than 40 percent of the AFDC recipients in the Burgess and Price study.[84]   A fourth of public assistance recipients in the state of New York were found to have had parents who had received assistance, half of them having been long-term recipients (from ten to fifteen years).[85]   A 1969 study by the Greenleigh Associates for the Human Resources Administration of New York City, based on a relatively small sample, reveals that 10 percent of the recipients had received welfare assistance as children. In a random sample, Greenleigh Associates found that the likelihood of receiving assistance was one in four for persons whose families had received aid when they were children and one in

[79] *Manpower Report,* 1968, p. 97.

[80] Burgess and Price, *op. cit.,* p. 50.

[81] "AFDC" *Children,* 16 (May–June 1969), p. 122.

[82] Sydney E. Bernard, "Fatherless Families: Their Economic and Social Adjustment," *Papers in Social Welfare,* No. 7, Florence Heller Graduate School for Advanced Studies in Social Welfare, Brandeis University, 1964.

[83] *Ibid.*

[84] Burgess and Price, *op. cit.,* p. 158.

[85] Moreland Commission Report, *Public Welfare in the State of New York* (Albany: State Capital, 1963), p. 50.

seven for those who had not.[86]   No third-generation dependency was reported. While the present research evidence is somewhat conflicting, it is clear that our knowledge is insufficient and generational dependency does not exist for the majority of welfare recipients.   According to President Nixon, in 1968, 600,000 families, out of an average caseload of 1.4 million, left the welfare rolls.[87]   We do not know the number of families who were able to become economically independent because they were able to receive assistance when they needed it. We do not have any knowledge of the number of families remaining on welfare because of the failure of other social institutions (e.g., education, employment, low wage scales, lack of resources for help with family problems).   The question is where to direct our concern and how to be of genuine help to families who are caught temporarily, sporadically, or more or less permanently in the welfare system.

MYTH OF REHABILITATION.   It is common to assume that the proper approach is to rehabilitate those on welfare, to cure them of their dependency and rid society of the burden of public assistance.   This was the assumption behind the 1962 Amendments to the Social Security Act and the one that prompted many congressmen to vote for the antipoverty programs under the Economic Opportunity Act.   In the words of one such congressman: "We sold this theory (antipoverty program) to the Congress on the theory we were going to phase out the dole and everything else, in order to make taxpayers out of tax-eaters. . . ."[88]   It is desirable to get rid of the dole, the stigmatized means of transferring income, but it is neither possible nor desirable to rid society of some mechanism for providing for income security and a greater measure of income equality.   The assumption that all those on welfare can be economically self-supporting ignores the obvious: Most of the public assistance recipients are aged, blind, disabled, dependent children, and mothers who are heads of households.   Indeed the proper aim might be to increase dependency on social provisions, not decrease it.   Four out of every ten children we call poor live in families in which the head is employed year round.   To promote their well-being requires greater, not less, dependency on social provision of income. Public assistance reaches only a portion of those in need, and some who are entitled to benefits receive none.   The notion that welfare recipients must be rehabilitated rests in part on the moral-flaw theory of poverty that views dependency as a form of personal pathology.   It ignores the extent to which dependency in modern industrial societies is a structural, not an individual, problem and the degree to which racism and class inequalities are additional social barriers to securing adequate income through employment.   Where opportunities are readily available there seems to be no difficulty in getting welfare clients to respond.   The findings based on a project in New Haven, Connecticut, question the whole myth of rehabilitation, the justification of as-

---

[86] *New York Times,* August 10, 1969.

[87] President's Message to Congress on Welfare, August 11, 1969.

[88] Congressman Carey of New York, *Hearings Before Subcommittee on War on Poverty Programs,* House Committee on Education and Labor, 89th Congress, 1st sess. (Washington, D.C.: Government Printing Office, 1965).

sociating welfare status with personal incapacity. The residents on welfare in this training project were more successful in employment outcomes than those having other sources of income.[89]

Welfare recipients are those for whom society has provided no rewarding social roles. They are the outsiders, functionally cut off from the larger society. It is proper to speak of enhancing skills for economic and social participation provided society intends to make room for these outsiders through genuine opportunities for employment and for decision-making. Unless we are prepared to solve the basic problem of work for the underclass by expanding job opportunities that offer something beyond menial work, we may, through our various manpower training programs, aid particular individuals but leave the structural causes of dependency untouched.

Daniel Patrick Moynihan observes that we have never solved the problem of employment, especially for Negroes, and consequently we prefer to pay short-run costs in welfare payments rather than undertake the basic economic reforms required to attain a full-employment economy. In his view, despite the outcry against the rising costs of welfare expenditures, the public is not prepared to pay the cost of required social reforms that might significantly reduce the number of people relegated to the welfare system. In this sense, as he puts it, the welfare system works at least in the short run to the benefit of the powerful since it makes ". . . few difficult or dangerous demands on those who run the society." It is less costly than the price of major structural changes that would involve ". . . not only the distribution of wealth, but probably also the distribution of power." [90] Although our knowledge of the exact structural sources of dependency is extremely limited, total commitment to achieving the maximum possible degree of economic self-reliance would probably entail the following: (1) a full-employment economy with low levels of cyclical unemployment and a massive effort to create new forms of work, upgrade job skills, and eliminate artificial credential barriers, (2) expansion of social provisions of income, other services, and minimum-wage standards that would establish an acceptable floor below which no citizen may fall, in this way replacing the dole with institutionalized rights, (3) national standards of education, adequate day care, and other social services, with special attention being given to those with the least access to resources and opportunities—those in the rural South, Appalachia, inner cities, Indian reservations, Puerto Rico, etc.—with the most deprived requiring social investment capital sufficient to launch them into a new level of functioning, (4) assurance of freedom of access to birth control knowledge and practice, (5) special community concern with the welfare of all children and a readiness to pay the cost of equalizing life opportunities, and (6) an end to racism.[91] There is little readiness to support structural changes of this magnitude, some of which would undoubtedly conflict with values regarded as more important than the problem of dependency. Given the fact that Negroes represent an increasing proportion of those on

[89] Bernard Neugeboren, *"Evaluation of Unified Social Services,"* mimeographed (New Haven, Conn.: Community Progress, Inc., 1967), p. 10.

[90] Daniel P. Moynihan, "The Crisis in Welfare," *The Public Interest,* No. 10 (Winter 1968), p. 7.

[91] These are modifications of eight points made by Moynihan, *ibid.,* pp. 9–10.

welfare, and in view of the fact that two-thirds of the Negro poor still reside in the South, it is clear that the issue of welfare dependency is an issue involving the distribution of power between whites and Negroes. It goes far deeper than the myth of rehabilitation would have us believe. Social rehabilitation of those in power might be a more appropriate statement of the problem before us.

At the same time there is a positive sense in which one may speak of rehabilitation as a goal. Perhaps habilitation is a better term, if by this we mean making available maximum resources and opportunities for the enhancement of social competence and social participation instead of concentrating narrowly on presumed defects to be corrected. Economic independence is desired by a significant proportion of mothers on AFDC. An unknown number can be helped to secure decent employment provided we are willing to make available essential education, training, job opportunities, and supportive resources. Yet no welfare program in the country has a budget for enough day care centers to permit able-bodied mothers on welfare to be employed.[92] It is estimated that perhaps from 200 to 300 thousand AFDC mothers might be self-supporting if provided with adequate education and if adequate day care services were available. In the view of the Advisory Council on Public Welfare, most recipients "cannot realistically be expected ever to become self-sustaining." [93] This means that in all likelihood from two-thirds to three-fourths of AFDC mothers and their children will continue for the foreseeable future to require some social provision of income. For those who do manage to secure employment, some form of income supplementation may be required. Given their limited education and job skills, most are not likely to secure work that will produce income above the poverty line. To assume that the rehabilitation of welfare recipients is the answer to economic dependency is a convenient rationalization of our resistance to the decent provision of income and to basic structural reforms that would permit the welfare poor to enter the society of the relatively affluent. We need to see the extent to which dependency is a normal consequence of the functioning of our social system, not a form of individual pathology.

Functions and Dysfunctions of Welfare

The welfare myths effectively prevent awareness of the structural causes of dependency. Thus they have a certain social utility, providing as they do a justifying ideology for a society that is not ready to treat the poor as citizens and to pay the cost of making this possible. Instead welfare functions primarily to keep the cost of assistance as low as possible. "The welfare system is designed to save money instead of people and tragically ends up doing neither." [94] The public welfare programs are caught in a dilemma, seeking to meet at least

[92] *Building the American City,* National Commission on Urban Problems, 91st Congress, 1st sess., House Document 34 (Washington, D.C.: Government Printing Office, 1968), p. 3.

[93] *Having the Power We Have the Duty,* Advisory Council on Public Welfare, *op. cit.,* p. 10.

[94] *Report,* National Advisory Commission on Civil Disorders, *op. cit.,* p. 252.

minimum needs of the welfare poor and to fend off a hostile community and seeking to provide money and services to the "consumer" public and to assure the supporting public that it is not wasting tax dollars or encouraging dependency and immorality. It represents a mixture of public charity and social control, the good samaritan and the sheriff; it insists on regulating the life of the client along with relieving poverty, in this way functioning to keep the welfare poor in a state of relative powerlessness. As a residual program it functions to maintain the discipline of work, or more accurately, the discipline that assures that some will be available to do the dirty work. In some places administration of public welfare is openly a system of enforced labor. Mary S. Larabee, reviewing a report from a field supervisor in a southern state at the 1939 National Conference of Social Work, said:

> The number of Negro cases is few due to the unanimous feeling on the part of the staff and board that there are more work opportunities for Negro women and to their intense desire not to interfere with local labor conditions . . . there is hesitancy on the part of lay boards to advance too rapidly over the thinking of their own communities which see no reason why the employable Negro mother should not continue her usually sketchy seasonal labor or indefinite domestic service rather than receive a public assistance grant.[95]

Winifred Bell also reports on the use of welfare regulations that ". . . required that able-bodied mothers and older children accept employment whenever it was available," a policy that affected Negro women the most.[96] In California assistance to unemployed fathers has been restricted when men were needed as farm laborers, for there was ". . . little disagreement from representatives of county (welfare) boards that . . . public welfare had a role to play in providing a pool of needy workers on whom growers could draw." [97] In Muncie, Indiana, AFDC mothers were threatened with the loss of welfare support for their children if they did not accept work for $1.25 an hour in local tomato-canning factories. As the Director of the County Welfare Department put it, in this way the women might ". . . say thanks to the community for its welfare help to them in the past." [98] From the English Poor Law to the present the public assistance programs have been primarily designed not to aid the poor but to force them to work. Conditions of public relief have been deliberately created to discourage people from remaining on assistance and to prompt them to seek work, no matter how debasing or disagreeable. "Less eligibility" was the rule, that is, the principle that the life circumstances of those on relief should be less eligible (less desirable) than the circumstances experienced by the lowest wage earner in the community. Ironically, this form of work incentive often turned out to be a work disincentive. Rules that required that grants be reduced in the amount of wages earned have discouraged

---

[95] Quoted in Bell, *op. cit.*, pp. 34–35.

[96] *Ibid.*, p. 107.

[97] Russell E. Smith, "In Defense of Public Welfare," *Social Work*, 2 (October 1966), p. 93.

[98] *Ibid.*

some welfare recipients from seeking economic independence. Further, the availability of a pool of marginal workers ". . . forced by public assistance policy and other means to labor at onerous, repetitive, and inhuman tasks—and for substandard wages. . ." means that we avoid automating much of these activities and thus fail ". . . to free human beings to perform human kinds of work." [99] To some degree, public assistance functions to subsidize a marginal labor force. Perhaps its main function now is to maintain our belief in the Protestant ethic, to sustain the American conviction that nothing is attained in this life without hard work. The poor are judged by standards of economic and sexual asceticism. Reuben G. King, Alabama Commissioner of Pensions and Security, said (referring to women whose AFDC grants had been stopped because of the "substitute father regulation") that a woman could always choose "to give up her pleasure and act like a woman ought to act like and continue to receive aid." [100]

The consequences of our residual public assistance program may be quite mixed. Public assistance relieves economic distress, destroys self-respect, and enables white children to remain in school but encourages Negro children to drop out. [101] It maintains a cheap supply of labor, yet through work programs it may also restore some to self-respect by providing new opportunities to work. It keeps the poor in their place and, by the depreciated status of the welfare recipient, the struggling upwardly mobile are reminded that they are "one up" on the poor. [102] In the absence of alternatives, AFDC has enabled mothers and children to remain together. Conservative critics have avoided specifying the alternatives they would provide to care for the several million children now receiving AFDC.

We seem to need the welfare poor to maintain the morality play involving the esteemed and disesteemed, to assure those with preferred status that success and self-reliance are one, and to keep clear the distinction between those who have made it and those who have failed. At this point, however, the welfare system has become so recognizably damaging to the poor and so dysfunctional for the larger society that we face a welfare crisis.

The "Welfare Crisis"

Calling for a complete revision of the nation's welfare system in 1967, Mitchell I. Ginsberg, then Welfare Commissioner in New York City and one of the country's outstanding social workers, declared that public assistance was "bankrupt" as a social institution. He proposed basic modifications in the

[99] Edward E. Schwartz, "Public Welfare In An Urbanizing America," in Thomas D. Sherrard (ed.), *Social Welfare and Urban Problems* (New York: Columbia University Press, 1968), p. 206.

[100] Walter Goodman, "The Case of Mrs. Sylvester Smith," *The New York Times Magazine*, August 25, 1968, p. 62.

[101] On the last point *see* Robert A. Dentler and Mary Ellen Warshauer, *Big City Dropouts and Illiterates* (New York: Center for Urban Education, 1965), pp. 31–35.

[102] *See* Adam Walinsky, "Keeping the Poor in Their Place: Notes on the Importance of Being One-Up," in Arthur B. Shostak and William Gomberg (eds.), *New Perspectives on Poverty* (Englewood Cliffs, N.J.: Prentice-Hall, 1965), pp. 159–168.

current program and development of new approaches to income maintenance that would reduce public assistance to a truly residual program for about 5 percent of those on the rolls.   Among his suggestions were to substitute a declaration of need for the investigation of means; encourage employment of welfare recipients by permitting them to retain part of their earnings; expand training programs; increase the number of day care facilities to enable mothers to work; integrate health, educational, and social service centers in low-income neighborhoods; and allow recipients to participate in the administration of the welfare program.   In addition he recommended that the government be the "employer of last resort," thus assuring everyone the right to work.   He also suggested that the aged, blind, and disabled be removed from public assistance and placed under the social security system; that a family allowance program be created; and that an expanded social service system of housing, health, day care, and education available to all regardless of income be developed.[103]   Criticisms of the present system, if not the same recommendations for reform, have been echoed by national political figures, major study commissions, scholars, social workers, prominent civic leaders, and welfare recipients.   No less a figure than the President of the United States declared:

> The welfare system today pleases no one.   It is criticized by liberals and conservatives, by the poor and the wealthy, by social workers and politicians, by whites and by Negroes in every area of the nation.[104]

He accompanied his remarks with an order creating a nineteen-member commission to study the "outmoded welfare system" and to recommend changes.

If there is general agreement that something is wrong with welfare there is not, necessarily, agreement on the nature of the ailment.   In reacting against a group of welfare mothers who staged a sit-in on Capitol Hill protesting relief restrictions, Russell B. Long, senator from Louisiana, where 80 percent of welfare recipients are black, indignantly declared: "If they can find time to march in the streets, picket and sit all day in committee hearing rooms, they can find time to do some useful work." [105]   Louisiana had its own special welfare crisis in 1960, when it saw fit to arbitrarily withdraw assistance from almost 6,000 families involving over 22,000 children.   The state took this action under a "suitable home" provision that made illegitimacy or consensual union a basis for ineligibility.   Since no alternative action was taken to provide for the needs of children, 95 percent of whom were Negro, their plight prompted national and international donations of money and clothing to meet their emergency needs.[106]   The incident is worth recalling since it reflects the complex ways that the Protestant ethic has been interwoven with racism to create an attitude, not confined to the southern community, that justifies a restrictive and repressive welfare system.   Another remark from Senator Long is also worth recording, since he serves as Chairman of the Senate Committee that handles all legislation related to public welfare.   His position of power and his

[103] *The New York Times,* May 10, 1967.

[104] *The New York Times,* January 29, 1968.

[105] *Ibid.*

[106] Bell, *op. cit.,* Chap. 9.

views, which reflect sentiments shared by others, reveal something of the nature of the conflict that surrounds efforts to reform the welfare system. Referring to proposed public assistance legislation he is quoted as saying: "There is no doubt that we will fight that battle again this year, of whether we are going to provide money to pay people to be worthless, to be useless, to be of no account." [107]

Harsh as these remarks are, they point to two key dimensions of the welfare crisis: a rising number of cases and rising costs and the social role, current and potential, of those we label welfare recipients. The fact is that welfare is the "cycle to nowhere." It has made recipients feel "worthless, useless and of no account." The question is, how can income and opportunity be provided that assures dignity and social participation to the casualties of our social system? The real crisis in welfare is the human cost of this inhuman system.

RISING COST OF RISING CASELOADS. To some, the major crisis is one of rising caseloads and expanding welfare expenditures. Caseloads in public assistance have increased, primarily in the AFDC programs where the number of recipients rose from 3 million in June 1960 to more than 8 million in June 1970. In the same period expenditures for this program more than tripled from a little under a billion to 3.5 billion. Annual costs of money payments to all public assistance recipients came to $6.2 billion in 1969. A major increase has been in the cost of medical care, largely as a result of the introduction of Medicaid. Medical expenditures were $589 million in 1967 and increased about eightfold to $4.4 billion in 1969, reflecting a beginning effort to meet the long-neglected health needs of the poor. Total expenditures for public aid, significant as they are, represented less than 1.5 percent of the 1969 GNP and less than one-third of our annual support for the war in Vietnam.

Although the number of public assistance recipients is large, it has actually declined as a percent of total population, from 54 per 1000 population in 1940 to 50 in 1969, largely because of expansion of coverage and benefits in Old Age, Survivors, and Disability Insurance. In the same period, equivalent figures for children receiving AFDC rose from 20 to 68 per 1000 population under 18. Clearly, it is the AFDC Program that is the bone of contention.[108] A variety of factors contribute to the increase in the number of AFDC recipients, not the least of which, in our view, is the continued failure to solve the problem of work for the lower-class male. Yet it must be granted that the link between employment and welfare is not entirely clear. From 1948 to 1962 the size of the AFDC caseload was directly correlated with rates of unemployment for men 20 years and over. From 1962 to 1968 the trend in AFDC continued upward despite declining rates of unemployment. As we have emphasized, however, subemployment may be the more significant variable. The relative inability to successfully perform the breadwinner role coupled perhaps with an increasing rejection of menial work helps to produce the female based household that represents the primary recipient of AFDC.

---

[107] Quoted by Elizabeth Wickenden, "The 1967 Amendments: A Giant Step Backward for Child Welfare," *Child Welfare,* Vol. 48 No. 7 (July 1969), 391.

[108] Social and Rehabilitation Service, Trend Report, 1968, *op. cit.,* p. 29.

At the same time, other factors also account for the rise in caseloads.   The following seem to be among the most important factors.

(1) Changes in the AFDC program involving broadened eligibility requirements and more liberal standards have extended coverage to more of the poor. Since 1961 Federal legislation has permitted states to extend assistance to families headed by unemployed parents, to older children if attending school and to a second adult in the family.   In addition, liberalization of standards of need in many states has expanded the number of those eligible for assistance.

(2) Supreme Court decisions—as in the case of King *v.* Smith, which denied the right of a state to refuse assistance on the grounds of a mother's relationship with a male not her husband, and the Shapiro *v.* Thompson case, which declared unconstitutional the one-year residence requirement—have also broadened eligibility.

(3) The rural-urban migration associated with the decline in agricultural employment and subsistence farming has increased the number of potential applicants for assistance.   To a degree difficult to assess, some of this has been migration from the south where restrictive regulations have denied assistance to the poor, to states where more liberal standards permit more people to be eligible for more adequate grants.

(4) A change in the political climate accompanied by the development of a militant welfare rights movement encourages the acceptance of a citizen right to social provisions established by law.   As the stigma of assistance is attenuated, more of the poor are prepared to apply for aid.   As the right to assistance is emphasized, fewer applicants are turned away.

Indeed, it may be that the increase in AFDC recipiency is in large measure a political phenomenon.   We are witnessing a redefinition of dependency.   For many, dependency is no longer viewed as a form of social pathology or a mark of personal failure.   Instead, public assistance is defined as a social right, a means to participate in the consumer society in the absence of alternative sources of adequate income or decent employment opportunities.   The demand of the National Welfare Rights Organization for an adequate income plan that would provide a $5500 minimum for a family of four is an indication of this redefinition of dependency.   Furthermore, the recognition that the poor are denied access to adequate income through no fault of their own is clearly evident in the proposal for a universal income supplement program made by the President's Commission on Income Maintenance Programs.   While staunch adherents of the Protestant ethic may find this difficult to accept, an increasing number of the poor, especially those in the black ghettos, are acting on this view of reality, rejecting the definition of welfare recipients as something less than full members of society.   Other factors are also involved, not the least of which has been the positive transformation in the self-concept of some members of the underclass as a result of increasing Negro militancy and the related development of the welfare rights movement, which encourages the demand for citizen rights to social provisions established by law.   Barriers of stigma and restrictive regulations are giving way reluctantly as public charity is increasingly being democratized with the aid of the law and organized political action.

The Negro revolt against welfare colonialism makes visible the extent to which we have used the AFDC program as a way of relegating Negroes to the limbo of economic dependency and the degree to which we have avoided recognizing this fact. In the period from 1948 to 1961, when Negroes accounted for 60 percent of the increase in AFDC, there was almost no recognition of the social significance of this fact, no analysis of its meaning, and no realistic attempt to mount a program that might offer an alternative to welfare.[109] Part of the failure to see what was happening ironically stemmed from the liberal desire to be "color blind," to see individual rather than racial characteristics. However worthy an objective, this meant ignoring the meaning of racial membership in a racist society. A further dilemma stemmed from the understandable fear that to focus attention on the high incidence of Negro dependency would only fan the flames of prejudice and have the unintended consequence of providing support for stereotyped views of the Negro. Social facts about rates of illegitimacy and family disruption that could lead to analysis of economic and social causes are commonly converted, by a public bent on exclusion of the Negro, into moral judgments about his character that rationalize such exclusion.

In any event we find now that a Negro child has at least six times the risk of being an AFDC recipient as compared with a white child, which ought to tell us something about the social process that underlies the selection of people for the role of welfare recipient. The data reveal that the problem is related to class more than it is to race. If one looks at the composition of welfare recipients in New York State, for example, one finds that in 1964 Puerto Ricans had an even higher incidence of welfare dependency than had Negroes. Puerto Ricans made up 4.53 percent of the population and 26.5 percent of the welfare recipients. Negroes in the same year made up a little over 10 percent of the population and 46 percent of the welfare recipients. It should be made perfectly clear however that the defects in public assistance mirror the structure of society and its values. It functions largely as we intend it to, seeking to cope with problems created by failures of our other institutions—economic, educational, and political. That it in turn also fails, despite the dedication of many genuinely concerned public welfare workers and administrators, is hardly surprising. It accomplishes what society is willing to pay for—some amelioration of destitution, but not the promotion of social security or justice.

WELFARE AS ILLFARE. The National Advisory Commission on Civil Disorders has clearly spelled out the failures of public assistance. Noting that the program is indispensable so long as it is the only way we have to meet basic needs for millions, most of whom are children, it calls for basic reforms directed at the following inadequacies in the current welfare system: (1) It excludes large groups of people in need. ((2) For those who are "included, it provides assistance well below the minimum necessary for a humane level of existence and imposes restrictions that encourage continued dependency on welfare and undermines self-respect." [110] We have already noted that at least half of those we define as poor receive no public assistance, and we have documented the below-poverty levels of assistance provided. The charge that a program designed to deal with the problem of dependency may contribute to further dependency needs some clarification. That welfare destroys self-respect seems self-evident, but this too may need some elaboration.

---

[109] Moynihan, *op. cit.*

[110] Report of the National Advisory Commission on Civil Disorders, *op. cit.*, p. 252.

The policy in public assistance has been to provide a subsistence level allowing barely enough to survive. Too few resources are available to enable a family to achieve a more adequate level of functioning. The fear that too generous assistance might pauperize recipients has restricted efforts to aid the poor. Ironically this lack of generosity has discouraged rather than encouraged economic independence. Regulations that require all earned income to be deducted from public assistance grants have functioned as a 100 percent tax on wages, a disincentive rather than an incentive to employment. As one AFDC mother put it:

> Before I drew the first check they had automatically cut my [welfare] check. Yet they want . . . [welfare recipients] to improve themselves. If they are going to take the money from you before you can help yourself, how are you going to be able to do it? [111]

The 1967 Amendments to the Social Security Act made at least a partial effort to meet the problem by requiring that the states disregard the first $30 and one-third of all additional earned income. Thus a mother who earns $60 a month may now keep $40 in addition to her regular grant. Though an improvement, it is considerably less generous than a special provision that previously enabled an AFDC recipient employed in an OEO project to retain the first $85 plus one-half of the remainder.

The most incredible aspect of our welfare approach is the failure to provide adequate programs for an unemployed father. Our failure to provide jobs and decent financial assistance has been demoralizing to men and to their families. In areas such as Appalachia, where no work is available, men have been forced into developing some form of illness or disability that might qualify them for welfare payments. A study of mental health in Appalachia made the following important observations in 1965:

> For many men today in eastern Kentucky and parts of West Virginia, the only means of survival is to be classified as disabled under one of the welfare programs. It is understandable that these men develop illnesses that are not always physically based. It is also understandable that their children drop out of school, when they see nothing to hope for. This situation is so widespread that it presents a motivation and a mental health problem of major proportions.[112]

Men without work and with no way of obtaining financial aid may be forced to leave their families if their absence is a condition of eligibility for public assistance. Although the Unemployed Parent provision of the AFDC program (AFDC-UP) was designed to meet this problem, about half the states have failed to appropriate funds for it. In those states that have the program there has been a tendency to restrict its availability. The 1967 amendments further curtailed the program by establishing certain conditions that limit its availabil-

---

[111] *"A time to listen,"* U.S. Commission on Civil Rights, *op. cit.,* p. 35.

[112] *Mental Health in Appalachia,* National Institute of Mental Health (Washington, D.C.: Government Printing Office, 1965), p. 6.

ity: requiring a thirty-day waiting period without employment and demanding a substantial and recent work history (i.e., at least six quarters of employment in the thirty-nine months ending within the year preceding application for assistance). In 1968, the average monthly number of families receiving assistance under this program was 66,000. Of the 130,000 applications received for such assistance in that year, less than two-thirds were accepted, compared to an acceptance rate of almost three out of four in the previous seven years.[113] Instead of strengthening the capacity of the male to carry out his breadwinning responsibility a program was developed that took over his economic function, one which in many ways assured low-income women a more steady source of economic support than they could expect from the men in their milieu. Acting under the image of providing resources to enable women to remain at home with their children, and reacting against the common public notion that women should be forced to work, public welfare administrators and social workers failed to strive for true freedom of choice for low-income women in the decision regarding work. Such freedom of choice involves access to decent employment opportunities and provisions for adequate day care of children along with the right to refuse employment if one's preference is for a maternal role. Lacking such a choice, dependence on welfare for some is increased along with denial of opportunities for expanded social participation that may accompany employment.[114] To be sure, given the lack of decent day care services, the limited employment opportunities, and the restricted education and training resources available, decent employment for women who wished it would not have been an easy goal to implement.

It still is not, despite the proclaimed goal of the 1967 amendments to assure economic independence for all employable persons sixteen and over in the AFDC program. For fiscal 1969, $118 million were appropriated for a special Work Incentive Program (WIN) to finance training for about 100,000 recipients. At the same time, funds for only limited day care services were made available. Apparently we shall continue to condemn mothers for being dependent and at the same time restrict their freedom to choose economic independence. Paradoxically, some of the decent intent of the public assistance program may also increase dependency. Provision of medical care to public assistance recipients under the Medicaid program means that some women cannot afford to work, given the low wages they are likely to earn, because they would risk losing the medical protection offered under public assistance. In the absence of a general program of medical care available to all, it is too expensive for some AFDC mothers to work, especially if they must also pay for the care of their children. Day care services are shamefully lacking everywhere. Thus the program tends to limit rather than enlarge opportunity, restrict rather than build hope. As one mother put it:

> Everyone has a deep-down feeling of lostness. There's no hope out here in Watts, we're stranded. We want something to look forward to. It's no fun cashing a county [welfare] check every week. We . . . don't want relief . . . we'd much rather have hope . . . a program to train us for

---

[113] *Trend Report, 1968,* Social and Rehabilitation Service, *op. cit.,* p. 55.
[114] Safa, *op. cit.,* p. 172.

work . . . I'd be proud to go to work if I could make enough to pay for a baby-sitter.[115]

Most important, self-respect is destroyed in a society in which to receive help is defined as debasing and in which methods of administering aid are designed to inform the recipient of his little worth to society. The means test is the degradation ceremony which casts the client into the debased role of the welfare recipient. Following is a graphic description of this process:

> . . . an applicant becomes eligible for assistance when he exhausts his money, gives a lien on his property to the Welfare Department, turns in the license plates of his car, and takes legal action against his legally responsible relatives. When he is stripped of all material resources, when he "proves" his dependency, then and only then, is he eligible. Welfare policies tend to cast the recipient in the role of the propertyless, shiftless pauper. This implies that he is incompetent and inadequate to meet the demands of competitive life. He is then regarded as if he had little or no feelings, aspirations or normal sensibilities. This process of proving and maintaining eligibility in combination with the literal adherence to regulations and procedures tends to produce a self-perpetuating system of dependency and dehumanization.[116]

There we have it. It is the dehumanization that is at the heart of the welfare problem.[117] The agency structure, even when public welfare workers are kind, understanding, and sympathetic, functions ". . . to reinforce and thereby perpetuate recipients' conceptions of themselves as suppliants rather than rights-bearing citizens." [118] The recipient is placed in a stigmatized and powerless role; subjected to a complex and humiliating determination of need; offered an assistance grant arrived at through an elaborate budgeting procedure open to a considerable degree of arbitrary administrative discretion; cast into the status of a public welfare client toward whom rehabilitative services may be directed without his consent; and converted into an object of agency decision-making which, however benign, is invisible and at times incomprehensible and at worst may involve invasion of privacy and violation of constitutional rights. It is the rejection of this dehumanizing process and a corresponding quest for citizenship status that have mobilized a militant attack on the public welfare system.

Although there has been increasing recognition of the defects in our public assistance programs, it also should be added that the programs have their positive value in addition to the ill fare they distribute. A measure of security is provided. In states in which grants are more nearly adequate there have been some positive outcomes, at least as measured by a decrease in school withdrawal (true, however, only for white students).[119] Some useful services in addition to

[115] *San Francisco Chronicle*, September 23, 1965.

[116] Moreland Commission Report, *op. cit.*, p. 53.

[117] Scott Briar, "Welfare From Below: Recipients' Views of the Welfare System." *California Law Review*, 54 (May 1966), p. 384.

[118] For an alternate point of view *see* Nathan Glazer, "Beyond Income Maintenance—A Note on Welfare in New York City," *The Public Interest*, No. 16 (Summer 1969), pp. 102–120.

[119] Dentler and Warshauer, *op. cit.*, p. 12.

income are offered, a point we elaborate on later. Improvements in the program have been made in various places, for example, the introduction of a declaration of need to replace the humiliating investigation of means. Our problem is that we are deeply conflicted about welfare. Nowhere is this more clearly seen than in the 1967 amendments, legislation that is once punitive and restrictive, yet providing in a modest way for a work incentive program, exemption of earnings, expansion of social services, and the training and use of welfare recipients as paraprofessional staff in public assistance.[120] The trouble is, as Mitchell I. Ginsberg pointed out, that ". . . the good things were in for the wrong reasons." He is correct when he adds that this is still ". . . the most punitive piece of welfare legislation passed in the history of the United States Congress." [121] The hostility toward AFDC recipients is particularly seen in the provision that would have set a ceiling on the number of children of absent fathers that could be aided with federal funds.[122] This was clearly an anti-Negro gesture, one that would simply have denied federal aid to needy children beyond a given state quota. As it turned out the provision was never implemented. In 1969 it was repealed because of the considerable public outcry against it, which says something about the basic decency of many Americans. Yet some of the punitive features remain, in particular the provision that denies to AFDC women the freedom of choice in decisions about work. Mothers may be required to work or to accept training, provided a determination is made that appropriate child care facilities are available. As the Council of Economic Advisers noted, this raises fundamental social issues of whether a child is better off in a child care center or at home with his mother and whether mothers should be required to work while also performing household tasks.[123] The most critical issue, however, is freedom of choice. The 1967 legislation deprives an AFDC mother of the right to determine the best interest of herself and her children. Responsibility for the decision regarding work is transferred from the person to the public welfare agency. Sanctions in the form of denial of assistance in cash are imposed for refusal to obey the judgment of an administrative official. Such punitive action poses a fundamental issue: Is the need for financial assistance a condition that should deprive an individual of freedom of action available to other citizens? Should social control accompany social provision? As Gilbert Steiner has correctly observed, "the overriding policy conflict in public assistance is between those who would impose constraints on the behavior of relief recipients and those who focus on need as the sole

[120] Wilbur J. Cohen and Robert M. Ball, "Social Security Amendments of 1967 and Legislative History," *Social Security Bulletin,* 31 (February 1968), especially pp. 17–19. The reader should also *see* Wickenden, *op. cit.,* for a critique of the public welfare amendments.

[121] Mitchell I. Ginsberg, "Changing Values in Social Work," transcript of the first Ann Elizabeth Neely Memorial Lecture, Sixteenth Council on Social Work Education Annual Program Meeting, New York, January 26, 1968, p. 5.

[122] Cohen and Ball, *op. cit.,* p. 17.

[123] *Economic Report of the President* together with *The Annual Report of the Council of Economic Advisers,* House Document No. 28, 91st Congress, 1st sess. (Washington, D.C.: Government Printing Office, 1969), p. 166.

issue." [124]   The continuing attempt to police the welfare poor is an index of their second-class citizenship, a status that the welfare rights movement now rejects.

Poor Law to Welfare Rights

Perhaps we are witnessing the final assault on the Elizabethan Poor Law and the special pauper status it established.   The attack comes from many directions, including an organized welfare rights movement and action through the courts that seeks to establish the poor as persons under the law, entitled to full citizenship rights and benefits.   It may be said that the welfare poor have only recently discovered their right to citizenship and are now mobilizing to make it a reality. As one delegate to the nation's first Welfare Rights Convention declared, ". . . we've just discovered that we're American citizens after all.   We have rights nobody ever bothered to tell us about.   So we're finding out and telling each other." [125]

Unfortunately the precise rights available to welfare recipients are not clear, for their special welfare status makes them subject to public regulation and deprivation of freedom, which undermine the notion of full citizenship.   Not until we have resolved the issue of the right to life will the poor achieve full membership in society.   This is an issue that is revealed in the unsettled question: Is public assistance a form of public gratuity, a conditioned benefit that permits regulation of the behavior of the recipient, or is it a legal right?

Public assistance has its origin in the Elizabethan Poor Law and, unlike social insurance, rests on the police power of government to promote public welfare through regulation and restraint.[126]   While the Poor Law accepted limited public responsibility for meeting the needs of the poor, its provisions were not an expression of the obligation of the state to its citizens.   Indeed to accept pauper supplies was to forego full claim to citizenship.   Moreover relief of the poor and their regulation as the "dangerous classes" are interwoven themes in both the early Poor Law and in its transformed version, our contemporary public assistance measures.   The early Poor Law aimed at the relief of destitution, the regulation of labor, the control of vagrancy, and the suppression of social disorder stemming from poverty and dislocations that accompanied the collapse of the feudal system.   Despite the increasing democratization of society through extension of citizenship rights, those at the very bottom, particularly if they had to resort to poor relief, continued to remain beyond the pale.

The development of our social welfare measures has involved a gradual removal of categories of individuals from the Poor Law stigma and devalued status.   The most significant departure, of course, was the development of our social insurance programs and the assurance of social security as a statutory right.   (As already noted, this is not entirely correct, given the Supreme Court decision in *Flemming v. Nestor.*   Yet for most purposes social insurance is

---

[124] Gilbert Y. Steiner, *Social Insecurity* (Chicago: Rand McNally, 1966), p. 112.

[125] *The New York Times,* September 9, 1966.

[126] A. Delafield Smith, *The Right to Life* (Chapel Hill, N.C.:   University Press, 1955), p. 68; Karl de Schweinitz, *England's Road to Social Security* (New York: A. S. Barnes, 1961).

treated as though it were a right, and it supports rather than undermines the notion of citizenship.) Social insurance originates under the taxation power of government to collect and disburse revenues for the general welfare, a point made by the Supreme Court when it settled the question of the constitutionality of the Social Security Act. The establishment of the special federal-state categorical programs of public assistance authorized under this legislation also partially removed recipients of these programs from the shadow of the Poor Law. Categories of individuals who could meet eligibility requirements under the new public assistance statutes no longer needed to depend on local poor relief (general assistance), the direct descendant of the Elizabethan Poor Law. In fact, a conception of limited rights to public assistance is embodied in the Social Security Act and in federal administrative regulations such as the right to apply for assistance, to prompt determination of eligibility, to receive assistance in money payments, and to have access to a fair hearing.[127] At the local level, with considerable regional variation, there is a continuation of the Poor Law philosophy of minimum assistance, repressive regulation, and social rejection of recipients—a philosophy that views the poor as a "threat and a burden," which most Americans continue to accept as perfectly consistent with their ideal of a free society. Humanitarian public welfare workers and administrators in many areas of the nation strive to humanize a basically inhuman system. In perhaps small but important ways they succeed in many instances.

At the national level, officials in the Department of Health, Education, and Welfare charged with the administration of federal participation in the public assistance programs have striven to provide guidelines to the states that will assure that public assistance recipients are treated with dignity and respect. For example, a policy statement issued on March 18, 1966 relates to the protection of the individual's legal and constitutional rights in eligibility determination. Among requirements that became effective July 1, 1967, were the following:

> Policies for eligibility determination must conform with all legal and constitutional protection and shall ". . . not result in practices that violate the individual's privacy or personal dignity, or harass him, or violate his constitutional rights.
>
> Specifically, States must especially guard against violation in such areas as entering a home by force, or without permission, or under false pretenses, making home visits outside of working hours, and particularly making such visits during sleeping hours; and searching in the home, for example, in rooms, closets, drawers, or papers, to seek clues to possible deception.[128]

An illustration of the problem this policy statement seeks to control is provided by a director of the Legal Services Unit of Mobilization for Youth: "the investigator comes, doesn't say hello and starts turning mattresses, rummaging in closets and drawers and accusing the woman of keeping a man in the house." [129]

A 1966 court action sought to enjoin intrusive investigatory methods as

---

[127] *Rights of Public Assistance Recipients,* Publication No. 3 (New York: National Conference of Lawyers and Social Workers, 1966).

[128] *Welfare Law Bulletin,* No. 4 (June 1966), p. 2.

[129] *The New York Times,* July 19, 1966.

carried on by the Department of Public Welfare in Washington, D.C. The plaintiffs, recipients of Aid to Families with Dependent Children, complained of ". . . unreasonable searches, harassing surveillance, eavesdropping, and interrogation concerning plaintiffs' sexual activity by certain investigators." In deciding against the plaintiffs, a U.S. federal district court maintained, among other things, that administration of relief funds is absolutely on the discretion of the agency and not subject to judicial review. The court relied primarily on the assumption that public assistance is a gratuity not a legal obligation and that the government has a clear right to make investigations to determine whether funds are secured through misrepresentation or spent improvidently. As the *Welfare Law Bulletin* observed: "The sweeping ruling of the District Court that availability of welfare funds is purely discretionary is fundamentally inconsistent with the new concept of entitlement." [130]

In a similar case in California, the state supreme court ruled that receipt of welfare benefits could not be conditioned upon a waiver of Fourth Amendment rights.[131]

Despite the HEW policy statement, raids on AFDC recipients continue, some of them in clear violation of standards established in the directive regarding such things as entering the home without permission and home visits outside working hours. An example involves an AFDC mother whose grant was discontinued because she refused to allow a complete search of her home by investigators who visited on two Sunday mornings.[132] The structure of public welfare tends to defeat even the most compassionate and dedicated public welfare workers and administrators. It ends up demoralizing the poor. The full citizenship of the welfare poor awaits the further democratization of society through clearly established rights to social benefits.

Such rights are now demanded by an organized movement of welfare rights recipients, the National Welfare Rights Organization. It seeks to change the welfare system and ultimately to overthrow it.[133] The goals are clear: decent jobs with adequate wages for those who can work; adequate income for those who cannot work, provided in a manner that assures dignity and justice; and the right to participate in decisions that determine how they must live.[134] In some measure the strategy underlying the movement was suggested by Richard A. Cloward and Frances Fox Piven, who elaborated on George Bernard Shaw's proposal for destroying the system of poor relief. As Shaw put it: "If we were

[130] "Welfare: Recipients' Right to Enjoin Intrusive Investigation Methods Denied," *Welfare Law Bulletin,* No. 6 (December 1966), p. 4, reporting on Smith v. Board of Commissioners, No. 1447 (D.D.C. October 1966).

[131] "Fourth Amendment Applies to Mass Welfare Search," *Welfare Law Bulletin,* No. 8 (May 1967), p. 2, reporting on Parrish v. Civil Service.

[132] "Preliminary Injunction Obtained Against District of Columbia Welfare Search Consent Provisions," Commission of the County of Alameda, 35 U.S.L.W. 2583 (Cal. Sup. Ct.), *Welfare Law Bulletin,* No. 12 (April 1968), p. 5, reporting on Steward v. Washington, Civ. No. 40. 432–68 (D.D.C. February 16, 1968).

[133] Joseph E. Paull, "Recipients Aroused: The New Welfare Rights Movement," *Social Work* (April 1967), pp. 101–106; and Martin Eisman, "Social Work's New Role in the Welfare-Class Revolution," *Social Work,* 14 (April 1968), 80–86.

[134] Poverty Rights Action Center, *Goals for a National Welfare Rights Movement* (Washington, D.C., 1966).

reasoning, far-sighted people, four fifths of us would go straight to the Guardians for relief, and knock the whole social system to pieces with most beneficial reconstructive results." [135]

The Cloward and Piven proposal advocated a massive campaign to enroll all the eligible poor for welfare aid and to assist recipients to obtain full benefits contained in the law but in practice rarely provided. These include such things as minimum standards of furniture, household equipment, clothing for children, and expenses for graduation from school. Overloading the system it was thought would produce bureaucratic disruption in welfare agencies and fiscal disruption in local and state governments, leading to a political crisis that would force a national administration to institute a Federal guaranteed income. It is not clear the extent to which the welfare rights movement has been influenced by this strategy. It appears that the National Welfare Rights Organization has preferred to focus on obtaining more benefits for current recipients rather than recruiting more of the potentially eligible.

It is too early to assess the success of the welfare rights movement. It is now part of the broader black movement for full citizenship rights and part of the democratic revolution that challenges all forms of social inequality. In the view of Martin Eisman the welfare rights movement is a welfare client revolt seeking the overthrow of the repressive welfare system. The social worker, he asserts, should assist in this revolt by aligning himself with the aims of the welfare rights movement, encouraging the welfare client to become conscious of and take pride in his class position and to build on the strengths of his group and style of life to be an effective instrument of social change. Social workers are active in the welfare rights movement and some have developed a Social Welfare Worker's Movement to promote the cause. Cooperation and conflict characterize the relationship between the National Welfare Rights Organization and the profession of social work. In May 1969, led by their director, Dr. George A. Wiley, NWRO took over the opening session of the National Conference on Social Welfare, demanding a greater voice in the conference for black and poor people.

The welfare rights movement has enabled many of the poor to acquire a new concept of their rights to benefits. In insisting on receiving such benefits in a way that does not violate their sense of dignity, some have acquired a new perception of themselves as citizens. Protection and extension of the citizen rights of welfare recipients and the poor in general have been aided by the development in the late 1960s of an entirely new legal approach to the problems of the disadvantaged. Relatively ignored by the legal profession in the past, in recent years the poor have become a focus of concern for an increasing number of practicing attorneys and legal scholars, who have developed a new field of social welfare law.

The pioneer in this effort was the legal aid services of the special demonstration project, Mobilization for Youth. The use of lawyers as advocates of the poor was vastly extended by the OEO-sponsored Legal Services. Special university welfare law centers and the activities of such organizations as the American Civil Liberties Union and the NAACP Legal Defense Fund have contributed

---

[135] G. B. Shaw, "Man and Superman," in Bernard Shaw, *Complete Plays with Prefaces* (New York: Dodd, Mead, 1963), Vol. III, p. 586.

to the development of social welfare law, which is helping to establish a new "bill of rights" for the poor. The focus of attention is on substantive and procedural rights of persons entitled to public benefits, including public assistance, social security, unemployment insurance, workmen's compensation, public housing, training programs, child welfare services, and education. A great many cases have been brought to state and federal courts. Some have reached the U.S. Supreme Court. A number of other lower court decisions have also protected and expanded the legal rights of the poor, including a 1968 decision of a federal court that halted the funding of a $100 million urban renewal project until an acceptable plan was approved for relocating uprooted families.[136] In the view of one lawyer involved in the case, the decision was "perhaps the most significant in the new national effort to establish legal rights for the poor." [137]

Two major Supreme Court decisions have required states to alter restrictions on eligibility for public assistance: *King v. Smith* (1968), which held Alabama's substitute father regulation invalid, and *Shapiro v. Thompson* (1969), which declared unconstitutional the one-year residence requirement common in many states. The Alabama substitute father rule, and similar ones in nineteen states and the District of Columbia, denied welfare benefits to children of women who engaged in extramarital sexual relations on the assumption that a substitute father was thereby available to provide support for the children.[138] By use of this provision Alabama had reduced its AFDC caseload by one-fourth between 1964 and 1967, denying assistance to 16,000 children and their mothers. Nationally some 400,000 children were affected by the Smith decision, but its significance extends even further because the "great issue at the center of the Smith case and the cases that will follow is whether individuals are diminished in the eyes of the law because they are poor and need help." [139]

In declaring residence requirements unconstitutional on the grounds that such provisions violate freedom of interstate travel the U.S. Supreme Court also noted the violation of equal protection of the laws. While recognizing that a state had a valid interest in "preserving the fiscal integrity of its programs . . . a State may not accomplish such a purpose by invidious distinctions between classes of its citizens." [140] In light of the common attitude that views with suspicion the motive of travel to another state to secure higher welfare benefits the following observation by the Court is noteworthy: Writing for the majority,

[136] *Law in Action,* 3 (April 1969), p. 5.

[137] *The New York Times,* December 29, 1968.

[138] The case was brought to the Supreme Court by Mrs. Sylvester Smith with the aid of Martin Garbus of the Roger Baldwin Foundation, an arm of the American Civil Liberties Union organized to assist the "disinherited." When Mrs. Smith's public welfare worker suggested that she give up the relationship that made her ineligible for assistance she refused saying, "if I end with him, I'm gonna make a relationship with somebody. . . . If God had intended for me to be a nun I'd be a nun." (Goodman, *op. cit.*)

[139] *Ibid.*

[140] Justice William J. Brennan, Jr., quoted in "Supreme Court Holds Durational Residence Requirements Unconstitutional," *Welfare Law Bulletin,* No. 17 (June 1969), p. 2.

Justice William J. Brennan, Jr., declared that a mother who "considers . . . the level of a State's public assistance is no less deserving" than someone who might move to a state to take advantage of better educational facilities.[141] Between 100 and 200 thousand individuals were affected by this decision in some forty states that had restricted eligibility by a residency requirement.

Not related to public assistance but of significance in the broad movement to extend the protection of the law to the poor is the Supreme Court decision in *Levy v. Louisiana* (1968). In this case the Court overruled a state court decision that illegitimate children were not "children" in the eyes of the law, thus denying them the legal right to sue a state charity hospital because of the alleged negligence in the death of their mother.[142] Writing for the majority, Supreme Court Justice William O. Douglas asserted: "We start from the premise that illegitimate children are not 'non-persons.' They are humans, live and have their being." [143] Of major significance too are such Supreme Court decisions as Gault (1967), which held that the due process clause of the Fourteenth Amendment required proceedings in juvenile courts that "measured up to the essentials of due process and fair treatment"; [144] and the Gideon decision, which provided for the right of counsel for indigent defendants.[145] These and other decisions have moved us closer to the notion of the poor as citizens entitled to equal protection of the laws.

The Right to Life

Another key issue is the right to life. In June 1969, on the third anniversary of the birth of the National Welfare Rights Organization, local groups in twenty-five cities sought to focus national attention on the need for a guaranteed adequate income and to dramatize to affluent Americans that poor people have a "right to live." Many Americans were hardly aware of this event, but the issue raised is central to social welfare. It symbolizes the transition from charity to justice. The issue may be posed in the following way: May a state constitutionally permit its poor to die from starvation or from exposure to the elements? [146] If not, then benefits provided to avoid destitution are a right, not a gratuity, since they represent the absolute difference between life and its deprivation. On the other hand the issue may be posed in a modified form. It may be argued that the Constitution in no way requires that the government provide for relief of need, but that once a system of welfare is established citizens have a

---

[141] *Ibid.*

[142] Levy v. Louisiana, No. 508, 36 U.S.L.W. 4458 (May 20, 1968).

[143] "Supreme Court Bars Discrimination Against Illegitimates Under Louisiana's Wrongful Death Statute," *Welfare Law Bulletin,* No. 13 (June 1968), p. 3.

[144] Application of Gault 87 S. Ct. 1428 (1967).

[145] "Juveniles Given Due Process Rights in Delinquency Proceedings," *Welfare Law Bulletin,* No. 9 (July 1967), p. 1; "Juvenile Delinquency and Youth Crime," President's Commission on Law Enforcement and Administration of Justice (Washington, D.C.: Government Printing Office, 1967), pp. 57–76; Anthony Lewis, *Gideon's Trumpet* (New York: Vintage Books, 1964).

[146] James J. Graham, "A Poor Person's Right to Life, Liberty and Property," *Welfare Law Bulletin,* No. 17 (June 1969), p. 31.

right to receive benefits in a manner consistent with their status as citizens.   In this event they have a right to benefits without invasion of privacy, discrimination, or interruption, except under conditions governed by due process that require a fair hearing and evidence of good cause.   As we shall attempt to demonstrate, in the context of the society in which we now live, the constitutional right to life is the preferred way to pose the issue for both pragmatic and ethical reasons.

Edward Bellamy, among others, promoted the ideal of the right to life, arguing that one's humanity is sufficient claim on society for resources essential for survival.[147]   In the *Right to Life,* A. Delafield Smith, a man with legal training, keen social awareness, and humane vision places this ideal in the context of law and society.[148]   The nature of our social organization and the due process clause of the Fourteenth Amendment, which assures that no one may be deprived of life, liberty, or property without due process of law, is the core of his reasoned argument for a legally established principle of the right to life.   Central to his thesis is the undeniable fact that man has experienced a great shift from dependence on nature to dependence on society for his economic survival.   He saw clearly what others have also pointed out—that in the modern world economic dependency is a social phenomenon, and increasingly so.   Industrialization and urbanization deprive individuals of any direct access to the means of survival. Life itself is dependent on socially structured opportunities for work and income made possible by a complex and interrelated system of production and distribution over which the individual exercises no control.   In this context, economic self-reliance is meaningless.   The basis of self-reliance in an agricultural economy is that, within limits, nature is predictable.   Effort does produce results, and one may indeed enjoy and feel entitled to the fruits of his labor.   Thus an essential basis for freedom of action, as A. Delafield Smith saw, is predictability.[149]   Such predictability must be socially structured, as dependence on society replaces dependence on the laws of nature.   Moreover, law must guarantee to the individual the right to what he needs to survive and to attain some acceptable level of living in a world not of his own making.

To a degree largely concealed by our ideology of individualism, we are increasingly dependent on the state; this dependency, however, is relative to our social class position and the resources at our command.[150]   We have emphasized several times that unemployment and consequent lack of income to assure survival are direct consequences of action or inaction on the part of government. This is clearly evident in conscious social policy to control inflation by action that results in increased unemployment for the poor.   In the context of a relatively managed economy, with further possibilities for its direction open to government through the science of economics and technological abundance, the state now has the power to determine the number and distribution of jobs

[147] Edward Bellamy, *Looking Backward* (Houghton Mifflin, 1888; reprint ed., Cleveland: World Publishing, 1945).

[148] A. Delafield Smith, *op. cit.*

[149] *Ibid.,* p. 130.

[150] Charles A. Reich, "The New Property," *Yale Law Journal,* 73 (April 1964), pp. 733–787.

and the allocation of income—in short the power to provide or withhold life opportunities.

It was possible at one time to blame the poor for their poverty, but in this era we know that the impersonal forces of changing technology and economy are simply beyond the control of individuals. The rationale for the right to life rests on an awareness of the social process that allocates life opportunities. Charles A. Reich puts it in the following way:

> It is closer to the truth to say that the poor are affirmative contributors to today's society, for we are so organized as virtually to compel this sacrifice by a segment of the population. Since the enactment of the Social Security Act, we have recognized that they have a right—not a mere privilege—to a minimal share in the commonwealth.[151]

The notion of entitlement rather than privilege or gratuity provides for the predictability so essential for freedom of action, an assurance against arbitrary limitations on assistance and against the submission of the individual to the discretionary authority of those who control the very means of his survival. The idea of entitlement obligates society to provide resources sufficient to assure an individual some reasonable standard of health and decency and endows the individual with the right to such resources when he can acquire them in no other way.[152] A major evil of the public welfare system is the degree to which it subjects individuals to bureaucratic discretion, exposes economic survival to ambiguous and changing standards of eligibility, and places the recipient in constant jeopardy of losing benefits through periodic investigatory and even inquisitorial visits.[153] The experience of the Legal Unit of Mobilization for Youth makes this clear. From 1964 to 1967 it handled more than 500 cases in welfare law. Approximately 85 percent originated in arbitrary, unreasonable, or illegal decisions of welfare workers. By mid-1967 over 300 fair hearings were filed by the Legal Unit, and an estimated 95 percent were settled in favor of the client before the fair hearing was held:

> No program in the welfare state better illustrates the need for definition of rights, clarification of procedures, control of administrative discretion, and a means of enforcing rights and protecting recipients than does the welfare-relief program.[154]

In short an individual must have an enforceable right to what he needs to assure security and independence. Our national phobia regarding economic

---

[151] Charles A. Reich, "Individual Rights and Social Welfare: The Emerging Legal Issues," *Yale Law Journal,* 74 (June 1965), pp. 1245–1257.

[152] *Ibid.*

[153] *Ibid.*

[154] Michael Appleby, "Overview of Legal Services"; Michael Appleby and Henry Heifetz, "Legal Challenges to Formal and Informal Denials of Welfare Rights," in Harold H. Weissman (ed.), *Justice and The Law in the Mobilization for Youth Experience* (New York: Association Press, 1969), pp. 26, 89 and 92.

dependency blinds us to the truth that A. Delafield Smith uncovers in the following statements: "There is only one proved method of avoiding the growth of the sense of dependency. . . . That method is to make him who is dependent the legal master of that on which he depends."¹⁵⁵   Often ignored is the fact that a major function of property rights is to assure this freedom and independence since the right to property means that an individual's survival is not dependent on the will of another individual or public authority.   The positive welfare state extends to the dispossessed this same basis for freedom, providing a property right to welfare benefits.   As Charles Frankel understood, here lies the moral originality of the welfare state and its moral challenge to the Protestant ethic.¹⁵⁶ Thus social security means not only economic security provided through societal means; it implies security against arbitrary human will, the assurance of freedom and independence through the right to life rather than through public charity.   It is based on a positive regard for individuals and a belief in releasing rather than repressing their powers of action.   As A. Delafield Smith puts it, ". . . until we stop trying to strengthen the human will by suppressing it, we will still see human welfare entrusted to the unloving arms of the police power."¹⁵⁷

The rationale for the right to life is to be found not in charity or even in humanitarianism but in recognition of the relationship of social structure to the possibilities of human freedom and the development of human capacities.   The amount of resources to which the individual has access and the conditions attached to their availability influence self-esteem and self-development.   Our mistake is to rely too heavily on the allocation of resources on the basis of capacity rather than needs.   Even the degree to which the needs of children are met depends primarily on the capacities of parents to secure resources through the market, when often the market has no place for them.   People must be driven, we seem to think, to contribute to society.   But A. Delafield Smith has another view:

> Willed action is not compelled action.   Life is not driven by its necessities. It is lured by its hopes.   Needs and capacities must be separated.   Needs demand gratification.   Capacities require opportunities for growth.   Insisting that needs be gratified to the extent of one's capacities is to destroy not build character.¹⁵⁸

Neither the family nor the market can in today's world adequately meet the economic needs of those effectively isolated from rewarding participation in society.   These structures of supply fail.   The defect is there, not in the individual.   The remedy lies with the power of the state to assure the right to life. The claim is one's citizenship in a society that has the capacity to secure a decent level of living for all and the power to exclude individuals from a decent share in the common wealth.   In a free society no citizen may be so excluded.   One's

---

¹⁵⁵ A. Delafield Smith, *op. cit.,* pp. 3 and 7.

¹⁵⁶ Charles Frankel, *The Democratic Prospect* (New York: Harper & Row, 1962), pp. 125–144.

¹⁵⁷ A. Delafield Smith, *op. cit.,* p. 71.

¹⁵⁸ *Ibid.,* p. 20.

". . . rights must be written in terms of social capacity, not in terms of individual capacity." [159]

At this point the quest for social security meets the quest for social justice, for they are inseparable. The right to life includes both. The claim is for equal protection of the laws in a society in which the economic fate of the individual resides in the uses of political power. In this light Bernard Evans Harvith has suggested the need for a constitutional right to the necessities of life

> . . . based upon the federal government's role as influencer of the economy, the fifth amendment bar on taking life without due process, and on interpretation of federal equal protection as requiring that every person must be given some minimum protection if the government is acting in regard to the economy and is committed to a war on poverty.[160]

It might seem that we were on the verge of establishing such a right when the Supreme Court in its March 1970 decision in Goldberg v. Kelly declared that "public assistance . . . is not mere charity", but a means to "promote the general Welfare, and secure the Blessings of Liberty to ourselves and our Posterity." [161] Indeed the Court declared that welfare is a right and not a mere gratuity, a ruling which it has been suggested may be a precursor of a constitutional "right to life" binding the State to guarantee the basic needs of its citizens.[162]

In the case of Goldberg v. Kelly the Court held that a recipient of public assistance was entitled to a hearing prior to any termination of benefits in any case involving controversy over eligibility. It was not the "right to life" but the right to procedural due process which the Court maintained required a pretermination evidentiary hearing. Such due process was essential to assure appropriate "balancing of interests" for in the words of the Court

> the interest of the eligible recipient in uninterrupted receipt of public assistance, coupled with the State's interest that his payments not be erroneously terminated, clearly outweighs the State's competing concern to prevent any increase in its fiscal and administrative burdens.[163]

Of great importance was the Court's recognition that entitlement to public assistance may be analogous to property rights. Drawing on Charles A. Reich's article "The New Property" which we discussed in Chapter Two, Justice Brennan declared: "It may be realistic today to regard welfare entitlements as more like 'property' than a 'gratuity'." [164]

[159] *Ibid.,* p. 49.

[160] Bernard Evans Harvith, "Federal Equal Protection and Welfare Assistance," *Albany Law Review,* 31 (June 1967), pp. 248–249.

[161] Quoted in Craig W. Christensen, "Of Prior Hearings and Welfare as 'New Property,'" National Institute for Education in Law and Poverty, *Clearinghouse Review,* 3 (April, 1970) pp. 333, 334.

[162] *Ibid.* pp. 334–335.

[163] *Ibid.,* p. 333.

[164] *Ibid.,* p. 334.

Yet, this was written in behalf of a slim majority of five-to-three. Only two weeks later in Dandridge v. Williams the newly established welfare "property right" was severely constricted when the Supreme Court granted to the states wide discretionary powers to set maximum public assistance grants.[165] Summing up the significance of the Kelly and Dandridge decisions Craig W. Christensen writes:

> . . . *Kelly* limits the right of the state to take the welfare recipient's 'property' without the safeguards of procedural due process, but *Dandridge* (italics in both cases) goes far to negate what is thereby given through the granting of complete license to the state to define the contours of the 'property'. If the constitutional 'right to life' is to be delivered up by judicial decision, it thus appears likely that it will be some time in coming.[166]

The fact is that the Court has not confronted the issue squarely. It is an interesting commentary on our values, as James J. Graham has observed, that in declaring resident laws unconstitutional the Supreme Court chose to rest their decision on the right to travel, as if that were ". . . any more important than the right to stay alive." [167] Perhaps the right to life is an issue that cannot be decided by the Court but must come through the political process, involving even a modification of the Constitution itself. In the meantime there are proposals for basic modifications of the welfare system, for development of new forms of income maintenance, and for the use of other means that would reduce poverty and promote greater equality. All of these can be critically examined in the light of the right to life.

Toward the Right to Life: Proposals for Reform

The welfare crisis has prompted a reconsideration of our current income maintenance programs. Various proposals for some form of guaranteed income are being advanced, and at least one—the negative income tax—is being tested in a three-year experiment in New Jersey under a 1968 federal antipoverty grant. While suggestions for a guaranteed income are not new, what is startling in the light of the American ethic of self-reliance is the serious consideration being given to such proposals by individuals in all walks of life. National attention was first focused on the question of a guaranteed income by the Ad Hoc Committee on the Triple Revolution, a group of prominent economists, scholars, and public figures who in March 1964 sent to the President of the United States a document analyzing the revolutions in weaponry, human rights, and cybernation. In their view, these vast social changes, especially the anticipated alarming increase in unemployment resulting from the new technology, required a constitutionally guaranteed income as one means of adapting to a revolutionary era in which the relationship between work and income could no longer be sustained. An assured income for all would help promote ". . . a

[165] *Ibid.*, p. 335.

[166] *Ibid.*, p. 336.

[167] James J. Graham, *Welfare Law Bulletin*, No. 17 (June 1969), p. 31.

true democracy of participation, in which men no longer need to feel themselves prisoners of social forces and decisions beyond their control or comprehension." [168]

Within two years, a presidential commission dismissed the notion that automation was accelerating the rate of unemployment, but expressed the conviction ". . . that rising productivity has brought this country to the point at last when all citizens may have a decent standard of living at a cost in resources the economy can easily bear." [169] In its 1966 report, the President's Council of Economic Advisors recognized that a system of universal payments to families based on a gap between their income and some minimum subsistence level was the most direct approach to reducing poverty and urged that this be given consideration along with other proposals. [170]

Within the social work profession, Edward E. Schwartz focused attention on the question of a guaranteed income by his proposal for a family security program that would provide, as a constitutional right, ". . . income sufficient to maintain a level of living consonant with American standards for the growth and development of children and youth and for the physical and mental health and social well-being of all persons." [171] The literature on this issue is now voluminous. [172] Even though a 1968 Gallup Poll showed that 58 percent of all Americans opposed and 36 percent favored a guaranteed annual income to assure each family a minimum income of $3,200 a year, it is clear that the idea is at least in the public arena for discussion. The question of how to assure the poor a more adequate level of income will continue for some time to be a major political issue. The variety of proposals may be classified in the following way: (1) reform of public assistance and social insurance, (2) new proposals for transferring income (e.g., family allowance, negative income tax, social divi-

[168] *The Triple Revolution,* Ad Hoc Committee on the Triple Revolution (Santa Barbara, California, 1964), p. 13.

[169] *Technology and the American Economy,* National Commission on Technology, Automation, and Economic Progress (Washington, D.C.: Government Printing Office, 1966), p. 59.

[170] *Economic Report of the President,* 1966, *op. cit.,* p. 115.

[171] Edward E. Schwartz, "A Way to End the Means Test," *Social Work,* 9 (July 1964), pp. 3–12, 97.

[172] A few references of particular interest to readers of this book are: Scott Briar, "Why Children's Allowances?," *Social Work,* 14 (January 1969), pp. 5–12. Eveline M. Burns (ed.), *Children's Allowances and the Economic Welfare of Children* (New York: Citizen's Committee for Children of New York, 1968); Irwin Garfinkel, "Negative Income Tax and Children's Allowance Programs: A Comparison," *Social Work,* 13 (October 1968), pp. 33–39; Christopher Green, "Guaranteed Income Plans—Which One is Best," *Trans-action,* 5 (January–February 1968), pp. 45–53; Moynihan, *op. cit.;* Alvin Schorr, *Poor Kids* (New York: Basic Books, 1966); Vera Shlakman, "Income Maintenance Alternatives," *Social Work,* 14 (January 1969), pp. 126–129; Robert Theobald (ed.), *The Guaranteed Income* (Garden City, N.Y.: Doubleday, 1966); James Tobin, "Do We Want A Children's Allowance?," *New Republic,* November 25, 1967, pp. 16–18; James C. Vadakin, *Children, Poverty and Family Allowance* (New York: Basic Books, 1968); Alan D. Wade, "The Guaranteed Minimum Income: Social Work's Challenge and Opportunity," *Social Work,* 2 (January 1967), pp. 94–101.

dend), (3) expansion of provisions in kind (e.g., food, housing, medical care), (4) tax reform, and (5) an employment policy that assures the right to work at adequate wages.

Improvement of Current Income Maintenance Programs

PUBLIC WELFARE.   A major proposal for the reform of the public welfare system came from the Advisory Council on Public Welfare.   It recommended a national minimum standard of public assistance based on a single criterion of need, accompanied by a universal comprehensive system of social services, all to be provided as a citizen right.   The means test would be modified to permit establishment of eligibility through ". . . personal statements or simple inquiry relating to . . . financial situation and family composition, subject only to subsequent sample review conducted in such manner as to protect . . . dignity, privacy, and constitutional rights." [173]   The federal government would establish national standards for adequate and equitable financial assistance and social services and share the cost of the total program in a way that would adequately reflect each state's relative fiscal capacity.   These are all desirable goals.   Yet they could have the effect of converting all the poor into public welfare recipients, enlarging caseloads, and expanding the public welfare bureaucracy.   Despite the laudable intent of defining public welfare as a right, it is doubtful that this can be done within the present system.   The high visibility of a dependent welfare class and the long tradition of stigma associated with public assistance are likely to be intensified by adding other poor to the welfare rolls.   The recommendations would reduce poverty but enlarge the welfare class unless public attitudes toward welfare change remarkably.   At best, public assistance is meant to be a residual program meeting the needs of a relatively small number of those whose specialized circumstances cannot be dealt with through other means.   It is not meant to be a mass program.   The proposals for a universal system of social service is another matter and will be discussed later.

It seems reasonably clear that some basic changes will be made in the welfare system.   What is not clear is the degree to which financial assistance will be provided as a right, free of "poor law" stigma and of arbitrary controls.   Some of both, along with significant departures from the tradition of public assistance, are found in the Family Assistance Plan proposed by the Nixon Administration. We shall review this plan in a later portion of this chapter.

SOCIAL INSURANCE.   Overcoming the gaps in our social insurance programs would go a long way toward eliminating poverty.   About a third of the poor, or some 8 million individuals, could be removed from poverty through higher social security benefits under the OASDHI program.[174]   Since the bulk of social

[173] "Having the Power We Have the Duty," Advisory Council on Public Welfare, *op. cit.,* p. xiii.

[174] Wilbur J. Cohen, "A Ten-Point Program to Abolish Poverty," *Social Security Bulletin,* 31 (December 1968), pp. 3–13.

security payments go to the nonpoor, the use of social security as an anti-poverty measure would be relatively expensive, although increased benefits to the near-poor would also have their value. It is estimated that it would cost about $11 billion to remove one-half the aged poor from poverty through increasing social security benefits.[175] Wilbur J. Cohen sees a 50 percent increase in the general benefit level and a minimum benefit level of at least $100 a month as a relatively immediate practical goal; it would enable over 4 million of the retired, widows, disabled workers, and dependents to have incomes above the poverty line. The further our social security program is expanded to provide for universal coverage and adequate benefits the less tenable is the image of insurance and earned benefits. If the major concern is with social adequacy, health insurance could be expanded to cover all. In fact, as Eveline Burns has observed, in all major countries except the United States the provision of health insurance has overcome one of the chief obstacles to a decent floor on income.[176] Although Medicare and Medicaid legislation move in this direction large segments of the population remain unprotected.

Ironically, despite the existing knowledge concerning the critical years in infancy and childhood, we have no means of assuring all children decent attention to their health needs. The Child Health Act of 1967 (amending Title V of the Social Security Act) calls for a single state plan to combine Maternal and Child Health, Crippled Childrens Services, and various project grants. Authorizing $250 million in 1969, increasing to $350 million by 1973, the act essentially continues existing objectives, adding emphasis on the prevention of infant mortality and screening for early identification of health problems of children eligible for Medicaid and dental care.

A national comprehensive health insurance provision would go a long way toward protecting all citizens against the increasingly high cost of medical care and assuring more equitable access to health services. Expansion and radical reorganization of the delivery of health services are also urgently required because the availability of medical care cannot be solved by health insurance alone. Other risks not covered might also be included. Alvin Schorr, for example, has suggested a "fatherless child insurance" that would protect children against the risk of losing a father for reasons other than death.[177] Coverage and benefits also need to be increased in unemployment insurance and workmen's compensation. In France, West Germany, Sweden, and the Netherlands unemployment insurance payments almost always provide for more than 50 percent of lost earnings, whereas in the United States benefits average about 35 percent. In addition dependents' allowances, now provided in ten states, should be universally available. Other inadequacies in our social insurance programs have already been noted. A children's allowance program may be seen as a form of social insurance and is now being seriously proposed as one of the new forms of providing income for the poor.

---

[175] Christopher Green, *Negative Taxes and the Poverty Problem* (Washington, D.C.: Brookings Institution, 1967), p. 173.

[176] Burns, "Social Security in Evolution," *op. cit.*

[177] Schorr, *op. cit.*, pp. 112–127.

New Proposals for Transfer of Income

CHILDREN'S ALLOWANCE. In some sixty-two nations of the world there is some form of child allowance program providing payments to all families with children in specified age groups, irrespective of income. This universal provision is a response to the reality of industrial societies, in which wages are distributed on the basis of work while family responsibility depends on family size and the special needs of children. Such a program can be seen as an expression of community regard for children and a willingness to share the cost of their proper care. The problem may be illustrated by noting that in March 1967 the spendable average weekly earnings in private nonagricultural employment for workers with no dependents were $81.37. For workers with three dependents the amount was just about $1 a day more, or $88.75. On a fifty-two-week basis workers with no dependents earned $4,231; those who had three dependents to support earned an additional $284.[178] A children's allowance would supplement family income. Depending on the level of payments it has the potential of reducing the number of poor and near-poor, 40 percent of whom are children. It is estimated that, at payments of $50 per month for each child under eighteen, three out of four children would be removed from poverty. The net cost after taxes might be a little over $28 billion dollars.[179] Suggested advantages in this approach are the elimination of the means test and the stigma associated with assistance because everyone would receive a benefit; the relative ease of administration; special assistance to large families; and avoidance for the most part of the issue of work incentive because it supplements rather than replaces earnings. It is possible that if benefits are high enough the issue of work incentives could arise for some large families. Some critics of the children's allowance stress its possible effect on the birthrate and express doubt about the ability of poor parents to spend benefits wisely and on behalf of their children. Alvin Schorr has pretty well disposed of the issue of the birthrate by demonstrating that there is no evidence from other countries that the children's allowance has any appreciable effect on it at all.[180] On this last point, evidence from Canada indicates that most parents spend the money in a manner consistent with the intent of the program.[181] Evidence regarding this country is sparse, but this in no way inhibits the popular conviction that the poor will only squander their benefits. A disadvantage of the children's allowance is its relatively high cost, since money goes to the nonpoor. A portion of this, however, may be recouped through changes in the tax structure. Those who favor the children's allowance tend to argue that the cost is well

[178] Moynihan, *op. cit.*

[179] Mollie Orshansky, "Benefits and Costs of Children's Allowances," in Burns, *Children's Allowances, op. cit.*

[180] Alvin L. Schorr, "Income Maintenance and the Birth Rate," *Social Security Bulletin,* 28 (December 1965), pp. 22–30.

[181] Bernice Madison, "Canadian Family Allowances and Their Major Social Implications," *Journal of Marriage and the Family,* 26 (May 1964), pp. 134–141.

worth what it purchases: the elimination of the stigma of public assistance and the establishment of a citizen right to payments.[182]

This is correct to the extent that a children's allowance program can eliminate public assistance as a significant source of income for the poor and to the degree that the concept of legal right cannot be established just as well in some other way. There is some doubt on both scores, as Irwin Garfinkel has clearly noted.[183] He demonstrates that even the most liberal children's allowance being proposed would require retention of public assistance for a significant group of the poor. Since over half of all families on AFDC have no source of income other than public assistance, a number of them would continue to require AFDC even with a $50-a-month children's allowance. For them the stigma of welfare would remain. This is made clear in the following observation:

> A family consisting of a mother and three children would receive, after taxes, $1,620 from the children's allowance. This is slightly lower than the 1961 national average income figure for an AFDC family of four. More important, it is $1,510 below the 1964 poverty line. Unless the size of the allowance is much larger than $50 a month, it would not constitute an adequate minimum income.[184]

It is doubtful that the public, in the near future, would accept a $50-a-month allowance at an estimated net cost of a little over $28 billion. The lower the benefit the greater the number of those who would continue to need public assistance. Even with the most liberal children's allowance proposal, about 28 percent of all poor families with children would remain in poverty, roughly a million families. An additional 10.2 million people who live alone or are childless would remain in poverty. An estimated $12 billion would be required to remove 70 percent of these from poverty, through expansion of social security.[185] While the children's allowance would abolish stigma for those who could do without public assistance, attention needs to be given to the size of the public assistance caseload that would remain. An unknown factor is the number of women who could be helped to obtain decent employment and then, with a children's allowance, would no longer need public assistance. The value of a children's allowance would be enormously increased through social provision of medical care and housing. A major virtue of a children's allowance is that it is a universal program that makes no invidious distinctions among citizens. Some maintain that the concept of legal right could be established equally as well through a negative income tax that would also more effectively and economically abolish poverty.

NEGATIVE INCOME TAX. The major controversy regarding new income programs involves the relative merits of a children's allowance as opposed to some

[182] Alvin Schorr, "Alternatives in Income Maintenance," *Social Work,* 11 (July 1966), pp. 22–29.

[183] Garfinkel, *op. cit.*

[184] *Ibid.,* p. 36.

[185] *Ibid.,* p. 39.

form of a negative income tax.[186]   Proposals for a negative income tax (NIT) vary, but they all contemplate using the internal revenue system for disbursing money to those whose income falls below some established minimum.   Proponents argue that this is the simplest and most economical way to assure a minimum income for all.   Since most proposals contain a work incentive feature, NIT turns out to be more complicated and more expensive than a direct cash grant to bring everyone up to the poverty line.[187]   This can be illustrated by the experiments now being conducted to test the outcomes of various kinds of negative income tax plans.   These seek to overcome the disincentive features of the welfare system that tend to restrict the amount of earnings a recipient may retain.   Until relatively recently a "tax" of 100 percent was imposed on such earnings, since all earned income was deducted from the grant.   One of the plans being tested involves a 50 percent negative income tax.   This means that benefits are reduced by \$.50 for every \$1 the recipient earns.   In other words he may keep half of what he earns until some break-off point is reached.   For example, a family of four persons with no income receives a payment of \$3,300 a year.   Should the family earn \$2,000, \$1,000 would be deducted from the \$3,300, providing a benefit of \$2,300 and a total family income of \$4,300.   Should the family earn \$6,600, it reaches the break-even point (50 percent of \$6,600, or \$3,300, is deducted from the payment of \$3,300, leaving 0).

Because of this work incentive feature some of the subsidy goes to the nonpoor, but most of this would go to the near-poor.[188]   This adds to the cost of the program; yet it is less expensive than an adequate child allowance.   One proposal estimates that poverty could be eliminated through a NIT program with a 62 percent negative tax rate (allowing retention of 62 percent of earnings up to a break-even point of \$6,000 for a family of five) at a cost of \$22 to \$28 billion.   This is estimated to be some \$12 to \$17 billion less than the cost of a combined children's allowance and social insurance program that would still leave 30 percent of the poor below the poverty line.[189]   A major argument against the NIT is that it is the stigmatizing welfare approach in a new guise.   Alvin Schorr puts it this way:

> . . . even a substantial negative income tax would, like public assistance, provide the money payment in a poor law framework.   It would be paid not for past work, not because of childhood or old age, not for any of the dozens of reasons that have been converted into social rights, but for the one reason we have so far failed to make into a right—want. . . .   The

[186] James Tobin, "The Case for an Income Guarantee," *The Public Interest*, No. 4 (Summer 1966), pp. 31–41; Alvin Schorr, "Against a Negative Income Tax," *The Public Interest*, No. 5 (Fall 1966), pp. 110–117; James Tobin, "A Rejoinder," *The Public Interest*, No. 5 (Fall 1966), pp. 117–119; Shirley Buttrick and Alan Wade, "Negative Income Tax: A Step Forward," *Social Work*, 14 (April 1969), pp. 104–106; Vera Shlakman and Scott Briar, "Briar and Shlakman Answer Their Critics," *Social Work*, 14 (July 1969), pp. 108–110.

[187] The Council of Economic Advisers estimates that in 1967 the poverty gap was \$9.7 billion. *Economic Report of the President*, 1969, *op. cit.*, p. 153.

[188] Garfinkel, *op. cit.*, p. 38.

[189] *Ibid.*, p. 39.

writer's impression is that poor people would, if they were consulted, reject the negative income tax.[190]

Just how the poor feel about the NIT is not known. Some indications are available, however, from the Gallup Poll of attitudes toward a guaranteed annual income. This revealed that the lower a person's income, the more likely he is to support such a plan. On the other hand, almost an equal number of the poor support and oppose the idea. Of those families with yearly incomes of $3,000–5,000, 47 percent supported and 48 percent opposed the idea. For families earning under $3,000 the corresponding figures are 48 percent and 45 percent. The overwhelming majority preferred a plan of guaranteed work rather than guaranteed income.[191] Since work alone, however important, cannot provide adequate income for all, some plan for income distribution based on a citizen right is essential. The argument that NIT cannot be defined as a social right is disputed by Irwin Garfinkel, who notes that the feeling of entitlement may be derived from a variety of sources: contributions, absence of a means test, or from the way a program is administered. All citizens undergo an impersonal means test through the income tax mechanism, but it does not contain the degradation associated with public assistance. A congressional act declaring the right to a decent standard of living implemented through a NIT plan could conceivably enable people to feel they are receiving benefits as a right.[192] Public support for such a declaration does not seem imminent. What does seem likely is Congressional enactment of some version of the Family Assistance Plan proposed by the Nixon Administration.

FAMILY ASSISTANCE PLAN. The Family Assistance Plan, a version of the NIT, was first proposed by President Richard M. Nixon in an address to the nation on August 9, 1969. Two days later, he sent a message to Congress entitled "Reform of the Nation's Welfare System." Declaring the present welfare system a failure, he offered a plan for a nationwide minimum payment to families with children. After extensive hearings by its Ways and Means Committee, the House of Representatives voted to accept a modified plan as presented in H.R. 16311. Following is a summary of the major provisions of that Act. Because the bill has been revised and is subject to further revision, and because its fate in the Senate is uncertain, only a bare outline will be provided to illustrate the kind of proposal being made.

The federal-state program of AFDC and AFDC-UP (Unemployed Parent) program is altered with the creation of a new Family Assistance Plan (FAP) whose purpose is the provision of "a basic level of financial assistance throughout the nation to needy families with children, in a manner that will strengthen family life, encourage work training and self-support, and enhance personal dignity." All needy families are eligible for direct federal payments. Included are the working poor families headed by an employed male. Coverage is also extended to families with an unemployed parent in those 29 jurisdictions without an AFDC-UP program. Not included are childless couples and single

190 Schorr, "Alternatives in Income Maintenance," *op. cit.*, p. 27.

191 *The New York Times,* June 15, 1968.

192 Garfinkel, *op. cit.*, p. 39.

individuals. The three categorical programs of public assistance for the aged, blind and disabled are combined into a single adult program with a requirement that states provide grants sufficient to assure a total income of $110 a month per recipient, or the standard already prevailing, should that be higher.

The plan establishes a federally financed income floor of $1600 for a family of four with no regular earnings. The first two family members receive $500 each, while $300 is provided for each additional member. Families may retain the first $720 of annual earnings and one-half of the remainder. The cut-off point is $3920 for a family of four and $5720 for a family of seven. (See Tables 20 and 21.) Thus a family of four that has no earned income (except for irregular income not to exceed $30 in any quarter) receives a benefit of $1600. Similarly a family of seven receives $2500. A family of four earning $1000 may retain $720 and one-half the remainder. Their total income is therefore $2460. In this way it is assumed that incentive to work will be encouraged by the application of a 50 percent marginal tax on nonexempt earnings instead of the 100 percent tax that has for the most part prevailed in public assistance.

The work incentive provision in the benefit schedule is accompanied by a work requirement. All able-bodied adults, including children sixteen and over not in school, are to register with the local public employment office for manpower services, training and employment. Exempt from this provision are mothers or other relatives caring for a child under the age of six, or any adult caring for an ill or incapacitated member of the family. Also exempt are mothers in families with a male breadwinner subject to this regulation. Payments are not to be made to those who fail to register as required or who refuse without good cause to accept employment or manpower training and services. In that event, other family members continue to receive their allotted portion of the family benefit. To encourage participation in manpower training programs an incentive allowance of $30 per month is provided for each family member participating in such a program. To facilitate the training and employment of mothers, funds are authorized for provision of child care.

Presumably employability is also to be enhanced by a requirement that the Secretary of Labor assure the preparation of an employability plan prescribing the manpower services, training and employment essential to enable each person to become not only self-supporting but prepared for job advancement. A separate bill to promote more adequate and better coordinated manpower programs was also presented to Congress by the Nixon Administration, as part of a general effort to transform "welfare" into a "workfare" program. The total estimated cost of the FAP is about 4 billion—less, said the President, in presenting this program, than the cost "of creating a permanent underclass in America." In his words the plan would establish the following "firsts"—(1) a minimum standard payment based upon uniform and single eligibility standards for all American families with children; (2) help for over two million families who are the "working poor"; (3) work opportunity with effective incentives; (4) relief for state governments of financial burden of welfare; (5) encouragement for families to stay together. At this point how might one evaluate this effort at welfare reform?

Unquestionably the plan is significant for what it proposes, and for what it fails to propose as well as for the rhetoric used to describe and justify the basic

Table 20. Proposed FAP Payment Schedule for Family of Four (Assuming Annual Payments of $500 Each for First Two Family Members and $300 Each for Additional Members, a $720 Income Exemption and a 50 Percent Marginal "Tax" on Nonexempt Income)

EARNINGS	NONEXEMPT EARNINGS	"TAX" AT 50%	NET PAYMENT	NET INCOME
$ 0	$ 0	$ 0	$1,600	$1,600
720	0	0	1,600	2,320
1,000	280	140	1,460	2,460
1,500	780	390	1,210	2,710
2,000	1,280	640	960	2,960
2,500	1,780	890	710	3,210
3,000	2,280	1,140	460	3,460
3,500	2,780	1,390	210	3,710
3,920	3,200	1,600	—	3,920

SOURCE: Legislative Analysis: The Bill to Revamp the Welfare System (Washington, D.C.: American Enterprise Institute, 1970) p. 15.

Table 21. Summary of Proposed FAP Payment Schedule

	PAYMENTS BY NUMBER OF MEMBERS PER FAMILY					
Income	Two	Three	Four	Five	Six	Seven
$ 0	$1,000	$1,300	$1,600	$1,900	$2,200	$2,500
720	1,000	1,300	1,600	1,900	2,200	2,500
1,000	860	1,160	1,460	1,760	2,060	2,360
1,500	610	910	1,210	1,510	1,810	2,110
2,000	360	660	960	1,260	1,560	1,860
2,500	110	410	710	1,010	1,310	1,610
3,000	—	160	460	760	1,060	1,360
3,500	—	—	210	510	810	1,110
4,000	—	—	—	260	560	860
4,500	—	—	—	10	310	610
5,000	—	—	—	—	60	360
5,500	—	—	—	—	—	110
6,000	—	—	—	—	—	—
Break-even income	$2,720	$3,320	$3,920	$4,520	$5,120	$5,720

SOURCE: Legislative Analysis: The Bill to Revamp the Welfare System (Washington, D.C.: American Enterprise Institute, 1970), p. 14.

changes in the welfare system. In essence, the Family Assistance Plan as presented by President Nixon expands the obligations of the welfare state but justifies the proposed reforms on the basis of a conservative ideology, moving people from the "welfare rolls to the payrolls." The fact is that the Family Assistance Plan will double the size of the public assistance caseload and increase from 5 to 12 percent the proportion of this population on welfare. The rhetoric of removing people from the welfare rolls conceals the fact that the new financial assistance plan will add not diminish the number receiving public aid, particularly in view of the fact that the stable working poor previously excluded from such benefits are now added to the welfare rolls. Whether we can abolish a separate "welfare class" regarded with suspicion and scorn will depend in large measure on the socially created attitudes toward those receiving payments. In this regard the image of welfare recipients projected by the President's message is most unfortunate. Throughout, the image of the welfare recipient as "sturdy beggar" choosing "handouts" in preference to work is projected in such statements as "there is no reason why one person should be taxed so that another can choose to live idly." On the other hand there is also clear recognition of the federal government's responsibility to assure economic security and to promote opportunities not only for employment, ". . . but for good jobs, that provide both additional self-respect and full self-support." What seems to be missing is sufficient commitment to assuring decent income or decent job opportunities. There is also a failure to confront the public with the dilemmas of full employment and price stability. It is extremely doubtful that a sufficient number of jobs will be created to match the skills of FAP beneficiaries either by the private sector or through government intervention, or that there will be a sufficient investment in manpower programs and supportive services to significantly enhance employment opportunities for this group. Other priorities appear to command national resources while pressure for price stability in the face of increasing inflation tends to produce public policy that increases the number of unemployed. This is revealed by the proposal of the Nixon Administration to train 150,000 welfare recipients in the first year of the Family Assistance Plan, although its own efforts to combat inflation had helped to increase the number of unemployed by one million in the period 1969–1970.

In this light, reliance on forced registration for employment and manpower services, particularly for mothers whose labor is not required by the realities of the job market, seems misplaced and unjustifiably coercive. It is the structure of opportunity as determined by economic policy and manpower policy, not individual motivation, that largely controls dependency on public aid for that small proportion of the current welfare caseload who can be expected to work. A modern work requirement as Alvin Schorr has proposed would recognize this fact. While men would be expected to work it would be understood that ". . . their capacity to work depends on the effectiveness of manpower programs and the availability of jobs they can fill." [193] For mothers, work would be regarded as essential to self-fulfillment if women so viewed it, but not essential to the economy. Thus mothers would not be expected to register for work as a condition for receiving assistance unless they chose to avail themselves of manpower services.[194] In like manner, The President's Commission on Income Maintenance Programs rejects ". . . the coercion involved in requiring poor mothers to work regardless of their skills, abilities and desires." [195] The Commission further rejects the notion that day care for children, however

---

[193] Alvin L. Schorr, "The President's Welfare Program and Commission," Paper prepared for delivery to the American Public Welfare Association Round Table Conference in Dallas, Texas, December 10, 1969, mimeo, p. 8.

[194] *Ibid.*

[195] *Ibid.*, p. 74.

justifiable on other grounds, should be provided so that women on welfare can be required to work, arguing that provision of day care for that purpose is ". . . costly, narrowly conceived, and coercive." [196] Thus the rhetoric of "workfare" and the measures proposed to enhance employment opportunities fail to deal with the realities of the problem of work as it presents itself to the poor, however effectively both of these may deal with the politics of winning short-run public support for welfare reform. Neither the right to work nor the right to adequate income are to be assured by FAP.

For the first time, however, income supplements are available to intact working poor families. Still, the cut-off point at $3,920 leaves a working class family of four struggling on incomes considerably below the Department of Labor's estimated cost of living for a moderate standard or even the lower standard (roughly $10,000 and $6,500 in spring of 1969), without benefit of public aid. Nonetheless the recognition of income needs of the employed poor is a significant advance. Of importance too is the establishment of a national income floor even though the guaranteed minimum is considerably below the official poverty line. The proposed $1,600 for a family of four compares unfavorably with the $2,400 per year recommended by the President's Commission on Income Maintenance Programs, even though in FAP the value of food stamps may bring total family real income up to this level. It is even less adequate when compared to the demand of the National Welfare Rights Organization for a guaranteed minimum of $5,500 a year, a demand that has been incorporated into the Adequate Income Act of 1970 (S-3780) and introduced into the 91st Congress by Senator Eugene McCarthy. It is in the latter Act, one hardly likely to receive more than passing notice, that the issue of relative deprivation is squarely faced in the following assertions that get to the heart of the matter. "As a wealth distribution system employment has never worked well for the poor, especially the black poor. Even if all eligible Americans were employed today, the poverty rate would not be seriously affected." Here too, it is the right to life that justifies the transfer of income in order ". . . to insure that every American will have at least the minimum income required to express freely the fundamental rights and liberties expressed in the Constitution." The FAP minimum, even with its work incentives and required state supplementation, cannot meet the problem of poverty or touch the more fundamental issue of income redistribution, which alone will get at the core of the problem of relative deprivation. Even the more modest goal of attaining the poverty line for all Americans seems inhibited rather than advanced by FAP, which provides for no plan to raise benefit levels by stages. Moreover the marginal tax rate of 50 percent may discourage rather than encourage lifting the minimum family income to the poverty line. As Alvin Schorr has observed, if the floor for a family of four were set at $3,555 this would require continued assistance to families with incomes up to $7,800 a year even though the amount of aid would be only $165 a year.[197] A conservative Congress is likely to retain a low payment level rather than raise benefits that would disburse money to those whose incomes appear to be so much above the poverty line. It might be better as Schorr suggests to substitute a 33 percent incentive formula or

---

[196] *Ibid.,* p. 74.

[197] Schorr, The President's Welfare Program and Commission, *op. cit.,* p. 6.

devise an alternative to FAP itself.[198]   Moreover, since FAP has been presented as a means of controlling rising welfare caseloads, its success will depend on keeping benefits low in order to restrict the number of families who become eligible.

Finally total national administration and financing of a basic income plan seems essential to deal with continuing inequities inherent in the varying willingness and capacity of states to supplement the federal contribution to the income needs of the poor.   FAP requires state supplementation with the aid of 30 percent federal matching.   The act as passed by the House specifies the January AFDC level of payments, or a congressionally defined poverty level. Later modifications gave the secretary of the H.E.W. authority to set the level for each state.   Moreover state supplementation does not cover intact families of the working poor and thus discriminates against this group.   In fact it appears that intact families with employed or unemployed fathers will be discriminated against if certain amendments to the House bill proposed by the administration are enacted.   In the act passed by the House and sent to the Senate Finance Committee, families eligible for AFDC-UP are entitled to federally subsidized state supplementation while families with a full-time breadwinner are not.   The Senate Committee complained, among other things, that with state supplementation, Medicaid and other benefits, a man with a family could be better off by working less than full time or not at all.   The choice before the administration was to propose supplementation for the working poor at a cost of an additional one billion dollars or to eliminate it for families with an unemployed father.   It chose the latter.   Should this amendment be adopted it remains possible for families with a deserting father to be better off than families with an employed or unemployed male breadwinner.   Other Administration proposals have been presented to meet the objections of the Senate Finance Committee that the FAP was not sufficiently related to other major welfare programs such as food stamps, Medicaid, public housing and rent supplements.   The Senate Committee saw disincentives built into FAP that were not immediately apparent.   The basic FAP benefit coupled with a certain level of earning might mean loss of eligibility for one or more welfare programs.   Rather than risk losing rent supplements, public housing or Medicaid a family might choose to keep earnings below a given level.   In response the Administration has proposed some new administrative measures and some new legislation which if enacted would constitute reforms considerably beyond the scope of the original FAP.   These include a Family Health Insurance program to replace Medicaid for low-income families with children with coverage to include the working poor; changes in public housing rentals to permit those with increased income to continue occupancy by paying a higher portion of their income as rent; a similar modification in the food stamp program to permit tapering off eligibility more gradually at upper income levels.

Thus, FAP may have set the stage for some reform of our system of social provisions.   If enacted, it will provide modest benefits to the working poor and to the public assistance recipients in some Southern states.   It will not solve the welfare crisis.   Moreover poverty and inequality will remain serious

[198] *Ibid.*

sources of conflict for no reform of the welfare system being given serious political consideration seems responsive to the revolution of rising expectations and to the measure of social justice essential to heal the deep and growing division of this society.   In the meantime more radical proposals for income distribution, such as the social dividend, are offered for consideration.

SOCIAL DIVIDEND.   The social dividend is a universal payment made to all without regard to income or status.   An originator of this idea was Lady Juliet Rhys Williams, who based her notion on the idea of a new social contract

> . . . whereby the State would acknowledge the duty to maintain the individual and his children at all times and to assure for them all of the necessities of a healthy life.   The individual in his turn would acknowledge it to be his duty to divert his best efforts to the production of the wealth whereby alone the welfare of the community can be maintained.[199]

Some productive effort thus is expected from all who can contribute to society. The idea of a social dividend can be justified on the basis of one's citizen right to share in socially produced income.   The notion that each individual produces his own income is about as fallacious as the assumption that each man produces his own knowledge.   Like knowledge, income is in large measure socially produced and each generation benefits from the contribution of previous generations to the pool of riches available.   As technology expands its capacity to produce, there is less and less a direct ratio of income to productive effort. This can be clearly seen in the data that reveal that between 1947 and 1961 the real output of the private economy in the United States increased by 59 percent; in the same period, the man-hours worked rose by only 3 percent.   Thus each hour of work today, as Herman P. Miller observes, produces 50 percent more than it did fifteen years ago.[200]

A more recent proponent of a universal payment is Robert Theobald, who assumed that, given the revolutionary possibilities of cybernation, the idea of work for everyone or at least work for wages was obsolete.[201]   Unlimited abundance produced by the new technology could remove the curse of Adam and free men from earning their bread through the sweat of their brow.   Freely chosen human endeavor could replace toil if we are willing to pay the price. The cost of an adequate guaranteed income for all could be as high as $165 billion and is beyond serious consideration at present.   Robert Theobald himself has changed his proposal to a more modest plan not unlike that of NIT, but without the complicated concerns around work incentive features.   His basic philosophy remains the same.[202]   The issue, as he sees it, is not the appro-

---

[199] Quoted in Schwartz, "A Way to End the Means Test," *op. cit.,* p. 7.

[200] Herman P. Miller, *Rich Man, Poor Man* (New York: Signet Books, 1965), pp. 213–214.

[201] Robert Theobald, *Free Men and Free Markets* (New York: C. N. Potter, 1963).

[202] Robert Theobald, "The Guaranteed Income: A New Economic and Human Right," *The Social Welfare Forum, 1966* (New York: Columbia University Press, 1966), pp. 138–150.

priate instrument for transfer of income but the goals toward which we are striving. For him the challenge is to free people from toil and enable as many as possible to do what they desire, rather than continue to structure the economic system so that an individual has no choice but to take whatever job is available to him. His more modest proposal would assure everyone an income up to the poverty line, based on a new constitutional right to prevent the government from using the benefit as a means of controlling the individual. Most people would continue to work because ". . . Americans have an almost pathological desire to toil." Some would work for incentives other than financial. Some would be released from bondage to the wage economy to join together to do what they find valuable. Our problem, Theobald believes, is not lack of resources so much as the values and institutions that prevent us from sharing our resources more equitably and keep us from allocating them in ways that might enable man to live in freedom and dignity.[203]

However unrealistic in terms of their current political feasibility, such ideas deserve consideration. To release man from the discipline of wage-related work would require a radical alteration of our image of man and a major reconstruction of our social order. It may be that our "mind-forged manacles," as William Blake put it, will keep us enchained in meaningless work and meaningless consumption to sustain a social drama that retains only its power to coerce us into obedience and to deprive us of our chance to become more fully human. On the other hand, there are now opportunities to humanize work, to offer new kinds of satisfying careers to those confined to unemployment and subemployment. A further consideration is our obligation to the family of man: What are the human uses of technology and resources and what manly work should we be doing to free all mankind from the bondage of poverty?

DILEMMAS. There seems to be no perfect income maintenance program. In the context of a society reluctant to bear the burden of eliminating poverty and fearful of any critical examination of its goals, the dilemmas that might be present in any event are multiplied. The dilemmas are real enough. There seem to be no adequate ways to reconcile the conflicting aims of social adequacy, economy, equity, and work incentive. Social adequacy means a decent income provided in a manner that enhances individual dignity and social participation. To achieve this, benefits need to be at some level that permits, when combined with other income, an average way of life not too far below the national median. The method of income transfer must embody the concept of a citizen right. A universal family allowance or social dividend could accomplish this purpose, but at costs that are now unacceptable because, as benefits are raised, an increasing portion goes to those who do not need them. A negative income tax would be more economical, but there is doubt that we can define this as a social right. Questions are also raised about equity. Should a family entirely supported through earnings have a level of living no higher than one supported in part through public subsidies? This is the traditional issue of "less eligibility" derived from the Poor Law concern with assuring that no one receiving public assistance has a level of living higher than that enjoyed by

[203] *Ibid.,* pp. 147–148.

the lowest wage earner in the community. Other issues of equity have to do with the moral justification for the wide disparities in income distribution, a political question we successfully avoid but one that is intimately related to the ultimate goals of the society. Most proposals tend to suffer from uncertainty about their possible impact on work incentive. As work incentive features are added, as for example in the NIT, the cost increases and administration becomes more complex.

Public anxiety about discouraging work motivation makes it difficult to design a program that provides adequate income as a citizen right. Actually, little is known about the relationship between income adequacy and work incentive. There is, however, some evidence that challenges popular assumptions. Preliminary reports from the New Jersey Urban Experiment, an OEO research project testing the impact of a guaranteed income, indicate that breadwinners in families receiving government cash payments continue to work as hard as ever. Some may be stimulated to work even harder than before. Those who are convinced that assistance reduces work incentive will need to explain how it happens that in this study earnings increased for 53 percent of the families receiving cash grants as compared with 43 percent of the families who were not recipients. At the same time, 31 percent of families not getting aid experienced a decline in income compared to 29 percent of those participating in the program.[204]

The problem is obscured by our refusal to face the issue of disciplining people to do the dirty work that has been the traditional lot of the poor.[205] It is clear that men do not work for money alone, especially when work is satisfying beyond the material rewards it provides.[206] Recent preliminary reports from a longitudinal study of labor force behavior reveals that over four-fifths of the white and slightly over one-half of the Negro workers stated that enjoyable work is more important than good wages. More than three-fourths of all those studied reported they would continue to work even if they got enough money to live comfortably without working.[207] This supports Harold Wilensky's contention that a primary motivation to work is the need to feel like a participant in the mainstream of society, to be "among the living." [208]

It is possible that, for some individuals, public assistance is a disincentive when work is not attractive and when regulations prohibit the retention of little if any earned income above the public assistance standard. Here, too, evidence is lacking. Whether real or mythical, fears about work incentive are a political consideration and will affect public consideration of any proposed reform in income maintenance. This is clearly evident in the Nixon administration's proposal for reform of the welfare system, with its frequent reiteration of the

[204] Fred J. Cook, "When You Just Give Money to the Poor," *The New York Times Magazine,* April 26, 1970, p. 110.

[205] Herbert J. Gans, "Income Grants and 'Dirty Work,' " *The Public Interest,* No. 6 (Winter 1967), pp. 110–113; and Frederick Herzberg, *Work and the Nature of Man,* (New York: World Publishing, 1967).

[206] Harold L. Wilensky, "Work As a Social Problem," in Howard S. Becker (ed.), *Social Problems: A Modern Approach* (New York: Wiley, 1966).

[207] *Manpower Report of the President,* 1969, *op. cit.,* pp. 168–170.

[208] Wilensky in Becker, *op. cit.,* p. 136.

theme of getting people "off the welfare rolls on to the payrolls." [209]   The public anxiety over releasing some people from the discipline of work prevents rational public consideration of the issue surrounding work incentives.   To what extent are we dealing, not with the issue of incentives, but of coercion, of structuring life so as to foreclose any dignified choice but to work for wages at those jobs that are available?   The 1967 amendments and portions of the Nixon administration's proposal that would require adults not caring for preschool children to work as a condition for receiving assistance are examples of a system that prevents serious consideration of alternatives to work, as we narrowly define that term.   The 1967 amendments required a case plan for each member of the family that would assure to the maximum extent possible that all adults sixteen and over ". . . will enter the labor force and become self-sufficient. . . ." Society may choose to do this, but incentives may not be quite the word to describe the process that seeks to convert all adults into employees, binding them into the present occupational structure and wage system, foreclosing any creative effort to imagine alternative uses of human time and energy.

We are still in the grips of the nineteenth-century economist's narrow world view of society as a giant producing machine and man as a commodity of production to be processed and manipulated to fit into the industrial system.   If he will not willingly find his niche he must be "motivated."   In this world view man, it seems, is inherently lazy or recalcitrant.   He must be goaded by the stick or the carrot or some judicious combination of both.   The image in any event is demeaning and it is false, as many contemporary economists understand.   Man is naturally active and growth motivated.   Little external force is required to motivate individuals to engage in pursuits that interest them and enrich their sense of self-hood.   To toil is another matter.   Man naturally avoids drudgery if unrelated to some transcending purpose.   To this extent, men are indeed lazy, quite properly and admirably so.   To the extent that society must manipulate people to do work they would not otherwise choose, institutionalized coercion disguised as incentives may be necessary.   What we do not face is the squandering of human energy, talent, and imagination on countless useless, meaningless, and even destructive tasks defined as work.   We are not quite ready to examine the extent to which work itself may be a problem. The quality of work available may be the problem, not how to motivate people to work by finely tuning the mechanism of incentives to discover the point at which the maximum number of people can be directed into the labor force. There is a dehumanized image of man underlying much of our discussion of work incentives: man as an object to be manipulated by discovering that point at which the pain of work can be offset by the rewards of wages sufficient to overcome a natural disinclination to be productive.   Much of our work is actually counter-productive, and it is work and its discontents that constitute a major social problem.[210]   It is the creation of human forms of work that actualize the best that is in all of us that should command our attention.   When work as a career complements the individual's desire for maximum self-development, the

---

[209] President's speech, August 8, 1969, and Message to Congress, August 11, 1969.

[210] Wilensky, in Becker, *op. cit.;* Daniel Bell, "Work and Its Discontents," *The End of Ideology* (New York: Free Press, 1960), Chapter 12, pp. 222–262; Jules Henry, *Culture Against Man* (New York: Vintage Books, 1965), pp. 25–37.

current issue of work incentive may turn out to be another old wives' tale we can finally put to rest. A movement in this direction is the effort to establish new careers in the human services, an effort that would establish ". . . a new Bill of Rights that includes the right to a permanent job, to a career, and to an income." [211] Other positive efforts are to humanize the work environment and to think in terms of strategies that would enable individuals to move from conception of work as a job to that of work as a career.[212] This is not to suggest that satisfying careers can be developed for all individuals, but it does suggest that serious attention to the problem of work would require massive investments in education, training, and development of new kinds of employment opportunities, including possibly guaranteed employment through government as the employer of last resort for those who cannot find work through normal channels.

The great anxiety about work incentive does not stem from legitimate doubts about the desire of most people to be productive. The problem largely centers around social control of those who reject menial work, a problem that may increase as Negroes continue to refuse jobs that are identified with their now-rejected inferior status and as general affluence undermines the values that support the discipline of work as the only means of survival. It is difficult to impose dirty work in a society undergoing a revolution in rising expectations. The anxiety about who will do the dirty work is revealed in a comment on the part of a conservative economist, Henry Hazlitt, who, in rejecting the idea of a guaranteed income, reveals the basis for his fears about work motivation. He writes: "Who would work? . . . shine shoes, wash cars, cut brush, mow lawns, act as porters at railroad or bus stations or do any number of necessary jobs." [213]

Viewing the idea of guaranteed income as alien to the spirit of free enterprise, Hazlitt also declares:

> This system maximizes production because it allows a man freedom of choice of his occupation, freedom in his choice of those for whom he works or who work for him, freedom in the choice of those with whom he associates or cooperates, and, above all, freedom to earn and to keep the fruits of his labor.[214]

There is freedom in the system for those who have access to preferred occupations but little freedom, if any, for those for whom opportunity consists of a series of dead-end jobs. We are not likely to develop creative responses to the problem of menial work if we do not recognize it as a central issue. Such responses might include incentives to automate certain tasks, thus freeing people for education and job training; extra compensations for essential but

[211] Frank Riessman, *Strategies Against Poverty* (New York: Random House, 1969), p. 28.

[212] *Manpower Report, op. cit.,* pp. 47–56; Marc A. Fried, "Is Work a Career?," *Trans-action,* 3 (September–October 1966), pp. 42–47.

[213] Henry Hazlitt, "Income Without Work," *Perspective on Important Issues,* Report No. 34 (Chicago: Illinois Bell Telephone Co., December 1966), as quoted in *Guaranteed Annual Income Newsletter.*

[214] *Ibid.*

distasteful work; and recruiting youths for temporary engagement in routine employment.   To face the problem of who is being recruited for the dirty work might force greater attention to efforts now under way to develop new opportunity structures consisting of new career ladders linked to appropriate education, training, and supportive resources.[215]   To focus attention on developing human forms of work would place the issue of work incentive in an entirely new perspective.

Work could be redefined to include paying people to go to school to work at the socially essential task today, self-development.   We already do this in some measure through various stipends provided to people who enter education and training programs.   A learning society requires that an increasing number of its citizens undertake the social obligation of continuous learning. New definitions of work might also include the essential political activity of citizens.   More important than restoring people to work at jobs now available to them might be the restoration of politics as a major preoccupation of citizens.[216]   We are threatened not by the indolence of individuals but by the concentration of power and authority in giant bureaucracies, with litttle participation in decision-making on the part of those whose lives are controlled. If we understand the danger bureaucracy poses to a free society and adopt as a goal the enhancement of a democratic society, the role for which we might be preparing people is that of politics in the Athenian sense.   For this purpose income might be provided to free people for the arduous task of learning how to participate as responsible citizens in the political life of their community. For example, in assessing how the dangers of bureaucracy might be overcome, Peter M. Blau offers the following suggestion: Perhaps, the challenge posed by bureaucratization can be met only if all citizens are able and motivated to devote a considerable portion of their time and energy to activities in the political life of their communities.[217]   Clearly resources must support such an endeavor, and the political role of citizen must be honored and facilitated in a way not yet fully developed in this society.

The current search is for a politically feasible reform of the present public assistance program—one that seems to promise economy and maximum preservation of the present work-oriented system.   These are clearly themes in the Nixon administration's proposal for development of a new family assistance plan.   On the other hand the proposal for a national floor on income, however modest, is a new departure that may have unforeseeable consequences.   Other proposals have also been made that would meet the test of economy and political feasibility.

In all likelihood a mixture of programs rather than any single one will be economically and politically feasible.   For example, an HEW task force has proposed the following to lift the non-aged poor out of poverty by 1972: (1) a children's allowance of $25 per month for all children under eighteen, (2) a reformed, noncategorical, federalized public assistance program, (3) ex-

[215] Riessman, *op. cit.,* Chap. 3, "New Careers."

[216] Harvey Wheeler, *The Restoration of Politics* (Santa Barbara, Calif.: Center for the Study of Democratic Institutions, 1965).

[217] Peter Blau, *Bureaucracy in Modern Society* (New York: Random House, 1956), p. 118.

pansion of existing benefits and employment programs.   The net cost is estimated at $13.2 billion.   This proposal is based on the assumption that there will be a $7.8 billion income poverty gap for the non-aged poor by 1972.[218]   To what extent our conception of the poverty line will have increased by that time to make this estimate far too conservative remains to be seen.   None of the proposals currently under consideration attempts to get at the far more complex problem of income inequality and the politically explosive issue of serious income redistribution.   It might be technically possible to do this through a negative income tax that assures income at one-half the national median, with appropriate tax offset on earned income to provide work incentive—but that hardly seems a realistic possibility.   A combination of income maintenance programs, expansion of other social provisions, tax reform, and a true full employment policy may well be the most effective way to assure adequate income and opportunities.   We turn now to other social provisions: food, housing, and medical care.

Social Provisions in Kind

Cash is not the only way of promoting social security and social justice.   It may not be the best way in some instances, but income to spend at one's discretion may generally be preferred as a means of assuring freedom of choice. At the same time, one's real income is expanded to the degree that desirable community resources are available.   These may be in a variety of forms: food, housing, medical care, recreation and leisure-time facilities, education, subsidized transportation, and so on.   The more social provisions available free or at moderate fees, the less income it takes to live above the poverty line.   The test of social adequacy needs to apply however; that is, provisions must be free of the Poor Law stigma, must measure up to an acceptable standard of quality, and must be readily available to all who wish to use them or to those who have special entitlement on the basis of some noninvidious criteria (e.g., meals on wheels for the aged, school lunch program for all children, recreation facility for teen-agers).   The following is a brief review of some essentials available as social provisions in this society:

> A man says: "I am hungry."
> The government official responds: "We produce enough food each year to feed every American.   And we have a sufficient array of welfare and food assistance programs to insure that no American need go hungry, regardless of income."
> The hungry man answers: "Your programs don't work.   The food is not enough to nourish me.   The food stamps cost more than I can pay.   The school lunch programs are for children in suburban schools.   The welfare check is too small for survival.   I am still hungry." [219]

This is a brief assessment of the state of our food programs for the poor in 1968, taken from a report by the Citizens' Board of Inquiry into Hunger and

[218] Briar, "Why Children's Allowance?," *op. cit.*

[219] Citizens' Board of Inquiry into Hunger and Malnutrition in the United States, *Hunger, U.S.A.* (Washington, D.C.: New Community Press, 1968), p. 50.

Malnutrition in the United States. The board concluded that the hungry man was right and that in truth the situation was even worse. Only 18 percent of the poor had access to even the inadequate surplus commodities and food stamp programs, two of the major means by which food is directly made available to those with low incomes. The board of inquiry reported that it had found ". . . concrete evidence of chronic hunger and malnutrition in every part of the United States where we have held hearings or conducted field trips."

Board members were struck by the high incidence of anemia, growth retardation, protein deficiencies, and other signs of malnutrition among the poverty population. Noting "a shocking absence of knowledge in this country about the extent and severity of malnutrition," they suggested that a conservative estimate includes 10 million Americans.[220] Since the publication of the report by the Citizens' Board of Inquiry, the nation's attention has been focused on hunger and malnutrition. In June of 1969, President Nixon appointed Dr. Jean Mayer, professor of nutrition at Harvard, as his special consultant with responsibility for organizing a White House Conference on Food, Nutrition, and Health. The Conference was held in December of 1969 and produced a report that made the following assertion: [221]

> Hunger and poverty exist on a disgraceful scale in the United States. The Nation's conscience will no longer stand for the toleration of these conditions. Funds must be provided to get food to needy people on an emergency basis. The President and Congress must supply the leadership in closing the hunger gap.

The value of the Conference is open to question, regarded by some as a way of evading the problem of hunger by substituting talk for effective action. It has been ridiculed as a "carnival" that wasted $900,000 that might better have been spent to purchase school lunches for 196,000 needy children for one full month.[222] In June of 1970, two investigators commissioned by the White House to study the Federal food distribution system, declared that the federal food assistance programs create a "cruel illusion that effective action is being taken against hunger." [223]

While sufficient income is the preferred way to assure an adequate diet, we have relied on the commodity distribution program and food stamps as residual measures to feed the poor. The commodity distribution program, however, was originated primarily to promote the interests of the farmer not those of the poor consumer. Section 416 of the Agricultural Act of 1949 directed the Secretary of Agriculture to donate commodities acquired through price support operations to needy persons in order to prevent waste. In general, the food made available has depended on commodities that happen to be

[220] *Ibid.,* pp. 9, 32.

[221] White House Conference on Food, Nutrition and Health, *Final Report,* (Washington, D.C.: Government Printing Office, 1970), p. 17.

[222] The National Council on Hunger and Malnutrition in the United States, *Action Report,* Vol. I, Number 5, December 1969, p. 2.

[223] Jack Rosenthal, "Food Programs Called Deceptive," *The New York Times,* June 3, 1970.

in surplus, not on the nutritional requirements of the low-income consumer. Despite some attempts to expand the variety of food distributed, the general conclusion is that the commodity program does not provide for minimal nutritional requirements.[224] The board of inquiry concluded that the commodity distribution program was a failure for the following reasons: (1) The Department of Agriculture had permitted the states to impose restrictive eligibility requirements. (2) Too few of the hungry participate—over 300 of the poorest counties had no food program at all in 1968. (3) The department had failed to exercise its power to institute commodity distribution programs when the counties chose not to apply. (4) Those who do participate receive too little food and inadequate nutrition.[225] The major failure, as many have observed, is due to the conflict of interest within the Department of Agriculture, whose primary responsibility is to help the farmer, not feed the poor. Economic policy, not social welfare policy, has dictated the kind and amount of food made available. Recognizing that the Agriculture Department and related congressional committees were primarily concerned with maximizing farm income, the board of inquiry recommended that food programs be removed from the jurisdiction of the Department of Agriculture.

In theory, the food stamp program was intended to overcome the deficiencies of the commodity program. In some respects it does. The programs, however, are mutually exclusive, so that a county with one cannot have the other. Both are optional so that local determination often means the freedom to exclude the poor from provisions intended to benefit them. The 1964 act establishing the food stamp program, in characteristic congressional rhetoric, declares that it is the policy of Congress

> in order to promote the general welfare, that the nation's abundance of food . . . be utilized . . . to the maximum extent practicable to safeguard the health and well-being of the nation's population and raise levels of nutrition among low-income households.[226]

Families in need (with each state establishing its own eligibility standards) are provided an opportunity to purchase food stamps at rates equivalent to their normal expenditure for food. The program was designed to reach families irrespective of whether they happened to meet requirements of other welfare programs. The food stamps, by providing a bonus, expand the purchasing power of the family. For example, a family of four with a monthly income of a $100 a month could purchase $78 dollars worth of food stamps for $44. With an income of $140 they might have $86 worth of stamps for $56. With an income of less than $30 a month, $8 will purchase $52 worth of stamps. The stamps replace cash in grocery stores and, with some restrictions, consumers are free to purchase what they wish. The program, however, has its serious limitations and has failed to live up to the congressional intent. The amount the poor are required to pay for the stamps frequently does not reflect their normal expenditure for food, meaning that either they cannot afford the

[224] *Hunger, U.S.A., op. cit.,* p. 56.

[225] *Ibid.,* p. 56.

[226] Food Stamp Act of 1964, P.L. 88–525.

stamps or that they have too little cash left over after the stamp purchase for other necessities. As one woman put it, "Well the first time I was glad for the food stamps to come in and when I went down there I wasn't getting but $102 a month and I had to pay $48 for $114 worth and I can't afford to buy food stamps." [227]

A survey conducted by the Department of Agriculture to discover why families were not participating revealed that most felt the stamps cost too much or they did not have enough money to purchase them. Preliminary reports for the department indicated that the change from surplus food to stamps in the South caused a 40 percent drop in participation, and in 1966 a food source was cut off for at least 75,000 people.[228] The Citizen's Board of Inquiry concluded in 1968 that the Food Stamp Program failed to fulfill its promise because prices were set at prohibitively high levels, food stamp allotments were set too low to provide the purchasing power necessary to secure an adequate diet, and families without income were given no special consideration. Administrative red tape, insensitivity, and federal deference to "local initiative," which meant that communities indifferent to the needs of the poor could prevent their access to benefits intended for them, also accounted for the failure. Consequently the board recommended a free food stamp program to be administered by the Internal Revenue Service.[229]

The poor are not the only recipients of food programs. Indeed the school lunch program operates primarily for the benefit of the middle-class, another instance of the "iron law of welfare"—those in need get the least.[230] The fact that school lunches are available to the middle class is itself no condemnation of the program. It might be seen as a progressive step toward universal social provisions. Indeed, the establishment of school lunch programs in other countries was part of the separation of welfare from Poor Law stigma. School meals established in England in the nineteenth century for "necessitous children" were by 1945 being offered irrespective of income as a universal provision "promoting solidarity and the unity of the nation." [231] Norway, Denmark, Finland, Sweden have for some time provided school meals as a universal provision, although there too their origin lay in residual efforts to aid needy children. Perhaps only in the United States are school meals used to aid the rich and discriminate against the poor. Some needy children do receive the benefits of the school lunch program. Estimates are that, at most, one-third of poor children attending public schools participate in a program clearly intended to benefit them. The national school lunch act declares that they shall "be served without cost or at a reduced cost." Yet ". . . a majority of poor children are forced to pay the full price for school lunch or go without.

[227] *Hunger, U.S.A., op. cit.*, p. 58.

[228] Thorkelson, H., "Food Stamps and Hunger in America," *Dissent*, 14 (1967), pp. 479–484.

[229] *Hunger, U.S.A., op. cit.*, p. 66.

[230] Martin Rein, "The Strange Case of Public Dependency," *Trans-action*, 2 (March–April 1965), pp. 16–23.

[231] Asa Briggs, "The Welfare State in Historical Perspective," in Mayer N. Zald (ed.), *Social Welfare Institutions* (New York: Wiley, 1965), p. 42.

The school lunch in fact operates for the benefit of the middle class." [232] Local communities determine eligibility for the free lunch. The fee of $.25 to $.35 a day is too costly for many children from poor families. In some instances children deprived of lunch are forced to sit in the cafeteria while other children are eating to "avoid supervisory problems during the lunch hour." [233] In some schools where poor children do receive free lunches they are made to stand in a special line, indicating their welfare status. Mitchell I. Ginsberg described this degradation ceremony in New York City:

> New York City provides free lunches to the children of welfare families. If you're not on welfare, you pay 35¢. To ease the administrative problems in some of our schools when lunch time comes, the teacher says: "Those of you on welfare, go on that side of the room; and those of you paying for your lunch, go on the other side of the room." [234]

Of course $.35 does not quite pay for the lunch but it provides the sense of entitlement to the federal and state subsidy that supports this provision. Unfortunately the program is financed in a way that invites discrimination against those who cannot afford the price charged for the school lunch. For every dollar of federal money the state must put up three. The amount charged to children contributes to the state share.[235] Although the federal law requires that poor children get free meals or meals at reduced price, this provision is simply not enforced, partly because states do not wish to bear the cost, partly because there are no clear standards to determine inability to pay, and partly because the discretion is left to the local community, sometimes to the homeroom teacher. Lack of cafeteria facilities, especially in low-income schools, is also an obstacle. Despite a congressional act authorizing funds to construct cafeteria facilities, too little has been appropriated to sufficiently expand the capacity to feed schoolchildren. Although the school is a natural setting for the delivery of a variety of social provisions to poor children that could materially contribute to their welfare, we have failed to assure to all children even so basic a thing as their daily bread.

HEALTH AND MEDICAL CARE. Deep value conflicts also inhibit adequate social provision of medical care and other resources to meet the health needs of our population. Again we are not quite able to fully agree that medical care is a citizen right to be available to all, nor are we able to organize the financing and delivery of our medical services accordingly. We seem, however, to be moving in this direction. In passing the 1966 Comprehensive Health Planning and Public Health Services Amendment Act, Congress declared that ". . . fulfillment of our national purpose depends on promoting and assuring the highest level of health attainable for every person, in an environment which contributes

---

[232] *Hunger, U.S.A., op. cit.,* p. 68.

[233] *The New York Times,* June 20, 1969.

[234] Ginsberg, "Changing Values in Social Work," *op. cit.,* p. 11.

[235] *Hunger, U.S.A., op. cit.,* p. 68.

positively to healthful individual and family living." [236]   Federal financial support was directed toward this end, "to assure comprehensive health services of high quality for every person, *but without interference with existing patterns of private professional practice of medicine, dentistry, and related healing arts."* [Emphasis added.]

Here is as good an example as one can find of the conflict between the organizational and the humanitarian mores. Yet it appears that national awareness of a crisis in medical care will bring about some major reorganization of financing and delivering health services that cannot help but interfere with existing patterns of private medicine.

The crisis in the delivery of health care comes at a time when most Americans are enjoying a longer life span and improved health as compared with previous generations. In 1966 life expectancy was 70.1 years compared to 49.2 at the turn of the century. Infant mortality rates sharply declined in the first half of the twentieth century (but have changed little in the past decade), and there have been major reductions in the incidence of acute illness and communicable diseases. Today the leading causes of death are cardiovascular diseases and cancer. For those under age thirty-five, however, accidents are the great killer.

Although advances in medical science and rising standards of living have produced striking improvements in health and life expectancy, this nation does not compare favorably with other developed countries in a number of indices of health. People in at least fifteen nations have a longer life expectancy at birth than those in the United States; some twenty-seven countries, at the beginning of the 1960s, had lower age-adjusted death rates for heart disease among males than had the United States; more than a dozen countries have lower rates of ulcers, diabetes, cirrhosis of the liver, hypertension without heart involvement, and accidents, and at least fourteen nations in 1963–1964 had lower rates of infant mortality.[237]

The infant mortality rate is an important measure of the health of our people and of the relative equality of life circumstances. If the Swedish infant mortality rate (14.8 per 1,000 live births compared to our 25 in 1963–1964) prevailed in this country, at least 40,000 fewer infant deaths would have been recorded annually in the early 1960s. The latest available figures reveal an infant mortality rate of 21.7 for the United States in 1968 and 12.9 for Sweden in 1967.[238] While mortality rates have dropped considerably for both white and nonwhite mothers and infants over the past two and a half decades, the disparities are still evidence of unequal life circumstances and unequal access to resources related to health. As Table 22 reveals, the nonwhite maternal mortality rate was more than three times the white rate in 1966. Mortality rates for nonwhite infants (one month to one year) were almost three times

[236] Comprehensive Health Planning and Public Health Services Amendments of 1966, PL 89–749.

[237] *Toward a Social Report,* U.S. Department of Health, Education, and Welfare (Washington, D.C.: Government Printing Office, 1969), p. 67; Metropolitan Life Insurance Co., *Statistical Bulletin,* 48 (May 1967), 6.

[238] Frank Faulkner, "Infant Mortality: An Urgent National Problem," *Children,* Vol. 17 (May–June 1970), p. 82.

that of white infants. Low-income children in general have twice the risk of dying before their first birthday as do the children of more affluent parents. The findings of the National Health Survey clearly confirm the link between poverty and ill health, supporting the oft-quoted remark of Dr. Charles W. Mayo that "sickness makes people poor and poverty makes people sick." The survey reveals that, in spite of the increased level of illness of low-income people and their greater need for health care, they "receive fewer health services than people with higher incomes." [239] The relevance of ill health to the problem of

Table 22. Maternal and Infant Mortality Rates, Selected Years, 1940–1966

| | MATERNAL (PER 1,000 LIVE BIRTHS) | | INFANT (PER 1,000 LIVE BIRTHS) | | | |
| | | | LESS THAN 1 MONTH OLD | | 1 MONTH TO 1 YEAR | |
	Nonwhite	White	Nonwhite	White	Nonwhite	White
1940	7.7	3.2	39.7	27.2	34.1	16.0
1950	2.2	0.6	27.5	19.4	17.0	7.4
1960	1.0	0.3	26.9	17.2	16.4	5.7
1961	1.0	0.2	26.2	16.9	14.5	5.5
1962	1.0	0.2	26.1	16.9	15.3	5.5
1963	1.0	0.2	26.1	16.7	15.4	5.5
1964	0.9	0.2	26.5	16.2	14.6	5.4
1965	0.8	0.2	25.4	16.1	14.9	5.4
1966	0.7	0.2	24.8	15.6	14.0	5.0

SOURCE: "Recent Trends in Social and Economic Conditions of Negroes in the United States," *Current Population Reports,* Series P–23, No. 26, U.S. Bureau of the Census, and Bureau of Labor Statistics Report No. 347 (Washington, D.C.: Government Printing Office, 1968), p. 21.

economic dependency is revealed by a recent study conducted by HEW that estimates that one-fifth to one-fourth of recipients of Aid to Families with Dependent Children are in need because of the illness or physical disability of the family wage earner.[240]

The problem of ill health extends beyond the question of availability of medical care, important though this is. We are increasingly aware that health cannot be separated from one's social environment and the style of life it nurtures. For the poor, increases in levels of income, improved housing, decent employment, education, and opportunities for self-respect may contribute more to alleviating problems of health than extension of medical care.[241]

[239] Forrest E. Linder, "The Health of the American People," *Scientific American,* 214 (June 1966).

[240] *Manpower Report,* 1969, op. cit., p. 170; U.S. Department of Health, Education, and Welfare, SRS news release, June 24, 1969.

[241] Philip R. Lee, "Health and Well-Being," in Bertram M. Gross (ed.), *Social Intelligence for America's Future* (Boston: Allyn & Bacon, 1969), p. 435.

For all of us, the style of life that our social system offers or forecloses has implications for the pursuit of some positive goal of health. Health is not simply the absence of disease and infirmity but an integral part of our interest in the quality of life, and it is the style of life we lead that seems to underlie many major contemporary health problems.[242]   To Dr. Jean Mayer our shockingly high rates of auto accidents and homicides reflect a "carelessness regarding human life which characterizes our society." Arteriosclerosis, as he notes, will respond better to a change in our sedentary mode of life and in our diet than to improvements in medical care. Planned communities that encourage people to exercise by providing walkways, parks, recreation areas, and such facilities as swimming pools and community tennis courts are health-related measures if we think beyond the treatment of illness and disability. Promotion of health requires an ecological view of the community, the supports it offers to life, and the values it upholds that express our conviction of the worth of individuals. In his book, *Equality,* R. H. Tawney recognizes this when he quotes a physician as follows:

> Health . . . is a purchasable commodity, of which a community can possess, within limits, as much or as little as it cares to pay for. It can turn its resources in one direction and fifty thousand of its members will live who would otherwise have died; it can turn them in another and fifty thousand will die who would otherwise have lived.[243]

As it turns out the poor are likely to make up a disproportionate number of the victims of a system that turns its resources away from life and the nurture of life. Poverty, as already noted, is the third leading cause of death in American cities.[244]

A small-scale, but very hopeful, development has been the establishment of neighborhood health centers under the Economic Opportunity Act. Centers, organized in a variety of ways to meet the needs of particular localities, have common approaches that differ vastly from the traditional delivery of health services to the poor—primarily in that they are run for the convenience of the patients. They offer comprehensive health services emphasizing prevention, all facilities for all family members under one roof, treatment of the family as a unit, outreach, no humiliating means investigation, choice of doctor, evening and weekend appointments, and so forth. They are equipped for emergencies and each is allied with a local hospital. The goal of the Office of Economic Opportunity was to have fifty centers operating by the end of 1968, but it is estimated that 850 health centers are needed to serve the poor alone.[245]   All of

---

[242] *Toward a Social Report, op. cit.,* pp. 7–8; Stanley A. Rudin, "The Personal Price of National Glory," *Trans-action,* 2 (September–October, 1965), pp. 4–9; Jean Mayer, "The Doctor's First Job—Preventing Sickness," *The New York Times Magazine,* November 28, 1965.

[243] R. H. Tawney, *Equality* (New York: Harcourt Brace, 1931), p. 179.

[244] Joseph T. English, M.D., "Health Among the Poor: The Challenge to U.S. Medicine," *Poverty and Health* (New York: National Tuberculosis and Respiratory Disease Association, 1969), p. 1.

[245] Judith Randal, "The Bright Promise of Neighborhood Health Centers," *The Reporter,* (March 21, 1968), pp. 15–18.

the centers emphasize employment of the poor in a variety of health roles including family health workers, home health aides, laboratory aides, assistants to physicians and nurses, and family planning aides.

A relatively new development in the direction of comprehensive health care is government sponsorship of family planning services. It was not until the second half of the decade of the sixties that the federal government became involved in the provision of birth control information and contraceptives. Concern over population growth, recognition of a link between poverty and family size, awareness of the personal and social ill-effects of unwanted children, and increasing sensitivity to the issue of freedom of low income women to exercise the same choice in control of births available to more affluent women—all helped to overcome traditional taboos against public support of family planning. By 1969 some 800,000 poor women had obtained family planning assistance through a variety of federally sponsored programs. Estimates are that as many as five million low income women may be in need of family planning services.

The heavy burden of child care is itself a cause of poverty and a barrier to equal opportunity for the poor. For example, in 1966 poor adults of working age (18–64) had more than double the number of children to support and care for as did more affluent adults.[246] The arrival of children before one is prepared to care for them may close off opportunities for personal growth and career development, not to mention the harm that may be inflicted on an unwanted child. There is no evidence that in general the poor desire more children than the non-poor. Between 1960 and 1965 however, low income women of child-bearing age (15–44) had an average of 153 births per 1,000 women compared to 98 for non-poor women. Given equal access to family planning it may be assumed that low income women would have a fertility rate similar to that of other women. If that assumption is correct, low income women gave birth to more than 400,000 unwanted children in 1966 whose conception might have been prevented at an estimated cost of $300 per unwanted birth. Apart from more significant human and social gains, the economic benefit to a family in avoiding the birth of one unwanted child is estimated to be approximately $7800. This is an average figure that takes into account the cost of child care and wages earned by some women who might be free to work, and represents a ratio of benefits to costs of 26 to 1. Although we do not fully know the degree to which the higher fertility rate of low income women is related to lack of access to birth control, such evidence as we have indicates this is a significant factor. The ready acceptance of family planning services by many of the poor seems to support this, despite fears expressed by some black militants that publicly supported family planning is a form of genocide.

In government circles there is an increasing readiness to expand support for family planning. In July 1969 President Nixon proposed a major expansion of federal birth control programs. Included in his special message to Congress

---

[246] Unless otherwise noted, the data cited in this section in support of family planning services is derived from Arthur A. Campbell, "The Role of Family Planning In The Reduction of Poverty," reprinted in *Congressional Record,* Vol. 115, No. 194, November 24, 1969, pp. S 14923–14927.

was a proposal to establish a commission to study the implications of population growth in the United States. The message also contained a pledge that birth control programs would not be "allowed to infringe upon the religious convictions or personal wishes and freedom of any individual." [247]   In July of 1970, one year following the President's message, the Senate adopted, without debate or dissent, a bill providing for comprehensive family planning services for all women in the United States who cannot afford them, including birth control pills, and other means of contraception, along with consultations, examinations, and referral to other medical services.[248]   Since similar legislation was under consideration in the House, such extended family planning services appears to be reasonably certain of enactment by Congress.

Access to family planning as part of comprehensive medical care is an essential part of the overall attack on poverty. But access to quality medical care is not simply a problem for the poor. It is increasingly a national crisis affecting all citizens. A White House Report on Health Care Needs sees a ". . . breakdown in the delivery of health care unless immediate concerted action is taken by Government and the private sector." [249]   A National Advisory Commission on Health Manpower affirms a "crisis in American health care." In its report it maintains that the crisis lies in the system for the delivery of health services, not solely in the lack of funds or trained health manpower:

> Unless we improve the system through which health care is provided, care will continue to become less satisfactory, even though there are massive increases in cost and in numbers of health personnel. . . . Because the present system channels manpower into inefficient and inappropriate activities, added numbers by themselves cannot be expected to bring much improvement.[250]

The heart of the crisis is the inability of the private system of medical care to meet the demands of a scientific and democratic revolution that calls for expanded services and new structures for the delivery of health care. The failure is political too—the inability of society to respond to early signs of a pending crisis and to take planned and rational steps to expand the capacity of the medical care system to meet the needs of its citizens. An example of this was the rejection of a 1948 proposal put forth by Oscar Ewing, administrator of the Federal Security Agency, for a comprehensive plan for federal support of the extension of medical care geared to gradual planned expansion of medical schools, hospitals, and other medical resources.[251]   The opposition of the medical profession and the general American phobia about intelligent planning

[247] *The New York Times,* July 19, 1969.

[248] Harold M. Schmeck, Jr., "Wide Family Planning Aid For Poor Passed in Senate," *The New York Times,* July 15, 1970.

[249] *The New York Times,* July 11, 1969.

[250] *Report of the National Advisory Commission on Health Manpower,* Vol I. (Washington, D.C.: Government Printing Office, 1967), p. 3.

[251] Oscar Ewing, *The Nation's Health: A Ten Year Program* (Washington, D.C.: Government Printing Office, 1948).

for the future permitted development of the current situation, in which citizen demand clearly exceeds the capacity of the system to respond. The result is a critical inflation, with costs of medical care rising over twice that of the general cost of living. Doctors' fees increased at the annual rate of 3 percent prior to 1965; since that time they have risen at the rate of 6 percent. The cost of one day of hospital care has increased from $44 in 1965 to $70 in 1969 to an anticipated cost of $100 by 1972.[252]

In part, the crisis stems from poorly conceived efforts to extend medical care without corresponding efforts to increase the capacity of the medical care system to meet the demand. Both the Medicare and Medicaid legislation of 1965 expanded the funding of medical care but not the number of personnel and medical facilities.[253] In 1969 federal expenditures for Medicaid were $2.5 billion, more than twice the estimates made at the time of its passage.[254] Hailed at the time of its passage as a significant advance in health care for the poor, it has more recently been described as ". . . one of the largest abortions ever produced by a centralized agency" by Dr. John H. Knowles. He maintains that it has simply perpetuated a system of welfare medicine for the poor. Medicaid is part of our public welfare system and, as Melvin A. Glasser warned shortly after passage of the act, it does tend to maintain a dual system of medical care to the detriment of the poor.[255] Medicare and Medicaid "enacted into law the worst features of prevailing arrangements" and "dumped hundreds of millions into the fee for service, solo practice market economy." [256] The insurance feature (Medicare) does not encourage preventive care; in fact it promotes the more costly alternative of hospitalization. The welfare feature (Medicaid) "exerts economic bids in favor of acute episodic care and interposes an obnoxious means test between the patient and the care needed." [257]

It has, however, extended medical care to some of those unable to pay for it. Like our other public assistance programs, it is a grant-in-aid provision in which the federal and state (and sometimes local) governments share the costs of services for low-income people. For those receiving public assistance the state must provide the following services: (1) inpatient hospital services (other than

[252] "White House Report on Health Care," *New York Times*, July 11, 1969.

[253] The Hill-Burton Act of 1946, originally intended to stimulate construction of rural hospitals, was revised in 1964 (PL 88–443) to include modernization—especially in urban slums. Under this legislation, by 1967 the government had helped build over 2,600 clinics, public health centers, and rehabilitation centers and had added some 388,000 hospital and nursing home beds. (*See* "What are the Pay-Offs from our Federal Health Programs?" [New York: National Health Education Committee, 1968], p. 27.) Several pieces of legislation in the 1960s were intended to increase health manpower, such as the Health Professions Educational Assistance Amendments of 1965 (PL 89–290) and the Allied Health Professions Personnel Training Act (PL 89–751). None of these have been sufficient in scope to meet the need.

[254] *The New York Times*, July 11, 1969.

[255] *Portland* (Maine) *Press Herald*, June 23, 1969.

[256] Melvin A. Glasser, "Extension of Public Welfare Medical Care: Issues of Social Policy," *Social Work*, 10 (October 1965), pp. 3–9.

[257] Gerard Piel, "An End to Welfare Medicine," *Trustee* 21, an undelivered speech at Cornell University Medical School, December 1968, quoted in "Notes and Comments," *Social Service Review*, 43 (March 1969), p. 90.

services in an institution for tuberculosis or mental disease), (2) outpatient hospital services, (3) other laboratory and X-ray services, (4) skilled nursing home services (other than services in an institution for tuberculosis or mental diseases) for individuals twenty-one or older, (5) physicians' services, whether furnished in the office, the patient's home, a hospital, a nursing home, or elsewhere.

All states are required to have the program by 1970. Those receiving public assistance as well as some other low-income individuals who would be eligible except for restrictive state requirements must be covered. By 1970 all "medically indigent" were to be included. While states set their own standards to define the medically needy, in the 1967 Amendments to the Social Security Act Congress set a maximum income level for federal financial participation in the cost of medical assistance at a level no higher than one-third above the usual public assistance level. For example, if a four-person AFDC family is allowed a total monthly public assistance grant of $120, a medically needy family of the same size in that state cannot have an income above $160 and still receive medical services. This has caused serious cutbacks in the availability of even this limited program to the poor. In New York State the legislature responded by reducing appropriations for medical assistance and by requiring certain Medicaid patients to pay 20 percent of their medical costs before they could receive government aid. In New York City alone some 200,000 low-income residents faced the loss of Medicaid benefits. In New York as elsewhere, when the budget was tight the easiest things to cut were the resources that go to the poor. It was, as one state legislator described it, "a sock-the-poor budget." [258]

It is not likely that medical care for the poor can be solved without solving the problem of medical care for all citizens, although delivery of medical services to the poor may still pose some special problems. An increase in allocation of resources to health, new methods of financing expansion in the number of medical care personnel, and a basic restructuring of the delivery of health services are required.[259] Both the citizen aspiration for comprehensive high-quality medical care and the scientific-technological revolution have made the "cottage industry" model of private medical care obsolete. As Eveline Burns has noted, the "solo practice" of medicine is outmoded:

> It is impossible for a single physician now to provide the range of modern medicine; practice becomes rapidly obsolescent; and new structures are required for the effective linkage of knowledge, skills and equipment requiring a greater degree of teamwork, coordination of specialists, and organization of medical practice related to a hospital or medical center.[260]

[258] *The New York Times,* March 30, 1969.

[259] Changes in methods of delivery and financing health care are on the horizon as indicated by the promise of the Nixon Administration to present to Congress by February 15, 1971 a proposal for restructuring and improving the medicaid program and by its commitment to introduce a family health insurance plan.

[260] Eveline M. Burns, "The Challenge and the Potential of the Future," *Report on Comprehensive Community Health Services for New York City* (New York: Commission on the Delivery of Personal Health Services, 1967).

Clearly the delivery of health services must become more social rather than individual in its orientation, both in terms of its structure and in terms of its purpose. The extent to which the medical care system can adapt to the new reality is an open question. The White House Report on Health Care Needs put the challenge in this way: "What is ultimately at stake is the pluralistic, independent, voluntary nature of our health care system. We will lose it to pressure for monolithic Government-dominated medical care unless we can make the system work for everyone in this nation." [261] The emphasis is misplaced, however much there are indeed legitimate concerns about monolithic government-dominated medical care. What is at stake is the individual's right to life and society's obligation to find the structures and resources most suited to meeting the needs of the person, not the preservation of any given system. The social provision of medical care can in all likelihood develop through some new synthesis of the public and private sectors, but only if the interests of the consumer—not those of the profession—and allied vested interests are given priority. The reconstruction of medical care, like all social reconstruction, requires some moral vision of the goal we are seeking. Richard Lichtman has offered the following: "The true moral justification for a program of social medical care lies in the fact that health is a fundamental constituent of a fully realized human life, and that each of us is responsible to his fellows for the highest development of that life." [262]

HOUSING. We may approach the problem of housing from the same moral perspective because, for all the enormous economic, political, and technical complexities involved, housing turns out to be essentially a value problem. We are concerned here with far more than the provision of decent shelter. The housing we make available symbolizes the value we attach to individual dignity and to the quest for community. No one has understood this better than Alvin Schorr, who sees clearly that housing policy must help ". . . create and support a sense of community." [263] A community assures to each individual a respectable place to live, work, and carry on the responsibilities of citizenship. What makes a slum is not simply the physical characteristics accompanying substandard housing, but the demoralization associated with occupying a dwelling that symbolizes one's social rejection. The recipient of welfare, the patient of charity medicine, the occupant of a slum dwelling or of a stigmatized public housing project, may each experience an assault on self-esteem. It is the symbolic meaning, the sign of deviance, that society attaches to these modes of experience that is of critical importance. The housing problem then may be seen as a *social* problem from three perspectives: (1) It stems from the failure of a social institution, the market system, to produce the number and quality of houses required. (2) It can be solved only through expanded social responsibility for allocating resources sufficient in scope to close the housing gap.

[261] *The New York Times,* July 11, 1969.

[262] Richard Lichtman, *Toward Community* (Santa Barbara, Calif.: Center for the Study of Democratic Institutions, 1966), p. 26.

[263] Alvin L. Schorr, "National Community and Housing Policy," *Social Service Review,* 39 (December 1965), p. 433.

(3) Its solution depends on providing housing that identifies the occupant as a member of the community.

Income, medical care, and housing cannot be adequately provided through the free market. Some social provision in direct or indirect subsidy is essential. So far as housing is concerned, the Commission on Urban Problems writes that, ". . . to expect the free market to supply housing for all Americans without subsidy requires a flight from reality."[264] As we already observed in Chapter Two, most Americans have benefited from some form of housing subsidy through income tax deductions or the low interest rates available under FHA or Veterans Administration loans. It is estimated that in tax deductions alone, middle- and high-income groups have received about three and a half times as much in housing subsidies than have the poor in direct housing subsidies to them.[265] The simple fact is that, while our housing policy has been extremely successful in enabling the majority of American families to benefit from improved housing, the poor and a significant group above the poverty line have been left out. They are without personal or social resources sufficient to attain the American norm of a desirable house.[266]

Estimates on the percentage of the population who might be described as "housing poor" vary. A conservative estimate by the President's Committee on Urban Housing is that approximately 7.8 million families (one in every eight) are priced out of the market for standard housing that would cost them no more than 20 percent of their total income.[267] Of central importance is the fact that nonwhites must earn one-third more than whites to afford standard housing.[268] If a family is poor, nonwhite, and large, most likely it is living in substandard housing. Estimates are that 11 million housing units are substandard and overcrowded. Over 6 million are substandard. The President's Committee on Urban Housing recommended that 26 million units be built or rehabilitated by 1978, including 6 to 8 million with federal subsidies for families needing housing assistance.

But nothing of this order seems likely despite the Housing Act of 1968, described by President Johnson as the "Magna Carta to liberate our cities"; it could, if implemented, go a long way toward solving our housing problem. The act reaffirms the goal of the 1949 Housing Act: "a decent home and suitable environment for every American family." Yet in the two decades since that pledge we have built fewer units of public housing for low-income families than Congress declared in 1949 were needed in the next six years. Moreover many that were built do not qualify as decent homes; nor do they provide a suitable environment, mostly because they were designed as residual

[264] *Building the American City*, National Commission on Urban Problems, *op. cit.*, p. 10.

[265] *Ibid.*, p. 27.

[266] Nathan Glazer, "Housing Policy and the Family," *Journal of Marriage and the Family*, 29 (February 1967), p. 163.

[267] *Building the American City*, *op. cit.*, p. 9; and *A Decent Home*, President's Committee on Urban Housing (Washington, D.C.: Government Printing Office, 1969), p. 7.

[268] *A Decent Home, ibid.*, p. 8.

social provisions and have tended to become, as Michael Harrington once said, the twentieth-century equivalent of the poorhouse. Throughout most of the history of public housing Congress has insisted that projects have few amenities. The Housing Act of 1954 promoted the building of ". . . high density, min-imum-amenity projects . . . now looked upon by many as 'horror' cases demonstrating a lack of understanding that adequate housing means more than four walls, a roof, and a door." [269]

In countries like Sweden, subsidized housing for those with low incomes is designed to be indistinguishable from dwellings occupied by the average family. The insistence on maintaining their second-class citizenship status goes a long way toward explaining the failure of our housing program for the poor. Federal effort has met about one-tenth of the nation's subsidized housing need in over a third of a century.[270] It is a failure of our political economy. The market responds very well to the needs of those with effective demand, those with incomes that can assure construction at a profit. The distribution of political power and our political philosophy cannot seem to produce the moral commitment and the matching resources to overcome the intricate network of banking interests, real estate interests, zoning regulations, construction industry, labor unions, and overlapping governmental units that affect the production and allocation of housing.[271] Commenting on the frustration of reformers who sought to rid Chicago of its tenements, Edith Abbott wrote, ". . . gradually it became clear that the housing problem is almost as immovable as the Sphinx." [272]

In recent years urban renewal, highway construction, code enforcement, and demolition for other purposes have destroyed more housing for the poor than government at all levels has built. The outlook for the future, short of a new sense of national priorities, seems pessimistic. The Housing Act of 1968, how-ever, contains the authorization and many of the tools for making a major impact on the problem. It contains provisions for improved public housing, additional assistance to large families, special consideration for enabling low-income families to purchase homes, improved tenant services, upgrading of personnel in public housing administration, restraints on the construction of high-rise apartments, greater freedom in public housing design, major ex-perimental housing to reduce costs, and means to facilitate a better partnership between the public and private sectors to attract private resources to low and moderate housing.[273] Even so, it lacks a level of appropriation equal to its intent: the development of programs to eliminate in a decade all the sub-standard housing in this country.

The 1965 Housing Act provision for rent supplements to subsidize improved housing for the poor by providing grants that would make up the gap between the rent and 20 to 25 percent of the family income has been continued. Al-

---

[269] *Ibid.,* pp. 57, 61.

[270] *Ibid.,* p. 53.

[271] *Ibid.,* p. 115.

[272] Edith Abbott, *The Tenements of Chicago: 1908–1935* (Chicago: University of Chicago Press, 1936).

[273] *A Decent Home,* (President's Committee on Urban Housing,) *op. cit.,* p. 66.

though the rent supplement was called by President Johnson "the most crucial new instrument in our effort to improve the American City," it barely passed Congress in 1965 after a bitter fight and received only the most meager appropriations.[274]   The modest sum of $65 million requested for this measure in 1968 was reduced by Congress to an appropriation of $30 million.   Funds requested for the implementation for the entire 1968 Housing Act were reduced by almost one-half, from approximately $2.6 to $1.4 billion, the bulk of this going for Model Cities and Urban Renewal programs not directly related to housing the poor.   To achieve the goal of 6 million subsidized low-income units would require 600,000 units a year or about twenty times the annual volume of public housing in the past decade; the estimated cost would be about $12 billion a year, or well over a total cost of $100 billion.   Moreover, housing costs are likely to rise sharply in the next decade, which will inflate this figure.   In addition to public reluctance to make this kind of investment, other obstacles to solving the housing problem are restrictive building codes, union work rules, and the failure to apply modern technology to housing construction. In the view of Ada Louise Huxtable, the ". . . hard truth is that there is absolutely no way, with current tools, procedures and appropriations, of solving America's basic shelter problem." [275]

None of this takes into account what is perhaps the greatest obstacle of all— the racial and social class prejudices that create barriers to community integration and help maintain the ghettos of the poor, the discriminated against, and the excluded.   As the Committee on Urban Problems observed: "A lot of the rules of our society will have to be changed before anything meaningful can be done to right the wrongs of our most disadvantaged and helpless citizens." [276]   Some meaningful things are being done and are worth continuing.   Almost everywhere in the field of social welfare, however, we confront the same moral problem: the failure of community, the uncritical celebration of the values of a commercial industrial society, the subordination of man to science and technology, and the acceptance of the social and human costs of a social system that cannot find a dignified place for all its citizens.   No one denies that to provide every American family with "a decent home and suitable environment" would be an extraordinary feat, about as "unlikely," as Tom Wicker has observed, "as putting a man on the moon." [277]   It would require increasing the income of the poor, cutting the costs of housing, providing large amounts of subsidies for low income dwellings.   It would mean a readiness to pay the costs, as Alvin Schorr has written, in money, status and security, that are the price of community; the money costs for decent housing, the status costs of accepting the poor as equals, and the cost in security to enable the poor to have a greater voice in political decisions.[278]

---

[274] Message to Congress, March 2, 1965.

[275] *The New York Times,* April 21, 1969.

[276] *A Decent Home, op. cit.,* p. 27.

[277] Tom Wicker, "In the Nation: The Far Side of the Moon," *New York Times,* July 22, 1969.

[278] Schorr, "National Community and Housing Policy," *op. cit.*

Poverty, Inequality, and Economic Policy

Issues of poverty and inequality and the quest for social security and social justice are inseparable from the contemporary thrust for further democratization of society. This renewed democratic revolution requires an economic base for the attainment of a more egalitarian society, one in which gross disparities of income are reduced and decent employment opportunities are assured. Economic policy promoting growth of the economy could assure that resources for expanded income maintenance programs and other important programs of social development are available with potentially less divisive political conflict than might otherwise be the case. Economic growth alone will remove some from poverty. In the past two decades almost all our progress in reducing poverty occurred in periods of economic prosperity. During 1949–53, 1954–56, and 1961 to the present, the annual decline in the number of individuals in poverty has averaged two million or more a year. If we were to continue at this rate poverty as we now measure it could be eliminated in about 10 years (5½ years at the 1968 rate).[279] Unfortunately, a great bulk of today's poor—the female-headed household, children, the disabled and the elderly—are least affected by economic growth. Thus, some redistribution of income is essential not only to lift them out of poverty but to deal with remaining issues of inequality for others who have attained the poverty line. Expanded economic growth eases if it does not guarantee the possibility of raising the income of the poor. At the present rate of economic growth federal revenues rise by $15 to $16 billion a year, some of which, particularly if combined with reductions in the amount expended for the military budget could be available for expanded social provisions. An increased rate of economic growth would make it even easier. The outcome of political conflict among competing interests will, however, determine the allocation of expanded resources. Economic growth, particularly if aimed at producing goods to meet social needs, can also help produce the jobs required for decent employment of the poor.[280] An improved manpower policy that guarantees the right to work, that directs attention to structural obstacles to employment, and that assures education, training, and supportive services to all those who wish to work or who might appropriately be expected to be in the labor force, is also an essential component of an overall strategy for enlarging social participation.

Unhappily, economic growth has its costs in destruction of the environment. It is doubtful that we can meet the ecological crisis without radically altering our conception of economic progress and our commitment to an overexpanding Gross National Product. This is graphically reflected in Kenneth Boulding's proposal, which wins the support of Robert Heilbroner, that the GNP now be renamed the Gross National Cost.[281] Instead of cheering every increment in

[279] United States Congress, *Economic Report of the President,* 1969, *op. cit.* pp. 155, 156, 159, and 160.

[280] Leon H. Keyserling, "Employment and the 'New Economics' " in Bertram M. Gross (ed.), *Social Intelligence for America's Future* (Boston: Allyn & Bacon, 1969), p. 341.

[281] Robert L. Heilbroner, "Ecological Armageddon," a review of *Population,*

economic growth we seem to have arrived at a point where a more ascetic way of life may have to replace the culture of high mass consumption, if man is not to utterly destroy the planet's capacity to support life.   In this event, reliance on unfettered economic growth to help solve the problems of poverty and inequality is self-defeating.   It is doubtful that the environmental crisis and the urban crisis can be met without a large measure of economic planning, significant income redistribution, expanded population control and a major reorientation in values supporting a consumer society.

Since the democratic revolution cannot be denied, values that affirm the individual's right to social participation and self-actualization must be embodied in new structures.   Social provisions of income, medical care and housing are among the resources that must be more equitably distributed and provided in a manner consistent with the claims of citizenship.   They are among the means for attainment of a more secure and just society.   Whether we are willing to pay the cost of developing such a society depends on the kind of human being we value and the social order we want.

Resources, Environment by Paul and Anne Ehrlich (W. H. Freeman, 1970) in *The New York Review of Books,* April 23, 1970, p. 6.

SEVEN

Social Welfare and Human Development: The Quest for an Adequate Socialization Structure

Socialization and the Ideals of a Democratic Society

From our democratic values we derive an answer, both simple yet enormously complex, to the question we posed at the end of the last chapter: What kind of human being do we value and what kind of society do we seek? Free men living in a community of free and equal men is the democratic ideal. Since ideals are, by their very nature, aspirations toward which we may continually strive rather than descriptions of reality, they offer a basis for criticism of existing social institutions, including our socialization structure. Socialization is the process by which we develop or fail to develop the capacity of individuals to participate effectively in society and to thereby contribute to its continuing renewal so as to enlarge the scope of human freedom.

Freedom is the exercise of choice among alternative possibilities. It requires socially structured opportunities to choose and capacities to exercise effective choice consistent with individual purpose and the shared goals of a community of free and equal men. Freedom means the existence of the widest possible range of choice, an ideal that demands that all internal and external constraints be justified as essential for the maintenance of democratic order. To expand freedom is to take into account new knowledge of the imperatives of human development and requirements for adapting to changing social reality. Continual renewal of social institutions is essential to foster the true self-reliant man, as Emerson so notably presented him to us. Emerson saw beyond the nineteenth-century narrow vision of economic self-reliance and recognized that the storing up of property was but "the want of self-reliance," the measuring of self-esteem ". . . by what each has, and not by what each is." Like Socrates, who taught us that the unexamined life was not worth living, Emerson revealed that self-reliance meant independent judgment of the values around which life is organized. The social sciences now support Emerson's image of self-reliance, revealing that it is not economic dependence that keeps man from attaining his full human stature, but slavish social dependence. This is the uncritical acceptance of the cultural fiction, that social script which provides us with our symbolic sense of self and the cues to our social performance in the drama we call society.[1] Freedom includes the degree of our participation in the creation of the social drama as well as the autonomy permitted in our role performance. It is more than the freedom of the market place or the freedom of the ballot box. The possibilities of freedom as well as its constraints are embedded in our social structure, in the way we socialize, educate, or miseducate our children, in the roles they can anticipate occupying, and in the ideals we uphold as worthy of our best energies. The free man is ethical man as distinct from moral man. In this context, morality is uncritical conformity to social definitions of right conduct. It is the culturally programmed behavior of social man, who adheres to group mores learned in childhood or who responds to the norms of whatever group happens to control the symbolic rewards required for a positive sense of self-value. It is the morality of W. H. Auden's *Unknown Citizen* and, in the extreme, that of an Eichmann ready to carry out any task provided it is imposed by an authority perceived to be legitimate.[2]

Ethical behavior involves independent judgment. It is autonomy in the face of established tradition, flexibility in determining conduct appropriate to unique situations. It is Huckleberry Finn choosing to violate the mores of a slave-holding society and acting ethically in order to behave toward Jim as a friend and fellow human being. The degree of freedom possible in any society will rest in large measure on the capacities of its citizens to contribute to the development of a community of free and equal men. Toward this end a democratic society

---

[1] Ernest Becker, *Beyond Alienation* (New York: George Braziller, 1967), p. 139; and Erving Goffman, *The Presentation of Self in Everyday Life* (Garden City, N.Y.: Doubleday, 1959).

[2] W. H. Auden, *The Collected Poetry of W. H. Auden* (New York: Random House, 1945), pp. 142–143; and Hannah Arendt, *Eichmann in Jerusalem: A Report on the Banality of Evil,* rev. ed. (New York: Viking Press, 1964). *See also* the report of research conducted by Stanley Milgram in *Trans-Action,* 6 (May 1969), 7–8. Adolf Eichmann was a Nazi bureaucrat who expedited the mass murder of Jews. When accused of genocide, his defense was that he was not personally responsible since he was only following the orders of his superiors. Milgram set up an experiment to discover how many people would follow orders to commit an inhuman act in order to learn to what extent any one of us might behave like Eichmann. In his ingeniously simulated experiment, subjects were ordered by a researcher to administer slight to severe and dangerous shock (from a realistic looking but actually a fake generator) to a man who presumably was participating in a study to test the effectiveness of shock in promoting learning. The conclusions of this pilot study indicate that ". . . a substantial proportion of people do what they are told to do, irrespective of the content of the act and without limitations of conscience, so long as they perceive that the command comes from a legitimate authority."

must critically assess how it goes about developing the potentialities of its members, and it must be prepared to commit its resources to their fullest realization. How to socialize human beings to have the capacity to participate in a free society and how to create those structures that provide maximum opportunities for the exercise of freedom are among the enduring questions that face a democratic society.

The Concept of an Adequate Socialization Structure

All societies must establish some orderly way of equipping their members with the values, attitudes, knowledge, and skills that will enable them to perform functions essential for maintaining the society and for adapting to changing reality. This is the definition of an adequate socialization structure from the point of view of any given society. In relatively stable societies governed by tradition, the extended family supported by a community of shared sentiments can effectively transmit to the growing child the values, attitudes, norms, and skills essential for social participation. In dynamic societies, as we noted in Chapter Three, the rapidity of change, the complex nature of life problems to be solved that defy established cultural prescriptions, and the decline of a community of shared morality undermines the capacity of the family to appropriately socialize the young. This is not to side with those who in a global way speak of the decline of the family for, as we shall point out in the next chapter, the actual situation is far more complex than that phrase can capture. It ignores the variations in family structures and resources; new societal functions of the family; lack of community supports for family responsibilities that may be at the source of its apparent "weakness"; and rising demands for human competence that the family alone cannot meet, not because it has declined in importance, but because it cannot alone command the resources in knowledge, personnel, and skills required for the challenge of human development in this era.

To some degree the responsibility for socialization shifts to formal organizations, particularly the schools. Other social services are given the responsibility for the control, treatment, and prevention of deviant behavior that tends to increase in all societies undergoing the related processes of industrialization, urbanization, and secularization. The school and other social services supporting, supplementing, and substituting for the family represent the quest for a socialization structure adequate to the needs of advanced industrial societies and to the goal of assuring to all individuals maximum opportunities for the development of their capacities. An adequate socialization structure, from the perspective of democratic values that place man at the center of concern, is one that prepares people with the competence to participate in society, to cope with changing reality, and to alter social institutions to more effectively promote the fullest development of all. We immediately confront a dilemma. Social system needs and human needs are both complementary and conflicting. The imperatives of our technological society may support and yet also undermine structures essential for the maximum development of our human potential, representing both a promise and a threat to human freedom. To socialize children to adapt to the needs of our social system is to both expand and constrict their freedom to develop their unique capacities for self-actualization.

Socialization and the Destruction of Self-Realization

If one accepts the judgment of Jules Henry, our socialization process is essentially destructive of the child's quest for self-realization. In Henry's view, it is the school in the service of processing children to fit into a technologically driven society that is the dominant instrument of socialization. Its primary function is the creation in children of the kind of self the culture demands, one organized around the ". . . competitive, achievement, and dominance drives." Toward this end, the major goal of the school is to instill in children the ". . . essential cultural nightmare fear of failure, envy of success, and absurdity."

> The early schooling process is not successful unless it has accomplished in the child an acquiescence in its criteria, unless the child *wants* to think the way the school has taught him to think. He must have accepted alienation as a rule of life. What we see in the kindergarten and the early years of school is the pathetic surrender of babies. How could it be otherwise? [3]

This perspective leads to the conclusion that a competitive, achievement-driven culture creates essential feelings of inadequacy that it then seeks to remedy through the mental health professions, whose function, in part, it is to ameliorate the excess stress of competition, to cushion failure, and to restore individuals to participation in the cultural game.[4] Many families have already prepared their children for this kind of acquiescence. As they enter school they are only too ready to continue to exchange their autonomy for the family-stimulated need for adult love and approval. Fearing most of all the loss of love, they handle the anxiety created by a competitive classroom situation by learning how not to learn, as my son once perceptively informed me. Instead they learn to give the teacher what she wants, adopting docility for personal growth in exchange for the assurance of being inside "the warmth of the inner circle of the teacher's sheltering acceptance." [5] On the other hand, Albert K. Cohen helps us to see that lower-class children who have not been prepared to adjust to the demands of the middle-class school system react by truancy and delinquency.[6] Whether through docility or through destructive rebellion, we have the human cost of our socialization mechanism, ill adapted to developing our individual potential. In the words of Edgar Z. Friedenberg, one finds in both suburban middle-class and inner-city lower-class schools a common ". . . banal, shabby, manipulative and utter dishonest environment in which both scholarship and

[3] Jules Henry, *Culture Against Man* (New York: Vintage Books, 1965), pp. 291, 292, and 305.

[4] *Ibid.*, p. 292; Edgar Z. Friedenberg, *Coming of Age in America* (New York: Random House, 1965); Edgar Z. Friedenberg, *The Vanishing Adolescent* (New York: Dell, 1962); Donald G. McKinley, *Social Class and Family Life* (New York: Macmillan, 1964). It should be pointed out that the best among the mental health professionals go beyond helping the individual to accommodate to the society. They seek to assist him in his efforts at self-actualization through a critical awareness of self and society.

[5] Jules Henry, "Docility, or Giving the Teacher What She Wants," *Journal of Social Issues,* 11 (April 1955).

[6] Albert K. Cohen, *Delinquent Boys: The Culture of the Gang* (Glencoe, Ill.: Free Press, 1955).

personal relationships are so deeply falsified and vulgarized that the question of discrimination becomes pure irony, since it is clear that those who succeed are as profoundly violated as those who fail." [7]

At the same time, there are crosscurrents of change, both reinforcing this surrender of self and militating against it. Our rapidly changing society needs people with the creative capacity for adaptation and for autonomy in the face of traditional cultural prescriptions that are ill suited to the new problems that must be solved.

Pro-life and Anti-life

This social need for people capable of renewing our social institutions seems consistent with the developing knowledge of man's intrinsic need for autonomy and self-directed growth. Here is the basis for some optimism and a clear direction for alteration in our socialization process, however difficult this may be to bring about. On the other hand, the deathly grip of tradition and the imperatives of our increasingly bureaucratized, rationalized, and technologically oriented society may set so narrow a limit on the kind of self-development functional for the postindustrial society that severe restrictions may be imposed on efforts to create a socialization structure oriented to the development of persons capable of open, spontaneous, creative responses to the demands of an organizational society. Such persons Erich Fromm and Michael Maccoby have chosen to call "life-loving" as distinct from those whose predominant orientation may be said to be "anti-life." [8] The former is primarily characterized by an intense love of life, an attraction to that which is alive, which grows, which is free and unpredictable. Such a person has an aversion to sterile, rigid order, to violence and destruction. At the other end of the continuum are those most attracted to the mechanical and to that which is not alive. They prefer rigid order, are uncomfortable with the free and unpredictable, and tend to feel that people ought to be controlled for their own good and the good of others. While most people are a blend of both orientations, it is the predominant tendency that seems to govern a person's behavior. The anti-life orientation tends to fit the "authoritarian personality," characterized by relatively poor self-image, inadequate mastery of coping skills, intolerance for ambiguity, an aversion for racial and ethnic differences, and a strong preference for the use of force in solving problems. There is some indication that such authoritarian orientations may tend to be inversely associated with socioeconomic position and levels of education.[9] It would seem that to humanize our social order requires that we learn how to develop people toward a pro-life orientation and to simultaneously develop a culture that celebrates life rather than the orderly and efficient destruction of life now symbolized by the power and the purpose of the giant military-indus-

[7] Edgar Z. Friedenberg, "What Are Our Schools Trying to Do?," *The New York Times Book Review*, September 14, 1969, p. 56.

[8] Erich Fromm, *The Heart of Man* (New York: Harper & Row, 1964); and *The New York Times*, August 14, 1968.

[9] Thomas S. Langner and Stanley T. Michael, *Life Stress and Mental Health* (New York: Free Press, 1963), p. 465; and James G. Martin, *Tolerant Personality* (Detroit: Wayne State University Press, 1964).

trial complex. Although personality alone does not explain behavior, since it is inseparable from socially structured roles that direct action, and although society undoubtedly requires a variety of personality types including the authoritarian, the kinds of human being we develop and their distribution in positions of leadership have enormous consequences for the level of decency and civility that will characterize our lives.[10]   The direction of socialization tends to be consistent with the dominant functional demands of society for individuals capable of filling its primary roles and achieving its major values.

Socialization for Living in a Culture of Science and Technology

Let us consider then the shape of our society and its requirements for maintenance and adaptation to change.   It is commonplace to note the complexity of our society.   Along with other Western nations, we are rapidly moving toward a postindustrial society organized around a culture of science and technology that requires for its maintenance and expansion an increasing pool of individuals with ever higher levels of competence in decision-making and problem-solving abilities.   Such a society is constrained to develop all its human resources to meet the needs of an occupational structure that requires an increasing number of scientists, professionals, managers, and technical workers.   All Western nations now experience critical shortages of trained manpower, which sets limits on the capacity for technological development; this creates pressures toward expanding educational and other opportunities to all social classes to maximize upward mobility.[11]   All institutions that limit the universal development of an achievement drive, appropriate cognitive skills essential for performing work requiring the mastery of language and mathematics, and a general capacity for continual learning may be said to be dysfunctional for such a society.   The family and the school come under critical scrutiny as it is increasingly recognized that their traditional structures may be poorly adaptive for socializing and educating for optimum cognitive development.   Class subcultures that may inhibit educational aspirations and attainment may be similarly dysfunctional for solving the manpower problem.   Efforts to expand educational and social opportunities for the fullest development of those human talents demanded by an advanced technological society lead to an emphasis on investments in human resources and on distributive justice.   In this sense a postindustrial society commits itself to social progress seeking to alter those social institutions that limit maximum development and efficient use of specialized skills required for technological advance.   At the same time, serious social policy dilemmas are raised regarding the right of families and groups to socialize their young in their own way regardless of social consequences.   This brief description of trends that seem apparent in all advanced technological societies

[10] Richard Christie and Marie Jahoda, *Studies In The Scope and Method of "The Authoritarian Personality"* (Glencoe, Ill.: Free Press, 1949), pp. 48–49; and Alex Inkeles, "Personality and Social Structure," in Robert K. Merton, Leonard Broom, and Leonard S. Cottrell, Jr. (eds.), *Sociology Today* (New York: Basic Books, 1962), pp. 249–275.

[11] John Porter, "The Future of Upward Mobility," *American Sociological Review,* 33 (February 1968), p. 5.

is of course only an approximation of social reality.   While some of these trends are discernible in the United States clearly they do not fully describe the American pluralistic, democratic, Calvinistic, commercial, capitalistic, individualistic society, which has some tendencies that support and some that resist the ever-increasing expansion of a culture of science and technology.

Humanist Rebellion Against Depersonalization of Life

In the United States and throughout the world there are humanist reactions against accommodating to the demands of an increasingly technological and rationalized society, with its heavy reliance on narrow functional intelligence, values that uphold productive efficiency as the chief end of life, and its tendency toward a mechanistic image of man.   A humanist renaissance, according to Erich Fromm, is taking place in the United States, in Western Europe, in some of the communist nations outside the Soviet Union, and in Latin America.   It affirms a belief in the essential unity of the human race, the dignity of the individual, and the need for a resacralization of life.   It rejects man as automaton and upholds a conviction of his self-actualizing potentialities consistent with the creation of the world order based on reason, objectivity, and peace.[12]   The goal of the humanist movement is not to escape science and technology but to subordinate it to human purpose.   Indeed, there may be only two major ideologies in the world today—the technological and the humanist.   Contrary to appearances, the capitalist and the communist worlds are in large measure ideological brothers, each committed to the same materialistic, managerial values of maximum productive efficiency and technological development.   All the advanced industrial nations are caught up in the same imperatives, dictated by ". . . the newest and most ruthless social game of all, the game of rational man—the game of numbers, calculation, efficiency: the uncompromising logic of modern bureaucracy."[13]   Max Weber, more than Karl Marx, has proven to be the prophet of the twentieth century.   The true subversion of a democratic society in the United States comes less from radicals who would overthrow it than from the efficient operation of formal organizations so structured as to deprive individuals of the power to exercise freedom of choice.   Our schools function less to enable individuals to understand and effectively cope with such concentration of power than to process children to surrender to organizational demands.   The school is the archetype of the bureaucratic system; it is designed to teach the child the docile surrender of self.

Humanizing a Technological Society

Needless to say the outcome of an accommodation between the imperatives of an advanced technological society and the humanist protest against its depersonalization of life is of crucial importance.   From this perspective an adequate socialization structure is one that prepares individuals to cope with an advanced technological system, for that seems inescapable, and yet at the same time, to

[12] Erich Fromm, lecture delivered at the University of California, Berkeley, 1966.

[13] Becker, *op. cit.,* p. 133; *see also* Donald Michael, *The Next Generation* (New York: Vintage Books, 1965).

work toward its increasing humanization, for that is desperately essential. While no such ideal structure exists anywhere and may be attainable only within limits, an effort to sketch even in barest form some of the features of such a structure is important if we are to nurture the development of human potential. It is clear that we are intervening in the socialization process in any event and shall continue to do so.   Much depends on our image of the kind of human being we are trying to develop and the knowledge and values we can bring to bear to justify the socialization structure we tolerate or create.

We know that to develop our human potential requires that we live in a learning environment, one that continually encourages us to go beyond any narrow and fixed view of ourselves, of social reality, of the values to which we commit our energies.   Our regard for the dignity and worth of all individuals requires that we prepare people to behave in ways that give concrete expression to democratic ideals, an obligation we accept in principle but for which we lack any adequate structure and process.   As Urie Bronfenbrenner observes, we have yet to develop a way of teaching children the ethics of a democratic society through the experience of living up to clearly defined expectations that require the exercise of responsibilities ". . . consistent with the welfare of all and the dignity of each." [14]   In our pluralistic society adequate socialization means, in part, the development of the ability to understand differences and to deal creatively with conflict—capacities we sadly lack, as Herbert Gans reveals in his study of Levittown.[15]   Unprecedented social change and the militant demand that we live up to our democratic ideals throws into question the socialization and education we have all experienced.   We see now that socialization is not a process to be confined to childhood or to be restricted to the family.   It involves a lifetime process of learning and unlearning.   The notion that most people are normally socialized and that some suffer from defects in socialization that make them the proper subjects of rehabilitation by social workers, psychiatrists, and others whose purpose it is to help deviants and the culturally deprived adjust to society entirely misses the point.   However much some individuals may require the therapeutic services of the mental health professions, we need to see the extent to which exclusive focus on deviants and their treatment is part of society's scapegoat mechanism, designed to deflect attention from a critical assessment of our culturally created style of life—the true source of our ailments.   This can be seen, for example, in a comprehensive study by the President's Commission On Law Enforcement and Administration of Justice, which reveals that the crime problem is deeply rooted in our way of life and that an effective approach requires ". . . a revolution in the way Americans think about crime":

> Many Americans take comfort in the view that crime is the vice of a handful of people.   This view is inaccurate.   In the United States today, one boy in six is referred to the juvenile court.   A Commission survey shows that in 1965 more than two million Americans were received in prisons or juvenile training schools, or placed on probation.   Another

[14] Urie Bronfenbrenner, "Introduction," in A. S. Makarenko, *The Collective Family* (New York: Doubleday, Anchor Books, 1967), p. xix.

[15] Herbert Gans, *The Levittowners* (New York: Pantheon Books, 1967), pp. 413–414.

Commission study suggests that about 40 percent of all male children now living in the United States will be arrested for nontraffic offenses during their lives. An independent survey of 1,700 persons found that 91 percent of the sample admitted they had committed acts for which they might have received jail or prison sentences.[16]

Noting that crime and delinquency is far more extensive than generally recognized and that many offenses go unreported, the commission relates the problem to the structure of society and recognizes that methods of treatment and control alone cannot suffice to make a significant impact on the problem.

> The Commission doubts that even a vastly improved criminal justice system can substantially reduce crime if society fails to make it possible for each of its citizens to feel a personal stake in it—in the good life that it can provide and in the law and order that are prerequisite to such a life. The sense of stake, of something that can be gained or lost, can come only through *real opportunity for full participation in society's life and growth.* [Emphasis added.] [17]

While improved methods need to be developed to assist those with special social handicaps, we are all in need of self-renewal—to use John W. Gardner's way of saying that in these critical times we must all gain new perceptions of social reality to make possible continuing democratic social development.[18] Part of the difficulty lies in our family experience. Socialization in childhood tends to create a prison in which we are protected from the anxiety of freedom of choice and the opportunity to develop our power of self-mastery and self-actualization. We do, however, require some such security in childhood, some ordered perception of the world, some definition of our place in the scheme of things. Man's very nature requires a socially defined sense of self. His quest for freedom rebels against the limited cultural definition of what he is and can become. Man is the undetermined animal who becomes determined by society. His powers are thereby both released and constricted. Unlike other animals, man is equipped with few if any instincts to direct his response to his environment. Social institutions substitute for instincts and may become just as mechanical and restricting. Through social institutions man derives his desperately needed symbolic sense of self-value and his definitions of the meaning of life. It is this reliance on others for one's sense of self that accounts for the paradox of freedom and social order. Martin Buber helped us to see this when he wrote, "Man is an audacity of life, unfixed and undetermined. He therefore requires confirmation." [19] Such social confirmation of selfhood re-

[16] *The Challenge of Crime in a Free Society,* President's Commission on Law Enforcement and Administration of Justice (Washington, D.C.: Government Printing Office, 1967), p. v.

[17] *Juvenile Delinquency and Youth Crime,* President's Commission on Law Enforcement and Administration of Justice (Washington, D.C.: Government Printing Office, 1967), p. 41.

[18] Gardner, *op. cit.*

[19] Will Herberg (ed.), *The Writings of Martin Buber* (Cleveland: World Publishing, 1956), p. 94.

lieves man's basic anxiety and at the same time makes man dependent on the social group. Ernest Becker highlights this tension between the individual and society when he observes that man has a desperate need for a symbolic sense of self-value but that society, in granting it to him, makes him the ". . . slave of habit and a narrow world view." [20]   In the words of William Blake, ". . . man has closed himself up, till he sees all things thro' the narrow chinks of his cavern." As Becker notes, it was Freud who helped us to see the critical significance of early training that exploits the anxiety of the child to mold him into a cultural artifact. Of course it is not that simple. The child and parent are actors in a transactional process. The child, receiving cues from parents, shapes himself into patterns of perception and action that will avoid anxiety stemming from the loss of parental love and approval. In this way the child learns to cope with the problem of winning parental support and to maintain his sense of self-value. There are, of course, enormous variations. However, the key problem that stems from early socialization, particularly in a dynamic society in which tradition is no longer an adequate guide to action, is the gap between coping mechanisms and social definitions learned in childhood and the reality demands that face the adult. The narrow and frequently distorted perceptions acquired in the family and in school may not be functional for the flexible adaptations required for coping with new and ambiguous situations that characterize changing social reality. They are also the inner constraints to personal freedom, self-reliance, and continued self-actualization.

Socialization and Social Structure

Socialization, however, is inseparable from the total social environment and the values embedded in our institutions. It is related to the family's place in the social system and the resources available to it for the performance of its responsibilities; the school's function in preparing people for the social roles they will carry; and the structure of roles that provide opportunities and constraints for freedom of action and development of self. To enlarge freedom of choice and to promote the development of man means a critical examination of the family, peer groups, schools, mass media, social agencies—all the components of our socialization process. It means discovering how to provide learning experiences based on knowledge of human development. It requires, in addition, values and roles that reward and facilitate human transactions oriented to the fullest self-development of all people.

Through social roles society distributes those functions (e.g., work, parental care of children, etc.) that must be performed if society is to maintain itself and realize values embodied in its institutions. Thus social order is possible when individuals do what is more or less expected of them in given social situations. In a dynamic society roles are rarely clearly defined and are often conflicting. Order, at least to some extent, is a necessary but not sufficient condition for a free society. There is a continuing tension between the claims of human freedom and the need for some minimum degree of social order, a conflict that needs always to be open, explored, and resolved in favor of the

[20] Ernest Becker, *The Structure of Evil* (New York: George Braziller, 1968), p. 275; and Becker, *Beyond Alienation, op. cit.,* p. 198.

maximum possible enlargement of individual autonomy.   Just as an orderly society is not synonymous with a good society, individual identity is not synonymous with social role, although it is inseparable from one's position in the social structure.   Ward Hunt Goodenough makes this clear:

> Identity is thus rooted in the social order. This is true both in the cognitive and substantive sense of who and what a person is and in the evaluative sense of how he is affectively regarded by his fellows and how he feels about himself. These things derive from his place in the social order, and from his ability to conduct himself according to the role relationships attaching thereto.[21]

This is clearly illustrated in the account of Dr. Poussaint, a Negro psychiatrist, describing his own feelings of impotence, rage, and humiliation at having to overtly genuflect by a "yes sir" response to a southern policeman's derogatory reference to him as "boy."

> "Alvin, the next time I call you, you come right away, you hear?   You Hear?" I hesitated.   "You hear me boy?"   My voice trembled with helplessness, but following my instincts of self-preservation, I murmured, "Yes sir."   Not fully satisfied that I had performed and acquiesced to my "boy status," he dismissed me with, "Now, boy, go on and get out of here or next time we'll take you for a little ride down to the station house." [22]

No amount of pride in self and in professional accomplishment could erase the socially sanctioned power of the police official to accord Dr. Poussaint an identity as less than a man.   Although identity is rooted in the social order, the roles available may fail to offer a satisfying basis for self-value.   They may constrict rather than free the individual to develop his unique potentialities by providing a definition of self that is fragmented, narrow, or debasing.   Societal roles may impose a heavy cost in self-esteem and in autonomy, illustrated by the role of racial outcast and welfare recipient and by occupational roles that subordinate the individual to an authority over which he can exercise no effective control.

A very hopeful trend is the redefinition of work as a career involving continuing self-development and the movement toward humanizing the work environment.   In the view of Marshall McLuhan the possibility of cybernating the production of material goods allows us to think of jobs in a new way.   "The job is whatever occupation, by demanding the full exercise of all our faculties, hastens our further development as human beings." [23]   This concept of work, as Bertram Beck has observed, is consistent with the organism's thrust toward full development, a characteristic that J. McVicker Hunt describes as the

[21] Ward Hunt Goodenough, *Cooperation in Change* (New York: Russell Sage Foundation, 1963), p. 177.

[22] Alvin F. Poussaint, "A Negro Psychiatrist Explains the Negro Psyche," *The New York Times Magazine,* September 20, 1967.

[23] Quoted in Bertram Beck, "Recreation and Delinquency," *Juvenile Delinquency and Youth Crime,* President's Commission on Law Enforcement, *op. cit.,* p. 339.

organism's inherent growth motivation.[24]   We are beginning to see that the problem of social reconstruction is to create those roles that permit and encourage self-development, meaning that we can rely (much more than our Calvinistic image of man would dare) on intrinsic motivation rather than external control. No clearly defined or rewarding roles may be available at all. Youths may be the major victims of this defect in social structure, which may account for a good deal of their alienation and for much of juvenile delinquency. As Eli Ginzberg has observed, we seem to be ". . . the only society in the world that cannot use the labor power of sixteen-and-seventeen year-olds, and this adds tremendously to their difficulties." [25]   It also adds to our difficulties, especially since we seem relatively unable to find a socially constructive way to use the idealism and energy of youths for social reconstruction.

When they are not excluded from social participation, the roles available to individuals may conflict or they may exert demands beyond personal and social resources available for adequate social performance. This point may be understood in terms of overloading individuals and family units with social expectations exceeding adaptive capacities and/or supportive resources, as suggested by the Midtown Manhattan study of mental illness and other research.[26] Such role strains create problems in social functioning around which we tend to organize our social services. These services are a part of a quest for a more adequate socialization structure that ideally requires altering role demands, designing new roles, enhancing personal competence, and the assuring of enabling resources.

As we have already noted and as we shall specify in greater detail later, many of our social services, until recently, have focused primarily on changing individuals rather than on altering the social structure to deal with system strains. We have tried to help individuals cope with stress without adequate attention to the social source of stress, that is, the damaged, conflicted, or residual roles and the deficits in social resources that fail to support and facilitate adequate social functioning. We see more clearly now that social competence is a function of developed individual capacities, enabling social resources, and facilitating role structures. Adequate social performance in a democratic society requires developmental experiences that equip the individual with the capacity for autonomy. Opportunities must be available to play roles that are compatible with the individual's need for self-esteem and his capacities for growth. Enabling resources and social rewards must encourage creative social participation, that is, the performance of essential functions and the innovations without which any society deteriorates into empty forms. Thus the

---

[24] *Ibid;* and J. McVicker Hunt, "The Psychological Basis for Using Pre-School Enrichment as an Antidote for Cultural Deprivation," *Merrill-Palmer Quarterly,* 10 (July 1964), p. 234.

[25] Child Study Association of America, *Children of Poverty—Children of Affluence* (New York: Child Study Association of America, 1967), p. 26.

[26] Leo Srole, Thomas S. Langner, Stanley T. Michael, Marvin K. Opler, and Thomas A. C. Rennie, *Mental Health in the Metropolis: The Midtown Manhattan Study* (New York: McGraw-Hill, 1962), Vol. I; Shirley Jenkins and Mignon Sauber, *Paths to Child Placement* (New York: Community Council of Greater New York, 1966).

quality of life and the level of personal well-being depend on the individual's capacity and opportunity to play vital social roles in work, in the family, and in the community in personally satisfying and socially rewarding ways.   This concept of social functioning enables us to ask what kind of developmental experiences, nurturing resources, and significant roles are available that enlarge freedom, contribute to personal growth, and enhance one's sense of dignity.   Although man is plastic, he is not infinitely so.   Not all social arrangements are compatible with the imperatives of human development.

If basic needs are not met, if dignified work is not available, if some are excluded from participation or allowed to participate only in ". . . arrangements which insult their self-respect and impair their freedom," we see the need for changes in the social structure itself.[27]   Thus human development and social development are inseparable.   For the purpose of discussion only, we pay primary attention to the former in the remainder of this chapter.   In a later chapter we shall consider social welfare from the perspective of social development.   Identity may be the key linking concept.   This refers to the individual's need for a positive sense of self that permits him to be self-reliant in the face of group pressure to conform to moral judgments he would reject.   If we can understand the sense in which identity is a major social problem, possibly the key problem, we have a ground for social protest and a guide for social reconstruction.   Erik Erikson identifies two pathological aspects of identity: identity diffusion and identity foreclosure.   In the first, the individual is without a firm sense of self; in the latter, he defines his self too narrowly, shutting out variety and change that would threaten a rigid yet fragile world view.[28] It may be that a society can involve itself in creative self-renewal to the degree that it learns how to enable individuals to acquire a secure identity to permit exploration of new values and new social arrangements for their realization. Educating people for an open and flexible attitude toward self and society and creating roles that provide the support people need to face the anxiety of change may well be problems in socialization and in social structure.[29]

Social Welfare and Human Development

Human Development and Social Structure

The need for social reconstruction and the direction of desirable change may be indicated by our increasing understanding of the relationship between human development and social structure.   Man is free to develop his powers of self-

[27] R. H. Tawney, *Religion and the Rise of Capitalism* (New York: Harcourt, Brace & World, 1926), p. 233.

[28] Erik H. Erikson, "The Problem of Ego Identity," in Maurice Stein, Arthur J. Vidick, and David Manning White (eds.), *Identity and Anxiety* (New York: Free Press, 1960), pp. 37–87.   *See also* the introduction to this volume, pp. 17–33.

[29] Some indication of this may be found in experiments using sensitivity training groups designed to enable individuals to gain greater awareness of self and of others and to alter behavior in the direction of enhanced social competence.   Critical features of such efforts are the creation of a sense of community, elimination of status differences and threats to self-esteem, and group support for self-awareness and individual autonomy.

reliance to the extent that social institutions nurture such development.   The science of man that teaches us that human nature is learned offers us a positive affirmation of the Eighteenth-century Enlightenment vision of human possibilities.   This is a vision our society claims as its highest value.   It is the vision that defines the positive goals of social welfare.   It is one toward which social intelligence, aided by a science of man dedicated to the progressive realization of human well-being, could realistically aspire.   Despite all the cruel and unjust disparities between this ideal of a free society and our current social arrangements, and despite all the ambiguities and complexities that stand in the way of its further realization, the Enlightenment vision is still a compelling one.   It is still the one around which we may hope to get democratic consensus and the one that offers hope of humanizing our social order.   However, we remain, as Ernest Becker so forcefully reveals, ". . . still stretched out upon the rack of uncritically functioning social institutions, which means that we have never really heeded the Enlightenment program." [30]   This is so partly because we shy away from critical evaluation of our social institutions in the light of our democratic beliefs.   The notion that we have a democracy to defend rather than one to continually develop is a major handicap.   Consider the statement of the President's Commission on National Goals cited in Chapters Two and Three.   Take another look at the following assertion:

> . . . All our institutions—political, social, and economic—must further enhance the dignity of the citizen, promote the maximum development of his capabilities, stimulate their responsible exercise, and widen the range and effectiveness of opportunities for individual choice.

What a breathtaking, affirmatively subversive idea, perfect for a society that would renew itself by paying serious attention to its proclaimed ideals.   We are only now beginning to give serious consideration to converting such ideal statements into instruments for social criticism.   Yet this is hopeful.   As William Gorham and Daniel Bell have observed, no society in history has ever made a comprehensive effort to assess those aspects of its structure ". . . which facilitate and which bar each individual from realizing to the fullest extent possible his talents and abilities, in order to allow him to . . . live a full and healthy life equal to his biological potential." [31]

We have not lost the Enlightenment vision, and now we have the resources to think seriously about the means for the progressive realization not of human perfection but of perfectability.   Yet without an image of human possibilities to focus attention on the ways in which social institutions constrict human freedom, foster dependence on obsolete social rules, and impair our potential for creative self-reliant adaptation to change, we lack an intelligent basis for social criticism, consensus, and directed change.

---

[30] Becker, *Structure of Evil, op. cit.,* p. 34.

[31] William Gorham and Daniel Bell, quoted in Bertram M. Gross, (ed.), *Social Intelligence for America's Future* (Boston: Allyn & Bacon: 1969), p. 23.

The Self-Actualizing Conception of Man

We are hobbled most of all by our image of man. The self-fulfilling prophecy of economic man, or man as social product, binds us into a mechanical shaping of ourselves in the very mold that constricts our freedom to become the authentic persons we have the power to be. An ideological rather than a scientific image of man embodied in our social institutions, imperceptibly translated into child-rearing and educational practices, and supported by concentrations of power that fear the release of human energy and creativity prevents us from acting on a new, more hopeful, scientifically grounded image of man.

This is not to say that all social and behavioral scientists agree on man's nature. Far from it. Indeed we may well be wary of accepting on the authority of science an image of ourselves that fails to enlarge our view of human possibilities or one that undermines our faith in human dignity. Consider, for example, one image of man that behavioral science purports to reveal to us. After reviewing current findings of behavioral scientists, Bernard Berelson and Gary A. Steiner summarize the image of man as he seems to be revealed by research. Behavioral science man tends to replace, through the compelling authority of science, the variety of images inherited from the past: the philosophical image of the ancient world, the Christian image, the political image of the Renaissance, the economic image of the eighteenth and nineteenth centuries, and the psychoanalytic image of the twentieth. Now the "real" nature of man has been revealed. He is

> . . . social man—social product, social producer, and social seeker . . . he adjusts his social perception to fit not only the objective reality but also what suits his wishes and his needs; he tends to remember what fits his needs and expectations, or what he thinks others will want to hear; he not only works for what he wants but wants what he has to work for; his need for psychological protection is so great that he has become expert in the "defense mechanisms"; in the mass media he tends to hear and see not simply what is there but what he prefers to be told, and he will misinterpret rather than face up to an opposing set of facts or point of view; he avoids the conflicts of issues and ideals whenever he can by changing the people around him rather than his mind. . .[32]

Berelson and Steiner are not distorting. They are faithfully reporting the results of scientific research. They admit that the image is incomplete, that most of the findings are based on Western man, particularly Americans, and may not be based on a truly representative sample of them. Furthermore, they note important omissions from the image of social man as he seems to unfold through current research. Their perceptive comment is worth quoting:

> As one lives life or observes it around (or within himself) or finds it in a work of art, he sees a richness that somehow has fallen through the present screen of the behavioral sciences . . . (which) has rather little to say about central human concerns: nobility, moral courage, ethical torments,

[32] Bernard Berelson and Gary A. Steiner, *Human Behavior: An Inventory of Scientific Findings* (New York: Harcourt, Brace & World, 1964), pp. 664–667.

the delicate relation of father and son or of the marriage state, life's way of corrupting innocence, the rightness and wrongness of acts, evil, happiness, love and hate, death, even sex. (On such matters, the behavioral sciences, with a focus on evidence, and psychoanalysis, with attention to the human stuff itself, should learn to make common cause more successfully than heretofore.) [33]

This description, which includes only a portion of their summary, does indeed reveal much about ourselves.

What is wrong then? What is missing is an image of man and his human possibilities. We have instead a picture of social man uncritically engaged in performance that maintains the social drama, anxiously defending his narrowly conceived conception of self and society, dancing to the tune of a cultural medley learned in childhood and reinforced by his group. Ironically, this version of social man in a period of rapid change may be socially incompetent man, incapable of perceiving the world accurately and responding to it creatively. We are not now describing the poor and the culturally deprived, the presumed misfits of society. The research reported by Berelson and Steiner describes most of us, including those who think of themselves as most fit and many who are in positions of responsible leadership. It documents the essential dilemma, inherent in socialization, that proceeds to reduce the anxiety of nonbeing by offering social definitions of selfhood in exchange for the individual's freedom to make independent judgments. Such socialization functions to conserve the cultural fiction and to preserve social order, but it fails to develop the capacities for critical social awareness and independent judgment essential for a free society. Indeed, in some respects, social man is ill suited for participation in a democratic society. The paradox, as Ernest Becker has put it, is that the self-reliant qualities democracy needs most are those that come ". . . least naturally to man." [34] Man's natural dependence on the group for self-value hinders the freedom with which he can judge group-supported norms and values. "Society, then, must cultivate . . . autonomous people who encourage the autonomy of others." [35] Daniel Bell recognized that the image of man revealed through the Berelson and Steiner volume was ". . . an indictment of contemporary society," one that required that universities fulfill their responsibility for developing the best in man by strengthening liberal education.[36] This is not the place to discuss the role of universities in this regard, although without question their contribution could be great. The problem clearly lies in our total society and in our entire approach to the development of our human potential. At the core of the problem is the controlling image of the kind of human being we are trying to develop and the social order we are trying to realize. If science is to assist in the struggle to progressively develop a democratic order it must provide us with an image of man that is scientifically grounded yet consistent with our faith in the creative power of the individual

[33] *Ibid.,* p. 666.

[34] Becker, *Beyond Alienation, op. cit.,* p. 198.

[35] *Ibid.,* p. 199.

[36] Daniel Bell, *The Reforming of General Education* (New York: Columbia University Press, 1966), p. 151.

to live in and contribute to a free society. As John R. Seeley has observed, "what is human nature except that which we draw out of man by the very image we project of his potentialities as we carry out our daily transactions with him." What we require from science is an image of man's possibilities, one that would provide a guiding vision of the best that man might become, and a direction for social reconstruction that would continually explore the limits of the possible.

Our image of man has consequences for the way we view people and problems and the alternative courses of action we may take in behalf of human welfare. We must choose between two images of man offered to us by science: the mechanistic and the organismic. In the former view, man is analogous to a machine and as such he is completely determined by forces over which he has no control. This is a view implicit in the stimulus-response school of psychology and in some measure in the oversocialized concept of man as a determined product of society. Both deprive us of a language for making essential moral judgments about the adequacy of social institutions, leading only to a pragmatic "cultural relativity." Man as machine can presumably be shaped to adapt to any social environment that those in power, including scientists, choose to create. This could lead to a science of the control of man, as B. F. Skinner's *Walden Two* makes all too plain.[37] A competing view sees man as organism, as a "self-maintaining, self-repairing, self-moving system."[38] Man is seen as holistic rather than dualistic (e.g., no separation of mind and body), dynamic rather than static, responding rather than merely reacting to stimuli.[39] This positive and hopeful view of man also has roots in humanistic biology. Rene Dubos puts it in the following words:

> From one end of the spectrum, man appears as an ordinary physicochemical machine, complex, of course, but nevertheless reacting with environmental forces according to the same laws that govern inanimate matter. From the other end man is seen as a creature that is rarely a passive component in the reacting system; the most characteristic aspect of his behavior is the fact that he responds actively and often creatively. . . . *Man is the more human the better he is able to convert passive reactions into creative responses.* [Emphasis added.] [40]

Now we have it. Man is both machine and creative organism, determined yet free. There is no necessary conflict between these complementary views, yet for social policy a choice must be made. To emphasize the former con-

[37] B. F. Skinner, *Walden Two* (New York: Macmillan, 1948); and Carl R. Roger and B. F. Skinner, "Some Issues Concerning the Control of Human Behavior," *Science,* November 30, 1956, pp. 1057–1066.

[38] Ludwig von Bertalanffy, *Robots, Men and Minds* (New York: George Braziller, 1967), p. 127; *see* especially Floyd W. Matson, *The Broken Image: Man, Science and Society,* (New York: Anchor Books, 1966), for a scholarly discussion of the shift from a mechanistic to an organismic model.

[39] Laura Thompson, *Toward a Science of Mankind* (New York: McGraw-Hill, 1961), Chaps. 5 and 6.

[40] Rene Dubos, "Humanistic Biology," *The American Scholar,* 34 (Spring 1965), p. 185.

cept is to restrict man's capacity to be more than a machine. To act on the latter is to free and encourage him to become more human. For this we require a more explicit model of human needs that might guide social policy.

Abraham Maslow offers us such a concept. While far from definitive, his theory of self-actualizing man provides an image of human possibilities that might be realized through intelligently planned social change. It directs our attention to the ways we might create and support a structure of socialization more consistent with the developmental needs of the individual and the social needs of this revolutionary era. It offers a human image of man that respects his social nature by indicating how social forms may liberate rather than constrict his development. There are three basic ideas in his conception of human needs: (1) the hierarchy of needs, (2) the prepotency of basic needs, and (3) the identity of self-actualization and health. In his view, our needs tend to arrange themselves in a hierarchy "from basic biological needs to learned self-esteem, to the highest expression of human personality, the actualization needs, which are productive of man's creativity." Such needs, in order of their prepotency, are (1) physiological (hunger, thirst, sex), (2) safety (protection against danger, security in gratification of basic needs and predictability in one's environment), (3) love and belongingness, (4) self-esteem, and (5) self-actualization.[41] Basic needs are prepotent in the sense that individual behavior will tend to be dominated by them until gratified, which means that only after gratification of basic needs can the individual begin to actualize his full potentialities. Until such needs are met, the individual is characterized by "deficit-motivation," seeking to reduce the tension that accompanies frustration of ungratified primary needs. Once relatively assured of their satisfaction, he is free to develop his higher potential, whereupon he is characterized by "growth motivation." To Abraham Maslow, this is equivalent to health, for ". . . a healthy man is primarily motivated by his needs to develop and actualize his fullest potentialities and capacities." [42] Included in such potentialities and capacities are the cognitive and aesthetic needs for intellectual inquiry, order, beauty, and meaning.

A great many scientists, philosophers, and theologians hold views similar to those of Abraham Maslow. Despite important differences, all see a reasonable basis for a new image of man, one consistent with our belief in his dignity and capacity for freedom. The image has its earlier roots in the Enlightenment's view of man's perfectability. Now, however, we have greater scientific understanding of the nature of man and his possibilities, a view that challenges the image of man embodied in our social institutions. As J. McVicker Hunt has observed, the theory of human motivation we are now deriving from behavioral science conflicts with the assumptions around which we organized our legal, political, and economic institutions.[43] Such institutions incorporated

[41] Abraham H. Maslow, *Motivation and Personality* (New York: Harper & Brothers, 1954), pp. 80–92; and Abraham H. Maslow, *Toward A Psychology of Being* (New York: Nostrand, 1962).

[42] Maslow, *Motivation and Personality, op. cit.,* p. 105.

[43] J. McVicker Hunt, "Intrinsic Motivation and Its Role in Psychological Development," in David Levine (ed.), *Nebraska Symposium on Motivation* (Lincoln, Neb.: University Press, 1965), pp. 189–282.

much of the Calvinist doctrine of the evil nature of man and the assumption that he had to be controlled, shaped, and motivated by external rewards and punishments. The Poor Law philosophy that regarded man as naturally lazy, driven to do useful work only through hunger and fear of starvation, is an extreme example of this. It is possible that societies characterized by scarcity require an image of man that will justify social discipline required to get necessary but distasteful toil accomplished. Affluent societies can afford wider freedom of choice and can facilitate the development of new views of man more consistent, perhaps, with his true nature.

Child Development and Intrinsic Motivation

New understanding of child development suggests the need to respect the child's intrinsic motivation to learn and alerts us to the importance of providing rich learning environments so matched with unique organismic potential as to promote self-directed growth. Indeed as one looks at some of the research findings, as presented by Hunt, one is impressed with the support provided for a self-actualizing view of man.[44] Such findings, as he observes, force us to alter our concept of the nature of man and his development. Following is an all too brief summary of his key points. The development of each child's potential for the acquisition of skills in handling linguistic and mathematical symbols and for the analysis of causal relationships depends on a continuous informational interaction with his environment. One develops his capacities by living in an environment that offers appropriately abundant stimuli related to phases in motor, affective, and cognitive development. To maximize the adult's capacity for effective problem-solving is to assure in infancy appropriate sensory stimulation and to respect the child's intrinsic motivation for cognitive growth. This requires special sensitivity to the problem of matching the learning encounter with the child's own interest. It is the "problem of the match," as Hunt puts it, that is critical in nurturing cognitive development. The basis for believing in spontaneous learning is the child's quest for the right degree of incongruity between the information already stored within the nervous system through previous encounters with the environment ("organismic standards") and new informational encounters that have a degree of complexity sufficiently challenging and interesting without being overwhelming.[45] Too little incongruity produces boredom, too much causes avoidance. Optimum incongruity provides "continuous cognitive growth with joy." [46] The "problem of the match," as Hunt presents it, conceptualizes in a new way the long concern with individualizing the learning experience of every child, a concern rarely carried out in practice. Most striking of all, it provides some scientific support for the self-actualizing model of man and for the value of optimal freedom for the child to direct his own learning. Since we cannot know enough about each unique organism we cannot arrange the match from out-

[44] Hunt, "The Psychological Basis," *op. cit.;* and J. McVicker Hunt, "Introduction," Maria Montessori, *The Montessori Method* (New York: Schocken Books, 1964).

[45] Hunt, "The Psychological Basis," *op. cit.*, pp. 228–242.

[46] Hunt. "Introduction," *The Montessori Method, op. cit.*, p. xxvii.

side. Instead, as Hunt puts it, "It would appear that the child must have some opportunity to follow his own bent. Thus, we come to the importance of that liberty emphasized by the Rousseau-Pestalozzi-Froebel tradition and by Montessori." [47]

The great significance of Maria Montessori in this regard is that her educational approach to children solved the problem of the match.[48] By developing a learning environment where a child relatively free of adult interference could learn to work in accordance with the laws of his own development, she broke with the public school lockstep tradition of having every child working on the same task at the same time. Although her approach needs to be refined, expanded, and related to newer developments, her basic understanding of and respect for the intrinsic growth motivation of the child and her understanding of the need to design learning environments that afford each child an opportunity to find his optimal "incongruity," or challenge to overcome, now seem to have considerable scientific support. The evidence for intrinsic growth motivation in children, the knowledge we are deriving about the kind of required nurturance and stimulation appropriately related to the epigenesis of child development, and the insight into the special importance of the proper match between the unique organism and environmental encounters have tremendous implications for efforts to create a socialization structure that will assure to the fullest extent possible that all children have the fullest opportunity to develop their capacities.

Human Development and the Social Environment

All social institutions come under critical scrutiny given this perspective. Class inequalities result in unequal environments for the development of human capacities because biological and social competence are distributed in relation to the family's position in the social structure and its access to resources that permit the physical, emotional, and intellectual nurturance of the child. Mass media, the school system, and other agencies of socialization may be judged in terms of the kind of environmental encounters they make available to the child. There are serious dilemmas as we ponder the problem of adapting institutions to this perspective of human development, none more perplexing than those we confront in assessing the capacity of the family to promote the development of children. As we become more knowledgeable about the importance of the early years, we recognize that to promote equality of opportunity may suggest radical alteration in our view of the capacity of the family to assure those learning experiences that will promote a child's continuous development. In the words of Robert Morison, ". . . it (is) quite clear that it is idle to talk of a society of equal opportunity as long as the society abandons its newcomers solely to their families for their most impressionable years." [49] We have a new understanding of the sense in which the family is ". . . an

---

[47] *Ibid., p. xxviii.*

[48] Hunt, "The Psychological Basis," *op. cit.,* p. 240.

[49] Robert S. Morison, "Where is Biology Taking Us?," *Science,* January 27, 1967, p. 432.

educative environment with its own curriculum." [50] We are only in the early stages of exploring how we may strengthen and supplement the family's capacity to provide each child with an abundant learning environment without invading family privacy or violating parental rights. The value conflicts are not easily resolved, for parental rights and the rights of children in this regard are not necessarily synonymous.

Recent efforts to provide preschool enrichment for the so-called culturally deprived, based on the recognition that participation in a technological society requires mastery of cognitive skills, have produced renewed interest in the learning environments available to all preschool children. Our expanding knowledge of links between the inborn potential of the child and the responsiveness of the environment in providing the appropriate stimulating inputs has significance for all children, not only those we label deprived. Jerome S. Bruner, for example, sees a major revolution in our conception of man, which ". . . forces us to reconsider what it is we do when we occupy man's long growing period in certain ways now familiar as 'schooling.' " [51] Although the school especially is undergoing critical scrutiny since we recognize its central importance as an agency of socialization and education, we are now aware that a child's total social milieu constitutes his learning environment, one that dictates the kind of informational and ethical encounters he will have available to him.

Paul Goodman, in *Growing Up Absurd,* shows a perceptive awareness of the degree to which the daily encounters of many children and youths are senseless regardless of their social class.[52] Concern with socialization focuses attention on the social environment, on the process of growing and learning, rather than on the function of any single institution—family or school. Our tendency is to think in terms of entities rather than transactional process, of *the* family or *the* school, rather than the quality of social interactions made possible by our social arrangements and by our moral ideals. It seems reasonably clear, for example, that structures that emphasize status, competition, and class inequality are dysfunctional for learning and therefore for the development of our human potential. Since man learns to become human through social interaction, the nature and quality of the social forms through which reciprocal human action and development take place are put to the test. Which social forms facilitate and which constrict man's capacities to become self-reliant through the mastery of those skills and the acquisition of those values and attitudes that enable him to effectively cope with his environment and to alter its form toward the progressive realization of free society? Here is a question for the science of man. According to Jerome Bruner, the cognitive skills that make for effective adaptation and competent problem-solving are being identified. These are skills in handling, in seeing, imaging, and in carrying out

---

[50] Benjamin S. Bloom, "Twenty-Five Years of Educational Research," in Patricia Cayo Sexton, (ed.), *Readings on the School in Society* (Englewood Cliffs, N.J.: Prentice-Hall, 1967), p. 232.

[51] Jerome S. Bruner, "Education as Social Invention," *Saturday Review,* February 19, 1966, p. 70.

[52] Paul Goodman, *Growing Up Absurd* (New York: Random House, 1960).

symbolic operations.[53]   Moreover, we are discovering some principles in the epigenesis of learning that have implications for how we structure learning encounters.

> Mental growth is not a gradual accretion either of associations or of stimulus-response connections or of means-end readiness or of anything else. It appears to be much more like a staircase with rather sharp risers, more a matter of spurts and rests than anything else. The spurts ahead in growth seem to be triggered off when certain capacities begin to unfold . . . certain capacities must be matured and nurtured before others can be stimulated into being . . . rich environments can hasten or slow rates of growth . . . until a child can hold in mind two features of a display at once . . . he (cannot) deal with their relationship.[54]

To optimize learning is to enhance the child's capacity for freedom, for freedom involves a progressive release from control by one's immediate environment to a competent mastery of it. Such mastery involves, along with and inseparable from cognitive development, the acquisition of affective and social skills, all of which contribute to a sense of competence and self-esteem.[55]   What is exciting and hopeful is that for the first time in history we are acquiring an understanding of human development along with the technological and scientific resources that could allow us to give increasing priority to designing a human environment.

Human Development and the Science of Man

If such an effort is to be directed by social intelligence we need a scientifically based image of man that will provide a guiding vision of human possibilities, one against which we can measure our current social arrangements and one that will indicate desirable goals for change. Such a theory of man would be prescriptive rather than simply descriptive, telling us, for example, not only how human beings learn but how we might optimize learning. We would know how man behaves under current conditions and could evaluate his behavior against an image of the range of human possibilities. The image we select depends on the kind of person we value and the social order we are trying to develop. If we value a free man living in a free society we need an image that leads us to a continual exploration of ways to expand human freedom. This is the direction of the humanistic psychologies led by Abraham Maslow and others; these psychologies are based on a regard for the human being as a self-initiating and self-actualizing organism.[56]   Rejecting the notion of a value-free science of man, this school of thought accepts the ethical obligation to devote itself to discovering ways to promote the growth of the human person. Its goal must be the expansion of human freedom by showing

[53] Bruner, "Education as Social Invention," *op. cit.,* p. 30.

[54] *Ibid.,* p. 25.

[55] Terry Borton, "Reach, Touch, and Teach," *Saturday Review,* January 18, 1969, pp. 56–58, 69–70.

[56] Abraham H. Maslow, "Some Educational Implications of the Humanistic Psychologies," *Harvard Educational Review,* 38 (Fall 1968), pp. 685–696.

man how societal forms constrict the development of his self-powers and by a continuing exploration of ways of designing social life to promote "maximum individuality within maximum community."[57] In this way human development and social development proceed together, but the test of the society is its ability to expand human freedom and to promote the fullest development of man.

Whether it is possible to move in this direction is unclear. Without a vision of an experimental democracy making a continual effort to renew itself to promote the fullest development of human potential we are at the mercy of science and technology, which are driven to play out their pragmatic imperative: that which is technically possible will be done. To place man and his needs at the center of concern is to humanize our society, to subordinate science and technology to human purpose, and to provide a guiding vision for social reconstruction.

Social Welfare and Human Needs

The basic question for inquiry for those interested in social welfare is how social institutions may be altered to more effectively meet human needs. As Gardner Murphy has written, "The realization of human potentialities . . . lies in studying the directions in which human needs may be guided, with equal attention to the learning powers of the individual and the feasible directions of cultural evolution."[58] Maslow provides a model of human needs that might guide social policy. Although all the evidence is not in regarding human needs and although one might dispute the extent to which the principle of need hierarchy operates in quite the way he suggests, one may with confidence insist on the importance of assuring the satisfaction of basic needs for survival, security, self-esteem, and self-actualization. A society concerned about human development cannot ignore the compelling evidence that the prior satisfaction of basic needs is necessary before human beings are free to develop their highest potential. Social institutions may then be critically evaluated in terms of how they allocate resources and experiences. Particularly in early childhood, basic provisions and socialization experiences that nurture growth must be assured. The imperatives of child development, not the market place, must determine the flow of nurturing resources. Given our knowledge of human development it may be possible to speak of the appropriate input of resources and experiences for children at different stages of development, allowing us to critically examine what we do to nurture or damage a child's capacity to grow.[59]

The promotion of positive mental health, broadly defined, is synonymous with human development that involves efforts to nurture persons so they can relate creatively to the world and contribute their energies and talents for the enrichment of all. As Matthew Dumont makes clear, the required perspective

[57] Becker, *Structure of Evil,* op. cit., p. 251.

[58] Gardner Murphy, *Human Potentialities* (New York: Basic Books, 1958), p. 13.

[59] Harry C. Bredemeier, "Proposal for an Adequate Socialization Structure," *Urban America and Planning of Mental Health Services* (New York: Group for the Advancement of Psychiatry, November 1964), Symposium V, No. 10, pp. 447–469.

is not one of therapy for sick individuals so much as a community development focus that is concerned with creating those social environments that assure to all the meeting of such essential needs as sensory stimulation, self-esteem, mastery, and community.[60]   Thus, while human needs are variously described, there is a remarkable degree of consensus on some essential requirements for a human environment.   Less important than consensus on the nature of human needs is agreement that our goal ought to be to progressively discover how to create those environments that promote the optimal development of man.   The challenge before us is to specify the kinds of physical, psychosocial, and socio-cultural resources and experiences required and the structures most appropriate for making them available.   This is not as utopian as it sounds provided we keep in mind the need for plural approaches, continuing experimentation, and the sobering realization that, at best, ideals can only be approximated.

The concept of humanizing our environment is not an idle one.   For example, the notion of humanizing the work environment is gaining consideration, and many experimental schools have been developed around the concept of the child's intrinsic motivation to grow and learn.[61]   A suggestion has been made by Charles Hamilton that centers be established in black ghettos to give parents a new opportunity to build on their own learning capacity.[62]   We are becoming aware of the importance of creating those social environments that nurture rather than limit or destroy human potential.   This focuses attention on social provisions that assure satisfaction of basic needs; socialization and education that enlarge rather than constrict the individual's cognitive and affective powers; social and political roles that enhance self-esteem and facilitate self-directed action; and values that endow life with dignity and encourage the quest for ever richer symbolic meaning.

The perspective is the one suggested by Hadley Cantril—"the individual's demand on society," which proceeds from an understanding of the needs of the human being and the requirements for his maximum development.[63]   Despite our vaunted individualism, we have in fact subordinated the individual to uncritically examined social institutions.   Our definition of individualism continues to reflect an ideology of economic self-reliance, not the autonomy and social competence required for a free society.   The evidence of this is clear from the Berelson and Steiner summary of findings regarding behavioral man. We have not yet discovered how to socialize man for participation in a free society, to develop self-critical and socially critical man capable of exercising choice and freely directing his energies and talents toward some shared purpose.

[60] Matthew Dumont, *The Absurd Healer* (New York: Science House, 1968), pp. 54–66.

[61] *Manpower Report of the President,* U.S. Department of Labor (Washington, D.C.: Government Printing Office, 1968), pp. 47–66; A. S. Neill, *Summerhill* (New York: Hart, 1960); George Dennison, *The Lives of Children* (New York: Random House, 1969).

[62] Charles Hamilton, "Race and Education: A Search for Legitimacy," *Harvard Educational Review,* 38 (Fall 1968), pp. 669–684.

[63] Hadley Cantril, "The Individual's Demand on Society," in Seymour M. Farber and Roger H. L. Winston (eds.), *Conflict and Creativity* (New York: McGraw-Hill, 1963).

Perhaps the key human need to which we must pay attention, as Ernest Becker suggests, is man's need for self-esteem maintenance, gained through experiencing one's self as the locus of power to act and accomplish some valued end. As he puts it, if ". . . I do not experience the free exercise of my own powers . . . I do not feel I have any value." [64] This is essentially what all of those related to humanistic psychology are saying. The evidence seems clear: to deprive anyone of his sense of mastery is to deprive him of his humanity.[65] Freedom, as John Dewey suggested, is the freedom to do specific things; that is, it involves the ability to master one's environment, to solve problems, to cope with change. We may discover that much of the behavior we call deviant, whether in the form of mental illness or delinquency, is but the protest of those denied an opportunity to actualize themselves. Problems of mental illness and delinquency from this perspective are issues related to our failure to develop effective coping behaviors and to facilitate their responsible exercise through roles that link individual potential to some socially valued purpose. Part of the human rights revolution is a protest against this inhuman denial of the opportunity to discover and develop self-powers and to use them in a social performance that is meaningful and dignified. While we have been ready to accuse the poor of lack of self-reliance we have not been so ready to see the sense in which the individual is so embedded in society that he cannot develop his capacities as a person without social resources and opportunities that promote competence. Moreover we have not seen the degree to which all of us might have developed a larger measure of the kind of interpersonal competence it takes to live effectively in this era. The attributes of such interpersonal competence have been identified as health, intelligence, empathy, judgment, autonomy, and creativity. These, according to Foote and Cottrell, can be specified in some detail and social institutions can be critically examined with respect to their positive or negative impact on the development of such human capacities.[66] Most important is their definition of competence:

> Competence denotes capabilities to meet and deal with a changing world, to formulate ends and implement them. . . . At the level of theoretical speculation, interpersonal competence as a general phenomenon appears to be based on what certain existentialist philosophers call transcendence. This term summarizes the uniquely human processes of suspended action, memory, revery, foresight, reflection, and imagination, by means of which a person from birth onward escapes progressively from the control of his

---

[64] Becker, *Structure of Evil, op. cit.,* pp. 277–278.

[65] In the famous Coleman study of school achievement, a major finding had to do with the relationship between self-confidence and school performance. In explaining differences between Negro and white achievement scores, Dr. Coleman notes that "perhaps the most important" result of the survey was the finding that "Negroes who gave responses indicating a sense of control of their own fate achieved higher on the tests than those whites who gave the opposite responses. This attitude was more highly related to achievement than any other factor in the student's background or school." James S. Coleman, "Equal Schools or Equal Students," *The Public Interest,* No. 4 (Summer 1966), p. 75.

[66] Nelson N. Foote and Leonard S. Cottrell, Jr., *Identity and Interpersonal Competence* (Chicago: University of Chicago Press, 1955).

immediately given environment and begins to control it. It is by this freedom from the irresistible instincts and external stimuli, which chain the responses of lower animals, that the human being is enabled to modify his surroundings, to plan and create, to have a history and a future. His detachment from the present situation provides both the opportunity and the necessity for him to declare his own identity and values as an adult.[67]

An adequate socialization structure would direct itself toward creating this kind of human competence. In the rapidly changing world in which we live, interpersonal competence is required to cope effectively with new situations and to make it possible to renew our social institutions. All social institutions would need to be oriented toward the enhancement of such competence.

> It appears to us that a community which organizes its activity so that it maximizes the number of healthy, intelligent, self-directing citizens, capable of viewing situations from perspectives other than their own, of weighing alternatives and making decisions, of defining new goals and inventing new ways of achieving them, is in fact a democratic community and is producing members who can sustain it against all more pessimistic theories of human nature and social order.[68]

Here is an agenda for social reconstruction for a society that aspires to develop free men capable of living in a community of free men. All our social institutions may be critically examined in terms of their contribution to the development of this kind of social competence. To develop a socialization structure adequate for a democratic society that aspires to the fullest development of its human potential requires nothing less. We know now that socialization cannot be confined to any single institution. The family alone cannot provide all the resources and learning opportunities essential for children; neither can the school.

Required is a total learning environment for children and adults that would include attention to mass media, the role of the neighborhood and peer groups, and the various institutions that structure social interaction. It would include the design of our cities to consider ". . . the developmental function of environment and . . . ways to improve it." [69] In this regard Buckminster Fuller is worth quoting at some length.

> In the next decade society is going to be preoccupied with the child because through the behavioral sciences and electrical exploration of the brain we find that, given the right environment and thoughtful answers to his questions, the child has everything he needs educationally right from birth. We have thought erroneously of education as the mature wisdom and over-brimming knowledge of the grownups injected by the discipline pump into the otherwise "empty" child's head. Sometimes parents say "don't" because they want to protect the child from getting into trouble. At other times when they fail to say "no" the child gets into trouble. The child,

[67] *Ibid.,* p. 40.

[68] *Ibid.,* p. 60.

[69] Stephen Carr and Kevin Lynch, "Where Learning Happens," *Daedalus,* 97 (Fall 1968), p. 1280.

frustrated, stops exploring.   It is possible to design environments within which the child will be neither frustrated nor hurt, yet free to develop spontaneously and fully without trespassing on others.   I have learned to undertake reforms of the environment and not to try to reform Man.   If we design the environment properly, it will permit child and man to develop safely and to behave logically.[70]

This may seem utopian.   Perhaps it is, but the function of utopian visions is to direct our energies toward the ideal in order that we may more nearly attain the possible.   Our more positive image of man offers some basis for modest optimism, provided we can learn to devote our resources to his fullest development.   For this purpose critical attention must be given to our hierarchy of values.   Man is self-actualizing, but it is the image toward which he aspires that determines the human qualities he will tend to develop and the social order he will create.   Social myths once useful for the release and direction of human energy later become shackles on intelligence and imagination.   A critique of the human cost of the values to which we now commit ourselves might reveal that our central goals are not those we would freely choose.

A guiding vision of man and society is central to social reconstruction.   We may then ask what action is possible, what difficulties stand in the way, what costs are involved in action or failure to act, and what conflicts and contradictions may keep us from fully realizing the ideal.   We have suggested that such an ideal is the one we proclaim—the free man living in a free society.   What we are only now beginning to do is to apply our scientific understanding of societal constraints on freedom to understand how we may create those social forms that release our potential to become more fully human.

Since the family first introduces the child to his humanity, let us next consider its contribution to the socialization process and the means by which society may support, supplement, or substitute for the functions performed by this important institution.

[70] R. Buckminster Fuller, "How Little I Know," *Saturday Review,* November 12, 1966, p. 70.

EIGHT

From the Welfare Family to the Welfare Society

Family and Social Change

Social Welfare may be seen as the effort of society to deal with three interrelated and overlapping problems: economic deprivation or insecurity, family instability, and the decline of community. Much of social welfare activity may be understood as attempts to support, supplement, and substitute for functions traditionally performed by the family. In preindustrial societies, the extended family was relied upon to meet the various needs of its members. The family, supported by its communal ties, performed all the welfare functions that an industrial society, in some measure, assigns to specialized agencies. Industrialization disrupts community, uproots individuals, deprives families of control over means of subsistence while placing them at the mercy of an uncertain wage economy, alters family structure, creates new social environments for which traditional patterns of behavior and socialization mechanisms are inappropriate, and thus develops the need for formal welfare organizations that may sustain the family, share in, or replace its functions.

It is possible to suggest a historical transition from the welfare family to the industrial welfare state, developed in varying degrees in different societies to meet basic needs of individuals and to assure some measure of equality of opportunity. Beyond the welfare state lies the image of a welfare society whose goal is the full and equal realization of the potentialities of all of its members. As already noted, in the United States we have yet to attain the modest goals of the welfare state, that is, a political right to a minimum standard of economic well-being. Moreover, despite the transfer of many family functions to public and voluntary formal organizations, we are reluctant to accept the family welfare ethic, that of *caritas* rather than demeaning charity. In a family resources tend to be allocated on the basis of individual need and regard for the person as a member of the unit. The American emphasis on individualism, our cultural heterogeneity, the lack of a sense of community, and the strong

319

attachment to the distribution of rewards on the basis of competitive achievement limit the extent to which sentiments of the family can be extended to the larger society. At the same time there probably will always remain some tension between the ethic of meeting needs and rewarding accomplishment. The differential distribution of rewards is likely to persist, but if families are so located in the reward system as to be denied access to resources essential for performance of family functions it is not surprising that we find various indices of family breakdown.

Radical changes taking place focus attention on the link between family and society. As we have already noted, families can perform only those functions that resources and capacities permit. If we value family life and wish to strengthen its capacity to carry out those functions that it can perform, we shall need a sensitive awareness of changes taking place that call for new kinds of communal supports for new roles for family members. For this reason, a look at some of the changes taking place is in order.

The Decline of the Family: Myth or Reality?

It is common to note the decline of the family as if that were an established and irreversible fact. As we have already observed, the actual situation is far more complex than can be suggested by that phrase, which ignores changing functions of and higher aspirations for family life; social class variations in family structure and resources; and a historic decline of community that may be the source of the apparent weakness of the family itself. That the family has changed and is perhaps undergoing a revolution in form and function is a safe enough observation. Yet nothing we know allows us to speak with confidence about the future direction of the family. At the same time, a sentimental model of family life may prevent critical awareness of some radical alterations that may be essential if it is to remain a viable institution. Although commonly regarded as a foundation of society and a natural environment for the optimal development of children, there are some observers of the contemporary scene who conclude that the family, at least in its present form, is incapable of performing its major societal function or of assuring its members the gratification of their needs.

To Barrington Moore, the family is an obsolete institution. He assumes that in advanced industrial societies, individuals capable of exercising choice, free of the burden of guilt and anxiety, would dispense with the family and would substitute ". . . other social arrangements that impose fewer unnecessary and painful restrictions on humanity." [1] Harvey Wheeler asserts that the socialization process ". . . has been gradually abandoned by the middle-class family, as it became more urbanized, more mobile, more loosely knit, more easily dissolvable." [2] Observing that the middle-class family may "go down in history

[1] Barrington Moore, "Thoughts on the Future of the Family," in Maurice R. Stein, Arthur J. Vidick, and David Manning White (eds.), *Identity and Anxiety* (Glencoe, Ill.: Free Press, 1960), p. 392.

[2] Harvey Wheeler, *The Restoration of Politics* (Santa Barbara, Calif.: Center for the Study of Democratic Institutions, 1965), p. 20.

as one of the most unsatisfactory institutions in human experience," Wheeler assumes that ". . . the degree of success with which we reshape and prepare the new functions of the post-industrial family system may determine our survival as a race." [3] In his view nothing short of planning the socialization process will suffice. The present style of family organization, according to Margaret Mead, is a "massive failure," as evidenced by youthful rebellion and by increasing deviance in a variety of forms, in response to which our proliferation of community-supported social services can have at best only an ameliorative effect.[4] However one responds to such strong indictments there is no likelihood that Americans are about to abandon the family nor is there compelling evidence that they could or should. It is nonetheless clear that the family is undergoing some major changes linked with the broader social revolution taking place. These changes challenge certain fundamental assumptions we have long held about the role of the family in our personal lives and its functions as a basic mode of social organization.

The family confronts us with a paradox. It is a social unit that may truly individualize the child, yet by the same token it has the power to deny him his individuality. In an impersonal society of large-scale organizations, the family remains the major primary group allowing for intimacy and expression of personal feelings, yet its structure of reciprocal obligations may restrict the range of desirable human experiences. It may protect the child and assure him access to society, yet as an institution the family supports social inequality and denial of social participation to some. It may be the foundation of a nation, yet the narrow loyalties the family tends to engender undermine identification with the family of man, an identification necessary for our survival. Finally, the family is a source both of the love that constricts our humanity and the love that has the power to lead us toward self-transcendence. Perhaps the family is obsolete and will give way to other social forms that will enlarge human freedom; or, as Ralph Linton suggests, it is more likely that the ancient trinity of father, mother, and child will survive if mankind survives and, if not, then ". . . in the Gotterdamerung which overwise science and over-foolish statesmanship are preparing for us, the last man will spend his last hours searching for his wife and child." [5] Given our deep, although ambivalent, emotional commitment to the family, it is difficult to view it with detachment. Although the future of the family is unclear two observations may be made with considerable certainty: (1) its functions are changing, and (2) the family in some form is likely to persist, and must persist. The issue is not the survival of the family but our capacity to determine those functions that the family can and should perform and our readiness to make available essential supportive resources. First one must see that the family is inextricably linked with the functioning of the larger social system.

[3] *Ibid.*

[4] Margaret Mead, "The Life Cycle and Its Variations," *Daedalus,* 96 (Summer 1967), p. 872.

[5] Ralph Linton, "The Natural History of the Family," in Ruth Nanda Anshen (ed.), *The Family: Its Function and Destiny* (New York: Harper & Brothers, 1949), p. 37.

Changing Functions of the Family

We may think of society as a system of interrelated institutions (or sub-systems) that function more or less adequately to attain certain valued ends. Institutions refer to patterned interaction organized around norms or role expectations (e.g., mothers shall care for their children) that apply to a particular category of reciprocal role relationships (e.g., mother-child) structured to carry out one or more functions (e.g., socialization of children) in pursuit of socially valued ends (e.g., maintenance of the system through acculturation of children).

A social system view, provided we do not extend it too far, is useful. It focuses attention on the interrelatedness and interpenetration of units in a system. It alerts us to the possibility that a change in one part of a system will cause change in another and enables us to think of causation as a process involving functional relationships among units in a system. For example, if the social and economic system functions to deprive lower-class males of adequate jobs, this limits opportunities for stable marriages for lower-class women, thus increasing the risk of illegitimacy and female-based households. Families deprived of stable breadwinners adapt to economic insecurities through female-based structures that enable men and women to enter and dissolve a relationship in accordance with change in economic circumstances.[6] While such structures may be functional for adapting to occupation-earner problems, they may not be suited to socializing children for effective functioning in the family and occupational roles in a society. Moreover, such children are likely to suffer from the stress of poverty, unrelieved by adequate welfare grants and services in a society that believes the poor are responsible for their own plight. Disparagement of the poor may also be reflected in the failure of the public school to meet the special learning needs of economically and socially deprived children, thus adding its contribution to their invidious social exclusion. This systematic process prepares children for school failure, for marginal employment, for family instability, and for selective recruitment for a variety of stigmatized roles as clients of residual welfare and correctional programs. Thus we initiate and maintain the cycle of intergenerational misery and waste in human potential.

A view of such functional interrelationships enables us to see that effective change may come from manipulation of distant variables in the system rather than from direct efforts to modify the behavior of a target population presumed to be in some way deviant or inadequate. For example, it is possible that the problem of family disorganization is likely to respond best to changes in the environment and resources available to the family, in particular to new and hopeful employment opportunities, to new rewarding roles, to changes in status. Dysfunctional child-rearing practices are more likely to be altered as parents attain a different concept of themselves and of the future of their children. The so-called culture of poverty, to the extent that this overused and abused phrase accurately describes values at variance with those essential for escaping poverty, is more likely to be altered indirectly through new life

[6] Hyman Rodman, "Family and Social Pathology in the Ghetto," *Science,* August 23, 1968, pp. 756–762.

opportunities rather than through direct efforts to socialize the poor into middle-class values. In any event, it is the web of social life, the relatedness of events, and the ethical implications of our interdependence that we may better appreciate through a social system view of the family. Values are central, for systems are goal directed. Alter the goals and you alter the system.

The values or goals toward which a social system is directed tend to be arranged in some hierarchy. Since all values cannot be simultaneously maximized, the importance of any social institution tends to be determined by its contribution to the dominant goals of society. This may mean that some subsystems are primarily evaluated in terms of their input into other systems more directly concerned with the attainment of society's preferred goals. Thus, in a society that gives priority to economic goals and technological advancement, the educational system will be evaluated not so much in terms of its contribution for developing the unique potentials of each individual, but to its success in processing people to fill positions in the occupational system. However much humanistic education may be valued, this cannot be the primary goal of the school system so long as its contribution to the efficiency and effectiveness of the technological society is a measure of its success and of its public support.[7] Thus, some subsystems are at least in part evaluated in the light of their contribution to the functioning of other more valued institutions. This is not only true of the public school system but of the family as well.

The family may be seen as a subsystem that functions to meet the needs of its members and the requirements of a given social order. Families traditionally are assigned such functions as reproduction, biological maintenance, socialization, emotional maintenance, social control, sexual gratification, and status placement. A common assumption is that there has been a gradual transfer of functions to other institutions, thus heralding a decline in the importance of the family itself. An alternate view holds that the form and content of family functions have changed with industrialization and urbanization but that the family remains a major and irreplaceable social institution. This view seems closer to the truth. In the first place, family functions are not simply transferred. Instead they may be shared with other institutions. For example, despite the major shift of education from the family to the school, families continue to perform an important educational function through the kind of learning environment they provide in the home, through helping children with homework, and through their capacity to expose children to new and stimulating experiences outside the home. Given the increasing importance of education, it is possible that families are more important in this respect than they ever were in the past. Indeed one may see a trend toward returning to the family an increasing responsibility for education, ". . . because people are already becoming interested in early learning, in the role of the family as an agent for human development and for personal growth."[8] It is the family as a learning environment, not the formal teaching role of parents, that is being

[7] Thomas F. Green, "Schools and Communities: A Look Forward," *Harvard Educational Review,* 39 (Spring 1969), pp. 221–252.

[8] Richard E. Farson, "Behavioral Science Predicts and Projects," by Richard E. Farson, Philip M. Hauser, Herbert Stroup, Anthony J. Wiener, in *The Future of the Family* (New York: Family Service Association of America, 1969), p. 61.

rediscovered and reemphasized. Thus, functions once relinquished by the family may be transferred back to it in new forms. This may also be seen, for example, in recent efforts to shift some responsibility for the care of the mentally ill back to the family. Nonetheless certain functions are especially characteristic of the family.

Unless otherwise noted the key ideas on family functions in this section are borrowed from Clark Vincent's article.[9] The family may be seen as a subsystem performing functions for other subsystems (e.g., the economy) and for the society as a whole. From this perspective, the family performs a major adaptive function, contributing to other social institutions by bearing the major burden of adjustment to change. For example, industrialization in all societies forces a basic change in family structure from an extended kinship system to some version of the nuclear family to meet the needs for a mobile and adaptable labor force. This little understood and unappreciated adaptive function of the family has a heavy human cost, inequitably distributed. Change imposes stress. In the absence of adequate societal supports, disorganization of family life may be the consequence. As Richard Titmuss observes, many of the social welfare programs seeking to cope with family "pathology" may be dealing with the consequences of the strain industrialization has imposed on family life. He writes:

> Viewed in terms of the long-drawn cycle of family life, the violent industrial upheavals of the 19th century, the poverty, the unemployment, the social indiscipline, the authoritarianism of men and the cruelty to children are by no means as remote today in their consequences as some economists and historians would have us believe.[10]

The vulnerability of the family to the stress of social change has policy implications if we wish to prevent family disorganization. Stress associated with change may be conceptualized as a crisis in role transition calling for enabling social resources and coping abilities that facilitate adaptation to new societal demands. For example, Marc A. Fried has identified the great rural-to-urban migration as a crisis in role transition calling for the development, on the part of the breadwinner, of new work attitudes and skills. Failure at this critical point might lead to severe family disruption, an eventuality that could be prevented by providing resources in the form of income, training, and supportive services to facilitate adaptation to the new social environment.[11] We shall return to this point.

A further function that the family performs for society is not commonly recognized: It is society's scapegoat; it takes much of the blame for social problems such as delinquency, dependency, mental illness, school failure, and

[9] Clark E. Vincent, "Mental Health and the Family," *Journal of Marriage and the Family,* 29 (February 1967), pp. 18–39.

[10] Richard M. Titmuss, "Industrialization and the Family," *Social Service Review,* 31 (March 1957), pp. 54–62.

[11] Marc A. Fried, "Is Work a Career?," *Trans-action,* 3 (September–October 1966), pp. 42–47; Marc A. Fried, "The Role of Work in a Mobile Society," in Sam Bass Warner, Jr. (ed.), *Planning for a Nation of Cities* (Cambridge, Mass.: Massachusetts Institute of Technology Press, 1966), pp. 81–104.

so forth. In this way attention is deflected from defects in other institutions whose organization and power make them less vulnerable to criticism. This is not to suggest that at a certain level of analysis the family may not be found to be causally implicated in all of the above problems. The common tendency to blame the family for social ills seems more politically than scientifically inspired. Scientists are themselves divided on the emphasis to be placed on the family as the source of such problems as delinquency.[12] The tendency of many sociologists to deny the central importance of the family in juvenile delinquency, as reported by Bordua, conflicts sharply with the research findings of the McCords, who write that ". . . our investigation of the origins of criminality reveals that the roots of crime lie deep in early familial experiences—so deep that only the most intensive measures, applied very early in life, can offer hope of eradicating them."[13]

The conflict between these two views may be more apparent than real. One may find delinquency rooted in early family experiences and still seek the social sources of the family's inability to properly socialize children. For purposes of primary prevention, focus might be on the larger social structures and the strains they impose on family life. For purposes of secondary prevention, early intervention in vulnerable families might be essential.[14] Although there is evidence for recognizing the importance of the family's role in social pathology, key social issues have to do with the way other social institutions may undermine the family's capacity to fulfill its responsibilities.[15] An exclusive focus on the family inhibits a radical critique of the society and the possible need for basic social reforms that would enable the family to function more adequately. Such reforms would probably involve a redistribution of income, power, and status and a reordering of major values—reforms so deeply

[12] David J. Bordua, *Sociological Theories and Their Implications for Juvenile Delinquency: A Report of a Children's Bureau Conference,* U.S. Department of Health, Education, and Welfare (Washington, D.C.: Government Printing Office, 1960), p. 15; and William McCord and Jean McCord, *Origins of Crime* (New York: Columbia University Press, 1959), Preface and pp. 166–172.

[13] McCord, *ibid.*

[14] Primary, secondary, and tertiary prevention are concepts from public health. The first refers to prevention of a disease at its source prior to the onset of any ailment. Thus fluoridation of the water permits basic prevention of tooth decay. Secondary prevention involves early case-finding and treatment, as illustrated by periodic dental checkups. Tertiary prevention is effective treatment after the onset of the problem to prevent further deterioration and to guard against a relapse. The terms may be usefully applied to approaches to social problems. *See* Council on Social Work Education, *Public Health Concepts in Social Work Education,* (New York: Council on Social Work Education, 1962); and Ludwig L. Geismar, *Preventive Intervention in Social Work* (Metuchen, N.J.: Scarecrow Press, 1969).

[15] This was the basis for the controversy underlying the Moynihan Report, which sought to focus attention on inequality and a presumed breakdown in Negro family life. *The Negro Family: The Case for National Action,* U.S. Department of Labor, Office of Policy Planning and Research (Washington, D.C.: Government Printing Office, March 1965). The political dimensions of this controversy are explored by Lee Rainwater and William L. Yancey in *The Moynihan Report: The Politics of Controversy* (Cambridge: Massachusetts Institute of Technology Press, 1967).

resisted that a natural preference exists for allowing the family to carry the burden of blame for social ills.   Society is more willing to support social services designed to change families than it is action aimed at reforming the economic and political system.   It is the family that is expected to adapt to society's needs.

The significance of the family to society may rest not on the priority attached to the family as such, but frequently on its subordination to the needs of other major institutions.   This is clearly seen in the relationship between the family and the economy.   The economic role of the family breadwinner has priority over the spouse and parental roles.   Most often the family has no choice but to adapt to the requirements for mobility, hours of work, and changes in occupational skills.   Role reversal may take place to accommodate the special demand for women in the labor force, particularly if adequate work opportunities are not also made available to men.   Occupational achievement requires primary loyalty to the role of breadwinner in the distribution of time and energy.   The changing needs of a technological society are ". . . translated and incorporated into the ongoing socialization of all members of the family, both children and adults." [16]   Thus the family performs a major function of mediating between individual needs and society's demands and goals, seeking to socialize its members to meet changing social expectations.   The family facilitates social change by bearing the major burden of adapting itself to the changing requirements of other social institutions.   In some measure such adaptation is reciprocal.

Institutions also adapt to family needs, but as Clark Vincent has observed, this is likely only to the extent that the central goals of such institutions are furthered by this process.   Thus in a profit economy, the housing industry will adapt its product to the changing housing needs of the family to the degree that it can maximize profits by so doing.   When there is a conflict between the goals of the family and other institutions, it is the family that is expected to adapt, and it does so since it lacks any other alternative.   The autonomy of the family is limited by its general lack of power.   In a society of competing interests, the family has no effectively organized advocate.   Some social welfare agencies attempt to perform this function, but in general they are relatively powerless in competition with other groups who are in a position to make decisions irrespective of consequences for family life.   The individual family is a fragile unit compared to the powerful forces arrayed against it.   The lower the occupational status, the more limited are the ties to economic and political collective bargaining groups and the more slim are the resources available to any family to promote its own interests.   For this reason a society that wishes to preserve and promote family life must articulate a family policy and provide structures and resources for its implementation.

Despite much change in family life, considerable stability also persists.   Although the nuclear family is often taken to be the modal type, much extended kinship in fact prevails in a modified form.   This is seen, for example, in the degree to which, contrary to common belief, the aged continue to be part of a family configuration; they share households, visit children, or maintain significant contacts through the telephone and other means.   While the aged have

[16] Vincent, *op. cit.,* p. 24.

critical unmet social needs, the degree of their isolation from family ties appears to have been somewhat exaggerated.[17] Many families continue to give financial assistance and care in other ways for the elderly. Given the increase in the life span it is possible that there are more families today providing some care for an aged person than at any time in our history.

Often ignored in discussions of the presumed decline of the family is the degree to which families are now carrying new responsibilities at almost every stage of the life cycle without adequate social provision of supportive and facilitating resources. The higher aspirations for personality development of every child place a heavier obligation than ever on parents to provide early nurturing and developmental experiences. Extended adolescence instead of early absorption into the work force, as was true in the past, means that families have prolonged responsibility for their teen-age and young adult children, with heavier burdens for social placement through college and other forms of advanced education. As already noted, a prolonged life span means that families must cope with problems in the care of the aged to a greater degree than at any time in the past. Each of these new responsibilities is a strain on family life. In the absence of adequate communal supports, they may represent risks to family stability.

A major function of the contemporary family, one that attests to its continuing importance, is to provide a setting for the free and spontaneous communication of human feelings, for the experience of the intimacy that comes with the shared release of fears and hostilities in an accepting and understanding relationship not easily found elsewhere. Indeed, as Dr. Otto Pollak has suggested, this may now be the primary function of the modern family, one for which it must develop a specialized competence. The necessity for this function stems from the impersonal, highly organized bureaucratic society with its rationalized roles and its constraints, its faceless authority, and its power to command the destiny of individuals. Otto Pollak writes:

> If we extend the meaning of the Latin root, "intimacy" means a relationship in which one enters the fears of the partner. In our society, where one comes more and more to realize to what degree his destiny is determined by impersonal and unpredictable forces such as atomic warfare, occupational obsolescence, and simply bureaucratic career mishap, the need for family members' willingness to enter into one's fears will become urgent and demanding. It will probably be one of the most important functions of the family in our time. In the past the ministry met such needs to a degree. In our times psychiatrists and social workers have met it. But no manpower extension in the helping professions is likely to ever attain coverage in meeting these needs. It is the family which is available and may increasingly be ready to do so.[18]

How to develop the social competence that will enable families to perform the functions of sympathetic understanding and the absorption of anger, fear,

[17] Alvin L. Schorr, *Filial Responsibility in the Modern American Family,* Department of Health, Education and Welfare (Washington, D.C.: Government Printing Office, 1960), p. 16.

[18] Otto Pollak, "The Outlook for the American Family," *Journal of Marriage and the Family,* 29 (February 1967), p. 199.

and other emotions is an important question. Nowhere do we adequately prepare people for sensitive awareness of and creative capacity to deal with human feelings. If anything our culture, by the isolation of art, religion, and ritual from the center of our lives, by the excessive rationalization and commercialization of daily existence, deprives us of those symbols that might evoke and richly express human emotions.[19] In the middle class the tendency is to intellectualize feelings. Among blue-collar families, according to Mirra Komarovsky, there seems to be relatively little capacity to reflect upon feelings or to communicate them. Such families have considerable difficulty, she reports, in exchange of thoughts and feelings. The men are especially inarticulate, partly because of an ideal of masculinity that derides emotional expression as unmanly. They are, as she puts it, "untrained in a capacity to share":

> . . . childhood and adolescence spent in an environment in which feelings are not named or discussed gradually strengthens these inhibitions, with deleterious affects upon the man's ability to give and receive emotional support and to cope with family conflicts. The most frequent reaction to conflict on the part of the less educated husband is repression and withdrawal, interspersed with violent quarreling. As one man put it, "You don't know quite what you feel. You are just sore and mad, so you don't say anything, and it gets worse. After a while, you blow up." [20]

Effective education for adults and children offered as part of general education and self-development rather than as treatment for emotional disturbances may be the appropriate way to prepare families for enhanced interpersonal competence. Throughout the country there are new programs being developed to promote such interpersonal competence, involving sensitivity groups and a variety of other experiences designed to increase self-awareness and sympathetic awareness of others. These are defined as educational programs for normal people rather than treatment programs for the emotionally ill. Although treatment programs will continue to be required, it is possible that universal social education of this sort, introduced early in life, may enhance interpersonal competence of the population and to some degree limit the need for later therapy. As already noted, experiments with affective education schools are now being conducted.[21]

[19] In the view of Jules Henry this neglect of human feelings is, however, an idictment to be made against all culture. He writes:
. . . no organized society has stipulated the procedures and guarantees for emotional gratification between husband and wife and between parents and children, but all societies stipulate the relationships of protection and support. . . . Meanwhile, the orientation of man toward survival, to the exclusion of other considerations, has made society a grim place to live in, and for the most part human society has been a place where, though man has survived physically, he had died emotionally. Jules Henry, *Culture Against Man* (New York: Vintage Books, 1965), p. 12.

[20] Mirra Komarovsky, in Child Study Association of America, *Children of Poverty —Children of Affluence* (New York: Child Study Association of America, 1967), pp. 42–44. *See also* Mirra Komarovsky, *Blue-Collar Marriage* (New York: Random House, 1962), Chaps. 7 and 8.

[21] Terry Borton, "Reach, Touch, and Teach," *Saturday Review,* January 18, 1969, pp. 56–58, 69–70; Max Birnbaum, "Sense and Nonsense About Sensitivity Training,"

Another important function of the family in the contemporary world, with its large-scale specialized and fragmented bureaucratic services, is that of social broker mediating between the organization and the needs of family members and negotiating with agencies to be sure that individualized services are provided to the extent possible.

> The "adequate" family of these days may be "adequate" not so much because of its internal relationships as because of its links with other socializing agencies. The "adequate" suburban family may be "adequate" because it knows about, and can successfully negotiate with, the school, the cub pack, the teen center—regardless of the quality of the relationship within the family itself. The urban areas in which serious group delinquency is most apparent are precisely those occupied by adults least able to master the dominant culture and with fewest extra-familial agencies to rely on.[22]

Social work has traditionally played a social broker role. More recently its importance has been reemphasized. However, families also need to learn how to function independently in this capacity. They need to be aware of the nature of the organizational society within which they operate and the kinds of actions they can take to promote the well-being of their members. We increasingly see that the knowledge possessed by the human service professions regarding personal and social functioning is to a considerable degree the knowledge all citizens require. It must be made available through efforts to promote new forms of social education that teach people the coping skills required for living in and for recreating their social order. Given such education and the supportive resources required, the family is likely to remain a basic institution, at least for most children, performing some functions shared with formal organizations and some that remain uniquely its own.

Changing Roles of Men and Women

Changing technology coupled with aspirations for equality of the sexes is having a powerful repercussion on the roles of men and women and therefore on family structure. Relationships between men and women are changing through the continuing economic and social emancipation of women that accompanies industrialization and through the biological emancipation made possible through the application of science to birth control. This scientific and technological support given to equality undermines the traditional basis for male and female identity and forces men and women to search for new ways to relate to one another.

A manpower revolution continues to draw more women into the labor force and into higher education. Work outside the home is increasingly accepted as a normal role for married women, so much that the President's Commission on the Status of Women seems to minimize the importance of women's traditional

Saturday Review, November 15, 1969, pp. 82–84; William C. Schutz, *Joy* (New York: Grove Press, 1967); Leland Bradford, J. Gibb, and K. Benne, *T-Group Theory and Laboratory Method* (New York: Wiley, 1965).

[22] Bordua, *op. cit.,* pp. 15–16.

roles as wives and mothers and their special feminine contribution of love and nurture.[23] It is possible that the movement of married women into the labor force has been the single most important change affecting American families in recent years. From 1961 to 1968, the number of married women in the labor force increased by more than one-fourth to a total of 17 million, a figure that represented more than three times their population increase.[24] By 1967 almost 37 percent of the married women with husbands present were working, compared to less than 15 percent in 1940.[25]

There has also been an increase in the number of mothers in the labor force. In families with both parents present there were 8.65 million working mothers (35 percent of the total number of such mothers) with almost 20 million children under age eighteen in March 1967. Five million of these children were under six. In addition over one-half of the 5.2 million female family heads were in the labor force.[26] Nowhere have we been able to keep up with the demand for suitable day care services. As of March 1968 licensed day care facilities were available for 531,000 children.[27] There were, however, more than 12 million children under twelve with mothers in the labor force that year. In spite of the proclaimed objective of getting mothers off welfare, the provision of day care for this purpose has lagged. The 1967 amendments to the Social Security Act authorized funds for day care of children of AFDC parents being trained for employment under the Work Incentive Program (WIN). The Department of Health, Education, and Welfare estimated that 1 million children would receive day care by 1972. The Bureau of the Budget requested $35 million for day care for the first year of WIN. Congress, however, appropriated half that amount, and less than $11 million of this was spent for day care for 85,000 children.[28] A major factor in improvements in family income is the labor force participation of women. In 1966 the median family income for a husband-wife family in which the wife was working was $9,246, almost a third higher than for families in which the wife was not employed. The insecurity of a wife's income needs to be emphasized, particularly in the absence of social provisions for meeting such a contingency as pregnancy. At least eighty-five other countries have some kind of maternity benefit program.

Studies indicate that women work primarily because they or their families need the money. At the same time, women have yet to attain equal employment opportunities. They share with Negroes and other minority group members some of the same discriminatory barriers: denial of jobs, less pay for identical work, and confinement to jobs in low-paying categories. In nine

[23] Margaret Mead and Francis B. Kaplan (eds.), *American Women:* The Report of the President's Commission on the Status of Women and other publications of the Commission (New York: Scribner, 1965). *See also* Edward D. Eddy's review in *The New York Times Book Review,* August 1, 1965.

[24] *Manpower Report of the President,* U.S. Department of Labor (Washington, D.C.: Government Printing Office, 1969), p. 54.

[25] *Statistical Abstract of the United States: 1968,* U.S. Bureau of the Census (Washington, D.C.: Government Printing Office, 1968).

[26] *Manpower Report of the President,* 1969, *op. cit.,* pp. 54, 56.

[27] "Day Care," *Children,* 16 (May–June 1969), pp. 122–123.

[28] *Saturday Review,* September 20, 1969, p. 75.

Standard Metropolitan Statistical Areas, women account for "one-fourth to one-third of the total work force and from one-third to one-half of the total white-collar work force, yet they held (in 1967) only a small percentage of higher echelon managerial or professional jobs." [29]

For lower-class women, as Gisela Konopka has observed, the relatively menial work opportunities available is an indication of their continued link to "a tradition of exploitation" and a constant reminder that their emancipation is incomplete.[30] Too little attention has been paid to the link between family life problems and unresolved issues of the status of women.

Women represent a great untapped resource of human talent. Given the pressures of an advanced technological society for developing its human resources, the trend toward the employment of women is likely to continue and education and employment opportunities are likely to be increasingly equalized. Attention needs to be given to the facilitating community resources and social policies required to assist women who choose to or who are required to enter the labor force. The President's Commission on the Status of Women suggests (among other things) that the following be implemented: child care services for all income levels; tax deductions for child care expenses of working mothers; public and private family services; professionally supervised homemaker services; comprehensive health and rehabilitation services, including easily accessible maternal and child health services; extension of minimum-wage legislation and unemployment insurance; paid maternity leave; equal employment opportunity; and provisions to encourage utilization of part-time employees.[31] The extent to which women will in fact seek full equality is not clear. Such research as we have does not indicate that women in general are prepared to support any radical reorganization of society required to promote their full equality in all spheres of life.[32] At the same time, Women's Liberation groups appear more than ready to make militant demands for full equality which have far-reaching implications for family life and for society as a whole.

Perhaps the second major change that may in the long run have the greatest impact on family structure is the revolution in the control of conception, which effectively separates sex from reproduction, undermines traditional sexual morality, and offers women the same opportunity for sexual freedom that men have historically enjoyed. The family as a social institution developed to a considerable degree as a link between sexual gratification and reproduction, with the consequent need to structure the cycle of birth and child care. The economic and biological emancipation of women may produce relatively different life styles from those traditionally associated with notions of family responsibility. To the degree that population control continues to be viewed as a critical problem, society's need for fewer child-bearing families may create a climate for greater acceptance of life styles for men and women independent of child-rearing responsibilities. Some indication of trends in this direction may

[29] *Ibid.*, pp. 198–199.

[30] Gisela Konopka, *The Adolescent Girl in Conflict* (Englewood Cliffs, N.J.: Prentice-Hall, 1966) p. 73.

[31] Mead and Kaplan, *op. cit.*, pp. 210–213.

[32] Jesse Bernard, "The Status of Women in Modern Patterns of Culture," *The Annals,* 375 (January 1968), p. 10.

be seen in marriage and family statistics that indicate the likelihood of continued major increases in the proportion of unmarried individuals who maintain their own households, a rise in the average age of women at first marriage, and some decline in the average size of households and families.[33] The need for fewer child-bearing families, the availability of relatively effective contraception, and the individual's desire to postpone obligations of parenthood to further other self-actualizing goals may lead to the acceptance of Margaret Mead's proposal that society sanction two kinds of marriage—one "individual," the other "family" oriented. Social arrangements would accommodate the sex drive and yet not require a binding marriage at an early age, which evidence indicates has a high-risk factor. Individual marriages for sexual gratification and companionship might be arranged and dissolved with relatively few social controls. Family marriages for the purpose of having children would be subjected to somewhat greater legal restrictions.[34] More permissive sexual unions and ready access to birth control are likely to reduce rates of illegitimacy and divorce rates in youthful marriages. What other consequences may follow remain to be seen.

Radical change in the status of women produces a sexual identity crisis as women acquire new identities and as ". . . males continue to depend for sense of their identity on the social differences no longer faced in social reality." [35] Efforts to resolve this problem and to discover new patterns for mutually satisfying modes of sexual relationships may be part of a cultural revolution that will transform family life and release human capacity from the narrow framework of the traditional family structure. The trend, particularly noted in middle-class families, toward a democratic companionship family is an indication of this. Family unity is maintained more by mutual regard and reciprocal exchange of satisfactions than by tradition and the exercise of authority.

The paradox is that marriage today may be both more satisfying and more fragile. As expectations for personal gratification and happiness increase, greater demands are placed on the marital union for self-fulfillment of both partners, and this is accompanied by greater readiness to dissolve the union as disappointments are encountered. Thus, as Richard E. Farson has noted, "frustration arises, essentially from the *improvement* in family life." [36] The paradox too is that the expectation of happiness in marriage may mean a greater risk of instability and unhappiness for children of a divorce as individual adult gratification is given precedence over family stability. On the other hand it appears that rates of divorce are highest in groups characterized by low income and low occupational status and lowest in groups with high occupation and income.[37] While each year a substantial number of marriages end in

---

[33] R. Parke and T. C. Glick, "Prospective Changes in Marriage and the Family," *Journal of Marriage and the Family*, 29, (May 1967), pp. 249–256.

[34] Harley L. Browning, "Timing of Our Lives" *Trans-action*, 6 (October 1969), p. 27.

[35] Mead, *op. cit.*, p. 875.

[36] Farson, *et. al., op. cit.*, p. 65.

[37] Hugh Carter and Alexander Plateris, "Trends in Divorce and Family Disruption," *Health, Education, and Welfare Indicators*, September 1963, p. xiii.

divorce, most divorced people eventually remarry. Moreover, the current level of divorce is considerably below the peak of 1945. It is well to point out that the common assertion that one marriage in four ends in divorce is a distortion because, in that statement, current divorces are related only to marriages, occuring within a given year while in fact current divorces occurred to marriages that took place at any time to persons still living. A more accurate measure is the divorce rate per 1,000 married females aged fifteen years and over. This has been under 10 (or 1 percent) each year since 1953. Thus, out of total married couples only one in every 100 obtained a divorce in 1960.[38] This rate has been rising very slowly since 1960; in 1965 the divorce rate per 1,000 married females was 10.6, which is still considerably below the 14.4 rate of 1945.[39] Improvements in education and socioeconomic position of the population in general may be reflected in greater stability and satisfaction in marriage as the democratic companionship relationship becomes the norm.

For some, even this model may seem too constricting. There have been renewed efforts at emancipation on the part of some women and experimental attempts to create new modes of communal living that express the need for affiliation beyond the boundaries of marriage and family. These are likely, however, to be peripheral. They might even provoke a "counter-revolution," as Margaret Mead anticipates, that may seek to ". . . refocus attention on the home, limit sexual freedom, curtail the individual development of women and subordinate the creative capacities of the individual adult to the needs of the group for docile parents, workers, and citizens." [40] Rapid change, new awareness of class and ethnic variations in family structures, and declining consensus regarding family norms make it difficult to determine what constitutes family disorganization as distinct from merely different or emerging forms of marital and family relationships. Families with an absent father need not necessarily be identified as disorganized; [41] the notion of "bachelor mothers" has been gaining some currency in England. It is possible that treating relatively unconventional family structures as deviant may contribute to their problems and that social acceptance of varied forms of family life, along with appropriate resources and supports, may enable such units to function adequately.

Changing Parent-Child Relationships

Change also characterizes the relationship of parents to children. Families tend to be characterized by a smaller number of children than in the past; more intensive economic and emotional investment in their well-being; prolonged dependency of children as additional years of education are required for adult social participation; and increasing parental anxiety and confusion about appropriate methods of child rearing, as change undermines traditional notions of child care and discipline. Reliance on experts in child development and family life education may compound the problem because theories conflict and

[38] *Ibid.,* p. v.

[39] *Statistical Abstract,* 1968, p. 61.

[40] *Ibid.,* p. 874.

[41] Elizabeth Herzog and Cecelia E. Sudia, "Fatherless Homes: A Review of Research," *Children,* 15 (September–October 1968), pp. 177–182.

are subject to change. Middle-class parents in particular may confront a dilemma in deciding on the kind of social world they are preparing their children to enter.

On the one hand we are a technologically driven society moving in the direction of a meritocracy of talent, seeking to mobilize human resources toward the single goal of maximum productive efficiency. On the other hand there are reactions against the ideology of technology on the part of the "non-accommodators," as Erik Erikson puts it, who are in quest of new modes of human relationships and new ways of socializing and educating their children for a positive affirmation of life and its possibilities.[42] Whether the humanistic preparation for the life they seek for their children does in fact enable them to adapt to requirements for living in an achievement-driven society is part of the dilemma. Middle-class families, according to Dr. Richard Flacks, can be classified into two types: those who continue to adhere to the capitalistic ethic of occupational achievement and those who stress a humanist perspective on life. The suggestion is made that the humanist family orientations are more likely to occur when the breadwinner is involved in a human relations profession.[43] The meritocracy toward which we seem to be moving requires of a family those socialization experiences in the early years that prepare the child to compete with his peers for educational attainment. Competition for status has moved from the marketplace into the classroom. The entire ". . . family-child world is changing because of the ever increasing importance of schooling in determining one's life chances." [44] This has led S. M. Miller to observe that to enhance the social functioning of the family in this era is to concentrate on increasing their educational competence.[45] The family contributes to the child's equal opportunity to compete for preferred status partly by providing a learning environment that stimulates the development of cognitive skills in the service of a "mobility ethos." In describing the mobility ethos, John Porter said that, along with the school, the family's function is to socialize a child to ". . . desire to acquire material possessions, to achieve, and to postpone gratification in favor of the irksomeness of learning." [46]

The degree to which learning is indeed irksome may depend on the extent to which learning in the service of a drive for status is compatible with the child's

[42] Erik H. Erikson, "Memorandum on Youth," *Daedalus,* 96 (Summer 1967), pp. 860–870. *See also* Estelle Fuchs, "The Free Schools of Denmark," *Saturday Review,* August 16, 1969, pp. 43–44 and 53. This article describes a similar quest for a humanistic education with doubts, however, about whether this is functional for living in a technological world.

[43] *The Acquisition and Development of Values,* National Institute of Child Health and Human Development (Washington, D.C.: Government Printing Office, 1969), pp. 6–7.

[44] Eli Ginzberg, "New Perspectives on the Family," in Child Study Association, *op. cit.,* p. 25.

[45] S. M. Miller, "Poverty and Inequality in America," in Frank Riessman, Jerome Cohen, and Arthur Pearl (eds.), *Mental Health of the Poor* (New York: Free Press, 1964), p. 15.

[46] John Porter, "The Future of Upward Mobility," *American Sociological Review,* 33 (February 1968).

own growth motivation; it may also depend on the degree to which a match exists between the child's own interest and the learning encountered. There may well be an inherent tension between love of learning for its own sake and learning as "creature of drive, exploited largely for survival and for prestige." [47] The family's dilemma in socializing children, in part, has to do with the kind and quality of drive for achievement it will seek to develop in the young child, assuming of course that it is in a position to be conscious of such a choice and to exercise options. What seems to be clear is that the child's life chances are heavily influenced by the family environment. In turn, the social-class position of the family is a strong determinant of what that environment will be like.

Social Class and Family Life

If vast changes are taking place they clearly do not affect all families the same way. Families vary enormously. To a significant degree variations are related to the family's position in the social structure. There is some evidence to indicate that family stability and perhaps the quality of family life are inversely related to social class. Rates of divorce and desertion occur more frequently among the lower class. Family solidarity appears to increase with additional income, education, leisure, and the security and satisfactions that may accompany work as a career. Families who make their way to the suburbs by way of fairly solid upward mobility may enjoy not only the comforts of middle-class life but the self-esteem that derives from social acceptance. Home ownership symbolizes such status and achievement. According to Herbert Gans pride and satisfaction in owning one's own home is reflected in greater family solidarity.[48] In large scale organizations, new forms of transactional work involving exchange of information and requiring human relations skills may be reflected in greater interpersonal competence in family relations as well. Thus it may be that family life is improving in quality and in stability for the upwardly mobile. It may be getting worse for those toward the bottom of the social-class system as families find themselves without the personal and social resources to participate as full members in society. Yet this is largely conjecture. The rejection of middle-class values and middle-class family life by a significant number of youths indicates that economically and socially successful families may be afflicted with a malaise that is concealed by the outward appearance of stability and harmony.

Even the greater instability of the lower-class family may require reexamination as we recognize that families with an absent father may represent a different rather than a deviant or pathological family structure. Although it is generally agreed that a good two-parent family is more conducive to healthy child development, the evidence does not indicate that a one-parent family is necessarily harmful or that it cannot, especially with adequate social supports, function adequately as a child-rearing unit.[49]

[47] Henry, *op. cit.*, p. 319.

[48] Herbert Gans, *The Levittowners* (New York: Pantheon Books, 1967).

[49] Elizabeth Herzog and Cecelia E. Sudia, "Family Structure and Composition: Research Considerations," in Roger R. Miller (ed.), *Race, Research, and Reason* (New York: National Association of Social Workers, 1969); Herzog and Sudia,

Lower-class families do not, however, have adequate social supports in the form of assured income, decent employment, adequate housing, quality medical care, day care, access to recreation and leisure time activities, or the opportunities for rewarding social participation that develop a sense of competence and self-respect. It is not surprising then that family disorganization, delinquency, mental illness, and other forms of social maladjustment are more heavily concentrated among the poor. For example, while severe and disabling forms of mental illness are found among all social classes, a disproportionate number of mental patients come from the lower end of the socioeconomic scale.[50] While the causal link between social class and mental illness is not fully known, it is reasonable to assume that deprivations and devaluations associated with inferior social-class position are significantly related to the higher incidence of mental illness and other problems in social functioning.

Yet to speak of family disorganization and related problems among the lower class is to ignore important variations in family structures, life styles, and coping abilities among the poor. The term lower class itself fails to distinguish between the stable working class and the unstable lower class.[51] Even within these two broad classifications there are significant subgroups and tremendous individual variations, still little understood. Of special note are the problem families—those families displaying the most severe forms of disorganization. Characteristics associated with such families have been identified as (1) chronicity of need, (2) multiplicity of problems, (3) resistance to treatment, and (4) handicapping attitudes.[52] Such characteristics, however, are descriptive rather than explanatory. Despite a long history of concern with multiproblem families, our knowledge regarding etiology, treatment, and prevention remains at best fragmentary.[53] In Hylan Lewis' terms, these are the "clinical families" having severe forms of pathology, who must be distinguished from other poor families whose problems are rooted more in their social environment than in their personal functioning. This is not to suggest that there are no societal factors in the development of multi-problem families, for in all likelihood such families are as much socially created as other forms of family life. Precisely how society is involved is obscure.

---

op. cit.; Hylan Lewis, "Race, Class, and Culture in the Sociopolitics of Social Welfare," in Roger R. Miller, *op. cit.* A different viewpoint cites the "growing body of research evidence" pointing "to the debilitating effect on personality development in Negro children, particularly males, resulting from the high frequency of father absence in Negro families." Urie Bronfenbrenner, "The Psychological Costs of Quality and Equality in Education," *Child Development,* 38 (December 1967), p. 914.

[50] S. M. Miller and Elliot G. Mishler, "Social Class, Mental Illness, and American Psychiatry: An Expository Review," in Riessman, *et al., op. cit.,* p. 22.

[51] S. M. Miller and Frank Riessman, "The Working Class Subculture: A New View," *Social Problems,* 9 (Summer 1961), pp. 86–97.

[52] Roland L. Warren, "A Multi-Problem Confrontation," in Gordon E. Brown (ed.), *The Multi-Problem Dilemma* (Metuchen, N.J.: Scarecrow Press, 1968), p. 89.

[53] Brown, *op. cit.;* Eleanor Pavenstadt (ed.), *The Drifters* (Boston: Little, Brown, 1967); Geismar, *op. cit.*

Family and the Quest for Community

A focus on social disorganization is likely to help us understand the contemporary strains in family life more than any assumption about the decline of the family. Social reconstruction would then be seen as essential for fostering healthy family and social development. Perhaps a better way of putting it would be to speak in terms of a community of shared meaning and purpose, our lack of it, and our great need for it.

In "The Eclipse of Community," Maurice Stein analyzed the malaise that characterizes middle-class suburbia. Though the outward forms of suburban life are remarkably different from those in the anomic slums, it is possible that a sense of powerlessness and lack of dignified purpose is common to two seemingly different social environments.[54] Industrialization supplanted a sacred with a secular view of life's purpose, thus freeing man of the constraints of tradition while binding his energies toward the shallow goal of a "worldly paradise based on material acquisitions."[55] The quest for status as an end in itself has meant the acceptance of an instrumental view of human relations and a narrow anxiety-ridden identity based on occupational achievement. Children have become valued for what they could accomplish rather than for themselves, despite parental insistence to the contrary. The human need for meaningful relationships with others as persons rather than as objects has become subordinated to a never-ending struggle for upward mobility. Husbands have become trapped in careers that have drained them of their best energies. Wives educated for careers but confined to subordinate domestic roles have kept compulsively busy as a way of denying the vacuum in which they lived. Since status could never be secure or necessarily attached to some self-transcending purpose that might make the struggle meaningful, a pervasive existential anxiety has prompted the resort to various forms of psychotherapy in a quest for self-realization. Psychological experts have become the ". . . modern shamans exorcising the tribal ghosts so that the routines of living can be kept up without interference. But these shamans cannot touch the underlying causes of the anxiety they temporarily allay."[56] Youths, forecasting their own life prospects on the basis of models around them, have learned to ". . . submerge the specter of a life that lacks rooted values and creative meanings by throwing themselves into the struggle for status."[57] Transforming themselves into objects and treating others in like manner has become the price for the quest for " . . . an ephemeral and empty sense of status." In this way the malaise of bourgeois society identified by Marx as alienation and by Durkheim as anomie has been achieved.[58] Such is the much-abbreviated analysis of Stein's

[54] Maurice Stein, "The Eclipse of Community," in Warren G. Bennis *et al.* (eds.), *The Planning of Change* (New York: Holt, Rinehart & Winston, 1962), pp. 38–43. This is an excerpt from a book by the same title, Maurice Stein, *The Eclipse of Community* (Princeton, N.J.: Princeton University Press, 1960), pp. 279–289.

[55] *Ibid.,* p. 39.

[56] *Ibid.,* p. 42.

[57] *Ibid.,* p. 41.

[58] *Ibid.*

thesis. He depicts the agony of middle-class society, a theme elaborated on by many others whose diagnosis of our times is essentially the same.[59]

However, not all observers of the American scene find this kind of malaise in suburbia.[60] The apparent revolt of a possibly small but significant minority of middle-class youths reflects a quest for new values and a rejection of the single-minded pursuit of status as the goal of life. Such a revolt indicates the inability of the family to win the loyalty of its children to existing institutions; but such symptoms of anomie as revealed by parental confusion and youthful rebellion clearly has roots in the larger social system. If there is failure it is not so much in the family as in our economic and political institutions, in our educational system, and in our central values and goals as they are reflected in national policies. The failure seems to be a basic incapacity for self-renewal sufficient in scope to meet the challenge of revolutionary social change. The family's capacity to transmit traditional norms and values is undermined in this period of change by nagging doubts on the part of adults as to the value of their commitment to the empty struggle for status and by the awareness on the part of youths that they have options their parents could not or would not exercise to search for other definitions of life's purpose. One may find in this the decline in family authority, but the root of the problem and the solution, if there is one, is to be found elsewhere.

The essential problem, as Urie Bronfenbrenner defines it, is the alienation of children from a sense of community. Although the problem may be in some respects more severe for lower-class children, in his view it is not restricted to the nation's poor: "So far as alienation of children is concerned, the world of the disadvantaged simply reflects in more severe form a social disease that has infected the entire society."[61] Children suffer, he thinks, from a decline of parenting both on the part of their parents and on the part of the community. They grow up in a relatively narrow and sterile world with too little of the stimulating and nurturing interaction with a wide variety of adults that was characteristic of the extended kinship family and small communal societies. Middle-class parents, preoccupied with the struggle for status, and lower-class parents, constrained by the struggle for survival, are without the resources in time, energy, and capacity to devote to their children. Barriers of social class, race, and age, combined with the extreme individualism characteristic of American life so isolates families from one another that children grow up without having a sense of community. Their impoverished social world deprives them of expanded intellectual horizons and of opportunities to experience regard and responsibility for others. The isolation of youths from adult society and the relative autonomy of peer groups prevent the constructive use of peer-group influence in character development, accounting in part for juvenile delinquency.

To Bronfenbrenner, the solution lies in efforts to recreate a sense of commu-

[59] *See,* for example, Erich Fromm, *Escape from Freedom* (New York: Holt, Rinehart & Winston, 1941); Erich Fromm, *The Sane Society* (New York: Rinehart, 1955); and Maurice Stein *et al., Identity and Anxiety* (New York: Free Press, 1960).

[60] *See,* for example, Herbert Gans, *The Levittowners* (New York: Pantheon, 1967); *Identity and Anxiety, op. cit.*

[61] Urie Bronfenbrenner, "The Split-Level American Family," *Saturday Review,* October 7, 1967, p. 66.

nity through experiences of shared purpose, which may overcome barriers of class, age, and race. Family and child development centers based on a collective regard for the welfare of all children can offer, he believes, a structure for the communal extension of parenting. Devotion to the common task of rearing children by all groups provides the common effort in behalf of a superordinate goal required for a sense of community. In his view, Head Start provides a model that might be extended to the middle class, for its purpose is not remedial education ". . . but the giving to both children and their families of a sense of dignity, purpose, and meaningful activity without which children cannot develop capacities in any sphere of activity, including the intellectual." [62]

What is clear is that the family cannot be understood apart from society, nor can it be strengthened in social isolation. Family and society are linked at all stages of the life cycle. The biological and social competence of family members reflects the family's social-class position and its access to social supports and resources. The family today is being asked to carry new responsibilities for which resources have not been made available and for which parental capacities have not been developed. From this perspective we confront not so much a failure of the family as new demands being made on it that call for new social provisions and services. As Margaret Mead noted long ago, "we now expect a family to achieve alone what no society ever expected an individual family to accomplish unaided. In effect, we call upon the individual family to do what a whole clan used to do." [63] If we are serious about our efforts to strengthen the family we will need to focus on the social context of family life and develop social policy that reflects a regard for this basic social institution.

Social Welfare Efforts to Strengthen Family Life

Issues in Family Policy

We have extolled family life but have rarely nurtured it in this society. We have sought to strengthen family life without providing the basic institutional supports essential to enable the family to perform its basic functions. We have, in short, relatively little in the way of a national family policy. Instead we focus on individual and social problems. So powerful is our emphasis on the individual that, for the most part, our programs designed to deal with social problems have tended to ignore the fact that the individual is part of a family unit. Even the program whose official rhetoric proclaims the goal of strengthening family life—Aid to Families with Dependent Children—is actually cast in the framework of individual needs and dependency rather than family needs and the goal of family stability and development. Grants were originally provided to dependent children without regard for the needs of the mother in the family. As late as 1969 most states made no provision for a needy family with an unemployed or subemployed father in the home.

Clark Vincent, among others, has noted our tendency to perceive social problems in terms of the individual. For example, he observes that the Eighty-ninth

---

[62] *Ibid.,* p. 66.

[63] Laura L. Dittman (ed.), *Early Child Care* (New York: Atherton Press, 1968), p. 3.

Congress in 1965 enacted fifty-nine laws that had some implications for the broad field of mental health. Yet the family is not included in any of the titles or subject areas of those pieces of social legislation. The 1965 OEO *Catalog of Federal Programs for Individual and Community Improvement,* containing 393 pages, does not contain any reference to family in its title. Moreover, the index contains only 3 indirect references to the family in 262 topical references and only 13 such references in 563 subheadings.[64] Despite extensive operations of the U.S. Department of Health, Education, and Welfare no major unit within that vast bureaucracy has the primary responsibility of considering the welfare of all American families. Advanced welfare states as Sweden and Norway, however, have well-defined family policies. In the United States we tend to rely more heavily on residual social services to cope with family breakdown rather than on broad social policy to assure all families essential social supports. We assume that the family should be self-reliant and that it requires an expression of social concern primarily at the point of breakdown. The relative lack of family policy in the United States might be made more clear by a brief reference to the variety of provisions made to support family life in one advanced welfare state—Sweden.[65]

A striking feature of family policy in Sweden is the extended income supports made available for all families. For example, a Swedish family with three children (mother not gainfully employed) and a taxable income of roughly $3,281 in American dollars (1964) receives a direct and indirect subsidy of some $840, an increase in disposable income of about 31.7 percent. For the bulk of Swedish families, such subsidies compensate for anywhere from 30 to 50 percent of the cost of rearing children. That is, they replace 30–50 percent of the decline in income such families would experience relative to childless couples in the same income bracket if no subsidies were available.[66] Such subsidies include the following:

(1) There are children's allowances, paid quarterly to all families regardless of income or number of children for each child under sixteen, and student allowances for youths attending school.

(2) Prenatal maternity and child health care benefits are available for all women who require such services. A provision in the law also requires that employers may not fire a woman because of maternity and that she must be permitted to return to her job. (Swedish families whose standard of living is based on two earners are therefore not exposed to the risk incurred by similar American families.)

(3) Children receive free dental care and almost-free medical care and checkups until school age. In addition free health care and free lunches are provided for children of school age.

(4) Loans enable a young couple to receive as much as $770 to establish a household. Home loans at 4 percent for thirty years are available. Families

---

[64] Vincent, *op. cit.,* pp. 18–19.

[65] The material on family policy in Sweden is drawn from Carl G. Uhr, *Sweden's Social Security System,* Social Security Administration, Research Report No. 14 (Washington, D.C.: Government Printing Office, 1966), especially Chap. 2, "Sweden's Social Policy for Families and Children," pp. 9–35.

[66] *Ibid.,* p. 31.

with children receive rent subsidies or rebates, varying with income and number of children. In 1961–1962, 5 percent of Swedish families received rent rebates, amounting to about a 10 percent reduction in rent. If similar arrangements had been in effect in the United States, a family of four with an income under $6,000 would have qualified for a rent rebate.

(5) A network of day nurseries, play centers, and nursery schools makes it feasible for mothers to work. There are also government-subsidized children's camps and special tax deductions for gainfully employed mothers. Low-income mothers with children under fourteen are entitled, at least once a year, to a free round-trip vacation anywhere in Sweden and at least a ten-day stay at a communal vacation home, where room and board is provided at a nominal cost. Home caretakers are provided, on request, to care for husbands and children.[67]

There has been no adequate evaluation of the impact of this policy on family life, but it is clear that Sweden has gone a long way toward solving its problem of poverty and toward assuring to all families a reasonably decent floor on income as well as other supports required in an industrial society. Some problems remain. Housing, for example, is still in short supply; it is estimated that about a third of the urban population is living in crowded substandard housing.[68]

If equivalent programs were available in the United States, it is estimated that they would require annual expenditures of $12–15 billion for cash allowances and for health and related services for nonindigent and nonrelief families. If we were to spend a proportion of our Gross National Product equivalent to what Sweden spends for family-oriented programs, we would allocate at a minimum some $16 billion. There are critics of the Swedish family policy who argue that provisions made for other than the needy limit resources that might be concentrated on helping the more deprived families. Here we meet the problem of universal versus special services. In Sweden, however, there is a strong desire to avoid any means test, which in that society is considered ". . . a stigma which a progressive democratic community should not inflict on less fortunate of its citizens."[69] Nonetheless, Sweden has been forced to work out a compromise between the principle of universal services and special programs for the needy. In 1969, Sweden rejected a plan to tax child allowances in order to preserve the universal nature of this program. However, a large increase in housing allowances on a means tested basis was accepted as a way of extending benefits to 40 percent of families with children.

It should also be noted that the common assumption that large expenditures for social welfare guaranteeing a minimum level of economic security invariably depress the economy and destroy initiative does not seem to be the case in Sweden. Expenditures for social welfare are about 12 percent of the Gross National Product and represent a relatively sizable portion of government expenditures and a rather heavy tax burden. Yet these expenditures have not impeded economic growth. If anything they seem to have facilitated it. Along with other factors, they have helped to maintain economic stability. Real Gross

[67] *Ibid.,* pp. 9–16.

[68] To allocate sufficient resources for housing would take away from the production Sweden needs for its international trade, which would create a serious balance-of-payments problem. *Ibid.,* p. 25.

[69] *Ibid.,* p. 21.

National Product grew at an annual rate of 4 percent in the eighteen years from 1946 to 1963.[70]

In addition to social welfare programs specifically aimed at supporting family life, Sweden also maintains a progressive and rational policy of full employment, which also has a positive impact on families. It operates, for example, a nation-wide network of labor placement services in conjunction with public employment offices. Labor mobility is stimulated by grants of money to enable workers to move to new areas where employment is available; this includes travel grants to seek work. If work is obtained grants are made available to provide for moving expenses and to maintain families if temporary separation is necessary. In addition, allowances consisting of a mixture of loans and grants enable a family to get settled in a new location. If the breadwinner keeps a new job more than six months, he does not have to repay the loan. There are also extended unemployment insurance benefits for those undergoing retraining. Through other measures, the government exercises control over the economy in order to maintain optimal levels of employment and to anticipate areas of unemployment and make essential provisions for this contingency.

There are signs in the United States that we may be moving in the direction of articulating a family policy as new programs are added and old programs are revised. Such is the view of Hylan Lewis, who sees a national family policy emerging as we move toward a universal income maintenance program, planned parenthood, comprehensive health services, manpower development training, and so forth.[71]

Family Policy: An Ideal Model

To have a maximum impact on family development a family policy would need to take into account (1) the family in its sociocultural context, (2) personal and social resources required for various stages in the family life cycle, (3) the desirability of an appropriate mix of strategies and programs, and (4) measures for replacing residual with institutional provisions and services.

Social policy concerned with the enhancement of family life must start with a recognition of the social context of family functioning, the inseparable link between family and community, and the interrelatedness of all social institutions. Special attention would be paid to the family's position in the social structure. Although too little is known about this, there is a growing body of evidence that suggests that family organization, child-rearing patterns, and the prevalence of various interrelated social ills are associated with social class and, in particular, with the occupational status of the breadwinner.[72] Although our understanding of the causal links between social class and family functioning is limited, some hypotheses are provided by Leo Srole's analysis of the relationship between social class and mental illness. Reviewing the evidence from the study *Mental*

[70] *Ibid.,* p. 153.

[71] Hylan Lewis, "The Family: New Agenda, Different Rhetoric," in Child Study Association of America, *op. cit.,* pp. 1–16.

[72] *See* works by Elliot Liebow, Hyman Rodman, Donald McKinley, and Mirra Komoravsky; *see also* Melvin L. Kohn, *Class and Conformity: A Study in Values* (Homewood, Ill.: Dorsey Press, 1969).

Health in the Metropolis—one of several studies that reveal a negative correlation between social-class position and rates of mental illness—Srole suggests that the data might be explained by three sociocultural dysfunctions.[73] These three "potentially malignant, socially linked phenomena" are (1) the poverty complex, (2) the stigmatize-rejection mechanism, and (3) the role discontinuity predicament. Of special significance is the suggestion that "if these can be demonstrated to be pathogenic for family functioning they are potentially open to the social process of correction." [74]

The first refers to the stress produced by economic and social deprivation. Although the actual link between mental illness and such deprivation remains obscure, there is sufficient evidence that family development suffers under the handicap of a poverty of resources required for functioning at some socially acceptable level. It seems fairly clear that in a money economy with relatively high expectations for family functioning, an adequate level of income is required to meet the basic needs of family members and to facilitate social participation. In this connection, some major points (most of them already introduced in previous chapters) may be summarized in the following way:

(1) Economic poverty associated with malnutrition and inadequate prenatal care means a high risk of complications in pregnancy, prematurity, and congenital defect. Inadequate income and deprivation of other nurturing resources may result in a biological insult for the newborn child in the form of mental retardation, cerebral palsy, epilepsy, behavioral disorders, and reading disability.[75]

(2) Basic needs must be met before individuals can develop higher-level functions.[76]

(3) Stable nonstigmatized income is related to stable family life. Moreover the amount and security of family income affects child-rearing priorities. Families with low incomes tend to devote major energy to survival needs. Too little

---

[73] Leo Srole, Thomas S. Langner, Stanley T. Michael, Marvin K. Opler, and Thomas A. C. Rennie, *Mental Health in the Metropolis: The Midtown Manhattan Study* (New York: McGraw-Hill, 1962), Vol. I. *See also* Thomas S. Langner and Stanley T. Michael, *Life Stress and Mental Health* (New York: Free Press, 1963). For other studies of the relationship between social class and mental illness *see* August B. Hollingshed and Frank K. Redlich, *Social Class and Mental Illness* (New York: Wiley, 1958) and A. H. Leighton, et al., *Sterling County Study of Psychiatric Disorder and Sociocultural Environment*, Vols. I, II, III (New York: Basic Books, 1959). For a critique of where we are in our understanding of this phenomenon *see* S. M. Miller and Mishler in Reissman, et al., *op. cit.*, pp. 16–36.

[74] Srole, *op. cit.*, p. 359.

[75] Bronfenbrenner, "The Psychological Costs," *op. cit.*; Gerald Caplan (ed.), *Prevention of Mental Disorders in Children* (New York: Basic Books, 1961), p. 91; Alfred H. Katz and Jean Spencer Felton (eds.), *Health and the Community* (New York: Free Press, 1965), pp. 199–211; Nevin S. Scrimshaw, "Infant Malnutrition and Adult Learning," *Saturday Review,* March 16, 1968, pp. 64–66 and 84; Florence Haselkorn (ed.), *Mothers-At-Risk* (New York: Adelphi University School of Social Work, 1966).

[76] Benjamin J. Bloom, Allison Davis, and Robert Hess, *Compensatory Education for Cultural Deprivation* (New York: Holt, Rinehart & Winston, 1965), p. 8; Abraham H. Maslow, *Motivation and Personality* (New York: Harper & Bros., 1954).

may be left for the emotional, cognitive, and social development of children. This is not to suggest that income stability and adequacy alone determine the quality of family life or of child-rearing practices.

(4) Economic poverty leads to social impoverishment since money is required for almost all participation in social life (e.g., transportation, club dues, church collections, entertaining guests, etc.).

(5) Money is freedom and power, freedom to exercise choice and power to make decisions governing one's life. For example, the feeling of being forced by economic circumstances to live in a slum adds to the demoralization of its residents.[77] Money, of course, is neither freedom nor power if it is provided in a way that debases and constricts the recipient. Clearly one must feel an entitlement to income either through earning it or through transfer payments provided as a citizen right.

(6) Research on efforts to assist the most deprived and most disorganized families suggests that adequate income may be an essential precondition for the effective use of other social services.[78]

(7) Significant capital investment may be necessary to move families out of poverty.[79]

(8) Relative deprivation, not the absolute amount of income, is the key to understanding the life style of the poor. So long as a group of people are forced to live at levels significantly below that of average citizens, ". . . we will continue to have the misery and the problems of an underclass." [80]

The last point draws attention to the fact that poverty in this society is not simply a lack of the basic essentials of life. It is fundamentally a demeaned status, a social position insulting to self-esteem, requiring the development of various defensive, protective, and compensating life styles that are sometimes captured in the ill-suited phrase, the culture of poverty. It is possible that the relatively high prevalence of mental illness and other deviant behavior among the poor are different ways of coping with the stigmatize-rejection process inherent in our status allocation mechanism. It may be that the stigma that accompanies the damaged roles occupied by the poor, which institutionalizes their failure, is the greatest threat to mental health and to family stability. The shame of being poor in a society that equates poverty with personal inadequacy may help to account for the findings on social class and mental illness.

Our attention is also drawn to the way status is achieved in this society. Once again we are reminded of the link between occupational role, family structure, and child-rearing patterns. Some of the points previously made are worthy of brief review. Work is central since it is the major social role, the primary link between family and society, and the means by which the material, social, and psychic resources (e.g., money, status, self-esteem, power, and autonomy) essential for family formation, stability, and development are acquired. The poor

[77] Scott Greer, *Urban Renewal and American Cities* (Indianapolis: Bobbs-Merrill, 1965); "Pruitt-Igoe: Survival in a Concrete Ghetto," *Social Work,* 12 (October 1967), pp. 3–13.

[78] Brown, *op. cit.*

[79] Alvin Schorr, *Poor Kids* (New York: Basic Books, 1966), p. 47.

[80] Lee Rainwater, "Looking Back and Looking Up," *Trans-action,* 6 (February 1969), p. 9.

are effectively barred from decent work opportunities and, when forced to rely on welfare, they move from a damaged work role to a damaged welfare role. Often they occupy both. Mastery in work seems to be a prerequisite for further self-actualization and for the enhancement of family life.

On the other hand there is some evidence that an excessive occupational achievement orientation may be dysfunctional for some families and possibly for the society as a whole.[81] However, so long as work remains the major instrument for allocation of status, self-esteem, and resources, the deprivation of decent employment opportunities will result in family life styles that deviate from the commonly accepted norm of a stable two-parent household. Thus the lower-class, female-based family may be seen as a solution to the occupation-earner problem of the lower class, an adaptation to economic insecurity.[82] This family structure, however, may be dysfunctional for rearing children for upward mobility. On the other hand, while an adequate two-parent family may be preferred, a stable one-parent family is probably a better child-rearing unit than a conflict-ridden two-parent union. Moreover, as already noted, research evidence does not support the simple assertion that children are necessarily damaged by growing up in a fatherless family. Instead of viewing the female-based household as a form of family pathology, it can be studied ". . . as a family form in itself, rather than as a mutilated version of some other form." [83] Since over 6 million children now live in families without a father, and since most of these will continue to remain single-parent families, it makes sense to explore the positives as well as the weaknesses in this form of family organization. It may be capable of providing a suitable family environment, especially if appropriate social supports and alternative masculine role models are available and if the stigma associated with labeling the single-parent family as deviant is removed. It might be noted that many middle-class families are functionally single-parent units because fathers may be, so far as the children are concerned, absent—preoccupied as many are with business and careers that leave little or no time for effective family interaction. Nonetheless, to the degree that we wish to reduce the prevalence of female-based households among the poor, it would appear that altering employment opportunities for lower-class males is essential.

For the blue-collar stable working class, issues of family structure and child-rearing practices are of a somewhat different order.[84] Although there are enormous differences among families occupying more or less the same social class position, the relationship between occupational status and child-rearing practices seems to hold some fruitful implications for social policy. It appears that child-rearing values and practices reflect the education and occupational status of the major breadwinner. For a society concerned about promoting individual initiative and autonomy, the evidence that altering the occupation of

---

[81] *Ibid.,* p. 99; McKinley, *op. cit.*

[82] Rodman, *op. cit.;* Elliot Liebow, *Tally's Corner* (Boston: Little, Brown, 1966).

[83] Herzog and Sudia, "Fatherless Homes," *op. cit.*

[84] Komarovsky, *Blue-Collar Marriage, op. cit.;* Eleanor Pavenstadt, "A Comparison of the Child-rearing Environment of Upper-Lower and Very Low-Lower Class Families," *American Journal of Orthopsychiatry,* 35 (January 1965), p. 89; Miller and Riessman, *op. cit.*

the breadwinner may be the most potent way of changing child-rearing values and practices to support these objectives compels our attention.

At least this is the conclusion of Melvin L. Kohn, who conducted a study to try to discover why social class affects parental values.[85] He concluded that autonomy in work leads to child rearing that stresses autonomy and independence and that authoritarian attitudes in child rearing reflect the limited freedom characteristic of the occupational role of the working class, a conclusion also supported by the work of Donald Gilbert McKinley.[86] Starting with the recognition that research has documented the fact that middle-class parents tend to emphasize self-direction in children and that working-class parents conform to external standards, Kohn's search was for the specific circumstances of social-class life that accounted for the link between class and parental values.[87] Like McKinley, Kohn came to the conclusion that the occupational conditions of each class tend to be instrumental in determining the parental values incorporated in child-rearing practices. Middle-class occupations are more likely to deal with the manipulation of interpersonal relations and symbols in a context allowing and even demanding considerable autonomy. Occupations characteristic of the working class are more likely to deal with things, to be routine in nature and subject to direct control and supervision: "In short, middle-class occupations demand a greater degree of self-direction; working-class occupations require that the individual conform to rules and procedures established by authority." [88]

Of considerable interest is the fact that this general statement was found to be true for parents in Washington, D.C., and Turin, Italy.[89] Important too is the finding that, while education and other variables are involved in the link between class and child rearing, these appear to be "secondary and reinforcing," while ". . . the really critical variables seemed to be the degree of self-direction characteristic of occupations in the two social classes." [90] The import of this finding is that it is the *present position in the social structure,* not primarily class origin or early socialization, that seems to be the major variable. Though class origins are important, ". . . values and orientation come to agree with those of . . . achieved class positions." [91]

When the values learned in early family experience conflict with those required by present occupational task, it is the latter that is controlling.[92] To bring about change in life styles and behavior patterns then, it appears that altering the social position of families to the degree possible may be the most

---

[85] Kohn, *op. cit.,* p. ix.

[86] McKinley, *op. cit.*

[87] A caution should be introduced here about a too simple link between middle-class child rearing and the development of initiative and autonomy. *See* Urie Bronfenbrenner, "The Changing American Child," *Journal of Social Issues,* 17 (January 1961), and Chap. 7 of this volume.

[88] Kohn, *op. cit.,* pp. ix–x.

[89] *Ibid.,* p. xi.

[90] *Ibid.,* p. x.

[91] *Ibid.,* p. 137.

[92] *Ibid.,* p. 201.

potent way of dealing with the culture of poverty and dysfunctional child-rearing patterns, a conclusion supported in Donald Gilbert McKinley's following statement: "If our analysis is accurate, then non-hostile and relatively permissive child-rearing practices would not become accepted practice for low-status parents without some change in the over-all structure of social rewards." [93]

This point of view suggests that the interrelated problems of poverty, family disorganization, and deviant behavior can best be understood and dealt with as consequences of structural defects rather than as manifestations of a culture of poverty. The psychological characteristics often attributed to the poor of a sense of powerlessness, hopelessness, and present-time orientation mirror the objective reality they daily confront. They are relatively powerless to affect their environment; life prospects are far from bright; scarce and insecure resources permit only a concern with the here-and-now problems of daily survival. [94] Pragmatic adaptations to deprivation and to a sense of personal failure do not constitute a separate and distinct value system, a style of life that is preferred over the middle-class model. If anything it seems that the poor more or less share the aspirations of the middle class. Experience, however, teaches them they cannot expect to attain middle-class goals and that they cannot secure a positive sense of self-esteem in terms of middle-class values.

With regard to family life, Elliot Liebow has demonstrated that lower-class males aspire to marry, provide for a family, and succeed as husband and father in order to attain the essential attributes of manhood in this society. Almost invariably they fail, primarily because of limited opportunities made even more constricted for minority groups by racial discrimination. Consequently, according to Liebow, lower-class males begin to organize their lives around the "shadow values" of street-corner life, with its emphasis on whiskey and the exploitation of women—values that are a defense against failure, providing an illusion of manhood. [95] Such patterns of repeated failure are not primarily a consequence of a cultural transmission of values and attitudes alien to a middle-class way of life but a direct consequence of the limited opportunity structure within which lower-class males find themselves. The implications for change, according to Liebow, are clear. The immediate conditions confronting the lower class must be altered, not their values, attitudes, and beliefs. [96] Others (e.g., Rodman and McKinley), as we have noted, arrive essentially at the same conclusion.

The matter is complicated now by the possibility that vast changes are taking place in the values of both the middle and lower classes so that it is difficult to

[93] McKinley, *op. cit.,* p. 81.

[94] For an explanation of the culture of poverty as introduced by Oscar Lewis, *see Children of Sanchez* (New York: Random House, 1961), pp. xxiv–xxxi and his article, "The Culture of Poverty," *Scientific American,* 215 (October 1966), pp. 19–25. For a discussion of this concept, *see* Elizabeth Herzog, "Some Assumptions About the Poor," *Social Service Review,* 37 (December 1963), pp. 389–402; and Charles A. Valentine, *Culture and Poverty* (Chicago: University of Chicago Press, 1968).

[95] Elliott Liebow, *Tally's Corner* (Boston: Little, Brown), pp. 208–215.

[96] *Ibid.,* p. 223.

assert with any confidence what values are held with what degree of commitment by various subgroups. For example, Nathan Glazer suggests that a major shift in values is occurring among the lower class, one that accepts the legitimacy of welfare over menial employment and denies the obligation to accept jobs at prevailing wages or the responsibility to support wife and children through subordination to the discipline of work. Whereas Liebow finds acceptance of the work and family ethic but structured failure to attain such life goals, Glazer sees a "massive change in values which makes various kinds of work that used to support families undesirable to large numbers of potential workers today." [97] It is possible that the social discipline of work is being rejected by some members of the lower class and by some middle-class youths. For the lower class and particularly for blacks, as we have noted, it may not be employment that is being rejected so much as dirty work.

To the extent that the lower class aspires to upward mobility, or would aspire to it if they could perceive realistic opportunities, major attention needs to be given to the provision of opportunities through expanded employment and manpower development and training programs and to other structural changes that materially alter the life prospects of those at the very bottom. However, the issue of a structural versus a culture of poverty stance is not entirely dispensed with; but the weight of the evidence may be in the direction of the former. Nor are the two positions necessarily in conflict.[98] Early family socialization supported by peer-group interaction may well institutionalize patterns of coping with problems of survival that turn out to be self-defeating when new opportunities are made available. Elliot Liebow recognizes this when he refers to the partly "self-fulfilling" failure of lower-class males who do not believe in their capacity to succeed.[99] For the most deprived and disorganized families, often referred to as the hard-core, multiproblem poor, early family experiences of deprivation, devaluation, and danger seem to be so harmful to social, emotional, and cognitive development of children that failure in all realms of life becomes self-perpetuating.[100] In this way the cycle of poverty, family disorganization, and related social ills may be sustained through the damage imposed on children by parents who are themselves the victims of familial and social deprivation.

What the evidence seems to suggest is that efforts to improve family life among the poor must start with priority attention to the deprivations and disabilities that accompany their inferior social position. We are dealing with the interrelated problems of economic deprivation, social isolation, and status deprivation, plus the destructive impact of these on the confidence and competence with which family members cope with life's problems. Although these problems are not easily resolved the goal of social policy is clear to Daniel P. Moyni-

[97] Nathan Glazer, "Beyond Income Maintenance—A Note on Welfare in New York City," *The Public Interest,* No. 16 (Summer 1969), p. 120.

[98] For a discussion of the complementarity between a structural and a culture of poverty thesis, *see* Ulf Hannerz, "Roots of Black Manhood," *Trans-action,* 6 (October 1969), pp. 13–21.

[99] Liebow, *op. cit.,* p. 208.

[100] Pavenstadt, *op. cit.*

han, who writes, "Urban policy must have as its first goal the transformation of the urban lower class into a stable community based on dependable and adequate income flows, social equality, and social mobility." [101] This would seem to suggest income redistribution sufficient in scope to enable all to have an "average" way of life; major changes in the educational system to promote learning at all age levels; decent employment opportunities; adequate housing; medical care; and other forms of capital investment in people that make an immediate and tangible difference in the life prospects of poor families. Yet nothing on the political scene suggests that we are ready to pay the cost of achieving the degree of social equality that the implementation of such proposals would require.

If Srole is correct that the poverty complex and stigmatize-rejection mechanism are linked to rates of mental illness and family malfunctioning, then money, status, and power are the costs of dealing with such dysfunctions of structured inequality. Our attention is thus drawn to the relationship between social class and family functioning. We see that economic and status deprivation are likely to have harmful consequences for family stability and for child-rearing practices. The altering of family functioning requires the altering of the family's position in the reward structure, which means a major redistribution of income and other resources that must be provided as a citizen right. In addition, massive efforts are required to open new and attractive employment opportunities for those toward the bottom of the social-class system. Programs for new careers in the human services might be especially recommended since they have the merit of offering a new opportunity structure in education and employment, with a mobility ladder geared to various levels of education and training. Such new careers meet a demonstrated critical manpower need in the human services. Moreover they offer occupational tasks that support the kind of value orientation consistent with child-rearing practices directed at promoting autonomy and self-initiated activity.[102] The transition from work as a job to work as a career alerts us to possible problems in role discontinuity, which brings us to Srole's third socio-cultural dysfunction, role discontinuity.[103]

Role discontinuity refers to the stress that accompanies a transition from a familiar role to a new role that makes demands one is unprepared to fulfill. Others besides Srole have also identified crises in role transition as a key concept, which alerts us to the need for education and social supports to facilitate transition into unfamiliar roles that require new coping capacities and skills. For example, Marc A. Fried sees the migration from rural to urban areas as a crisis in role transition calling for development on the part of the breadwinner of new work attitudes and skills. Failure at this critical point may lead to severe family disruption, psychiatric disorders, and other social ills, although our knowledge of this is incomplete.[104]

[101] Daniel P. Moynihan, "Toward a National Urban Policy," *The Public Interest,* No. 17 (Fall 1969), p. 8.

[102] Kohn, *op. cit.*

[103] For a discussion of problems in role transition from work as a job to work as a career, *see* Fried, "Is Work a Career?," *op. cit.*

[104] *Ibid.;* and Fried in Warner, *op. cit.,* p. 103.

We discussed in Chapter Four some of the human costs of the great migration of Negroes from rural to urban areas without the aid of facilitating social supports and resources. It is Fried's view that identification of the variety of crises in role transition, of which the migration crisis is only one, would permit the planning of supportive services related to high-risk situations rather than high-risk populations. The focus would be on the social structure and defects in the provision of adaptive resources rather than on defects in people.[105] For families facing migration or a similar effort to upgrade their occupational status, financial assistance, education, manpower training, and other supportive services would be necessary to launch them into a new level of functioning. This is the meaning of Alvin L. Schorr's notion of a significant capital investment required to move families out of poverty. He writes:

> The situation of families taking off from poverty is analogous to that of developing countries. Take-off awaits "the build-up of social overhead capital," together with the necessary skills and drive for improvement. Take-off for poor families requires surplus money for investment in self-improvement, as well as the skill and drive more usually asked of them. To support people at minimal income may represent responsible and even charitable public policy. If it does not pass the threshold of minimum subsistence and provide some surplus, however, it is not a functional anti-poverty program.[106]

This investment approach would require a policy that goes beyond minimal assistance to a family after the family's failure to deal with a crisis. An adequate policy would seek to make available enabling resources at such various stages in the family life cycle as (1) the beginning of marriage, (2) expectant parenthood, (3) parenthood, (4) the early school years, (5) the adolescent years and the launching of older children into marriage and careers, (6) the empty nest, and (7) the aging years. Some families of course would have greater need for such social supports than others, but all families might at one time or another want to avail themselves of universal provisions and services. For example, the newly married pair may require education and counseling to cope with the challenge of marriage and to help with decisions about further education, career choice, and plans to start or postpone a family. The more youthful the marriage, especially for those with poverty backgrounds, the greater the risk of marital failure and the greater the need for help at this point. As Alvin L. Schorr has made clear, the tendency of poor youths to drop out of school and marry early locks them into a series of other decisions that create a high risk of poverty and marital and family instability.[107] Early marriage may preclude further education that could enlarge earning power. The decision to marry early and to drop out of school invariably forces an occupational choice of limited prospects.

The stage is set, as Schorr notes, for the almost inevitable family-cycle squeeze as expanding family size exceeds resources, which leads to family stress, con-

---

[105] *Ibid.*

[106] Schorr, *Poor Kids, op. cit.,* p. 47.

[107] *Ibid.,* p. 27.

flict, and possible breakdown.[108] The occupational decision of lower-class youths is not likely to represent anything like a choice. Instead entry into the labor market tends to be a response to immediate necessity, more accidental than considered. By the time he has reached his mid-twenties the limits of a wage earner's lifetime income have been fairly well established.[109] If children come too soon and too frequently, lower-class couples are almost inevitably locked into poverty. Discouragement, tension, and conflict are likely consequences. Especially for lower-class youths, the first stage of family formation may require competent vocational and educational guidance and family planning services to permit freedom of choice around child-spacing. On the other hand, it should also be noted that youths are less likely to drop out of school if employment prospects are good and if staying in school is perceived as a realistic way of obtaining decent opportunities. "The high school dropout withdraws under the structural constraints of a social and economic context of low advantage." [110] Youths already out of school and married may offer a strategic target for socially structured supports and resources. For example, some young couples may apply for financial assistance early in their marriage. According to the St. Paul study, such couples may represent a high risk of developing into severely disorganized multiproblem families.[111] Optimal investment of resources in education, job training, planned parenthood, and supportive services, with adequate financial assistance to permit postponement entry into the job market may reap considerable individual and social benefits. Of course, this assumes a full employment economy and a willingness to create jobs for those otherwise excluded from the normal job market, since job training without jobs makes little sense.

The expectant parent also confronts a major role transition. For women least prepared for this experience and for the responsibilities of motherhood, education, counseling, and other services attached to good prenatal care are of central importance. Despite long recognition that preventive services might be strategically offered at this point, except for some important exceptions, too little has been done. We have yet to organize our approach to the expectant mother and to the mother at point of delivery to assist those most vulnerable to stress at this crisis in role transition.[112] During parenthood a children's allowance or some equivalent form of income maintenance that takes into account the special needs of families with children would go a long way toward assuring the economic security necessary for family stability.

The early school years represent for the child his crucial role transition; this is now recognized, however inadequately, through various preschool efforts at preparation. Basic changes in the school system to adapt to the special needs of children from different family learning environments are required. During

[108] *Ibid.,* pp. 36–45.

[109] *Ibid.,* p. 30.

[110] Robert A. Dentler and Mary Ellen Warshauer, *Big City Dropouts and Illiterates* (New York: Center for Urban Education, 1965).

[111] L. L. Geismar and Beverly Ayres, *Families in Trouble* (St. Paul, Minn.: Greater St. Paul Community Chest and Councils, 1958), p. 97.

[112] Marian Gennaria Morris, "Psychological Miscarriage: An End to Mother Love," *Trans-action,* 3 (January–February 1966), pp. 8–13.

their children's adolescent years, low- and moderate-income parents could be helped with a children's allowance that might enable them to launch their children into marriage and careers with less precipitous haste.[113]

The empty nest may be a period of trauma or an opportunity for women to enter new careers or continue former ones, provided society encourages this through various means such as opportunities for part-time employment while children are young, adequate day care, and programs for continuing education that are flexible and adapted especially for the mature woman. The aging years require their own special services as we have begun to recognize as evidenced by the Older American's Act and other measures.[114]

At any stage of the life cycle families may require a mix of strategies and programs for optimal functioning. Moreover, at each stage deprived families may require the greatest investment in services and resources, although any family may need to avail itself of such universally provided provisions and services. How to meet the priority needs of the poor through a system of universal provisions and services poses a continuing dilemma. We will return to this issue after considering the question of the appropriate mix of strategies and programs.

The Need for a Mix of Strategies and Programs

Families vary and their needs are multiple. It is clear that no single strategy or program will suffice to help families attain optimal functioning. As Alfred J. Kahn has observed, one always needs to ask "What mix of income policy, social utilities, case services, and institutional change would advance what social objectives?" [115] At the same time there are those who suggest that, as far as the needs of the poor are concerned, we would be wise to choose an income over a social service strategy. A spokesman for this point of view is Lee Rainwater.[116] Priority needs, he argues, are the redistribution of income and an adequate employment program to assure every citizen a level of income not too far below the median. Rainwater would seem to discount the value of including social services as an approach to poverty and related problems. Additional income, he thinks, would alleviate poverty and other social ills.

> There are good reasons from the social science information now available to us for believing that the most powerful and immediate resource to assist the poor to cope with their problems, not only the problems of economic

[113] Schorr, *Poor Kids, op. cit.,* p. 47; and Jean Aldous and Reuben Hill, "Breaking the Poverty Cycle," *Social Work,* 14 (July 1969), p. 10.

[114] Clark Tibbitts, *Middle Aged and Older People in American Society* (Washington, D.C.: Government Printing Office, 1964).

[115] Alfred J. Kahn, "Social Services as Social Utilities," *Urban Development: Its Implications for Social Welfare,* Proceedings of the 13th International Conference of Social Work (New York: Columbia University Press, 1967), p. 197. Kahn defines a social utility as ". . . a resource or facility, designed to meet a generally experienced need in social living." We draw on this concept in the latter part of this chapter.

[116] Lee Rainwater, "The Services Strategy vs. the Income Strategy," *Trans-action,* 4 (October 1967), pp. 40–41.

disadvantage, but all of the dependent problems of community pathology, individual lack of motivation, and the like—the most powerful resource is income.[117]

While the evidence we have offered would seem to argue for giving priority to an income strategy this does not quite dispense with the question of the need for social services. Rainwater seems to confine his arguments primarily to dismissing the value of residual services because they are stigmatizing and largely ineffective efforts to change the behavior of the poor while they continue to live under the very circumstances that call forth their strategies for survival. In this we concur. Given an adequate income strategy, however, it is likely that many of the poor would still need social services (as would the nonpoor).

It is a mistake, as Andrew Billingsley has observed, to pose the issue as income versus service.[118] In his view we have had an income rather than a service strategy, but our basic income program has been largely dysfunctional for family life and our social services, such as they are, have been poorly supported and largely ineffective. The AFDC program seems designed more to disrupt than to strengthen family life. The social service strategy in public welfare was given special impetus by the 1962 Amendments to the Social Security Act, but, in Billingsley's view, the focus on services was never given adequate support.[119] A major failure, he thinks, has been the inability of public welfare to recruit a sufficient number of professionally trained social workers to carry out the service function. Whether this is the primary source of the difficulty is open to question, for Billingsley himself poses a more troubling problem: "The fact is, however, we do not know in a professional way what services are required. We have not made sufficient efforts to find out from the people involved." [120]

Some recent studies have been conducted to discover the impact of social service efforts in New York City's public welfare program.[121] The findings are not hopeful for those who advocate increasing services in our present public welfare programs (e.g., the 1962 and the 1967 Amendments to the Social Security Act). In a sample of 1,777 female heads of public assistance households, one-half or less knew of the availability of social services other than medical care. A third or less reported receiving services other than special money grants during the ten-month study period; furthermore, a third or more reported they would not ask for a service even if they wanted it: ". . . the overall impression is not so much one of negative response to the service as it is to other factors, including confidence in the capability of the system *and* its representatives to effect service and the relevance of the service to the client." [122]

[117] *Ibid.*, p. 41.

[118] Andrew Billingsley, *Black Families In White America* (Englewood Cliffs, N.J.: Prentice-Hall, 1968), pp. 186–189.

[119] *Ibid.*, p. 187.

[120] *Ibid.*, p. 188.

[121] Richard Pomeroy, with Harold Yahr and Lawrence Podell, *Studies in Public Welfare: Reactions of Welfare Clients to Social Service* (New York: City College of New York, 1968).

[122] *Ibid.*, p. 72.

Our current services are woefully inadequate and more adequate income programs are needed. Not everyone, however, would give exclusive attention to these two strategies: there are also issues of institutional reform and the distribution of power. To some the question of power is of primary import, and they would give priority to social action strategies aimed at mobilizing the poor to achieve and exercise power over either an income or a service strategy. From this point of view, poor families would not be able to be more competent and self-directed until they act to alter their position of powerlessness and structured dependency.

This is the position that Warren C. Haggstrom argues persuasively.[123] It may be summarized as follows: Poverty is not simply a lack of money and money alone will not alter the psychological disabilities that afflict the poor (i.e., apathy, lack of regard for the future, feeling that one is not in control of one's fate). Instead, poverty is a relationship of the powerless to the powerful, a social situation of enforced dependency. Social services provided by the powerful community have sought to alleviate the negative consequences of this relationship without altering the relationship itself. Indeed, such programs ". . . presupposing the inferiority of the people in the area perpetuate and exacerbate the inequality."[124] The poor are relatively powerless to affect the institutions that control their lives both because of their lower-class socialization, which denies them the confidence and competence to act in their own behalf, and because of their lower-class social position, which denies them the opportunity and power to act. Instead of providing opportunities for the poor, they must be organized to secure opportunities for themselves. Consequently powerful conflict organizations are needed to assure that the poor participate in community decisions that allocate resources and opportunities. Successful organized self-help restores self-respect and reverses the subculture of poverty by enabling the poor to share in power and decision-making as citizens.

Community action programs aimed at political mobilization of the poor have been attempted; results have been uncertain at best.[125] Other community organization efforts aimed more at neighborhood and community integration than at the redistribution of power (sometimes referred to as community development rather than community action) have also sought to develop self-help group activity.[126] Such programs have not been designed specifically to deal with problems in family functioning, but they would have an impact on family life indirectly as they affected the self-image and attitudes of participants, their

---

[123] Warren C. Haggstrom, "The Power of the Poor," in Riessman, *et al., op. cit.,* pp. 205–223.

[124] *Ibid.,* p. 214.

[125] Frank Riessman, "Self-Help Among the Poor: New Styles of Social Action," *Trans-action,* 2 (September–October, 1965), pp. 32–36; Riessman, *Strategies Against Poverty, op. cit.,* Chap. 1; Charles Silberman, *Crisis in Black and White* (New York: Random House, 1964), Chap. 10, pp. 308–355; Peter Marris and Martin Rein, *Dilemma of Social Reform* (New York: Atherton Press, 1967); Kenneth B. Clark and Jeannette Hopkins, *A Relevant War Against Poverty* (New York: Harper & Row, 1969); Thomas Gladwin, *Poverty USA* (Boston: Little, Brown, 1967), chap. 7.

[126] Leighton, *et al., op. cit.*

position in the social system, the resources at their command, and the general integration of neighborhood or community life.[127]

One program involving a community organization component was specifically directed at improving family life. Entitled Project ENABLE (Education and Neighborhood Action for Better Living Environment), the project was funded under an OEO grant to the Family Service Association of America, the Child Study Association of America, and the National Urban League. Its goal was to train professional and paraprofessional people to conduct parent education in local community action programs. Such educational programs, however, were to be focused not only on the problems of parents but on the conditions in the community that helped to create the problems.[128] A number of Head Start programs also include some attention to community organization, a point we return to later.

Social provisions, social services, and action to alter conditionŝ in the community that undermine family life are all needed. What kinds of provisions, services, and action are required, which are feasible given our resources and political climate, how they are to be organized and administered for the most effective results, and most importantly, toward what social objectives they are to be directed are questions that are likely to challenge and plague policymakers for as long as one can foresee. Yet first things first seems to be the most sensible approach. In this society that means an adequate income strategy to provide everyone with the freedom and power that comes with money and decent employment. It is difficult to believe that we will be of much assistance to poor families until we have accomplished that, and it is romantic to believe that is all that will be required. A lesson perhaps can be learned from Norway, an advanced welfare state, where major emphasis in social policy has been placed on structural reforms to assure all individuals basic economic and social rights and opportunities. In the United States our emphasis has been upon treatment and cure of the individual so he can more effectively adjust to society's demands.

. . . . In Norway, on the other hand, it has become unfortunately obvious that even when society is "good," job opportunities favorable, wage levels

---

[127] Note the apparently successful effort of the Black Muslims to aid ghetto families. What membership in the Nation of Islam can do, it seems, is to provide group support, discipline, material assistance, and a religious identity that offers pride in self and dignified purpose in life. There are here the ingredients of community that are difficult if not impossible to duplicate through deliberate social policy. Essentially what we have here is further evidence of the power of group membership to influence behavior, a lesson we seem to have difficulty incorporating adequately in our various modes of social intervention. *See* "The Black Wasps," *Trans-action*, 6 (May 1969), pp. 8–9.

[128] Reports on Project ENABLE may be obtained from the Family Service Association of America, 44 East 23rd St., New York, N.Y. *See* Aaron Rosenblatt, *Attendance and Attitude Change: A Study of 301 ENABLE Groups* (New York: Family Service Association of America, 1968), pp. 360–416; Ellen P. Manser, *Project ENABLE: What Happened?* (New York: Family Service Association of America, 1968).

high, health maximal, education available to all, and the living standard conspicuously affluent, some people are nevertheless sick, youth is maladjusted, children neurotic, old people psychologically unwanted, and international relationships increasingly distrustful. . . . In other words, political science and social science must go hand in hand, and social welfare must provide both progressive social legislation and economic security as well as opportunity for individual treatment based on psychological and sociological insight.   It is this view that Norwegian social work supported by the government represents today.[129]

One need not accept entirely the assumption that an advanced welfare state is synonymous with a "good" society to recognize that even in the best of all possible worlds individual suffering will remain and that a variety of social services will be required.[130]   What kinds of social services are required, not only to assist individuals with problems of adaptation that are to be found in any society but to contribute to the development of those institutions that release and nurture human potentialities, is the pressing question.   One cannot avoid the conviction that, for all its benefits in redressing inequalities, an advanced welfare state is based on a misplaced definition of the good society and of life's purpose.   The welfare state can only redistribute the benefits of industrial technology.   It is essentially quantitative in its orientation and cannot deal with the spiritual malaise that stems from the very principles of modern society with its heavy emphasis on rationalism, individualism, and materialism.

The Role of Social Services

Like so much of our social welfare vocabulary the term social services is ambiguous.   We mean by it those efforts to restore, maintain, and enhance the social functioning of individuals and families through (1) enabling social resources (e.g., day care and homemaker services) and (2) processes that enhance the capacity of individuals and families to cope with stress and with the normal demands of social life.   Such processes (e.g., education, casework, psychotherapy, etc.) may be seen as "people-changing" efforts; they represent extensions of the family's traditional functions of socialization and social control.   Change occurs, however, not only through direct attempts to modify individual behavior but through alterations in one's social environment.   Consequently social services may also be seen as efforts to modify the social relationships in which an individual or family are embedded.   The ideal goal of the social services is the enhancement of social competence.   Such competence is a function of personal and social resources, that is, individual coping ability and enabling social resources and structures that develop individual capacities and facilitate their expression.

Social services may be seen as efforts to support, supplement, and substitute for functions traditionally performed by the family.   Education and counseling are efforts to strengthen the capacity of parents to perform their role obligations; day care and homemaker services may supplement child-rearing and

[129] Lilian Bye, "The Social Welfare Program of Norway," in *Urban Development, op. cit.,* p. 161.

[130] McGee, *op. cit.,* p. 178.

home management functions performed by the mother; foster care may temporarily or permanently substitute for the family environment. The above definition of the social services does not fully capture the range and variety of services, which may extend from simple information and referral to advocacy, to the provision of concrete services, to education, counseling and other efforts at modification of individual and group behavior. Although social work services are traditionally identified as *the* social services, other professional activities such as legal services, consumer education and counseling, employment counseling and manpower development, vocational rehabilitation, health education, and so forth increasingly make up the broad network of social welfare services.

Models of Social Service

Several different models may be suggested as a way of describing the complex and changing social service scene.[131] These are the (1) clinical model, (2) social broker model, (3) child and family development model, and (4) social self-help model. These are neither mutually exclusive nor exhaustive.

The Clinical Model

Until the 1960s the clinical model of the social services was the most widely prevalent. The focus was primarily on the individual; problems were perceived in terms of a medical model of pathology to be treated or cured; and strategies of intervention were fashioned largely in terms of some version of psychotherapy. Whether practiced by professional social workers as casework or by clinical psychologists or psychiatrists as therapy, the essential orientation was more or less the same. Individuals with problems were seen as sick, in need of help to cope more adequately with problems defined mostly as intrapsychic in origin. This might be called the mental health model, for dynamic psychiatry and its concern with treatment of psychological malfunctioning fashioned the approach of social work and other human service professions. The brilliant insights of Freud provided the major theoretical view of the suffering individual.

The transformation of the field of mental health from a clinical preoccupation with the sick individual to a concern with community mental health marked the rediscovery of man in society.[132] In social work, putting the "social" back into professional practice marked the decade from 1950 to 1960; it was a period of a rediscovery of social work's historic concern with the social environment,

---

[131] For a review of trends in the social services, *see* National Association of Social Workers, *Changing Services for Changing Clients* (New York: Columbia University Press, 1969).

[132] In some measure community psychiatry has not fully incorporated the social perspective. For a critique of community mental health efforts that represent "new wine in old bottles" *see* M. Brewster Smith, "The Revolution in Mental-Health Care— A 'Bold New Approach'?" *Trans-action,* 5 (April 1968), pp. 19–23. For an excellent statement on social psychiatry *see* Matthew Dumont, *The Absurd Healer* (New York: Science House, 1968). This is not to suggest that the psychiatric world view, and in particular the contribution of Freud, is to be discarded. Instead we are in a stage of reassessment and reintegration of the psychic and the social.

which has early roots in the social settlement movement. This is not to suggest that people do not experience psychological problems but rather that the source and the solution to such problems may be located in the social environment, in the poverty complex, in the role discontinuity and the stigmatize-rejection processes of society, as our review of Srole's sociocultural dysfunctions has already indicated. With regard to the poor, the social psychiatrist Robert Coles has made the point well:

> I have found in the most apathetic or lawless people enough unused energy and side-tracked morality to make of them different people, given different circumstances in their everyday lives. . . . The problems these people have is a psychological one only because it continues to be a social and political one.[133]

Concrete Services and the Social Broker–Advocate Model

To alter the circumstances in the lives of the poor is the concern of the social broker–advocate model. Its roots in social work precede the development of psychiatrically oriented casework, with its focus on altering the ego functioning of individuals. Environmental manipulation is the term given to efforts to help people improve their housing, locate employment, obtain welfare payments to which they may be entitled, secure legal assistance, use appropriate medical resources, or find a suitable nursing home for an aged parent. The service is to assist the individual and the family find its way through the labyrinth of specialized and fragmented programs, to link individual and family needs to community resources. Such concrete services for the poor tend to be ". . . related to the basic matters of existence." [134] The problem often is not one of simply linking needs to resources but one of advocacy, of intervening in behalf of a client to assure that the resources to which he is entitled are provided.

In New York City the Mobilization for Youth project reports that "Soon after service was begun, it became evident that part of the responsibility for people's problems lay with the very institutions on which they had to rely for their existence. A good many clients lack the basic survival requirements." [135] Agencies designed to meet needs have their own organizational inertia and constraints that may make them less than humanely responsive to requests for service, especially when the claimant lacks the power to demand the help he seeks. Advocacy is intervention on behalf of such a person to fill ". . . in the power deficit on his side of the transaction (with an official agency) by providing him with a defender who has specialized knowledge of the rules and regulations of the system." [136] Two illustrations from the Mobilization for Youth Experience may help make clear the need for such an advocacy service:

---

[133] Robert Coles, "Is Prejudice Against Negroes Overrated?," *Trans-action* 4 (October 1967), p. 46.

[134] Hettie Jones, "Neighborhood Service Centers" in Harold H. Weissman (ed.), *Individual and Group Services in the Mobilization for Youth Experience* (New York: Association Press, 1969), p. 43.

[135] *Ibid.,* p. 38.

[136] *Ibid.,* p. 45.

A fifty-four-year-old woman has been living in her one-room flat for three months with no lights. She cannot pay the electric bill, and the Department of Welfare, even after repeated requests, will not put her on its rolls because she cannot establish the legitimacy of her New York residence to its satisfaction. One day she complains of feeling ill and goes to the hospital; the hospital sends her home. She goes again when, after a few days, she feels worse, and is again sent home. Nothing is wrong; nothing shows on the x-rays. Three days later she returns to the hospital with a worker from NSC [Neighborhood Service Center] South. It is now noticed that the woman has a large tumor in her chest and is dying of bone cancer. Is it the three day's wait that has located the illness or the magic of the worker's demand, the power she wields as the representative of a social agency? And on whose conscience do those three months of darkness lie?

A woman whose son has been wounded in Vietnam wants to find out where he is and how he is. She has no address; she knows only that he has been taken from the Philippines to a hospital in Japan. She calls the Red Cross and is told that it is not possible to obtain such information. She comes to NSC South. A worker phones the Red Cross for her and is given an address to which one may write for the desired information. Where is the magic this time? Where is the failure? [137]

Case advocacy may produce concrete benefits for given individuals and families but may not result in basic institutional changes required to make programs and services more responsive to the needs of consumer groups. For this reason policy advocacy through organized community action may be necessary, a social action strategy to which we return in the next chapter. The social broker model of social services may include not only a focus on concrete services or advocacy on behalf of a client, but any form of intervention in the network of social relationships affecting an individual or family. Since role relationships are reciprocal, to alter the behavior of significant others toward a subject is likely to produce a change in the latter.[138] Thus for children with school behavior problems, changing the attitudes and behavior of teachers toward the children may be as essential as direct efforts to alter the behavior of the "deviants." In this sense the social worker or other helping person acts as broker between the individual and the relevant structure, helping him to adapt to the demands of a given social system and seeking to alter his immediate social environment to make it more responsive to his particular needs.

Child and Family Development Model

There is no single version of the child and family development model. Head Start may be taken as one prototype. This is a preschool enrichment program developed as part of the 1964 Economic Opportunity Act's War on Poverty effort. Despite the fact that Head Start programs vary considerably, ideally they provide a structure for comprehensive family centered services, linking

---

[137] *Ibid.*, p. 44.

[138] For a description of this concept of social service *see* Elliot Studt, Sheldon C. Messinger, and Thomas P. Wilson, *C-Unit: Search for Community in Prison* (New York: Russell Sage Foundation, 1968).

family, child, and community development. Potentially they represent a new and creative approach to families living in poverty. Unlike traditional social services for the poor that tend to place the consumer in a dependent and devalued recipient status, the emphasis in Head Start programs is on parent participation in agency decisions, in child development and self-development programs, and in action to improve community conditions.[139] The focus is educational rather than therapeutic, family and group activity centered rather than individually oriented, social rather than clinical; programs emphasize the acquisition of social skills rather than the treatment of psychological defects; they are achievement directed, stressing the development of strengths rather than the correction of weaknesses. Learning to enhance an individual's personal and social competence through exposure to new experiences and opportunities to play new roles might be said to be the central objective of Head Start centers, even though no perfect model of this may exist anywhere.

In recent years other child and family development programs have also been initiated. Parent and child centers have been developed that extend the philosophy of Head Start to disadvantaged families with children under the age of three, with the intent of preventing the development of social, emotional, and cognitive deficits.

A major concern of such centers is the enrichment of the early childhood environment, with attention being given to the development of language skills and perceptual and cognitive abilities and the provision of varied and stimulating experiences. What is essentially new about this approach is the deliberate attempt to prevent or remedy early the cognitive dysfunction that some believe lies at the heart of the problem for the most severely deprived and disorganized families.

The recognition that child-rearing practices among the poor, plus the stressful conditions of deprivation, may so impede the social, emotional, and cognitive development of young children as to seriously handicap them in efforts to break out of the cycle of poverty has stimulated the development of such centers. Deficits in the learning environment provided by the family, it is believed, contribute to social inequality. James S. Coleman writes:

> For those children whose family and neighborhood are educationally disadvantaged, it is important to replace the family environment as much as possible with an educational environment—by starting school at an earlier age, and by having a school which begins very early in the day and ends very late.[140]

Robert D. Hess writes:

> . . . behavior which leads to social, educational and economic poverty is socialized in early childhood, that is, it is learned; and . . . a long range

[139] *Parent Involvement: A Workbook of Training Tips for Head Start Staff,* Office of Economic Opportunity, Project Head Start, OEO Pamphlet 6108–12 (Washington, D.C.: Government Printing Office, May 1969).

[140] James S. Coleman, "Equal Schools or Equal Students?," *The Public Interest,* No. 4 (Summer 1966), pp. 70–75.

program of intervention cannot be effective unless it concerns itself with the socialization or re-socialization of the children of welfare families.[141]

On the basis of his study, Melvin L. Kohn also comes to the conclusion that the family

> ". . . functions as a mechanism for perpetuating inequality. . . . Class differences in parental values and child-rearing practices influence the development of the capacities that children someday will need for coping with problems and with conditions of change.[142]

A study conducted in the Soviet Union indicates that family influence tends to perpetuate an elite through a ". . . social process with a dynamic of its own, and state authority can . . . only influence and not control it." [143] In short the process by which the family contributes to social inequality is not clear. In the study by Melvin Kohn it would appear that the central variable is the occupational status of the breadwinner. Lower-class families tend to perpetuate inequality primarily because of a conformist value orientation in child rearing that fails to equip the child with the capacity to cope with new situations and to solve new problems, thus making him relatively incompetent to deal with change. From Kohn's study, however, one would not necessarily draw the inference that a preschool enrichment approach should have priority in efforts to alter the family's contribution to inequality. Instead attention should be given to changing where possible the occupational status of the breadwinner. Child-rearing practices change as the family's occupational status changes. It is possible that both structural changes (changes in the family's social position and in resources available to it) and direct efforts to alter the family's learning environment may be necessary, though the combination of these approaches will vary for different families. Several cautions are worth repeating. Poor families vary enormously; studies of social-class differences in child-rearing practices and their impact on the development of children are far from conclusive; strengths of poor children may be ignored through excessive preoccupations with deficits; and distinctions between various subgroups among the poor are not always made clear. Moreover, invidious comparisons of lower-class and middle-class child-rearing practices may impute to the middle class an optimum child-rearing environment that is not justified.

Martin Deutsch, who has made a notable contribution to identifying possible cultural deficits among poor children, observes that we may tend to ignore significant deprivations suffered by middle-class children. He writes:

> Middle-class people who work and teach across social-class lines often are unable to be aware of the negative aspects of the middle-class background because of its apparent superiority over the less advantageous background provided by lower-class life. We really have no external

[141] Robert D. Hess, "Educability and Rehabilitation: The Future of the Welfare Class," *Journal of Marriage and the Family*, 26 (November 1964), pp. 422–429.

[142] Kohn, *op. cit.*, p. 200.

[143] This is a reference to a study by Mervyn Matthews, described in "Problem for the Classless Society," *Trans-action*, 6 (October 1969), p. 11.

criterion for evaluating the characteristics of a milieu in terms of how well it is designed to foster development; as a result we might actually be measuring one area of social failure with the yardstick of social catastrophe.[144]

Maurice R. Stein makes a similar observation:

> . . . . what we really have in middle class life is the existence of pseudo-individualists who understand neither how they are connected with others nor how they are distinct from them at deeper levels, but who manage to control their role playing to maintain the impression of individuality.[145]

Nonetheless there is some evidence that the child-rearing practices more characteristic of those toward the bottom of the social-class system may be dysfunctional for child development and for upward mobility in a middle-class society.[146] Jerome S. Kagan, for example, makes the following observation:

> Longitudinal studies being conducted in our laboratory reveal that lower class white children perform less well than middle class children on tests related to those used in intelligence tests. These class differences with white population occur as early as one to two years of age. Detailed observations of the mother-child interaction in the homes of these children indicate that the lower class children do not experience the quality of parent-child interaction that occurs in the middle class homes. Specifically, the lower class mothers spend less time in face to face mutual vocalization and smiling with their infants; they do not reward the child's maturational progress, and they do not enter into long periods of play with the child. Our theory of mental development suggests that specific absence of these experiences will retard mental growth and will lead to lower intelligence test scores.[147]

A few experimental family and child development centers have been established that offer new learning opportunities to the poor with a focus on the educational and developmental needs of the entire family.

---

[144] Martin Deutsch, "The Disadvantaged Child and the Learning Process," in H. Passow (ed.), *Education in Depressed Areas* (New York: Teachers College Bureau of Publications, 1963), p. 164.

[145] Maurice R. Stein, "Socio-cultural Perspectives on the Neighborhood and the Families," in Pavenstadt, *op. cit.,* p. 317. For an illustration of a middle-class, popular, conforming boy with a shallow sense of self and limited capacity to relate, *see* Chaps. 4 and 5 in Edgar Z. Friedenberg, *The Vanishing Adolescent* (New York: Dell, 1962). For a study of narrow middle-class values assimilated by many children *see* Alice Miel, *The Short Changed Children of Suburbia* (New York: Institute of Human Relations Press, American Jewish Committee, 1967).

[146] Catharine S. Chilman, "Poor Families and Their Patterns of Child Care," in Dittman, *op. cit.,* p. 221. *See also* her review of studies of child-rearing among the poor in *Growing Up Poor,* U.S. Department of Health, Education, and Welfare, Welfare Administration Publication No. 13 (Washington, D.C.: Government Printing Office, 1966).

[147] Jerome S. Kagan, "Inadequate Evidence and Illogical Conclusions," *Harvard Educational Review,* 39 (Spring 1969), p. 274.

For example, the Family Education Center in Chicago has such a program; it offers adult education, prevocational and vocational training, and work experience programs. At the center mothers may attend classes while their preschool children are involved in a child development program. In the view of Charles V. Hamilton, such a center expanded to include educational and vocational programs for fathers and organized to function as a community school might become a central integrating institution in the ghetto. Parents would have new roles as teachers, volunteers, students, and policy-makers. The school ". . . would belong to the community. It would be a union of children, parents, teachers (specially trained to teach in such communities), social workers, psychologists, doctors, lawyers, and community planners." He continues:

> Absolutely everything must be done to make the system a functioning, relevant part of the lives of the local people. Given the present situation of existing and growing alienation, such involvement is essential. If it can be demonstrated that such a comprehensive educational institution can gain the basic trust and participation of the black community, it should become the center of additional vital community functions. Welfare, credit unions, health services, law enforcement, and recreational programs —all working under the control of the community—could be built around it.[148]

An additional feature included in some centers and other child development projects are home visits by specially trained teachers who educate parents into new ways of relating to their children by demonstrating different child-rearing techniques. Programs that combine home visits with opportunities for mothers to observe and participate in the nursery school report impressive success compared to counseling efforts to alter child-rearing practices. J. McVicker Hunt reports:

> Attempts to influence the child-rearing of parents of the lowest socioeconomic status by means of psychotherapy-like counseling have regularly failed. On the other hand, involving parents first as observers and then as aids in nursery schools, where they get an opportunity to see the effects of new (to them) ways of dealing with children and where these techniques are explained and tried out first in school and then in home demonstrations, all this appears to be highly promising.[149]

According to Hunt, several studies demonstrate that ". . . a substantial portion of parents of poverty can be taught . . . to be effective teachers of their young when they are given models to imitate, when the actions of the models are explained, and when home visits are provided to bring the new ways of child-rearing into the home." [150]

[148] Charles V. Hamilton, "Race and Education: A Search for Legitimacy," *Harvard Educational Review,* 38 (Fall 1968), pp. 682, 683.

[149] J. McVicker Hunt, "Black Genes—White Environment," *Trans-action,* 6 (June 1969), p. 21.

[150] *Ibid.,* p. 21–22; and J. McVicker Hunt, "Has Compensatory Education Failed? Has It Been Attempted?," *Harvard Educational Review,* 39 (Spring 1969), p. 294.

Of special significance is the fact that when parents are involved in the education of their young children they apparently manage to communicate their new knowledge to their neighbors, who, it seems, also adopt new child-rearing practices. Test scores revealed that neighbor children of the mothers receiving the home visits had higher test scores than children in a comparable neighborhood without such visits.[151]

In principle, parent participation extends to organized efforts to bring about changes in welfare, housing, education, medical care, and other conditions in the community required to promote family life and social well-being. In reality, social action that evokes major conflicts of interests and pits the powerless poor against more powerful segments of the community is rarely successful.[152] The Child Development Group of Mississippi (CDGM), a statewide Head Start project, eventually ran into resistance from more powerful segments of society who were not about to permit or support attempts at social reform. The words of an official of the Office of Economic Opportunity are revealing: "CDGM doesn't seem to be an agency or an organization as it's some kind of damn concept. It's supposed to be a school for small children; yet it seems to be a community project involving much more than that. That may be great, but we are only funding Head Start here." [153]

Issues involved in efforts at social reforms are discussed in the next chapter. Here it may be noted that, although the concept of the child and family development center has the attractive feature of integrating family and community development, the kind and degree of community change possible through such a structure is an open question.

The developmental approach to children and their families, with emphasis on educational experiences for the enhancement of personal and social skills as distinct from primary reliance on a clinical-therapeutic orientation to social services, can be extended to other programs as well. A notable illustration of an agency traditionally concerned with a casework and counseling service that has embarked on a developmental approach to youths may be found in the experience of the Family Service Association of Nassau County (Mineola, New York). It has fun-and-learn clubs, a thinking-skills project, a verbal interaction project, a nursery school and tutoring program, and other efforts to get at the basic problem, which is that

> . . . the children are not vitally connected with life; they have not been encouraged to see, hear, or participate." A sense of nothingness, detachment, and profound frustration and fear of new experiences comes from . . . limited encounter with life. They dip their toes in the water

[151] *Ibid. See also* Rupert A. Klaus and Susan W. Gray, "The Early Training Project for Disadvantaged Children. A Report after Five Years," Society for Research and Child Development, Monograph No. 120, 33 (1969).

[152] For an account of the demise of a program that acted on the assumption that basic changes in the community had to accompany new child development approaches *see* Polly Greenberg, *The Devil Has Slippery Shoes* (New York: Macmillan, 1969). This is a report of a creative and exciting child development and community action program [CDGM].

[153] From a review by Wallace Roberts of *The Devil Has Slippery Shoes, Saturday Review,* November 15, 1969, p. 93.

but cannot swim. This is true literally and figuratively and winds up in a progressive helplessness—an inability to give coherence and meaning to life's experiences . . . the children's difficulties have resulted not so much from neurotic conflicts—although these are in evidence—as from deficits in emotional development, support and guidance; social development and identification; and ability to conceptualize and solve problems. This underdevelopment is expressed by a compelling need for immediate satisfaction and physical action, poor attention span, weak controls, and the lack of motivation and capacity to assimilate life's experiences rewardingly.[154]

All families might profit from new learning experiences that enhance interpersonal competence. Family agencies that have narrowly focused on the provision of casework services for treatment of personality problems are now urged to concern themselves with enabling all families to attain optimal functioning.[155]

Direct efforts to improve family life are not without critics. To some, such efforts should be subordinated to major attempts to radically alter the social, economic, and political system. Living in more benign social environments, it is argued, families will naturally develop in more wholesome ways. We have already noted the evidence that suggests that for deprived families a basic change in material circumstances seems a prerequisite to changes in family patterns and child-rearing practices. Severe political controversy may develop around any suggested family policy that is perceived as an invasion of family privacy. Direct efforts on the part of government to influence family structure or child-rearing patterns carries heavy risks, which have been well stated by Nathan Glazer:

> There are parts of the society that are more legitimately subject to government intervention than the family—the economy, the educational system, the system of police and the courts and prisons—and we may hope to influence the family through these institutions. . . . We cannot interfere in the intimate spheres of life; we do not have the knowledge, and if we did, we should use it with restraint. We know the family makes the social conditions. We know too that social conditions make the family. But it is the latter knowledge that is the basis of social policy.[156]

This is not an argument against social services, which families are free to accept or reject, but against any organized effort on the part of government to

---

[154] Salvatore Ambrosino, "A Family Agency Reaches Out to a Slum Ghetto," *Social Work,* 11 (October 1966), p. 18. For an excellent theoretical discussion of the importance of focusing attention on the development of social skills as distinct from treatment of psychiatric disorders *see* Morton Beiser, "Poverty, Social Disintegration and Personality," *Journal of Social Issues,* 21 (January 1965), pp. 56–78.

[155] *See* especially Nelson N. Foote and Leonard S. Cottrell, Jr., *Identity and Interpersonal Competence* (Chicago: University of Chicago Press, 1955); and Farson, *et al., op. cit.*

[156] Nathan Glazer's foreword in E. Franklin Frazier, *The Negro Family in the United States* (Chicago: University of Chicago Press, 1966), quoted in Billingsley, *op. cit.,* p. 191.

directly alter the functioning of families. We face a serious dilemma. Society can hardly be indifferent to the consequences of family patterns that appear to be inimical to its survival, yet neither scientific knowledge nor our pluralistic values allow for any firm guides to action.

To the extent that knowledge may substantiate the claim that child-rearing practices among the working and lower classes are dysfunctional for upward mobility, to fail to alter family environments is to condemn children to inequality. As John Porter has noted, there are no easy answers to the moral questions involved, but ". . . we may have to accept further intrusions into the realm of the family through social policy, for there is also a moral problem in not providing working- and lower-class children with a chance to move up." [157] Perhaps a way out of this dilemma is indicated by the evidence that seems to suggest that structural changes that raise the educational and occupational status of parents also produce desirable changes in child-rearing practices.[158]

This is a view supported by S. M. Miller and Frank Riessman. They argue that efforts to promote greater social equality through early childhood education represents "the new preschool mythology." [159] Proponents of this myth espouse "child centered radicalism," believing that the world can be transformed through radical change in the way very young children are reared and educated. In contrast, sociological radicalism maintains ". . . that adult institutions must change first, and that child development may then reflect these basic institutional changes." [160] In our view, the weight of the evidence seems to support the latter position but it would be a mistake to assume the issue is closed. Probably it is a mistake to pose the issue in either-or terms.

Structures must change to facilitate new kinds of behaviors, but the kind and quality of behavior one may expect will surely depend in large measure on the kind of developmental experiences provided in the early years and throughout life. The central concern goes beyond issues of social equality to the more fundamental question of the development of our human potential. One is inclined to agree with J. McVicker Hunt ". . . that mankind has not yet developed and deployed a form of early childhood education (from birth to age five) which permits him to achieve his full genotypic potential." [161] At the same time, it is not likely that we shall either develop or deploy such forms of early childhood education until our major concern is with man and his fullest development. This calls for radical change in the structures and the values of our society.

With regard to the preschool enrichment strategy of overcoming inequality there are scientific issues regarding its effectiveness and political issues regarding allocation of resources to foster future over present alleviation of poverty and inequality. While current evidence does not support any major claim for success of Head Start and related programs it is argued that preschool programs have not been adequately developed or sufficiently tested to determine their

[157] Porter, *op. cit.*, p. 17.

[158] Kohn, *op. cit.*, pp. 137, 199, and 201.

[159] S. M. Miller and Frank Riessman, *Social Class and Social Policy* (New York: Basic Books, 1968), "The New Preschool Mythology," pp. 113–19.

[160] *Ibid.*, p. 113.

[161] Hunt, *Compensatory Education, op. cit.*, p. 292.

potential effectiveness. It may take a decade or two before we can determine the impact of altering the "ecological niche" of infants and young children.[162] Furthermore, critics of preschool programs maintain that efforts to change young children fail to consider the more basic problem of altering the public school system. The Head Start strategy has unquestionably been oversold as a relatively painless and inexpensive way of fighting poverty. Its focus is on the future generation and as such it avoids facing the political issue of the realloca- tion of resources sufficient in scope to permit children and families now living in poverty to live more decently and with greater hope. The attention given to Head Start thus supports a conservative political response to the needs of the poor. It may also be questioned on empirical grounds. It is the view of Morris Janowitz that the focus on early childhood is at best a partial strategy and at worst a basic error in priorities.

> A partial strategy of change which allocated highest priority to the pre- school youngster is a reflection of a concern for the management of the individual rather than with the management of the slum community. The counter strategy of intervention with the eldest school age groups is more plausible. In a slum community, the 14 to 18 year old males have the greatest impact on the moral and social climate of the school. In this group are opinion leaders in the slum youth culture and the effective bearers of the culture of the slum from one generation to the next. If these youngsters develop a sense of frustration and a group life in oppo- sition to the goals of the school, as they generally do, they are able to frustrate innovation. The case can be made that this group represents the highest priority, not the youngest group, if comprehensive change is to be effected.[163]

Furthermore, it is suggested that if preschool experiences are desirable they are desirable for all children. Quality programs should be provided as a universal right, available to all parents who choose to use them, and integrated with respect to race and class, thus avoiding the stigma and harmful segregation that accompany special programs for the poor.[164] Residual day care services and special preschool programs for the poor continue to isolate lower-class children from others, depriving them of the learning potential inherent in socially integrated peer groups. At the same time it is not clear whether the special learning needs of deprived children can be entirely met within a universal program. For the most severely deprived children special programs may be necessary.

---

[162] *Ibid.,* p. 296. For a discussion of the effectiveness of preschool programs *see* Arthur R. Jensen, "How Much Can We Boost IQ and Scholastic Achievement?," *Harvard Educational Review,* 39 (Winter 1969), pp. 1–123; and "Discussion" in *Harvard Educational Review,* 39 (Spring 1969), pp. 273–356.

[163] Morris Janowitz, "Institution Building in Urban Education," Working Paper No. 103, Center for Social Organization Studies, University of Chicago, February 1968, p. 44. Paper prepared for David Street (ed.), *Innovation in Mass Education* (New York: Wiley, 1968).

[164] Ivor Kraft, "Head Start To What?," *The Nation,* September 5, 1966, p. 181.

Self-Help Model of Service: Organized Mutual Aid

The term social service implies doing something for people, a provision of help through formal organization and a reliance on the professional delivery of some resource (e.g. counseling, education, day care, homemaker service, foster care, etc.). Such services substitute for or replace the informal mutual aid characteristic of families and communal life. Since the variety of services people require in an urban setting cannot be assured through informal networks of mutual concern and obligation (although these by no means are absent), new forms of mutual aid develop. Self-help groups have spontaneously arisen to meet common needs. In some instances they appear more successful than formally organized and professionally staffed services. Alcoholics Anonymous is such a self-help group. Synanon for drug addicts, Recovery, Inc., a self-help organization for ex-mental patients, and AFDC mothers' clubs are others among a growing list of similar efforts to create a "community of sufferers" who assist one another. Based on principles of reciprocity and group participation they stand in marked contrast to bureaucratic and professionally structured health and welfare services. Such self-help organizations have been encouraged and subsidized to a greater extent abroad than in the United States.[165] More recently, partly because of the impetus given to the "maximum feasible participation" of the poor in the War on Poverty and its attention to organizing the poor for self-help projects, and partly because of general trends toward "participatory democracy," increasing attention has been paid to a community development approach to shared needs and problems. In this approach, the role of the professional is that of catalyst and resource person, making it possible for those with common needs and interests to get together and to develop a group structure through which mutual aid can take place.

It is possible that social workers and other human service professionals will increasingly have this as their primary role. As Richard E. Farson sees it, those who work in family service agencies ". . . will become arrangers of experiences rather than a corps of professional helpers."[166] The fact is that we can never provide enough professionals to meet the need. Moreover, in Farson's view, the ". . . greatest resource for the solution of any social problem is the very population that has the problem."[167] Agencies wishing to help families might do well to experiment with ". . . developing networks of families in the community that can be helpful to each other."[168] Helping people to help themselves, as everyone knows, has been the most familiar way of describing social work; yet such self-help has been largely defined as individual self-reliance rather than socially organized mutual aid. It is the necessity of maintaining and re-creating social networks through which individuals and families can reciprocally aid one another that we have largely lost sight of.

An adequate family policy would recognize that, just as no man is an island, so no family may exist and thrive in social isolation. Families are vulnerable

[165] Alfred H. Katz, "Application of Self-Help Concepts in Current Social Welfare," *Social Work,* 10 (July 1965), pp. 68–74.

[166] Farson, *op. cit.*

[167] *Ibid.,* p. 69.

[168] *Ibid.,* p. 72.

to breakdown when they lack resources at critical points in family development and when they are isolated from supportive social networks. In her study, Helen Icken Safa demonstrated that AFDC families function more adequately when they have sustaining family ties.[169] When such extended family ties are not available, other social networks must be developed through self-help groups and other efforts at community development.[170] In this sense family development and social development proceed together.

Residual to Institutional: Social Services as Social Utilities

The kind of supportive resources and services that families require in an urban society that aspires to self-actualization of all its members is a critical question for social policy. Part of the answer lies in a reconceptualization of social provisions and services. We must abandon the residual and accept the institutional view, which regards social welfare as social inventions designed to enhance the common life of man. In this view social welfare programs meet social needs of an urban technological society and should embody the values we proclaim to be the ethos of a democratic community. Unhappily, the residual view continues to prevail. Nowhere has this been better documented than in Florence A. Ruderman's study of day care for children of working mothers.[171] As she notes, applying a residual framework to an institutional need has resulted in restricting the supply of services that are urgently required. While working mothers increase in number and the desire for quality child care expands, the number of day care centers throughout the country has remained constant or has even declined since the end of World War II. In her study two-thirds of all working mothers knew of no day care center easily available to them.[172] Some other consequences of this residual approach to a common need are (1) public apathy and absence of support, (2) social and psychological segregation, since children of the poor, of minority groups, and those from broken families tend to be concentrated in centers that have a "class and caste character," and (3) low standards and poor quality of care in both the socially provided day care for the poor and troubled and in the profit-oriented proprietary centers for the middle class. With regard to the last point, of special importance is the observation that to leave services to the marketplace for those with the ability to pay is based on an inadequate ". . . sense of the *social* development of institutions. Individuals or individual families, however 'adequate' do not by themselves create schools, hospitals, or other social services." [173] An inappropriate definition of day care in the framework of case-

[169] Helen Icken Safa, *Profiles in Poverty* (Syracuse, N.Y.: Syracuse University Youth Development Center, 1966), pp. 160–163.

[170] Ward Hunt Goodenough, *Cooperation in Change* (New York: Russell Sage Foundation, 1963); and Leighton, *et al., op. cit.*

[171] Florence A. Ruderman, *Child Care and Working Mothers* (New York: Child Welfare League of America, 1968).

[172] *Ibid.*, p. 344. This is changing with the present emphasis on preschool programs and the increased federal funds available for day care.

[173] *Ibid.*, p. 347. On the other hand, in Britain and in the United States there is increasing recognition that under certain circumstances services might be better provided through the market mechanism.

work services and fragmentation of services due to a social work pathology-oriented concept of child care are other harmful consequences of a residual view of an institutional need.[174]   Arbitrary distinctions between social work–sponsored day care, nursery schools, and special preschool enrichment programs need to give way to a concept of child care centers as providing a variety of programs based on the needs of children.   It is preferable to think of such child care centers as social utilities rather than as social services.

Alfred J. Kahn whose work is the basis of the following discussion, defined a social utility as:

> . . . a social invention, a resource or facility, designed to meet a generally experienced need in social living.   It is defined as so vital that the broader community suffers from the results of the deprivation faced by an individual.   Because of this, the provision is not left to the market economy even though some particularly affluent people may continue to resort to the market.[175]

Social services developed out of a residual tradition of social welfare.   The term connotes remedial help for the failures and misfits of the system.   Social utilities is a positive concept.   It reflects an awareness that to humanize our urban technological world is to design our social environment so as to contribute to individual, family, and community development.   In addition to such physical utilities as highways, transportation systems, power plants, sewage disposal, and a potable water supply, civilized life in an urban setting requires a variety of socially designed ways of meeting common needs.   Social utilities are those that support and facilitate social relationships.   They reflect the attention we give to the human dimension of our urban civilization.   They address needs that are rooted in the social reality with which we must daily cope, and they embody the values we attach to persons and their relationships with one another.   They are inventions through which we may progressively help to renew our social order.   The kind of social utilities that may be desirable are indicated in part by knowledge of the resources required to cope effectively with the urban environment and the supports essential for competent role performance in family, work, and civic life.   The following is an illustrative outline of social utilities.

INFORMATION, LIAISON AND ADVOCACY.   Any citizen might ask the following questions: Where can I find the resource I need?   How can I be assured of getting the service to which I am entitled?   Our bureaucratic society, with its fragmented, often inaccessible, and little-known services, and with consumers often powerless to get attention to their individual needs, requires an easily available source of information and direct assistance with the problem of negotiating one's way through the labyrinth of formal organizations.   Studies consistently show that few people have any accurate knowledge of the kinds of community services provided and where they are located.   There is a need for the social broker model of service, previously discussed, provided in a way

---

[174] *Ibid.,* p. 350.

[175] Alfred J. Kahn, in *Urban Development, op. cit.,* p. 193.

that is accessible to all citizens. The British Citizen's Advice Bureau (CAB) is a universal service with as many as 466 local units. It handles in a single year more than a million inquiries, provides ". . . information, advice, steering, and referral in a stigma-free atmosphere, open to all groups in society." [176] Information about educational benefits, social security payments, consumer rights, landlord-tenant issues, personal problems, opportunities to relocate one's business, and the range of inquiries regarding government- and community-sponsored programs and services are the concern of the CABs. In the United States the Neighborhood Multi-Service Centers in poverty areas have taken on both the information and the advocacy function. [177] In few communities, if any, does one find the universal provision of such a service. To assure that citizens are fairly and adequately treated by officials, there is increasing interest in the United States in the concept of the Ombudsman. [178]

EMPLOYMENT COUNSELING, MANPOWER AND CAREER DEVELOPMENT. In a society of rapidly changing technology individuals are exposed to a lifetime of continuous occupational and career development. Occupational and career choice itself poses a major social problem for many individuals for whom we have yet to provide adequate service. For lower-class youths the problem is particularly acute. Educational and vocational guidance in our public school system in many instances is more of a disservice than a service to youths. [179] Although the U.S. Employment Service acts as a job-screening and counseling agency it tends to be essentially a residual service. [180] Efforts have recently been made to upgrade the agency. Adequate job-training and retraining programs, decent financial and other supports for families during retraining periods, assistance with relocation to new communities, and the variety of supports required for the crisis in role transition make up part of the provision required to meet the social need for adapting to changing work requirements. [181] Innovations in the area of employment sabbaticals as a right for all workers for continued education and self-development and for subsidies analogous to the GI

---

[176] *Ibid.,* p. 200; *see also* Alfred J. Kahn, *Neighborhood Information Centers: a Study and Some Proposals* (New York: Columbia University School of Social Work, 1966); also Mildred Zucker, "Citizen's Advice Bureaus: The British Way," *Social Work,* 20 (October 1965), pp. 85–91.

[177] Hettie Jones, "Neighborhood Service Centers," in Harold H. Weissman (ed.), *op. cit.,* pp. 33–53; and Robert Perlman and David Jones, *Neighborhood Service Centers,* U.S. Department of Health, Education, and Welfare, Office of Juvenile Delinquency and Youth Development (Washington, D.C.: Government Printing Office, 1967).

[178] Franklin M. Zweig, "The Social Worker as Legislative Ombudsman," *Social Work,* 14 (January 1969), pp. 25–33.

[179] *See* Aaron V. Cicourel and John I. Kitsuse, *The Educational Decision-Makers* (Indianapolis: Bobbs-Merrill, 1963); and Harold Wilensky, "Careers, Counseling and the Curriculum," *Journal of Human Resources,* 2 (Winter 1967), pp. 19–40.

[180] Clair Wilcox, *Toward Social Welfare* (Homewood, Ill.: Irwin, 1969), pp. 315–320.

[181] For outstanding discussions of problems and programs in the general area of employment and manpower development the reader is referred to the annual *Manpower Report of the President,* published by the U.S. Department of Labor.

bill to enable anyone who wishes to return to school might some day be feasible.

PROVISION THAT MEETS BASIC NEEDS AND ASSURES AN ADEQUATE LEVEL OF ECONOMIC WELL-BEING FOR ALL AS A CITIZEN RIGHT. Attention has already been given to issues of income, housing, medical care, and other resources that meet basic needs that the market does not or cannot provide. A decent income, adequate medical care, and suitable housing are social utilities that at some point in this society will have to be regarded as citizen rights much as free public education is today. It is doubtful that we will go very far in addressing urgent domestic issues until we have made a serious commitment to the goals of social security and social justice for all.

DEVELOPMENTAL PROVISIONS FOR FAMILIES AND SPECIAL AGE GROUPS. Some one has said that we are the first generation in which cultural evolution takes place in a single lifetime. Rapid and accelerating social change requires new means for developing and continually renewing the social competence of individuals and families. The starting point in planning such provisions, as Kahn observes, is ". . . full comprehension of what it means to be mother, adolescent, retired adult, child with only one parent." [182] Personal and social resources required for adequate role performance and for critical role transitions provide the key to the kind of provisions that may be necessary. Our discussion of the family life cycle and its implications for family policy is relevant here. Child and family development centers, adequate homemaker services, subsidized family vacations, and special programs for youths and the aged are part of the total range of social utilities that might be required. Of special interest are the Social Security Centers for Family Welfare in Mexico. They represent a social utility, a normal provision for families covered by the social security programs, which by law is defined as a national public service.[183] Housed in attractive buildings, such centers make available a rich variety of educational, vocational, and leisure-time activities that far exceed anything the American social settlement movement was able to accomplish in its attention to the social needs of the poor. Preventive medicine, nutrition, home economics, general culture and citizenship education, organized sports, lectures, folk ballet and popular dances, music training, choral groups, and orchestra, theatre, and special programs for small children are some of the offerings of the centers. Few U.S. communities have anything equivalent to offer families: an attractive place where they and their children can go for individual and shared activities for the development of self and the enrichment of life.

RECREATION AND LEISURE TIME ACTIVITIES. Recreation and leisure probably should not be a separate item. We are moving into a new era of rediscovery of man as a playful animal. The sharp separation of work and play, education

[182] Kahn, in *Urban Development, op. cit.*, p. 202.

[183] Social Security Institution of Mexico, *Social Security Centers for Family Welfare* (Mexico, 1961), p. 13.

and recreation, family life and fun, is becoming obscured.[184] Specialized agencies concerned ". . . with constructive use of leisure time . . . become antiquated."

> If recreation programs are to have relevance in today's world, they must merge with others to create a total environment serving a central goal of human development. Reference is made not primarily to organization mergers but to mergers of concepts and disciplines so that we lose the Calvinistic insistence upon differentiation between work and play.[185]

Richard E. Farson sees a similar fusion of family development programs with recreation and entertainment. According to him,

> . . . the family service agency of the future will become an all-purpose "family fulfillment program" through which families will be able to achieve new heights in their lives. I did not say a *center* because the minute one thinks of a center he thinks of a building, some sort of structure—a connotation that should already be out of date for the family service agency. We are already seeing a beginning in the fusion of mental health, education, recreation, welfare, and entertainment, and they will be increasingly fused in the future.[186]

CASE SERVICES. In any social system people will have special problems and they will need special help. There will be failure, despair, maladjustment, personal crises of many kinds. Because individuals are unique, social institutions can never be perfectly adapted to all who must engage themselves in social life. Help with individual problems as a citizen right without stigma should be part of any human society. As more generous attention is given to other forms of social utilities one may anticipate a decline in the need for case services. In any event the field of social welfare will be seen as including far more in the way of socially provided opportunities and resources than counseling or therapy for people in trouble.

The notion of social utilities is based on an image of a welfare society, one which we have said assumes that all social institutions exist to serve the needs of man. It is a society in which the sentiments of the family are extended to all, at least in the sense that the individual's rightful claim to full membership is acknowledged and his demand for self-actualization is supported and nurtured. Social welfare as an ideal encompasses this view of man and society. Social reform toward this end is a theme we explore in the next chapter.

---

[184] For a perceptive discussion of this theme *see* Bertram M. Beck, "Recreation and Delinquency," in *Juvenile Delinquency and Youth Crime, op. cit.*

[185] *Ibid.,* p. 339.

[186] Farson, *op. cit.,* pp. 72–73.

NINE

Social Welfare as Social Development: The Quest for Community

Self-Renewal or Revolution?

Unprecedented and unsettling changes now taking place suggest that we shall be able to maintain a viable society only if we are prepared to reform our basic institutions. At the same time there are those who see social reform as an inadequate response to the crises of this era. A violent revolution must produce a new society according to some who no longer believe in the capacity of the American system to live up to its democratic ideals. We may still have time to renew our institutions, but time is running out. Failure to respond to the demand for social justice stimulates efforts at violent redress of grievances. In turn such violence may produce a repressive counter-revolution of iron resistance to the demands of dissident minorities. In any event a democratic society cannot be conserved in this era save through continuous adaptation to change.

Basic alteration of our social institutions is the order of the day, either through peaceful self-renewal, as John W. Gardner would have it, or through violent revolution.[1] The increasing tension between inequality of social class and equality of citizenship is a major dynamic calling for rearrangements of our social and economic institutions that will assure to all decent income and the capacity and opportunity to participate fully in the benefits and obligations of society. Our ability to rearrange our institutions and to reorder our priorities without being forced to do so through organized pressure is now being questioned. In the view of Roland L. Warren, ". . . this society is daily proving its own inability to renew itself . . ."[2] He believes the conventional

[1] John W. Gardner, *Self-Renewal: The Individual and the Innovation Society* (New York: Harper & Row, 1963).

[2] Roland L. Warren, "Social Work and Social Revolution," Colloquium paper given at the School of Social Service, St. Louis University, April 25, 1968, p. 15.

political processes have proved to be incapable of responding to the needs of increasing numbers of dissident groups in society who are prepared to use a variety of "norm-violating" disruptive tactics from civil disobedience to violent rebellion in efforts to force basic social reforms.[3]

We may be, as George Herbert Mead might have put it, in "cracking time," an era when our basic institutions seem to crumble in the face of radically new social needs.[4] Yet, despite evidence of this unraveling of our social fabric, we seem incapable of responding in a creative way. Our major problem from this perspective is not proverty, inequality, racism, and the compounded dilemmas wrapped up in references to the urban crisis. Instead we face a social breakdown, reflected in our inability to mount an effective effort to deal with the deep divisions and threats so thoroughly and authoritatively documented by several leading study commissions.[5] This inability to mobilize to cope effectively with clearly present dangers Nathan Goldman has designated as ". . . the crucial problem *of* the society," the ailment lying less in conditions defined as various forms of social pathology and more in society's ineffectual response.[6] John W. Gardner has declared that "the machinery of the society is not working in a fashion that will permit us to solve any of our problems effectively."[7] Perhaps no more dramatic warning of the critical condition of the body politic can be found than that issued by the National Commission on the Causes and Prevention of Violence. Failure to develop more effective public action, according to the Commission, will mean that our cities will deteriorate into "places of terror" and "fortresses." Massive police surveillance and other security provisions will be required to maintain public order. Even in the suburbs, ownership of guns will be commonplace as the climate of fear, hatred, and violence intensifies. To create "the great, open, humane city-societies of which we are capable" requires public and private action that maintains the values of a free society and assures "safety, security and justice for every citizen in our metropolitan areas."[8]

With problems of this scope, traditional welfare programs with their emphasis on rehabilitative services, however useful in individual instances, are totally inadequate to the need. Prominent social workers and social scientists agree on this.[9] Not only are the methods of traditional welfare programs in-

---

[3] *Ibid.*

[4] Paul E. Pfuetze, *Self, Society, Existence* (New York: Harper Torchbooks, 1961), p. 246.

[5] *See* reports of the National Commission on the Causes and Prevention of Violence; the National Commission on Urban Problems, and the President's Committee on Urban Housing, all listed in the bibliography; *see also* other commission reports cited in Chap. 2.

[6] Nathan Goldman, "Social Breakdown," in Bertram M. Gross, (ed.), *Social Intelligence for America's Future* (Boston: Allyn & Bacon, 1969), p. 401.

[7] John W. Gardner, "The Problem-Solving Society," The Godkin Lectures for 1969, Kennedy School of Government, Harvard University, March 24, 1969.

[8] *The New York Times,* November 24, 1969.

[9] Harold H. Weissman (ed.), *Justice and the Law in the Mobilization for Youth Experience* (New York: Association Press, 1969), p. 203; Kenneth B. Clark and

adequate, but their underlying definitions of social ills now come under serious question. Repression, rehabilitation, and political reform are three ways society may respond to its social problems. The welfare model emphasizes a therapeutic orientation. Thus deviant behavior is defined in terms that suggest personal pathology rather than unresolved political issues. Treatment of the individual, not political reform, is the suggested remedy. It is true that efforts at rehabilitation are more humane than punishment of offenders against the social mores. In both instances, however, it is the individual and not the social system that is defined as in need of change. Welfare programs that reflect a therapeutic world view are both humanitarian and politically conservative.

To illustrate the point, consider the problem of economic dependency. It continues for the most part to be defined as deviant behavior. Rehabilitation of welfare recipients is favored over punishment, although in places the crime of poverty is more than a relic of the past.[10] Today, however, it is the political issue of income redistribution and a citizen right to a decent share in the commonwealth that challenges the definition of economic dependency as a problem of individual maladjustment. We see now that society is so structured as to create and perpetuate a dependent class of welfare recipients. Only a significant redistribution of income in support of the ideal of one's right to life will be an adequate response to that condition we now define as economic dependency. In this light dependency is a political issue, not a social problem.

The same may be said for most of the interrelated social ills we are by and large dealing with so unsuccessfully. The answers, if there are any, lie more in political reform than in rehabilitative services, however much the latter may continue to be important.

The focus of attention is the total social system, its functions and dysfunctions, and the way it may be progressively altered. We are coming to realize that we are being overwhelmed by the human costs of our existing social system. No longer can we assume we are dealing with minor defects, with isolated social problems that can be controlled without fundamental alteration in the entire social structure. The fact is that the very social processes that produce our affluent society also create the deprived underclass; the same technology that adds to our expanding Gross National Product also pollutes our environment; the market economy that produces all the consumer goods and services that meet private wants of those who command effective demand inhibits the production of goods and services so urgently required to meet pressing public needs. Indeed, as Michael Harrington has put it, the ". . . diseconomies of private investment are becoming the controlling facts of our life." [11]   Decisions made in pursuit of corporate profit are not necessarily compatible with the public interest in livable cities, assuming of course that such

---

Jeannette Hopkins, *A Relevant War Against Poverty* (New York: Harper & Row, 1969), p. 67.

[10] Betty Mandell, "The Crime of Poverty," *Social Work,* 7 (January 1962), pp. 3–11.

[11] "A Center Report: Priorities in an Affluent Society," *The Center Magazine,* 3 (January 1970), p. 72.

public interest can be clearly identified.   What is increasingly clear is that we are dealing in large measure with a social system that has no adequate mechanism for establishing an ecological balance between private satisfactions and social imperatives.   We have reached the limit of a system geared primarily to economic development.   The next phase must be the creation of a system geared to social development, one that honors human values and one that places fellow man at the center of concern.   In the words of Kenneth Boulding, we have exhausted the possibilities of living in a "cowboy economy" based on the image of endless economic frontiers to be exploited for individual profit. We now confront the realities of the space economy, of finite resources, including the natural environment, available to the family of man.   Boulding's image of earth as a spaceship graphically reveals our interdependence and our common stake in preserving our environment.   Future trends seem clear; there shall be increasing pressure toward intelligent control over all of social life. We are entering a new phase of political consciousness and activity, one that spells both danger and promise for human liberation.

Over two decades ago Karl Mannheim wrote, "We are living in an age of transition from laissez-faire to a planned society."   The choice he saw was not between a planned or an unplanned society, but rather between one "ruled either by a minority in terms of a dictatorship or by a new form of government which in spite of its increased power, will still be democratically controlled." A complex mass society could not, he thought, be governed without a "series of inventions and improvements in the field of economic, political and social techniques." [12]   Planning may mean a regimented society.   Yet, if we are to humanize our urban technological society and deal with the critical problems that threaten to disrupt social order, democratic planning is essential.   The issue according, to Leonard Duhl, is how to "plan and optimize freedom of individuals, groups, and cultures."   Planning in an open dramatic society, he believes, can further democracy by reducing inequalities, educating people to make effective choices, and enlarging the range of available resources and opportunities for social participation.[13]   It is apparent that we are in the midst of a radical transformation of society, which is creating new problems and new resources for the development of human potential.   The transition from an economy of scarcity to one of relative abundance, a revolution of rising expectations giving rise to violent impatience with all forms of social exclusion, and the combined impact of uncontrolled scientific change and urban growth compel attention to the possibilities of rational and comprehensive planning.[14]

Urbanization and the problems associated with it have led Philip M. Hauser

[12] Karl Mannheim, *Diagnosis of Our Time* (London: Paul Kegan, 1943), p. 3.

[13] Leonard Duhl (ed.), *The Urban Condition* (New York: Basic Books, 1963), p. xi.

[14] This can be seen in a number of recent pieces of social legislation that, in a politically timid way, at least begin to flirt with comprehensive planning. A comprehensive state or regional plan formulated with some degree of citizen participation is required in the following federal laws: mental retardation (PL 88–156 and 89–105), mental health (PL 88–164 and 89–105), health (PL 89–239), demonstration cities and metropolitan development (PL 89–754), juvenile delinquency (PL 90–445).

to the conclusion that we have no alternative but to plan for the attainment of national goals.

By reason of the changed character of our society the time has come for the formulation of a comprehensive policy in respect of the development of our physical and human resources and a coordinated and integrated series of programs to achieve these goals. In brief, it is assumed here that the United States is a welfare state and that such a designation is neither pejorative nor dangerous. It is rather a badge of maturity—explicit recognition of the changed character of American society and the new requirements by reason of the change.

By reason of the above considerations the time has come to declare that:

> *It is the general social goal of the United States to provide each inhabitant of this nation with the opportunity, freedom and security to enable him to achieve optimal development of the human potential; and to contribute, as far as feasible, to attainment of this goal for all humanity.*[15]

In this statement we have the recognition of both a functional need to plan for the maintenance and stabilization of social order and an ideological commitment to planning for human freedom and fulfillment. There is no assurance that planning seized upon to ensure the former will of necessity contribute to the latter. As Samuel Mencher has observed, ". . . attention to welfare goals by government does not in itself guarantee a democratic value system."[16] Instead, the complexity of advanced industrial societies and the desire to maintain the stability of existing patterns of power and privilege may motivate concern with planning to deal primarily with threats to social order. Thus all attempts at social planning involve ideological issues concerning means and ends. A conception of social welfare as social development involves a democratic social philosophy as well as an effort to create a process for renewing social institutions to reflect a commitment to human well-being.

In a sense, social welfare as social development is part of the rediscovery of society. It represents an increasing, though belated, recognition that man must substitute intelligent political direction for the invisible hand of the free market and social responsibility for economic individualism. Collective decisions must help to establish social order and assure a greater measure of social justice when neither tradition nor the automatic operations of market forces are adequate to the task. A laissez-faire society could operate under the grand, though socially destructive, illusion of a natural harmony between individual and public interest.

Social welfare programs developed partly to cope with the consequences of an uncontrolled market. Social welfare posed no serious challenge to the legitimacy of the market mechanism as the primary instrument for controlling

[15] Philip N. Hauser, "The Challenge of Urbanization," in *Income Maintenance Programs,* Joint Economic Committee, Subcommittee on Fiscal Policy, 90th Congress, 2nd sess. (Washington, D.C.: Government Printing Office, 1968) Vol. II, p. 625.

[16] Samuel Mencher, "Ideology and the Welfare Society," *Social Work,* 12 (July 1967), p. 7.

production and allocation of goods and services.   Thus it has until recently stood in the shadow of the market, a residual rather than a primary instrument for decisions governing what we shall do with our natural and human resources and how the fruits of social production shall be distributed.   Social welfare as social development is a positive concept based on the recognition that all citizens in an industrial society may require a variety of socially provided goods and services to develop their capacity to participate in society and to achieve and maintain a desirable standard of well-being.   Such provisions and services contribute to the functioning of modern industrial societies and are not solely humanitarian efforts to aid individuals in distress.   They may be seen as social inventions to facilitate adaptation to an urban technological system and to improve the quality of life.   This concept recognizes that man adapts and develops through the creation of social institutions.   His capacity to deal with his social problems depends on his inventiveness and creativity in designing new structures that will enable him to achieve a quality of life consistent with the resources at his command and the goals to which he aspires.   Such a view challenges the primacy still given to market determination of the direction of our industrial system.   The unresolved conflict between the culture of capitalism and the moral ideal of social welfare determines the parameters of the possible in social reform, a theme to which we return later in this chapter.

Social welfare as social development recognizes the dynamic quality of urban industrial society and the consequent need to adapt to change and to new aspirations for human fulfillment.   It goes beyond the welfare state to a concept of a welfare society committed to a continuing renewal of its institutions to promote the fullest development of man.   It envisions not a static planned society but a society in continuous process of collaborative planning.   William H. Form has put it in the following way:

> Development differs from traditional planning in the sense that the design and execution of plans are conceived as continuing unified processes which are constantly refined by a number of participating organizations. Social and economic development is not considered as planning but as the way of life of a modern society.[17]

The notion of social development remains an ideal, perhaps at best imperfectly attainable.   It is sobering to note that over two decades ago Gunnar Myrdal thought he detected a "new way of thinking" in the proposals of the National Resources Planning Board for ". . . securing, through planning and cooperative action," a variety of rights to work, economic security, and the amenities of life.[18]   He saw a gradual transformation of economic liberalism from "rugged individualism" to "a more social type" of "inalienable rights . . . gradually taking shape within the great political canon of America and . . . acquiring the respectability of common adherence even if not of immediate

---

[17] William H. Form, "Social Power and Social Welfare," in Robert Morris (ed.), *Centrally Planned Changed* (New York: National Association of Social Workers, 1964), p. 83.

[18] Gunnar Myrdal, *An American Dilemma,* 2 vols. (New York: Harper & Brothers, 1944), Vol. I, pp. 209–210.

realization." [19]   However, despite the expansion of social legislation and the development of some semblance of the welfare state, the concept of a citizen right to work, economic security, and the amenities of life envisioned over three decades ago remains rhetoric in the company of equally bold slogans about a "war on poverty" and the building of "model cities." Americans are not prepared to accept the basic structural changes required to deal with social ills in any comprehensive way. Though we intervene in all problem areas through an incredibly complex system of programs and services, intervention, as Harvey Wheeler has observed, is not planning.[20]   Our preference is for ameliorative services rather than basic social reform. Thus, in the words of Irving Louis Horowitz, our welfare state is ". . . an attempt to 'cool out' the marginal underclass and minimize the potential danger it poses. It is an attempt to avoid the consequences of large-scale marginality without making any social structural changes." [21]   The fatal error is that time is running out and the underclass, or at least a significant militant minority, plus other dissident groups now challenge the legitimacy of existing institutions.

This incapacity of society to respond adequately to its massive problems is frequently noted but often unexplained. It is simple to note that knowledge and resources are relatively scarce in comparison to the magnitude of the task of social reconstruction and that consensus on means and goals of social reform is difficult if not impossible to achieve. Moreover the zeal for social reform may be sobered by recognition of past failures and unintended consequences of similar efforts at directed change. The costs of reform are painful to those who would need to sacrifice money, power, and status. Although society is threatened by an urban crisis the majority of Americans in their daily lives do not experience the deprivations and inequalities that energize the minority revolt against social exclusion. Allocation of resources to meet the challenge of renewing our urban environment and restoring all persons to the status of citizen is constrained by the competing demands of the war in Vietnam, the arms race, and the imperative of controlling inflation—all of which have more powerful constituencies than do the residents of the inner city or the rural pockets of poverty. While the ethic of social justice argues for greater redistribution of income, status, and power, the pragmatic test of winning elections instructs political leaders to be mindful of the conservative preferences of those who vote for law and order rather than justice through law. Granted that these factors in some measure explain the national "paralysis of the will," as John W. Gardner has characterized the relative impotence of our attack on our social ills, still there is more to be said about the ideological and structural obstacles to social reform.[22]

Perhaps at the very root of our difficulty is the continuing American ideology, however modified in recent years, that continues to give primacy to the market system, to economic individualism, and to a conception of government as a

[19] *Ibid.,* p. 209.

[20] Harvey Wheeler, *The Restoration of Politics* (Santa Barbara, Calif.: Center for the Study of Democratic Institutions, 1965), p. 18.

[21] Irving Louis Horowitz, *Professional Sociology* (Chicago: Aldine Press, 1968), p. 124.

[22] *The New York Times,* December 10, 1969.

reluctant and begrudging welfare state, more to be feared and distrusted than empowered to act in behalf of the commonweal. While the classical free market and its laissez-faire philosophy of a natural harmony between acquisitive self-interest and social well-being have given way to a regulatory welfare state, still the primacy of the market, as Harvey Wheeler has observed, remains unchallenged. Consequently our efforts at social intervention are essentially ". . . ameliorative actions engrafted onto a basic market economy." [23]   We continue to depend on market decisions to achieve economic welfare, save for stabilizing and stimulating actions of government to promote full employment, maintain economic growth, or redress in some modest way the social insensitivity of the market mechanism. While many of our social ills can be attributed to the lack of an appropriate social balance between production of goods and services that meet private over public needs, Americans are in general politically indifferent to this issue.[24] Our economic system, so impressively tuned to producing goods and services that satisfy private wants, clearly cannot meet our social needs in the areas of health, education, housing, mass transport, urban redesign, and environmental control. Yet for the most part, Americans are not insisting on a basic reordering of priorities in allocation of our resources from the private to the public sector. We have unlimited private wants but little effective demand for public goods, backed up by a willingness to increase our taxes in order to purchase the amenities of a more civilized, more just, and more compassionate social order.

Unless the majority of Americans reorder their preferences and increase their taxes to demand a heavier reliance on public over private use of our collective resources we simply will not have the means to deal with the accumulated social neglect of human resources and the natural environment. Social scientists have paid too little attention to the process by which Americans come to value the satisfaction of private over public consumption of goods and services; they have not examined the degree to which the highly touted "consumer sovereignty" does indeed operate to express a free and educated choice among competing alternatives. While mass media and the advertising industry help to influence the expression of private consumption preferences, no equivalent mechanism is available to educate the public about alternative social uses of our technology. We are in the grips of an obsolete image of economic man and a market society that continues to perpetuate an ideology favorable to the established structure of power and privilege. Basic changes are not likely to occur without the adoption of new values based on an image of man and society radically different from the one now embodied in our social institutions. Little is known about how such changes take place, but it seems clear that if we are to reform our social institutions the targets of change no longer are primarily the victims and the casualties of our social system, but the vast majority who give it such unqualified support. A new ideology more consistent with the human and social imperatives of this era must replace economic individualism. The myth of equal opportunity accompanies the continuing belief in the ultimate beneficence of free enterprise. Since all are presumed to

[23] Wheeler, *op. cit.,* p. 18.

[24] John Kenneth Galbraith, "The Theory of Social Balance," *The Affluent Society* (Boston: Houghton Mifflin, 1958), Chap. 18, pp. 251–269.

have equal opportunity to compete for social position and its accompanying rewards, the distribution of material wealth and social status are seen as a consequence of individual initiative, competence, and social productivity. Thus the existing distribution of rewards appears to be inherently just.

The philosophy of economic individualism has made some accommodation to the welfare state, and liberal capitalism has been considerably transformed into welfare capitalism. Increasing numbers of Americans expect government to meet various social needs and to take care of the poor. We honor the vocabulary of laissez faire yet support vastly increased government activity. We are for the most part operational liberals and ideological conservatives, as Lloyd A. Free and Hadley Cantril inform us. While many of the old controversies about the welfare state have been pragmatically resolved at the level of government programs, on an ideological level the issue of the welfare state ". . . most definitely *has not* been resolved . . ." [25] Our political philosophy continues to regard government action in behalf of human welfare as a somewhat illicit extension of government power. We need, suggests Lawrence K. Frank, a new political theory, one that may legitimatize and justify ". . . these departures from our accepted beliefs about the limited powers and responsibilities of government." [26]

> The need for a political theory for this emerging "Service State" is . . . especially urgent. The Service State, not to be confused with the Welfare State with its aura of charity and philanthropy, is oriented to the enhanced "well-being" of everyone, as Halbert Dunn has expressed it. It marks the acceptance of human conservation as the basic democratic task . . .[27]

While we have vastly expanded government services in the areas of education, medical care, urban renewal, housing, and social security every

> . . . addition and enlargement is made as a separate program with no coherent and systematic commitment, no political theory to justify and rationalize these enlarged government activities, and no statement of policy for their extension and administration. We are improvising and operating by a series of piecemeal programs.[28]

Instead of this patchwork approach to social ills, we need a new image of the kind of society we are trying to create, one primarily committed to nurturing human potential. Our political theory must incorporate such a concept,

[25] Lloyd A. Free and Hadley Cantril, *The Political Beliefs of Americans* (New Brunswick, N.J.: Rutgers University Press, 1967), pp. 36, 40.

[26] Lawrence K. Frank, "The Need for a New Political Theory," *Daedalus*, 96 (Summer 1967), pp. 809–816.

[27] *Ibid.*

[28] *Ibid.* For an illustration of political recognition of the need to move away from a programmatic approach, in which a new program for each social problem is developed, toward a systematic approach that recognizes the need for some basic alteration in the structure of institutions *see* Abraham Ribicoff, "The Competent City: An Action Program for Urban America," *Congressional Record*, 113 (January 23, 1967), p. 5709.

out of which we may develop a social calculus to guide policy decisions. As Lawrence K. Frank has put it: ". . . we cannot avoid much longer the recognition that we live by and for what we believe, value, and aspire to, and that these beliefs must be translated into the choices and decisions that guide our individual and group living." [29] It is possible that essential to the development of this new political theory are some basic revisions in the Constitution. Since its framers had no conception of government obligation for ". . . welfare of citizens as welfare is now conceived," Rexford G. Tugwell proposes (among other changes) a new preamble to the Constitution:

> We the people in order to strengthen our nation, perfect its institutions, unite in common endeavors, provide freedom, justice, well-being, and good order for all, and with the purpose of promoting peace among people, do ordain this Constitution and establish the government whose fundamental law it is.[30]

Such a declaration would express a positive concept of the responsibility of government to contribute to human well-being. It establishes what Disraeli saw as the essential function of government announcing, as he did that "power has only one duty: to secure the social welfare of the people." [31] One is quick to note, however, that in a pluralistic society the social welfare of the people is subject to conflicting interpretations. The creation of a political structure that is adequately responsive to the needs and values of a heterogeneous society is an essential prerequisite for democratic social reform.

The Politics of Social Reform: Issues of Power and Participation

The deep ambivalence Americans have about government inhibits the development of a political theory adequate to the responsibilites now thrust upon government. The paradox of the nation is that it has potentially powerful resources but a political structure that effectively inhibits their use. As Peter Marris and Martin Rein point out, "no other nation organizes its government as incoherently as the United States." [32] The tradition of divided powers functions to prevent the abuse of excessive authority and yet also represents "an almost obsessive distaste for effective government." [33] The equation of local autonomy with personal freedom makes centralization of authority suspect. Even problems that are national in scope tend to be perceived as "a complex of local

---

[29] Frank, *op. cit.,* p. 816.

[30] Rexford G. Tugwell, "Rewriting the Constitution," *The Center Magazine,* 1 (March 1968), p. 19; Scott Buchanan, *So Reason Can Rule,* A Center Occasional Paper (Santa Barbara, Calif.: Center for the Study of Democratic Institutions, 1967), p. 5.

[31] Benjamin Disraeli, *Sybil or the Two Nations,* Vol. IX of the Bradenham Edition (London: Peter Davies, 1927; original publisher, Mayday, 1845), p. 318.

[32] Peter Marris and Martin Rein, *Dilemmas of Social Reform* (New York: Atherton Press, 1967), p. 7.

[33] *Ibid.,* p. 8.

difficulties to which national policy should offer support rather than direction." [34] At the same time our political structure is not sufficiently adapted to the needs of a pluralistic society. As Herbert J. Gans observes, our ideology of altruistic democracy successfully conceals such political realities as the uses of power to promote self-interest and the failure of government by majority rule to be sufficiently responsive to the needs of minority groups. [35] The belief in altruistic democracy had its origin in the application of primary group morality to politics, in the general American detachment from the political process, and in the isolation of political reality from our public school curriculum. [36] Americans have little understanding or acceptance of the political dimension of social reality and as a consequence tend to apply a primary group morality, with its rejection of motives of self-interest, to the political sphere of life. As events make it clear that self-interest is prevalent in political decisions, the consequence is a distrust of politics or a cynical attitude toward the process.

A more mature politicalization of the American people would involve, says Herbert J. Gans, the following: a recognition that politics is a universal phenomenon; that all matters about which disagreement exists are by nature political; an appreciation of the role of the politician as one who resolves disagreements; and an acceptance of the fact that such a role is guided by non-familial norms. [37] Altruistic democracy compels judgment of political events by private motives rather than social consequences. Americans are peculiarly ambivalent and confused in their attitudes toward self-interest. Economic individualism extols it; Christian idealism deplores it. The tendency to evaluate political activity in terms of this motive rather than in terms of outcomes prevents an acceptance of the fact that the political process is often directed by significant elements of group self-interest. This is not necessarily harmful provided the result is responsive to the pluralistic needs of the community. [38] According to Gans, our political structure and our insistence on majority rule inhibit attention to the pressing needs of minority groups. [39] In his view we will not successfully deal with poverty, racial inequality, and urban decay until the needs of the poor and minority groups are permitted political expression through structural changes that create a pluralistic democracy. [40] Government by majority rule means in effect a tyranny of the majority, who can ignore the needs of minority groups, leaving them no recourse save disruption as a means of pressing their claims on society. The notion of majority rule also conceals the degree to which the structure of American democracy ". . . allows affluent minorities to propose and the majority to dispose." [41] Issues of unequal alloca-

---

[34] *Ibid.,* p. 9.

[35] Herbert Gans, *The Levittowners* (New York: Pantheon Books, 1967), p. 351; *see also* Herbert J. Gans, "We Won't End the Urban Crisis Until We End 'Majority Rule,' " *The New York Times Magazine,* August 3, 1969, pp. 12–15, 20–28.

[36] Gans, *Levittowners, op. cit.,* p. 351.

[37] *Ibid.* For a somewhat different view *see* Wheeler, *op. cit.*

[38] Gans, *Levittowners, op. cit.,* p. 358.

[39] Gans, "We Won't End the Urban Crisis," *op. cit.*

[40] *Ibid.,* p. 24.

[41] *Ibid.,* p. 14.

tion of power are not confronted when decision-making in the "public interest" through the exercise of majority rule is the simplistic model conveyed by our schools and other institutions.

In Gans' view, the power to gain adequate attention to the needs of minority groups must be assured through such measures as an extension of the one man, one vote principle to all levels of government and to political parties; the abolition of the seniority system in all legislatures; government funding of all political campaigns; a provision for increasing the responsiveness of public and private bureaucracies through citizen and consumer participation on policy-making boards; a constitutional amendment to assure all citizens decent jobs and income; the establishment of a cabinet-level department to represent the interests of minority groups; an equalization formula in disbursement of public funds that allocates a larger share to low-income areas; heavier public subsidies for such things as mass transit; and alteration of political boundaries to facilitate decentralization and greater community control of local institutions.[42]   While such structural changes would go a long way toward assuring that the wishes of the poor and other minority groups are more adequately represented, unanswered is the question of the source of power to produce such changes.

Until relatively recently social welfare ideology and practice have operated to avoid confronting issues of power and its distribution.   Social welfare has been an integral part of a world view that proclaimed a natural harmony between the interests of the powerful elites and those of the "community."   Consensus, not conflicting interests, characterized the community of men, or so it seemed.   Those who gave to the community chest or served on boards of social agencies were promoting the common good, not preserving a system of power and privilege that they enjoyed at the expense of the excluded, a system whose very structure of inequality helped to create the social problems toward which their apparent humanitarian effort was directed.   Some sociologists have contributed to this consensus view of society that tends to disguise the reality of power and authority and the degree to which social order is in fact maintained by the sanctions the relatively powerful can impose on the relatively weak.[43] The consensus and the constraint image of society, as Ralf Dahrendorf has insisted, are complementary—not conflicting—views.[44]   Recognition of the coercive nature of social structure and the sense in which relations of power and authority invariably lead to clashes of group interest enables us to confront the inevitability of social conflict and its useful function in promoting social change.[45]   The acceptance of power and conflict as normal social processes avoids either a sentimental or a conspiratorial view of society.   It allows us to ask how power may be shared and how conflict may be directed creatively. Social development requires both consensus on some superordinate values that bind men together and opportunities for the expression of group conflict that

---

[42] *Ibid.*

[43] Ralf Dahrendorf, *Class and Class Conflict in Industrial Society* (Stanford, Calif.: Stanford University Press, 1959).

[44] *Ibid.,* p. 163.

[45] *Ibid,* especially pp. 165–240; *see also* Simon Slavin, "Concepts of Social Conflict: Use in Social Work Curriculum," *Journal of Education for Social Work,* 5 (Fall 1969), pp. 47–60.

may move organizations toward more creative adaptation to their environment. As Daniel Katz has observed, "organizations without internal conflict are on their way to dissolution." [46]   The observation of Ralf Dahrendorf is worth quoting:

> Everywhere . . . the struggle between freedom and totalitarianism may be regarded as one between different attitudes toward social conflict.   Totalitarian monism is founded on the idea that conflict can and should be eliminated, that a homogeneous and uniform social and political order is the desirable state of affairs.   This idea is no less dangerous for the fact that it is mistaken in its sociological premises.   The pluralism of free societies, on the other hand, is based on recognition and acceptance of social conflict.   In a free society, conflict may have lost much of its intensity and violence, but it is still there, and it is there to stay.   For freedom in society means, above all, that we recognize the justice and the creativity of diversity, difference, and conflict.[47]

The American tendency to insist on a consensus view of society fosters an artificial harmonizing ideology, one that ill prepares us to deal effectively with the reality of conflicting group interests and with the structure of power and privilege.   To the degree that power is not confronted and that groups with varied interests have unequal power to control their participation in social life, to that degree we are less free and democratic than we think.   In the following discussion power is defined as: ". . . the ability of one social unit (group or person) to influence the behavior of another social unit and thereby condition its access to social values." [48]   Social scientists are divided in their view of the distribution of power in society between the "stratification" theorists and the "pluralists."   Among the former are such scholars as Floyd Hunter and C. Wright Mills, who believe that power is concentrated among elites who are at the apex or command posts of our social, economic, and political structures.[49] The pluralists believe that power is dispersed among a fairly broad range of groups, depending on the particular issue at hand.   This view is supported by such people as Robert A. Dahl and Edward C. Banfield.[50]   It has been noted by Cloward and Piven, however, that even though ". . . influence is dispersed, it is not dispersed among all classes but chiefly among those located in the middle and upper reaches of the social structure."   They elaborate on this point by observing that participation in decision-making increases with education, income, and social status:

[46] Quoted in Slavin, *ibid.,* p. 50.

[47] Dahrendorf, *op. cit.,* p. 318.

[48] Harold L. Wilensky and Charles N. Lebeaux, *Industrial Society and Social Welfare* (New York: Free Press, 1965), p. 265.

[49] Floyd Hunter, *Community Power Structure* (Chapel Hill: University of North Carolina Press, 1953); and C. Wright Mills, *The Power Elite* (London: Oxford University Press, 1956).

[50] Robert A. Dahl, *Who Governs? Democracy and Power in an American City* (New Haven: Yale University Press,, 1961); and Edward C. Banfield, *Political Influence,* (Glencoe, Ill.: Free Press, 1961).

In short, while sociologists and political scientists may differ regarding the structure of influence in American communities, their disagreement actually centers upon the question of how influence is distributed within the middle and upper levels of the social order. Whatever the answer to this question, low-income people have consistently less of the various requirements for influence.[51]

The 1960s saw increasing attention paid to the powerlessness of the poor and a heightened awareness of the distribution of power in society. From this perspective, existing social welfare measures could be understood in terms of the ". . . politics of pressure groups and expediential alliances," as Norton Long has put it.[52] The most politically powerful, namely organized labor, big farmers, and the middle-class aged, became the prime beneficiaries of the New Deal social legislation, joining the veterans ". . . as members of a highly selective category of relief recipients." [53] The poor benefited least from the social security programs, but welfare was available on conditions that institutionalized the demeaned and powerless status of its recipients.

The passage of the Economic Opportunity Act of 1964, with its provisions for the development of Community Action Programs, had a new ". . . welfare theory . . . in search of a welfare politics." [54] The proclaimed target was now the powerlessness of the poor, not their economic needs. In fact, OEO-sponsored Community Action Programs had no clear and consistent goals. Most often they attempted a variety of conflicting functions: organizing the community for better delivery of social services, organizing the poor in community development self-help projects, and political mobilization of the poor to increase their influence over decisions that affected their lives.[55] What was new, however, was the amount of attention given to the dimension of powerlessness as a factor in poverty and of the political nature of the relationship of the poor to the remainder of society. The idea of organizing the poor was not new, and the model for the Community Action Programs had already been developed by Mobilization For Youth, perhaps the single most ambitious effort to chart a new course in social work with the poor.[56] The early effort of Mobilization For Youth to mobilize the poor for political action taught an object lesson

[51] Richard A. Cloward and Frances Fox Piven, "Politics, Professionalism and Poverty," Paper prepared for Columbia University School of Social Work Arden House Conference on "The Role of Government in Promoting Social Change," Harriman, New York, November 18–21, 1965, p. 8.

[52] Norton E. Long, "The Politics of Social Welfare," delivered at St. Louis University School of Social Work, St. Louis, Missouri, November 6, 1969.

[53] *Ibid.,* p. 4.

[54] *Ibid.,* p. 8.

[55] *See* Marris and Rein, *op. cit.;* Daniel P. Moynihan, *Maximum Feasible Misunderstanding* (New York: Macmillan, 1969); Clark and Hopkins, *op. cit.;* John C. Donovan, *The Politics of Poverty* (New York: Western Publishing, 1967).

[56] For a rationale for political mobilization of the poor by one of the earliest advocates of this strategy, *see* Saul Alinsky, *Reveille for Radicals* (Chicago: University of Chicago Press, 1945). For a comprehensive review of the experience of Mobilization for Youth, *see* Harold H. Weissman (ed.), *The New Social Work,* 4 vols. (New York: Association Press, 1969).

other community action programs were destined to learn as well. Bertram M. Beck, director of Mobilization For Youth, writes:

> As time passed we received our first practical lesson in the unwillingness of government to supply funds to pay the salaries of persons who are attempting to alter basic political and social institutions. Like so many lessons it took a long time to sink in.[57]

A study by Kenneth B. Clark and Jeannette Hopkins indicates that the Community Action Programs generally are unsuccessful in redistributing power on behalf of the poor.[58] Instead, despite continued adherence to a vocabulary of social action, most such programs found it more expedient to revert to the provision of traditional social services.

Obstacles to effective political action on the part of the poor are many and complex. In some respects, however, the problem may be simply understood. Groups do not give up power willingly. They use their superior resources to protect their share of influence and to punish those who threaten their advantages. Thus the threat of backlash is one of the possible costs of any serious challenge to the status quo. Yet efforts to organize the poor fail for reasons more complex than this. For one thing we have no adequate "theory of the effective uses of social power." [59] Moreover, although the poor are relatively powerless, this does not mean they are necessarily ready and eager to struggle for the opportunity to exercise power, as some of the early community action strategists assumed.

> The strategy assumes that the poor themselves desire power and will enlist in efforts to gain it. In fact the poor man is much more concerned about money and purchasing power than he is in wielding power over malfunctioning social institutions. His interest in community action is therefore episodic, related to the short-run prospects of immediate gain, and unsuited to a long-range strategy of developing a political power base. The only really successful community-action campaign at MFY was related to welfare, and money was a central factor in this campaign.[60]

The fact is that the poor have few personal and social resources for the exercise of influence. Organizations tend to be powerful when they have an economic base and are functionally related to the larger society. The contemporary poor are increasingly marginal, both economically and politically. Their labor, while not yet fully expendable, has little value to the economic system. Except for special instances of concentrated black votes, the poor are relatively unimportant to those who seek political office. With little in the way of resources to bring to bear on community decision-making, ". . . advocates of the poor are driven to employ, more or less exclusively, tactics of disruption

---

[57] Bertram M. Beck, "Mobilization for Youth: Reflections About Its Administration" in Weissman (ed.), *Justice and the Law, op. cit.,* p. 148.

[58] Clark and Hopkins, *op. cit.*

[59] *Ibid.,* p. 259.

[60] Weissman, *Justice and the Law, op. cit.,* p. 201.

and dramatic protest—all of which further offends and antagonizes members of middle-class political culture." [61]   It is not surprising then that the director of Mobilization For Youth, Bertram Beck, has concluded that neighborhood organization of the poor cannot be relied on to produce major social change.[62] In his view society is not prepared to support any major redress of grievances; consequently much that passes for social action in antipoverty programs is "a tragic sideshow."   Had the nation a genuine commitment to a war on poverty, programs would have been built on an economic base leading to some redistribution of wealth, which in turn would have produced some redistribution of power.   The overall conclusion of at least a half dozen years of experience with Mobilization For Youth is that, in our society, power is to a considerable degree grounded on an economic base; community action is a doubtful strategy for attainment of power; and ". . . if poverty is to be eradicated, the economic problems of the poor must take precedence over their social and political problems." [63]

Yet to write off the political mobilization of the poor may be somewhat premature.   The association of blacks with welfare provides a source of political power in the movement for welfare rights.   Unattractive as the prospect is, violence and the threat of violence may turn out to be a potent political resource that might force basic social reforms.   An interest in social peace may be more compelling than an appeal to democratic ideals.   However, massive repression may seem to those with limited vision to be the less costly response.   In any event the issue of participation and integration of the poor and minority groups will not be avoided.

The idea of the maximum feasible participation has taken root in some communities and cannot now easily be withdrawn.   The poor, particularly organized blacks, are having some impact on community decision-making.[64] It appears, however, that such general labels as the poor and the disadvantaged conceal unique issues of class and caste, whose resolutions are likely to lead in different directions.   The participation of blacks may mean the development of "a community of black people who have finally claimed for themselves the difference which has been thrust upon them by hundreds of years of American racism." [65]   Participation of blacks may not move in the direction of the liberal ideal of assimilation but toward "compartmentalization of communities along racial lines," with blacks insisting on and enjoying the power and autonomy of black communalism.[66]

[61] Cloward and Piven, *op. cit.,* p. 21.

[62] Beck in Weissman, *Justice and the Law, op. cit.,* p. 148.

[63] *Ibid.,* p. 201.

[64] Roland L. Warren, "Model Cities First Round: Politics, Planning, and Participation," *Journal of the American Institute of Planners,* 35 (July 1969), pp. 245–252; and Melvin B. Mogulof, "Black Community Development in Five Western Model Cities," *Social Work,* (January 1970), pp. 12–18.

[65] Melvin B. Mogulof, "Federal Support for Citizen Participation in Social Action," *The Social Welfare Forum, 1969* (New York: Columbia University Press, 1969), p. 106.

[66] *Ibid.,* p. 107.

In any event we seem to be moving toward the creation of a new society, toward political rather than an exclusively therapeutic orientation to social problems. Attention is now on the relationship between the advantaged and the disadvantaged, whites and blacks, young and old. The structure of these relationships, in particular the distribution of power and privilege inherent in these relationships, is now being challenged. We are able to see, if we wish to, that many of our social problems are a consequence of social isolation and relegation of segments of our population to inferior, deprived, and meaningless roles. The structure of inequality is now a major target of social reform. Resistance to giving up power and privilege is still the major barrier to the creation of a more just society. Social development in this direction means structural changes that allow for citizen participation in new economic, social, and political roles. Such participation must be broadly conceived: "Participation means participation in every dimension of life, of culture, or of our economy, our educational system, our political system, our decision-making processes. It means full enfranchisement with respect to the totality of society's activities." [67] Through such participation it is possible that much of the adaptive deviance that represents efforts to cope with failure, stigma, and alienation may be overcome.

Obstacles to such expanded participation, in addition to those already noted, may be found in (1) the direction of our technology, which suggests that increasing numbers of the least educated and skilled will be regarded as economically expendable, and (2) our resistance to paying the cost of creating new forms of work or of redistributing income to those who will not be able to participate in any meaningful way in the occupational structure. The fact is that we have no program adequate to the task of dealing with large groups of people who, under our present arrangements, are defined as marginal and are treated accordingly. Yet our failure to provide for participation of ". . . certain groups whose contribution to the control of the society and the management of its technical system is minimal leads to various types of 'crises.' " [68] We can anticipate continued crises in the form of organized protest against inequality, alienation, and exclusion. These can have positive outcomes for, as Edgar S. Cahn and Jean Camper Cahn have written, protest may be viewed ". . . as a first affirmative step toward full citizenship for an electorate which before has spoken largely in the language of withdrawal and alienation—of crime, of violence, delinquency, and dependency—but which now seeks other, more positive forms of expression and involvement." [69] A study of those who participate in the welfare rights movement, for example, revealed that such participation overcomes a sense of powerlessness. [70] Furthermore, organized protest, conflict, and even violence

[67] Edgar S. Cahn and Jean Camper Cahn, "Citizen Participation," in Hans D. C. Spiegel (ed.), *Citizen Participation in Urban Development* (Washington, D.C.: NTL Institute for Applied Behavioral Science, 1968), 1, p. 223.

[68] John W. Dyckman, "Some Conditions of Civic Order in an Urbanized World," *Daedalus* Vol. 95, No. 3 (Summer 1966), p. 807.

[69] Cahn, in Spiegel, op. cit., p. 219.

[70] Helen Levins, "Organizational Affiliation and Powerlessness: A Case Study of the Welfare Poor," *Social Problems,* 16 (Summer 1968), pp. 18–32.

may under certain circumstances provide a social system with essential feedback and "corrective insights" that enable it to adapt more effectively and attain a new equilibrium better suited to the varied and changing needs of its members. Social institutions are maladapted when they are malinformed. Even violence provides information, indicating a societal defect that must be modified to establish a new equilibrium. The danger of massive repressive counterviolence of course bears repeating.

The notion of counterviolence draws attention to the interrelationships that characterize a social system. Attention given to the needs of the disadvantaged without regard for other segments of society, in particular those whose precarious social position makes them most fearful of loss of status, is likely to produce a counterreaction. If we do not enrich the lives of all, can we meet the needs of the deprived? In some measure the pressure for social reform today appears to come from those toward the top and those at the bottom of society. As Max Frankel has suggested, the poorest, along with the affluent and educated upper classes, press for social change whereas deep resistance comes from that "large body of middle-class Americans, newly prosperous or still striving, who fear the loss of what they have acquired or intend to achieve if the ways and priorities of life are to be seriously altered." [71] So long as a sense of self-worth is dependent on the existence of the deprived and the despised, it is doubtful that the vast majority of middle-class Americans will voluntarily support the radical reforms required to bring the marginal groups into the society.

Perhaps nothing short of a cultural revolution will ultimately suffice, one that provides a new definition of life's purpose and new symbols for identity that do not require the invidious status distinctions we have come to accept as the very definition of our being. It is possible that such a revolution is now in process. Richard Goodwin has perceptively analyzed the malaise that afflicts middle-class America, noting that the sense of powerlessness is not confined to the ghetto and that our need for a shared and ennobling purpose will not be satisfied by continuing adherence to the cult of economic growth. [72]

The concept of participation appears to be taking on broad meaning that goes beyond expanding opportunities for the deprived. For many economically secure Americans the sheer size and complexity of society has driven them to search for ways to regain ". . . a degree of personal mastery over their lives and their environment." [73] The felt need to participate in decisions, to overcome social isolation, to share in some dignified purpose, to be part of some communal life seems to characterize the lives of many. [74] It is possible, as

[71] Max Frankel, "Introduction," *Rights in Conflict,* The Walker Report to the National Commission on the Causes and Prevention of Violence (New York: Bantam Books, December 1968).

[72] Richard N. Goodwin, "Reflections, Sources of Public Unhappiness," *The New Yorker,* January 4, 1969, pp. 38–58.

[73] *Ibid.,* p. 41.

[74] A different view is suggested by Herbert J. Gans, who sees the current effort to create a participatory democracy as likely to fail. The middle class, he thinks, has little need to participate since the system works well enough for them without their active involvement. Gans, *Levittowners, op. cit.,* p. 359.

Daniel P. Moynihan has suggested, that we are witnessing a general rejection of the larger community and a quest for participation in specific communities, smaller in size, which would involve a voluntary association of people with common goals and values.[75]   One may see this in a positive light as a quest for a society that honors, not the one-dimensional value of equal opportunity and the single-minded goal of occupational success, but the fullness of opportunity as Dorothy Lee understands that term—a true pluralistic society.[76]

The quest for participation is partly an effort to overcome the sense of alienation produced by large-scale organization and the concentration of decision-making in the hands of distant experts and officials and partly a response to the failure of social institutions to function adequately.   Where institutions provide the services people want there may be less demand for citizen participation.   For example, in Sweden, according to Gunnar Myrdal, where there is general consensus on the goals of the welfare state and fairly wide satisfaction with the way the government functions to meet the needs of the people, the problems in attaining collective goals are defined as essentially technological and organizational.   Consequently there appears to be little need for radical protest and little room for citizen participation.   Private concerns, not public issues, appear to preoccupy the people of Sweden.

We are not suggesting that there is in America a massive demand for participation in policy decisions.   It may be that at all times only a small minority are politically active.[77]   The requirement, points out John W. Gardner, is not that all should participate but that the opportunity for participation be available.[78]   The opportunity to participate in decisions appears to be an increasingly important requirement for the establishment of a new social contract.[79]   As Harvey Wheeler has observed, however, we face a dilemma because "participational democracy occurs for political reasons just at the time when it has been rendered dysfunctional for technological reasons."[80]   Complex decisions facing society require a level of sophisticated knowledge ordinarily unavailable to most persons.   We are in a position of having to create new structures that will make democratic participation a possibility in the postindustrial society. Among these are new means to make access to knowledge widely available, for knowledge today is the new basis for social power.   Those who control access to knowledge are in a position to shape the future society.

[75] Daniel P. Moynihan, "Toward a National Urban Policy," *The Public Interest,* No. 17 (Fall 1969), pp. 3–20.

[76] Dorothy Lee, *Freedom and Culture* (Englewood Cliffs, N.J.: Prentice-Hall, 1959).

[77] Evidence indicates that limited participation has always been the case.   In most organizations it appears that ". . . a limited 'elite' . . . run things for a complacent general membership."   William Bruce Cameron, *Modern Social Movements* (New York: Random House, 1966), p. 166.

[78] Gardner, Godkin Lectures, *op. cit.*

[79] Cahn, in Spiegel, *op. cit.,* p. 222.

[80] Harvey Wheeler, *The Rise and Fall of Liberal Democracy* (Santa Barbara, Calif.: The Center for the Study of Democratic Institutions, 1966), p. 26.

Social Science and Social Development

Knowledge as Power

The postindustrial society may become the first society actively guided by scientific knowledge. In this event knowledge would replace capital as the new basis of social power. Those who can control the production and application of bureaucratic and computerized knowledge may control the shape of society, the uses to which its resources are put, and the fate of the individual. Science is not merely a body of knowledge with which man may embellish his social life: it is a means by which man attains increasing control over his physical and symbolic environment. Such control may expand human freedom or become a source of tyranny. Such tyranny may be subtle and bloodless—not the application of force but a genteel coercion based on the illusion of freedom.[81] To aspire to democratic participation in this era is to search for methods that might make it possible to counteract the tendency of the wealthy, especially government and industry, to monopolize the use of social science while the poor, the racial minorities, and other relatively powerless groups have limited if any effective access to social science information.[82]

As political decisions increasingly determine the allocation of resources and life opportunities, power will to a considerable degree be determined by the relative access competing groups have to the control of information. In this context social welfare becomes concerned with the redress of imbalances in the competent use of knowledge. New kinds of social utilities involving such things as multiple-access computer systems, subsidies to citizen groups to enable them to employ specialists to interpret social policy implications of knowledge, and innovative educational structures for the "positive cultivation of the common mind" are essential to preserve and expand democratic participation during this scientific revolution.[83] The degree to which such participation will be possible, given the increasing dependence of decision-makers on highly specialized knowledge and the decreasing capacity of even educated citizens to become adequately informed about key public issues, is unknown. A free society, however, will need to find ways to enable all citizens to share in the power that accompanies access to knowledge. This is especially true as science becomes the basis for social policy and as social policy increasingly guides the direction of social change.

Toward the Active Society

Societies may drift with social change or seek to actively guide societal processes toward goals determined by powerful elites or influenced by broad participation in decision-making. It may be that we are moving in the direction of an active society, to use Amitai Etzioni's way of describing social units that are relatively capable of guiding their own processes.[84] A major factor

[81] Horowitz, *op. cit.,* p. 336.

[82] *Ibid.,* p. 333.

[83] *Ibid.;* and Wheeler, *Restoration of Politics, op. cit.,* p. 26.

[84] Amitai Etzioni, "The Active Society," in Sara Jane Heidt and Amitai Etzioni (eds.), *Societal Guidance: A New Approach To Social Problems* (New York: Crowell, 1969), p. 7.

determining the capacity to be in control of social change is the cybernetic capacities of the society, that is, its ability "to collect, process and use knowledge." [85] Wide access to cybernetic capacities and the ability of the social unit to attain consensus on goals that genuinely incorporate the perspectives and interests of its various subgroups determine the extent to which the direction of the active society is democratically determined.

While there are some indications of a trend toward the active society, we continue, in Etzioni's view, to be more accurately described as a "drifting" society.[86] Capitalist democracies in general are so characterized; they show little capacity to act except in response to a crisis. Even then the accommodations made are not likely to produce the structural changes required. The inability or unwillingness of powerful segments to share power and resources with those whose interests would reshape the social order not only keeps the system inherently conservative, but prevents it from actively guiding its own social development.[87]

In response to such resistance to change, students, clergy, civil rights leaders, antipoverty workers, and others seek to mobilize relatively powerless groups in the struggle for a "more egalitarian and active society." [88] Social integration that overcomes a high degree of alienation is now possible only through greater equality in social participation.[89] The degree to which we move in this direction will depend on social science, values, and politics.

Social Science as Ideology: The Union of Knowledge, Values, and Politics

In some respects social science embodies knowledge, values, and politics, disclaimers regarding the objectivity and neutrality of social science notwithstanding. Social scientists invariably play a political role. They define and redefine social reality, influence judgments regarding social policy, and invariably help to conserve or change the social system.[90] They may choose to produce "stable knowledge" that accepts the basic assumptions upon which a society rests, preferring to elaborate and revise its "secondary assumptions"; or they may provide "transforming knowledge" that critically examines the basic assumptions of a given system.[91] Producers of stable knowledge are likely to be more generously rewarded since they provide the symbols that help to protect the system from radical political scrutiny. Decision-making elites prefer stable to

[85] *Ibid.,* p. 8.

[86] *Ibid.,* p. 28.

[87] *Ibid.,* p. 28.

[88] *Ibid.,* p. 30.

[89] *Ibid.,* p. 28.

[90] *Ibid.,* p. 11; John R. Seeley, "Crestwood Heights: Intellectual and Libidinal Dimensions of Research" in Arthur J. Vidick, Joseph Bensman, and Maurice R. Stein (eds.) *Reflections on Community Studies* (New York: Wiley, 1964), p. 180. *See also* Chapter One of this volume.

[91] Etzioni, in Heidt and Etzioni, *op. cit.,* p. 12.

transforming knowledge and are not likely to encourage too thorough an examination of the fundamental premises of a social system that assures their continued power and privilege.[92]   This helps to explain Alvin Gouldner's observation that ". . . academic sociology since Comte has always been ready to lend support to any established social system. . . ."[93]   Recent radical movements among social scientists are in part an effort to give active critical expression to the inescapable political character of their disciplines.   This is reflected, for example, in the founding of a new action-oriented social science journal, *Social Policy,* that commits itself "to the search for radical change in our society."[94] The overt or covert link to politics characterizes all the sciences in a world in which the imperatives of science and technology are the driving forces that alter our environment, our way of life and our very image of ourselves.   No one has seen this more perceptively than Harvey Wheeler.   In his profound analysis of the social implications of the scientific revolution he observes: "Science has become society's legislature."[95]   If we are to humanize our social order and achieve the ideal goals of social welfare we shall need to find ways to link science to the pursuit of those values we want reflected in our social institutions and to develop those political means that will assure that all have an opportunity to participate in deciding what those values are to be.

Social Science and Human Progress

The fundamental purpose of a science of man is to provide that critical social perspective that might enable human beings to liberate themselves from obsolete and constricting social forms.   The knowledge man needs is knowledge that will guide him toward creating those social institutions that expand his self-powers with the least cost in injury to others.   Society is held together by a social myth, a social fiction that rationalizes and justifies our institutional arrangements, defines the meaning and purpose of life, and orders our existence accordingly. Man needs critical reason to free him from narrow and shallow conceptions that limit his image of life's possibilities, yet he also needs to create new values, richer symbolic definitions of reality.   Science must be an instrument in the service of man, treating him as an end and committed to his fullest development. This means that knowledge must identify means to expand the freedom to choose those social arrangements that more nearly express human aspirations. In short, science must expand social intelligence and social imagination. William J. Goode has put it in the following way:

> Perhaps by ascertaining both our values and the possible organizations for achieving them, we might learn that the costs of many contemporary pat-

[92] *Ibid.,* p. 12.

[93] Alvin W. Gouldner, "Toward the Radical Reconstruction of Sociology," *Social Policy,* May–June 1970, p. 23.

[94] Editorial statement in the first issue of *Social Policy,* May–June 1970, p. 2, International Arts and Sciences Press, 901 North Broadway, White Plains, New York.

[95] Harvey Wheeler, *Democracy In A Revolutionary Era,* A Center Occasional Paper, The Center For The Study Of Democratic Institutions, Santa Barbara, California, 1970, p. 119.

terns are too great . . . we may be able to demonstrate that many desirable but presently nonexistent arrangements are also possible.[96]

A value-directed science would operate on Morris Raphael Cohen's dictum, already alluded to in Chapter One, that what is socially significant can only be determined by the contemplation of social ends.[97]   The ends that appear to be most consistent with our scientific understanding of the requirements of human development and our democratic aspirations for full and equal opportunity for all are captured in the phrase offered us by Ernest Becker: "maximum individuality within maximum community." [98]   The central problem to which science must address itself appears to be one of ". . . integrating the human family while preserving the integrity of the individual members." [99]   Individual freedom and social order—those ancient polarities—now pose the social dilemmas that require the aid of science.   At the same time, only a science oriented toward maximizing human freedom through social development can provide both the critical perspective and the guides to social action.   All social institutions come under scrutiny in the light of social justice, the principle that appears to be the essential link between individual liberty and social order.[100]

As we have noted several times, justice refers to each man's right to affirm and actualize himself, to draw from society those sustaining and nurturing resources and experiences that permit his fullest human development.   From social welfare as charity to social welfare as justice is the agenda for scientifically grounded social reform.

Goals of Social Reform

For those social welfare leaders with vision social reform has always been the goal.   As early as 1910 Jane Addams, in her presidential address to the National Conference of Charities and Corrections, expressed it in the following way: "The negative policy of relieving destitution, or even the more generous one of preventing it, is giving way to the positive idea of raising life to its highest value." [101]   Some ideal image of the kind of society that would raise life to its highest value is essential if we are to strive for human progress rather than the mere amelioration of existing social ills.   In a volume addressed to social workers, Lawrence K. Northwood commented on this need:

> We must know what we are moving toward as well as what we are moving away from: the lack of an inspiring image for tomorrow perhaps is equally

[96] William J. Goode, "The Protection of the Inept," *American Sociological Review,* 32 (February 1967), p. 19.

[97] Morris R. Cohen, *Reason and Nature* (New York: Harcourt, Brace, 1931) p. 343.

[98] Ernest Becker, *The Structure of Evil,* (New York: George Braziller, 1968), p. 251.

[99] Pfuetze, *op. cit.,* p. 307.

[100] *Ibid.,* p. 315.

[101] Jane Addams, *A Centennial Reader* (New York: Macmillan, 1960), p. 85.

as serious a deficiency for social workers as the failure to recognize current social problems, and to work for their amelioration.[102]

To engage in directed social change is to make moral choices about the kind of human being we value and the social order we want. In some measure we have no choice, for the scientific revolution that is upon us requires that we abandon old concepts and reconstruct our image of man and society. To decide the kind of social order we wish to promote requires some clarity about what it is we are leaving behind or should try to leave behind. We have all been introduced time and again to the notion of cultural lag, which suggests that obsolete social symbols have a way of dictating the minds of men long after they have ceased to serve any useful purpose. Social structures incorporating such symbols persist even in the face of radically new circumstances that require social arrangements more adequate to the needs of the time. The scientific revolution makes a museum piece of values and institutions designed to solve the problem of economic scarcity, but we persist in believing in the vitality of liberal capitalism. We have essentially solved the problem of production, but our images of economic man and the market society remain as powerful symbols and continue to define our human nature and our social existence. If one discounts the human and social costs of this ideology but grants its impressive material and technological achievement, it has clearly functioned to create the resources that now permit us to go beyond its narrow vision of human motivation and social responsibility.

The ideology we inherited from Hobbes, Locke, and Smith, among others, informs us that man is ". . . essentially 'homo economicus' and social justice is essentially the fulfillment of contractual obligations." [103] Since the natural state of man, according to the Hobbesian view, is that of a "war of all against all," human nature is clearly evil, and man is not to be trusted. The primary function of the state is to ". . . assure that neither the powerful cheat the weak, nor the shiftless take advantage of the industrious." [104] Within these ground rules a society based on contract, leaving each man free to bargain for his own best advantage, is the best assurance of freedom and social harmony. Those who cannot provide for themselves through participation in this natural order of market activity may be aided through charity. This laissez-faire philosophy that limited state regulation of the market has in part been abandoned in favor of a modest version of the welfare state. As we have already noted, however, the ideology of the free market remained paramount and that of the welfare state suspect. Yet the moral ideal of welfare also has roots in the values of equality and dignity, and these have served to support the expansion of social responsibility for meeting human needs. Social welfare modifies the play of market forces. Its historical trend has been toward assuring an enforced mini-

---

[102] Lawrence K. Northwood, "Deterioration of the Inner City," in Nathan E. Cohen (ed.), *Social Work and Social Problems* (New York: National Association of Social Workers, 1964), p. 247.

[103] Bernard J. Coughlin, in a review of Donald S. Howard, *Social Welfare: Values, Means, Ends* (New York: Random House, 1969), in *Journal of Education For Social Work,* 5 (Fall 1966), p. 76.

[104] *Ibid.,* p. 76.

mum of civilized life as society has become more affluent and as the concept of citizen rights has democratized our notions of charity. The social response to the continuing tension between equality of citizenship and inequality of class may ultimately lead to the "elimination of the market altogether, at least as a force influencing human relationships." [105]

What we are leaving behind, or should be, is our concept of economic man and our image of a society with limited obligations of social responsibility. Man is now seen as unlimited in his potential, not narrowly construed as an acquisitive maximizer of economic gain. The obligation of society extends to promoting his fullest development, not merely to meeting his subsistence needs. The structure of inequality is the immediate target of social reform because the maldistribution of income, status, and power not only undermines the commitment of deprived groups to the preservation of social order but represents major barriers to full citizenship status.

One way to conceptualize the goal of social reform is to speak in terms of moving from an image of economic man to one of political man. The term political is used broadly here to refer to participation in the political quest for the good society, in an ongoing critical examination of social issues, and in the determination of decisions about the kind of social order we shall create. The political forum replaces the market as the central institution, and new structures are established to empower the citizen with the knowledge, resources, and decision-making apparatus to help shape the commonweal.[106] The decisions made would have increasingly less to do with the allocation of resources to promote creature comforts, a decent level of which we might learn to take for granted, and more to do with the promotion of "culture comforts . . . the traditional goals of humanism . . . the only goals worthy of man." [107]

The goals of social reform would not be cast primarily in the image of the Great Society, with its belief that all that is required is a more equitable distribution of the good things of this society, a better share of the pie for everyone. Instead the concept of the missing community better outlines the long-range direction of social progress. Neither expanded economic growth nor the more equitable and social distribution of the Gross National Product alone will satisfy man's urge for personal significance and for human fellowship. Equality of opportunity is not the only key to social ills. There are deprivations other than the denial of opportunity for occupational success. "The lack of purpose and the lack of social love and approval," as Donald Gilbert McKinley has written, "are perhaps even more strongly felt deprivations in our very secular and impersonal society." [108] Loneliness, social isolation, and a sense of being trapped in a meaningless routine of life may be more keenly felt by the disadvantaged, but alienation is part of the human condition in a depersonalized, fragmented, bureaucratized society. Even for the relatively successful, the ethic of work and family is no longer an adequate definition of life's purpose. We are dealing

[105] Asa Briggs, "The Welfare State in Historical Perspective" in Mayer N. Zald (ed.), *Social Welfare Institutions* (New York: Wiley, 1965), pp. 44–46.

[106] Wheeler, *Restoration of Politics, op. cit.*

[107] Wheeler, *The Rise and Fall of Liberal Democracy, op. cit.*, p. 25.

[108] Donald G. McKinley, *Social Class and Family Life* (New York: Macmillan, 1964), p. 268.

not only with the problems related to denial of opportunity but to those that afflict the participants in the American Dream. Material welfare as the basis for the good life has simply lost its appeal for many. Now it is our relationships with one another and the meaning of our living together that is problematic. The point has been well made by George Dennison:

> We Americans have suffered such losses of humane communality that we cannot allow ourselves to see the waste of life that stares us in the face. Our very sense of crisis is nothing more than a refined technique of avoidance. Thus we have "a problem of the schools" and talk to each other solemnly about improved facilities, better methods of instruction, more supervision, ignoring all the while the painful truth that what children need most is for the lives of their elders to make sense. We are our children's problems. To the extent that we are isolated from each other our children have no world.[109]

The goals of social welfare must now include the quest for community. As Richard Lichtman has written, "a community is not a corrective but a constructive system of human existence . . . it organizes itself affirmatively for the sake of human well-being." [110] Social welfare as salvage and repair, as a residual concept of treating or rescuing the casualties of the system, would give way to a positive affirmation of all as persons with entitlement to full development of their capacities. Man is social, but it is the quality of social relationships that determines his capacity to be a free individual sharing in the creation and enrichment of symbolic order. "To be free, to be responsible, to be a real person, and to be in mutual relation with all otherness—all these mean the same thing." [111]

While science may guide action in the quest for community in which social welfare is the expression of equal and mutual regard for one another, only art and religion can provide the aesthetic and ethical symbols such a society requires. It is from the poets, as John Dewey observed, that we obtain the imaginative vision that may direct our quest for an ethical community.[112] Man as symbolic animal is ultimately *homo religioso,* seeking self-transcendence through identification with superordinate values that religion may provide. The resacralization of life, the confirmation of man as an end, the resistance to the dehumanizing scientific and technological imperative, the subordination of reason and technique to human purpose may well require the creation of a new religious mythology. Such a "mythology of adulthood," suggests Henry A. Murray, is needed to celebrate interdependence and creation and to rescue us from symbols that confine us to a puerile view of the world.[113] Symbolic man

---

[109] *The New York Times,* January 12, 1970.

[110] Richard Lichtman, *Toward Community* (Santa Barbara, Calif.: Center for the Study of Democratic Institutions, 1966).

[111] Pfuetze, *op. cit.,* p. 249.

[112] Joseph Ratner (ed.), *Intelligence in the Modern World: John Dewey's Philosophy* (New York: Modern Library, 1939), pp. 999–1000.

[113] Henry A. Murray, "Beyond Yesterday's Idealisms," in Crane Brinton (ed.), *The Fate of Man* (New York: George Braziller, 1961), p. 16.

lives and grows by the images he creates. In the words of Lewis Mumford, he "grows in the image of his gods and up to the measure they have set." [114]

A radical critique of society is an assault on the social myths upon which social order rests. This should not be understood to mean that man can escape society or avoid creating new and more meaningful definitions of reality. A society stands condemned to the degree that it deprives its citizens of the capacity and opportunity to participate in the free creation of meaning. Invariably the degree of such freedom that is possible is historically conditioned. Societies in early stages of economic development depend on a disciplined labor force to overcome the problem of scarcity and on social fictions that bind men to existing structures. Critical awareness is a luxury societies can afford only when resources permit and even demand the creation of alternative styles of life. The measure of danger and challenge we confront in the United States at this moment is precisely the extent of our arrival at the point at which old symbols cease to assure order. We are threatened either by anarchy or by repressive measures to bolster the status quo. By the same token we are in an exciting period for the re-creation of our culture; we have the resources that make it possible for us to ask what values we shall honor and a political and spiritual crisis that demands an answer.

For the time being efforts at social reform proceed for the most part without attention to such ultimate questions as the moral ends of social action. The ends are largely taken for granted and perhaps this is unavoidable. Immediate pressing issues—income distribution, jobs, housing, racial discrimination, education, participation in decision-making—provide the agenda for social reform. To be sure each issue raises questions of values. How we shall make income available to those who cannot adequately participate in the economy, for example, poses a moral issue that strikes at the very heart of a society organized around the ethic of work. Very likely changes will take place in our income maintenance program. It is not likely, however, that a public debate on the quality of life, dictated by our commitment to the notion that people must either be employers or employees involved in a system primarily geared to maximizing corporate profit, will provide an informed basis for judgments on the merits of alternative income programs. No such public forum exists to make possible such reasoned inquiry into the very structure of our society or ways we may wish to alter it.

Social reform, as distinct from social revolution, seeks to improve the operation of a social system, not create a new one. It accepts certain basic premises upon which the system rests. Such premises, however, may represent competing principles of social organization, thus providing the dynamics of conflict and change. Out of such conflict the social system evolves and may develop into a qualitatively new form of social organization. The culture of capitalism and the culture of democracy are such competing principles, and they have been, as T. H. Marshall has observed, "at war" with each other. [115] Democracy implies equality of citizenship, and this idea is a continuing challenge to inequality of

[114] Lewis Mumford, *The City in History* (New York: Harcourt, Brace & World, 1961), p. 575.

[115] T. H. Marshall, *Class, Citizenship, and Social Development* (Garden City, N.Y.: Anchor Books, 1965), p. 93.

class, upon which capitalism rests.[116]   While no industrial society functions without a system of stratification, the degree of inequality in the distribution of opportunities and rewards and the manner in which such inequality is expressed are subject to attack.   The legitimacy of the reward system that produces a degree of inequality that John Kenneth Galbraith chooses to call "obscene" is likely to be increasingly questioned, not only by those who suffer from its abuses but by others whose ethical commitment is to the egalitarian ideal.[117]   Inequalities in status and in distribution of opportunities for self-esteem are as keenly felt deprivations as inequality in material resources, although all of them are almost inseparable in a society in which material resources represent such important symbols of self-regard and social approval.   Social differentiation without stigma, status without invidious imputation of personal inferiority, and a democratic share of political power may be utopian goals.   The notion of equality, however, as Harold Laski declared, ". . . points the way to the essence of the democratic ideal . . . the effort of men to affirm their own essence and to remove all barriers to that affirmation." [118]

The unfinished business of democracy is the business of social welfare, we suggested in Chapter One.   While social welfare had its origin in the concern with dependency and poverty, we see now that the evil was and is inequality. The early concern with pauperism and the current concern with poverty are ways of defining the problem that draw attention away from the central issues, the right of all men to a full and equal realization of their common humanity and the right to opportunities to participate in society in ways that make this possible.   The problem lies in the structure of inequality, the relationship of the powerful to the powerless, of the advantaged to the disadvantaged.   Poverty and associated problems are consequences of this relationship.

To some extent social welfare programs have moved away from the mere amelioration of poverty to a concern with the social integration of the poor. If the poor are indeed to be participants in society we must, as Richard M. Titmuss has suggested, "widen our frame of reference.   We shall need to shift the emphasis from poverty to inequality; from *ad hoc* programs to integrated social rights; from economic growth to social growth." [119]   Social growth involves a basic shift in the allocation of our resources of income, medical care, housing, education, and social services to favor the disadvantaged in order to overcome gross inequalities in the conditions of life and the debilitating consequences they produce.[120]   Ultimately the test of social development is the development of man, of all men, and of our highest capacities as human beings.   Institutions exist to serve the needs of man.   When they no longer function adequately men have the right and the obligation to change them.   Social welfare as social development proceeds on this assumption.

[116] The author is mindful that this may imply too simple a notion of social class and class conflict.   For a more sophisticated analysis *see* Dahrendorf, *op. cit.*

[117] "A Center Report, Priorities in an Affluent Society," *op. cit.,* p. 74.

[118] Harold Laski, "Democracy," *Encyclopedia of the Social Sciences,* (New York: Macmillan, 1931), Vol. V, p. 76.

[119] Richard M. Titmuss, "Social Policy and Economic Progress," *The Social Welfare Forum* (New York: Columbia University Press, 1966), pp. 25–39.

[120] *Ibid.*

Paradoxes of Social Welfare

There are "dilemmas and moral ambiguities" in the ideal of social welfare, as Charles Frankel has helped us to understand.[121]   To speak of changing institutions to meet the needs of men conceals both the difficulties of social reform as well as conflicts over whose needs are to be given primary consideration.   Moreover, directed social change has its costs.   Even the attainment of the ideal goals of social welfare, assuming for a moment that we might agree on these, may have its unwelcome price.

While radical reforms are necessary to produce a more equal and more just society, only incremental reforms may be politically feasible.   Short of revolution, any social system probably can be changed only within limits set by its structure of power and privilege and by its ideology, which defines the range of permissible deviation.   To press for change that goes beyond the tolerance of those who have the power to resist is to risk loss of support for those modest changes that might be acceptable.   The fact is that the social ills we deplore are created by the same social system that produces the benefits the majority have come to accept as worth preserving, on the assumption—real or imaginary—that radical social change would offer them no compensating gains.   If we have a disadvantaged population, there are others who enjoy advantages.   Those who think they gain from the system are not eager to change it on behalf of those who are its victims.

In order to win support for some change, radical criticism of social institutions may be attenuated by those who design programs in behalf of the disadvantaged.   For example, Peter Marris and Martin Rein have noted that the poverty cycle theory underlying the Community Action Programs functioned to avoid too open and direct a challenge to middle-class values.   Since the projects depended on the cooperation of middle-class community leaders and professionals identified with institutions that needed to be changed in behalf of the poor, criticisms of such institutions could not be made too explicit.[122]

When criticism is explicit it is likely to be ignored.   For example, the National Advisory Commission On Civil Disorders made it crystal clear that the ghetto was created by the very organization of white-dominated society.   "White institutions created it, white institutions maintain it, and white society condones it." [123]   When the criticism is pressed too forcefully it may lead to a dangerous polarization of society, with opposing factions acting out of a sense of righteous indignation and accepting the legitimacy of violence.   Perhaps this is what is happening already.   A country as disparate as ours, with little sense of community, with deep and divisive discontents, and with a history steeped in violence risks falling apart either if it fails to make radical reforms to promote a greater sense of justice or if such reforms are forced too rapidly upon an unwilling majority.

[121] Charles Frankel, "Some Paradoxes in the Ideal of Welfare," The Elizabeth Wisner Lecture, Tulane University School of Social Work, New Orleans, Louisiana, October 19, 1965.

[122] Marris and Rein, *op. cit.*, pp. 53–54.

[123] *Report,* National Advisory Commission on Civil Disorders (Washington, D.C.: Government Printing Office, 1968), p. 1.

There are further dilemmas. All social action has its unintended consequences, "some of which may be regarded as incidental cost, some of which may be unexpected benefits, and others of which represent substantial inversions of the original action." [124] Efforts at reform rarely turn out the way people intend. Although some of the spin-off may be beneficial, other consequences pose new problems that must be dealt with. An illustration of this may be found in the support given by the Ford Foundation to the school decentralization plan in New York City in 1968–69. As a consequence of its support of greater community control of local school systems, a conflict was engendered between some members of the black community and school teachers and administrators, a significant portion of whom were Jewish. As a result it appears that some black anti-Semitism was stimulated. Francis Keppel, former U.S. Commissioner of Education and one of the persons responsible for drafting the Ford Foundation School Decentralization Plan remarked as follows:

> I confess not to color blindness but to insufficient acuity on anti-Semitic prejudice . . . Personally I don't think I was sensitive enough to the prejudice issue. In formulating plans for a greater community control in schools we made a conscious choice, that professional administrators and teachers would have to adjust to more local involvement. We felt it was in the interest of the community as a whole. But we had not counted on the fall-out of prejudice it produced.[125]

The fact is that we do not possess the knowledge we need to deal in any fundamental way with our social problems; yet often we cannot avoid acting, using the best knowledge at our command. It may be that eventually we shall have more sophisticated action theories that will also permit us to design programs of social reform and adequate techniques for anticipating and correcting the unintended consequences. Even when we possess knowledge we may not be able to put it to use. It would not be difficult to design a way to radically redistribute income, for example. Our values and our distribution of power do not, however, appear to support anything but a modest change in the structure of income inequality. Thus solutions to social problems even when available may not be regarded as economically or politically feasible. This is not because the forces of evil outweigh the forces of good. Instead our moral ideals conflict and all values cannot be simultaneously maximized. A society totally without social problems would require a degree of totalitarian control inconsistent with any concept of a free society. Freedom and a considerable degree of social disorder are associated phenomena, as Irving Louis Horowitz has made clear:

> The dilemma for those who consider social problems obstacles to be overcome is that any true overcoming of social problems implies a perfect social system. And this entails several goals; first, the total institutionalization of all people; second, the thoroughgoing equilibrium between the parts of a system with respect to their functioning and the functioning of other sectors; and third, the elimination of social change as either a fact

[124] Raymond A. Bauer, "Societal Feedback," in Gross, *op. cit.,* p. 64.

[125] *The New York Times,* January 26, 1969.

or value. Thus, the resolution of social problems from the point of view of the social system would signify the totalitarian resolution of social life.[126]

There is the further problem of scale. It may be possible, for example, to design an educational experience for preschool children that would make a significant difference in their cognitive and emotional development. On a small scale it may be possible to provide the ideal setting for such an experience. On a vast scale the situation may be quite different. One has only to look at the crisis of our public schools to see the failure of mass education, though we grant that here the problem is not simply one of scale. Instead we are confronted with the conflict between aggregate and distributive values, to use the language of Thomas F. Green.

> By an aggregate value, I mean a good to be maximized for society even though it may not be maximized for each individual within the society. By a distributive value, I mean one which is to be maximized for each individual, though not necessarily for the society as a whole.[127]

As Green notes, proposals to reform the schools to provide for a humanistic education that would ". . . cultivate the independence of each 'individual' and develop each person to the fullest" is an expression of distributive values. Such proposals, he insists, run counter to the aggregate values of a managerial society that sees the school as "a productive enterprise, preparing people to take a functional role in an increasingly orderly, rational, and productive society." [128] Efforts to change the educational institution in ways that run counter to its primary function for the larger social system are likely to fail unless the larger system itself can be changed. Much of social welfare effort is in behalf of distributive values. The same conflict with the functional needs of the larger social system are present. We have already seen this in the discussion of proposals for various forms of guaranteed income in Chapter Six. Invariably fears regarding work incentive that might deprive the system of its assured supply of marginal workers prevail against the right of individuals to a decent level of living. As the supply of "dirty workers" is no longer needed, or their retention is regarded as too costly, we are likely to get greater support for modest income programs that free some people from the discipline of work without the stigma of the dole. The conflict between aggregate and distributive values, however, is likely to be present in any society. All systems seek to maintain and enhance their functioning. The well-being of the total system is not necessarily compatible with that of any given individual. The wealthier the society the more tolerant it can be of the individual who deviates and the more generously it can meet individual needs.

The aspiration contained in the moral ideal of welfare, though far from unambiguous, surely includes, among other possible goals, the creation of those social conditions that free the individual to develop his full powers as a person.

---

[126] Horowitz, *op. cit.,* p. 125.

[127] Thomas F. Green, "Schools and Communities: A Look Forward," *Harvard Educational Review,* 39 (Spring 1969), pp. 221–252.

[128] *Ibid.*

"To be a person is to be an autonomous source of action," as Emile Durkheim clearly understood.[129]   Yet such autonomy is never unfettered, even under optimal conditions, and always requires in addition to the individual capacity to choose an equivalent capacity to conform to some structure that makes social order possible.   The tension between freedom and order is thus a basic polarity of social life.   Moreover freedom is not an unmixed blessing, as Dostoevsky reveals in the story of "the grand inquisitor" and as Erich Fromm depicts in *Escape From Freedom*.[130]   It represents a burden as well as a blessing.   If it were possible to achieve a society without injustice, one that assured to each individual all he could possibly demand in the way of opportunity for self-determination, a price would be exacted in the form of personal responsibility that not all would welcome.   This is what Charles Frankel means when he asserts that there is a harsh ethic in the moral ideal of welfare that rarely is made clear.   Society is unjust and condemns many to deprivations that should be overcome.   To reverse this state of affairs and to achieve welfare, declares Frankel, is to create a world in which we have no one to blame but ourselves if we do not like what we have done with our own life.[131]

However, as Frankel goes on to point out, the moral ideal of welfare contains conflicting values of charity and justice that require constant efforts at balance and adjudication.   Charity here is the Christian concept of love or *caritas,* not bourgeois benevolence.   It is accepting of individual faults, inclined to excuse failure, and generously responsive to individual needs out of recognition that one's membership in the human family is sufficient ground for a claim on collective resources and sympathetic attention.   On the other hand justice, as Frankel defines that term, accords men their rights and holds them accountable for their behavior.   It rewards excellence and condemns failure because it acts on the assumption that men are capable of exercising individual responsibility.   After all, as Frankel observes, if we cannot blame a man for being bad we cannot praise or admire a man for being good.   No society that wishes to uphold the ideal of individual autonomy can accept an extreme position on social determination of behavior that excludes all notions of individual freedom and responsibility.   The truth is that we must live by both charity and justice in a state of continuing tension, each acting to offset the excesses of the other.   "Fanaticism is the price we pay when we forget charity; sentimentality is the price we pay when we forget justice." [132]

To strive for a balance between *caritas* and justice is to strive for a community of men that goes beyond contemporary welfare liberalism, one that overcomes the inequality inherent in the very structure of contemporary society, whose fundamental principles of social organization run counter to the moral ideal of welfare.   Love and justice are the ethics of social welfare and the values of

[129] George Simpson, *Emile Durkheim on the Division of Labor in Society* (New York: Macmillan, 1933), p. 403.

[130] Fyodor Dostoevsky, *The Brothers Karamazov* (New York: Modern Library), Part 2, Book 5, Chap. 5, pp. 255–274; Erich Fromm, *Escape From Freedom* (New York: Farrar & Rinehart, 1941).

[131] Charles Frankel, *op. cit.,* p. 7.

[132] *Ibid.,* p. 9.

true community. The dilemma is that these cannot be realized within our present social system nor can true community be other than an ideal beyond perfect attainment. This is not a counsel of despair. The function of ideals is to direct our efforts and to give nobility to our strivings. Max Weber helped us to see this when he wrote, "Certainly all historical experience confirms the truth—that man would not have attained the possible unless time and again he had reached out for the impossible." [133]

Postscript: The Future of Social Welfare

The central idea of welfare is humanitarian regard for our fellow-man. This can be expressed in the form of benevolence that seeks to reduce suffering without upsetting class inequality. In this case we have an exchange system that allows us to dole out benefits to the poor and disadvantaged provided they do not claim these as rights or question the legitimacy of the reward system. Such a system functions to maintain a status-oriented society in which our very sense of self-esteem may require the denigration and even the annihilation of the personality of others.

Humanitarian regard may also mean an identification with the family of man, an expansion of one's loyalty beyond the narrow confines of family and group to include ever wider segments of humanity. It incorporates the religious notion of a common brotherhood now confirmed by our scientific understanding of the interrelatedness of all social systems. We are in fact interdependent. Our behavior has inescapable consequences for others for which we must bear moral responsibility. The better science can trace the consequences of our actions the less we can escape the ethical implications of the way we organize our social life. Definitions of social welfare that are narrow and parochial must be expanded to embrace the entire family of man.

Social problems are now being defined in international terms. Poverty, inequality, and the human consequences of social systems organized around power and competitive advantage are on the agenda of international social welfare. Issues of the warfare state are now inseparable from issues of human welfare. Our science and our technology is transforming the world, yet the direction of our scientific revolution is not necessarily consistent with the needs of man. There are some signs that this may change. A joint conference of the American Association for the Advancement of Science and the British Association for the Advancement of Science, held in Boulder, Colorado, in 1969, addressed itself to the relationship of science to critical world problems. One of the conclusions was that scientists must carry out large-scale studies to "relate national goals, formulated in terms of human needs, to the growth of science and technology, and to the allocation of resources." [1] Yet the power of science and technology can contribute to human well-being only if science itself becomes committed to this ethical goal, for "knowledge without love will lead mankind

[133] Dennis H. Wrong, "Max Weber: The Scholar as Hero," *Columbia University Forum,* 5 (Summer 1962), p. 34.

[1] H. Bentley Glass, "Letter From the President," American Association for the Advancement of Science *Bulletin,* Vol. 14 (September 1969).

to destruction." [2]   The same may be said for the social sciences.   Some social scientists are recognizing that involvement in the human condition is inescapable.   Through default or through design their studies have consequences they cannot avoid.   Perhaps the scientific revolution committed to guiding the human revolution, a linking of reason with a passion for human freedom, offers grounds for hope.

All around us there are signs that human beings are coming alive to new and exciting potentialities in the nature of man and the possibilities for social life. The Protestant ethic has outlived its usefulness.   Man was made for joy, for creation of meaning, for ritual and drama, for love, for poetry and mystery, for self-transcendence, and for union with all mankind.   There is more, much more, to man than the narrow image of him that we have incorporated into our economic and political life.   Here lies the hope for human welfare.

[2] Paul E. Pfuetze, *Self, Society, Existence* (New York: Harper Torchbooks, 1961), p. 307.

Bibliography

Abbot, Edith. *The Tenements of Chicago, 1908–1935.* Chicago: University of Chicago Press, 1936.

Abel, Lionel. "Is There a Tragic View of Life?," *Commentary,* December, 1964.

The Ad Hoc Committee on the Triple Revolution. *The Triple Revolution.* Santa Barbara, Calif.: 1964.

Addams, Jane, *The Spirit of Youth and the City Streets.* New York: Macmillan, 1909.

———. *The Second Twenty Years at Hull House.* New York: Macmillan, 1930.

———. *A Centennial Reader.* New York: Macmillan, 1960.

———. *Twenty Years at Hull House.* New York: Signet Classics, 1961.

Advisory Council on Public Welfare. *Having the Power We Have the Duty.* Washington, D.C.: Government Printing Office, 1966.

Albee, Edward. *The American Dream and the Zoo Story.* New York: Signet Books, 1959.

Aldous, Joan, and Reuben Hill, "Breaking the Poverty Cycle," *Social Work,* Vol. 14 (July 1969), pp. 3–12.

Alinsky, Saul. *Reveille for Radicals.* Chicago: University of Chicago Press, 1945.

Allen, Steve. *The Ground Is Our Table.* Garden City: Doubleday, 1966.

Altshuler, Alan. "The Potential of 'Trickle Down,'" *The Public Interest,* No. 15 (Spring 1969), pp. 46–56.

Ambrosino, Salvatore. "A Family Agency Reaches Out to a Slum Ghetto," *Social Work,* Vol. 11 (October 1966), pp. 17–23.

"The American Underclass: Red, White and Black." *Trans-action,* 6 (February 1969).

Anshen, Ruth Nanda. *The Family: Its Function and Destiny.* New York: Harper & Brothers, 1949.

Arendt, Hannah, *Eichmann in Jerusalem: A Report on the Banality of Evil.* rev. ed. New York: Viking Press, 1964,

Atkinson, Brooks (ed.). *The Selected Writings of Ralph Waldo Emerson.* New York: Modern Library, 1950.

Auden, W. H. *The Collected Poetry of W. H. Auden.* New York: Random House, 1945.

Ball, Robert M. "Social Security Perspectives," *Social Security Bulletin,* Vol. 31 (August 1968), p. 3.

Banfield, Edward C. *Political Influence.* New York, Free Press, 1961.

Barr, Sherman. "Budgeting and the Poor," *Public Welfare,* Vol. 23 (October 1965), pp. 246–250, 293–294.

Becker, Ernest. *The Revolution in Psychiatry.* New York: Free Press, 1964.

———. *Beyond Alienation.* New York: George Braziller, 1967.

———. *The Structure of Evil.* New York: George Braziller, 1968.

Becker, Howard S. (ed.). *Social Problems: A Modern Approach.* New York: Wiley, 1966.

Beiser, Morton. "Poverty, Social Disintegration and Personality," *Journal of Social Issues,* Vol. 21 (January 1965), pp. 56–78.

Bell, Daniel. *The End of Ideology.* New York: Free Press, 1960.

———. *The Reforming of General Education.* New York: Columbia University Press, 1966.

———. "Notes on the Post-Industrial Society (1)," *The Public Interest,* No. 6 (Winter 1967), pp. 24–35. This material has appeared in *A Great Society?,* ed. by Bertram Gross (New York: Basic Books, 1968).

———. "Notes on the Post-Industrial Society (11)," *The Public Interest,* No. 7 (Spring 1967), pp. 102–118. This material has appeared in *A Greaty Society?,* ed. by Bertram Gross (New York: Basic Books, 1968).

Bell, Winifred. *Aid to Dependent Children.* New York: Columbia University Press, 1965.

Bellamy, Edward. *Looking Backward.* Cleveland: World Publishing, 1945; first published by Houghton Mifflin, 1888.

Bennett, John W. "Communal Brethren of the Great Plains," *Trans-action,* Vol. 4 (December 1966), pp. 42–47.

Bennis, Warren. "Beyond Bureaucracy," *Trans-action,* Vol. 2 (July–August 1965), pp. 31–35.

————. "Post-Bureaucratic Leadership," *Trans-action,* Vol. 6 (July–August, 1969), pp. 44–51, 61.

————, Kenneth D. Benne, and Robert Chin. *The Planning of Change.* New York: Holt, Rinehart & Winston, 1962.

Bentrup, Walter C. "What's Wrong with the Means Test?," *Public Welfare* Vol. 23 (October 1965), pp. 235–242.

Berelson, Bernard, and Gary A. Steiner. *Human Behavior: An Inventory of Scientific Findings.* New York: Harcourt, Brace & World, 1964.

Berg, Ivar. "Rich Man's Qualifications For Poor Man's Jobs," *Trans-action,* Vol. 6 (March 1969), pp. 45–51.

Bernard, Jessie. "The Status of Women in Modern Patterns of Culture," *The Annals,* Vol. 375 (January 1968).

Bernard, Sydney E. "Fatherless Families: Their Economic and Social Adjustment." In *Papers in Social Welfare,* No. 7. Waltham, Mass.: Florence Heller Graduate School for Advanced Studies in Social Welfare, Brandeis University, 1964.

Bertalanffy, Ludwig von. *Robots, Men and Minds.* New York: George Braziller, 1967.

Billingsley, Andrew. *Black Families in White America.* Englewood Cliffs, N.J.: Prentice-Hall, 1968.

Birnbaum, Max. "Sense and Nonsense About Sensitivity Training," *Saturday Review,* November 15, 1969, pp. 82–84.

"The Black Wasps," *Trans-action,* Vol. 6 (May 1969), pp. 8–9.

Blau, Peter. *Bureaucracy in Modern Society.* New York: Random House, 1956.

Bloom, Benjamin S., Allison Davis, and Robert Hess. *Compensatory Education for Cultural Deprivation.* New York: Holt, Rinehart & Winston, 1965.

Bonen, Gil, and Philip Reno. "By Bread Alone, and Little Bread: Life on AFDC," *Social Work,* Vol. 15 (October 1968), pp. 5–11.

Boorstin, Daniel. *The Americans: The National Experience.* New York: Random House, 1965.

Bordua, David J. *Sociological Theories and Their Implications for Juvenile Delinquency: A Report of a Children's Bureau Conference.* U.S. Department of Health, Education, and Welfare, Washington, D.C.: Government Printing Office, 1960.

Boroff, David (ed.). *The State of the Nation.* Englewood Cliffs, N.J.: Prentice-Hall, 1965.

Borton, Terry. "Reach, Touch, and Teach," *Saturday Review,* January 18, 1969, pp. 56–68, 69–70.

Bradford, Leland, J. Gibb, and K. Benne. *T-Group Theory and Laboratory Method.* New York: Wiley, 1965.

Bremner, Robert H. *From the Depths—The Discovery of Poverty in the United States.* New York: New York University Press, 1964.

Briar, Scott. "Welfare From Below: Recipients' Views of the Welfare System," *California Law Review,* Vol. 54 (May 1966), pp. 370–385.

———. "Why Children's Allowances?," *Social Work,* Vol. 14 (January 1969), pp. 5–12.

Brinton, Crane. *Ideas and Men.* New York: Prentice-Hall, 1950.

——— (ed.). *The Fate of Man.* New York: George Braziller, 1961.

"British White Paper on Social Security Reform," *Social Security Bulletin,* Vol. 32, (May 1969), pp. 3–15.

Bronfenbrenner, Urie. "The Changing American Child," *Journal of Social Issues,* Vol. 17 (January 1961).

———. "The Split-Level American Family," *Saturday Review,* October 7, 1967, pp. 60–66.

———. "The Psychological Costs of Quality and Equality in Education," *Child Development,* Vol. 38 (December 1967), pp. 909–926.

Brown, Gordon E. (ed.). *The Multi-Problem Dilemma.* Metuchen, N.J.: Scarecrow Press, 1968.

Brown, Stuart Gerry (ed.). *We Hold These Truths.* New York: Harper & Brothers, 1948.

Browning, Harley L. "Timing of Our Lives," *Trans-action,* Vol. 6 (October 1969), pp. 22–27.

Bruner, Jerome. "Character Education and Curriculum," in Jerome Bruner (ed.) *Learning About Learning.* U.S. Department of Health, Education, and Welfare. Washington, D.C.: Government Printing Office, 1966.

———. "Education as Social Invention," *Saturday Review,* February 19, 1966.

Buber, Martin. "I and Thou," in Will Herberg (ed.), *The Writings of Martin Buber.* New York: Meridian Books, 1956, pp. 43–62.

Buchanan, Scott. *So Reason Can Rule.* Santa Barbara, Calif.: Center for the Study of Democratic Institutions, 1967.

Burgess, Elaine M. "Poverty and Dependency: Some Selected Characteristics," *Journal of Social Issues,* Vol. 21 (January 1965), pp. 79–97.

Burgess, Elaine M., and Daniel O. Price. *An American Dependency Challenge.* Chicago: American Public Welfare Association, 1963.

Burns, Eveline M. "Social Security in Evolution: Toward What?," *Social Service Review,* Vol. 39 (June 1965), pp. 129–140.

———. "The Role of Government in Health Services," *Bulletin of the New York Academy of Medicine,* Vol. 41 (July 1965), pp. 1–42.

——— (ed.). *Children's Allowances and the Economic Welfare of Children.* New York: Citizens Committee for Children of New York, (1968).

Buttrick, Shirley, and Alan Wade. "Negative Income Tax: A Step Forward," *Social Work,* Vol. 14 (April 1969), pp. 104–106.

California Law Review, Vol. 54 (May 1966); also published as ten Broek, Jacobus, (ed.) *The Law of the Poor.* San Francisco: Chandler Publishing Co., 1966.

Cameron, William Bruce. *Modern Social Movements.* New York: Random House, 1966.

Cantril, Hadley, and Lloyd A. Free. "Hopes and Fears for Self and Country," Supplement to the *American Behavioral Scientist,* Vol. 6 (October 1962).

Caplan, Gerald (ed.). *Prevention of Mental Disorders in Children.* New York: Basic Books, 1961.

———. *Principles of Preventive Psychiatry.* New York: Basic Books, 1964.

Caplovitz, David. *The Poor Pay More.* New York: Free Press, 1963.

Carr, Stephen, and Kevin Lynch. "Where Learning Happens," *Daedalus,* Vol. 97 (Fall 1968), pp. 1277–1291.

Carter, Hugh, and Alexander Plateris. "Trends in Divorce and Family Disruption," in Department of Health, Education, and Welfare *Indicators* (September 1963).

Caudill, Harry M. *Night Comes to the Cumberlands.* Boston: Little, Brown, 1962.

"A Center Report—Priorities in an Affluent Society," *The Center Magazine,* Vol. 3 (January 1970), pp. 72–83.

Chein, Isidor. "The Image of Man," *Journal of Social Issues,* Vol. 18 (October 1962), pp. 1–35.

Child Study Association of America. *Children of Poverty—Children of Affluence.* New York: Child Study Association of America, 1967.

Chinitz, Benjamin. "New York: A Metropolitan Region," *Scientific American,* Vol. 213 (September 1965), pp. 134–148.

Christensen, Craig W. "Of Prior Hearings and Welfare as New Property,"

National Institute for Education in Law and Poverty, *Clearinghouse Review,* Vol. 3 (April 1970).

Christie, Richard, and Marie Jahoda. *Studies in the Scope and Method of the Authoritarian Personality.* New York: Free Press, 1949.

Cicourel, Aaron V., and John I. Kitsuse. *The Educational Decision-Makers.* Indianapolis: Bobbs-Merrill, 1963.

Citizen's Board of Inquiry into Hunger and Malnutrition in the United States. *Hunger, U.S.A.* Washington, D.C.: New Community Press, 1968.

Clark, Kenneth B., and Jeannette Hopkins. *A Relevant War Against Poverty.* New York: Harper & Row, 1969.

Clinard, Marshall B. *Slums and Community Development.* New York: Free Press, 1966.

Cloward, Richard A. "Social Class and Private Social Agencies," in *Education for Social Work, 1963.* New York: Council on Social Work Education, 1963, pp. 123–137.

————, and Lloyd E. Ohlin. *Delinquency and Opportunity.* New York: Free Press, 1960.

————, and Frances Fox Piven. "A Strategy to End Poverty," *The Nation,* May 2, 1966, pp. 510–517.

Cohen, Albert K. *Delinquent Boys: The Culture of the Gang.* New York: Free Press, 1955.

Cohen, Eli E., and Louis Kapp (eds.). *Manpower Policies for Youth.* New York: Columbia University Press, 1966.

Cohen, Morris R. *Reason and Nature.* New York: Harcourt, Brace, 1931.

Cohen, Nathan E. (ed.). *Social Work and Social Problems.* New York: National Association of Social Workers, 1964.

Cohen, Wilbur J. "Social Policy for the Nineteen Seventies," in Department of Health, Education, and Welfare *Indicators* (May 1966).

————. "A Ten-Point Program to Abolish Poverty," *Social Security Bulletin,* Vol. 31 (December 1968), pp. 3–13.

————, and Robert M. Ball. "Social Security Amendments of 1967 and Legislative History," *Social Security Bulletin,* Vol. 31 (February 1968), pp. 3–19.

Coleman, James S. "Equal Schools or Equal Students?," *The Public Interest,* No. 4 (Summer 1966), pp. 70–75.

————. "Toward Open Schools," *The Public Interest,* No. 9 (Fall 1967), pp. 20–27.

————, et al. *Equality of Educational Opportunity.* Washington, D.C.: Government Printing Office, 1966.

Coles, Robert. "Is Prejudice Against Negroes Overrated?," *Trans-action,* Vol. 4 (October 1967), pp. 44–45.

———. "Like It Is in the Alley," *Daedalus* Vol. 97 (Fall 1968), pp. 1315–1330.

Commager, Henry Steele. *The Search for a Usable Past.* New York: Knopf, 1967.

——— (ed.). *Lester Ward and the Welfare State.* Indianapolis: Bobbs-Merrill, 1967.

Cook, Fred J. "When You Just Give Money to the Poor," *The New York Times Magazine,* April 26, 1970, p. 110.

Coser, Lewis A., and Bernard Rosenberg (eds.). *Sociological Theory: A Book of Readings.* New York: Macmillan, 1957.

Council on Social Work Education. *Public Health Concepts in Social Work Education.* New York: Council on Social Work Education, 1962.

Dahl, Robert A. *Who Governs? Democracy and Power in an American City.* New Haven, Conn.: Yale University Press, 1961.

Dahrendorf, Ralf. *Class and Class Conflict in an Industrial Society.* Stanford, Calif.: Stanford University Press, 1959.

———. "Recent Changes in the Class Structure of European Societies," *Daedalus,* Vol. 93 (Winter 1964), pp. 225–270.

———. *In Praise of Thrasymachus.* The Henry Failing Distinguished Lecture, Eugene, Ore.: University of Oregon, April 25, 1966.

Dalton, George (ed.). *Primitive, Archaic and Modern Economies: Essays of Karl Polanyi.* Garden City: Anchor Books, 1968.

de Jesus, Carolina Maria. *Child of the Dark.* New York: Dutton, 1962.

Dennison, George. *The Lives of Children.* New York: Random House, 1969.

Dentler, Robert A., and Mary Ellen Warshauer. *Big City Dropouts and Illiterates.* New York: Center for Urban Education, 1965.

Dependency and Poverty. Colloquia 1963–1964, Waltham, Mass.: The Florence Heller Graduate School for Advanced Studies in Social Welfare, Brandeis University, 1965.

de Schweinitz, Karl. *England's Road to Social Security.* New York: A. S. Barnes, 1961.

de Tocqueville, Alexis. *Democracy in America.* 2 vols. New York: Vintage Books, 1962.

Devine, Edward T. *Social Work.* New York: Macmillan, 1922.

Dexter, Lewis Anthony. *The Tyranny of Schooling.* New York: Basic Books, 1964.

Disraeli, Benjamin. *Sybil or The Two Nations.* Printed as Vol. IX of the Bradenham Edition. London: Peter Davies, 1927; originally published by Mayday in 1845.

Dittman, Laura L. (ed.). *Early Child Care.* New York: Atherton Press, 1968.

Donovan, John C. *The Politics of Poverty.* New York: Western Publishing, 1967.

Dostoevsky, Fyodor. *The Brothers Karamazov.* New York: Modern Library.

Drucker, Peter F. "The Sickness of Government," *The Public Interest,* No. 14 (Winter 1969), pp. 3–23.

Dubos, Rene. "Humanistic Biology," *American Scholar,* Vol. 34 (Spring 1965), p. 185.

Duhl, Leonard (ed.). *The Urban Condition.* New York: Basic Books, 1963.

Dumont, Matthew. *The Absurd Healer.* New York: Science House, 1968.

Dyckman, John W. "Some Conditions of Civic Order in an Urbanized World," *Daedalus,* Vol. 95 (Summer 1966).

Eisman, Martin. "Social Work's New Role in the Welfare-Class Revolution," *Social Work,* Vol. 14 (April 1969), pp. 80–86.

Elazar, Daniel J. "Are We a Nation of Cities?," *The Public Interest,* No. 4 (Summer 1966), pp. 42–58.

Elkins, Stanley M. *Slavery.* New York: Grosset & Dunlap, 1963.

Ellul, Jacques. *The Technological Society.* New York: Knopf, 1965.

Erikson, Erik (ed.). *Youth: Change and Challenge.* New York: Basic Books, 1963.

——. *Insight and Responsibility.* New York: W. W. Norton, 1964.

——. "Memorandum on Youth," *Daedalus,* Vol. 96 (Summer 1967), pp. 860–870.

Etzioni, Amitai. *Modern Organizations.* Englewood Cliffs, N.J.: Prentice-Hall, 1964.

Ewing, Oscar. *The Nation's Health: A Ten Year Program.* Washington, D.C.: Government Printing Office, 1948.

Farber, Seymour M., and Roger H. L. Wilson (eds.). *Conflict and Creativity.* New York: McGraw-Hill, 1963.

Farson, Richard E., Philip M. Hauser, Herbert Stroup, Anthony J. Wiener. *The Future of the Family.* New York: Family Service Association of America, 1969.

Ferry, W. H., Michael Harrington, and Frank L. Keegan. *Cacotopias and Utopias.* Santa Barbara, Calif.: Center for the Study of Democratic Institutions, 1965.

Fine, Sidney. *Laissez-faire and the General-Welfare State.* Ann Arbor, Mich.: University of Michigan Press, 1964.

Fleisher, Belton M. *The Economics of Delinquency.* Chicago: Quadrangle Books, 1966.

Foote, Nelson N., and Leonard S. Cottrell, Jr. *Identity and Interpersonal Competence.* Chicago: University of Chicago Press, 1955.

Frank, Lawrence K. "Research for What?," *Journal of Social Issues,* Supplement Series No. 10, 1957, Kurt Lewin Memorial Award Issue.

———. "The Need for a New Political Theory," *Daedalus,* Vol. 96 (Summer 1967), pp. 809–816.

Frankel, Charles. *The Democratic Prospect.* New York: Harper & Row, 1962.

———. "Some Paradoxes in the Idea of Welfare," The Elizabeth Wisner Lecture, New Orleans, La.: Tulane University School of Social Work, October 19, 1965.

Free, Lloyd A., and Hadley Cantril. *The Political Beliefs of Americans.* New Brunswick, N.J.: Rutgers University Press, 1967.

A "Freedom Budget" for All Americans. New York: A. Philip Randolph Institute, October 1966.

Freud, Sigmund. *The Mind of the Moralist.* New York: Viking Press, 1959.

Fried, Marc A. "Is Work a Career?," *Trans-action,* Vol. 3 (September–October 1966), pp. 42–47.

Friedenberg, Edgar Z. *The Vanishing Adolescent.* New York: Dell, 1962.

———. *Coming of Age in America.* New York: Random House, 1965.

———. "What Are Our Schools Trying To Do?," *The New York Times Book Review,* September 14, 1969, p. 56.

Friedman, Rose D. *Poverty: Definition and Perspective.* Washington, D.C.: American Enterprise Institute for Public Policy Research, 1965.

Friedlander, Walter A. *Introduction to Social Welfare.* 3rd ed. Englewood Cliffs, N.J.: Prentice-Hall, 1968.

Fromm, Erich. *Escape from Freedom.* New York: Farrar & Rinehart, 1941.

———. *The Sane Society.* New York: Rinehart, 1955.

———. *The Heart of Man.* New York: Harper & Row, 1964.

Fuchs, Estelle. "How Teachers Learn to Help Children Fail," *Trans-action,* Vol. 5 (September 1968), pp. 45–49.

———. "The Free Schools of Denmark," *Saturday Review,* August 16, 1969.

Fuchs, Victor R. "The First Service Economy," *The Public Interest,* No. 2 (Winter 1966), pp. 7–17.

Fuchs, Victor R. "Redefining Poverty and Redistributing Income," *The Public Interest,* No. 8 (Summer 1967), pp. 88–95.

Fulbright, William J. "The Uses of Flexibility," *Saturday Review,* May 8, 1966, p. 19.

Fuller, R. Buckminster. "How Little I Know," *Saturday Review,* November 12, 1966.

Galbraith, John Kenneth. *The Affluent Society.* Boston: Houghton Mifflin, 1958.

————. *The New Industrial State.* New York: Houghton Mifflin, 1967.

Gans, Herbert J. "Income Grants and 'Dirty Work,' " *The Public Interest,* No. 6 (Winter 1967), pp. 110–113.

————. *The Levittowners.* New York: Pantheon, 1967.

————. "We Won't End the Urban Crisis Until We End Majority Rule," *The New York Times Magazine,* August 3, 1969, p. 12.

Gardner, John W. *Self-Renewal: The Individual and the Innovative Society.* New York: Harper & Row, 1963.

Garfinkel, Irwin. "Negative Income Tax and Children's Allowance Programs: A Comparison," *Social Work,* Vol. 13 (October 1968), pp. 33–39.

Gass, Oscar. "The Political Economy of the Great Society," *Commentary,* October 1965, pp. 31–36.

Gavin, James M., and Arthur Hadley. "The Crisis of the Cities," *Saturday Review,* February 24, 1968.

Geismar, Ludwig L. *Preventive Intervention in Social Work.* Metuchen, N.J.: Scarecrow Press, 1969.

————, and Beverly Ayres. *Families in Trouble.* St. Paul: Greater St. Paul Community Chest & Councils, Inc., 1958.

Gerth, H. H., and C. Wright Mills (eds.). *From Max Weber: Essays in Sociology.* New York: Oxford University Press, 1946.

Gettleman, Marvin E., and David Mermelstein (eds.). *The Great Society Reader: The Failure of American Liberalism.* New York: Random House, 1967.

Ginsberg, Mitchell I. "Changing Values in Social Work," transcript of the first Ann Elizabeth Neely Memorial Lecture, Sixteenth Council on Social Work Education Annual Program Meeting, New York, N.Y., January 26, 1968.

Ginsberg, Morris. *On Justice in Society,* Ithaca, N.Y.: Cornell University Press, 1965.

Gladwin, Thomas. *Poverty USA.* Boston: Little, Brown, 1967.

Glasser, Melvin A. "Extension of Public Welfare Medical Care: Issues of Social Policy," *Social Work,* Vol. 10 (October 1965), pp. 3–9.

————. "Problems and Prospects for Mental Health Coverage Through Collective Bargaining Agreements," *American Journal of Orthopsychiatry,* Vol. 36 (January 1966).

Glazer, Nathan. "Paradoxes of American Poverty," *The Public Interest,* No. 1, (Fall 1965), pp. 71–81.

————. "Housing Policy and the Family," *Journal of Marriage and the Family,* Vol. 29 (February 1967), pp. 140–163.

————. "Beyond Income Maintenance—A Note on Welfare in New York City," *The Public Interest,* No. 16 (Summer 1969), pp. 102–120.

Goals of Public Social Policy. Rev. ed. New York: National Association of Social Workers, 1966.

Goffman, Erving. *The Presentation of Self in Everyday Life.* Garden City, Doubleday, 1959.

Goldberg, Gertrude S., with Carol Lopate. "Strategies for Closing the Poverty Gap," *IRCD Bulletin,* Vol. 5 (March 1969), pp. 1–8.

Goode, William J. "The Protection of the Inept," *American Sociological Review,* Vol. 32 (February 1967), pp. 5–19.

Goodenough, Ward Hunt. *Cooperation in Change.* New York: Russell Sage Foundation, 1963.

Goodman, Leonard H. (ed.). *Economic Progress and Social Welfare.* New York: Columbia University Press, 1966.

Goodman, Paul. *Growing Up Absurd.* New York: Random House, 1960.

Goodman, Walter. "The Case of Mrs. Sylvester Smith," *The New York Times Magazine,* August 25, 1968, p. 28.

Goodwin, Richard N. "Reflections, Sources of Public Unhappiness," *The New Yorker,* January 4, 1969, pp. 38–58.

Gordon, Margaret S. *The Economics of Welfare Policies.* New York: Columbia University Press, 1963.

Gottman, Jean. "The Corrupt and Creative City," *Center Diary: 14,* Center for Study of Democratic Institutions, September–October 1966, pp. 34–37.

Gouldner, Alvin W. "Toward the Radical Reconstruction of Sociology," *Social Policy,* May/June 1970, pp. 8–25.

Graham, Hugh Davis, and Ted Robert Gurr (eds.). *Violence in America.* 2 vols. A report to the National Commission on the Causes and Prevention of Violence, Washington, D.C.: Government Printing Office, 1969.

Green, Christopher. "The Economics of a Guaranteed Minimum Income," *GAIN,* Vol. 1 (February 1967), pp. 1–3.

————. *Negative Taxes and the Poverty Problem.* Washington, D.C.: Brookings Institution, 1967.

Green, Christopher. "Guaranteed Income Plans—Which One Is Best," *Trans-action,* Vol. 5 (January–February 1968), pp. 45–53.

Green, Thomas F. "Schools and Communities: A Look Forward," *Harvard Educational Review,* Vol. 39 (Spring 1969), pp. 221–252.

Greenberg, Polly. *The Devil Has Slippery Shoes.* New York: Macmillan, 1969.

Greenfield, Meg. "The 'Welfare Chiselers' of Newburg, New York," *The Re-porter,* August 17, 1961.

Greenleigh Associates, Inc. *Facts, Fallacies and Future.* New York: Green-leigh Associates, 1960.

————. *Public Welfare: Poverty-Prevention or Perpetuation?* New York: Greenleigh Associates, December 1964.

Greer, Scott. *Urban Renewal and American Cities.* Indianapolis: Bobbs-Merrill, 1965.

Gross, Bertram M. (ed.). *A Great Society?* New York: Basic Books, 1966.

———— (ed.). *Social Intelligence for America's Future.* Boston: Allyn & Bacon, 1969.

Group for the Advancement of Psychiatry. *Urban America and the Planning of Mental Health Services.* Symposium No. 10, Vol. V (November 1964).

Gutman, Herbert G. "The Failure of the Movement by the Unemployed for Public Works in 1873," *Political Science Quarterly,* Vol. 80 (June 1965), pp. 254–277.

Haber, Alan. "Poverty Budgets: How Much Is Enough?" *Poverty and Hu-man Resources Abstracts,* Vol. 1 (May–June 1966), pp. 5–22.

Hamilton, Charles V. "Race and Education: A Search for Legitimacy," *Harvard Educational Review,* Vol. 38 (Fall 1968), pp. 669–684.

Hamilton, John A. "The Politics of Hunger," *Saturday Review,* June 21, 1969.

Hannerz, Ulf. "Roots of Black Manhood," *Trans-action,* Vol. 6 (October 1969), pp. 13–21.

Harlem Youth Opportunities Unlimited, Inc. *Youth in the Ghetto.* New York: HARYOU, 1964.

Harrington, Michael. *The Other America.* New York: Macmillan, 1962.

Harris, Richard. *Sacred Trust.* New York: New American Library, 1966.

Harvith, Bernard Evans. "Federal Equal Protection and Welfare Assistance," *Albany Law Review,* Vol. 31, (June 1967), p. 210.

Haselkorn, Florence (ed.). *Mothers-at-Risk.* New York: Adelphi University School of Social Work, 1966.

Heidt, Sara Jane, and Amitai Etzioni. *Societal Guidance: A New Approach to Social Problems.* New York: Crowell, 1969.

Heilbroner, Robert L. *The Worldly Philosophers.* Rev. ed. New York: Simon & Schuster, 1964.

———. *The Limits of American Capitalism.* New York: Harper & Row, 1965.

Henry, Jules. "Docility, or Giving the Teacher What She Wants," *Journal of Social Issues,* Vol. 11 (April 1955).

———. *Culture Against Man.* New York: Vintage Books, 1965.

Hentoff, Nat. *The New Equality.* New York: Viking, 1964.

Herberg, Will (ed.). *The Writings of Martin Buber.* Cleveland: World Publishing, 1956.

Herzberg, Frederick. *Work and the Nature of Man.* Cleveland: World Publishing, 1966.

Herzog, Elizabeth. "Some Assumptions About the Poor," *Social Service Review,* Vol. 37 (December 1963), pp. 389–402.

———, and Cecelia E. Sudia. "Fatherless Homes: A Review of the Research," *Children,* Vol. 15 (September–October 1968), pp. 177–182.

Hess, Robert D. "Educability and Rehabilitation: The Future of the Welfare Class," *Journal of Marriage and the Family,* Vol. 26, (November 1964), pp. 422–429.

Hiestand, Dale I. *Economic Growth and Employment Opportunities for Minorities.* New York: Columbia University Press, 1964.

Hoffer, Eric. *The Ordeal of Change.* New York: Harper & Row, 1963.

Hoffman, Martin L. and Lois Wladis Hoffman (eds.). *Review of Child Development Research,* Vol. I. New York: Russell Sage Foundation, 1964.

Hofstadter, Richard. *The American Political Tradition.* New York: Vintage Books, 1948.

Hollingshed, August B. and Frederick K. Redlich. *Social Class and Mental Illness.* New York: Wiley, 1958.

Horowitz, Irving Louis (ed.). *The New Sociology.* New York: Oxford University Press, 1964.

———. *Professing Sociology.* Chicago: Aldine Press, 1968.

Howard, Donald G. *Social Welfare: Values, Means, Ends.* New York: Random House, 1969.

Huizinga, Johan. *Homo Ludens.* Boston: Beacon Press, 1950.

Hunt, J. McVicker. "The Psychological Basis for Using Pre-School Enrichment as an Antidote for Cultural Deprivation," *Merrill-Palmer Quarterly,* Vol. 10 (July 1964), pp. 209–248.

———. "Has Compensatory Education Failed? Has It Been Attempted?," *Harvard Educational Review,* Vol. 39 (Spring 1969), pp. 278–300.

Hunt, J. McVicker. "Black Genes–White Environment," *Trans-action,* Vol. 6 (June 1969), pp. 12–22.

Hunter, David R. *The Slums: Challenge and Response.* New York: Free Press, 1964.

Hunter, Floyd. *Community Power Structure.* Chapel Hill, N.C.: University of North Carolina Press, 1953.

Hutchins, Robert M. "The Nurture of Human Life," *Bulletin* of the Center for the Study of Democratic Institutions, (March 1961).

Huyck, Earl E. "White-Non-White Differentials: Overview and Implications," *Demography,* Vol. 3, 1966, pp. 548–565.

Jackson, Luther P. *Poverty's Children.* Washington, D.C.: Cross-Tell, 1966.

Jeffers, Camille. *Living Poor.* Ann Arbor, Mich.: Ann Arbor Press, 1967.

Jenkins, Shirley, and Mignon Sauber. *Paths to Child Placement.* New York: Community Council of Greater New York, 1966.

Jensen, Arthur R. "How Much Can We Boost IQ and Scholastic Achievement?," *Harvard Educational Review,* Vol. 39 (Winter 1969), pp. 1–123.

Kagan, Jerome S. "Inadequate Evidence and Illogical Conclusions," *Harvard Educational Review,* Vol. 39 (Spring 1969), pp. 274–277.

Kahn, Alfred J. "The Social Scene and the Planning of Services for Children," *Social Work,* Vol. 7 (July 1962), pp. 3–14.

———. "New Policies and Service Models: The Next Phase," *American Journal of Orthopsychiatry,* Vol. 35 (July 1965), pp. 652–662.

———. "The Societal Context of Social Work Practice," *Social Work,* Vol. 10 (October 1965), pp. 145–155.

———. *Neighborhood Information Centers: A Study and Some Proposals.* New York: Columbia University School of Social Work, 1966.

Kahn, Gerald, and Ellen J. Perkins. "Families Receiving AFDC: What Do They Have to Live On?," reprint from *Welfare in Review,* Vol. 1 (October 1963).

Kaplan, Abraham (ed.). *The New World of Philosophy.* New York: Random House, 1961.

Kaplan, Berton H. "Social Issues and Poverty Research: A Commentary," *Journal of Social Issues,* Vol. 21 (January 1965), pp. 1–10.

Kaplan, Saul. *Support from Absent Fathers of Children Receiving AFDC.* Public Assistance Report No. 41, Washington, D.C.: Government Printing Office, 1960.

Katz, Alfred H. "Application of Self-Help Concepts in Current Social Welfare," *Social Work,* Vol. 10 (July 1965), pp. 68–74.

————, and Jean Spencer Felton (eds.). *Health and the Community.* New York: Free Press, 1965.

Katz, Daniel, and Robert L. Kahn. *The Social Psychology of Organizations.* New York: Wiley, 1966.

Keil, Charles. *Urban Blues.* Chicago: University of Chicago Press, 1966.

Kelman, Herbert C. "The Social Consequences of Social Research," *Journal of Social Issues,* Vol. 21 (July 1965), pp. 21–40.

Kenniston, Kenneth. *The Uncommitted: Alienated Youth in American Society.* New York: Harcourt, Brace & World, 1967.

Keyserling, Leon H. *The Role of Wages in a Great Society.* Washington, D.C.: Conference on Economic Progress, 1966.

Klaus, Rupert A., and Susan W. Gray. "The Early Training Project for Disadvantaged Children: A Report After Five Years." Monographs of the Society for Research in Child Development Serial No. 120, Vol. 33, No. 4, 1969. Chicago: University of Chicago Press, 1969.

Kluckhohn, Clyde. *Mirror for Man.* New York: Whittlesey House, 1949.

————, and Henry A. Murray (eds.). *Personality in Nature, Society, and Culture.* New York: Knopf, 1954.

Kohn, Melvin L. *Class and Conformity: A Study in Values.* Homewood, Ill.: Dorsey Press, 1969.

Komarovsky, Mirra. *Blue-Collar Marriage.* New York: Random House, 1962.

Konopka, Gisela. *The Adolescent Girl in Conflict.* Englewood Cliffs, N.J.: Prentice-Hall, 1966.

Kozol, Jonathan. *Death at an Early Age.* Boston: Houghton Mifflin, 1967.

Kraft, Ivor. "Head Start To What?," *The Nation,* September 5, 1966, pp. 179–182.

Langholm, Magne. *Family and Child Welfare in Norway.* Oslo: Norwegian Joint Committee on International Social Policy, 1963.

Langner, Thomas S., and Stanley T. Michael. *Life Stress and Mental Health.* New York: Free Press, 1963.

Lasch, Christopher. *The New Radicalism in America.* New York: Knopf, 1965.

Laski, Harold. "Democracy," in *Encyclopedia of the Social Sciences.* Vol. V, pp. 76–84. New York: Macmillan, 1931.

Lebeaux, Charles N. "Life on ADC in Detroit, 1963," *Newsletter* of the Metropolitan Detroit Chapter National Association of Social Workers, March 1964.

Lee, Dorothy. *Freedom and Culture.* Englewood Cliffs, N.J.: Prentice-Hall, 1959.

Leighton, Alexander H., et al. *Sterling County Study of Psychiatric Disorder and Sociocultural Environment.* Vols. I, II, III (New York: Basic Books, 1959).

Levine, David (ed.). *Nebraska Symposium on Motivation.* Lincoln, Neb.: University of Nebraska Press, 1965.

Levins, Helen. "Organizational Affiliation and Powerlessness: A Case Study of the Welfare Poor," *Social Problems,* Vol. 16 (Summer 1968), pp. 18–32.

Lewis, Anthony. *Gideon's Trumpet.* New York: Vintage, 1964.

Lewis, Harold. "Parental and Community Neglect," *Children,* Vol. 16 (May–June 1969), pp. 114–118.

Lewis, Oscar. *The Children of Sanchez.* New York: Random House, 1961.

———. "The Culture of Poverty," *Scientific American,* Vol. 215 (October 1966), pp. 19–25.

Lichtman, Richard. *Toward Community.* Santa Barbara, Calif.: Center for the Study of Democratic Institutions, 1966.

Liebow, Elliott. *Tally's Corner.* Boston: Little, Brown, 1966.

———. "Fathers Without Children," *The Public Interest,* No. 5 (Fall 1966), pp. 13–25.

Linder, Forrest E. "The Health of the American People," *Scientific American,* Vol. 214 (June 1966), p. 21.

Little, Malcolm. *The Autobiography of Malcolm X.* New York: Grove Press, 1965.

Loch, Charles Stuart. "Charity," in *The Encyclopedia Britannica.* Vol. V, 11th ed., pp. 860–891. Cambridge, England: University of Cambridge, 1910.

Lopata, Helena Znaniecki. "The Secondary Features of a Primary Relationship," *Human Organization,* Vol. 24 (Summer 1965), pp. 116–121.

Low, Seth. *America's Children and Youth in Institutions.* U.S. Children's Bureau Publication 435, Washington, D.C.: Government Printing Office, 1965.

Lubove, Roy. *The Professional Altruist.* Cambridge, Mass.: Harvard University Press, 1965.

———. "Social Work and the Life of the Poor," *The Nation,* May 23, 1966, pp. 609–611.

Lundberg, George R. *Can Science Save Us?* New York: Longmans, Green, 1947.

Lynd, Robert S. *Knowledge for What?* Princeton, N.J.: Princeton University Press, 1939.

Maas, Henry S., and Richard E. Engler, Jr. *Children in Need of Parents.* New York: Columbia University Press, 1959.

McClelland, David. *The Achieving Society.* Princeton, N.J.: Van Nostrand, 1961.

McCord, William, and Joan McCord. *Origins of Crime.* New York: Columbia University Press, 1959.

MacIver, Robert M. *Politics and Society.* New York: Atherton Press, 1969.

McKinley, Donald G. *Social Class and Family Life.* New York: Macmillan, 1964.

MacLeish, Archibald. "The Great American Frustration," *Saturday Review,* July 13, 1968, pp. 13–15.

———. "The Revolt of the Diminished Man," *Saturday Review,* June 7, 1969.

Madge, John H. *The Tools of Social Science.* New York: Longmans, Green, 1953.

Madison, Bernice. "Canadian Family Allowances and Their Major Social Implications," *Journal of Marriage and the Family,* Vol. 26 (May 1964), pp. 134–141.

Makarenko, A. S. *The Collective Family.* Garden City: Anchor Books, 1967.

Malik, Charles. "Reflections on the Great Society," *Saturday Review,* August 6, 1966, pp. 12–15.

Mandell, Betty. "The Crime of Poverty," *Social Work,* Vol. 7 (January 1962), pp. 3–11.

Mann, Thomas. *Confessions of Felix Krull.* New York: Knopf, 1955.

Mannheim, Karl. *Diagnosis of Our Time.* London: Paul Kegan, 1943.

Manser, Ellen P. *Project ENABLE: What Happened?* New York: Family Service Association of America, 1968.

Marcuse, Herbert. *One-Dimensional Man.* Boston: Beacon Press, 1964.

Marris, Peter, and Martin Rein. *Dilemmas of Social Reform.* New York: Atherton Press, 1967.

Marshall, T. H. *Class, Citizenship, and Social Development.* Garden City: Anchor Books, 1965.

Martin, James G. *Tolerant Personality.* Detroit: Wayne State University Press, 1964.

Martz, Helen E. "Illegitimacy and Dependency," Reprint, Health, Education, and Welfare *Indicators,* September 1963.

Maslow, Abraham H. *Motivation and Personality.* New York: Harper & Brothers, 1954.

———. *Toward a Psychology of Being.* New York: Van Nostrand, 1962.

———. "Some Educational Implications of the Humanistic Psychologies," *Harvard Educational Review,* Vol. 38 (Fall 1968), pp. 685–696.

Matson, Floyd W. *The Broken Image: Man, Science and Society.* Garden City: Anchor Books, 1966.

Mead, Margaret. "The Life Cycle and Its Variations," *Daedalus,* Vol. 96 (Summer 1967), pp. 871–875.

———, and Francis B. Kaplan (eds.). *American Women.* The Report of the President's Commission on the Status of Women and other publications of the Commission. New York: Scribners, 1965.

Mencher, Samuel. "Ideology and the Welfare Society," *Social Work,* Vol. 12 (July 1967), pp. 3–11.

———. *Poor Law to Poverty Program.* Pittsburgh: University of Pittsburgh Press, 1967.

Merriam, Ida C., Alfred M. Skolnik, and Sophie R. Dales. "Social Welfare Expenditures 1967–68," *Social Security Bulletin,* Vol. 31 (December 1968), pp. 14–27.

Merton, Robert K., Leonard Broom, and Leonard S. Cottrell, Jr. (eds.). *Sociology Today.* New York: Basic Books, 1962.

Meyer, Henry J., Edgar F. Borgotta, and Wyatt C. Jones. *Girls at Vocational High.* New York: Russell Sage Foundation, 1965.

Michael, Donald. *The Next Generation.* New York: Vintage Books, 1965.

———. "Urban Policy in the Rationalized Society," *Journal of the American Institute of Planners,* Vol. 31 (November 1965), pp. 283–288.

———. "On Coping with Complexity: Planning and Politics," *Daedalus,* Vol. 97 (Fall 1968), pp. 1179–1193.

Miel, Alice. *The Short Changed Children of Suburbia.* New York: Institute of Human Relations Press, The American Jewish Committee, 1967.

Miller, Herman P. *Rich Man, Poor Man.* New York: Signet Books, 1965.

Miller, Roger R. (ed.). *Race, Research, and Reason: Social Work Perspectives.* New York: National Association of Social Workers, 1969.

Miller, S. M. "Stupidity and Power," *Trans-action,* Vol. 1 (May 1964).

———. "The Credential Society," *Trans-action,* Vol. 5 (December 1967), p. 2.

———, and Martin Rein. "Change, Ferment and Ideology in the Social Services," in *Education for Social Work.* New York: Council on Social Work Education, 1964.

————, and Frank Riessman. "The Working Class Subculture: A New View," *Social Problems,* Vol. 9 (Spring 1961), pp. 86–97.

————, and Frank Riessman. *Social Class and Social Policy.* New York: Basic Books, 1968.

Miller, Walter B. "Implications of Urban Lower-Class Culture for Social Work," *Social Service Review,* Vol. 33 (September 1959), pp. 212–236.

Mills, C. Wright. *The Power Elite.* London: Oxford University Press, 1956.

———— (ed.). *Images of Man.* New York: George Braziller, 1960.

Mogulof, Melvin B. "Federal Support for Citizen Participation in Social Action," pp. 86–107, in *The Social Welfare Forum, 1969.* New York: Columbia University Press, 1969.

————. "Black Community Development in Five Western Model Cities," *Social Work,* Vol. 15 (January 1970), pp. 12–18.

Mondale, Walter F. "Reporting on the Social State of the Union," *Trans-action,* Vol. 5 (June 1968), pp. 34–38.

Montessori, Maria. *The Montessori Method.* New York: Schocken Books, 1964.

Moore, Wilbert E. "A Reconsideration of Theories of Social Change," *American Sociological Review,* Vol. 25 (December 1960), pp. 810–818.

More, Sir Thomas. *Utopia.* New York: Everyman's Library, 1951.

Moreland Commission Report. *Public Welfare in the State of New York.* Albany: State Capital, 1963.

Morgan, John S. (ed.). *Welfare and Wisdom.* Toronto: University of Toronto Press, 1968.

Morison, Robert S. "Where Is Biology Taking Us?," *Science,* January 27, 1967, pp. 429–433.

Morris, Marian Gennarea. "Psychological Miscarriage: An End to Mother Love," *Trans-action,* Vol. 3 (January–February 1966), pp. 8–13.

Morris, Robert (ed.). *Centrally Planned Change.* New York: National Association of Social Workers, 1964.

Moynihan, Daniel P. "Employment, Income, and the Ordeal of the Negro Family," *Daedalus,* Vol. 94 (Fall 1965).

————. "A Crisis of Confidence," *The Public Interest,* No. 7 (Spring 1967), pp. 3–10.

————. "The Crisis in Welfare," *The Public Interest,* No. 10 (Winter 1968), pp. 3–29.

————. *Maximum Feasible Misunderstanding.* New York: Macmillan, 1969.

————. "Toward a National Urban Policy," *The Public Interest,* No. 17 (Fall 1969), pp. 3–20.

Muller, Herbert J. *The Uses of the Past.* New York: Oxford University Press, 1957.

———. *Freedom in the Modern World.* New York: Harper & Row, 1966.

Mumford, Lewis. *The City in History.* New York: Harcourt, Brace & World, 1961.

Murphy, Gardner. "Human Potentialities," *Journal of Social Issues,* Supplement Series No. 7, 1953.

———. *Human Potentialities.* New York: Basic Books, 1958.

Musgrove, F. *Youth and the Social Order.* Bloomington, Ind.: Indiana University Press, 1964.

Myers, Robert J. *Social Insurance and Allied Government Programs.* Homewood, Ill.: Irwin, 1965.

Myrdal, Alva. *Nation and Family.* New York: Harper & Brothers, 1941.

Myrdal, Gunnar. *An American Dilemma.* 2 vols. New York: Harper & Brothers, 1944.

———. *Value in Social Theory.* Edited by Paul Streeten. New York: Harper & Brothers, 1958.

———. *Challenge to Affluence.* New York: Pantheon, 1964.

Nathan, Richard B. *Jobs and Civil Rights.* Prepared for U.S. Commission on Civil Rights by the Brookings Institution, Clearinghouse Publication No. 16, Washington, D.C.: Government Printing Office, 1969.

National Advisory Commission on Civil Disorders. *Report.* Washington, D.C.: Government Printing Office, 1968.

National Advisory Commission on Civil Disorders. *Supplemental Studies.* Washington, D.C.: Government Printing Office, 1968.

National Association of Social Workers. *Changing Services for Changing Clients.* New York: Columbia University Press, 1969.

National Citizens' Committee for Community Relations and the Community Relations Service of the U.S. Department of Justice. *Putting the Hard-Core Unemployed into Jobs.* Part I, Washington, D.C.: Government Printing Office, 1967.

National Commission on Community Health Services. *Health is a Community Affair.* Cambridge, Mass.: Harvard University Press, 1966.

National Commission for Social Work Careers. *Manpower: A Community Responsibility.* 1968 Annual Review. New York: National Commission for Social Work Careers, 1968.

National Commission on Technology, Automation, and Economic Progress. *Technology and the American Economy.* Vol. I. Washington, D.C.: Government Printing Office, 1966.

National Commission on Urban Problems. *Building the American City.* 91st Congress, 1st sess., House Document 34. Washington, D.C.: Government Printing Office, 1968.

National Institute of Child Health and Human Development. *The Acquisition and Development of Values.* Washington, D.C.: Government Printing Office, 1969.

National Institute of Mental Health. *Mental Health in Appalachia.* Washington, D.C.: Government Printing Office, 1965.

Neill, A. S. *Summerhill.* New York: Hart, 1960.

Nelson, George R. (ed.). *Freedom and Welfare.* The Ministries of Social Affairs of Denmark, Finland, Iceland, Norway, Sweden, 1953.

Neugeboren, Bernard. "Evaluation of Unified Social Services." Mimeographed. New Haven, Conn.: Community Progress, Inc., 1967.

New York City Youth Board. *Proceedings of the Metropolitan New York Conference on Religion and Race,* 1964.

Niebuhr, Reinhold. "Some Things I Have Learned," *Saturday Review,* November 6, 1965.

Nolan, Martin. "A Belated Effort to Save Our Cities," *The Reporter,* December 28, 1967.

Office of Economic Opportunity, Project Head Start. *Parent Involvement: A Workbook of Training Tips for Head Start Staff.* OEO Pamphlet 6108–12. Washington, D.C.: Government Printing Office, May 1969.

Olson, Philip (ed.). *America as Mass Society.* New York: Free Press, 1963.

Orshansky, Mollie. "More About the Poor in 1964," *Social Security Bulletin,* Vol. 29 (May 1966), pp. 3–38.

———. "The Shape of Poverty in 1966," *Social Security Bulletin,* Vol. 31 (March 1968), pp. 3–31.

Orwell, George. *The Orwell Reader.* New York: Harcourt, Brace & World, 1956.

Owen, David. *English Philanthropy, 1660–1960.* Cambridge, Mass.: Belknap Press, 1964.

Parke, R., and T. C. Glick. "Prospective Changes in Marriage and the Family," *Journal of Marriage and the Family,* Vol. 29 (May 1967), pp. 249–256.

Parker, Jo Goodwin. "What Is Poverty?," *Congressional Record.* House Vol. 112, No. 155 (September 14, 1966), pp. 21617–21618.

Passaw, H. (ed.). *Education in Depressed Areas.* New York: Teachers College Bureau of Publications, 1963.

Paull, Joseph E.   "Recipients Aroused: The New Welfare Rights Movement," *Social Work,* Vol. 12 (April 1967), pp. 101–106.

Pavenstadt, Eleanor.   "A Comparison of the Child-Rearing Environment of Upper-Lower and Very Low-Lower Class Families," *American Journal of Orthopsychiatry,* Vol. 35 (January 1965), pp. 89–98.

—— (ed.).   *The Drifters.* Boston: Little, Brown, 1967.

Pearl, Arthur, and Frank Riessman.   *New Careers for the Poor.* New York: Free Press, 1965.

Perlman, Robert, and David Jones.   *Neighborhood Service Centers.* U.S. Department of Health, Education, and Welfare, Office of Juvenile Delinquency and Youth Development. Washington, D.C.: Government Printing Office, 1967.

Pettigrew, Thomas F.   *A Profile of the Negro American.* Princeton, N.J.: Van Nostrand, 1964.

Pfuetze, Paul E.   *Self, Society, Existence.* New York: Harper Torchbooks, 1961.

Polanyi, Karl.   "Our Obsolete Market Mentality," *Commentary,* February, 1947, pp. 109–117.

——. *The Great Transformation.* Boston: Beacon Press, 1957.

Polier, Justine Wise.   "Problems Involving Family and Child," *Columbia Law Review,* Vol. 66 (February 1966), pp. 305–316.

Pollak, Otto.   "The Outlook for the American Family," *Journal of Marriage and the Family,* Vol. 29 (February 1967), pp. 193–205.

Pomeroy, Richard, with Harold Yahr and Lawrence Podell.   *Studies in Public Welfare: Reactions of Welfare Clients to Social Service.* New York: Center for the Study of Urban Problems, 1968.

Pope Paul VI.   *On the Development of Peoples.* Encyclical Letter, Papulorum Progessio. Boston: St. Paul Editions, 1967.

Porter, John.   "The Future of Upward Mobility," *American Sociological Review,* Vol. 33 (February 1968), pp. 5–19.

Poussaint, Alvin F.   "A Negro Psychiatrist Explains the Negro Psyche," *The New York Times Magazine,* August 20, 1967.

Poverty-Rights Action Center.   *Goals for a National Welfare Rights Movement.* Washington, D.C., 1966.

President's Commission on Income Maintenance Programs.   *Poverty Amid Plenty: The American Paradox.* Washington, D.C.: Government Printing Office, 1969.

President's Commission on Law Enforcement and Administration of Justice. *The Challenge of Crime in a Free Society.* Washington, D.C.: Government Printing Office, 1967.

President's Commission on Law Enforcement and Administration of Justice. *Juvenile Delinquency and Youth Crime.* Washington, D.C.: Government Printing Office, 1967.

President's Commission on National Goals. *Goals for Americans.* New York: Prentice-Hall, 1960.

President's Committee on Urban Housing. *A Decent Home.* Washington, D.C.: Government Printing Office, 1969.

President's National Advisory Commission on Rural Poverty. *The People Left Behind.* Washington, D.C.: Government Printing Office, 1967.

President's Panel on Mental Retardation. *National Action to Combat Mental Retardation.* Washington, D.C.: Government Printing Office, 1962.

"Pruit-Igoe: Survival in a Concrete Ghetto," *Social Work,* Vol. 12 (October 1967), pp. 3–13.

Rainwater, Lee. "The Services Strategy vs. The Income Strategy," *Trans-action,* Vol. 4 (October 1967), pp. 40–41.

———. "Looking Back and Looking Up," *Trans-action,* Vol. 6 (February 1969), p. 9.

———, and William L. Yancey. *The Moynihan Report: The Politics of Controversy.* Cambridge, Mass.: MIT Press, 1967.

Raison, Timothy. "The British Debate the Welfare State," *The Public Interest,* No. 1 (Fall 1965), pp. 110–118.

Randal, Judith. "The Bright Promise of Neighborhood Health Centers," *The Reporter,* March 21, 1968, pp. 15–18.

Ratner, Joseph (ed.). *Intelligence in the Modern World: John Dewey's Philosophy.* New York: Modern Library, 1939.

Reich, Charles A. "Midnight Welfare Searches and the Social Security Act," *Yale Law Journal,* Vol. 72 (June 1963), p. 1347.

———. "The New Property," *Yale Law Journal,* Vol. 73 (April 1964), pp. 733–787.

———. "Individual Rights and Social Welfare: The Emerging Legal Issues," *Yale Law Journal,* Vol. 74 (June 1965), pp. 1245–1257.

Rein, Martin. "The Social Service Crisis," *Trans-action,* Vol. 1 (May 1964), p. 3.

———. "The Strange Case of Public Dependency," *Trans-action,* Vol. 2 (March–April, 1965), pp. 16–23.

Report on Comprehensive Community Health Services for New York City. New York: Commission on the Delivery of Personal Health Services, 1967.

Reps, Paul. *Zen Flesh, Zen Bones: A Collection of Zen and Pre-Zen Writings.* New York: Anchor Books, 1961.

Ribicoff, Abraham. "The Competent City," *Congressional Record,* Vol. 113 (January 23, 1967), p. 5709.

Richmond, Mary E. *Social Diagnosis.* New York: Russell Sage Foundation, 1917.

Riesman, David. "Notes on Meritocracy," *Daedalus,* Vol. 96 (Summer 1967), pp. 897–908.

Riessman, Frank. "Self-Help Among the Poor: New Styles of Social Action," *Trans-action,* Vol. 2 (September–October 1965), pp. 32–36.

———. *Strategies Against Poverty.* New York: Random House, 1969.

———. Jerome Cohen, and Arthur Pearl (eds.). *Mental Health of the Poor.* New York: Free Press, 1964.

Rights of Public Assistance Recipients. New York: National Conference of Lawyers and Social Workers, 1966.

Robinson, Reginald. *Community Resources in Mental Health.* New York: Basic Books, 1960.

Rodman, Hyman. "Family and Social Pathology in the Ghetto," *Science,* August 23, 1968, pp. 756–762.

Roger, Carl R., and B. F. Skinner. "Some Issues Concerning the Control of Human Behavior," *Science,* November 30, 1956, pp. 1057–1066.

Rosenblatt, Aaron. *Attendance and Attitude Change: A Study of 301 EN-ABLE Groups.* New York: Family Service Association of America, 1968.

Rosenthal, Robert, and Lenore F. Jacobson. "Teacher Expectations for the Disadvantaged," *Scientific American,* April, 1968, pp. 19–23.

Ross, Aileen D. "Philanthropy," in *International Encyclopedia of Social Sciences.* Vol. XII, pp. 72–80. New York: Macmillan and Free Press, 1968.

Rostow, W. W. *The Stages of Economic Growth.* Cambridge, Eng.: Cambridge University Press, 1960.

Ruderman, Florence A. *Child Care and Working Mothers.* New York: Child Welfare League of America, 1968.

Rudin, Stanley A. "The Personal Price of National Glory," *Trans-action,* Vol. 2 (September–October 1965), pp. 4–9.

Rustin, Bayard. "A Way Out of the Exploding Ghetto," *The New York Times Magazine,* August 13, 1967.

Safa, Helen Icken. *Profiles in Poverty.* An Analysis of Social Mobility in Low-Income Families. Syracuse, N.Y.: Syracuse University Youth Development Center, 1966.

Sanford, Nevitt. "Social Science and Social Reform," *Journal of Social Issues,* Vol. 21 (April 1965), pp. 54–70.

————. *Self and Society.* New York: Atherton Press, 1966.

Schlesinger, Arthur M., Jr. *The American As Reformer.* Cambridge, Mass.: Harvard University Press, 1950.

Schorr, Alvin L. *Filial Responsibility in the Modern American Family.* U.S. Department of Health, Education, and Welfare. Washington, D.C.: Government Printing Office, 1960.

————. *Slums and Social Insecurity.* Washington, D.C.: Government Printing Office, 1963.

————. "Income Maintenance and the Birth Rate," *Social Security Bulletin,* Vol. 28 (December 1965), pp. 22–30.

————. "National Community and Housing Policy," *Social Service Review,* Vol. 39 (December 1965), pp. 433–443.

————. *Poor Kids.* New York: Basic Books, 1966.

————. "Alternatives in Income Maintenance," *Social Work,* Vol. 11 (July 1966), pp. 22–29.

————. "Against a Negative Income Tax," *The Public Interest,* No. 5 (Fall 1966), pp. 110–117.

————. *Explorations in Social Policy.* New York: Basic Books, 1968.

————. "Social Services Are No Substitute for Economic Policies," *Social Work,* Vol. 14 (April 1969), p. 2.

Schottland, Charles I. *The Social Security Program in the United States.* New York: Appleton-Century-Crofts, 1963.

Schutz, William C. *Joy.* New York: Grove Press, 1967.

Schwartz, Edward E. "A Way to End the Means Test," *Social Work,* Vol. 9 (July 1964), p. 3.

Scrimshaw, Nevin S. "Infant Malnutrition and Adult Learning," *Saturday Review,* March 16, 1968, p. 64.

Sexton, Patricia Cayo. *Education and Income.* New York: Viking, 1961.

———— (ed.). *Readings on the School in Society.* Englewood Cliffs, N.J.: Prentice-Hall, 1967.

Shannon, David A. *The Great Depression.* Englewood Cliffs, N.J.: Prentice-Hall, 1960.

Shaw, George Bernard. *Selected Plays.* New York: Dodd, Mead, 1948.

Sherrard, Thomas D. (ed.). *Social Welfare and Urban Problems.* New York: Columbia University Press, 1968.

Shlakman, Vera. "Income Maintenance Alternatives," *Social Work,* Vol. 14 (January 1969), pp. 126–129.

————, and Scott Briar. "Briar and Shlakman Answer Their Critics," *Social Work,* Vol. 14 (July 1969), pp. 108–110.

Shostak, Arthur B., and William Gomberg (eds.). *New Perspectives on Poverty.* Englewood Cliffs, N.J.: Prentice-Hall, 1965.

Sidenbladh, Goran. "Stockholm: A Planned City," *Scientific American,* September 1965, p. 107.

Silberman, Charles. *Crisis in Black and White.* New York: Random House, 1964.

————. *Crisis in the Classroom* (New York: Random House, 1970).

Simpson, George. *Emile Durkheim on the Division of Labor in Society.* New York: Macmillan, 1933.

Skinner, B. F. *Walden Two.* New York: Macmillan, 1948.

Skolnik, Alfred M. "Twenty-Five Years of Workmen's Compensation Statistics," *Social Security Bulletin,* Vol. 29 (October 1966), pp. 3–26.

Slavin, Simon. "Concepts of Social Conflict: Use in Social Work Curriculum," *Journal of Education for Social Work,* Vol. 5 (Fall 1969), pp. 47–60.

Smith, A. Delafield. *The Right to Life.* Chapel Hill, N.C.: University of North Carolina Press, 1955.

Smith, M. Brewster. "The Revolution in Mental Health Care—A 'Bold New Approach'?" *Trans-action,* Vol. 5 (April 1968), pp. 19–23.

————, and Nicholas Hobbs. *The Community and the Community Mental Health Center.* Washington, D.C.: American Psychological Association, 1966.

Smith, Russell E. "In Defense of Public Welfare," *Social Work,* Vol. 11 (October 1966), pp. 90–97.

Social Action Guide. New York: National Association of Social Workers, 1965.

Social and Rehabilitation Service. *Trend Report, 1968.* National Center for Social Statistics Report A–4. Washington, D.C.: Government Printing Office, 1969.

Social Security Administration. *Widows with Children under Social Security.* Social Security Administration Research Report No. 16. Washington, D.C.: Government Printing Office, 1966.

Social Security Institution of Mexico. *Social Security Centers for Family Welfare.* Mexico, 1961.

Spiegel, Hans D. C. (ed.). *Citizen Participation in Urban Development.* Washington, D.C.: NTL Institute for Applied Behavioral Science, 1968.

Srole, Leo, Thomas S. Langner, Stanley T. Michael, Marvin K. Opler, and Thomas A. C. Rennie. *Mental Health in the Metropolis: The Midtown Manhattan Study.* Vol. I. New York: McGraw-Hill, 1962.

Stein, Herman D., and Richard A. Cloward (eds.). *Social Perspectives on Behavior.* New York: Free Press, 1958.

Stein, Maurice. *The Eclipse of Community.* Princeton, N.J.: Princeton University Press, 1960.

————, Arthur J. Vidick, and David Manning White (eds.). *Identity and Anxiety.* New York: Free Press, 1960.

Steiner, Gilbert Y. *Social Insecurity.* Chicago, Ill.: Rand McNally, 1966.

Stern, Philip M. *The Great Treasury Raid.* New York: Random House, 1964.

Street, David. "Educators and Social Workers: Sibling Rivalry in the Inner City," *Social Service Review,* Vol. 41 (June 1967), pp. 152–165.

———— (ed.). *Innovation in Mass Education.* New York: Wiley, 1968.

Studt, Elliot, Sheldon C. Messinger, and Thomas P. Wilson. *C–Unit: Search for Community in Prison.* New York: Russell Sage Foundation, 1968.

Sumner, William Graham. *The Forgotten Man.* Reprint. New Haven, Conn.: Yale University Press, 1919. (Speech delivered at Yale in 1833.)

Tawney, R. H. *The Acquisitive Society.* New York: Harcourt, Brace & Howe, 1920.

————. *Religion and the Rise of Capitalism.* New York: Harcourt, Brace & World, 1926.

————. *Equality.* New York: Harcourt, Brace, 1931.

tenBroek, Jacobus, and Floyd W. Matson. "The Disabled and the Law of Welfare," *California Law Review,* Vol. 54 (May 1966), pp. 809–840.

Theobald, Robert. *Free Men and Free Markets.* New York: Potter, 1963.

———— (ed.). *The Guaranteed Income.* Garden City: Doubleday, 1966.

————. "The Guaranteed Income: A New Economic and Human Right," in *The Social Welfare Forum, 1966.* New York: Columbia University Press, 1966.

Thernstrom, Stephan. *Poverty and Progress.* Cambridge, Mass.: Harvard University Press, 1964.

Thompson, Laura. *Toward a Science of Mankind.* New York: McGraw-Hill, 1961.

Thorkelson, H. "Food Stamps and Hunger in America," *Dissent,* Vol. 14 (1967), pp. 479–484.

Thurz, Daniel. *Where Are They Now?* Washington, D.C.: Health and Welfare Council of the National Capital Area, 1966.

Tibbitts, Clarke. *Middle Aged and Older People in American Society.* Washington, D.C.: Government Printing Office, 1964.

Tillich, Paul. "The Ambiguity of Perfection," *Time,* May 17, 1963, p. 69.

Titmuss, Richard M. "Industrialization and the Family," *Social Service Review,* Vol. 31 (March 1957), pp. 54–62.

————. *Essays on the "Welfare State."* London: George Allen & Unwin, 1958.

————. "The Welfare State: Images and Realities," *Social Service Review,* Vol. 37 (March 1963), pp. 1–11.

————. "The Role of Redistribution in Social Policy," *Social Security Bulletin,* Vol. 28 (June 1965), pp. 14–20.

————. "Social Policy and Economic Progress," in *The Social Welfare Forum.* New York: Columbia University Press, 1966.

————. *Commitment to Welfare.* New York: Pantheon, 1968.

Tobin, James. "The Case for an Income Guarantee," *The Public Interest,* No. 4 (Summer 1966), pp. 31–41.

————. "A Rejoinder," *The Public Interest,* No. 5 (Fall 1966), pp. 117–119.

————. "Do We Want a Children's Allowance?," *New Republic,* November 25, 1967, pp. 16–18.

Townsend, Joseph. "A Dissertation on the Poor Laws," in J. R. McCulloch (ed.), *A Select Collection of Scarce and Valuable Economic Tracts.* London, 1859.

Trilling, Lionel. *Freud and the Crisis of our Culture.* Boston: Beacon Press, 1955.

Uhr, Carl G. *Sweden's Social Security System.* Social Security Administration Research Report No. 14. Washington, D.C.: Government Printing Office, 1966.

United Nations. *The Universal Declaration of Human Rights: A Standard of Achievement.* Special 15th Anniversary Edition. New York: United Nations, 1965.

United Nations Department of Economic and Social Affairs. *Report on the World Social Situation.* New York: United Nations, 1963.

United Nations Department of Social Affairs. *Training for Social Work: An International Survey.* New York: United Nations, 1950.

U.S. Bureau of the Census. *Historical Statistics of the United States, Colonial Times to 1957.* Washington, D.C.: Government Printing Office, 1960.

————. Herman P. Miller. *Income Distribution in the United States.* A 1960 Census Monograph. Washington, D.C.: Government Printing Office, 1966.

————. *Population Estimates.* Series P–25, No. 359, Washington, D.C.: Government Printing Office, February 20, 1967.

————. "Family Income Advances, Poverty Reduced in 1967," in *Current Population Reports.* Series P–60, No. 55. Washington, D.C.: Government Printing Office, 1968.

————. *Statistical Abstract of the United States: 1968.* Washington, D.C.: Government Printing Office, 1968.

————. "Trends in Social and Economic Conditions in Metropolitan Areas," in *Current Population Reports,* Series P–23, Special Studies, No. 27. Washington, D.C.: Government Printing Office, 1969.

———— and Bureau of Labor Statistics. "Social and Economic Conditions of Negroes in the United States," in *Current Population Reports.* Series P–23, No. 24, Bureau of Labor Statistics Report No. 332. Washington, D.C.: Government Printing Office, 1967.

———— and Bureau of Labor Statistics. "Recent Trends in Social and Economic Conditions of Negroes in the United States," in *Current Population Reports.* Series P–23, No. 26, Bureau of Labor Statistics Report No. 347. Washington, D.C.: Government Printing Office, 1968.

U.S. Commission on Civil Rights. *Children in Need.* Urban Studies: Cleveland. Washington, D.C.: Government Printing Office, 1966.

————. *Racial Isolation in the Public Schools.* Vol. I. Washington, D.C.: Government Printing Office, 1967.

————. *a time to listen . . . . a time to act.* Washington, D.C.: Government Printing Office, 1967.

————. Paul Good. *Cycle to Nowhere.* Clearinghouse Publication No. 14. Washington, D.C.: Government Printing Office, 1968.

U.S. Congress. *Economic Report of the President* together with *The Annual Report of the Council of Economic Advisors.* House Document No. 28, 91st Congress, 1st sess. Washington, D.C.: Government Printing Office, 1969.

————, House Committee on Education and Labor. *Hearings Before Subcommittee on War on Poverty Programs.* 89th Congress, 1st sess. Washington, D.C.: Government Printing Office, 1965.

————, House of Representatives. *Problems and Future of the Central City and Its Suburbs.* Message from the President of the United States. House Document No. 99, 89th Congress, March 2, 1965.

————, Joint Economic Committee. *Twentieth Anniversary of the Employment Act of 1946.* 89th Congress, 2nd sess. Washington, D.C.: Government Printing Office, 1966.

————, Joint Economic Committee. *Old Age Income Assurance.* 90th Congress, 1st sess., Part III, Public Programs. Washington, D.C.: Government Printing Office, 1967.

U.S. Congress, Joint Economic Committee. Written by Dick Netzer for the National Commission on Urban Problems. *Impact of the Property Tax.* 90th Congress, 2nd sess. Washington, D.C.: Government Printing Office, 1968.

————, Joint Economic Committee. *Income Maintenance Programs.* 90th Congress, 2nd sess., Vol. II. Washington, D.C.: Government Printing Office, 1968.

U.S. Department of Health, Education, and Welfare. *Closing the Gap in Social Work Manpower.* Washington, D.C.: Government Printing Office, 1965.

————. *1965 Social Security Amendments, Welfare Provisions.* Washington, D.C.: Government Printing Office, 1965.

————. *Programs and Services.* Washington, D.C.: Government Printing Office, 1966.

————. *Social Development: Key to the Great Society.* Washington, D.C.: Government Printing Office, 1966.

————. *Social Security Programs in the United States.* Washington, D.C.: Government Printing Office, 1966.

————. *Social Security Programs Throughout the World, 1967.* Social Security Administration. Washington, D.C.: Government Printing Office, 1967.

————. *Health, Education, and Welfare Trends.* 1966–67 ed., Part I, National Trends. Washington, D.C.: Government Printing Office, 1968.

————. *Toward a Social Report.* Washington, D.C.: Government Printing Office, 1969.

U.S. Department of Labor. *The Negro Family: The Case for National Action.* Office of Policy Planning and Research. Washington, D.C.: Government Printing Office, March 1965.

————. *America's Industrial and Occupational Manpower Requirements 1964–75.* Bureau of Labor Statistics. Washington, D.C.: Government Printing Office, 1966.

————. *Manpower Report of the President.* Washington, D.C.: Government Printing Office, 1966.

————. *The Negroes in the United States.* Bureau of Labor Statistics, *Bulletin 1511.* Washington, D.C.: Government Printing Office, 1966.

————. *Manpower Report of the President.* Washington, D.C.: Government Printing Office, 1967.

————. *Manpower Report of the President.* Washington, D.C.: Government Printing Office, 1968.

————. *Manpower Report of the President.* Washington, D.C.: Government Printing Office, 1969.

————. Manpower Administration. *Summary Tables for Evaluation of Coverage and Benefit Provisions of State Unemployment Insurance Laws as of December 31, 1965.* Bureau of Labor Statistics V–256, July 1966.

Urban Development: Its Implications for Social Welfare. Proceedings of the XIII International Conference of Social Work. New York: Columbia University Press, 1967.

Vadakin, James C. *Children, Poverty and Family Allowances.* New York: Basic Books, 1968.

Valentine, Charles A. *Culture and Poverty.* Chicago: University of Chicago Press, 1968.

Van Den Berghe, Pierre L. "Poverty as Underdevelopment," *Trans-action,* Vol. 6 (July–August, 1969), p. 3.

Verga, Giovanni. *The House by the Medlar Tree.* New York: Grove Press, 1953.

Vernon, Glenn M. *Human Interaction: An Introduction to Sociology.* New York: Ronald Press, 1965.

Vidich, Arthur J., Joseph Bensman, and Maurice R. Stein (eds.). *Reflections on Community Studies.* New York: Wiley, 1964.

Vincent, Clark E. *Unmarried Mothers.* New York: Free Press, 1961.

————. "Mental Health and the Family," *Journal of Marriage and the Family,* Vol. 29 (February 1967), pp. 18–39.

"Vocational Rehabilitation of the Disabled: The Public Program," in Health, Education and Welfare *Indicators.* December 1965. Reprint. Washington, D.C.: Government Printing Office, April 1966.

Wade, Alan D. "The Guaranteed Minimum Income: Social Work's Challenge and Opportunity," *Social Work,* Vol. 2 (January 1967), pp. 94–101.

Waller, Willard. "Social Problems and the Mores," *American Sociological Review,* Vol. 2 (December 1936), pp. 922–933.

Warner, Sam Bass, Jr. (ed.). *Planning for a Nation of Cities.* Cambridge, Mass.: MIT Press, 1966.

Warner, Sylvia Ashton. *Teacher.* New York: Simon & Schuster, 1963.

Warren, Roland L. "Model Cities First Round: Politics, Planning and Participation," *Journal of the American Institute of Planners,* 35 (July 1969), pp. 245–252.

Wasserman, Harry R. "Socio-economic Effects of Unemployment." DSW dissertation, University of California at Berkeley, 1965.

Watts, Alan W. *The Two Hands of God: The Myths of Polarity.* New York: George Braziller, 1963.

Weinberger, Paul E. (ed.). *Perspectives on Social Welfare.* New York: Macmillan, 1969.

Weisbrod, Burton A. "Investing in Human Capital," *Journal of Human Resources,* Vol. 1 (Summer 1966), pp. 5–21.

Weissbourd, Bernard. *Segregation, Subsidies and Megalopolis.* Santa Barbara, Calif.: Center for the Study of Democratic Institutions, 1964.

Weissman, Harold H. (ed.). *The New Social Work.* 4 vols. New York: Association Press, 1969.

Welter, Rush. *Popular Education and Democratic Thought in America.* New York: Columbia University Press, 1962.

Wheeler, Harvey. *The Restoration of Politics.* Santa Barbara, Calif.: Center for the Study of Democratic Institutions, 1965.

————. *The Rise and Fall of Liberal Democracy.* Santa Barbara, Calif.: Center for the Study of Democratic Institutions, 1966.

————. *Democracy in a Revolutionary Era.* Santa Barbara, Calif.: Center for the Study of Democratic Institutions, 1970.

White House Conference. "To Fulfill These Rights," in *Council's Report and Recommendations to the Conference.* Washington, D.C.: Government Printing Office, 1966.

Wickenden, Elizabeth. *Social Welfare in a Changing World.* U.S. Department of Health, Education and Welfare. Washington, D.C.: Government Printing Office, 1965.

————. "The 1967 Amendments: A Giant Step Backward for Child Welfare," *Child Welfare,* Vol. 48 (July 1969), pp. 388–394.

Wilcock, Richard C., and Walter H. Franke. *Unwanted Workers.* New York: Free Press, 1963.

Wilcox, Clair. *Toward Social Welfare.* Homewood, Ill.: Irwin, 1969.

Wildavsky, Aaron. "The Empty-head Blues: Black Rebellion and White Reaction," *The Public Interest,* No. 11 (Spring 1968), pp. 3–16.

Wilensky, Harold. "Careers, Counseling and the Curriculum," *Journal of Human Resources,* Vol. 2 (Winter 1967), pp. 19–40.

————, and Charles N. Lebeaux. *Industrial Society and Social Welfare.* New York: Free Press, 1965.

Wilkinson, John, *et al.* *Technology and Human Values.* Santa Barbara, Calif.: Center for the Study of Democratic Institutions, 1966.

Willhelm, Sidney M. "Elites, Scholars and Sociologists," *Catalyst,* No. 2 (Summer 1966), pp. 1–10.

————, and Edwin H. Powell. "Who Needs the Negro?," *Trans-action,* Vol. 1 (September–October 1964), pp. 3–6.

Wilson, James Q. "The Urban Unease: Community versus City," *The Public Interest,* No. 12 (Summer 1968), pp. 25–39.

Wolins, Martin, with Jerry Turem. "The Societal Function of Social Welfare." *New Perspectives, The Berkeley Journal of Social Welfare,* Vol. 1 (Spring 1967), pp. 1–18.

Woodard, Calvin. "Reality and Social Reform: The Transition from Laissez-Faire to the Welfare State," *Yale Law Journal,* Vol. 72 (December 1962), pp. 286–328.

Wrong, Dennis H. "The Failure of American Sociology," *Commentary,* November 1959, pp. 375–380.

———. "The Functional Theory of Stratification," *American Sociological Review,* Vol. 24 (December 1959), pp. 772–782.

Young, Whitney M., Jr. *To Be Equal.* New York: McGraw-Hill, 1964.

Zald, Mayer N. (ed.). *Social Welfare Institutions.* New York: Wiley, 1965.

Zetterberg, Hans L. *Social Theory and Social Practice.* New York: Bedminster Press, 1962.

Zucker, Mildred. "Citizens Advice Bureaus: The British Way," *Social Work,* Vol. 10 (October 1965), pp. 85–91.

Zweig, Franklin M. "The Social Worker as Legislative Ombudsman," *Social Work,* Vol. 14 (January 1969), pp. 25–33.

Index

443